Robin Harris worked for the Conservative Party from 1978, and increasingly closely with Margaret Thatcher herself from 1985, writing her speeches and advising on policy. By the close of her premiership, he was probably the most trusted member of her political team at Downing Street, and he left Number Ten with her. As a member of her personal staff, he then drafted the two volumes of her autobiography and a further book on her behalf. After Margaret Thatcher's retirement from public life, Robin continued to see her regularly. He has also written a history of Dubrovnik and an acclaimed biography of Talleyrand. He lives in Cornwall.

THE CONSERVATIVES

A HISTORY

Robin Harris

CORGI BOOKS

TRANSWORLD PUBLISHERS
61–63 Uxbridge Road, London W5 5SA
A Random House Group Company
www.transworldbooks.co.uk

THE CONSERVATIVES
A CORGI BOOK: 9780552170338

First published in Great Britain
in 2011 by Bantam Press
an imprint of Transworld Publishers
Corgi edition published 2013

Addresses for Random House Group Ltd companies outside the UK
can be found at: www.randomhouse.co.uk
The Random House Group Ltd Reg. No. 954009

The Random House Group Limited supports the Forest Stewardship Council® (FSC®),
the leading international forest-certification organisation. Our books carrying the FSC
label are printed on FSC®-certified paper. FSC is the only forest-certification
scheme supported by the leading environmental organisations, including Greenpeace. Our
paper procurement policy can be found at www.randomhouse.co.uk/environment

Typeset in Erhhardt by Falcon Oast Graphic Art Ltd.
Printed and bound by CPI Group (UK) Ltd, Croydon, CR0 4YY.

2 4 6 8 10 9 7 5 3 1

CONTENTS

ACKNOWLEDGEMENTS

I am delighted to honour several debts of gratitude. I was given an early steer towards sources by Professor Robert Tombs. I then benefited from the efficiency and professionalism of the staff of the British Library and the London Library. Similarly, my thanks go to Jeremy Mcilwaine, the Conservative Party archivist at the Bodleian Library. I am especially grateful to Professor Richard Shannon and Professor Vernon Bogdanor, both of whom read through large sections of the text and offered invaluable suggestions and corrections. (Naturally, the opinions, and any remaining mistakes, are my responsibility alone.) I was assisted at various points by Lord Black of Brentwood, Chris Collins, Simon Heffer, Sheila Lawlor and Lord Lexden. Finally, I thank Eddie Bell, my agent, for his good-humoured encouragement, and Doug Young and the team at Transworld for their expert advice.

INTRODUCTION

The case for a new history of the Conservative Party is not difficult to make. In the first instance, it rests on current political circumstances. After almost two decades of being either discredited, while in office, or out of office altogether – and, in either case, of only marginal interest and importance – the party has returned to government, albeit as the dominant element in a coalition. Quite what that will mean for the country or the party is as yet unclear: I briefly examine the record so far towards the end of this book. But the turn-round in Conservative fortunes, if rather less sharp than many were predicting a year before the 2010 election, should certainly remind political commentators how quickly lazy assumptions dissolve under new conditions. More importantly – for it is the intention of this book to reach beyond the cognoscenti – recent events should lead anyone with a sense of history, or even of curiosity, to wonder how the resilient, adaptable organization that is the Conservative Party has survived so long, overcome so many crises, and, yet again, come out (more or less) on top.

Second, and perhaps surprisingly, there is no up-to-date, readable, referenced, single-volume history of the Conservative Party in print. To say this is not to ignore the indispensable multi-volume Longman history.[1] It is not to diminish the significance of Robert Blake's marvellous Ford Lectures, subsequently updated to take into account later developments. Nor do I question the value (though I do question some of the judgements) of John Ramsden's résumé, *An Appetite for Power*.[2] Finally, it is not to belittle the studies of individuals and events that together tell aspects of the Conservative Party's story. Some of these, not least the biographies, are among the best of their kind, and I have drawn heavily on them, as the notes to the following pages will show.[3] But none of these volumes, long or short, quite fills the gap that I now try to plug. In any case, as any perusal of those earlier studies confirms, each generation views the past differently, because more recent historical experience explodes some certainties and promotes others, while suggesting a host of nuances in between. Perhaps that is especially so when viewing the past of a political party, because parties themselves are in the business of re-interpreting and, less creditably, re-inventing history. My own experience, once stressfully on the inside and now contentedly on the outside, allows me – even compels me – to appreciate that process of airbrushing and embellishing more than most.

Third, the Conservative Party is an especially complex historical phenomenon. Depending on some contestable dating, it is probably the oldest right-of-centre party with a continuous existence anywhere in the world. It is also probably the most successful political party in the world (except for the Communist Party, which is not really a party at all, in that it does not respect the legitimacy of multi-party systems). Broad generalizations about a political organism with such a long and often contradictory existence must, therefore, be few or qualified. Those that emerge from these pages should not be construed as 'lessons' for the present, though they may constitute indications for it.

The need for the Conservative Party to win over moderate opinion, the need at the same time to stay connected to its roots, the need to encourage new talent, the need to change the wrong and pick the right leaders, the need to move with the times while continuing to influence them, most relevantly perhaps the need to manipulate and to survive coalition – all these obviously sensible imperatives become strangely difficult to reconcile and apply in the practical circumstances of real political life. Were that not the case, of course, the Conservatives would never have been out of power; for their leaders – despite J. S. Mill's suggestion that most stupid people are Conservative – have rarely been stupid. In the last chapter some of these threads will be brought together. But the result may still look, to those seeking applicable lessons, distressingly tatty. My defence is that political histories, as opposed to political handbooks, offer few neat conclusions and plenty of loose ends.

The Conservative Party is, in one particular and little-noted respect, not like other modern parties at all. As a result, this book will not read like, say, a complementary companion to the various histories of the Labour Party. A recent if forgettable example may illustrate this point.

In June 2009 James Purnell, the Work and Pensions Secretary, sent a highly damaging letter of resignation to the Prime Minister of the day, Gordon Brown. In order to assert his nobility of intention, not least in the eyes of Labour Party supporters, Mr Purnell – with what degree of sincerity it is difficult to gauge – echoed a sentiment often heard on the left:

> Dear Gordon,
> We both love the Labour Party. I have worked for it for twenty years and you far longer. We know we owe it everything and it owes us nothing [etc.].

No Conservative politician at any stage of the party's history would have written such a letter. No one has ever pretended to 'love' the Conservative Party. It is doubtful if even the most sentimental member of the Primrose League, let alone a backbench MP, would have claimed to 'owe' the party 'everything'. Any serious Tory figure adopting such a pose would incur immediate ridicule. The Conservative Party exists, has always existed and can only exist to acquire and exercise power, albeit on a particular set of terms. It does not exist to be loved, hated or even respected. It is no better or worse than the people who combine to make it up. It is an institution with a purpose, not an organism with a soul.

That said, it would be foolish to write the history of the Conservative Party as if ideas or (in the broader sense) ideology were a mere device, and as if organization were all that mattered. The Conservative Party is more than an instrument. It has an identity. It even professes, in its own fashion, some modest ideals. Conservative politicians who parade their cynicism have not usually profited from it. Ambition curbed, or at least controlled, is a better route to the top. The Conservative Party has its own traditions, habits and passions, even if these are not guaranteed permanency, any more, of course, than is the party itself. And again, Tory politicians who ignore them, or their significance, often slip up.

A satisfactory history of the party has to concern itself with all these elements and to try to avoid fitting them into a rigid frame-work of dates and periods that conceal rather than illuminate – particularly when it comes to describing the proto-party's nebulous beginnings, as I do in the first two chapters.

A final caveat. There have long been competing tendencies, on the one hand to exaggerate, and on the other to ignore, the role of (lower-case) 'conservatism' as a philosophical outlook in the life of the (upper-case) Conservative Party. Both risks should be minimized by getting the relationship clear.

The single best definition of what it means to be conservative remains that offered some years ago now by the philosopher Michael Oakeshott. The well-known passage runs:

> To be conservative ... is to prefer the familiar to the unknown, to prefer the tried to the untried, fact to mystery, the actual to the possible, the limited to the unbounded, the near to the distant, the sufficient to the superabundant, the convenient to the perfect, present laughter to utopian bliss. Familiar relationships and loyalties will be preferred to the allure of more profitable attachments; to acquire and to enlarge will be less important than to keep, to cultivate and to enjoy; the grief of loss will be more acute than the excitement of novelty or promise. It is to be equal to one's own fortune, to live at the level of one's own means, to be content with the want of greater perfection which belongs alike to oneself and one's circumstances. With some people this is itself a choice; in others it is a disposition which appears, frequently or less frequently, in their preferences and aversions, and is not itself chosen or specifically cultivated.[4]

Perhaps the most important observation about this outlook is that – to the extent that such a thing is possible in this world – it is one that should make us happy. This is because it is sane; it offers a reliable purchase on reality; and sanity and reality are the only basis for sustainable happiness – or so conservatives would argue.

It hardly needs emphasizing that conservatism, thus understood, is not in itself a political programme. The link between the conservative mind and Conservative politics is indirect, and it stems from the conservative person's attitude to change – namely that he or she is suspicious of it. This psychological and historical fact helps explain why the Conservative Party has lasted. Lasting, enduring, surviving is what conservatives value. But this predisposition can also lead to difficulties, not least when change is what the party leadership demands, as in one form or another it has from Peel to Cameron. Such recurring tension is, therefore, also a recurring theme of this book. At the time of writing these difficulties are once again evident. So perhaps, despite my fastidiousness, this book may prove practically useful after all.

Three further and final points need to be made by way of explanation of the approach pursued.

First, the history of the Conservative Party is presented in what follows with the emphasis on its leaders. Biography is often, anyway, more fun than institutional history; but that is not, in fact, the governing rationale. The internal constitution of the Conservative Party, the instincts of the members, the qualities expected of those who reach the top, all help to make it, more than other British political parties, something akin to an elective dictatorship. The Conservative Party's internal revolutions are ruthless, but infrequent. Between such times, the leader's hands are largely free. (Of course, in practice, only some leaders succeed in leaving an abiding mark: others are too briefly incumbent or variously deficient to do so.) The decisive role of the party leader in Conservative politics is reflected in my chapter titles, many of which are duly composed along the lines of 'Peel's/Disraeli's/ Churchill's [etc.] Party'. Other approaches, for example stressing ideas or organization, would be possible. But personality is the focus preferred here, and I would argue that it conveys the dominant reality.

Second, tracing the history of any institution from the distant past to the present day runs up against the problem of distorting perspective. Not just changing sources but changing judgements – among them an author's own – make it difficult to treat events through which we have passed and people whom we have known as if we had encountered them only in books and reflected on them at a distance. For this reason, the reader will find that I have resisted the temptation to go into great detail about the politics of the Conservative Party during the last quarter-century or so. In the relatively new field of study known as Contemporary History practitioners tread a tightrope between mere record and opinionated journalism. Had I lingered further I might have fallen off. So there is at least as much here about the nineteenth as about the twentieth century, and substantially more than about the early twenty-first.

Third, the chapter about Margaret Thatcher (which incorporates, for reasons explained in the text, the subsequent tenure of John Major) is obviously less detailed than I could – or in other circumstances, given my knowledge, would – have written. This, though, is not because of the self-denying ordinance outlined above. It is, rather, because I had completed a full-length biography of Mrs Thatcher which was only to be published on her death. Sadly, that occurred in April 2013. My book, *Not For Turning: The Life of Margaret Thatcher* (Bantam Press, 2013), now tells her story in detail.

For Rhetoric he could not ope
His Mouth but out there flew a Trope
publishd 6th april 1782 by C Bretherton)

The 'father of conservatism', Edmund Burke, in a cartoon of 1782. The polemics celebrated in the artist's note were first deployed against royal power and then, decisively, against the forces of Revolution.

1

TORY BEGINNINGS

Conservative-minded people are always likely to be conscious of, touchy about, and generally fascinated by their past. This mentality may to critics seem like snobbery, and sometimes it is. But it reflects something arguably nobler and certainly deeper – namely the desire for roots. It received a memorable justification from Edmund Burke, who notes in his *Reflections on the Revolution in France* that 'people will not look forward to posterity who never look backward to their ancestors'.[1] Certainly, from the organized beginnings of the party, Conservatives have been happy to exhibit their political genealogy. This has been done sometimes to justify some current stance, but even more frequently to deplore it. Thus the young Benjamin Disraeli, in his novel *Sybil* (1845), writes, in the shadow of his increasing disgruntlement with Peel:

> Sir Robert Peel is not the leader of the Tory party ... In a parliamentary sense that great party has ceased to exist; but I will believe that it still lives in the thought and sentiment and consecrated memory of the English nation. It has its origin in

great principles and in noble instincts; it sympathises with the lowly, it looks up to the Most High; it can count its heroes and its martyrs; they have met in its behalf plunder, proscription and death. Nor, when it finally yielded to the iron progress of oligarchical supremacy, was its catastrophe inglorious ... Even now it is not dead, but sleepeth; and in an age of political materialism, of confused purposes and perplexed intelligence, that aspires only to wealth because it has faith in no other accomplishments, as men rifle cargoes on the verge of shipwreck, Toryism will yet rise from the tomb.[2]

Naturally, Disraeli already considered himself the animator of this resurrection.

Disraeli deliberately, and in this case accurately, describes the party as Tory, and not Conservative. The word 'Tory', like its counterpart 'Whig', stems from the abuse of enemies, a bitter insult turned, as is frequently the way in England, into a badge of honour. Both terms were first used in the seventeenth century; both refer to outlaws defined, significantly, by their religion. 'Tory' is derived from the Irish *tóraighe*, meaning a 'pursuer', and refers to the dispossessed Catholic Irish, who preyed off Protestant English settlers. The 'Whigs' were Dissenting Protestants in the Scottish Lowlands who rebelled against the imposition of the 1662 Act of Uniformity.[3] The names acquired their wider political significance somewhat later – Tories as enthusiasts for monarchy and the Church of England, Whigs as proponents of parliamentary authority and religious toleration (or at least toleration of Protestant Dissent). In both cases, this was as a result of the Exclusion Crisis of 1679–81, when an unsuccessful attempt was made to bar the Roman Catholic James, Duke of York (later King James II), from the British throne.

In an important sense, however, the Tory and Whig parties were never mirror images of each other. Parties that uphold the highest authorities of the land and those that challenge them weigh differently in the balance of advantage. In the eyes of a seventeenth-century Tory, an ideal political world would have had no room for organized political parties at all. The King, not his subjects – not even his most loyal subjects – ruled, and he did so by a divine dispensation, a mysterious and exalted 'Divine Right', which it was at worst blasphemous, at best bad manners, to question. Charles I's speech from the scaffold succinctly summarizes the doctrine:

> For the people – and truly I desire their liberty and freedom as much as any body whomsoever – but I must tell you that their liberty and their freedom consists in having of government those laws by which their life and their goods may be most their own. *It is not for having share in government, Sirs; that is nothing pertaining to them. A subject and a sovereign are clean different things*.[4]

Within such a framework, the political party has no justification.

Of course, that view was already outdated by the time the King uttered it. Charles's alienation from current political realities and assumptions was, indeed, one of the reasons why he lost his head. But such a philosophical and sentimental starting point meant that, for Tories, engaging in overt party politics did not come naturally. This reticence went, and to some extent still goes, beyond constitutional theory. It corresponds to a deep-seated psychological reality. The attitudes of Toryism, which find an echo in philosophical conservatism, are essentially defensive and centre on authority, allegiance and tradition.[5] These things may be worth fighting or even dying for – as many did in the cause of the Stuart monarchy – but they are not obvious parts of an active political programme.

The cause of 'Church and King' which the first Tory Party took as its own was, therefore, an inadequate creed for that jostling of competing but compatible interests which is the ordinary condition of politics. So, unsurprisingly, although both Whigs and Tories made their appearance on the national scene at about the same time, the Whigs were from the first more tightly organized, and soon more politically developed.

The Glorious Revolution of 1688–9, which overthrew James II and substituted William III and Mary (James's daughter), made a further large and enduring difference to the early parties. The Revolution, for all its re-interpretation by later conservative-minded thinkers like Burke (minimizing its populism, exaggerating its continuity), threw more than one political spanner into the Tory works.[6] It was the first time since the fall of the Cromwellian Commonwealth that tradition-minded royalists found themselves radically out of sympathy with the reigning monarch. True, this did not for the most part push Tories into the wilder reaches of conspiracy. The number of hard-core Tory Jacobites was limited, and the active Jacobite cause soon became captured by forces in Scotland, Ireland and continental Europe with which few English Tories could associate. In any case, Tory High Church Anglicanism implied no sympathy for the Roman Catholicism which the Pretender, James Edward Stuart, to his personal credit but political disadvantage, refused to disown. It was, anyway, at a pinch possible, even after 1688, for Tories to concentrate their loyalties on the authentically Stuart Queen Mary, and forget her unwelcome Dutch husband. Yet, all that said, Tories were unmistakably on the back foot. The example of the 'Non-Juror' Anglican bishops – who refused to swear allegiance to William and Mary and suffered for it – served, even for many unprepared to go so far, as a troubling moral reproach. And troubled consciences made, as so often, for uncertain politics.

It was still, however, the Crown that mattered. William himself was uninterested in British politics, except in so far as British politicians were prepared to support and, above all, finance his continental wars. He was thus quite happy to govern through ministries led nominally by either a Whig or a Tory. Indeed, as a foreigner and frequent absentee, he allowed home-grown politicians freer range than had any previous monarch. This in turn led to polarization in Parliament between Whigs and Tories, while the Government itself navigated its way, in conducting the King's business, between, through and over them, avoiding over-dependence on either group.[7]

In any case, if upholding royal authority now seemed to many Tories a less attractive cause than in the great days of Charles I and Charles II, there was, happily, the other traditional cause to fall back upon – upholding the Church of England. After all, the Church, more specifically the English episcopacy, just as much as Divine Right, had been among the articles of faith for which King Charles 'the Martyr' had died.[8] The Tories, therefore, remained the 'Church Party' throughout the period of Stuart rule, and by the end of Queen Anne's reign the cry of 'the Church in Danger' had become the most potent and reliable weapon in the Tory Party's propaganda arsenal.[9]

Reference to the final and, as it turned out, terminal crisis for the early Tories as a party of government requires consideration of the last old Tory Party leader, Henry St John, first Viscount Bolingbroke. Bolingbroke's reputation has over the years risen and fallen – the ascents becoming shallower and shorter and the declines more precipitate and enduring. Born into an ancient county family of which he was passionately proud, but brought up in Battersea, Henry St John impressed contemporaries from an early age by his looks, his wit and his eloquence. His friends, acquaintances and admirers included, at one time or another, such luminaries as Jonathan Swift, Alexander Pope, Voltaire and the Earl of Chesterfield. He was, in fact, a natural celebrity. And, like many such, he had enormous personal faults. He was an immoral, impious, bibulous, scheming, loquacious, mercurial figure (indeed, he was known as 'Man of Mercury' – and embraced the soubriquet); manipulative, self-indulgent and, for all his fire, a bit of a coward.

The Tories had, at this time, under Anne, almost ideal conditions in which to flourish. As an acceptably legitimate Stuart, and one with neither Catholic proclivities nor the will to intervene over-much in the regular business of government, this monarch was highly acceptable to Tories. They in turn, or most of the intelligent and ambitious ones – and St John was both highly intelligent and wildly ambitious – were prepared to make compromises. They had already dropped attachment to Divine Right, limiting themselves to a high view of the royal prerogative; they had also dropped (or at least suppressed) their Jacobitism; and for reasons of expedience St John strove, albeit in the end unsuccessfully, to consolidate that shift.

Instead, Tories stressed their commitment to High Anglicanism. It was a practically useful cause, because it provided the justification for purging and intimidating their Whig opponents, who had links to the Dissenters. The Tories promoted Occasional Conformity Bills in 1702, 1703 and 1704, aimed at those who met the legal conditions to hold public office by occasionally taking Anglican holy communion, while regularly worshipping elsewhere. In 1714, through the Schism Act, they aimed at eviscerating the Dissenters' education system. St John promoted these moves – albeit on strictly partisan grounds, for he was an occasional conformist himself. Indeed, as his later works show, he was a Deist rather than an orthodox Christian of any variety.

The Tories also settled upon a distinctive view of foreign policy. This was to support in principle the wars against France – with extreme reluctance in the case of the Tory backbench squires, who bore the burden of the hated land tax levied to pay for them. But they would advocate, instead of the land-based, continental campaigning favoured by the Whigs, a less expensive and, it was hoped, more commercially profitable maritime strategy.

For a time, St John made himself indispensable. But in the end his plans collapsed, and the Tory Party's fortunes with them. It was partly bad luck. Anne remained childless. The succession of the Hanoverians, which proved impossible to prevent, was bound to renew in an acute form the problems of allegiance which the Tories had experienced in the wake of the earlier Glorious Revolution.

Hardly less important were St John's own misjudgements. He manoeuvred to keep out George I. When that failed, he sought a return to influence, which also failed. He then fled to join the Old Pretender. But, in remarkably short order, he abandoned the Jacobite cause too. These serpentine tactics so damaged his reputation and tainted that of his followers that they prevented serious rehabilitation, let alone a return to power.

Bolingbroke is a recognizable Tory type, a rightist *frondeur* of great brilliance and no ballast. An unlikely Tory leader and, despite his eminence, an improbable member of the Tory Party pantheon, his claims to greatness have been asserted.[10] In his 'Vindication of the English Constitution' (1835), Disraeli would portray Bolingbroke as central to a Tory movement, itself synonymous with 'the English nation', engaged in an apocalyptic struggle with the Whigs – the 'anti-national party', led by 'Venetian Magnificoes' bent on imposing their oligarchic interests.[11]

More significant, however, coming from a nearer contemporary, are Edmund Burke's views of Bolingbroke; and they are wholly negative. Burke's first book, *A Vindication of Natural Society* (1756), was indeed an anonymous, tongue-in-cheek send-up of Bolingbroke's opinions about the merits of 'natural' (i.e. non-doctrinal) religion. In his book, Burke defends orthodox religious truth by showing what would be the disorderly consequences of extending Bolingbroke's philosophical approach to political and social institutions. Even in later life, when concerned with

15

altogether different questions, Burke's scorn remained: 'Who now reads Bolingbroke, who ever read him through?', he asks in the *Reflections*.[12] The best that can be said of St John, and it is not much, is that he was a nostalgic, 'reactive conservative', whose reaction got him, and his party, nowhere.[13]

Toryism survived Bolingbroke. The Tory Party even survived George I and George II. But it did so as a depleted and marginalized body of opinion. It had an often vocal body of parliamentary support. But it could never be the party of government, which under the first two Hanoverian monarchs was securely in the hands of the Whigs. Above all, Toryism now represented the creed of the Country against the Court, the 'outs' against the 'ins', the squires against the moneyed men and the metropolis. It was as near a creed of perpetual, and thus hopeless, opposition as can be imagined. Significantly, it finds its most notable representative not in a real politician but in a comic anti-politician, Squire Western, created by Henry Fielding in *Tom Jones*. The Squire's Tory prejudices and limited intellectual accomplishments are perfectly clear in, for example, the following exchange of insults with his Whig-sympathizing sister:

> 'Sister,' cries the Squire, 'I have often warned you not to talk the court gibberish to me. I tell you I don't understand the lingo: but I can read a journal, or the London Evening Post. Perhaps, indeed, there may be now and tan a verse which I can't make much of, because half the letters are left out; yet I know very well what is meant by that, and that our affairs don't go so well as they should do because of bribery and corruption'. – 'I pity your country ignorance from my heart', cries the lady. 'Do you?' answered Western; 'and I pity your town learning; I had rather be anything than a courtier, and a Presbyterian, and a Hanoverian too, as some people, I believe are.'[14]

Even so, Tory attitudes were in the first half of the eighteenth century not so much the exclusive preserve of the uneducated as of the powerless. So even clever Tories had to be cautious, if their Toryism was not to destroy their prospects; and no Tory was ever cleverer than Samuel Johnson. The Doctor's timeless Tory mindset is recognizable from his quips at the expense of fashionable opinion, his gloomy piety, his black humour. His Toryism was sincere; it fully corresponded to the creed's requirements; and it accurately reflected the incremental changes taking place in Tory outlook. Johnson, while rejecting royal Divine Right, was a passionate believer in royal hereditary right. He was in private a Non-Juror, refusing any office that required the oath to the Hanoverians. But, like other Tories, from the 1760s he became increasingly committed to the ruling dynasty. He rallied to George III, vigorously defending in speech and print the royal prerogative and the policies associated with its exercise.[15]

Johnson's friendship with and admiration for the Whig Burke illustrate the degree to which, even before the French Revolution, party labels failed adequately to sum up political attitudes. In particular, the Whigs were so ubiquitous in politics at this period that Whiggism was an inadequate definition of a man's political persuasions. As Sir Lewis Namier demonstrated – though his conclusions have since been qualified and contested – party affiliation was not the only, or even in many cases the principal, driver of political action. The web of personal and local interests and connections was often more important, though the precise balance between ideology and interest differed at different times.[16]

What is beyond doubt is that as the reign of George III progressed, the stasis that had characterized politics under the first two Hanoverians cracked and splintered. The lack of any strong party opposition – in this case, any Tory opposition – encouraged the growth of factionalism among the governing élite – in this case, the Whigs. One Whig faction, grouped around the Marquess of

Rockingham, broke off altogether and went into opposition. This faction, through the political imagination and inspired polemic of Rockingham's secretary, adviser and agent, Edmund Burke, then began to evolve into something like a political party.

Burke's ideas about the purpose of party, contained in his *Thoughts on the Cause of the Present Discontents* (1770), have about them a time-less quality: 'Party is a body of men united for promoting by their joint endeavours the national interest upon some particular principle in which they are all agreed.'[17] And his moral defence of political com-bination is equally memorable: 'When bad men combine, the good must associate; else they will fall, one by one, an unpitied sacrifice in a contemptible struggle.'[18] But one must recall that Burke writes self-consciously as a Whig, looking back to the 'Old Whigs' of Queen Anne's reign; that he does not suggest that any particular party, even Rockingham's, should have a permanent existence; and that his purpose in writing is essentially defensive. The *Thoughts* are framed as an answer to those (notably the 'King's Friends' and, on occasion, the Elder Pitt) who denounced all factions and demanded government based on 'Men not Measures'.

The Rockingham Whigs regarded their distinctive purpose as the resistance to and the reduction of royal influence on government. But they soon found themselves defined by something quite differ-ent, namely their opposition to the American War. This was for some years a very unpatriotic and unpopular stance. But when the war was finally lost, and America with it, and when Lord North's Government duly fell, Rockingham was called by the King to form his (second) ministry.[19] This was an uneasy, fragile affair – and then Rockingham himself suddenly died. After restlessly under-mining Rockingham's successors, George III finally took the momentous gamble of entrusting his political fortunes to the Younger Pitt. Pitt then successfully defended his minority Government in the Commons and sealed his authority by triumph-ing in the following year's general election.[20]

These events of 1783–4, whose full significance no one at the time could properly judge, represent one of the markers from which historians sometimes date the beginning of the new Tory (or even the future Conservative) Party. In Victorian times such an assertion was, indeed, commonplace.[21] In truth, the thesis as it stands is not convincing, and few modern commentators would defend it. But that said, the establishment around Pitt of a body of men who would hold the political ground that any future Conservative Government would 'naturally' claim to hold is of great significance. The Pittites – if not Pitt himself – have a good claim to be considered proto-Tories of the new school that would, in time, evolve into the Conservatives.

Pitt himself was not a Tory. He was a Whig. In some respects he was, indeed, a more liberal Whig than his great Whig opponent, Charles James Fox. But Pitt had also shown what any Tory, before or later, would recognize as a distinctively Tory sense of duty (as well as an entirely human opportunism) in answering the King's summons to serve. The belief that the King's business must be done, whatever personal or political interest demanded, provided one significant mark of continuity between early and later Tories and, indeed, between both and the Conservatives.

Two further factors had, however, to be brought to bear before Pitt's new ministry could form the nucleus of a Tory movement. The first was simply its longevity. Time and the exercise of office and patronage worked in favour of the creation of a recognizable party as the basis of Pitt's Government. As the years passed, and successive crises were overcome, Pitt grew in stature and authority, and – despite the manner in which he had first been called into office – his and his colleagues' standing depended less on the will and whims of the King.

The second and more important factor in the creation of a new political paradigm was the French Revolution. The year 1783 has no great importance in the realm of political ideas. The same cannot be said of 1789. In the early 1790s the British political class, animated largely by Burke, became polarized on new lines determined, at least initially, according to views of events in France.[22] Among the manifestations of this reconfiguration was a split, at first tacit but later formal, in the ranks of the Whigs. Those conservative-minded Whigs gathered around the Duke of Portland and other magnates who in 1794 joined the administration have even been seen as 'the real nucleus of the Tory Party'.[23]

Burke's concerns were never just or even primarily with what was happening in foreign parts. He was horrified by what he saw in France because he believed that the ideas and attitudes generated there found an echo in and posed a threat to Britain. Despite his evocation of the sufferings of the French royal family (in one of his less well-received passages) and his excoriation of the French mob, the main targets of criticisms in his *Reflections on the Revolution in France* (1790) were home-grown British troublemakers. These were the fellow-travelling, radical liberal, Dissenting critics of the British constitution, of the Anglican Church, and of the country's wider social and economic system.[24]

In any history of conservative thought – and not just English conservative thought – Burke must hold pride of place. Not, of course, that even now Burke considered himself a Tory, or that his friend Johnson would have thought him one.[25] On the face of it, his association with the long campaign to reduce Crown influence and his support for the claims of the American colonists are proof positive of his Whig credentials. Yet, while true as regards labels, that conclusion misleads, for Burke's was an intensely conservative mind from the outset.

Even during his first, 'liberal', pre-Revolution period, he was more often than not to be found arguing in terms that are strikingly conservative, even reactionary. This is not to say that his liberalism was a sham. He would not have argued for religious and even (limited) sexual tolerance had it been so. But he always thought liberty could go too far. He was a critic of atheism and Deism and an outspoken supporter of the Church of England. He opposed shorter, more frequent parliaments, which radicals wanted, because he feared that they would lead to more corruption and demagogy. He was, indeed, hated by the radicals long before the French Revolution. He went out of his way to court unpopularity by rejecting the populist notion of the 'mandate', and gave to his Bristol constituents the fullest and earliest expression of the classic doctrine of parliamentary representation, by which 'your Representative owes you, not his industry only, but his judgement; and he betrays instead of serving you if he sacrifices it to your opinion'.[26]

The most effective exponents of conservative politics have often been outsiders. Burke was an outsider's outsider. Namier describes him as a 'solitary, rootless man who preached party; and a party politician with such a minority mind that (however much he denied it) he relished being in opposition'.[27] Such paradoxical people are apt either to pass into oblivion or else, borne along by events, to create a revolution – in Burke's case, a counter-revolution. Despised as an Irish adventurer, suspected (wrongly) of being a covert Catholic – hostile cartoonists portrayed him as a Jesuit – never losing his accent, surrounded by suspect friends and family, usually in debt, Burke is, on one reading, a supremely unlikely defender of the ancient constitutional and social order of England. So marked is the anomaly that some have suspected, then and since, that in his conservatism he was merely playing a tune composed by his aristocratic paymasters. But while Burke almost always needed money, he was not venal; and his patrons were anyway too idle and untalented to dictate his opinions or construct his reasoning. Burke was able to understand, justify and defend Britain's aristocratic system precisely because he came from outside it. He had the intuitions and insights of the parvenu. Being Irish was part of this. Burke understood France because he had witnessed the fragility of order in Ireland. He believed what complacent Englishmen could not imagine: that 'it could happen here'. He was conscious that civilization was founded upon restraints, assumptions, conventions, rules and habits that are the work of centuries, but can be discredited or destroyed in a fit of absence of mind. So while Burke was in favour of justice he was hostile to levelling. He was sometimes privately critical of the aristocracy, but his criticism was not that they were overbearing, over-mighty or over-privileged; it was that they were so often feckless and idle, more interested in the Turf than in Parliament. They should, he thought, have been more attentive to their duty. Vigour, he felt, not constitutional reforms or innovations, was what was required in coping with the domestic agitation of radicals. Above all, it was required in fighting the war with France – a war that Burke increasingly saw as an apocalyptic struggle, with the forces of evil unleashed against European and Christian civilization.

Burke never thought that he had abandoned the Whigs. He thought that they had abandoned him – though he had to stretch some points to prove the argument.[28] Unlike his reactionary counterparts in Europe, and unlike the eighteenth-century Tories, his starting point was a limited monarchy, a strong Parliament and the rule of law – in English historical terms, the constitutional settlement of 1688 and the political, social and economic settlement based on it. He could not have become a conservative prophet, in the circumstances of the time, if he had not started out a Whig.

Pitt used Burke, but he did not in these matters agree with him. Like Fox, Pitt did not think that French ideas, as opposed to French armies, were a threat to Britain. He was constantly hopeful that an accommodation with France could be made – and constantly disappointed, while Burke's gloomy predictions proved correct. Pitt adopted anti-Revolution rhetoric when it was expected and expedient. But privately he spoke scornfully of Burke's denunciations of Revolutionary ideas, dismissing his final *Letters on a Regicide Peace* (1796) as 'rhapsodies in which there is much to admire and nothing to agree with'.[29]

It was the memory of Pitt, not Burke, that the Tories chose later to exalt. Burke's disciple William Windham was disgusted at the way in which not just Whigs but Pittites shied away from honouring his mentor's contribution to the national struggle against Revolutionary France. The desire to glorify Pitt would lead Tories into absurd attempts to re-invent him, not least as a committed Christian.[30] Yet it was Burke's mind, not Pitt's, that wrestled with the larger questions that have since faced conservatives (and often Conservatives). How to cope with profound challenges to social stability? How to defeat not just a hostile power but a hostile ideology, above all when both are combined in the form of what Burke called 'an armed doctrine'?[31] How to secure people's allegiance to the state? How to justify, above and beyond utilitarian argument, the sacrifices and inconveniences required of those living at the bottom of the social pile, in order to sustain an uncomfortable and imperfect world? His answers to these and other dilemmas can be compressed into eight interdependent propositions:

Always respect 'prescription' – that is, the presumption in favour of arrangements, institutions and attitudes that have stood the test of time. Avoid change – particularly constitutional change – unless it is strictly necessary, and then reform piecemeal, in ways that conform to the spirit and tradition of existing practice. Hold to the principle of inheritance, in both politics and society, as a means of entrenching institutions. Always defend property, for it is the basis of ordered liberty and prosperity. Suspect 'abstract' thinking, meaning all attempts to make the world conform to idealistic, utopian notions of perfect justice, based on the coercive application of, for example, natural rights. Prefer to rely on what Burke called 'prejudice' – a term now irretrievably tainted, but by which he meant recourse to the accumulated, pre-rational wisdom absorbed through tradition and manifesting itself as instinct.[32] Nurture and respect the organic links between the practical circumstances – the 'little platoon' – in which a man finds himself, and the greater national and international entities.[33] Finally, remember that man is by instinct a religious animal, and do not forget that any true religion needs to be organized around a hierarchy and an identifiable body of doctrine.[34]

Certain aspects of Burke's thesis (as of his language) have weathered better than others. In some cases, as with the application of his thinking about the Revolution to the threat of Soviet communism in the Cold War, Burkean principles were invoked for their own (legitimate but distinct) purposes by later conservatives.[35] In others, as with the emphasis on the rights of property, economists have radically developed what Burke just touched upon.[36] Burke's arguments for convention – 'Manners are of more importance than laws. Upon them in a great measure the laws depend' – have been taken to heart by most politicians on the cultural and social right.[37]

By contrast, Burke's arguments in favour of constitutional immobility, which were adopted by his and Pitt's successors, proved within a few decades to be a blind alley – one that would lead the early, and by now self-styled, Tories into a major and nearly fatal smash-up. Burke did not, it is true, rule out absolutely and for ever all constitutional change. In a passage sometimes quoted out of context he even writes: 'A state without the means of some change is without the means of its conservation. Without such means it might even risk the loss of that part of the constitution which it wished the most religiously to preserve.'[38] But this is nothing more than an ad hoc defence of the Glorious Revolution, which Burke also does his best to represent as a minor deviation rather than a new turning. His arguments, from a High Whig perspective – one which would later be adopted by Tories, while the Whigs abandoned it – were framed in terms which ruled out even modified democracy. What mattered was property (with property serving, in Burke's view, as a proxy for 'virtue and wisdom, actual or presumptive') not numbers; not the opinions of what he once imprudently described as the 'swinish multitude'.[39] In fact, he would have preferred a more limited, not a larger, electorate than that represented in the unreformed British Parliament.[40]

In practice, argument about electoral or any other institutional reform was long overshadowed by the war with France. Even when the threat of imported revolution diminished, the pressures and dangers of the war itself kept the authorities uneasy and the propertied classes frightened. Order was, in these circumstances, the priority. From 1792 a series of repressive measures was introduced, habeas corpus suspended, seditious writings banned, treason trials launched.[41] One can argue – and historians continue to do so – that the threat of revolution in Britain was exaggerated to excuse an authoritarian crackdown. The fact remains that rather few articulately opposed repression, and those few found themselves highly unpopular. In such an atmosphere, alterations to the existing franchise seemed to represent subversion of the constitution. Burke had urged Englishmen to 'approach the faults of the state as to the wounds of a father, with pious awe and trembling solicitude'.[42] Pitt now agreed. Once a strong supporter of reform, he became its opponent.

Parliamentary reform would return, with a vengeance, to the centre of British politics. In the meantime, though, it was the Catholic question that was more pressing. The reason why had nothing to do with the inherent justice of the cause and everything with the need to maintain British rule in Ireland, where it was faced with conspiracies, disorders, a major revolt and the threat of French intervention. On the question of shelving parliamentary reform, Pitt and his Tory successors in government were broadly united. On the question of Catholic 'emancipation', however, they were split.

Pitt had regarded emancipation, that is, the removal of the legal disabilities that burdened Catholics and prevented their sitting in Parliament or holding government office, as an essential part of his

plan to bind Ireland closer to England.[43] The 1800 Act of Union –
a reaction to the dangerous Irish uprising of 1798 – had abolished
the separate Irish Parliament; full enfranchisement of the Catholics
(constituting three-quarters of the Irish population) might sugar
that bitter pill. In the absence of such a move, the Anglo-Irish
Protestant Ascendancy's situation looked still more vulnerable. For
the ruling families, the temptation to spend their time and employ
their talents in England, rather than at home in Ireland, would only
increase, while the frustrations of the Catholic majority were not
appeased but inflamed. Meanwhile, the black legend of London's
historic perfidy would become yet more deeply entrenched,
poisoning future generations.[44]

In the event, George III refused to accept emancipation, and Pitt
resigned. There followed an uneasy truce on the matter among
Pitt's successors, which would be preserved with increasing
difficulty as time went by.

Pitt's departure in 1801 (he would return to form a ministry, but
only briefly, from 1804 to 1806) provides a suitable point at which
to consider how far the new political entity that had grown up
under his and Burke's shadow had taken definite shape. Did an
identifiable Tory Party now exist? The answer is that it did, but not
in the manner in which it had formerly done, or would do in the
future.

Although nomenclature lagged behind substance, it is significant
that the Pittites, by the first decades of the nineteenth century, had
ceased to call themselves Whigs. As late as 1812, it is true, Lord
Liverpool was to be found assuring the Prince Regent that his new
ministry had been formed on 'Whig principles'. But this was a
defensive and, indeed, disingenuous declaration. Well before then,
the Opposition, that is the successors of Fox and associates of
Grenville, had acquired an effective monopoly of that term.
Independent MPs and some commentators had already begun
calling the Pittites 'Tories'.

That said, some Tories were more Tory than others. Views of the Catholic question were the main measure applied. The term was most likely to be used to refer to what were also known as Ultra-Tories – hard-line, irreconcilable Protestants, mainly but not exclusively to be found in the Lords and on the Government's back benches, who regarded the challenge to the Protestant settlement of 1688 as tantamount to a threat to the state itself. (There was a certain historical irony involved in this, since the old Tories had been High Church and more indulgent towards Catholicism than to Dissent.)[45]

So there was, by this time at least, a definable sense of what being Tory meant – or, above all, what it did not mean, since in political life enemies are usually more obvious than friends. Quite where Toryism began and ended, though, was debatable, and this uncertainty reflected two further circumstances.

First, there was until the very eve of the Great Reform Bill no distinctive, separate Tory party organization. There were local political clubs. There was also a network of local interests in constituencies, where power was exercised by patrons of varying political views, or of none at all. The decisive national influence, however, was that exercised through the control possessed by the Government of the day of preferment to offices, salaries and pensions. Consequently, governments in this unreformed system did not, as a rule, lose elections. They were made, unmade and remade at Westminster. Those decisions were then ratified, with different degrees of enthusiasm reflected in differently sized majorities, by a highly unrepresentative electorate.

During the first decades of the nineteenth century, the extent of this disposable Crown patronage shrank. This partly reflected the general reduction in the personal influence of the monarch in politics – George III being in later life usually mad, George IV (the former Prince Regent) irresponsible and addicted to laudanum, and William IV eccentric and politically incompetent. But the change also reflected specific reforms effected, under outside pressure, to make government less corrupt and more efficient. For example, the secret service money (under Treasury control), which in the eighteenth century had been liberally spent to influence elections, was left untouched by Lord Liverpool. Some positions in the Treasury, the Customs and the Church were also becoming depoliticized. One immediate result of this trend was that it was harder to exert discipline over one's supporters in the House of Commons – as Liverpool found to his embarrassment. More power duly fell to groups and personal connections and, more generally, to independent-minded backbenchers. This fluidity could not and did not last. But it now opened a space for more modern parties to develop. These would in due course provide a new basis of orderly government (and opposition) – but not yet.[46]

The second reason why the Tory party was easier for people at this time to perceive than to delimit was that its loose tribal loyalties were made looser still by ideological and personal difference. 'Liberal Toryism' as a concept is a slippery expression and one subject to somewhat different definitions. But it remains an indispensable (and contemporaneously used) description of a particular viewpoint. It increasingly prevailed under Liverpool's Government. It then defined but destroyed Canning's. And then, in an altered form and many years later, it became the mark of Peel's second ministry – before helping to wreck the Tory Party, still more catastrophically, on the reef of the Corn Laws.

Liberal Toryism was characterized less by a desire to remove specific injustice (though not every Tory's heart was hard, and an evangelical conscience was at work) than by a wish to establish the affairs of the nation on those liberal principles that were assumed to lead to prosperity and stability. Its proponents had been influenced, directly or at variable removes, by the economic writings of Adam Smith and David Ricardo. They accepted that minimal intervention by the state in the economy and society was the most prudent and progressive rule to follow. This had its counterpart in foreign affairs, where national self-interest rather than the construction of grand (and, as it happens, illiberal) pan-European systems was taken to be the dominant concern of statesmanship. These approaches reflected, in turn, a powerful intellectual tendency, a 'spirit of the age'. It was not confined to the Tory (or later Conservative) Party. Indeed, it received its classic political exposition from the Tories' opponents.[47] Liberal Toryism, though, was in tone hostile to the optimism and utopianism of otherwise similar views enunciated by radicals. Free market economics, and social policies based on self-help not state-help, were adopted by liberal Tories because they seemed the pragmatic, practical answer to the problems of the day. The main conflicts between leading Tory figures (as opposed to the backwoodsmen and bigots) were about these policies' implementation, not their underlying purpose.[48]

Given the difficulties raised by the need to accommodate modern liberal policies with old illiberal prejudices, the Tory administrations of the period were by no means unsuccessful. Looking back on the period, that well-connected diarist Charles Greville notes that the 'old Tory Ministry . . . was the strongest and longest that we have seen for many years'.[49] In fact, Robert Banks Jenkinson, Lord Liverpool (succeeding to the earldom on the death of his father in 1808), is the longest-serving Prime Minister of the United Kingdom. He has a good claim to have won the war against France under Napoleon, to have secured Britain's interests in the peace, to have resisted successfully (if coercively) major threats to order, and to have laid the grounds for Britain's Victorian prosperity.

But he also had the misfortune to fall foul of Disraeli's polemical talents. In *Coningsby*, which contains a wealth of memorable and misleading political observation, Liverpool appears as 'the arch-mediocrity [who] presided rather than ruled over [a] cabinet of mediocrities':

The arch-mediocrity had himself some glimmering traditions of political science. He was sprung from a laborious stock, had received some training, and though not a statesman, might be classed among those that the Lord Keeper Williams used to call 'statemongers'. In a subordinate position his meagre diligence and his frigid method might not have been without value; but the qualities that he possessed were misplaced; nor can any character be conceived less invested with the happy properties of a leader. In the conduct of public affairs his disposition was exactly the reverse of that which is the characteristic of great men. He was peremptory in little questions, and great ones he left open.[50]

Jenkinson had, indeed, a shambling appearance, an unimpressive manner, uneven health, a habit of worrying and a disconcerting inclination to weep. (Having said which, a tendency to the lachrymose was not uncommon at this time. Canning's successor, Goderich, wept copiously in 1827, as he told the King that he had been unable to form a government; George IV dismissed him as a 'blubbering fool'.)[51] In any case, though more obviously substantial than Goderich, 'Jenky', as Liverpool was known, was not at all Disraeli's (or perhaps anyone's) idea of a charismatic leader. Yet he was not by any means a nonentity either. His best biographer describes him as 'a great conservative statesman'.[52] But perhaps Canning summed him up most tellingly: 'not either a ninny – or a great and able man'.[53] Liverpool had a fierce hatred of Revolutionary principles, inspired by an early visit to France. His competence earned the respect of Pitt, whom he devotedly followed and whose legacy he strove to continue. After Pitt's death, he proved himself, under Spencer Perceval, an excellent Secretary for War in support of Wellington's Peninsular campaign. And it was in large part because of a well-merited reputation for effectiveness that he unexpectedly, and hesitantly, succeeded Perceval as Prime Minister, on the latter's assassination by a madman at Westminster in 1812.

The early years of the new administration were primarily taken up with foreign affairs. As Prime Minister, Liverpool supported Castlereagh's prudent and effective conduct of policy in the last stages of the war and at the Congress of Vienna. But with peace, as often happens, domestic political difficulties multiplied and the common will to confront them evaporated. There was a sharp economic downturn. Widespread social and political disturbance culminated in the so-called Peterloo Massacre at Manchester in August 1819, which was met by the notorious Six Acts aimed at repressing potentially seditious activity.[54]

The facts that his preferred style as Prime Minister was that of a chairman rather than a commander, and that he sat in the Lords (as he had done, indeed, since 1803), meant that Liverpool's policies were usually enacted by and attributed to others.[55] In some respects, his Toryism can hardly be described as 'liberal' at all. For example, he opposed abolition of the slave trade and was hostile to Catholic emancipation. He was, though, a strong free trader and a rigorous 'monetarist' a century and a half before that term was current. With Peel, he pressed through in 1819 the policy of a return to 'cash payments', that is, the return to a gold standard for sterling. The same prudent financial and liberal economic views would have led him, had he not been frustrated by Parliament, to keep the income tax (which was ended by the Commons in 1816) and to preserve free trade in grain (which was lost with the introduction of the Corn Law in the previous year). Liverpool did, though, insist on a break with profligacy. He demanded budget surpluses, ending the ruinous build-up of debt. While it is not true that Liverpool's later ministerial changes marked the beginning of liberal Toryism, they undoubtedly accelerated it. In 1822 Frederick 'Prosperity' Robinson (the later lachrymose Viscount Goderich) became a popular, if incompetent, Chancellor of the Exchequer, and William Huskisson became an unpopular, but brilliant, President of the Board of Trade. And Canning became Foreign Secretary.

Of these later ministerial changes made by Liverpool, it was Canning's assumption of the Foreign Secretaryship (on Castlereagh's suicide) that had the greatest impact on the Tory Party and on politics. Canning's personality and career exercised a unique fascination upon his contemporaries, and though his practical achievements were few he remained for future generations of Tories (and not just Tories) by far the most exciting politician of his time.[56] In some respects, his rise to the top prefigures that of Disraeli, the ultimate Tory outsider. Canning was a commoner – the only untitled politician to be Foreign Secretary until Ramsay MacDonald. His background was (relatively) impoverished. He was of Anglo-Irish Protestant stock, but without useful Irish connections. He was the son of an actress, which the snobbish Whig (and future Prime Minister) Earl Grey publicly declared should have been quite sufficient to prevent Canning becoming Prime Minister. He rose initially because Pitt favoured him, but later because he was simply the best debater and public speaker of his day. So great was his talent in the House of Commons that even his critics could not deny it, or his colleagues overlook it. His enemy Wellington conceded that Canning 'was the finest speaker he had ever heard'.[57]

Canning was also an inspired polemicist, the first (and for long one of the few) in the Tory camp who understood the need to use the press, pamphlets, speeches and – a complete shock to the world of diplomacy – published diplomatic dispatches to rally opinion. In October 1797 Canning had founded, with Pitt's encouragement, a short-lived but highly effective weekly paper entitled the *Anti-Jacobin*, designed to attack 'French', liberal ideas. Twelve years later, in 1809, he was connected with the foundation of the most important and influential Tory/Conservative journal ever produced: the *Quarterly Review*, launched in answer to the Whig *Edinburgh Review* (1802). The *Quarterly Review*'s success represented a striking confirmation of Canning's conviction that the

Tories should fight for public opinion – which he described in a speech in Liverpool in 1822 as similar in its dynamic effects to the power of steam.[58]

Canning's political verse constitutes a powerful indictment of a particular kind of liberal mind. On the sort who bends over backwards to excuse the enemy's action, while 'candidly' admitting the faults of his own side, Canning wrote:

> Too nice to praise by wholesale, or to blame,
> Convinced that all men's motives are the same;
> And finds, with keen discriminating sight,
> Black's not so black; – nor white so very white.
> . . .
> Give me th'avow'd, th'erect, the manly foe;
> Bold I can meet – perhaps may turn his blow;
> But of all plagues, good Heav'n, thy wrath can send,
> Save, save, oh! save me from the Candid Friend!

And on self-righteous internationalism:

> Through th'extended globe his feelings run
> As broad and general as th'unbounded sun!
> No narrow bigot he; his reason'd view
> Thy interests, England, ranks with thine, Peru!
> France at our doors, he sees no danger nigh,
> But heaves for Turkey's woes the impartial sigh;
> A steady patriot of the world alone,
> The friend of every country – but his own.[59]

To the end of his life, Canning gathered around him an identifiable group of personal and political friends. But he also had a rare gift for making enemies. People disliked him for the usual reasons – because he was clever, witty, good-looking, eloquent, too aware of his abilities and unwilling to conceal them, low-born and, above all, indefinably but unmistakably flashy. He greatly enjoyed annoying important people. He shocked George IV by offering to form a ministry without first being asked. He wrote an insulting letter to Wellington, whom he needed at the time to join his Government. He told funny, wounding stories. But among his many foes pride of place went to Robert Stewart, Viscount Castlereagh.

The modern consensus is that Castlereagh was unfairly vilified by his contemporaries and underrated by the older historians.[60] The consensus is probably correct, but it is still true that in terms of the history of the Conservative Party Castlereagh really figures only as Canning's foil. Although Canning, too, was Irish by birth, he had no lasting connection with the place. By contrast, Castlereagh's political role in Ireland was crucial to his later career. It was he who, as Acting Chief Secretary, was instrumental in (and later blamed for) the crushing of resistance in 1798 and later in using mass bribery and corruption to induce the Irish Parliament to abolish itself – for which he was also heavily blamed. In all this, he was doing Pitt's bidding. Unlike Canning, who had cheekily sought out Pitt to get into the House of Commons, Castlereagh had been sought out by Pitt, because the Government needed him to help govern Ireland. Also unlike Canning (and like Jenkinson), Castlereagh followed Pitt's urging and did not go into opposition after Pitt's resignation in 1801. Castlereagh was then made President of the Board of Control (with responsibility for India). This aroused the envy of Canning, who was at this point unsuccessfully urging on Pitt a direct challenge to the Government, and even fighting an unauthorized campaign on Pitt's behalf. When Pitt did, briefly, return to power, Castlereagh began his first spell as Secretary for War. Canning meanwhile received the junior post of Treasurer of the Navy.

After a spell out of office, during the chaotic 'Government of All the Talents', both Castlereagh and Canning came back under the

Duke of Portland in 1807. Castlereagh resumed his duties at the War Office, while Canning received the prize of Foreign Secretary. The still greater prize of leader in the Commons – 'Leader of the House'– though, was given to Spencer Perceval. The significance of that post was that when the Prime Minister, as now, was a peer, the Leader answered for the Government as a whole in the Commons. Both Castlereagh and Canning wanted the job. On grounds of common sense, neither should have had it – Castlereagh because he was one of the worst speakers on the front bench, Canning because, despite his brilliance in debate, he had work enough to do in directing foreign policy.

The Portland administration endured increasing difficulties: Portland was ill; the Peninsular War was going badly. Canning convinced himself that the war effort was failing because of Castlereagh's incompetence and threatened to resign if Castlereagh were not moved. Portland agreed to move him. But through weakness and confusion nobody actually informed Castlereagh. The mess was then compounded by the disastrous Walcheren expedition, for which Castlereagh was heavily blamed.[61] Portland's health collapsed completely. Canning resigned. Castlereagh belatedly learned of what he insisted on considering a plot and of Canning's role in it, and he too resigned. And while the war effort stumbled, and the Government sank into confusion, Castlereagh challenged Canning to a duel and shot him in the leg on Putney Heath. Opinion quickly hardened against Canning. A more measured judgement, however, is that Castlereagh's reaction was so extreme as to cast doubt on his mental health – a suspicion which his later horrible end and the speculations of the modern medical profession render all the more plausible.[62]

Three years after the duel, however, Castlereagh was back in the Government, now as Foreign Secretary, and soon to combine the post with Leader of the House in the wake of Perceval's assassination. Canning had tried to stop the appointment. He had answered Liverpool's invitation to rejoin the Government by demanding that he should be not just Foreign Secretary – which Castlereagh was prepared to yield – but Leader – which he was not. Canning had overreached himself. For the next decade it was Castlereagh, not Canning, who was the main public face of the Government.

Not that it burnished his reputation at home. Castlereagh was blamed for the repression of dissent after Peterloo, though it was not he who designed the legislation or enforced it. He was also criticized for supporting the European Congress system after 1815, which in the eyes of the British Government was aimed at ensuring stability, but which was designed by the Holy Alliance powers (Russia, Austria and Prussia) to crush liberal and national movements. In fact, Castlereagh was pursuing a pragmatic not an ideological line, and by the time of his death had begun distancing Britain from the other powers. Castlereagh's own state paper of 1820 was, indeed, the basis upon which his successor, Canning, claimed to conduct policy.[63]

The facts, though, could not compete with perceptions. Castlereagh was a politician whom ordinary people loved to hate. When a grandee's windows were to be broken by the mob, they somehow had to be Castlereagh's.[64] To radicals and even to moderate liberals, Castlereagh was irredeemable. When he committed suicide by cutting his throat, having convinced himself that he was facing exposure by a male transvestite prostitute, there was little public sympathy. Mrs Arbuthnot, Wellington's intimate confidante, wept for the loss of a 'dear and valued friend'.[65] But Greville found that people he met in London 'assumed an air of melancholy, a *visage de circonstance* ... they did not care; indeed if they felt at all, it was probably rather satisfaction at an event happening than sorrow for the death of the person'.[66] Others did not limit themselves to hypocrisy. Byron's indecent verse written on hearing the suicide is more often quoted than anything that Castlereagh himself ever said:

So he has cut his throat at last! He? Who?
The man who cut his country's long ago.[67]

Castlereagh's death in 1822 opened the way for Canning's return as Foreign Secretary and, finally, Leader of the House.[68] For the next five years he used his political imagination and powers of communication to reshape Toryism. One can argue that this was mainly a matter of style, not substance. But in high politics, style – if sufficiently distinctive – can sometimes constitute substance, and Canning's did. His decision to fight an urban parliamentary seat in Liverpool in 1812, itself a bold decision for a Tory, was a sign not only of his self-confidence but of the potential for Tories to reach out to urban middle-class support. The Whigs were shaken by what they described as 'The Triumph of the Tories'. Like so much in Canning's career, his Liverpool campaigns – he held the seat for a decade before moving to a less demanding one – were devoid of practical long-term effect. But they showed that a new style of politics, incorporating vigorous campaigning, was open to Tories, even while they defended – as did Canning – the merits of an un-reformed constitution.

Canning also brought, along with formidable intellectual range, his new and aggressive rhetorical style to the Foreign Office.[69] This robust populism would later be abandoned by the Tories, but triumphantly practised by the Whig (and ex-Canningite) Palmerston, before being dusted down, drained of its liberalism and repainted in the colours of romantic imperialism by Disraeli. (Having said which, Canning's agent in Liverpool was John Gladstone, the father of Disraeli's nemesis, and the connection is important, because W. E. Gladstone always professed admiration for Canning, as the antithesis of Castlereagh.[70] Whether he actually understood his hero is another matter.)

By the end of Liverpool's long ministry, the warning signs were already evident. But they developed into a crisis on his resignation, the consequence of a massive stroke, early in 1827. In April the King asked Canning to form a new ministry. Six members of the old Cabinet (including Wellington and Peel) and thirty-five other holders of government posts refused to serve. Many distrusted Canning personally; some loathed him. Almost to a man, the defectors explained their decision, when they explained it at all, on grounds of Canning's support for Catholic emancipation. This was disingenuous, because Canning officially left the question 'open'. More subtle was Peel's variant that Canning's appointment fundamentally shifted the balance away from the 'Protestants' to the 'Catholics' (by which they meant emancipationists) in the Cabinet. There is, of course, some substance to that charge.[71] But the effect of their action was to advance, not obstruct, the emancipationist cause, since Canning had to rely on his Tory 'Catholic' friends and on a section of the Whigs led by Lansdowne (also 'Catholics') to fill the gaps in his Government. Within four months of forming it, Canning was dead – probably the victim of cancer, but with its effects hastened by standing for two hours in the icy cold at St George's Chapel, Windsor, for the Duke of York's funeral. (The Bishop of Lincoln also died of the ordeal; the Dukes of Wellington and Montrose were left seriously ill.)[72]

Doubtless, too, Canning was a victim of the strains created by the Tory defection. Years later Lord George Bentinck (Canning's nephew and private secretary, and by now leader of the protectionists) would claim that Peel had 'chased and hunted [Canning] to death' over Catholic emancipation.[73] That was a grotesque exaggeration; but Peel and Wellington certainly killed liberal Toryism as Liverpool and Canning had understood it. Significantly, during this crisis, and indeed from now on, the 'Protestants' alone adopted the Tory name.

The nature of the new political alignment that emerged is evident from the diaries of Mrs Arbuthnot. Thus she wrote on 22 March 1827 that 'the King's delay in naming a successor for Lord

Liverpool has been advantageous to the *Tory cause*; it has given them time to reflect upon the consequences of Mr Canning's being placed at the head of affairs'. (In fact, she was over-optimistic there.)[74] A few weeks later, on 1 May, she noted that Canning's invitations to join his Government had 'been refused by Whigs *and Tories*'.[75] And as Canning was at the point of death, she allowed herself to pity him, despite recollection of how 'he has behaved towards *our party*'.[76]

This 'party' can hardly be said to have entertained any sophisticated ideas. But at least it satisfied, in an implicit rather than articulated fashion, Burke's definition of a 'body of men united for promoting by their joint endeavours the national interest upon some particular principle'. The Tories now stood for the Protestant settlement, the Church of England, an unreformed House of Commons, a powerful House of Lords, the royal prerogative and – of increasing importance as the years went by – the landed interest. Most importantly, in practical terms, they stood against whomever and whatever challenged these pillars of state and society.

Canning himself did not last long enough to create a separate new identity with his Whig allies; and after his death all the Canningites, sooner or later, defected. So could Canning have saved the Tories? Possibly not, but he had a better chance of doing so than his successors. Canning was in favour of one liberal cause – Catholic emancipation – but staunchly against the other – parliamentary reform. Tory backwoodsmen opposed both. But if the Tory leaders, notably Wellington and Peel, had overcome their personal feelings, and if Canning himself had lived to argue his case, he might have bought time for the Tories to adjust. Instead, they careered, more or less oblivious, towards the precipice.

Robert Peel

Robert Peel, the first Conservative leader and Prime Minister. His death, after being thrown from his horse in 1850, shocked the nation. But Peel's own party had already cast him aside.

2

PEEL'S PARTY

Goderich's inability to form an administration sufficiently strong to face Parliament meant that the obvious choice of Prime Minister was the Duke of Wellington. When the Duke answered the King's summons, George IV was, as usual, in bed. 'Arthur,' said the King, 'the Cabinet is defunct!' The monarch insisted that the question of Catholic emancipation remain open, that both 'Catholics' and 'Protestants' be included in the ministry, and that Lord Grey, leader of the Whigs, whom he hated, be kept out. Otherwise Wellington had a free hand. The Duke proceeded to exercise it, initially, in a sensible manner.[1] Four long-time supporters of Canning retained the offices they had briefly held under Goderich, including the most able and committed liberal Tory, Huskisson. Peel would be Leader of the House and Home Secretary. The Duke himself was almost exclusively interested in foreign policy, where he sought to reverse Canning's 'liberalism'. But his troubles were to come from quite different directions. These were eminently predictable; but, for various reasons, neither Wellington nor Peel, the two most powerful Tories, was equipped to deal with them.

Wellington has often been seen as unpolitical, and his political mistakes attributed to that fact. But this is so in only a very limited sense. He was, in truth, highly partisan, having a visceral dislike and distrust of the Whigs which influenced his later ministerial choices.[2] He had always, indeed, been a politician. He was a member of the Irish Parliament before he made his name as a soldier. He then showed political skills of a certain kind in getting himself out of scrapes – notably when he was nearly disgraced for signing the Convention of Cintra (1808), which allowed a defeated French army to sail away with their weapons, baggage and booty.[3] He was later shrewd enough to retain the confidence of Secretaries of War while he fought his great campaigns – no easy task. Military life does not, though, encourage the accommodations important in politics, and anyway Wellington, though an inspiring leader, was by nature solitary and by temperament harsh. In later life he seemed more out of touch than he was because he became increasingly deaf, as a result of a howitzer explosion on the parade ground in 1822.[4] But he was never a fool – except, perhaps in his disastrous marriage, which (significantly) he made through jilted pride. And he was not politically naïve.

Wellington's supreme asset in politics was that he was Britain's greatest living hero. His distinction was such that all but the radicals and the mob (and a few Ultras: he even fought a duel with the Earl of Winchilsea) were respectful or at least frightened of him. His greatest deficiency – and a fatal one – was a lack of imagination. He was quick-minded, able to see on most occasions the immediate course to take, but he lacked foresight. Although not dishonest, he thought that, having argued a case ferociously in private and public, he was then perfectly entitled to reverse his position when circumstances required. He could not remotely understand why others thought this culpable.[5]

In the matter of Catholic emancipation, the shoal upon which Canning's administration had been stranded, the Duke's personal and political traits were shown in their worst light. His real views were far removed from what they were publicly believed to be. Like others from the Anglo-Irish ascendancy – Castlereagh, for example – he had always been a pragmatist on the issue, which he saw as determined by the problems of ruling Ireland. By 1825 he had reluctantly decided that Catholic emancipation should be conceded, though with 'safeguards' for the Protestant establishment. He drew up a paper to that effect. It even proposed a concordat with the Pope. But before it could be discussed one of the King's brothers, the Duke of York, delivered a violent denunciation of any compromise on the question. So it was sharply dropped. And Wellington's real views remained private.[6] When, three years later, the Duke became Prime Minister, his public utterances could be, and were, interpreted differently by the different sides. But that spring his Government did not oppose the repeal of the Test and Corporation Acts, which bore on the Dissenters (albeit lightly). Perceptive observers now grasped that the Government's will to resist similar moves in favour of the Catholics had dissolved.

What actually prompted the Duke to bring forward the measure when he did was the outcome of an election in County Clare. It was occasioned by the rule which then obtained that appointment to a place in Government required re-election, in this case, ironically, the re-election of a pro-Catholic. The Irish leader of the Catholic Association, Daniel O'Connell, stood and routed the Government's candidate.[7] This suggested that henceforth no Irish MP could be given office without causing a by-election that the Government of the day would lose. The anomaly whereby Irish Catholics could be electors (as the so-called forty-shilling county freeholders, given a vote by the 1793 Franchise Act), and even candidates – but not MPs, because of the impossibility of their taking the oath, was shown to be not just absurd but unworkable. Wellington felt he must act.

But he had other business to transact first. He was reshaping his ministry. What was probably an innocent mix-up over voting on a matter of electoral reform led Huskisson to offer his resignation. The Duke cheerfully accepted it, upon which the Canningites left en bloc. So, paradoxically, it was a Tory Government purged of its more liberal members that now sought to put through the liberal policy of Catholic emancipation.

The policy was finally announced in February 1829. In the short term, this was good tactics. Ultra-Tory Protestants found it more difficult to attack a ministry of red-blooded Tories than one tainted by allies of Canning. But the wider public impression – one of politicians who had recently and publicly argued against a measure suddenly proposing it – was damaging.

The unreformed Commons, returned by a small and un-representative electorate, was, in religious matters at least, more enlightened than the country as a whole. Anti-Catholic prejudice outside the Westminster élite now fuelled a ferocious popular back-lash. 'Brunswick Clubs' were established which whipped their supporters into fury at the betrayal. (The Elector of Hanover was also Duke of Brunswick – hence the name.) Monster meetings were held. Anglican and Methodist clergy harangued their flocks. The feeling against emancipation was less violent in its expression than in the previous century – there was no parallel to the Gordon Riots of 1780 – but the movement was still politically dangerous. It joined in an odd embrace the lowest with the highest classes, culminating in the Duke of Cumberland's ranting at his brother, the King, demanding he refuse consent to the measure.

In the House of Commons, though, emancipation was bound to pass. Feeling had long been moving in that direction, and practical men with no tenderness towards Catholics thought that the time had come to concede the point. Among these realists was by now Robert Peel.[8] But Peel had his own problems, which would over the coming years become those of the Tory (and then Conservative) Party.

Robert Peel was by instinct a time-server. But these were unpredictable times. He had followed with some distinction the career path expected of him. His father (Sir Robert), having made his money as a manufacturer in printed calico, bought himself a property in Tamworth (Staffordshire) and climbed into a Commons seat in the constituency he now controlled. His son, young Robert, duly followed the same pattern, abandoning his business background to become an MP – and going further, rising to the ranks of Government. He rose fast, because he was hard working, sober and prudent. Byron recalled their time together at Harrow: 'I was always in scrapes, Peel never.'[9] He was also brilliant. He gained the best double first (in Classics and Mathematics) at Oxford in his year, and his memory and analytical ability were remarked on by contemporaries throughout his life.

But as Disraeli tellingly noted, Peel was very shy.[10] He was uneasy, even late in life, when mixing in Court circles.[11] Wellington thought it worse than shyness. He remarked: 'I have no small talk and Peel has no manners.'[12] This gaucheness even extended to table manners.[13]

Peel was prickly, oversensitive, self-obsessed (albeit in a moralistic fashion), sometimes difficult, off-puttingly pompous. He was a superb parliamentarian, though there was something 'a trifle sermonic' (the expression is Bagehot's) about his speeches.[14] He had his whimsical and amusing moments, but not many encountered them.[15] Robert Peel was a loving husband, a good father, and a firm friend – unless you crossed him, in which case (as the Tories' chief propagandist, John Wilson Croker discovered), he was unforgiving.[16] Peel was no philistine. He was a patron of artists, and he acquired a remarkable collection of work, which he kept first in his newly built London house in Whitehall Gardens and then transferred to the opulently furbished pile he constructed on the site of the family house at Drayton.[17] He remained conscious, perhaps over-conscious, of his family's industrial background, describing himself, for example, in a speech in the City of London in 1834 as 'the son of a cotton-spinner'.[18] This was politics, of course, but revealing too. Disraeli's assessment at this point is waspish, but not inaccurate: 'Peel always pût a question and to the last he said "woonderful" and "woonderfully". He guarded his aspirates with immense care. I have known him slip. The correctness was not spontaneous. He had managed his elocution like his temper: neither was originally good.'[19]

In such a politician, with such a personality, an early misjudgement can become the root of an obsession. In Peel's case it was on the Catholic question. He had served as an effective Chief Secretary in Ireland since 1812. He might have concluded – as did others – that some concessions to the majority faith were necessary. But, to the contrary, in 1817 he delivered in the House of Commons such a sweeping, devastating rebuttal of the arguments for emancipation that he was hailed and indeed lionized as an Ultra ('Orange Peel', in O'Connell's expression). Nor did he mind reaping the benefits. In 1818 he was selected to stand for the prestigious Oxford University seat in preference to Canning, and won it.[20] But there was a cost. Peel was publicly associated with what increasingly seemed – and, indeed, was – the wrong side. He was not really an Ultra Protestant, merely a fairly devout and doctrinally uninterested Anglican. In most respects he was a liberal Tory. He was, as has been noted, a sound money man. He was, above all, a reforming Home Secretary, his most famous achievement the advocacy and eventual creation of a civilian police force for London – the forerunner of the Metropolitan Police Force.

Through the 1820s Peel continued to oppose Catholic relief, but with decreasing enthusiasm. The trouble was that at every stage he was bound by his previously asserted opinions, which he felt unable to disavow, finally joining Wellington in pulling the rug from under Canning.

So when Peel and the Duke proposed their own Bill for

emancipation, there was uproar. 'Orange Peel' now went the whole hog, opposing in Cabinet any of the suggested safeguards as unworkable (which, in truth, they were). The only countervailing measures adopted were the suppression of the Irish Catholic Association and a reduction in the size of the Irish electorate, with the introduction of a £10 freehold qualification. The rage caught up with him. In chaotic circumstances, Peel was defeated in his Oxford seat by the Protestants and had ignominiously to be found a seat at Westbury, a notorious 'pocket borough' in the grubby hands of the corrupt Sir Manasseh Lopes. This incident would not be forgotten when the focus shifted to parliamentary reform.[21]

It would certainly not be forgotten by the Tory Ultras. There is a tendency to regard the opponents of *bien pensant* liberal measures as inevitably and irredeemably stupid. This was – and, incidentally, is – by no means the case. When the Dowager Duchess of Richmond decorated her drawing room with stuffed rats named after Wellington and Peel, she had a point. They had, indeed, ratted. Nor did the Ultras just huff and puff. They mounted an effective, if ultimately futile, press campaign. Their leaders even toyed with supporting parliamentary reform – the Marquess of Blandford advanced a remarkably radical set of proposals – in despair at what had been done by the unreformed House of Commons. This was not mere foolishness. The country was much more Protestant than the political élite. People like the young Cornish backbencher Sir Richard Vyvyan – philosopher, metaphysician and arch-reactionary – who tried to forge a link with the Whigs through Palmerston, were certainly not 'blockheads' (to adopt the current terminology of abuse).[22]

Catholic emancipation rectified a great injustice. But equally, judged by the purpose for which it was enacted – as a way of solving the Irish problem – it was worse than useless. It allowed a large body of Catholic Irish to put their grievances directly in the House of Commons and, in due course, to exert a crucial influence on decisions affecting the rest of the Kingdom, not least parliamentary reform. And when the Ultra Lord Falmouth, defending the Protestant settlement, demanded to know: 'Upon what principle will you talk of preserving the tree of the constitution, when you have laid your axe to the root?' he asked an unanswerable question.[23]

Catholic emancipation split the Tory Party deeply and, as it turned out, fatally. But its legacy would also haunt the Conservative Party that emerged from the Tory wreckage, because of its effect on Peel – both his view of himself and the view that others took of him. Denounced as a traitor to the cause with which he was most publicly linked – the Protestant supremacy – he now alternated between threats of resignation, partial disengagement and endless self-justification. Above all, he was appalled at the prospect of any more public U-turns. So the Tories could not look to the one man who might just possibly have saved them, when the still more dangerous question of parliamentary reform arose.

Catholic emancipation was indeed enacted – but at a high political price. The Bill was opposed in the Commons by 173 supporters of the Government on second reading, and 142 on third. In the Lords, 109 Tories voted against it. These were substantial, determined minorities.

Wellington and his colleagues now suffered two pieces of bad luck. First, there was a sharp economic downturn. For a variety of reasons – structural, cyclical, social – the balance between (and interpretation of) which is disputable – the country in the second quarter of the nineteenth century faced tensions that were summed up by Thomas Carlyle as the 'Condition-of-England Question'.[24] Within this period, 1829–30 was a time of particularly severe recession. The resultant distress manifested itself, for emotional rather than logical reasons, in strident demands for parliamentary reform.

That cause itself had kept rumbling on. Differences over it had led, as noted above, to the departure of Huskisson and his friends.

In fact, hardly any one defended the existing system in its totality any more. Despite the argument of 'virtual representation' advanced by Burke and his successors, it is easy to see why. Acceptance of proprietary politics – the effective ownership of constituencies by wealthy and powerful patrons – was under pressure from public opinion nourished by an active press. Yet the system in the 1820s was frozen into much the same shape as in the 1760s. The anomalies were glaring. For example, Manchester, Birmingham and Leeds (each with a population approaching a million) had no parliamentary representation, while eleven seaboard counties plus Wiltshire contained more than half of all English seats.

The worst abuses, judged by all criteria, were to be found in the boroughs. Nomination or 'pocket' boroughs were controlled by a single individual, using the various means available. It was estimated in 1827 that 276 (out of 658) seats were held by direct nomination. The most notorious cases, though, were the 'rotten' boroughs, where electorates had shrunk over the years almost to extinction. Even the boroughs considered 'open', with a relatively large electorate that allowed some expression of opinion, were not fully so: even here, powerful corporations exercised control over eagerly corruptible electorates.

The English counties as a whole were much more open. Apart from Westmorland, none was controlled by a single magnate, though contests were often avoided by agreement between the main families. The Welsh seats were organized in similar fashion to the English, though more equitably. Scotland was more oligarchic than either. Ireland was, of course, a case apart. The boroughs there were in the hands of the Protestant Anglo-Irish ascendancy, while the counties were now, in practice, dominated by the Catholic Association.[25]

On 23 February 1830, Lord John Russell put forward in the Commons a motion to give representation to Manchester, Birmingham and Leeds. It was defeated by a solid majority. But inside the Government, a more important argument was taking place. The question was whether to endorse a compromise that might allow the Tories to sidetrack plans for comprehensive reform by allowing the seats in those boroughs judged indefensible under the present system to be given to the disfranchised cities, rather than to the counties. Such an approach might have been championed by Canning or, indeed, by any liberal Tory Government. It might have saved the Tories. But, at this eleventh hour, it was rejected by Wellington and Peel.[26]

And it was indeed the eleventh hour – for, in a second piece of bad luck for the Tories, on 26 June George IV died. This meant a general election. It also removed the obstacle created by the late King's refusal to allow Lord Grey, the most respected proponent of reform, to serve as Prime Minister. William IV, whose views, such as they were, can be described as moderate Whig, had no such objections.

As has been noted, governments did not under the unreformed system lose elections. But it was unheard-of for an administration enjoying the confidence of Parliament and the monarch to make no gains at all. This the Tories now achieved. Moreover, they did significantly badly where the contests were most open. It was a warning of the change in public opinion. Approaches were made to try to draw Canningites such as Palmerston and Melbourne into the Government. But their price was too high, and it included reform. Wellington therefore concluded that the best hope was to reunite the Tories by wooing back the Ultras. He would do this with a public pledge to oppose any reform whatsoever of the existing system.[27]

In the Lords, on the night of Tuesday, 2 November 1830, Wellington rose to answer a studiously moderate speech from Grey urging the general case for reform. He began urbanely enough, but then launched into a well-prepared but immoderate attack on the whole idea. The Duke declared:

I am fully convinced that the country possesses at this present moment a legislature which answers all the good purposes of legislation, and this to a greater degree than any legislature ever has answered in any country whatever . . .

I will go further and say that the legislature and the system of representation possess the full and entire confidence of the country . . .

I will go still further and say that if at the present moment I had imposed upon me the duty of forming a legislature for any country, and particularly for a country like this in possession of great property of various . . . descriptions, – I do not mean to assert that I could form such a legislature as we possess now, for the nature of man is incapable of reaching such excellence at once, – but my great endeavour would be to form some description of legislature which would produce the same results . . .

Under these circumstances I am not only not prepared to bring forward any measure of the description alluded to by the noble Lord [i.e. Grey] . . . I am not only not prepared to bring forward any measure of this nature, but I will at once declare that . . . I shall always feel it my duty to resist such measures when proposed by others.

The Duke sat down amid silence, followed by a murmur.

Turning to Aberdeen, the Foreign Secretary, Wellington asked: 'I have not said too much, have I?'

'You'll hear of it,' warned Aberdeen.

As the House emptied, someone arrived and asked what the Duke had said. Aberdeen replied: 'He said that we were going out.'[28]

Despite that gloomy prognosis, the full implications of Wellington's démarche were not generally obvious at the time. The reaction was simply astonishment that he had gone so far. Not everyone was prepared to sink with the ship. The Colonial Secretary, Sir George Murray, dissociated himself in the Commons from the Duke's words. Even Mrs Arbuthnot privately admitted she wished the speech had not been made.[29] But she reflected the Duke's frustrations when she complained in her diary:

> We have a large majority in both Houses, we have the large majority of the nation, the country is prospering, the taxes diminished, trade revived, all Europe looking to us as a reference and as the arbiter in all her quarrels and discussions; and we break down because we have not two or more members of the House of Commons who can speak. It is really vexatious.[30]

Vexatious or not, this analysis was quite unrealistic. Even before there was a vote on Reform, the Tory Government was defeated on a vote on the Civil List, mainly because of Ultra defections. Wellington promptly resigned and Grey was asked to form a ministry. A Government Reform Bill was now inevitable.

Wellington's own view was clear enough. He felt 'that beginning Reform is beginning Revolution'.[31] Certainly, there was Revolution in the air. That July, the last French Bourbon king, Charles X, was overthrown. The Government of his Orléans successor, Louis-Philippe, remained extremely fragile. News from abroad cast a shadow over disturbing events at home. Riots spread through the southern counties of England in August. News of agricultural risings filled the London newspapers. The King was advised not to risk dining at the Guildhall.

After fierce debates, the Reform Bill was carried on second reading in the Commons by just one vote, as a result of the Irish Members' support. But the Government was then defeated on an amendment put forward by the Tory General Gascoyne. This required that the representation of England and Wales not be reduced. It would later resurface and finally become law, and would prove very beneficial to the Conservatives, whose fortunes were dependent on their bedrock support in England. But at this point it precipitated a dissolution, which meant fresh elections – on the old franchise, of course, but in an atmosphere where the Tories were in a dreadful position, and the Whigs and Radicals in the ascendant. The result was predictable. The Tories hung on in some areas, but only where public opinion had least chance of being heard. The Bill returned to the new House and received a second reading by a decisive majority on 7 July 1831. If reform was now to be defeated, it would have to be in the Lords. But this tactic was replete with even more perils, not least for the aristocratic constitution which underpinned Tory power.

On its second reading in their House, on 8 October 1831, the peers threw out the Bill. The country was now plunged into renewed and still more violent ferment. Moderate middle-class reformers in the Political Unions struggled to contain the mob, often unsuccessfully. The worst outbreak was at the end of the month in Bristol. Order in the city entirely collapsed, and by the time troops eventually restored it, hacking down with their sabres the drunken rioters, many of the city's finest buildings were burnt-out shells. The propertied classes peered over the brink. Was this indeed revolution?

One might have imagined that the Tory leaders would at this point have drawn the lesson that a head-on refusal to accept reform risked destroying the very institutions the party existed to protect. One would be wrong. The Whig ministry threatened to seek the creation of sufficient new peers to outvote the Tory majority. The King's known reluctance to agree to this brought the standing of the monarchy, too, into question. Some Tory peers did seek compromise, and were accordingly christened, without affection, the 'Waverers'.[32] But neither Wellington nor Peel saw matters in that light. Peel, when not sulking back at Drayton, was urging the Tory peers not to compromise, though he was also personally resolved not to make lasting common cause with the Ultras. His attitude at this time disquieted those who had to do with him. Mrs Arbuthnot thought him 'supercilious, haughty, arrogant' – hating everybody and being hated in return – but she [i.e. her hero, the Duke] also accepted that it was 'not possible for anyone to lead [in the Commons] except [Peel]'.[33] This was shortly to be confirmed.

The Whig ministry was defeated in committee in the Lords. Grey and the Cabinet announced their intention to resign unless there were a large creation of peers, which the King resisted. So out went the Whigs. But the King also insisted, via his Tory emissary Lord Lyndhurst, that any new Tory ministry must introduce parliamentary reform. Wellington regarded any summons from the monarch to form a ministry as a command, but he could not by any means persuade Peel to accept office on these terms. In the end, in recognition of the absurdity of Wellington heading a pro-reform ministry, and in the absence of Peel, the ministry's putative leadership was given to the Speaker, Charles Manners Sutton. Even before the new Government faced its critics, some members had had enough of this leader-designate, dismissed by Lyndhurst as 'a damned tiresome old bitch'.[34] When it did face the House, on Monday, 14 May 1832, the ministry was simply hooted out of existence. Meanwhile, there was widespread disorder in the country. Even Wellington now recognized that the game was up, and the King was informed. Grey was summoned and returned to office, with royal agreement to a creation of peers if necessary. But at the monarch's request, the Tories in the Lords backed down to avoid it. The Bill finally went through, and Parliament was dissolved in early December.

Elections now took place on the new franchise. They resulted in the heaviest defeat the Tory Party ever sustained. Looked at in another way, and with the benefit of (a good deal of) hindsight, they marked the end of the Tories and the beginning of the Conservatives. The Conservatives (as for convenience we shall now call them) were reduced to fewer than 150 out of 658 seats in the Commons. History, it seemed, was on the march. The Whigs must rule, liberalism (or even radicalism) must triumph, and a reactionary rump of discredited and demoralized reactionaries must endure a prolonged and painful political kicking. But this is not how events turned out. It remains to examine how – and to explain why.

The Whig ministry was much less solidly based than appearances might suggest. The Whigs themselves were divided between those who had reluctantly taken up parliamentary reform in order to preserve the existing social, economic and political order, and those for whom reform, extending into wider and more controversial areas, was an end in itself.[35] Each new stage of reform offended new interests, exposed new divisions, demanded new arguments.[36] The most controversial issues were, as earlier, religious – in the first instance the Irish Church, but potentially the English Church too.

The more conservative Whigs soon started to withdraw support for the Government. In a sense, the first of these was William IV, whose doubts began even before the Reform Bill became law. Stanley, Sir James Graham, the Duke of Richmond and Lord Ripon (formerly Goderich) – members of the so-called 'Derby Dilly', the group around Stanley (later the Earl of Derby) – resigned in 1834.[37] Then Grey himself resigned. The Lichfield House Compact, the following year, successfully brought together Whigs, Liberals, Irish and Radicals to defeat Peel's short-lived ministry (as we shall shortly see). But it did so at the cost of establishing in the minds of the propertied classes the notion that the safe old Whig Party had only served as a bridgehead for all sorts of highly unsafe tendencies.

Significantly, from about this time the term 'Whig' began increasingly to give way to the term 'Liberal' to describe the main opposition grouping – and the country's liberalism definitely still had its limits. The leadership of the party also fell into less acceptable hands. Melbourne, who succeeded Grey, though charming and instinctively moderate, was also, as Greville observed, 'considered lax in morals, indifferent in religion, and very loose and pliant in politics'.[38] Lord John Russell, the Liberal leader in the Commons (and later Prime Minister), was, despite his brains, pluck and principle, instinctively radical, and anyway quite unable to inspire confidence – he was unimposing, and very short. Underlying these personal problems was the fissiparous tendency of all reforming parties and governments, which so often plays into the hands of their conservative (and Conservative) opponents. In a two-party system it is, indeed, one of the main drivers of political change. Although party divisions were not by the 1830s set in concrete, and although the system cannot, of course, yet be described as fully democratic, this tendency is one of the main reasons why the Conservatives made such progress at their apparently indomitable opponents' expense.

A further consideration is that while the changes effected by the Great Reform Act (which, on balance, deserves its epithet) were extensive, they did not constitute a political revolution. The Conservatives were, of course, heavily disadvantaged by them – the Tories had held a tight grip on most of the boroughs now abolished. But they had been even more disadvantaged through the unpopularity incurred by opposing reform – which most people thought was no longer an issue. In any case, a large number of nomination boroughs survived the Act. It was for one of these, under the patronage of the Duke of Newcastle (whose son, Lord Lincoln, was a friend of his), that the young W. E. Gladstone now entered Parliament. Beside the leftover opportunities for influence, there were other important – and politically useful – anomalies. London, for example, was still substantially under-represented. And although the size of the national electorate as a whole had increased by perhaps 80 per cent, one side-effect was actually to reduce the working-class electorate in a large number of towns.[39] Two amendments to the original proposals helped. The first – already mentioned – was the Gascoyne amendment, which preserved the number of English seats. The second was the Chandos amendment, which enfranchised the £50 tenants-at-will in the counties. This probably allowed the influence of (usually Conservative) landlords greater rein – or at least the Radicals thought it did.[40]

But the most important beneficial effect of the Reform Act was to force the Tories to adapt. One must not oversimplify. Wellington is often regarded as the last Tory Prime Minister and Peel the first Conservative one. But Wellington remained leader of the party after 1832, and Peel only replaced him in 1834 because Wellington voluntarily withdrew. There was no party rebellion.[41] That said, the Duke's earlier withdrawal – in order to allow the absurd Manners Sutton to emerge – showed that it was no longer possible to imagine his forming any administration in the new conditions. Wellington himself, one may add, had no sympathy with the dogmatic attitude taken by J. W. Croker, who had argued against reform and so felt it dishonourable to sit in a reformed House of Commons. The Duke replied tersely to his explanatory letter: 'I am very sorry that you do not intend again to be elected to serve in Parliament. I cannot conceive for what reason.'[42] The problem for the Duke was different: it was that people would not accept him as Prime Minister, and he knew it. They would, though, accept Peel. What proved most reassuring, though, was the combination. As the painter Benjamin Robert Haydon reflected: 'What a curious thing it is, I never feel comfortable with Sir Robert and the Duke out!'[43] But the order in which he mentioned them was, of course, significant.

Peel carried heavy psychological and political luggage. In the end it would prove too heavy for him and his party. But from the Tory crash of 1832 to the Conservative crash of 1846 he dominated politics. His weaknesses of character have been mentioned; but without the enormous strengths, he could not have created a Conservative Party, as he did, in his own image. Douglas Hurd sums it up: Peel (like Lord Hurd, one might add) was 'a man of government'.[44] Bagehot, less enthusiastic, hostile to his politics and contemptuous of his lack of originality, still had the highest regard for Peel in that single respect: 'He was a great administrator.'[45]

This was also part of the problem. For Peel, administration alone was what counted. His experience in the unreformed system, and his innate conviction of how government should be conducted, made him, though he did not recognize it, a transitional figure. His failure to manage that role – along with the excoriation he suffered at Disraeli's hands – was what undid him. Peel, like Wellington, took a high view of the executive. The King's (or Queen's) business must be done. He had an obligation, from which he only reluctantly, eventually, wriggled out, to answer the call to govern. But he was also dependent on a party, and he felt that his party should follow the same line of reasoning and fall in with his wishes. His reaction when it did not was – reflecting both his principles and his temperament – one of outraged contempt. The classic distinction (which like many such distinctions is oversimplified) is that whereas under the old system governments made parliaments, now parliaments made governments, and they did so through parties. This new dispensation meant that parties could never be mere instruments of government, and when expected to be so they would develop – as did the Conservatives under Peel – what have been well described as 'symptoms of neurosis'.[46]

This, though, is to anticipate. The ability to inspire and retain confidence, to radiate soundness, is a great asset. It is doubly important on the right, because so often the left is singing the more attractive political tunes. It was crucial at this juncture because the Conservatives had, above all, to look respectable. Peel was in constitutional terms old-fashioned; but, equally, he is the first and indeed the model practitioner of this kind of Conservative political leadership – a leadership which is all the more effective because it seems so humdrum, moderate and reasonable as to be above politics altogether. There is, of course, a drawback in placing compromise above coherence – one to which Disraeli alludes in an exchange between his two Conservative political hacks in *Coningsby*:

> 'Hush!' said Mr. Tadpole, 'The time has gone by for Tory governments; what the country requires is a sound Conservative Government'.
>
> 'A sound Conservative Government', said Taper, musingly. 'I understand; Tory men and Whig measures'.[47]

The cynical quip was prophetic of trouble to come, not least because its author made the trouble. For the moment, however, Peel's approach was exactly what was required. He refused the temptation (which others felt, though he did not) to engage in factional opposition. He neither systematically used the Tory majority in the Lords to block the Government's measures, nor did he align with the Radicals in the Commons to defeat them. He exerted discipline – and he waited.

The first opportunity proved premature. When Grey resigned in 1834 and William IV imposed on his successor, Melbourne, terms that the latter could not accept, the King then asked Wellington to form a ministry. Peel was away in Italy at the time and for a short while the Duke ruled the country almost alone. But Wellington had made it clear to the King from the first that he could only be a caretaker – Peel must be Prime Minister. At no point in his ensuing 120 days in power did Peel ever have a majority in the House of Commons, which was embarrassing. The episode also proved a humiliation for the monarch. But during those few months Peel showed that, contrary to what the party's critics had implied, it was competent to govern, and that he was, indeed, an alternative Prime Minister. He did more. At the ensuing general election he published the Conservative Party's – indeed, any British political party's – first manifesto, in the form of an address to the electors of his Tamworth constituency. (The first Liberal equivalent was Gladstone's programme of 1874.)[48]

The Tamworth Manifesto, approved by the Cabinet and released to the press, made a great impact. It was by no means a racy read. But it served its purpose admirably. This was to reassure the public that Peel would head no Ultra-Tory ministry, and that his party accepted the Reform Act (as he had already stated in the Commons) as 'a final and irrevocable settlement of a great constitutional question'. At the same time, Peel promised 'a careful review of institutions, both civil and ecclesiastical' and 'the correction of proved abuses', listing some specific measures, as well as voicing the usual generalities about good, economical government.[49] The ensuing election increased the number of Conservatives by about a hundred. But it was not enough. The ministry was defeated on Opposition demands for appropriation of revenues from the Irish Church for non-Church purposes. The religious question would just not go away, however much the former 'Orange Peel' sought to finesse it.

But by now a still larger change had occurred. Though consolidated by the recent campaign, its origins, yet again, lay in the Reform Act, which – even when in prospect – had forced the Tory Party to assert its identity and organize its activities on a new basis. The word 'conservative' employed in its modern sense was apparently first used in an article in the *Quarterly Review* in January 1830. The passage, revealing because of its self-conscious novelty, runs: 'We now are, as we have always been, decidedly and conscientiously attached to what is called the Tory, and which might with more propriety be called the Conservative Party.' The derivation is from the French *conservateur*. For a time the word 'Conservators' was used. But by 1831 the *Standard* was referring without apology or qualification to the 'Conservative Party'.[50] The French derivation is important, because it harks back to the Revolution – opposition to which in England, no less than France, and more successfully, was the original inspiration of conservatism. That keen and subtle observer of the English scene Charles Maurice de Talleyrand understood the nuances. Replying to accusations from his Liberal Whig friend, Lady Holland, in 1835, he defined his own position (accurately, as it happens) as being a *conservateur libéral* rather than *un tory déguisé*.[51] The distinction was already important.

A Conservative is, by definition, at least theoretically speaking, not a reactionary. He plans not to return to the past but to shape the future without losing sight of what is and what has been. The Tories were, by the time of their demise, an identifiable party with clear if unfashionable beliefs. But they had often behaved more like a faction. By contrast, Peelite Conservatism was intended to reach out beyond traditional Tory boundaries to all those who, whatever their past allegiances, wished to preserve the state of affairs in the country consolidated by the 1832 Act. Concern for the rights and protection of property was the single most important element of the Conservative case – even the bitter arguments about the Irish Church were quarrels about property.

Initially, the label Conservative did not figure largely in party campaigning. It appears nowhere in the Tamworth Manifesto and was not at this stage actively promoted by the party. But by the 1837 elections it was.[52] Greville's diaries catch the flavour of its evolution, starting to talk of the 'Conservatives' in 1833:

> The Tories are sulky and crestfallen; moderate men are vexed, disappointed, grieved; and the Radicals stand grinning by, chuckling at the sight of the Conservatives (at least those who so call themselves, and those who must be so *really*) cutting each others' throats.[53]

Two years later:

> Peel clearly does not intend that there shall be (as far as he is concerned as their leader) a *Tory* party, though of course there

must be a *Conservative* party, the great force of which is the old Tory interest, and his object evidently is to establish himself in the good opinion of the country and render himself indispensable – to raise a party out of all the other parties, and to convert the new elements of democratic power into an instrument of his own elevation, partly by yielding to and partly by guiding and restraining its desires and opinions.[54]

For this, better central organization was required. A Tory Committee was operating in 1830 to promote the party's cause in the press. But it had little success and finally sank into financial scandal. A much more important initiative which (just) preceded the Reform Act, and whose creation became a vigorous force afterwards, was the foundation of the Carlton Club.[55]

A new sort of gentlemen's club was now being formed, less exclusive than the old aristocratic political clubs of the previous century, like Brooks's and White's. These newer clubs were open to the wealthy middle classes and prized not just for their company but for their amenities. The Travellers, founded in 1819, was one of the earliest. Another was the Athenaeum, founded by Croker in 1824. What would be the Carlton Club had its origin in a meeting held on 10 March 1832 at the Thatched House Tavern, with the Marquess of Salisbury in the chair. A committee was appointed to find a property and draw up rules. A week later the Club received its name, reflecting the choice of premises: a short lease was taken on a house owned by Lord Kensington, No. 2 Carlton Terrace. Peel and Wellington were trustees. The club duly opened and functioned in that location till 1835. It then moved to a new building designed by Sir Robert Smirke in Pall Mall. Ten years later it expanded into adjoining property and was extensively altered by Sidney Smirke, Robert's brother. In 1854 the whole building was knocked down and replaced with another that was destroyed in a German air raid in 1940.

The Carlton Club has always been a party political club, though it did not require formal Conservative Party membership (perhaps because members of the royal family belonged to it). It has reflected the importance placed by Conservatives then and since on combining political and social activity. Disraeli understood this when he first embarked on his career in Conservative politics, lobbying energetically – and successfully – to become a member. He joined in 1836, three years after Gladstone (who at this stage was also aligned with the Conservatives). By 1839 membership stood at more than a thousand.

But the Club was not merely a place for gossip and self-advancement. Until the creation of the Conservative Central Office, in 1868, it was also the party's organizational headquarters. From 1835 the Carlton was home to the Conservative Party's election committee. This was the initiative of Francis Bonham, who served as the party's discreet and indefatigable chief agent (in fact, though not in name) until the break-up in 1846 (when he departed with the Peelites).[56] The committee's significance lies more in its existence, marking a step in organizational coherence, than in its executive power, which was limited by the independent-mindedness of patrons, MPs and party activists in the country. It would certainly have been of little value without the more or less spontaneous growth of Conservative associations in the constituencies.

There had always been political clubs that acted to support Tory candidates. But the new associations were different, because they were, in principle at least, constantly and not just sporadically active. They spread quickly up and down the country, but mainly in the boroughs, where the hardest battles for votes were fought.[57] Here the enfranchisement of £10 householders, small businessmen who were also frequently Dissenters, was a significant problem for the Conservatives, exacerbated by the reform of the old oligarchic corporations (through the Municipal Corporations Act of 1835), which had often previously kept potentially hostile boroughs in Tory hands. The new associations were not rivals but rather supplements to the now reduced influence of Tory patrons, though conflicts could unusually occur. The associations should not be regarded as manifestations of a trend towards 'Tory democracy' (however defined). They rarely took a hand in the choice of candidates, which remained in the grip of the great men of the area. Candidates were also expected to pay their election expenses. The purpose of the associations was limited and practical. It was to distribute literature aimed at countering the party's opponents and, above all, to fund and organize voter registration.

The latter task was a direct result of the provisions of the Reform Act. The law now required that voters pay a shilling to be registered – in the counties once only, in the boroughs every year. The system was not merely expensive but complicated. Registration could be and was challenged on many grounds. This opened up huge possibilities for both political activists and lawyers. Indeed, until later legislation changed the system this was the golden age of Conservative lawyers, who alone possessed the skills to act as election agents.

One more development should be mentioned, indicative of increasing central party oversight of elections. This was the establishment of central party election funds. Such funds are known to have existed from 1835, and were administered by the Earl of Rosslyn, with Peel and Wellington acting as trustees.[58] They were, of course, only supplementary to the great bulk of activity taking place in the constituencies. But they are not without importance.

Whether the growth of local and central organization actually helped the Conservatives win elections is unclear, since their opponents were organizing too. There was a steady increase in the number of Conservative MPs. But many of these were defectors from the ranks of the Government's supporters, rather than the

result of electoral triumphs. There was also, perhaps more significantly, an increase during the period in the number of Conservative
candidates. Contested elections were not a sure sign of changes in
opinion, since, particularly in rural areas, a seat might be left
uncontested simply in order to avoid expense. But they can be seen
as indications of party enthusiasm and effectiveness, which both
reflected and underpinned the campaign that the Conservatives
under Peel were waging at a national level.

That campaign was inexorably, but not swiftly, successful.
William IV died in 1837 and was succeeded by his eighteen-year-
old niece, Victoria.[59] At the obligatory general election the number
of Conservative MPs returned increased from 273 to 313. The
party now had a majority of English seats and Melbourne had to
rely on the Irish. Peel was not, in fact, anxious to take office too
soon, certainly not with a minority Government. In 1839, however,
Melbourne threw in the towel after a narrow victory on a secondary
colonial matter – suspension of the Jamaican Assembly. Peel was
conscious that the young Queen was dazzled by Melbourne and
surrounded by Whig appointments. In order to ensure it was known
that the incoming Conservatives enjoyed the monarch's confidence,
he sought the appointment of new ladies of the royal bedchamber.
The Queen threw a tantrum and refused, and Melbourne wearily
returned. The Conservatives could wait. Moreover, by the time
they did attain office they enjoyed what was almost as useful as a
large majority – the benefit of the influence over Victoria of her
new consort, Prince Albert, who approved of Peel.

Unfortunately for the party, another event occurred in 1839
which was to prove more troublesome. During a sharp manufacturing downturn that was depressing wages, a national Anti-Corn Law
League was founded. Led in Parliament by Richard Cobden and
John Bright, the league would be one of the most effective lobby
groups ever devised; and Cobden and Bright, whose campaigning
on matters ranging from free trade to non-interventionist foreign

policy, and from Ireland to the franchise, helped create a distinctive ideology of radical liberalism, would prove among the Conservative Party's most dangerous doctrinal enemies.[60]

In 1841 Melbourne's Government was defeated on sugar duties and went to the country on various free trade proposals, including a fixed 8s per quarter duty on foreign wheat. Whatever the country thought of that, electors knew what they thought of the Whigs, who were routed. The Conservatives scored a large overall majority – 367 to 291 – though they did significantly better in England and in the counties than elsewhere.

Peel was now the undisputed master of his party. No one could openly challenge him. He also dominated the House of Commons. But he could not control events. It often happens that a Government elected to deal with one set of problems is then confronted with a completely different set; and this was bound to be particularly the case for Peel's Conservatives. The movement of opinion that had brought them in was defensive of existing institutions, which the irresponsibility of the Whig–Liberal–Radical–Irish parliamentary majority seemed to threaten. Having a Conservative Government would ensure that changes would be moderately and competently managed, that roots would not be dug up. But not even Conservative governments can stand still. Moreover, in Peel the country had as Prime Minister an administrative activist.

Was Peel, as Disraeli charged in his great philippic at the time of repeal of the Corn Laws, someone who simply adopted current ideas? Was, indeed, Peel's political life 'one great appropriation clause'? Peel's own final speech as Prime Minister, with its odd (and, as Disraeli pointed out, unparliamentary) tribute to Richard Cobden, might suggest so.[61] But Peel was not in the ordinary sense pragmatic, let alone weak. He was, in fact, that strange combination, a doctrinaire technocrat.[62]

Peel's Government carried forward in the economic sphere the approach piloted under Lord Liverpool. Peel's 1842 budget – and it was indeed his budget, because his Chancellor (Goulburn) was a cipher – reintroduced the income tax. The tax had been first introduced by Pitt to pay for the war against France and then abolished in 1816. It was regarded as a measure of economic orthodoxy because it raised money by means other than tariffs, and at the same time it was regarded as socially responsible because it fell more heavily on the rich (or, more precisely, the higher earners). At the same time Peel lowered the protection against imported grain by a revision of the 1828 sliding scale of corn duty and continued the dismantling of tariff walls. He got away with it so easily because his backbenchers were relieved he had not gone further: income tax was set at quite a low level – 7d in the pound (it was also allegedly 'temporary') – and the level of protection afforded to home-grown corn might well also have been less.

The changes have a further significance for the history of the Conservative Party, because it was Gladstone, appointed by Peel to the Board of Trade, who was responsible for the detailed tariff reform measures in the 1842 and 1845 budgets. Gladstone had previously been a moderate supporter of the Corn Laws. He was very much on the traditionalist wing of the party, concerned particularly with issues of Church and State (giving precedence to the interests of the former) and incurring the suspicion of those (like Peel himself) on the liberal wing. But Gladstone's engagement with economics from this time, and his involvement with what would be seen as the Peelite project, would both transform his own politics and, through the struggles with Disraeli, have a determining impact on the Conservative Party's fortunes.

Eighteen forty-two was a time of great economic hardship, and Peel was genuinely moved by it. He was also concerned about the ability of British manufacturing to compete. On both grounds, he had now privately concluded that there was no case for corn duties, which forced up the price of food for the poor and pushed up the cost of labour for the manufacturers. It would have been more honest, and perhaps in the long run less politically harmful, if he had openly said so. But he did not; and, worse still, he said the contrary. Peel defended the Corn Laws in public and said that their repeal would just add to rural poverty, not help the urban poor. He did not, though, believe this. In truth, he took an absolutist – in fact, economically wrong – view of the effects of free corn imports. He thought that agriculture would benefit, because the country as a whole would benefit, from free trade. But that was not and could not be true.

By his last years there had grown up a good deal of suspicion of Peel among his party, which percolated widely.[63] His reputation ensured that. So did his known liberalism. People could see the progress made by the Anti-Corn Law League. How would Peel respond to it? His tactics made matters worse. Party discipline was greater than it had been for decades. There was a true party system operating.[64] But tightly organized whipping – and Peel was fortunate in having a good Chief Whip in Sir John Young – was a novelty. Votes could still be lost by governments formally enjoying a large majority. On two separate occasions, neither of which was a matter of great moment, Peel forced his backbenchers to reverse their votes by threatening resignation. His conviction that the party simply existed to do his will forms an explanation. But his manner rubbed in the salt.

The damage done by Peel's announcement of his intention to propose total repeal of the Corn Laws can only be explained by a number of different factors which came together to create a devastating political explosion. First, it was preceded – in an uncanny echo of the circumstances surrounding the introduction of parliamentary reform – by an old-fashioned religious quarrel which fatally damaged Conservative unity. Disorders in Ireland demonstrated that emancipation had not solved the underlying problems attached to British rule. Moderate men began to think that a deal with the Catholic Church would ease the situation – an idea that had attracted Wellington as long ago, it will be remembered, as 1825. Such a compact should, in Peel's view, involve a large increase in government grant to the Irish Catholic seminary of Maynooth. This, when announced, caused uproar, particularly among the Ultra-Tories. Peel carried the measure, but only on third reading and then only with opposition support. There would be a close correspondence between those of his party who rebelled over Maynooth and those who, the following year, rebelled against repeal of the Corn Laws.

Of Peel's many miscalculations, the Maynooth affair must be accorded pride of place. There was no reason to think that it would secure the support of Rome or the Irish hierarchy, let alone the bulk of the Irish – nor did it.[65] But it paved the way for all that followed.

The second factor related to the significance of the landed interest to the composition and indeed the identity of the party which Peel led. The overall economic arguments were on Peel's side – the case for free trade is ultimately unanswerable. In political terms, too, Peel's attempt to place his party on the side of cheap food was to be vindicated by all those occasions in later years when protection cost the Conservatives votes. As a result, modern commentators have usually supported Peel against his critics. Douglas Hurd, for instance, sees him as the initiator of globalization.[66] But this view overlooks the circumstances of the time. The party Peel led was not a bourgeois, urban party, though it was tentatively seeking middle-class support. It was a party largely based upon land, agriculture and the counties. Nor was the country yet transformed into anything approaching the 'workshop of the world'. Peel knew this. It was why he felt the need to argue that his measures would not harm the landed interest. It was also why he concealed his views for so long.

His critics were right in viewing Peel's approach as dishonest. By 1841 the Conservatives were the party of those who feared an end to protection. Peel did nothing to discourage that perception. Disraeli's later dissection of Peel's tactics was effective because it made sense to people who would much rather have sided with the sober Anglo-Saxon Peel than with the raffish Jewish Disraeli. Disraeli, certainly, already disliked Peel, mainly because he had not, in Disraeli's view, recognized and rewarded his talents. He also disliked him because he was temperamentally Disraeli's opposite in all respects. And he disliked him because it seems clear that, although polite relations had been maintained, he felt himself disliked, and had probably felt it from the beginning (though he did not admit as much). The first meeting was, apparently, at the unpropitious hour of breakfast, when the young Disraeli asked Peel to lend him some papers for a book he was writing. Peel 'buried his chin in his neck-cloth' and said not a word to him during the rest of the meal.[67]

Some years had passed since then. But usually deferential back-bench MPs would have howled Disraeli down, rather than cheered him on, if he had not with his wittily cruel invective expressed their sense of betrayal. They agreed with his comparison of Peel to a Turkish high admiral who, on being taxed with treason, replied: 'I have an objection to war. I see no use in prolonging the struggle, and the only reason I had for accepting the command was that I might terminate the contest by betraying my master.'[68] They warmed to his mockery of Peel's justification of his conversion – to ideas he had hitherto disowned – as a mark of statesmanship:

> My idea of a great statesman is of one who represents a great idea
> – an idea which may lead him to power, an idea with which he
> may connect himself, an idea which he may develop, an idea
> which he may and can impress on the mind and conscience of a
> nation. That, sir, is my notion of what makes a man a great states-
> man. I do not care whether he be a manufacturer or a
> manufacturer's son [i.e. like Peel]. That is a grand – that is,
> indeed, an heroic – position. But I care not what may be the

position of a man who never originates an idea – a watcher of the
atmosphere, a man who, as he says, takes his observations, and
when he finds the wind in a certain quarter trims to it. Such a
person may be a powerful Minister, but he is no more a great
statesman than the man who gets up behind a carriage is a
great whip.[69]

The country gentlemen hooted with derision as the Government
front bench squirmed, while Disraeli mocked their allegedly high-
minded acceptance of office. This, he suggested, simply concealed
their wish for a salary:

What an advantage to a country to be governed by a Minister who
thinks only of posterity! The right honourable gentleman has
before assured us that he and his colleagues are only thinking of
the future. Who can doubt it? Look at them . . . The only thing
is, when one looks at them, seeing of what they are composed,
one is hardly certain whether the 'future' of which they are thinking is indeed posterity, or the coming quarter day.[70]

Never had a Prime Minister and his colleagues been treated with
such open contempt in Parliament. Nor were they the victims of an
unrepresentative gaggle. The protectionists were not all Ultras
(though the Ultras were usually protectionists). Lord George
Bentinck, who now emerged as the head of the new protectionist
Tory Party, was in his manner and obsessions an extremist, but he
was not a card-carrying reactionary. His hero was Canning. Nor was
he an assiduous parliamentarian, preferring the Turf. Bentinck was
simply outraged by Peel's betrayal. He explained: 'I keep horses in
three counties, and they tell me I shall save fifteen hundred a year
by free trade. I don't care for that: what I cannot bear is being
sold.'[71]

But perhaps the most significant of Peel's critics was Edward

(Lord) Stanley, who knew Bentinck well because of their shared mania for horse racing – an important connection for the emerging party's future. Stanley's sharply defined character needs to be examined in the context of his later leadership of the Tories. But the important point here is that he was extremely liberal on other issues of the day. It was, indeed, his liberalism which had led him to join Grey's Cabinet. It long kept him out of formal membership of the Conservative Party – he only joined the Carlton in 1841, when he became Peel's Colonial Secretary.

Stanley and Peel had subsequently grown apart. Both had large egos. Both were intelligent. Peel was overbearing, Stanley ambitious and nobody's yes-man. Feeling marginalized, in 1844 he asked to go to the Lords, where he served his apprenticeship to succeed Wellington as leader.[72]

Stanley argued in detailed Cabinet memoranda against Peel's Corn Law proposals. He was not a deeply convinced protectionist. Until the last moment, he would even consider voting for Peel's measure, though mainly to keep the party together. What was decisive for him, now and later, was that the Government had been elected on the understanding that it would maintain agricultural protection, and now it was proposed, on quite unconvincing grounds, suddenly to abandon it. As he left the Cabinet, he told his colleagues: 'We cannot do this as gentlemen.'[73] It was a matter of honour.

Peel had claimed that he had to act with such speed because of the Irish potato famine. But this argument was bogus. He had been moving in favour of free trade since his 1842 budget. On the basis of the (now well-known) maxim 'Never let a crisis go to waste', he used the failure of the Irish potato crop in October 1845 to bounce his Cabinet, and then to try to bounce his party, into repeal.[74] In fact, the Irish could not afford to buy corn. Stanley later summed up the absurdity in his speech in the Lords, when he said that repeal of the Corn Laws would no more mitigate Irish distress than if

Parliament passed a law reducing the price of pineapples.[75] What was needed in Ireland was relief, not trade – and, to his credit, Peel provided some.

So he need not have proceeded as he did. He was faced by an opportunistic demand for repeal from Russell. But he could have resisted it. He could have suspended the Corn Laws, if he wished to test the water. He could have refused to take up office again, after briefly relinquishing it on Stanley's resignation, despite Russell's humiliating inability to put together a ministry. (That he did not made him particularly vulnerable to Disraeli's barbs.) Some Whig ministry would, after all, sooner or later have emerged. But Peel was determined not just to see the Corn Laws repealed, but to repeal them himself.

Peel exulted – the word is not too strong – in the prospect of forcing his party into the lobbies against their instincts to do his bidding, as they had meekly done before. There is testimony to his strange mood: hubris and the desire for martyrdom at odds in a psyche tortured by internal contradictions.[76] When Disraeli had finished with him in the House, the hubris had been replaced by barely suppressed tears. Now the only consolation left was the martyrdom.

Peel got his way with the Corn Laws, though two-thirds of his party voted against him. The embittered protectionists had organized themselves far more effectively than Peel ever envisaged possible. His contempt for his backbenchers had led him to mis-calculate. Now they had their revenge, joining opportunistically with the Opposition to defeat the Government the following day on an Irish Coercion Bill. Peel was out. He would never hold office again. Nor, for many years, would the Conservative Party.

The judgements one makes upon Peel and upon the rebels who unseated him inevitably reflect more than an assessment of the cold facts. They demand an assessment of what the task of politics – or, at a more exalted level, the task of statesmanship – actually is. Peel's friends and supporters, though they would sympathize and follow him on his lonely road, were appalled at what he was doing. Goulburn, Chancellor of the Exchequer, wrote:

> In my opinion the party of which you are the head is the only barrier which remains against the revolutionary effects of the Reform Bill. So long as that party remains unbroken, whether in or out of power, it has the means of doing much good, or of preventing much evil. But if it be broken in pieces by a destruction of confidence in its leaders (and I cannot but think that an abandonment of the Corn Law would produce that result), I see nothing before us but the exasperation of class animosities, a struggle for pre-eminence, and the ultimate triumph of unrestrained democracy.[77]

Peel expressed his own feelings after his resignation in a letter to a friend that shows his disdain for his old party and his temperamental unsuitability to lead it:

> So far from regretting the expulsion from office, I rejoice in it as the greatest relief from an intolerable burden . . . To have to incur the deepest responsibility, to bear the heaviest toil, to reconcile colleagues with conflicting opinions to a common course of action, to keep together in harmony with the Sovereign, the Lords and the Commons; to have to do these things, and to be at the same time the tool of a party – that is to say, to adopt the opinions of men who have not access to your knowledge, and could not profit from it if they had, who spend their time in eating and drinking, and hunting, shooting, gambling, horse-racing and so forth – would be odious servitude, to which I never will submit. I intend to keep aloof from party combinations.[78]

Many will find Peel's outlook admirable and that of Disraeli,

Bentinck and the others stupid, short-sighted or cynical. Disraeli's natural role as villain of the piece is given added piquancy by the exchange he had with Peel during the great debate, about whether he had ever sought office. Peel said he had; Disraeli, perhaps chancing his luck, but more likely caught off balance, denied it. Peel had all the time in his possession the wheedling letter of 1841 in which Disraeli had indeed asked for a job. But he never used it. The tale is a good one. But the implication that Peel could have destroyed his tormenter and saved himself, yet stayed his hand, is false. Peel was, indeed, in his personal dealings intensely honourable, even archaically so. He had on an earlier, similar occasion refused to reveal the existence of a damaging letter he had received from Russell. (In that instance it got out anyway.) But had he waved the offending paper at Disraeli across the Dispatch Box it would have been no more than a useful debating point. Peel could not have escaped; and Disraeli's character was not, after all, the issue.[79]

When in 1850 Peel died as the result of a riding accident, he was immediately regarded as a national hero. During his agony, as he lay in his house at Whitehall Gardens, the number of enquiring well-wishers grew so great that the police cleared the courtyard and a temporary gateway was built from which bulletins were issued every two or three hours. When news of the death was given out, tributes poured in. Mills stopped. Shops closed. It was genuine, unstudied national grief – though not everyone shared it. Referring to the (inaccurate) account that Peel had been less than stoical in his pain, one duke remarked: 'Well, he lived a coward, and he has died one.'[80] He was wrong, and doubly so. But for all Peel's governmental achievement and the accolades he received, he had been a bad political leader. To unpolitical people this does not seem to matter. But these people are also wrong. It did, and it does matter – especially if you are Prime Minister.

Under Lord Derby and his deputy, Benjamin Disraeli (right), the Conservatives scrambled back into power in 1866. But this time, with growing agitation for electoral reform (here represented by an insistent 'working man'), the government was in a quandary.

3

DERBY'S PARTY

In the battle over repeal of the Corn Laws what amounted to a new party came into being. This was understood by the participants at the time. But one should not exaggerate the immediate significance. In Victorian England parties still, to some extent, came and went. What was not predicted by any of the main players, probably not even by Peel in his gloomiest moments, was that the split between protectionists and Peelites would be permanent.

It was April 1846 before the protectionists in the House of Commons acquired an undisputed leader, in the form of Bentinck. His effective deputy, naturally, was his close friend Disraeli. (They were known sarcastically as 'The Jockey and the Jew'.) Stanley was elected leader of the protectionists in the Upper House. The election was made in his absence, and he initially declined a greater role – he was, indeed, at first opposed to any formal break. But his views changed along with events. In July, Bentinck publicly acknowledged Stanley's leadership of the protectionist party as a whole, and this was henceforth undisputed.[1]

At the subsequent general election the Conservative Party organization (such as remained of it) went with Peel, who had never
formally relinquished the leadership. A central election fund,
managed by Bonham and the Chief Whip Sir John Young,
supported a number of Peelite candidates. For their part, the protectionists were driven back to using the protection societies as a
base. But although the 1847 election was fought in a more than
usually chaotic fashion, the anger and resentment that characterized intra-Conservative relations in Westminster did not inevitably
spill out into the country. In so far as he could, Stanley personally
tried to discourage fights between Peelite and protectionist candidates. Local accommodations and the ever-present desire to avoid
the cost of unnecessary contests did much of the rest. Thus 236 of
401 constituencies were not contested at all, and there were, in the
end, only ten cases of Peelites and protectionists fighting one
another. Beyond the clear fact that the protectionists lost the
election, much of the outcome was also confused. This was because
of the difficulty of describing Conservative MPs' loyalties in the
new Parliament. The number of Peelites, for example, has been
variously put at between 80 and 120. The protectionists, by one
estimate, had 243 seats. It was not wholesale national rejection, but
the rump party was forced back to heavy reliance on the English
counties.[2]

In the wake of the Corn Laws, the House of Commons was an
odd place and, initially, presented an even odder sight. The protectionists, in their loathing of Peel and his colleagues, at first sat on
the government (that is, Whig/Liberal) benches. Though emotion-
ally satisfying, this proved highly impractical in the conduct of
House business. So in the 1847 session they moved over to the
opposition benches. Bentinck, Disraeli and the protectionist leaders
sat below the Dispatch Box, while Peel and his friends took the
places up to the Speaker's chair. In the Lords, all was appropriately
more decorous. No Peelite peer matched the standing enjoyed by

the protectionist Stanley. Peelites and protectionists sat alongside each other. Wellington's attitude was an important factor in the accommodation. Though he had followed Peel through loyalty, he did not fully approve of his conduct. He thought, indeed, that Peel had 'broken up a noble party' and argued that it was for Stanley 'to rally it again'.[3] (This, though, turned out to be a forlorn hope.) In any case, he now accepted Stanley's political seniority.

The 1847 result demonstrated that protection was most unlikely to provide a programme for Conservative victory. But how – and when – to ditch the policy? Stanley was reluctant to do so immediately, for fear of provoking the same accusations of bad faith that had brought down Peel. Bentinck would doubtless have agreed. But in December 1847 Bentinck resigned as a result of party dissatisfaction following his vote in favour of a Bill admitting Jews to Parliament. The following September, he suddenly died. Lord Granby, eldest son of the Duke of Rutland, tried and signally failed as Bentinck's successor. Granby's main qualification for the job, as with the other possible candidates, was really that he was not Disraeli. Stanley shared that distrust and never wholly lost it. But with Bentinck dead, keeping Disraeli out of the Commons leadership was still more difficult. Stanley managed to persuade him, very grudgingly, to accept the position of one of three joint leaders (alongside the dim Granby and the elderly, colourless J. G. Herries).[4] But the arrangement could not last. By early 1849, Disraeli was Stanley's deputy and effective leader of the protectionists in the Commons.

Disraeli's wider impact on the Conservatives is the central theme of the following chapter. But Gladstone summed up his significance in these years with pinpoint accuracy in describing him as 'at once Lord Derby's necessity and his curse'.[5] The party needed Disraeli, not just because it had so few talented speakers but because very few people have ever had Disraeli's extraordinary capacity for sustained political attack from a position of political weakness. He was, in fact, the greatest parliamentarian of his day – greater than Gladstone, though not his match as an outdoor speaker – and probably the greatest Commons opposition leader of all time. He had the courage, quickness and opportunism essential to that demanding role, which he filled for longer than any other politician. Disraeli was also extremely funny, and since he was known to be at least as funny in private life as in public, his audience in the House of Commons had the greater regard for his wit, because it seemed more natural.[6] In reality, it was the result of much preparation. He counselled others never to let a good line go to waste and obeyed his own injunction.[7] In fact, in public he was completely controlled, in every pose studiedly – and for his enemies, maddeningly – artificial. A contemporary observer recalled, for example, how he avoided neologisms, let alone what would today be regarded as 'slang'. His diction was exact to the point of pedantry: thus 'Parliament' had four syllables and even 'business' acquired three.[8] Having launched his political career as an outrageous dandy, he later dramatically reversed course and dressed in Parliament in an austere and rather old-fashioned manner. (He wore a brown suit.) Despite his sense of humour, he affected, like the best comedians, a withdrawn and slightly doleful look in public. Only his black-dyed beard and hair, showing tell-tale grey at the roots when regarded closely, confirmed that physical vanity was not dead.[9]

Disraeli had a well-modulated, attractive and finely controlled voice. He would begin a speech quietly and slowly but then rise to a loud and dramatic climax without any loss of tonal depth.[10] He learned and practised out loud his important speeches, and he never used notes. Sometimes, he admitted, this meant he forgot some point or line; but he added: 'If I once used notes, I would lean upon them.'[11] He was short-sighted from birth – in old age he could not see across a room – and regretted that he could not pick out faces in the House of Commons. But, like any actor, he made the most of his infirmities, using his eyeglass as a dramatic prop: when under particularly fierce attack, he would slowly place it in his eye and look at the clock (or appear to look at it) before returning to affected somnolence.[12] His mannerisms, in fact, became a ritual of which his supporters knew the secret code:

> Whenever he was about to produce a good thing, and his good things were very good, anyone in the habit of watching him knew precisely when they were coming. Before producing the point, he would always pause, and give a nervous cough: the action of his hands was remarkable. He carried a cambric handkerchief, of spotless whiteness, in his left [frock coat] skirt pocket. He would place both hands in both pockets behind him; then bring out the white handkerchief, and hold it in his left hand before him for a few seconds; pass it to his right hand: then with his right hand pass the handkerchief lightly under his nose, hardly touching it; and then with his left hand replace the handkerchief in his pocket, still holding his hand, with the handkerchief in it, in his pocket, until a fresh topic.[13]

Disraeli's strengths were not, however, always so evident. Some Tory MPs saw his idiosyncrasies not as stylish but as offensive. The Commons Chief Whip, William Beresford, hated Disraeli (as, indeed, he had hated Bentinck) and took every opportunity to attempt to undermine him with Stanley. Beresford remained a painful thorn in Disraeli's side until his removal was facilitated by an election corruption scandal. (It is, indeed, hard to see that Beresford had the temperament for a Chief Whip or, indeed, a politician at all: hooted on the hustings, he told the crowd that 'they were the vilest rabble he had ever seen, and he despised them from his heart'.)[14] Such, though, were the odd, mutually distrustful colleagues upon which the new party's fortunes hung.

In the early days, there was even uncertainty about its name. 'Conservative' seemed tainted to many. 'Country' or simply

'Protectionist' were both mooted. But sensibly (and thanks in part to Beresford) the old title was not quite abandoned. The immediate motive for its retention was hope of winning back the Peelites; but the decision was more important for other reasons. As Peel had seen, the long-term future of the party lay in attracting at least some of the urban vote. Economic and social realities were such that a wholesale, permanent retreat to the shires must eventually mean an abdication of power.[15] The trick was to retain the country while gradually winning the towns. This eventually happened, though when it finally occurred it would be more the result of social change than of deliberate political tactics.

Unlike Peel, Disraeli did not despise the landed interests and their representatives. But he often found the country gentlemen exasperating. They 'never read' – he complained – and they 'did not understand the ideas of their own time'.[16] They showed, for example, no interest in his schemes to influence the press, which was overwhelmingly hostile, or to set up a Tory newspaper, despising as they did all dealings with journalists.[17] Above all, Disraeli could not quickly persuade them to give up protection, and on this matter Stanley was no help. As for Disraeli's personal view on protection, there were well-founded doubts about his commitment to the policy. It was put about that he had even sought, on one occasion, to reassure Palmerston about his suitability for a job by declaring: 'Search my speeches through and you will not find one word of protection in them.' The story was malicious and probably, as to the facts, false; but Edward Stanley, the party leader's eldest son, who was also at this time Disraeli's friend and disciple, thought the sentiment itself true enough – as, doubtless, did others.[18] One should perhaps add that this in itself does not make Disraeli – any more than it made his leader, Stanley – a hypocrite. It was, after all, the conduct of Peel, not the abandonment of protection itself, which created the schism that rent the party.

Truth to tell, the late 1840s were in any case a bad time to push the proposal for relinquishing protection. There was a sharp agricultural depression. Protectionist demands revived and protectionist candidates achieved several by-election successes. Industrial protection, too, raised its head. Stanley slapped down Disraeli's attempts explicitly to renounce the policy in favour of special fiscal help for the landed interests. The party leader's caution probably made sense at the time. But it also meant that any remaining chance of winning back the Peelites receded further. Not till 1852 were the corn duties officially consigned to the sizeable Conservative dustbin of outmoded policies.

Stanley became the fourteenth earl of Derby on the death of his father in June 1851. In the same year, the Conservatives had their first opportunity to form a Government. In February, Stanley (as he still was) received his summons from the Queen on Russell's resignation. He was reluctant. The Conservatives were in a clear minority. Only if there were at least a partial reunion with the Peelites would a stable administration be possible – though with Peel himself now dead that should not have been unthinkable. Initially, Stanley declined altogether, as a matter of tactics, so as to show up the weakness of the alternatives. He later explained, in a characteristic metaphor: 'It is a bungling fisherman who strikes at the first nibble: I shall wait till the fish has gorged the bait, and then I am sure to land him.' Asked a second time, he agreed to try. Approaches were duly made to the Peelites. Disraeli, who was even more desperate for power than he was prickly about position, offered to serve under Gladstone, if necessary. But it was all to no avail. Later that evening (Tuesday, 25 February 1851) Edward Stanley found his father in a state of deep depression. Everything had gone wrong. There would be no Conservative ministry. Disraeli was highly critical, believing that Stanley should have gone ahead; not to do so was 'a confession of incompetence'. He then added, as he did on such occasions, that he intended to retire from public life and concentrate on his books. Wellington later unhelpfully, if accurately, explained the failure to the Queen: 'There are two sections of the Conservative Party: on one side officers without men, on the other men without officers.' The Duke then, even more unhelpfully, told everyone else what he had said.[19]

But Russell resigned once again on 21 February 1852, brought down by Palmerston and his supporters. (Russell had used Palmerston's unauthorized expression of support for Louis-Napoleon's coup as an excuse to get rid of him: but Palmerston soon had his revenge.) Summoned to the Palace, but still rebuffed by the Peelites, Derby this time went ahead and formed a protectionist Conservative administration. Wellington's contribution on this occasion was to christen the ministry. As the little-known and undistinguished names were read out in the Lords, the old man asked in the bellow of the nearly deaf: 'Who? Who?' And so the short-lived 'Who? Who' ministry acquired its place in history. Its members, with the exception of the Prime Minister, Derby, were certainly untried. Disraeli was amused by the number of dukes; but others were less amused by Disraeli's own complete lack of governmental experience – though he was now party leader in the Commons and Chancellor of the Exchequer. The Earl of Malmesbury, a friend of Derby's, took the Foreign Office, while the unimpressive Spencer Walpole became Home Secretary. The twin priorities of the Government were to show competence and to win a majority at the following dissolution. In neither was it successful.

Disraeli tried in his first financial statement to make a decisive move towards free trade. Derby, though, was outraged at what he considered 'a eulogy of Peel' by Disraeli and quickly restored in a speech at Mansion House what he considered the necessary degree of ambiguity.[20] In practice, any substantial protectionist measure was politically unthinkable. So it was on a distinctly fuzzy programme, supported by an undertow of anti-Catholicism, that the Conservatives fought the election. They made some gains in the English counties, but remained in a clear minority in the House of Commons.

Disraeli's budget, which he now introduced, was an attempt to square the circle created by protectionism without protection. But it was all too clearly a device to buy off the landed interest. The Whig MP (and historian) Thomas Babington Macaulay described it as 'nothing but taking money out of the pockets of people in the towns and putting it into the growers of malt'.[21] (Disraeli had halved the malt tax to help the agriculturalists.) Naturally, under fire Disraeli gave as good as he got. Indeed, his pulverizing of his critics in the House was ferociously funny. Even Gladstone conceded that the speech 'as a whole was grand; I think the most powerful I ever heard from him'.[22] It also contains one of the most famous lines in politics: 'England does not love coalitions.' The insight is memorable, but questionable. In any case, Disraeli's virtuosity probably contributed to the Government's undoing. Convention held that the Chancellor should have the last word; but an enraged Gladstone then intervened.

Gladstone felt provoked by Disraeli's personalized jibes, but he also had his own well-calculated reasons for making a mark at this point. He had, of course, been out of office since the fall of Peel, who – now that he was dead – increasingly became Gladstone's model. His aim was to carry through Peel's vision, and advance his own interests, as Chancellor of the Exchequer in the Government which looked like emerging from the 'coalition' against Disraeli's measures. His words in the debate were thus addressed at least as much to his fellow Peelite, Aberdeen, the future Prime Minister, as at Disraeli. The speech was a job application.

Gladstone put on a good show. A witness recalled that his 'usually calm features were livid and distorted with passion [and] his voice shook'. In a speech that seemed to veer between madness and brilliance, Gladstone energetically but forensically destroyed both the budget's concept and its detail. When he sat down, there was little left of it.[23] The budget was duly rejected by 305 to 286 votes, and the Government promptly resigned.

The Conservatives would not return to power for another six years. The Liberals, meanwhile, were still divided and their leader, Russell, widely despised. Hence the emergence of Aberdeen at the head of a Peelite–Liberal Ministry. The Peelites secured fifteen places in the Ministry, six of them in the new Coalition Cabinet, including Gladstone as Chancellor. The formation of the 1852 Aberdeen Government represents, in several senses, a turning point in Conservative fortunes: it also provides a useful vantage point for reflection on the party's still unresolved problems.

Until 1852, Derby, Disraeli and many other protectionists had hoped that a reunion of the old Conservative Party was imminent. By the time of Peel's death the Peelite organization was largely defunct, not least because after 1846 Peel refused to act as a party leader. The overall number of Peelite MPs declined quite rapidly – falling from 89 to just 45 after the election of 1852 (and to only 26 after 1857). Eighteen of the Conservative MPs who had voted for the repeal of the Corn Laws did later join the protectionists – but they included none of the leaders.[24] The most prominent of these were Sir James Graham, Henry Goulburn, Aberdeen, Gladstone, Lord Lincoln (later Duke of Newcastle), Sidney Herbert and Lord Dalhousie.[25] Of these, Gladstone would be by far the most important, as well as by far the oddest. Whereas only Graham was at this point positively inclined to the Liberals, the general sentiment of the Peelites was rather detached from other parties. In fact, they were, following the example of Peel in later life, inclined to be self-important and self-regarding, looking down from a great height on partisan disputes, concerned about supporting free trade and opposing religious intolerance, but having no wish for fusion with either Liberals or Conservatives.

Gladstone was, through ambition, or distrust of the Liberal secularism, or nostalgia, or probably for all three reasons, most inclined to rejoin the Conservatives. The end of protectionism as party policy in 1852 should have made it easier. But Gladstone's hatred of Disraeli personally, sharpened by his scorn for what he saw as the chicanery of Disraeli's budget, closed off that possibility.[26] Nor would the Conservatives now, in any case, have wanted him back. On the night of the vote, those Peelites who had opposed the budget wisely kept away from the Carlton Club.[27] But with characteristic lack of sense and sensitivity, Gladstone went there a few days later and had the misfortune to run into Beresford with a group of drunken protectionist MPs. They treated him so roughly he was forced to leave.[28]

Gladstone was one those fortunate politicians whose real convictions moved in parallel to his equally real interests. He had by now usefully convinced himself that the Liberals were not so much of a threat to the Church of England as he had once feared. The Aberdeen ministry, dominated by Peelites but including Liberals, then institutionalized the existing Conservative schism. Gladstone would not now shift, nor would the others. The resulting loss of only slowly replaceable talent goes a long way towards explaining the Conservatives' difficulties in winning elections and in forming a credible Government during these wilderness years.

The Conservative leaders look a better team now than they did to contemporaries. Derby provided weight and Disraeli fire. But the two were often at odds over tactics. Derby was against opportunistic stances and alliances, much as Peel had been in the 1830s. He disagreed, as has been noted, with Disraeli's wish to throw over protection quickly. Despite his 'Orange' credentials, he also warned his deputy about exploiting anti-Catholic feeling, and was in the event proved right.[29] Derby now wanted to 'kill [the Aberdeen coalition] with kindness' and let the different factions within it fall apart – which they disobligingly failed to do. He would not attack Aberdeen's engagement in the Crimean War, as Disraeli wanted, and as Disraeli's mouthpiece *The Press* in fact did – to Derby's fury.[30]

These differences partly reflected the different tactical requirements of opposition in the Lords and Commons. In the Lower House inactivity is viewed as a sign of weakness; in the Lords it can be a badge of statesmanship. But the differences were also ones of temperament. Disraeli was simply more aggressive than his aloof, increasingly ill, often depressive leader. And there could be no warmth between them. Derby was of a different generation, a different class and, of course (as both he and Disraeli accepted), a different race. He was unapproachable and intensely dignified; no one in the party lightly presumed on his intimacy. He was a cold, clever, unkind man. In contrast to Disraeli, he never gave encouragement to younger men new to politics.[31] He was jealous of Disraeli's hold over the affections of his shy, sensitive, unmarried son, and showed it in brutal fashion. Finding Stanley arrived at Knowsley unexpectedly, his father sneered: 'What the devil brings you here, Edward? Are you going to get married, or has Disraeli cut his throat?'[32] (It would be many years before Stanley – by then fifteenth earl of Derby – would finally break away from Disraeli's influence to join the Liberals, where by reason of his views and attitudes he should probably always have been.)

Derby never visited Disraeli's comfortable home in its beautiful setting at Hughenden, paid for by the Bentinck family. He would not have wished to. For his part, Disraeli first visited Derby's ancestral pile at Knowsley in December 1851. He thought it 'a wretched house'. Derby was clearly bored with Disraeli's company. He only wanted to discuss horse racing and hunting and Disraeli could only discuss politics.[33] In October 1859 Disraeli again stayed overnight at Knowsley with his wife, Mary Anne, en route to a banquet where he and Derby were due to speak. Over dinner, Derby made cruel fun of Mary Anne in front of his guests. (He liked doing this sort of thing.[34]) Mary Anne Disraeli was a ridiculous figure in many respects, her talk full of nonsense and indiscretions. But Derby's behaviour caused deep offence to

Disraeli, who was highly protective of his wife, and he never accepted Derby's hospitality again.[35]

Disraeli and Derby grumbled about each other incessantly. But Disraeli kept his complaints *sotto voce*, for Derby was always the unchallenged master of his party, no matter how much back-benchers chafed at his absences and his reticence. And anyway, Derby was always, when it mattered, formally loyal to Disraeli, whom he needed. When the Prince Consort expressed his private doubts about Disraeli's reliability, Derby countered: 'He has better reason than anyone to be attached to our constitutional system since he has experience how easily under it a man may rise.'[36] This was politic, shrewd and true.

Derby and Disraeli could collaborate because they were both political realists. When occasion demanded, Derby too could be opportunistic, and Disraeli knew how to practise restraint. The reality, which both men recognized, was that their options were extremely limited. The first limitation was imposed by Peelite refusals of reunion. The second, and more serious, was that imposed by Lord Palmerston. In the event, both Derby and Disraeli would essentially agree with their colleague Malmesbury's dispirit-ing assessment: 'My answer [to the impatient] has always been that the Conservative Party can never be an active one except in office, or in Opposition against a Minister who attacks our institutions, and that we are now without either of these stimulants and, there-fore, dormant.'[37]

Those words were written two years into Palmerston's first Government. Before he took office, at the age of seventy, the situation had, at least briefly, appeared quite different. The omens looked remarkably good. The ignominious collapse in January 1855 of Aberdeen's discredited ministry, in which Palmerston had served (though only as Home Secretary, so with no connection to the Crimean War), opened the way for Derby and the Conservatives to return to power. Summoned by the Queen, Derby invited

Palmerston, Gladstone and Sidney Herbert to join his embryo Government. Palmerston, however, was determined to take first prize, and held out. After much manoeuvring, Derby had to admit defeat: he did not even bother to consult his colleagues before doing so. From their opposing viewpoints, both Disraeli and Gladstone (who despised Palmerston's populism) concurred in being highly critical of Derby's decision. But it seemed the right one at the time – not only for the country, where Palmerston was lionized as a War Leader, but even for the Conservative Party, and for Derby: heading a minority Conservative Government that excluded the most popular foreign minister of his age, and at a time of war, was an uninviting prospect. In any case, there seemed a good chance that Palmerston would fail. And even if he succeeded, his age should guarantee that he could not stay long. Such, then, was the Conservatives' gamble. Of course, it went disastrously wrong. Disraeli might consider Palmerston merely 'an old painted pantaloon'.[38] But others did not; and Palmerston himself just went on and on. In doing so, he deprived the Conservatives of the chance of office because – as Malmesbury implied – he had also deprived them of both their target and their platform.

Palmerston was pre-eminently not just the man for the crisis but in a wider sense the man for the times. The 1850s and 1860s were, in Bagehot's phrase, 'the day after the feast' – a period of moderation, restraint and scepticism.[39] The issue of further parliamentary reform never completely disappeared from the political agenda: it merely seemed to most of the political class, and probably to most people outside it, a great deal less pressing than it had been. Similarly, the Chartist movement – in its formal sense a movement for democracy, but embracing at the margins a much more radical social and economic programme – that had terrified an earlier generation no longer had the power to alarm. After the failure of the great National Petition of 1842, and the suppression of strikes and protests the following year, Chartism lost its way. Finally, on

Kennington Common in 1848 police and volunteer constables successfully dispersed a great assembly of demonstrators. In Europe, the year 1848 was one of revolution. In Britain, by contrast, it signalled the defeat of the revolutionaries. Though violent agitation recurred, the governing class had shown it would not be shifted, and it would not be defied.[40]

It was easy for critics, then and later, to describe the country as enduring an 'age of stagnation'. Even accepting the (by no means acceptable) pejorative implication, this is an inadequate description. It was, above all, a period of substantial prosperity. Liberal economics – and thus those Tories Liverpool and Peel – had contributed. Yet the general upswing was not, in itself, the work of the politicians but rather of businessmen, whose achievements were celebrated at the Great Exhibition of 1851. Recent investigation suggests that the general rise in English living standards in the 1830s and 1840s was less pronounced than sometimes suggested. But these were decades when Britain was approaching the height of its economic greatness.[41]

At such times, the tone of politics changes. Confidence edges into complacency. Politicians are expected to hold the ring at home and to assert the national interest abroad, but not to court unnecessary risk on either front. This is classically the mode of politics that the Conservative Party prefers and which it practises most successfully. But in the mid-nineteenth century it was not the Conservative leaders, but rather Palmerston, who offered it.

Palmerston is, therefore, almost as much a part of the Conservative story as are Derby and Disraeli. He was no more interested than the Conservatives in most of what enthused the more liberal Whigs. Once the Great Reform Bill was carried, the whole subject of electoral reform bored him – to Russell's disgust. Palmerston, one should recall, had been a Canningite rather than a Whig, and he remained Canning's disciple. His foreign policy, with its stress on robust defence of national interest, combined with judicious promotion of liberal constitutionalism, all presented with enormous patriotic flair, was Canning's writ large. The only identifiably liberal cause which moved him was the suppression of slavery, and even this imperative was subject to manipulation when national interest required.[42] He would have found no difficulty in being a Conservative, if it had suited his interests. But at his age, and with the existing balance of political forces, it did not. Lady Palmerston, speaking for her husband during the abortive negotiations to bring him into Derby's ministry in 1852, explained his cynical view. He felt that 'in England change of principle was more easily forgiven than change of party'.[43] And he was probably right.

The hold that Palmerston had over his fellow countrymen, and the degree to which he had stolen the most powerful weapons in the Conservative arsenal, are perhaps best illustrated by his response to the attacks on his conduct in the Don Pacifico affair, when he was Foreign Secretary in Russell's Government in 1850. For excellent reasons he seemed destined for humiliation, and in other conditions that would have been his fate. The House of Lords, persuaded by a masterly speech from Derby, had censored Palmerston's use of the British Mediterranean Fleet to collect compensation from Greece for property of doubtful value destroyed in a riot. This property happened to be owned by a crooked Portuguese Jew, David Pacifico, who also happened to enjoy British citizenship, having been born in Gibraltar. On any ordinary grounds the military response was disproportionate. Palmerston was not rated – by what was, admittedly, an enormously exacting parliamentary audience – as one of the greatest orators of his day. He was not especially polished. But he had a cunning, winning way of making his fellow MPs feel that he confided in them, which usually worked.[44] On this occasion, though, something different was required, and he provided it, replying to his critics in a four-and-a-half-hour speech that destroyed his opponents in both Houses, enraptured the middle classes, was talked about in the taverns, and fully and finally enshrined his immortal reputation as 'England's Minister'.[45] The most politically significant passage relates not to the events at issue, but rather to the happy state of Britain and, by skilful elision, the patriotic duty of a British Government to defend British citizens wherever and whenever tyranny jeopardized their rights. Said Palmerston:

> While we have seen . . . the political earthquake rocking Europe from side to side – while we have seen thrones shaken, shattered, levelled; institutions overthrown and destroyed – while in almost every country of Europe the conflict of civil war has deluged the land with blood . . . this country has presented a spectacle honourable to the people of England and worthy of the admiration of mankind.
>
> We have shown that liberty is compatible with order; that individual freedom is reconcilable with obedience to the law. We have shown the example of a nation in which every class of society accepts with cheerfulness the lot which Providence has assigned to it; while at the same time every individual of each class is constantly striving to raise himself in the social scale – not by injustice and wrong, not by violence and illegality – but by persevering good conduct and by the steady and energetic exertion of the moral and intellectual faculties with which the Creator has endowed him. To govern such a people as this is an object worthy of the ambition of the noblest man who lives in the land; and therefore I find no fault with those who think the opportunity a fair one, for endeavouring to place themselves in so distinguished and honourable a position. But I contend that we have not in our foreign policy done anything to forfeit the confidence of the country . . .
>
> I, therefore, fearlessly challenge the verdict which this House, as representing a political, a commercial, a constitutional country,

is to give on the question now brought before it; whether the principles on which the foreign policy of Her Majesty's Government has been conducted, and the sense of duty which has led us to think ourselves bound to afford protection to our fellow subjects abroad, are proper and fitting guides for those who are charged with the Government of England; and whether, as the Roman, in days of old, held himself free from indignity, when he could say *Civis Romanus sum*; so also a British subject, in whatever land he may be, shall feel confident that the watchful eye and the strong arm of England will protect him against injustice and wrong.[46]

These sentiments are closer to an historically identifiable conservatism than Derby – or, at this time, even Disraeli – managed to utter. That is true, even though Palmerston's actual conduct of foreign policy as a whole was – and, given Britain's trading interests, had to be – a good deal more cautious than his rhetoric.[47]

Palmerston's Government fell in March 1857, because his allies deserted him over his belligerent tactics in China. But its demise did neither them nor the Conservative Opposition much good. The ensuing electoral contest was personalized, and the personality of Palmerston triumphed. The Tory vote slumped. Alarmingly for the Conservative leaders, a number of Conservative candidates explicitly declared their support for Palmerston. Paradoxically, what then forced him out again the following year was the accusation that he had been too willing to appease France by deporting plotters against Napoleon III. Old and unpopular, he seemed finished. And the Conservatives had another chance.

Derby was still personally reluctant to take office. But he frankly admitted to the Queen that, after what had happened in 1851 and 1855, he would have to accept it, if offered, because otherwise 'the Conservative Party would be broken up for ever'.[48] The ensuing Conservative ministry was very much a minority administration.

Accordingly, its measures were the mildly liberal ones any other ministry would have undertaken – removing property qualifications for MPs, allowing Jews to sit in Parliament, passing an India Act. The Opposition, meanwhile, pressed, abroad, the line of hostility to Austria in the continuing Italian independence struggle and, at home, the case for parliamentary reform. The Conservatives opposed the first but felt the need to respond to the second, and introduced their own Reform Bill.

But Disraeli's reform proposals, like his 1852 budget, were too obviously skewed in his party's interests to stand a chance in such a House. The Government envisaged harmonizing the suffrage requirement in counties and boroughs, but – and this is what really mattered to the Conservatives – as a quid pro quo it would have stripped borough dwellers of their county votes and effected a redistribution of seats in favour of the counties. (The latter proposal was, in strict numerical terms, perfectly justified – the counties were seriously under-represented – but in the prevailing atmosphere it was portrayed as partisan.) The Bill was duly defeated on 1 April 1859, by 330 to 291 votes. In the following election the Conservatives gained seats, but not enough.

Meanwhile the Opposition united against them. On 6 June 1859, in Willis's Rooms in St James's, a gathering of Whigs, Liberals, Palmerstonians, Radicals and Peelites publicly put aside their differences. Palmerston, in a display of comradely sprightliness, sprang on to the platform and hauled up the diminutive Russell after him. There were loud cheers and fulsome expressions of goodwill.[49] This meeting meant the end of Derby's ministry – defeated six days later in the Commons. It also can be seen to mark the origins of the reconstructed Liberal Party, which Palmerston and Russell would now lead, but which would only later be fashioned into a successful party of government by Gladstone (who was, in fact, cautiously absent that day from Willis's).

Derby's second ministry thus had nothing better to show for

itself than his first. Not surprisingly, the Conservatives now went notably quiet. They confined themselves to limited criticism, while lending support to Palmerston against his more radically minded colleagues (including Gladstone). Indeed, a series of specific undertakings was given to that effect.[50] Not even the temperamentally activist Disraeli contested the approach.

The problem with the Conservatives' strategy was simply Palmerston's longevity. There was, indeed, a morbid race between the demoralizing despair that gnawed at the entrails of the Conservative Party and the physical disintegration which affected the Prime Minister. In early August 1865 the now 61-year-old Disraeli wrote to Derby, declaring that he felt 'in the decline of life' and was fatigued with the 'the leadership of hopeless Opposition'. He offered to yield up his role to someone who might help Derby 'form an anti-Revolutionary Government on a broad basis'.[51] He was probably half sincere.

Summer passed into autumn. Then, on Wednesday, 18 October, just short of his eighty-first birthday, Palmerston suddenly died. All at once, the view from the Carlton Club looked brighter.

The Club, itself, after the departure of the Peelites, had once more become the main centre of Conservative Party activity. There had been modest improvements. Disraeli, with Derby's concurrence, had put the organization on to a new footing, appointing Sir William Joliffe as Chief Whip, in place of the disloyal and irascible Beresford, and Philip Rose as the party's election manager. Both were good choices. Joliffe was a country gentleman with useful contacts and no ambition. Rose was Disraeli's solicitor. In an attempt to safeguard his professional integrity (which did, in the end, become sullied), Rose insisted on being unpaid and remained based at the Carlton. Markham Spofforth, however, a junior member of the firm, did receive a salary and undertook much of the day-to-day party business, maintaining an office in Westminster. Disputed results were still good business for solicitors. But

Spofforth enjoyed no monopoly in party lawsuits. Perhaps the most important break with the past, however, was that neither Rose nor Spofforth (unlike Bonham earlier) sat as an MP.[52] This placed a ceiling on their ambitions.

It was something of an achievement to keep the party organization healthy during this period of impotence and frustration. The central organization of the Peelites had swiftly disappeared after 1846: that did not happen to the Conservatives in the 1850s and 1860s. The Conservatives had another advantage. They were much richer than their opponents. Derby himself was phenomenally wealthy and often generous.[53]

As in earlier years, by far the most important political activity at election time was organized locally. The task of the centre was to monitor and nudge it along. Since the 1832 Act, this activity had been concentrated on the boroughs, with a particular focus on the registration – and de-registration – of voters. That remained the case. The smaller and middling boroughs, where Conservative gains looked most likely, were the priority. But the counties also required attention, partly because borough dwellers spilled out into their electorates, and partly because it was obvious that, sooner or later, county electorates would be enlarged. The first initiative for a national effort at voter registration in the counties was unofficial and was, indeed, rejected by the party. But the plan later received official approval and support. It was one of a number of new departures in the late 1860s, which are considered in the next chapter.[54]

Despite the vital signs, this was an unhappy time for Conservatives at all levels. The party managers had to cope with a good deal of discontent. Much of it was directed at the leadership, even though, as is traditionally the way, it was expressed semi-privately, or in coded fashion. Joliffe complained that after Palmerston's return to power in 1859 Derby spent too much of his time at Knowsley – though that can hardly have surprised people, because it was simply what the aristocracy did when out of power. Unfortunately, Disraeli, too, was often away from Westminster, surrounded by a small and unrepresentative group of intimates in Hughenden.[55] This was deemed less excusable.

But now, with Palmerston – finally – dead, Tory self-doubts and grumbles fell away. Russell, as Prime Minister, was the immediate beneficiary; Gladstone proposed a new Reform Bill. But the Liberals were in fractious mood. The Bill was bitterly opposed by a conservative-minded section of the party, christened by the Radical John Bright the 'Cave of Adullam', and led by the brilliant, cantankerous, myopic albino Robert Lowe. Lowe's principled arguments against an extension of the electorate to what, as a classical liberal, he regarded as the all-too-biddable and bribable working class were a very different mix from those of Disraeli.[56] In this case, the Adullamites were decisive. Gladstone's measure was duly thrown out by the Commons. And so the Conservatives had yet another chance. But what were they to do with it?

What was not in doubt, this time round, was whether they would take power. They seized it; and the single thread of continuity in all that followed is their determination to hold on to it. This, in turn, meant that they would have to take up the issue of franchise reform.

There was, once again, an evident demand for change. On 29 June 1866, within a fortnight of the failure of Gladstone's Bill, an assembly of 10,000 gathered to protest. The following month a demonstration of double the size in Hyde Park ended in violence. Had they a working majority in the Commons, the Conservatives might just have ignored such pressure. But they were not in that happy position. They were in a minority, beneficiaries of the divisions of their opponents rather than their own electoral success. Disraeli, leading in the Commons for the new Conservative ministry, saw in these circumstances a unique opportunity, and – with Derby's complete agreement – resolved to exploit it.

There were some respectable philosophically conservative, as well as party-political Conservative, arguments for a Reform Bill at this juncture. Of the former, the most important was based on the assumed need to preclude the onset of thoroughgoing urban-based democracy. This, it was felt (following Burke's admonitions), must lead to threats to property and much else besides. Arguably, this defensive goal would be best pursued not by piecemeal resistance to individual proposals to widen the franchise, but rather by placing it, once and for all, on a uniform and intellectually defensible basis. This, it was thought, was most likely to be achieved by accepting household suffrage in the boroughs, but with some safeguards. As regards the Conservative (that is, partisan) arguments for change, the goals were more specific, and not at all high-minded. Trying to gain greater representation for the counties, limiting the urban electoral sprawl, and some useful gerrymandering through seat redistribution – all had their attractions. Finally, the Conservatives thought that it was just about acceptable to widen the franchise of the boroughs as long as they kept the counties out of that reform.

What actually happened is that politics prevailed over principle, and the pressure of events then prevailed over political calculation.[57] Finally, Disraeli sought, with some long-term effect, to persuade the world that the outcome was what he had intended all along and that it reflected a strategic, indeed a philosophical, response to the great problems of the day.

The variously complicated options came and went in the course of debate in the House of Commons, modified through wheezes and concessions devised, dropped or remodelled by Disraeli. The Cabinet was often – and deliberately – kept in the dark. But not all its members were stupid, and few politicians have been more intelligent than Robert Gascoyne-Cecil, Lord Cranborne (later third Marquess of Salisbury). General Peel (Sir Robert's brother), the Earl of Carnarvon (an intelligent but somewhat silly man, not helped by his school nickname of 'Twitters', much employed by Disraeli) and Cranborne himself all balked at the proposed household franchise, and understandably. They were, as they complained, being asked to accept what amounted to an electoral revolution, without any assurance, or even any serious discussion, of the outcome.

The prospect of this troika's imminent resignation from the Cabinet forced a furious Derby to amend his proposals. The compromise was a £6 rating franchise. This was then unconvincingly expounded by Disraeli to the House. Meanwhile, behind the scenes Disraeli stirred up the backbenchers. The view which then came out of an MPs' meeting at the Carlton Club was that it was preferable to revert to the original household franchise (with safeguards). The thinking is not difficult to fathom. It was not profound. But it was typical. The party wanted to prevail in the House. It was not too worried about details. It had no great hopes of electoral success in the boroughs on any franchise. So why not bow to Radical blackmail? Why not purchase some popularity by going all the way? Why not make one's opponents look foolish in the process? Why not *win*? And why not enjoy it? Equally typically, these apparently shrewd considerations turned out to be problematic in their results.

For now, however, they prevailed. At a special Cabinet on Saturday, 2 March 1867, Derby and Disraeli persuaded the majority to revert to the original plans. Strengthened by Cranborne, and unmoved by Derby's prediction that it would be 'the end of the Conservative Party', the three ministers resigned. Cranborne's subsequent resignation statement was moderately phrased: he wanted the Government to fall, but he did not wish, himself, to bring it down. Despite that, his speech denouncing Disraeli would have given pause to a better man, or a worse politician, than its target. Implicitly making the comparison with Disraeli's own attack on Peel's betrayal over repeal of the Corn Laws, Cranborne now excoriated an approach based on what he called 'the ethics of the political adventurer'.[58] All knew whom he meant. But Cranborne did not deign to conspire. This relieved the party leaders of the fear of serious rebellion from their own side. The difficulties they faced from the Opposition were, though, quite sufficient.

Disraeli's plans, in fact, soon fell apart. He tried to have borough household suffrage tempered by dual voting, based on special qualifications. But he failed. He also had to concede a lower qualification for the franchise (£12 ratepayers) in the counties than he wanted. More seriously, he had made much in Cabinet and in the House of the distinction between those in the boroughs who paid their rates personally and those who 'compounded', that is, did so through their landlords. The former were allegedly upstanding, independent-minded citizens worthy of enfranchisement, the latter not. But he then simply capitulated to an amendment moved by Grover Hodgkinson (the 'Hodgkinson Amendment'), which abolished compounding altogether. It was shameless, but in parliamentary terms effective. And so the Second Reform Act reached the statute book as what at least looked like a Conservative measure.[59]

Disraeli did not mind how many passes he had sold. He knew the significance of what he had done. After winning the first significant division on the measure, he walked into the Carlton Club coffee room in the early hours and, with a rare look of joy, announced: 'This is the greatest night since '41!'[60]

Whatever one thinks of that judgement, the passing of the Act was certainly important for the Conservative Party – but not for the reasons most Conservatives thought at the time. The 1868 election held on the new franchise was badly lost. This hardly suggests either that the new electors were impressed by the party's reforming credentials or that the reformers had mined any new conservative social seam. In fact, Cranborne's analysis in the scorching article he had contributed to the autumn 1867 issue of the *Quarterly Review* turned out to be correct. Disraeli and Derby had implemented a revolution whereby, henceforth, 'a clear majority of votes in a clear majority of constituencies [had] been made over to those who [had] no other property but for the labour of their hands'. They had, by accepting household franchise, 'fully hoodwinked' their parliamentary supporters; and the Conservative hope that the party had settled the question of democracy was vain, because 'there can be no finality in politics'.[61]

Derby himself revealed the frivolity and cynicism of the enterprise when he later acknowledged (in private conversation) that it was about 'dishing the Whigs'. As for the effects, these amounted to a 'leap in the dark'.[62] In fact, as a result of the Act – notably Disraeli's acceptance of the Hodgkinson Amendment – the size of the electorate approximately doubled.[63] Rather than sarcastically enquiring of Lady Cranborne whether 'Robert was still doing his sums', Derby (and Disraeli) might arguably have done more of their own.[64] But, of course, the sums did not matter to them. It was power that mattered.

One might object that this criticism is unjust. Why, after all, should the Conservatives not have embraced democracy earlier than they eventually did? But that is beside the point. No Conservative at the time did embrace it, and certainly not Disraeli. No Conservative thought that a major widening of the electoral base was even in the party's interests. It is true that, in the long run, the great Conservative revival of the late nineteenth and early twentieth centuries would be based on the cities, not the countryside. This may prove something about the Conservative Party's adaptability. But it proves little about the wisdom or otherwise of Disraeli and Derby in 1867.

Disraeli personally, however, was a beneficiary of the passing of the Act. His parliamentary sure-footedness, his brilliance in debate, and his verve and nerve in handling the Bill finally established him as a political leader in his own right – and, indeed, as the leader of the Conservative Party after Derby. The moment for that change was now approaching.

Derby's health had for years been bad. In 1861 and 1862 he had been for long periods a semi-invalid, laid low by gout and various infections, and afflicted by what seems to have been a stroke. Throughout 1863 his health was fragile. The summer of 1864 was made miserable by a recurrence of gout. In November he had an ulcerated throat. He spent too long at Knowsley, which was damp and depressing.[65] He was capable of revival. The prospects and exigencies of office electrified him. His enormous intellect was undimmed. His personality remained crushing. He could rouse himself to write a flawless memorandum, compose an incisive speech, or issue a terrifying rebuke. But he had aged by more than his years. He was ill, yet again, at the time of the Reform Act, nervously exhausted and drained by the pain of gout, for which he was now being treated with large and potentially lethal quantities of opium and alcohol. Sometimes he could hardly move and was carried up and down stairs. His complexion had acquired a deadly pallor.[66]

He was not yet seventy. But on Wednesday, 19 February 1868 he wrote to Disraeli informing him of the 'absolute necessity' of his resigning the premiership because of his health, and of his hope that Disraeli would accept the office that the Queen would in all probability ask him to undertake.[67] The assumption Derby made proved correct. It need not have been. The leader in the House of Commons was by this time bound to be the most likely candidate to lead the party and become Prime Minister, when the post fell vacant. Moreover, Disraeli's leadership in the Lower House had been that of a virtuoso performer. Yet it was still eventually lack of a suitable alternative that overcame doubts about him. He was not, after all, young – only five years younger than Derby – and his achievements, outside the Commons, were few. In truth, Disraeli was lucky that Derby's health finally collapsed when it did. Had Derby remained leader for a further year, and the party been out of power once again, matters would have been more complicated. As it was, it fell to the Queen, on the advice of the outgoing Prime

Minister, and not to the suspicious barons of the Conservative Party, to decide the matter. This helped smooth Disraeli's way. After a short delay, because Derby was keen to get through an embarrassingly large number of resignation honours, Disraeli duly received his appointment. At a celebratory reception, which he and his wife gave at the Foreign Office, the new Prime Minister declared: 'I have climbed to the top of the greasy pole.'[68] (He liked the expression and used it on several occasions.)[69]

Disraeli would stamp his identity on the Conservative Party in a way that Derby – despite being its longest-serving leader and thrice Prime Minister – simply did not. Disraeli undoubtedly took the credit for much of what Derby had achieved. During the years of their association, Derby was definitely the senior partner. If Derby had dropped him, Disraeli would have fallen – though, being a cunning and experienced politician, Derby always understood the benefits of avoiding that.

Only at the end, as Derby's always dull star waned, did Disraeli's truly begin to dazzle. Ill and bitter, finding it as hard as any power-ful leader does to draw back – in this case, back towards decline and death – Derby now resented Disraeli's swagger. He resented, in particular, the famous speech in Edinburgh in October 1867, in which Disraeli – even before he had taken the reins – with effrontery and in defiance of historical fact, but with a note of genius, claimed his place in a line of Tory reformists.[70] Referring to the 1867 Reform Act, and to his conduct during its passage, and enlarging on it, Disraeli claimed to have 'had to prepare the mind of the country, and to educate – if it be not arrogant to use a phrase – . . . our Party'. He also placed this mission within what might be termed a Tory reformist framework: 'In a progressive country change is constant; and the great question is not whether you should resist change which is inevitable, but whether that change should be carried out in deference to the manners, the customs, the laws, the traditions of the people, or in deference to abstract principles and arbitrary and general doctrines.'[71]

Derby lingered on. He spoke in the Lords, though without his old force. He then retired to Knowsley. Asked how he felt, he uttered his final words: 'Bored to the utmost powers of extinction.' He died on 23 October 1869.[72]

By then the Conservative Party was out of office again. But it was out of the wilderness too. It was also Disraeli's. And with Disraeli in charge, no one would be bored.

DISRAELI AT SYDENHAM.

*Disraeli's speech to a Conservative mass audience at the Crystal Palace,
Sydenham, in 1872, dwelt on the twin themes of Empire and social reform.
Both would figure even larger in party legend than in practice.*

4

DISRAELI'S PARTY, I – LEADER OF THE OPPOSITION

Disraeli's first spell as Prime Minister was short and its measures seize few historical headlines. Being in a minority, his ministry had to concentrate on non-partisan but, perhaps because of that, generally useful measures. The Corrupt Practices Bill, for example, was a step towards tackling bribery at elections. The appointment of a royal commission on the Sanitary Laws would have important consequences, not least when the Conservatives returned to power.

Disraeli was also to be found mulling over what to do about Ireland. Land tenure was currently the most difficult issue, with a large tenant class beholden to and resentful of a small landlord class. Somewhat more amenable to compromise appeared, at this stage, the religious question. The aim was a *modus vivendi* with the Catholic Church in a country where all official institutions were Protestant, but where Protestants were a minority. Derby and Disraeli tentatively settled on a scheme to set up a Catholic university in Dublin. The Irish hierarchy and, in England, Henry Manning, Archbishop of Westminster, appeared interested.

But then Gladstone up-ended the strategy. He had been shocked to lose office and appalled to find Disraeli as Prime Minister. He needed an issue to re-unite the Liberal Party. Above all, responding to Russell's declaration at Christmas 1867 that he would not again take office, Gladstone – already Liberal leader in the Commons – needed a way of demonstrating his capacity for outright leadership of the party. Terrorist incidents and disorders perpetrated by 'Fenians' now provided an opportunity to bring the question of Ireland to the table.[1] Gladstone argued that religious resentment lay at the root of the problem. On this, the Liberals could always hope to outbid the Conservatives. Gladstone now embraced calls for dis-establishment of the Church in Ireland and brought forward resolutions in the Commons to that effect.[2] This was even more to the Catholic and Irish taste than a university, and the Conservatives were duly outflanked.

Nor, in the matter of the Church of Ireland, did they have firm ground to stand upon. Almost everyone, even on the Conservative benches, understood that existing arrangements were indefensible. The real question was how Church resources could be deployed more sensibly without endangering its existence. But Disraeli could not now admit this. He also felt outraged at what he considered a stab in the back by Manning. In any case, Gladstone's resolutions were carried and the Government's case against them was put singularly feebly by Stanley, who – serving as Foreign Secretary under Disraeli as he had in his father's last administration – did not believe in it.[3] Disraeli's colleagues were, indeed, divided by their differing ecclesiastical allegiances. Cairns (Lord Chancellor) was a Low Church Ulsterman.[4] Gathorne-Hardy (Home Secretary) was High Church, as was (albeit outside the Cabinet) Cranborne, soon to be Salisbury. For his part, Stanley (soon to inherit his father's earldom) was an extreme if philanthropically minded progressive, a secularist who detested all kinds of churchmanship and in particular what he called sneeringly the *parti prêtre*.[5]

As for Disraeli, he greatly enjoyed debating religion, which he did in a passionate but wholly speculative manner. Years earlier, young Edward Stanley had described his mentor as highly interested in 'the philosophical discussion of religious questions, [meaning] the origin of the various beliefs which have governed mankind, their changes at different epochs, and those still to come'.[6] Disraeli was a philosophical and theological relativist; a sceptic, in fact, though he would have bridled at the description. But really what mattered to him, in any case, was the politics. On this ground he took great pleasure, and saw considerable advantage, in denouncing anything which seemed to pose a threat to the Anglican establishment. He was even-handed, disliking equally deviants on either wing, High Church 'Ritualists' and Broad Church rationalists ('Rits' and 'Rats', as he called them).[7] So now, having hung on long enough to ensure the franchise was in place and to exert the maximum ecclesiastical patronage, Disraeli went to the country on an only slightly updated version of the traditional Englishman's 'No Popery' platform.

Disraeli always retained a taste for conspiracies – like his interest in the philosophy of religion, it was part of his Continental mind-set. In this case, the role of principal plotter fell to the Catholic wing of the Anglican Church, the Ritualists, who were, so their cruder critics suggested, acting as Roman fifth columnists, bent on subverting England's Protestant heritage. Disraeli was certainly among these cruder critics (as was the Queen); and, as so often, he overdid it. Even in the overheated atmosphere created by so-called 'papal aggression' (the re-creation of the Catholic hierarchy in England) some years earlier, or at the height of the controversy over papal infallibility a little later, the language Disraeli now used in his election address would have seemed extreme. Under present conditions, it was plain absurd. He solemnly told the electors of Buckingham: 'Among the discordant activity of many factions there moves the supreme power of one Power . . . The ultimate triumph were our Church to fall would be to that Power which would substitute for the authority of our Sovereign the supremacy of a foreign Prince . . .'[8]

Whatever Disraeli and others might subsequently claim, in fighting the first election on the new, extended franchise which they had proudly introduced they showed no interest whatsoever in Tory democracy but placed their reliance instead on old-fashioned prejudice. Not having much else to offer, the tactics were better than nothing. They may have helped further strengthen the party's hold on Lancashire, where the Orange vote would remain of great significance for many years. But, taken as a whole, the throw failed. While the Conservatives made gains in the English counties, they sustained significant losses in the boroughs (though even here there were other straws in the wind – see below). The results for Scotland and Ireland then decisively reinforced those of England. Disraeli, recognizing the outcome, but incidentally creating a constitutional precedent, declined to meet the new Parliament and resigned. The Conservatives were out, and Gladstone's great reforming administration was in, with a large majority (387, to the Tories' 271).[9]

In modern conditions, Disraeli would almost certainly have had to resign as leader. It was he (now that Derby had gone) who bore chief responsibility for the radical widening of the borough franchise, and the new borough voters had shown no gratitude at all. It was then his personal decision, pursued against the instincts of key colleagues and encapsulated in his highly negative election address, to fight on a No Popery platform. In the conditions of the time, however, discontent with his leadership found other outlets.

There were moves to have Cranborne, now Salisbury (having succeeded to the marquessate on 12 April 1868), take over as leader in the Lords. His fellow rebel Carnarvon even suggested that in this role Salisbury need have no dealings with Disraeli, though this was hardly a practical option. The vacancy had arisen because Malmesbury, who had stepped into Derby's shoes, refused to continue. Disraeli desperately sought to twist the arm of Cairns to take the job and prevailed. But after one session Cairns withdrew.

Disraeli knew how disastrous it would be if he had to try to work with Salisbury. It was no secret how matters stood. Salisbury icily described his leader in a letter written at this time as 'an adventurer', 'without principles and honesty' and (to cap it all) not 'identified by birth or property with the Conservative classes in the country'.[10] One, or the other, or both members of such a partnership could not have survived it. In the event, the non-factional, reassuringly high-born, amiable Duke of Richmond accepted the post, with Cairns as his mentor. This was no more than a win on points for Disraeli. Cairns was a long-standing enthusiast for 'fusion' of Conservatives and Whiggish Liberals under the leadership of the young Derby. Fortunately for Disraeli – and fortunately for the Conservative Party – Derby did not fulfil the expectations placed in him. Initially, he was too loyal. Then, he was seen to be too liberal. Much later, he was exposed as temperamentally too feeble – at least in his detractors' eyes. (Another explanation, perhaps more accurate and certainly more charitable, was that as a principled Cobdenite, and believing in tranquillity through trade, he was radically opposed to Disraeli's assertive foreign policy.) Finally, under circumstances to be described below, he resigned and jumped political ship altogether.

In these difficult years of Opposition, Disraeli's leadership ultimately depended on just one man – himself. His self-belief, despite his depressions and distractions, kept him going. Though he would claim on several occasions to be willing to step down as party leader, he always insisted that he remain in the House of Commons. This condition rendered any attempt to replace him hopeless, because the prospects for any Conservative leader in the

Lower House, confronted with Disraeli's sardonic and electric presence, were bleak. Nor, at this point, would the party have been prepared to accept the only alternative leader from the Lords, namely Salisbury.

So the Conservatives, and their leader, struggled on. It was an unsatisfactory period for all concerned. Disraeli was often ill or absent. He spent more of his time writing his latest novel, *Lothair* (which gave him the satisfaction of getting back at Manning), than he did concentrating on parliamentary business. He rationalized his disengagement by explaining that all the Conservatives could do was wait and predicting that the Radicals would turn against Gladstone once he had served their purpose. This was, anyway, how Disraeli viewed politics.[11] One of his convictions, founded on many years of experience, was (as he put it) that 'the pendulum swings'.[12] And eventually it did.

So Disraeli survived to return to power. That he did is part of a larger mystery, which is how he managed to retain his political grip for so long and under such unpropitious conditions. This juncture, suspended between failure and triumph, seems an apposite place to examine the man behind the politician.

Salisbury's description of Disraeli as 'an adventurer' is apt. His life was, indeed, an adventure, in which fame was the constant goal, though the means of attaining it evolved. His chosen motto, *Forti nihil difficile* ('To the brave nothing is hard'), sums up the defiance which was at the base of his character.[13] He had the self-reliance and self-containment of an outsider, though the social aspects of this should not be exaggerated. His family was, by upper-middle-class standards, quite respectable.[14] His father, Isaac D'Israeli, acquired some minor literary distinction, inherited money and, finally, moved into a house in the country, at Bradenham in Buckinghamshire. Isaac was a non-practising, sceptical Jew, who fell out with the synagogue, and Benjamin was in due course baptized, at the age of twelve. Had he not been, of course, he could not have had a career in politics at all.

Young Disraeli might have attended a public school, even Eton, but for some reason he was sent instead to a private school run by a Unitarian minister. Ever afterwards, Disraeli romanticized Eton (and detested Unitarianism). His education continued to be un-conventional. He spent a year at home reading in his father's copious library and then, making no attempt for Oxford or Cambridge, was articled to a firm of City solicitors. He dropped the apostrophe in his name – the first and last time in his life that he played down his exoticism – and moved as much as he could, using his father's connections, in literary circles. Among this acquaintance was the publisher, John Murray. Murray not only flattered young Benjamin's literary ambitions: he was foolish enough to place confidence in his services when founding a newspaper, which failed, and when backing a speculative mining venture, which collapsed. Disraeli lost far more money than he possessed and sank deep into debt, from which he struggled for years to escape. Writing fashionable novels about high society (from a position of imaginative ignorance) seemed a good way back to the road of fame and wealth. And it would prove so, but not at first. Through his sister Sarah he found a publisher for his first book, *Vivian Grey,* in which he sent up Murray and lampooned the still more dangerous Croker. The book was, not surprisingly, badly received and, weighed down by his early failures, Benjamin suffered a severe and prolonged nervous collapse, which lasted from 1827 to 1830.

The prescribed cure was foreign travel, and it worked. Young Disraeli had already developed the taste. In 1826 he did a grand tour of Europe with friends. Travel was a pathway to Romance, and for Disraeli the Romantic ideal was summed up by the outrageous life of Byron. On this occasion, he was rowed on Lake Geneva at night by Byron's former boatman, Maurice. On his second, longer, therapeutic Eastern tour of 1830–1, he made the acquaintance of Byron's even more famous associate Tita, who had fought by

Byron's side at Missolonghi. (Tita was later installed by Disraeli as a servant at Bradenham, and after Isaac's death provided with the post of government messenger by the then Prime Minister, who later still obtained a pension for his widow.)[15] Benjamin's lengthy visit to the eastern Mediterranean heightened his appreciation of Oriental exoticism. It developed his sense of his own Jewishness within that context – something that would henceforth be a connecting theme in his novels. It has also been suggested, plausibly but not provably, that he came to terms in this new environment with an otherwise suppressed homosexual streak in his nature.[16] Of more importance for the future, however, is the sympathy Disraeli discovered for the Ottoman Empire. The Ottomans had, of course, over the centuries proved far more tolerant of Jews than had Christendom. But Disraeli's sympathy for the Turks and for the Middle East in general was primarily sensual. He liked the elaborate manners, relished the extraordinary costumes, and even took a perverse delight in the brutality. Writing to a friend, he described his time in the pashaluk of Albania:

> When I wrote to you last I had some thoughts, indeed I had resolved, to join the Turkish Army as a volunteer in the Albanian war. I found, however, on my arrival at Corfu . . . that the Grand Vizier . . . had proceeded with such surprising energy that the war, which had begun so magnificently, had already dwindled into an insurrection . . . I determined to turn my intended campaign into a visit of congratulation to headquarters . . . [at] Yanina, the capital of the province . . . For weeks I was in a scene equal to anything in the *Arabian Nights* – such processions, such dresses, such corteges of horsemen, such caravans of camels. Then the delight of being made much of by a man who was daily decapitating half the Province.[17]

Disraeli returned to England cured of his depression and with ideas and drafts for future novels in his knapsack. Above all, he came back determined to go into politics, news of the Great Reform Bill having reached him in Egypt.[18] Unlike his family, who were Tory diehards, Benjamin was enthusiastic for the cause of reform. He promptly threw himself into the task of finding a parliamentary seat. But he made the quest on his own terms. The two dominant elements in his newly assumed political identity – ones which would echo through his career – were his social radicalism and his Jewishness.

Disraeli stood three times as a Radical at High Wycombe, all without success. He championed far-reaching reform of the franchise. But he was an independent Radical, aligning himself with the Tories rather than the Whigs. This was in part because the Whigs would not have him anyway, and in part because he was by instinct a paternalistic populist rather than a utilitarian. But above all it was because he was beholden first to the local Tory magnate, Lord Chandos, and then, more closely, to the man who would become his mentor, model and protector, the Tory former Lord Chancellor, Lord Lyndhurst. (It was Lyndhurst who taught him the value of impassibility under pressure, summed up in Disraeli's famous advice – 'never complain and never explain'.)[19] It was, therefore, as a declared Tory that he stood in Taunton (1835), again unsuccessfully, and then – finally successfully – for Maidstone (1837). Another success followed. His fellow Member, Wyndham Lewis, died the following year and Disraeli re-established his finances by marrying his widow – though the money, for which (as he frankly admitted) he pursued her was soon supplemented by, on his side, affection and, on hers, devotion.[20]

Disraeli did not now leave behind his socially radical rhetoric. But he had to drop Radical politics. The theme of an alliance between the Crown, the landed aristocracy and the lower classes, all connected within an organic and traditional framework of duty, would become his political trademark. It was destined to appear and reappear in various nebulous and opportunistically selected shapes and sizes down the years. At this point it centred on the 'Young England' Group. Formed by three young Conservative MPs, George Smythe, Alexander Baillie-Cochrane and Lord John Manners, its idealistic, muddled identity was made up of romantic medievalism, High Church piety and social justice. Disraeli was asked to join and soon – because of his seniority and his abilities – he effectively led it. He never accepted the full programme (no sensible politician would have) and the piety he could, anyway, do without. The group did not last. Of its members, only Manners would enjoy a notable political career, largely thanks to Disraeli's patronage.

Disraeli made of Young England what he could for his own purposes. Visiting Paris, he button-holed King Louis-Philippe and offered it as a secret vehicle for French policy, in what has been aptly described as 'a mild form of treason'.[21] Disraeli went some way towards voting with the movement's convictions. He supported the Chartists and repeatedly attacked the new poor law. But Young England's most eloquent and influential expression is to be found in Disraeli's novels *Coningsby* (1844) and *Sybil* (1845). (The extent to which there is a connection between this legacy and the social legislation enacted by Disraeli's second ministry will be considered separately.)

The third book of the trilogy, *Tancred* (1847), while bearing traces of 'Young England', is notable for its development of Disraeli's other long-term obsession, the nature of Jewishness and the role of the Jews in history and society. From *Alroy* (1833), about a twelfth-century Jewish hero, through *Coningsby*, where the mysterious, fabulously wealthy Jew Sidonia first appears, to *Tancred*, where Disraeli's views on the interdependence of Judaism and Christianity are expounded at length, the theme was on constant display. Disraeli also tackles it in his biography of *Lord*

George Bentinck (1851) – Bentinck and Disraeli having fought side by side for Jewish toleration.

Why could he not leave the matter alone? And why did he adopt such an extraordinarily provocative line of argument in defence of Jewish rights? The answer to both questions, which says much about his character, is that he was determined to assert his – and by extension the Jewish people's – essential superiority, not ask for special favours. Perhaps he had been wounded by experience of anti-semitism, though there is not much evidence of that.[22] In any case, from the earliest times Disraeli asserted his claims in rather preposterous terms to superiority on grounds of birth – 'I am not disposed for a moment to admit that my pedigree is not as good as that of the Cavendishes.'[23] And, naturally, because Disraeli was a Conservative, the Jews had to be the most conservative people in the world. In *Lord George Bentinck*, he asserts: '[The Jews] are a living and most striking evidence of the falsity of that pernicious doctrine of modern times, the natural equality of man . . . all the tendencies of the Jewish race are conservative. Their bias is to religion, property and natural aristocracy.'[24]

Disraeli had little knowledge of and less interest in Judaism as a religion. He was not, after all, a practising Jew, but a baptized and occasionally practising Christian. Prominent Jews like the Rothschilds, though friendly and flattered, were also uneasy: here was a renegade Jew making claims for Jews that most practising Jews would prudently avoid.[25] Disraeli described himself to the Queen as 'the blank page between the Old and the New Testament'.[26] It was as the 'purest' branch of the semitic element of Caucasian stock that Jewry demanded respect. Such views, foolish even at the time, later did Jews harm, playing into the hands of dogmatic anti-semites. Their importance, however, as a factor in Victorian politics is different, and twofold. First, they reduced the credibility of Disraeli's religious campaigns on behalf of political Anglicanism. And second, they provided a handle, as will be seen later, for those wishing to damn the Conservatives' policy towards the Eastern Question.

In the early 1870s under Disraeli, just as in the late 1830s under Peel, the main force working for a Conservative revival was reaction against the radicalism of the party in power – both anger at what had already been done, and fear of what might be next.[27] But Disraeli was prepared to wait. He had acquired more patience with experience. Above all, he had had his fill of minority governments. If he was to govern, he wanted a working majority. And that meant more than a marginal Conservative advance in an election. It required a Liberal collapse. But how to achieve it? And how to know when the conditions for it had been reached?

Gladstone's ministry soon set about providing them. Having succeeded, without too much difficulty, in his plans for the Irish Church, the Prime Minister grasped the much more difficult issue of Irish land reform. He did so sooner than he wished, because it was patently – and predictably – clear that abstruse questions of the Irish Church Establishment were irrelevant to the wider settlement of the country. He had to act because of the continuing Irish agricultural crisis and, specifically, because of the threat posed by Fenian revolutionaries. But the response showed the strategy to be misguided. The Irish Land Act of 1870 did nothing to calm the storm – rather the contrary. It went some way towards compensating tenants for improvements they had made to their dwellings, if evicted from them. But many of those under threat of eviction were not, anyway, in this category of improvers.[28] And the rent controls offered did not meet tenants' demands either. The measure whetted expectations but failed to satisfy them, the classic fate of belated reforms. The only hope of solving the Irish land question was to turn the tenants into owners, allowing them to purchase land on affordable terms. It was left to the Conservatives under Salisbury to undertake this – under the Ashbourne Act of 1885 and the Balfour and Wyndham Land Acts of 1891 and 1903 respectively.[29] By then, however, it was too late to alter deep-seated Irish hostility to the Union. So Gladstone's legacy to Ireland was deeply unproductive. Nor was it politically advantageous at home. In Ireland, disillusionment with the Liberals would lead at the following general election to their virtual extinction, to the benefit of Home Rulers. In England, on the other hand, the challenge to the principle of property rights which the Irish Land Act implied was too strong for conservative-minded Whigs. Their leader, Lansdowne, resigned from the Government.

Gladstone also fell out spectacularly, and even more damagingly, as it turned out, with the Radicals and Nonconformists over education. Again, the Government's problems demonstrated the classic difficulty faced by reformers – from which Conservatives did not generally suffer – of raising expectations and then disappointing them. The National Education League, aimed at achieving nationwide secular education, had been formed in Birmingham in 1869, with the Radical Joseph Chamberlain to the fore. The Conservatives, as the Church party, were united in defending Church schools. They could also look for some support from Catholics. The Elementary Education Bill introduced by W. E. Forster, himself a Nonconformist turned Anglican, was a compromise. It did not make education formally either free or compulsory. But it plugged the gaps in the existing Church-dominated system by instituting a new category of rate-funded non-denominational local 'board schools' run by elected 'boards'. Grants were also provided to allow an expansion of Church schools, which were still, in theory, expected to be the main educational providers. No one was satisfied. Almost everyone was angry. But the significant political result was to alienate many Nonconformists from the Liberal Party, which they thought had betrayed them.

These two measures – on Irish land and education – were probably the most important in undermining Liberal support, to the benefit of the Conservatives, at the 1874 election. But they were also just the most controversial elements of the Gladstonian reforms, which disturbed a wide range of established interests. Army reforms (ending the purchase of commissions), the opening up of Oxford and Cambridge to non-Anglicans, the Civil Service reforms, the Licensing Act (regulating public houses) and the Ballot Act (introducing the secret ballot at all elections) – along with measures on trade unions, public health and courts administration – constituted a tidal wave of change. The sum was more than the parts, though many of the parts were disruptive enough, and all the while the political and moneyed classes were conscious of a rise in the influence and self-confidence of suspect Radicals, even Republicans like Sir Charles Dilke, demanding yet further change.[30]

Disraeli's tactics played well in such conditions. He adopted the traditional Conservative tactic of publicly supporting the Government against its Radical critics, saving his sharpest barbs for the most contentious and least popular measures, and usually sticking to generalities, while deploring the ministry's overall record. This did not require much activity. Indeed, there was widespread criticism of his somnolence. But foreign policy did help.

Gladstone was forced to wriggle when his handling of US demands for compensation for the depredations of the British-built Confederate warship *Alabama* threatened humiliation or even war. In fact, Disraeli came to life in 1871. He had spotted a strategically important shift in national affairs. The shock defeat of France in the Franco-Prussian War the previous autumn had, Disraeli realized, created a new European balance. This was brought home to the wider public when Russia used the occasion to repudiate the Black Sea clauses of the Treaty of Paris of 1856, prized in Britain as the only remaining trophy of the Crimean War. Disraeli spoke in warning tones to the House of Commons: 'This war represents the

German revolution, a greater political event than the French revolution of the last century ... The balance of power has been entirely destroyed, and the country which suffers most, and which feels the effects of this great change most, is England.'

In private his focus was less high-minded. While deploring any attempt (which he thought Salisbury's polemically anti-German commentaries in the *Quarterly Review* encouraged) to compromise British neutrality, he wrote to Derby giving his view of the domestic political impact of Prussia's triumph:

> I am not, however, sorry to see the country fairly frightened about foreign affairs. First, because it is well that the mind of the nation should be diverted from that morbid spirit of domestic change and criticism, which has ruled us too much for the last forty years, and that the reign of priggism should terminate. It has done its work, and in its generation very well, but there is another spirit abroad now, and it is time there should be.
>
> Second, because I am persuaded that any reconstruction of our naval and military systems that is practicable will, on the whole, be favourable to the aristocracy, by which I mean the proprietors of land: and thirdly because I do not think the present party in power are well qualified to deal with the external difficulties which await them.[31]

These were shrewd insights. But they were not combined with any new initiatives, and Disraeli's colleagues became increasingly discontented. He was sixty-seven. He was a survivor, but could he ever again be an inspirer, or, most problematically, a winner? While the odder features of his personality had either been modified or accepted, he still carried round with him something of the air of a mountebank. His divisive past rendered him unlikely to win over conservative-minded Whigs who now, like the Peelites of earlier days, were apparently ripe for recruitment. So it is easy to see why the party's senior figures thought that Derby – liberal, (relatively) young, aristocratic and highly respectable – would be a better bet, if the Conservatives were ever to make the required electoral break-through and return to power.

At the end of January 1872, at Burleigh, the seat of the Marquess of Exeter, and in the absence of both Disraeli and Derby, a tentative Tory putsch was launched. Gathorne-Hardy's diary records almost all that is known of it:

> [Cairns] boldly broached the subject of Lord Derby's lead and the importance of Disraeli knowing the general feeling. We all felt that none of his old colleagues could or would undertake such a task as informing him. John Manners alone professed ignorance of the existence of the feeling in or out of doors. I expressed the view that Disraeli had been loyal to his friends and that personally I could not say I preferred Lord Derby but that it was idle to ignore the general opinion. Noel [the Chief Whip] said from his own knowledge he could say that the name of Derby as leader would affect 40 or 50 seats.[32]

The plot failed, as such things do, mainly from cowardice and conflicting interests, rather than from any notable loyalty to the leader. Apart from Manners, only Sir Stafford Northcote (who arrived later) seems to have supported Disraeli directly.[33] The Chief Whip's observations, recorded here, were particularly treacherous – though the mutual dislike between Gathorne-Hardy and Derby, mainly on religious grounds, ensured the former's support for his current leader. It was enough. In any case, Disraeli soon began to demonstrate renewed vigour, both in his dealings with colleagues and, most importantly, in the public projection of his leadership.

This seems to have been more than a reaction to what he must have learned was afoot. Despite his courage, Disraeli suffered, like other politicians out of power, from depressive spells. His pride was an obstacle to retirement. But his hopes of a return to Downing Street were dim. Suddenly, he sensed he had caught the change in national mood he had privately foretold.

On 27 February the recovery of the Prince of Wales from a near-fatal bout of typhoid was celebrated with a service of thanksgiving in St Paul's Cathedral. It was a great national occasion. A reaction was evident against the sniping by critics of the monarchy, among whom Gladstone was, by association, unfairly numbered. The Prime Minister when he appeared was loudly booed. But Disraeli was cheered wildly by the crowds wherever he went. Unlike Gladstone, he was not used to popular demonstrations. This one had a profound effect on him. Afterwards, he was spotted in his distinctive long white coat in the Carlton Club, leaning against a table by the door and apparently listening to what was said, but wearing a strange expression. An observer who knew him well recorded the moment:

> I have heard it said by one who spoke to Napoleon I at Orange in France that his face was as that of one who looks into another world: that is the only description I can give of Disraeli's look at the moment I speak of. He seemed more like a statue than a human being . . . In the afternoon I said to [the Tory MP George Sclater-Booth, with whom he had been speaking], 'What was Disraeli talking about when I came into the room?' He replied, 'About some county business; I wanted his opinion'. I said, 'I will tell you what he was thinking about: he was thinking that he will be Prime Minister again!'[34]

Disraeli would shortly chance another popular demonstration. Though far from spontaneous, indeed tightly organized, it was not without risks. He disliked and discouraged exclusively working-class events. His style of oratory was framed for the Dispatch Box, not the soap box, nor even the elevated public platform of a mass meeting. Yet this was precisely what was now urged upon him. The event was planned for Manchester. The setting was important. It was the historic seat of Cobdenite Radicalism and a great manufacturing city – thus, in traditional Tory terms, enemy territory. On the other hand, Lancashire had in recent years become – under circumstances to be described – a heartland of Conservative strength. Manchester was also, of course, within the bailiwick of the house of Derby.[35] For these reasons, Disraeli moved cautiously, discussing with colleagues, especially with Derby, what he would say.

The tour lasted what Disraeli later described as a 'wondrous week'. It began on Easter Monday with a rousing welcome from enthusiasts pulling the visitors' carriage to their destination. The next day saw what was (for the Conservatives) an unprecedented parade. Members of the two to three hundred members of Conservative associations in the county, flags flying, undaunted by the incessant rain, filed past Disraeli and Mary Anne into the capacious ballroom of the Pomona Gardens. Wednesday was for serious politics, and judging by the length of his speech Disraeli felt that his audience deserved it, for he addressed them in Manchester's Free Trade Hall, with Derby by his side, from 7.30 to 11.00 at night. It was, of course, far too long. Much of it, particularly the first section on the constitution, must have flown way above the audience's head, and though it provided an intellectual justification of sorts for the twists and turns of his own political career, it offered few pointers to the future. The other two sections were of more significance, though in each case this can easily be – and has sometimes been – misunderstood.[36]

Disraeli argued that while there had been steady improvement in 'the condition of the people' in recent decades, and while its continuance required stability, prudent legislation could also be of assistance. Re-using a line he had first employed eight years earlier to Buckinghamshire Agricultural Association, he punned on the Vulgate version of a line from the book of Ecclesiastes, 'Vanity of vanities, all is vanity', to express a new concern for public health matters – 'Sanitas sanitatum, omnia sanitas'. The specifics he touched on were few – air, water and food purity, and factory conditions. He had, on that earlier occasion, explained more closely the philosophy behind his concern: 'The question [of health] is becoming both in town and country one of paramount interest. The greatness of the country depends on the race that fills it, and . . . if the race become inferior you lose all the results and all these blessings.'

The motivation, then, albeit expressed in Disraeli's peculiar language, was close to that which prompted the contemporary Prussian militarist state to concern itself with the well-being of the classes from which its soldiers and workers would be drawn. It did not have anything much to do with English philanthropic tradition. Moreover, the allusions made now in Manchester were to consolidation of existing public health Acts rather than to anything new. *The Times*, indeed, criticized the omission. Finally, the fact that (after his Crystal Palace speech later that year) Disraeli did not then return to the subject before the 1874 general election hardly suggests that, beyond deploying a useful theme, and one which had some evocative connection with his own past, social reform was in his view a great issue at stake between the parties.[37]

By contrast, what Disraeli said about foreign affairs did indeed engage with a seminal theme. This, too, was vague, and one would be hard pressed to relate it to measures which his later ministry actually implemented; but it was of importance to his own and to future Conservative thinking. He prefaced the passage with one of his best mocking metaphors: 'As I sat opposite the Treasury Bench, the Ministers reminded me of one of those marine landscapes not very unusual on the coasts of South America. You behold a range of exhausted volcanoes. Not a flame flickers on a single pallid crest. But the situation is still dangerous. There are occasional earthquakes, and ever anon the dark rumbling of the sea.' He then continued in a vein of romantic imperialism which no senior political figure had previously mined:

In answer to those statesmen, those mistaken statesmen, who have intimated the decay of the power of England and the decline of her resources, I express here my confident conviction that there never was a moment in our history when the power of England was so great and her resources so vast and inexhaustible. And yet, gentlemen, it is not merely our fleets and armies, our powerful artillery, our accumulated capital and our unlimited credit on which I so much depend, as upon that unbroken spirit of her people, which I believe was never prouder of the Imperial country to which they belong.[38]

The second major public address Disraeli made that year, on 24 June to a banquet organized by the Conservative National Union (of which more below) at the Crystal Palace, though it has its place in the development of the party's campaigning themes, was less noticed than the Manchester speech. It covered much the same subjects but, being tauter and shorter, it has provided more quotable copy. Again, the constitution and (at slightly greater length, but in no greater detail) public health and working conditions, figured; but it was, also again, the section on foreign affairs that contained evidence of most thought. Disraeli levelled a plausible – and, over the years, highly effective – charge against the party in power: 'If you look to the history of this country since the advent of Liberalism – forty years ago – you will find that there has been no effort so continuous, so subtle, supported by so much energy, and carried on with so much ability and acumen, as the attempts of Liberalism to effect the disintegration of the Empire of

England.' Disraeli offered, in place of an attitude which regarded the colonies as (in his own words many years earlier) 'a millstone round our necks', an alternative scheme of mutual defence and benefit.[39] He called for a policy of 'reconstructing as much as possible our Colonial Empire and of responding to those distant sympathies which may become the source of incalculable strength and happiness to this land'.

The year 1872 was, in political terms, a good one for Disraeli. It secured his shaky leadership. It saw the emergence of both the positive and negative themes which would help propel him towards power. But it was also marked by dreadful personal loss. Mary Anne had been even more delighted than her husband by the welcome given to his speech in Manchester. She ran to meet him afterwards crying, 'Oh! Dizzy, Dizzy, it is the greatest night of all. This pays for all!'[40] And she had, indeed, paid, not just financially but by putting up with numerous discomforts on his behalf. On one occasion, her hand was trapped and injured by a coach door when the couple were on the way to the Commons where he had a difficult speech to make: she said nothing, for fear she would disturb him before his own ordeal.[41] But Mary Anne was eighty and she was now slowly but evidently dying of stomach cancer. Over the summer Disraeli spent much of his time driving around London and the home counties with her. He saw places he had never before visited. He wondered at the 'miles of villas' in the new middle-class suburbs where the foundations of the new, middle-class Conservative Party were being laid, though there is no evidence that now or later he grasped their political significance. She lasted till mid-December.

Disraeli was floored by his wife's death. He was also rendered a great deal poorer because he lost their London house, held in her name, and the income that had been settled on her. He moved, when Parliament was sitting, into a hotel. Here the indispensable Monty Corry – his private secretary since 1866 – initially oversaw arrangements, though Corry then had to absent himself to care for his own sick father. Disraeli spent most of his evenings dining with political colleagues and their families. He was never a great eater or drinker – though he appreciated a bottle of burgundy or claret. Often he found the conversation much below par.

Fortunately, and despite his advanced age, he had lost none of his capacity for making female friends. Women had served Disraeli well over the years. There was, of course, his wife. There would be, on an altogether different level, the Queen herself. Mention should also be made of the elderly Jewish widow Mrs Brydges Willyams, living in Torquay, who left him a substantial legacy, apparently in appreciation of his defence of the Jews.[42] But Disraeli also retained a youthful capacity for indiscretion, and he now, in the late summer of 1873, fell hopelessly in love with Selina, Countess of Bradford. She was fifty-four, but still attractive, and no fool. One of five Forester sisters – another was Disraeli's close but platonic friend, the widowed Anne, Countess of Chesterfield – Selina had not always had a high view of him. 'Somehow he is a man I cannot respect', she had written more than twenty years earlier. Presumably it was easier now, and easier still when, the following year, Disraeli became Prime Minister. Whether her husband knew about the *affaire* – as Disraeli clearly regarded it – is not altogether clear. If Bradford suspected, it did not prevent his later introducing Disraeli to the House of Lords. Disraeli's letters were quite explicit. Selina urged him not to use the Number Ten seal on his *billets-doux*. He even proposed marriage to Anne, presumably as a ruse to cover physical closeness to Selina, which the former sensibly refused. Though it gave Disraeli heartache, and made him somewhat ridiculous into the bargain, the business – the subterfuge, especially – revived his spirits.[43]

So, suddenly, did politics. Gladstone's ministry – Disraeli's 'extinct volcanoes' – was exhausted. In particular (hence the 'rumbling') the factions within it were increasingly at war. Nothing daunted, in February 1873 Gladstone took up Ireland again, this time reviving the original proposal made by Disraeli for an Irish university, based on the principle of endowing equitably Protestant and Catholic institutions. In this case, it was the terms under which the new university, the counterpart for Catholics of the Protestant Trinity College Dublin, was to function which formed the political stumbling block. The Conservatives and many Liberals felt that the Catholic bishops had been given too great a say. But the bishops also turned against it, because the scheme required a religiously mixed student body. The Bill was narrowly defeated by Tory and Irish votes in the House of Commons, and Gladstone resigned.

Disraeli, however, was determined not to form another minority Government. So, in answer to the Queen's summons, he argued that where a measure had been defeated – even one regarded by the Government of the day as matter of confidence – by forces which, as in this case, had no common programme, the Opposition had no duty to accept office. He stuck to this line, even when it was made clear that the Queen would grant a dissolution if he requested it. He thought that although the Conservatives would have made substantial gains – they had already, he told her, gained some thirty seats through by-elections – those advances would be insufficient to give him a working majority. Because of the constitutional delicacy of the matter, Disraeli was required to give his full reasons in writing.[44] So, grumbling, Gladstone had to carry on.

It was clear, in any case, that an election would not be long delayed. Gladstone, as an activist Prime Minister, saw no attraction in hanging on to office without the power to implement reforms. But when he did decide to go to the country, he took the Conservatives by surprise.

Alongside institutional reform, Gladstone's passion was financial economy. His problem, as for so many reformers, was that his reforms cost money. This, in turn, forced him to economize in defence, which played into the hands of the Tories, who could and did portray him as weak. For now, Gladstone decided to return to his economically liberal roots. As long ago as 1853, when introducing his first budget, Gladstone had been committed to phasing out the income tax. The expense of the Crimean War had thrown his calculations awry. Other priorities had since intruded. But now he suddenly announced a dissolution (on 25 January 1874) and promised, on the basis of a planned budget surplus, to abolish the income tax entirely. (In truth, his hand had been forced by colleagues determined to resist cuts and keep up defence spending.) The reality of the apparent Conservative Party revival would now be tested.

Disraeli was, despite his prestige, still very much on trial. Attitudes towards him in the senior ranks of the party wavered. From thinking him too laid-back, people now wondered if he was too aggressive. A public letter written from the Bradfords' home in Weston on 3 October 1873 as a mini-manifesto for a by-election in Bath, struck a polemical note: 'For nearly five years the present Ministers have harassed every trade, worried every profession, and assailed or menaced every class, institution and species of property in the country . . . [T]he country has, I think, made up its mind to close this career of plundering and blundering.'[45] The tone was denounced as undignified, even by some Conservatives. And the Tories lost Bath. Disraeli affected to be unmoved – but, all the same, he felt it appropriate to defend his letter and his leadership in a speech to the University of Glasgow (where he was installed as Rector). In fact, his judgement was better than that of his critics, as events would show.

In his later years, Disraeli left practical decisions on matters of party organization to underlings, while expecting to be kept informed. The re-organization of the party that occurred under his leadership will therefore always, and rightly, be primarily associated with John Gorst.[46] Gorst retrospectively inflated his own importance. He was a menace as well as a genius, and before the end of Disraeli's reign his difficult side was much in evidence. But without his vision, drive and refusal to bend before influential mediocrities, it is difficult to imagine the Conservative Party having got itself into sufficiently good shape to win its landslide victory of 1874.

Gorst was a Lancashire man, from Preston. He had been a teacher, missionary and barrister before being returned as Conservative Member for Cambridge at a by-election in April 1866. In the House he took a high Tory line and objected to the 1867 Reform Act; but as soon as it was passed he showed an interest in organizational reforms to cope with its effects. Gorst became secretary of the most vigorous and important of the local party bodies, the Metropolitan London and Westminster Conservative Association. The Association, like Gorst himself, had large ambitions, and these initially bid fair to throttle at birth another potentially still more important body, the already mentioned Conservative National Union – about whose inauspicious origins something now needs to be said.

Like most of the party's organizational activity at the time, the National Union was the brainchild of Lord (William) Nevill (later Earl, and finally Marquess, of Abergavenny), known on account of his influence and energy as 'the Great Panjandrum of the Tories'. It was intended to bring together the existing borough associations, societies and working men's clubs, create more, and place them all under a single institutional umbrella. (The Conservative associations in the counties were gathered under Charles Keith-Falconer, secretary of the County Registration Association.) Nevill placed the organization of the boroughs in general and of the nascent National Union in particular in the hands of a young up-and-coming Lancashire barrister, H. C. Raikes. Raikes quickly discovered how thankless a task he had. He faced jealous opposition from the well-established Lancashire borough associations, and particularly from Gorst's instrument, the Metropolitan London and Westminster Conservative Association. The latter was due to hold a great banquet at the Crystal Palace, Sydenham, to celebrate the passing of the 1867 Reform Act. It seemed to Raikes that this was an ideal public occasion at which to launch the National Union. But Gorst and his colleagues were not at all pleased. They wanted the limelight for themselves, and they had no wish to share it with socially inferior upstarts. Nor (for rather different reasons), it turned out, was the party leadership keen on the proposal.

Difficult as it is to imagine now, the party's objection then was to any great public demonstration by Conservative working men. It was thought that the event was bound to be unruly and that this would worry the middle classes. Disraeli himself, when consulted, was opposed to the idea. Though not much concerned by the bourgeoisie's opinions about this or anything else, he had his own dislike of anything that smacked of class conflict. So the party leaders resolutely backed the Metropolitan London and Westminster Conservative Association's exclusive claims to its banquet, which was, indeed, a glittering success. Meanwhile, the National Union's launch was shunted into the obscurity of a tavern meeting the following day, with no fanfare and no dignitaries – and, ironically (for want of anyone more important) Gorst himself in the chair.

The early years of the National Union's history were equally undistinguished. There was, in fact, an air of timidity about it all. An attempt was even made to change its official title – National Union of Conservative and Constitutional Associations – by dropping the word 'Conservative' altogether, since the party affiliation was felt likely to deter working men from joining. ('Constitutional' was at the time considered less provocative.) This move failed. But there was a marked reluctance among Tory working men themselves to take any leading role in the National Union's affairs. At the other end of the party spectrum, while Disraeli gave his approval to the modest arrangements he was insistent that ministers should not become involved. The National Union continued to struggle, not least against its London rival.

Although Gorst was on the Council of the National Union, he still devoted his main efforts to the London Association. The party's defeat in the 1868 election indirectly helped resolve matters, because Gorst lost his parliamentary seat and needed a job, preferably one which would ease his way back into the House of Commons.[47] Well before the election, Spofforth's performance as principal agent had given cause for complaint. A separate committee effectively took over his duties in the election. But to spare his feelings, and his pocket, for the present he retained his title and pay – and, just as important for the future, he retained Lord Abergavenny's patronage. It was nevertheless clearly necessary that a full-time successor be found soon if the challenges of organizing a mass party in a mass electorate were to be met. Attention focused on Gorst. His experience was unique; his energies were proven and his character flaws as yet not fully revealed. So, with Disraeli's approval, in 1870 he was duly appointed by Gerard Noel, the Chief Whip, to the post of party principal agent.

Gorst was not just a party official, he was a politician: he took no salary and he made it clear that he intended to return as an MP. This independent-mindedness would create problems later, but for the present his political acumen was a boon. He concentrated his efforts on the boroughs, which were belatedly recognized as electorally crucial, while Keith-Falconer worked on the counties (also overseeing relations with Scotland). They formed a good partnership. It was Keith-Falconer, now joint secretary of the National Union and effectively Gorst's assistant, who would organize the great Crystal Palace event in 1872. But even before then Gorst had begun reconstituting the party organization in a more practical and professional shape. In 1871 he had, indeed, become secretary to the National Union, thus securing that organization's future, while also keeping it firmly under control. In 1872 Gorst set up a new principal agent's office at 53 Parliament Street. This was soon known as the party 'Central Office' – a title which would be attached to Conservative headquarters, during its various physical relocations, until after the 1997 election defeat. The offices of the National Union and of the Registration Association, under Keith-Falconer, were also brought into Central Office.

Gorst did not remain office-bound. He travelled around the country from seat to seat, concentrating on the big boroughs which had to be won, chivvying, exhorting and gathering information. He wanted to break the hold which traditional money and connection exerted on the constituencies, knowing that they bred inefficiency. New constituency associations were formed. Disraeli had always been keen to see as many seats fought as possible. This determination was more than echoed by Gorst. By 1873 the party's representatives were also equipped with *Hints for Candidates*. Another significant step was the presentation to Disraeli in 1871 of Central Office's report on the 1868 election. It was three years after the event. But from now on, Conservative Party leaders would regard it as an essential part of their role to read and comment on these reports.[48]

Naturally, what could be done on the basis of the data provided in order to increase the chance of winning elections was less clear. The degree to which good organization counts in parliamentary elections is something about which it is possible to argue, even today. The party organizers, like Gorst then, believe themselves the key to victory, and suspect that the politicians are the problem. The politicians, by and large, take the opposite view. (Fortunately for Gorst, he was no longer in charge of organization when scapegoats were needed.)

In these early years of professional party organization there was another imponderable. It was impossible to know scientifically what voters thought before they voted. There was no opinion polling, even of a primitive kind. Judging why electors voted as they did was, therefore, a matter of hunches. Given the huge increase in the borough electorates which would in due course, after Disraeli's death, be matched in the counties, and given that the politicians with few exceptions came from an altogether different social background from these voters, election outcomes were highly mysterious. Contemplating them, even so clear-minded a politician as Salisbury could sink into nebulosity. Reflecting on the 1880 election defeat, for example, he observed: 'The hurricane that has swept us away is so strange and new a phenomenon that we shall not for some time understand its real meaning. I doubt if so much enthusiasm and such general unity of action proceeds from any sentimental opinion – or from any academic judgement. It seems to have been inspired by some definite desire for change . . .'[49] (Of course, Salisbury had been in Biarritz at the time of the campaign.)

The one thing that predictions at this time, even predictions supported by professionally gathered and analysed data, had in common is that they were always completely wrong. Municipal elections offered some clues to changes in public opinion. Gorst tried to make sense of them. But local factors, then as now, introduced distortions. So it was parliamentary by-elections that were most closely scrutinized. Well before the 1874 general election these were providing the Conservatives with reasons for encouragement. The unanswerable question was how far the evident shift in opinion against the Liberal Government would, in the event, translate into seats.

Probably more important than any initiative launched by the Conservatives – and certainly more important than Disraeli's vague promises about improving the conditions of working men – was the party's increasing appeal to the middle classes. The *embourgeoise-ment* of what had been the party of the aristocracy and the landed gentry still had a long way to go. But it had begun. One can only speculate about the causes. The shift certainly reflected disgruntle-ment among men of property of all sorts, great and small, at the direction in which the Liberals had moved ever since the death of Palmerston. Gladstone might, in one guise, be the embodiment of a reassuring financial prudence. But he kept bad political company, and his Government seemed always ready to dance to a Radical tune – or, still worse, an Irish jig. One can, in any case, exaggerate the differences between the economic policies of the two parties. The contrast was clearer on foreign policy, at least in tone, with the Conservatives pledging to uphold Britain's interests as a great imperial power.

Even so, it is hard to know how well nascent imperialism went down with the middle classes – as opposed to the lower orders, who seem to have relished it. Disraeli himself told the Cabinet at the height of the crisis with Russia in 1877 that 'the middle classes would always be against a war: but fortunately the middle classes did not now govern'.[50] His implication that the middle classes would always oppose expensive foreign policies may have had some sub-stance. Or, of course, it may have just reflected his towering snobbery.

But probably the simplest and most general explanation of why the middle classes were turning to the Conservatives is also the truest: upwardly mobile people, particularly when they acquire a little capital and some property, rally to the security and relish the cachet offered by right-of-centre parties – at least as long as no overwhelming obstacle is placed in their way. This somewhat de-dramatizes the role of Conservative political leaders in winning elections, but it is widely demonstrable.

The otherwise disastrous 1868 election results had already pro-vided some readable writing on this particular wall. Lord George

A Uniform Whig.

"I preserve consistency, by varying my means to secure the unity of my end." Burkes Reflections VP 354.

Edmund Burke satirized by James Gillray (1791) for his alleged inconsistency – a Whig denouncing the French Revolution.

Portrait miniature of William Pitt the Younger (*right*), intense and somehow fragile, and (*below*) Pitt addressing the House of Commons on the French declaration of war in 1793.

George Canning (*above*), a superb Foreign Secretary but short-lived Prime Minister, whose death left the Tories floundering – not least in the face of agitation for electoral reform and an end to 'rotten boroughs' (*below*). Neither Wellington nor Robert Peel, here conferring in the 1840s (*right*), had Canning's brilliance, but, especially in tandem, they were more reassuring.

The Reformers' Attack on the Old Rotten Tree; or, the Foul Nests of the

Peel reintroduces the income tax in 1842, depicted (*above*) as a phoenix rising from the ashes of its earlier abolition after the Napoleonic Wars. Gluttonous John Bull (*below*) salivates over the prospect of cheap food as a result of repeal of the Corn Laws.

No. 1. Price 1d.   Coloured 2d.

A Race between the Old Protectionists Drag, and the Anti Corn Law League Fast Coach.

The cause of free trade ('Manchester') is shown (*above*) overtaking that of protection (the 'Derby Dilly') during the Corn Laws crisis. But Peel was the main political loser, resigning office amid widespread dismay (*right*), having been humiliated by the upstart Benjamin Disraeli (*below*, as a young MP).

SIR ROBERT PEEL RETURNING FROM THE HOUSE AFTER HIS RESIGNATION.

The interior of the rebuilt Chamber of the House of Commons in 1858 – the year of Derby's second premiership.

The fourteenth Earl of Derby (*right*), as Conservative leader in the party's wilderness years, established a productive but wary relationship with his deputy, Disraeli. In 1867 (*below*), year of the Tory Second Reform Act, Derby stands at one end of the Cabinet table and Disraeli at the other. A violent demonstration in Hyde Park by the Reform League the previous year (*bottom*) had shaken the authorities.

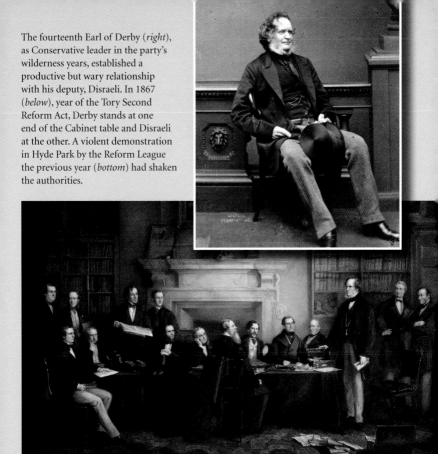

Disraeli (*right*), caricatured in 1869 by 'Ape' as 'The Reformist' – an allusion to his Edinburgh speech of October 1867, in which he claimed to have educated his party on the subject. At Hughenden (*inset*) Disraeli could relax with friends. Here, in 1874, the adored Selina Bradford sits on the left; devoted Monty Corry sprawls in the foreground.

Hamilton, who became a protégé of Disraeli, found himself returned as MP for Middlesex at the age of twenty-two. He explained how 'the constituency . . . unknown to the wire pullers, had during the past ten years been converted from Radicalism to Conservatism. Rapid extension of suburban railroads and the out-pouring of professional men, tradesmen, and clerical employees into the rural outskirts of London had steadily changed the tone and politics of the constituency.'[51]

Lord George was a true blue aristocrat, who had merely benefited from middle-class votes. But W. H. Smith, the news agency and bookstall proprietor, was a member – albeit an exceedingly wealthy one – of the class that voted for him. His story is famously illustrative of how the Conservative Party was becoming the party of government. Young Smith's social, religious and political career paths were all of a piece. He greatly expanded and developed his father's news agency business, mainly by shrewd use of the opportunities opened up by the rail network. He changed from Methodism to Anglicanism, though he retained a solemn streak of philanthropic enthusiasm and evangelical earnestness which, alongside his commercially shrewd decision to keep unsavoury material off his bookstands, earned him his later public nickname of 'Old Morality'. Smith had thought of standing as a Liberal in 1856 and 1857. But he was blackballed from the Reform Club: this helped divert his political sympathies. In 1865 he stood (and lost) at Westminster as a Palmerstonian Liberal against the Radical John Stuart Mill. But by 1868, with Gladstone now leading the Liberals, he had had enough. He stood again at Westminster, this time for the Conservatives, on the new franchise. He was elected, not least because his great wealth allowed him greatly to outspend his opponents. The arrival of such a figure with such a background in the House of Commons, representing a long-time Liberal seat, symbolized the growing rejection of Gladstone and Liberalism by the English urban and suburban middle class.[52]

A slightly different variation on the same theme is offered by the career of Richard Cross.[53] Cross was, from the start, a social and political step ahead of Smith. His was an affluent middle-class Lancastrian family, and Lancashire Toryism was, as it were, the first growth of the newer vintage. Cross had attended Rugby under Thomas Arnold and then Trinity College Cambridge. He was close to his schoolfriend Derby and was, indeed, the only middle-class Lancastrian allowed into Knowsley.[54] Richard Cross's father and grandfather were both lawyers, and he too became a highly success-ful barrister on the northern circuit, before becoming a banker. In 1857 Cross won Preston for the Conservatives. The only pledge on which his supporters insisted was that he was not to join the Carlton Club. He temporarily stood down as an MP in 1862 on becoming a partner in a bank in Warrington. But he went into local government, becoming chairman or deputy chairman of every sig-nificant body in the area – a useful basis for his future duties in Disraeli's Government. Cross was then returned to the Commons at the 1868 election, pushing out Gladstone himself in the new constituency of South-West Lancashire.

Cross's appointment as Disraeli's Home Secretary in 1874, though it owed much to his old friend Derby, who was anxious to stop Gathorne-Hardy getting the job, was a considered statement of the importance now attached to representatives of the upper middle class in Tory affairs. W. H. Smith's appointment in the same year as Financial Secretary and his elevation to the Cabinet in 1877 as First Lord of the Admiralty – a decision questioned by the Queen on social grounds but amply justified in practice – reinforced the same message. Disraeli might make jokes about the middle classes, but he knew he could not do without them.

Disraeli was now, in January 1874, taken completely by surprise when Gladstone suddenly went to the country. But even if he had had more time, it is doubtful whether he would have greatly altered the very narrow focus of his manifesto. It was a dour warning about the threats to the constitution and the Church posed by Gladstone's allies, and of unspecified dangers abroad. If Disraeli's plans included improving the lot of the workers, he said nothing about it.[55] Not that this was bad tactics. Even more than usual, the dictum that governments lose elections more than oppositions win them was applicable: Gladstone had managed to alienate both the Whigs and the Dissenters, the two strata of his bedrock support, while annoying nearly everyone else into the bargain. Attacking the brewers with his Licensing Act also ensured that Tory coffers were filled still higher, a favour which the party then repaid by easing the licensing provisions once in office. Naturally, this confirmed everything that Gladstone imagined about the wickedness of his enemies and of his Enemy-in-Chief. But by then it was too late.

The 1874 election results produced, despite the many earlier straws in the wind, a great shock to all concerned in the size of the Conservative majority. Gorst's calculations had suggested that the party would obtain an overall majority of just three. Disraeli did not dissent. When he learned that he had, in fact, a majority of over fifty, he observed that 'no party organisation could have caused this result', which was perfectly true, though undoubtedly organization helped.[56]

Two factors – over and above the uncertainties described earlier – may have made the outcome even harder than usual to predict in this case. The first was the cumulative effect upon national opinion – a concept which it now becomes sensible to discuss – of political information retailed by a national press. Gladstone's abolition of stamp duty in 1855 and repeal of the paper duty in 1861 sharply reduced the price of newspapers and accordingly increased their numbers and circulation. For their part, the Conservatives had made a major effort to influence political coverage. London was, obviously, particularly important. The *Globe* was purchased by Raikes. The *Standard* was anyway Conservative and Gorst was close to it – sometimes too close, when his tips were misleading. The *Morning Post*, under its editor Algernon Borthwick, a supporter of Palmerston, shifted in favour of Disraeli. In 1871, the Central Press Board in the Strand was purchased by the Conservatives to serve as its news agency for an increasingly important provincial press. It is reasonable to think that these initiatives now yielded results beyond those foreseen by the party hierarchy.[57]

The other factor was the introduction – again by Gladstone – of the secret ballot at elections by the Ballot Act (1872). Disraeli greatly disliked it and the Conservatives had resisted it. But Gorst's perceptions were shrewder. He saw that the removal of outside influence worked both ways. The intimidatory grip of Tory landowners in the counties might be put at risk. But, equally, in the secrecy of the polling booth, middle-class voters in those boroughs under Liberal control could now transfer their allegiance more easily, and in 1874 they clearly did so. The impact of the secret ballot was to increase political volatility.

The 1874 election was in one sense, and despite the remaining restrictions on the franchise, the first 'modern' election. As is the norm today, two great parties confronted one another with separate and opposing programmes and (with the exception of Ireland) fighting on much the same issues. The result was a sharp swing to the Conservatives, who increased their share of the vote from 31.6 per cent in 1868 to 36.6 per cent in 1874, while the Liberal share fell from 42.1 per cent to 36.2 per cent. In the English boroughs as a whole, there was a Conservative gain of more than thirty seats. The lion's share of this advance was in the middle-class constituencies, where the trend that saw W. H. Smith triumph in 1868 accelerated. The Conservatives swept all before them in London and the Home Counties: the City, suburban Surrey, Kent and Essex all changed their allegiance, while Middlesex and Westminster returned two Conservative Members each, all with substantial majorities.[58]

Henceforth the party's support rested crucially on a Home Counties–Lancashire axis.

The scale of the Liberal Party's national defeat was not, however, an unmixed blessing for the Conservatives. The Liberal wipe-out to the benefit of Home Rulers in Ireland, where Gladstone's measures signally failed to impress or appease, left the Conservatives as the only Irish party in favour of the Union.[59] And for the country at large it meant that if a Liberal Government again took office it could only rule by embarking on changes that threatened consti-tutional stability. For the present, though, fortune smiled on the Tories – and on the Queen, who was overjoyed to see the back of Gladstone.

PUNCH, OR THE LONDON CHARIVARI.—August 26, 1876.

EMPRESS AND EARL;

OR, ONE GOOD TURN DESERVES ANOTHER.

Lord Beaconsfield. "THANKS, YOUR MAJESTY! I MIGHT HAVE HAD IT BEFORE! *NOW* I THINK I HAVE
EARNED IT!"

*Disraeli went to the House of Lords as Earl of Beaconsfield in 1876 only
because of his failing health – he considered the Upper House a kind of death.
Wags, though, enjoyed the idea that his coronet was a reward for
gaining the imperial crown for Queen Victoria.*

5

DISRAELI'S PARTY, II – IN POWER

Disraeli was, at last, where he wanted to be: in power, with a large majority. But he now also faced two problems. The first, which he could not hope to overcome, was his age. He was seventy, and not at all well. 'It has come too late,' he remarked.[1] He still had enormous reserves of willpower and he was noticeably transformed when dealing with political business from a tired old man into a sharp and vigorous operator. But he had always been afflicted by fragile health, connected with his nerves. 'I am never well, save in action, and then I feel immortal,' he declared.[2] In later life he had what was described as gout, for which he received no more damaging remedies than did other contemporaries.[3] But it may, in reality, have been some other rheumatic condition, given its regular coincidence with inflammation of the lungs. His great fear was the east wind, and rightly so, for in the end it helped carry him off. In any case, as Prime Minister he was only intermittently able to devote to his work all the energy it required.

Disraeli's second problem was of a different order, though after the initial friction it was overcome more easily than he can have hoped: what do about Salisbury. The latter had ceased to declaim publicly against Disraeli in those regular, disobliging *Quarterly Review* articles which he penned during his summer holidays. But this did not imply any reconciliation. He was in Italy during the campaign and on his return was immediately faced with the unpleasant dilemma of either swallowing his pride or forgoing office. Carnarvon, as Salisbury told his wife:

> Pressed on me strongly that if I remained outside I should be a perfect cipher – which is entirely true; but slavery may be a worse evil than suicide. I urged that coming back into the same Cabinet with Disraeli as dictator would be practically a submission ... This evening I dined with the Derbys. [Lady Derby was Salisbury's stepmother.] He hinted much but said nothing directly. I gathered that they had not quite given up the idea of his having the first place. As far as I could, I encouraged it – for it would undoubtedly solve my difficulty.[4]

But there was no way out. Disraeli, not Derby, was Prime Minister. Through the intermediary of Lady Derby it was made clear to Salisbury that he could be Secretary of State for India. Salisbury was proud, but not too proud to serve either his own interests or those of his country (or indeed those of India, where a terrible famine had struck Bengal).[5] He and Disraeli eventually met to seal the agreement. Disraeli was all charm. But the discussion turned mainly on the uncomfortable topic for the High Church Salisbury of a Bill to suppress Ritualism, which was something the Archbishop of Canterbury and the Queen both demanded, and with which Disraeli happily went along. Salisbury seems to have misunderstood the reassurances he now received. Anyway, he was contemptuous of Disraeli's thoughts on the subject, of which, he observed, '[he] is sublimely ignorant'. Salisbury duly took office. But he lamented that he found Disraeli 'as enterprising as ever' (which was not a compliment) and 'that therefore the experiment will be a trying one'.[6] In this, though, Salisbury's habitual pessimism misled him. At least in its final stages, the synergy was one of the most productive ever achieved by two Cabinet colleagues.

The rest of the Cabinet then fell easily into place. Carnarvon, returning on the coat-tails of his master, Salisbury, took the Colonial Office. Derby was bound to have the Foreign Office – to which he was ill suited for reasons already described. Gathorne-Hardy was denied the Home Office, at Derby's insistence, and received the War Department instead. This was the beginning of his removal from the first rank of politics, for he had earlier been talked of as Disraeli's successor. Cross became Home Secretary. Northcote was Chancellor of the Exchequer.

Stafford Northcote's career saw him always close to great events and great men – from the time he was Gladstone's secretary in 1842–50 to his edging aside by Salisbury at the end of his life in 1887. But Northcote is the classic instance of a statesman who never made the top. His problem was not a lack of brains but a lack of personality, occasionally compounded by a lack of money, and never helped by what in Disraeli's eyes was the final inhibitor, a lack of style.

Disraeli's snobbish prejudices were evident in his insistence that six of his twelve-strong Cabinet be peers and that the aristocracy be amply represented in his Government as a whole. Most of these high-born public servants (excepting, obviously, Salisbury) were an embarrassment. But Disraeli did not repent. In 1878 he appointed the Duke of Northumberland to the Cabinet as Lord Privy Seal, in which capacity he proved superbly inadequate.

Like Peel in 1841, Disraeli had ridden the crest of a wave of opposition against reformist activism, or, as he had provocatively described it, against 'plundering and blundering'. Such a ministry as his, therefore, existed to resist or circumvent dangers, not solve controversial problems. This also satisfied Disraeli's personal preferences. Cross was taken aback to find that there was no legislative programme ready to give shape to the new Queen's Speech. But in this he was being naïve. Because of Gladstone's timing of the election, the 1874 session was truncated, and so not much could anyway be achieved.

There was, though, plenty of politics. Disraeli insisted that Northcote take a penny off income tax and give government relief for services provided on the rates – a final nod in the direction of the landed county interests offended by repeal of the Corn Laws. The Licensing Act was amended to please the brewers, and a Factory Act was introduced to satisfy the 'Nine Hours' movement, to which all the Lancashire Tories were committed. Most heat, however, was generated by the measure to 'put down Ritualism' (in Disraeli's unhappy phrase – though he borrowed it) and to end (in a worse one, for which he was solely to blame) 'the Mass in masquerade'.

Despite Disraeli's feelings on the matter, he would not have proceeded to legislate on Ritualism had Tait, the Archbishop of Canterbury, not pressed for it. Nor, in all probability, would he have sharpened his language as he did were he not under relentless pressure from the Queen. Disraeli's approach was heartily disliked by most of his colleagues and very nearly led to the break-up of the Cabinet. It was also, and most importantly, opposed by Salisbury, who referred in a bitter speech in the Lords to the need to ignore the pressure of 'bluster'. This was deemed insulting to the Commons. Then Disraeli, in the Lower House, and provoked by the Liberal Opposition, characterized Salisbury in a bitter-sweet response, as a 'great master of jibes and flouts and jeers'. But Disraeli wrote a letter of apology, and the two men quickly made up. Neither wished to escalate a secondary dispute into a crisis, at least not so early in the Government's life; and working together then proved easier than they thought. They were soon even exchanging gossipy letters about colleagues and events. Salisbury quickly became part of Disraeli's inner Cabinet, though he retained his suspicions of his chief.[7] The more serious consequence of the affair lay in the alienation of High Church opinion. This would manifest itself when the 'Atrocities' ferment shook Disraeli's Government two years later.

The 1875 session was almost wholly concerned with social legislation. The measures were well prepared and politically important, even if their uniqueness was later exaggerated. Disraeli took a closer personal interest in the drafting of that year's Queen's Speech than in any other's. This, though, was more because of the effect he wanted to create than because the details mattered to him. He liked in any case to say that most Bills proposed by incoming governments were first found 'in the pigeon holes of their predecessors'.[8] This was true now. For example, the Public Health Act of this year could certainly be seen as fulfilling the pledge contained in Disraeli's Manchester speech in 1872. But it was a measure that essentially consolidated earlier provisions, and one which a government of any colour could and probably would have introduced.

Another characteristic of Disraeli's measures in this session is that they were mostly 'permissive', as the jargon had it – that is, they provided a framework within which others, in practice local authorities, could act. He himself, speaking on the Agricultural Holdings Bill (which secured some compensation to tenants for improvements made), described 'permissive legislation [as] the character of a free people'.[9] A case in point was the Artisans Dwellings Act, introduced by Cross. This empowered municipal authorities to take over slum areas by compulsory purchase and provided for cheap loans to assist with the building of new housing.[10] It was a continuation of earlier measures, not the first step towards mass council housing. And, of course, it relied upon municipal authorities regarding slum clearance as a priority. Until the emergence of activists in the mould of Joseph Chamberlain in

Birmingham, this was not generally the case, though there was some construction of housing in London. Inertia subsequently became paralysis, once Northcote decided to cut back on Exchequer loans in order to control excessive public borrowing. The same conditions applied to the Sale of Food and Drugs Act. It was another fulfilment of a public pledge; but its operation too was restricted, in practice, by the squeeze on local authority budgets.

Not all the initiatives came from the Government. The Merchant Shipping Act, to tighten provisions against unseaworthy vessels, was implemented largely – and belatedly, because of a log-jam of Bills – in response to angry agitation by the Liberal MP for Derby, Samuel Plimsoll (of Plimsoll line fame). Plimsoll's tantrums caused Disraeli no end of disturbance. Plimsoll got his way, though practical implementation proved tardy.

Disraeli took particular pride in his labour legislation, though whether he understood its implications or foresaw its effects is doubtful. When the tedious details of Cross's measures were discussed in Cabinet, Disraeli (for the first time Derby could remember) actually fell asleep.[11] Perhaps, in the light of later history, he should have stayed awake. Of the Government's two measures, the Employers and Workingmen Bill was equitable, in that it removed the anomaly whereby breaches of contract by employers were a civil matter, but breaches of contract by employees a criminal offence. The second measure, the Conspiracy and Protection of Property Bill, was much more far-reaching and, arguably, set labour law in a wrong direction, from which after more than a century it would have to be rescued (by another Conservative Government, under Margaret Thatcher). The measure was devised in defiance of objections from employers and the majority report of a royal commission. It reversed Gladstone's 1871 Criminal Law Amendment Act and gave the unions the right to picket and legal immunities for doing so. The Bill was introduced in response to pressure from Northern Tory MPs, themselves under pressure from the unions (the predecessor of the Trades Union Congress had been founded in the late 1860s). Disraeli pompously boasted to Selina Bradford: 'We have settled the long and vexatious contest between capital and labour.'[12] More significantly, he predicted that his measures would 'gain and retain for the Tories the lasting affection of the working classes'.[13] Of course, they did neither.

In his Mansion House speech that August Disraeli claimed to have redeemed his pledges to elevate the 'condition of the people'. Others agreed. In 1879 Alexander Macdonald, one of the two Labour MPs, would declare to his constituents: 'The Conservative Party have done more for the working classes in five years than the Liberals have in fifty.'[14] But the pace now slowed. The Government's Education Bill in 1876 moved further towards – though it did not yet enact – universal elementary education. As a sign of what really mattered to the party, however, it was then hijacked by Tory backbenchers determined to restrain the growth of board schools.[15]

The question which must be asked, however, is: Why did Disraeli bother? Why did he invest so much political capital in social reform at all? A cynical response – and, on the subject of Disraeli, cynicism has its place – is that he did not have anything else to do. He half-believed that practical schemes of social improvement were an alternative to institutional upheavals of the sort advocated by con-stitutional radicals.[16] But this was little more than a rhetorical device. Constitutional changes like the secret ballot and curbs on corruption had not proved harmful to the Conservatives, and it was already clear that a further stage of reform in the county franchise was likely. So the strategic logic of social reform to avoid political reform cannot, even at the time, have seemed very convincing.

The obvious answer to the question posed is that Disraeli was reflecting current expectations. There was an international dimension. Prussian Germany was on the rise, with its approach of making effective soldiers by creating reliable, educated, healthy citizens. Still more important, the revolutionary disorders of the Paris Commune in 1871 suggested that ignoring the needs of the lower classes posed immediate threats to the upper ones. (There was a minor panic in London as news of events across the Channel came in.) But the pressures for action were, above all, home-grown. They emerged from the huge economic and social changes – above all, the pace of urbanization – which were transforming Britain itself. Government interventions of different kinds were clearly required to deal with these new conditions. Despite Disraeli's somewhat flimsy distinction between 'permissive' and 'coercive' measures, no clear philosophy of intervention had been worked out by the Conservatives or, indeed, by their opposite numbers. But a debate had begun on the subject, which would become more vigorous, and indeed acrimonious, as the years went by. It already encompassed public health and education. It would later stretch into other fields.

A crucial (though, as it turned out, temporary) contribution to this debate had been made by the New Social Alliance. This initiative, originating in the mind of the engineer and ship designer John Scott Russell, aimed at a programme of social reforms – a mixture of the wildly utopian and the strictly practical – and it attracted the sympathies, if not the explicit commitment, of leading Tory figures. Derby was sceptical. Disraeli was politely interested. Others were more enthusiastic. The schemes themselves petered out. But the movement both reflected and encouraged that public debate about social issues which Disraeli addressed in his speeches of 1872, and in his measures of 1875.[17]

A final, and intriguing, possible answer to the puzzle of why Disraeli was so concerned with social reform is that it actually mattered, in its own right and in philosophical terms, to him and his party. Conservative propagandists and apologists have often asserted as much. They did so in the rest of the nineteenth century.[18] They did so in the twentieth century.[19] They continue to do so today.[20] An impressive historical pedigree can be given to this argument. Alongside the broadly laissez-faire approach to economic and social policy which was dominant in conservative thinking and Conservative politics from Burke to Disraeli, there was always another view. This can best be described as that of Tory radicalism. It is closely associated with the campaigns for Factory Acts and against the poor laws waged by earlier Tory politicians such as Michael Sadler (1780–1835), Richard Oastler (1789–1861) and, most famously, Anthony Ashley-Cooper, seventh Earl of Shaftesbury (1801–85).[21] The impulse behind this brand of Tory politics was evangelical and paternalistic. It was strong, but it was limited. Its leading spokesmen were, for the most part, what is nowadays known as single-issue politicians – hence, in part, their restricted influence.

Disraeli, in his own radical and Young England days, echoed some of the rhetoric and occasionally embraced some of the policies associated with this group. But there is no evidence that in the 1870s he still thought he was fulfilling the objectives of Tory radicalism. His later statements about the welfare of the working classes were never more than trite, polite expressions of concern. In 1848 he had declared sententiously: 'The palace is not safe, when the cottage is not happy.'[22] But, by the 1870s at least, it was concern for the palace (that is, the monarchy) and for the landed aristocracy – the other two partners in Young England's harmonious social vision – which were at the forefront of his thoughts in government. Cottages came some way behind.

Disraeli probably had some hopes that Tory working-class support, of the kind he first witnessed in the Manchester demonstration in 1872, would increase, to the party's electoral benefit – and that, of course, he thought about a great deal. But *The Times*'s striking attribution of even this limited kind of Tory democratic thinking to Disraeli, in an editorial on the second anniversary of his death, misleads more than it illumines: 'In the inarticulate mass of the English populace [Disraeli] discerned the Conservative working man, as the sculptor perceives the angel prisoned in a block of marble.'[23] Disraeli was, indeed, a great and imaginative political artist. And Tory working men (and, in due course, women) would be of immense significance to the party. Without the third or so of the working class who voted Conservative from the 1880s to the present day, the party would never have secured its unique record of election victories.[24] But neither Disraeli's 1867 Reform Act nor his social legislation, let alone his Young England whimsies, had anything much to do with gaining that support.

Despite his personal peculiarities, Disraeli's view of government was, in fact, highly traditional and recognizably Tory. At home, the priority was the defence of the constitution and the aristocratic social system it reflected, and overseas it was the defence of the national (and increasingly the imperial) interest. Equally traditionally, despite a necessary preoccupation with those domestic political questions that made or un-made governments, Disraeli thought that the successful conduct of foreign policy was the supreme mark of a statesman. He did not have much experience in it. He had a host of romantic notions about foreigners in general and the East in particular, absorbed in his youth, and the prejudices then acquired still held some sway with him. But he had not seen the Orient since. His travels, even in Europe, were few. His knowledge of foreign languages was especially weak for a top-ranking British politician – indeed, his French was so basic that Corry briefed Lord Odo Russell, the British ambassador in Berlin, to persuade Disraeli not to address the Congress of 1878 in that traditional diplomatic language. (Russell told him that the others present would be disappointed if the greatest living English orator did not use his own mother tongue; the Prime Minister was persuaded. It was not just Disraeli who laid on flattery, in his words, 'with a trowel'.)[25]

All that said, Disraeli's character and mindset were in most respects well suited for foreign affairs. He had a sense of Britain's rightful position in the world. He had no illusions about human nature. He had no queasiness about the pursuit of *raison d'état*. He had, it is true, an overdeveloped taste for intrigue, believing that much of Europe was in the hands of secret societies, or Jewish financiers, or the Vatican. He also had a shaky hold on geography. But he was at ease in any court. He had some of the personal tastes and characteristics of that other great courtier-diplomat, Charles Maurice de Talleyrand.[26] Disraeli would probably have been more effective in his foreign policy if he had been younger, and so more energetic, and if he had not for most of his time as Prime Minister been inhibited by his Foreign Secretary Derby's passivity.

Disraeli intended, from the first, to pursue a more vigorous foreign policy than had Gladstone. He was, as far back as 1866, an enthusiast for the imperial cause.[27] He was equally worried about the marginalization of Britain in Europe. But it was by no means clear, at the time or even later, what this analysis implied for concrete policy. In Europe, he would have liked to stand up to, and preferably divide, the *Dreikaiserbund* – the alliance between imperial Germany, Austria and Russia – maintenance of which was the core of Bismarck's policy. But this proved impossible for Britain, a maritime power with the means neither to coerce nor to seduce the alliance's individual members. (When the *Dreikaiserbund* did split, it was because of Russian folly, not British initiative.) In all these schemes, France was no longer a useful ally after its crushing by Bismarck in the Franco-Prussian War. Its only role was as victim.

In 1875 Disraeli bought from under French noses (though with silent French acquiescence) the 44 per cent share in the Suez Canal company owned by the bankrupt Khedive of Egypt. It was a dramatic coup, performed in the cloak-and-dagger manner Disraeli always enjoyed, though at the cost of heavy interest on the £4 million loan advanced by Baron Rothschild. It did not do everything that Disraeli and the Queen pretended. But it was, all the same, a significant assertion of interest in an area increasingly important to Britain. And it turned into an excellent investment besides.[28]

The Liberals denounced the Suez deal. But they were even more inflamed the following year by the Royal Titles Bill, which bestowed on the Queen the title of Empress of India. It was Victoria, rather than Disraeli, who pressed for it, at this politically difficult juncture. But he was keen, nevertheless, because of his romantic enthusiasm for such adornments and because it was a studied declaration of Britain's enduring commitment to its Indian Empire (an open issue since the Mutiny). Disraeli defended himself effectively in the House of Commons – and had the added pleasure of destroying the reputation of his old enemy Robert Lowe in the process.[29] The real trouble for the Government lay not in the symbolism of Empire, but rather in the nuts and bolts of its admin-istration – above all, in controlling agents on the spot, as would shortly become evident.

But it was the Government's approach to the vexed and long-running Eastern Question – that is, the future of the Ottoman Empire in Europe – that was to leave its deepest mark on British politics. In 1875 the Ottoman Empire, already in a state of financial collapse, was faced by a serious rebellion of its Christian subjects, first in Herzegovina and then in Bosnia.[30] It seemed questionable whether this could be put down at all; and in any case it was assumed (quite rightly) that the Turks would perpetrate their usual horrors in attempting to do so. Disraeli was unmoved by the prospect of horrors but interested in the opportunities for states-manship. He optimistically remarked in a letter to Lady Bradford: 'I really believe "the Eastern Question" that has haunted Europe for a century, and which I thought the Crimean War had adjourned for half another, will fall to my lot to encounter – dare I say to settle?'[31] The three northern powers (Russia, Germany and Austria) intervened to insist on religious and administrative reform, first in December 1875 with the 'Andrassy Note', from the

Austro-Hungarian foreign minister of the same name, and then in May 1876, with the Berlin Memorandum. Disraeli grumblingly accepted the first but had the Cabinet publicly denounce the second. The British Mediterranean fleet was despatched to Besika Bay, outside the Dardanelles, as a show of strength and as a sign to Turkey of British support. It was the first time since Palmerston that such assertive action had been taken, and it was received at home with enthusiasm.

It would be too much to say that Disraeli had at this point a thought-through policy. He had been unsympathetic at the time to Palmerston's goal of preserving the Ottoman Empire against Russian inroads, though unlike Derby he had avoided saying so in public. But he had since changed his mind. He now revealed himself as a fierce adherent of Palmerston's assumption – which had since become the consensus of the British foreign policy establishment – that it was imperative to uphold Turkey at all costs. There were also temperamental factors at work. As already noted, he had harboured a degree of sympathy for the Turks from his youth. He had no sympathy for disruptive minorities raising the flag of religious or national liberties against them. (On this score it is worth quoting his observation in a letter to Selina Bradford, though more for its insight into British thinking than its inherent wisdom: 'Fancy autonomy for Bosnia, with a mixed population: autonomy for Ireland would be less absurd, for there are more Turks in proportion to Christians in Bosnia than Ulster v. the other three provinces [of Ireland].')[32]

Above all, now and later, Disraeli was determined not to have Britain treated as a second-rate power by the *Dreikaiserbund*. The accusation made by Derby, in a letter seeking (but not receiving) Salisbury's support in resisting Disraeli, to the effect that he 'believes thoroughly in "prestige" as all foreigners do, and would think it (quite sincerely) in the interests of the country to spend 200 millions on a war if the result was to make foreign States think more highly of us as a military power', was not too wide of the mark.[33] But, of course, what liberal statesmen of Derby's outlook failed (and still fail) to see is that whether a great power is feared is, indeed, a highly important question, as regards both its own interests and the wider balance of power. And, 'foreign' or not, Disraeli's prejudices in this matter were a good deal closer to those of the nation than were the impeccably English Derby's.

Despite that, during the successive stages of the Eastern crisis Disraeli was usually in a small minority in the Cabinet. Partly, Cabinet members reacted according to their respective religious positions, the High Church Carnarvon being the loosest of these cannons. Partly, colleagues followed their own reading of events, as well, of course, as calculation of their own interests. (In Salisbury's case, the distinction between the two was particularly difficult for others to discern.) Disraeli himself was wholeheartedly in favour of supporting the Ottomans against Russia and, if necessary, fighting a war to do so. At times, it is true, he considered the case for seizing elements of a dismembered Turkey, but this was not his considered course. In this Turcophile approach he was, for both better and worse, supported – indeed, egged on – by the Queen, whose resentment of Russia strained the bounds of propriety, even possibly (Disraeli feared) of sanity. Outside the political élite, the eruption of national bellicosity strengthened Disraeli's arm. But one must not exaggerate the effect. Whatever pleasure might be derived from breaking Gladstone's windows, the mob did not dictate events.

Derby's position was potentially more important than any external influences. But Derby was incapable of embracing any vigorous policy at all. He allowed his efforts at securing peace with Russia to lead him and, still more foolishly, his wife, into revealing secrets to the Russian ambassador, Shuvalov.[34] Salisbury, who had the mindset and intellect to disentangle diplomatic myths from reality, certainly had the clearest view. He did not believe that the Ottoman Empire had to be upheld, either to maintain the balance

of power, or to protect the route to India, or for any other con-
ventionally accepted reason. He had not agreed with Palmerston's
approach in the Crimean War. And whatever had been right then –
if it had, indeed, been right – applying it in some amended
fashion in current circumstances was pointless. He described his
thinking in a memorable passage of a letter to Lord Lytton:

> The commonest error in politics is sticking to the carcasses of
> dead policies. When a mast falls overboard, you do not try to save
> a rope here and a spar there, in memory of their former utility;
> you cut away the hamper altogether. And it should be the same
> with a policy. But it is not so. We cling to the shred of an old
> policy after it has been torn to pieces; and to the shadow of the
> shred after the rag itself has been torn away.[35]

But – unlike Derby – Salisbury did not in consequence favour a
policy of diplomatic pacifism. If Turkey were to fall, Britain must
protect its own interests, and it was indeed over the question of
annexing Cyprus as a base from which to assert those interests in
the eastern Mediterranean, which Salisbury strongly supported,
that Derby would finally resign.[36]

In the end, Salisbury lined up with Disraeli against Derby. This
was partly because he thought Russia should no longer be appeased
and partly because he wanted Derby's job, but above all because of
his contempt for the current policy and for the current Foreign
Secretary – which he later ventilated in the Lords, outrageously
comparing him, on hearing Derby's resignation speech, with the
perjurer Titus Oates.

The different stages of the crisis can be separately enumerated,
but in domestic political terms they all merged, with tumultuous
and polarising effect. In 1876 the Bosnian revolt started to ripple
outwards. The Serbian state declared war on the Ottomans in
support of the rebels, but was then crushed before Russia could

intervene. However, it was the Bulgarian uprising against Turkish rule in the same year, put down with extraordinary ferocity, that seriously jeopardized support for Disraeli's moderately assertive pro-Turkish stance. Initially he was badly informed, because of the deficiencies of the Foreign Office and the myopia of Sir Henry Elliot, Britain's Turcophile ambassador in Constantinople. But even as evidence accumulated, he did not want to believe the reports of atrocities (a word which in correspondence he always placed in quotation marks). He even referred scornfully in Parliament to such talk as 'coffee house babble'. But in private he was also angry at having been misled and not unaware of the political damage. So he was pleased to have the Government reach the end of the session relatively unscathed.

It was Disraeli's last appearance in the Commons. He was tired, ill and cantankerous. When his doctor had warned him he could not continue with his present workload, he thought of retiring altogether. But he chose instead to accept an earldom as Lord Beaconsfield (the title enjoyed, as Viscountess, by his late wife – and which he insisted be pronounced with a long 'ee', unlike the town).[37] He quickly inured himself to the staid conventions and slow debates of the Upper House. He was 'dead', as he put it – 'dead, but in the Elysian Fields'.[38]

Then politics suddenly came very much alive. In September Gladstone published a pamphlet, *Bulgarian Horrors and the Question of the East*, that created a political storm never previously seen on the rights and wrongs of foreign policy. It divided the country's élite into two mutually loathing camps, a schism which remained in being until Disraeli's death and, in different forms, well beyond it. This division had more direct impact on the Liberals than on their opponents. Indeed, the Liberal official leadership privately thought Gladstone's demagogy had dangerously exceeded proprieties. The Conservatives, by contrast, rallied strongly behind Disraeli's policy – with the exception of the High

Church faction, which had its own score to settle with him. Among the populace at large there was more suspicion of Russia than concern for the Ottomans' Christian subjects.

The high point of anti-atrocitarian activity was the 'National Conference on the Eastern Question', held in St James's Hall on 8 December under the chairmanship of the Duke of Westminster in the afternoon and Lord Shaftesbury in the evening. The great High Church preacher Henry Liddon summed up the feeling of those who rallied behind Gladstone – and, incidentally, demonstrated why it could never appeal to the masses: 'Perish the interests of England, perish our dominion in India, sooner than we should strike one blow or speak one word on behalf of the wrong against the right.' Others struck a lower tone. The leading historian Edward Freeman, referring to Disraeli's earlier speech at the Lord Mayor's Banquet in Guildhall, and in the presence of Gladstone and other dignitaries on the platform, speculated whether 'the Jew in his drunken insolence' would also 'fight to uphold the independence and integrity of Sodom'. The sentiment clearly came from the heart. Freeman had earlier written (of Russia): 'There is a nation in the freshness of a new life, burning to go on the noblest of crusades, and the loathsome Jew wants to stop them.' Disraeli had encountered a certain amount of anti-semitism in society. (He had to wait till he was over sixty before he was admitted to join Grillon's parliamentary dining club, whereas Derby and Gladstone joined before they were thirty.) But when Liberal self-righteousness legitimized illiberal prejudice all decencies were abandoned.[39]

Salisbury, who was at the time thought to be the most pro-Russian member of the Cabinet, was now sent as the Government's representative to a conference of the powers in Constantinople. (It was ostensibly to reinforce his mission that the St James's Hall meeting was staged.) Salisbury knew the attempt to find a compromise was likely to fail. He predicted 'sea sickness, much French and failure'.[40] The analysis proved correct. His chances of success were not helped by the facts that Elliot systematically undermined his negotiating stance, and that in doing so the ambassador was thought to represent Disraeli's real views.

The basic problem, however, lay in the diplomatic miscalculation at the heart of the Government's official policy. Salisbury recognized, as Disraeli and the Queen refused to recognize, that each gesture of support by the British for the Ottomans simply provided an excuse for the Sultan (or those around him) to refuse concessions. And without such concessions from the Porte the crisis admitted of no solution. So British policy was self-defeating. Nor did it offer salvation to the Ottomans, because in any conflict with Russia they were likely to face defeat.

This was soon put to the test. In April 1877 Russia duly declared war on Turkey. The Ottomans at first defied expectations, their armies holding the Russians off until the end of the year. But they then collapsed, and the way to Constantinople seemed open. The British Cabinet was still hopelessly divided about strategy, let alone tactics. Carnarvon was for resigning, because the policy was too bellicose, though Salisbury discouraged him. Disraeli was frustrated because the Cabinet would not accept his proposal that a Russian assault on Constantinople be considered a formal *casus belli*. The deadlock risked national and political humiliation.

Yet the difference between the two main figures, Disraeli and Salisbury, was, in fact, bridgeable. It stemmed from different assessments of danger, rather than different concepts of statesmanship. Both men, unlike Derby, were prepared to employ force, if the national interest required it. But whereas Disraeli wanted to use force to support Turkey, Salisbury had in mind partially dismembering it, seizing Crete, Cyprus or some other Ottoman possession as a British *place d'armes* or *pied à terre* (as the notion was quaintly described). Both notions were rejected as too aggressive by Derby and Carnarvon.

In January 1878 Salisbury decisively shifted his position.

Whatever view one took of the prospects of the Ottoman Empire, the Russian advance must be stopped. The Cabinet duly ordered the British fleet to approach the Dardanelles, while a special military credit vote was authorized and a defence treaty sought with Austria. Derby and Carnarvon resigned. Derby was due to be replaced by Salisbury. But then the Turks unexpectedly agreed to an armistice. The order to the fleet was countermanded, and Derby came back, though Carnarvon did not. (Disraeli knew that the loss of Derby was politically dangerous; Carnarvon, though, was dispensable.) It was only a brief, unsatisfactory respite. The Russians did not, in fact, seize Constantinople. But the rumours flew. In one panic, Disraeli, with strong support from Salisbury, ordered the British fleet to pass through the Straits, defying Russian threats and Turkish fears. It remained in front of Constantinople as a warning of possibilities throughout the rest of the crisis. Salisbury had scornfully described Derby's approach as 'to float lazily downstream, occasionally putting out a diplomatic boathook to avoid collisions'.[41] The time for boathooks had gone, and that for ironclads had arrived. The old approach could not last, and nor could its increasingly detached, and perhaps disturbed, practitioner.[42]

Disraeli seems to have set Derby up. On the one hand, he told his Foreign Secretary that he agreed there was no point in seizing an island, as Salisbury wished. On the other, he privately gave Gathorne-Hardy, the War Secretary, the strongest impression that this is precisely what he wanted. So Derby was encouraged to argue ever more strongly against the move, which he deplored, going ever further out on the limb which the Prime Minister intended to cut off.[43] The Russians still had the advantage, and they now used it – or, more precisely, abused it – compelling the humiliated Turks to sign the Treaty of San Stefano on 3 March 1878. When the outrageous terms of this *diktat* were known in Europe, the Russians were undone. A huge Greater Bulgaria under Russian control was to be carved out at the expense not just of the Turks but of the non-Bulgarian Slavs (as well as the Greeks), who hated the plan. The Austrians, Bismarck's closest allies, were even more furious at this blow to the balance of power in south-eastern Europe, their own backyard. The *Dreikaiserbund* was, for the moment, crucially split. Yet, facing this crisis, Britain was still effectively bereft of a Foreign Secretary, pursuing a foreign policy crafted and implemented without Derby's effective participation.

Although the details were later contested, it seems that on Wednesday, 27 March the Cabinet agreed the calling out of the Reserves. With Derby isolated, the Cabinet wrangled over and in principle agreed, but did not definitively endorse, proposals for the seizure of Scanderoon and Cyprus, and the sending of troops from India to Malta. Derby now resigned again, and this time was indeed replaced by Salisbury. Later, there was a bitter dispute between the new and old Foreign Secretaries in the House of Lords about the precise point on which Derby had gone. This made interesting politics but was of no substantive significance because, in truth, Derby had stayed far too long, feebly enacting while covertly obstructing a policy to which he was opposed.[44]

The change allowed a return to orderly Cabinet government, rather than government via intrigue. It also allowed the Conservatives to take full advantage of the plebeian patriotism, nurtured in London's music halls, which, after the popular song, was known as 'jingoism'.[45] (Ever since, working-class patriotism has sent shudders down the spines of the more refined Conservative politicians, but it has proved of enormous assistance to the party.) And it allowed Salisbury to emerge as Disraeli's likely heir.

Nevertheless, the loss of Derby, later followed by his defection from the Conservative Party to join the Liberals, was a small political revolution. Just a few months earlier he was still being seen in some quarters as a successor to Disraeli. The Stanley influence was enormous. Some of the damage done to the party would, it was hoped, be overcome by appointing Derby's brother, Frederick Stanley, to the War Office in place of Gathorne-Hardy. But this created another problem. Despite the efforts of 150 Tory back-bench MPs to persuade Gathorne-Hardy to stay in the Commons, he was now tired and disappointed and, on being appointed India Secretary in place of Salisbury, insisted on going to the Lords as Viscount Cranbrook.[46] Gathorne-Hardy's was not a great brain, but he was, in his way, a great Conservative politician – a vigorous debater, aggressive, with down-to-earth views and an iron constitution, and well able to hold his own against troublemakers. He had, in fact, only one political weakness, and that was uxorious-ness – he was so fond of his wife that he went home early from the Chamber. By contrast, Disraeli had made his mark by his near-perpetual presence. Gathorne-Hardy's departure to the Lords would later allow Gladstone to dominate the Chamber, the so-called Fourth Party to mock the Tory front bench, and the Home Rulers to create unopposed mayhem.

Salisbury's appointment as Foreign Secretary had its most important effect outside Britain. It helped convince the Russians and the other powers that Britain at last meant business. The 'Salisbury Circular' now set out to the great powers in incisive and authoritative style Britain's objections to San Stefano. A Congress was bound to be called, and Disraeli and Salisbury were bound to attend.

At the Congress of Berlin (which Bismarck now convened in his assumed role of 'honest broker'), Disraeli, old and often ill but always in his element, provided the face of British policy; Salisbury provided the mind. In any case, the outcome had been more or less secured by the agreements the new Foreign Secretary had made in advance of the Congress itself. Greater Bulgaria was cut down to size – trisected, in fact, with only the northern section falling under Russian control. Russia received other acquisitions: too many according to the jingoists, but less than the Tsar might have hoped.

In compensation for these limited Russian advances, Austria acquired Bosnia-Herzegovina, which stored up trouble in the long term but made good sense in the present. Britain received Cyprus, an important asset for British power in the eastern Mediterranean and, in broader terms, for assuring defence of the route to India in the not unthinkable event of total Turkish collapse.

On their return to England, Disraeli and Salisbury were feted wildly, with some assistance from Conservative Party impresarios. Disraeli proclaimed several times that he had brought 'peace with honour'. He accepted the Garter from the Queen, on condition that Salisbury accept it too, and that fastidious aristocrat agreed. At the celebratory banquet organized by Tories from both Houses at the Duke of Wellington's Riding School in Knightsbridge to laud the achievement, Disraeli uttered his famous rebuke of Gladstone as 'a sophistical rhetorician inebriated with the exuberance of his own verbosity'.

Eighteen seventy-eight was the year of Disraeli's triumph. But it preceded a year of troubles, which itself preceded a year of disaster. Perhaps most cruelly, 1879 saw a sharp reaction against the assertive imperial foreign policy which was his most distinctive creation. Nor was he blameless. It was Disraeli who had insisted on appointing Lytton, son of an old friend from his unrespectable youth, as Viceroy of India, and who then defended him as a man of 'imagination' until this quality ended in disaster. Lytton used the Prime Minister's protection, first against Salisbury, whom he initially beguiled but then alarmed, and then against the less watchful Cranbrook, in order to a pursue a forward policy against Russian influence in Afghanistan. The outcome was an unauthorized move to impose a British mission in Kabul. When this was repulsed, the Government recognized that the humiliation could not be endured and embarked on the unwanted but – thanks to the tactical brilliance of General Roberts – successful British campaign which has gone down in history as the Second Afghan War. The Amir of

Afghanistan fled and was replaced by his son. The Russians withdrew their mission from Kabul and did nothing too threatening. Disraeli appeared to take the credit by speaking in high-flown terms of Britain's imperial vocation in his Guildhall speech that November. In May 1879 a convention was signed by which a British mission under Sir Louis Cavagnari was triumphantly installed in Kabul.

Then, on 3 September, Cavagnari and his staff were murdered by rebel Afghan troops. General Roberts was now sent back on a punitive mission – The Third Afghan War. This too was successful. But in 1880 the British were faced by yet another revolt. Disraeli – who was privately furious with Lytton – was held responsible by the Opposition and by his many Liberal critics for the disaster and its messy aftermath. Gladstone later, to Salisbury's disgust, ordered the evacuation of Afghanistan altogether.

In the meantime, however, a still greater humiliation had been inflicted on British policy and arms in South Africa. It was the result of a toxic mix of high-mindedness, vacillation and stubbornness – exactly the sort of combination that leads to military mishaps. The high-mindedness in question came from the Colonial Secretary (until his resignation in 1878), Carnarvon. In his previous spell in that job, he had successfully masterminded the federation of Canada. Now he wanted the same outcome for South Africa (with the role of the French *québécois* played by the Dutch). It made some sense in theory, because the Boers needed help against the Zulus, and because the English wanted a secure hold on the recently discovered diamond fields. But it made little sense in practice, because the Boers hated the English, the Cape did not want to lose authority to a federal government, and the British Government underrated the threat posed by the Zulus – a threat now aimed, after annexation of the Transvaal in 1877, at Britain rather than the Boers.

The second element, the vacillation, came from London. The

new Colonial Secretary, Sir Michael Hicks Beach, was not well versed in South African affairs and, like his Cabinet colleagues at the time, far more concerned about the possibility of war with Russia. Disraeli was also distracted. This allowed room for the third factor, stubbornness, to engineer disaster. Sir Bartle Frere, formerly Governor of Bombay, a strong-minded, iron-willed proconsul who thought he could always get his own way, had been imported to South Africa in 1877 by 'Twitters' with an unavowed mission (as Disraeli angrily later noted). Frere understood that he was to head the new federation, which, however, it also fell to him to create. He believed – wrongly – that the main threat to the plan was posed by the Zulus, rather than the Boers. In any case, he was firmly instructed from London to avoid a Zulu war. The Government had too many other worries to fight one. Frere, though, blithely ignored his orders, issued an ultimatum to the Zulus, and began his war, while the Government failed to send in time the reinforcements required to win it. The result was the destruction of a British force at Isandhlwana on 22 January 1879.

The news, when it arrived in Britain, was politically devastating. Disraeli nearly collapsed. The British overall commander in South Africa, Lord Chelmsford, eventually proved capable of wiping out the Zulus at Ulundi, once reinforcements arrived. But this was not before the embarrassing demise of the French Prince Imperial (Napoleon III's son – 'that little abortion' as Disraeli unpleasantly described him), speared to death by Zulu assegais.[47]

The Government's foreign policy was intellectually defensible. Moreover, it could be argued that the reverses had themselves been reversed, and the happy memory of 'peace with honour' from Berlin still lingered. The cost of operations threw the public finances into deficit, which was embarrassing. But the main political problem was that these events brought back Gladstone. Giving up his Greenwich seat, he announced his intention to fight the Scottish seat of Midlothian. Wrongly imagining that a dissolution was imminent, he embarked upon what turned out to be a lengthy and highly personalized crusade against 'Beaconsfieldism'.

In the absence of psephological data it is impossible to be sure about the relative importance of the different factors in the following year's Conservative rout. Given public manifestations of support for Conservative foreign policy, it seems unlikely that the overseas setbacks were themselves of much electoral importance. Disraeli's summation of what finally sank him, contained in a letter to Salisbury after the event, is very probably correct – 'hard times'.[48]

The end of the 1870s marked the start of a period of deep, prolonged, and socially and politically destabilizing agricultural depression. This was when the worst fears of the agricultural protectionists, expressed three decades earlier, were finally realized. There were successive bad harvests, caused by appalling weather which destroyed crops. Livestock farms were hit by disease. The yields and acreage of wheat both fell sharply. One could have expected prices to rise. But because of access to foreign supply, they actually fell.[49] Disraeli was aware of the agricultural distress. One reason why he obtained a dissolution when he did, in early 1880, was because he feared the effect of the Farmers' Alliance, stirring up a rural revolt against the Conservatives in the county seats.[50] (He was altogether unaware, though, of equally worrying long-term problems in industry.[51])

Did organizational weakness worsen the election outcome? The answer is that it probably did, but not crucially. Gorst later had every reason to claim that it had, because that magnified his past achievements and increased his current importance. He had been succeeded as the party's principal agent in 1877 by William Baillie Skene – his opposite in all respects. Skene was the sort of amiable, well-connected, wealthy, well-born nonentity that the Conservative hierarchy is prone to appoint when it thinks it can get away with it. Gorst himself, back in the Commons later that year, loudly complained about failure to cultivate the boroughs. It was Gorst's agitation in the National Union which most infuriated the party managers, whom he in turn despised. What is certainly true is that the Liberals were moving ahead, both organizationally and in terms of public support. The emergence of the National Liberal Federation, based on Joe Chamberlain's Birmingham Caucus, pointed the way. By 1880 even Lady Salisbury was declaring: 'We must have caucuses.'[52]

In deciding when to seek a dissolution, Disraeli, like other leaders, relied heavily on the party whips. The obvious time to go to the country was in the wake of the Congress of Berlin. Sir William Hart Dyke, the Chief Whip, was consulted and in reply drew up a memorandum containing excellent, but mistaken, reasons against an immediate dissolution. The most important one was that income tax must first be got down – it had risen in both 1877 and 1878 to pay for military operations. But the one that probably weighed most heavily was the fact that Tory MPs were, as the Chief Whip noted, against an election – and the fact that Disraeli and the Cabinet were tired weighed heavily too. Governments with healthy majorities rarely go to the country early. Everyone wants to hold on to what they have. One estimate, necessarily inexact, suggests that had an election been called in 1878 Disraeli would at best have been returned with a greatly reduced majority.[53] This would have been a nuisance. But he did not have any radical legislative programme in mind; foreign policy, his main preoccupation, does not require regular legislative endorsement; and, anyway, such a result would have been a great deal better than what occurred.

On the basis of by-election results, the electorate was heavily polarized during 1876–7, with high turnouts reflecting the bitter controversies of those years, and with the Liberals slightly ahead. The following year the advantage reverted briefly to the Conservatives.[54] Indeed, there was a surprisingly (and misleadingly) good by-election result in Sheffield as late as January 1880.[55] The

1880 session was insignificant and truncated. The only notable legislation was an Electoral Practices Act, which extended from the boroughs to the counties the practice of hiring transport to take people to the polls (and so dubbed the 'Cabs' Bill). It did little good to the Conservatives, which was the object.

The announcement of a dissolution was made on 8 March. Disraeli's manifesto, in the form of a letter to the Lord Lieutenant of Ireland, the Duke of Marlborough, was uninspiring, though prescient in warning of future danger to the Union between England and Ireland. Having written that, Disraeli did remarkably little, the convention being that peers did not campaign. Salisbury, the other leading party figure, was recovering his shattered health in Biarritz. (In the meantime, Disraeli used Hatfield House as his little team's campaign headquarters: he alone, however, was allowed to drink the Château Margaux.[56]) Tory officials, supported by the Tory press, claimed to be confident of victory. There was certainly plenty of money available. Disraeli had no direct contact with feeling in the country and there is no reason to think that he foresaw the result. But he was not deceived, either, by the optimistic assertions from the party machine.

The results, when they came in, were stunningly bad. The party did poorly everywhere. It lost thirty-six seats outside England. But the most notably bad results were in the English counties, including the loss of four of the eight Lancashire county seats, where Derby's influence was now hostile. And to cap the humiliation, Gladstone won Midlothian. The previous election had returned 352 Conservatives, 243 Liberals and 57 Home Rulers. The new one had 352 Liberals, 238 Conservatives and 62 Home Rulers.[57] Not only was it a rout; it was such a rout that, as it appeared on the surface at least, all the gains of Disraeli's earlier triumph had been reversed.

The Queen wept. Disraeli did not. He was disappointed but phlegmatic. He again resigned without meeting the new House of

Commons, thus reinforcing the constitutional precedent. Though seventy-six, he carried on as leader, because that was his duty and because it was what the party clearly wanted.

He took pleasure in a final bout of patronage, awarding honours to friends in demonstration of, variously, his loyalties (a peerage for Corry, who became Lord Rowton), his defiance (an earldom for Lytton) and his enduring gratitude (a barony for the widow of a Bentinck). Unlike Salisbury, Disraeli had no squeamishness about dispensing the spoils of office. He had, so far as he could, re-politicized government appointments, earlier de-politicized under Gladstone. In fact, he never revised the view he expressed in 1858 that patronage was 'the outward and visible sign of an inward and spiritual grace, that is Power' – a formulation which would hardly have pleased Salisbury.[58]

Disraeli also completed the novel he had begun two years earlier, *Endymion*. For this he received the largest advance hitherto paid for a work of fiction – though with so many historical characters appearing in transparent disguise (Palmerston, Bismarck, Napoleon III, Cardinal Manning among others), 'fiction' is perhaps a misnomer.[59]

Severe and unexpected election defeats always bring poison in their wake. But the effects of this one were limited while Disraeli lived. No one wanted to act against him. No faction, anyway, yet felt powerful enough to challenge the others. At a meeting of the parliamentary party in Bridgewater House, off Green Park, on 19 May 1880, Disraeli set out his strategy. It was the familiar one of supporting the Liberal Government against its own Radicals, while opposing dangerous measures. The political considerations were familiar, too, because the Conservatives had once more in their sights a defection of Whigs from the government benches into their own ranks. But while professing loyalty to Disraeli and acceptance of his guidance, restive and far from disinterested spirits in the Commons were intent on pursuing other paths. (Since this group, the 'Fourth Party', reached the summit of their irritating importance later, the story is better told in the next chapter.) Northcote, 'the Goat', as he was mockingly called – because of his appearance, not his habits, being elderly and a model of pious rectitude – was unable to maintain his authority. This was more than tactically important, because as Leader of the House Northcote must at this stage be considered Disraeli's heir apparent. So his undermining had a subversive effect on the party's standing. Disraeli was not much help, because he was obviously amused by and privately sympathetic to the underminers. He told Henry Drummond Wolff, one of the chief miscreants: 'I fully appreciate your feelings and those of your friends, but you must stick with Northcote. He represents the respectability of the party. I wholly sympathise with you all, because I was never respectable myself.'[60]

In fact, the manoeuvring was not about tactics, let alone policy. It was, as usual in the Conservative Party, about power, which ultimately meant the leadership. Disraeli now wanted Salisbury to succeed him and made no secret of the fact.[61] And Salisbury wanted the leadership. But despite his seniority, experience and intellect, he was far from assured of the job. So it was in his interests that Disraeli continue for a while longer. That looked a real possibility, because his health had improved. On 3 February 1881 Disraeli addressed a party meeting in his house in Curzon Street; and he appeared in the Lords on 15 March, at a vote of condolence on the assassination of the Tsar. But the east wind he feared so much did its worst. He fell ill with pneumonia and died on 19 April – a date that would be of some significance for the mythology which grew up around it.

It was also a nightmare date for Gladstone, particularly when he learned of Disraeli's insistence that he be buried with a private funeral at Hughenden. Gladstone (wrongly) thought this an act of false humility that betokened the grossest vanity, and he was naturally furious. He was then forced to pay tribute in the

Commons to someone whom he hated and despised, while denying the fact. In private, according to Lord Acton, Gladstone described Disraeli 'as the worst and most immoral Minister since Castlereagh'.[62] No wonder that in preparing his response to his old enemy's demise he was racked with nervous indigestion and serial bowel malfunction.[63] Disraeli, had the roles been reversed, would not have suffered any such complaints, since he never concealed the depth of his dislike for Gladstone – and a final reflection is in order on that relationship.

Gladstone and Disraeli did not understand each other, though they both tried, at least in the early days. Gladstone even managed a kind word about Disraeli's sick wife.[64] But the efforts at amity were short-lived. Disraeli quickly concluded that Gladstone was a prig – which was true – and a hypocrite ('Tartuffe' in Disraeli-speak) – which, by most definitions at least, was not. (Disraeli was enjoyably enlarging on these themes in his new novel, *Falconet*, when death overtook him, and it.) The opprobrious term he used most frequently to characterize Gladstone was 'vindictiveness'. This was probably fair, though revenge and retribution are sufficiently similar to be confused.

The beginnings of Disraeli's and Gladstone's mutual opposition lie in the age of Peel. Disraeli destroyed Peel. Gladstone was a self-proclaimed Peelite to the end.[65] It was, though, the Eastern Crisis that set in concrete the low views they had of each other – and the views of their respective partisans. Gladstone thought that Disraeli, partly because of his Jewishness, was devoid of any sense of justice and rootedly hostile to constitutional liberty. For Disraeli – and for the Queen and others – the only unanswered question was whether Gladstone was clinically insane. In the end, Disraeli concluded that no such excuse was available, observing to Lady Bradford in 1877: 'What restlessness! What vanity! And what unhappiness must be his! Easy to say he is mad. It looks like it. My theory about him is unchanged: a ceaseless Tartuffe from the beginning. That sort of man does not get mad at seventy.'[66]

The division of opinion which the contest between the two great rivals engendered lives on. In Victorian times, outside a few (anti-Disraeli) High Church divines on the one hand and some (anti-Gladstone) secularist Whigs on the other, the line of division was recognizably party political. But with the destruction of Liberalism (in any Gladstonian form at least) and the later evolution of Conservatism the polarization becomes perhaps more interesting. Like that between temperamental Roundheads and Cavaliers, it distinguishes even those whose political opinions are otherwise similar. Thus, for example, the leading right-of-centre commentator Simon Heffer, writing in the *Daily Telegraph* on the two-hundredth anniversary of Gladstone's birth, argued that his hero 'in the 300 and more years between Cromwell and Mrs Thatcher . . . was the finest political leader this country had', and went on to deplore 'the moral cowards who revere the memory of the mountebank Disraeli'.[67] Heffer was then answered in equally robust language by another well-known right-of-centre commentator, Peter Oborne, writing in the *Spectator*, who described the present Conservative Party leader, David Cameron, as reaching back to 'a purer school of Conservatism . . . [which] reached its apotheosis with Disraeli'.[68]

At the root of these disagreements is a dispute over what the Conservative Party exists to do. One can argue that the ex-Peelite Gladstone is the Conservative Party's lost leader and that his recognizably 'Thatcherite' approach to finance and taxation is more conservative than Disraeli's. The difficulty is that this ignores the degree to which on all that mattered most to conservative-minded Englishmen of the day – the Church, property, the constitution, Ireland – Gladstone was either himself a Radical or at least willing to embrace Radical arguments. He was, it is true, the disciple of Peel. But he was not in the mould of that stolidly dull and prudently reserved figure in most respects that mattered. As such, the elevation of Gladstone to the conservative pantheon is unhistorical.

Equally unhistorical and more frequent have been the attempts by Conservative Party propagandists down the years to suggest a greater coherence, continuity, distinctness and substance to Disraeli's social reforms than they ever possessed. It is also debatable whether the impact of that propaganda, to the extent it had an impact, was positive. At important junctures, it has distracted the Conservative Party from more manageable economic questions and more pressing international ones – a recurring theme in the rest of this book.

What really mattered to Disraeli in the course of his career were the monarchy, the landed interest and, above all, national prestige. His stance on these matters defined and displayed his conservatism far more than did anything else. To the first of these three causes he devoted much of his diminishing energy but not, in the end, to very great effect. His reverence for the monarchy, which he focused on the person of the Queen, was exaggerated – and ridiculous: 'We authors, Ma'am . . .' the novelist Prime Minister was wont to remark en passant, in flattering reference to his sovereign's *Leaves from the Journal of Our Life in the Highlands*.[69] At times he went too far in humouring her. He revealed too much of the working of the Cabinet for the country's good. He was too accommodating to her pressure. He personalized the relationship between monarch and minister to an extent that endangered the orderly conduct of business, particularly when a less sympathetic minister was appointed.

Nor could he do much, in practice, for his second concern – preservation of the hereditary aristocracy. The landed interest long retained its influence. Upper-class members of Tory Cabinets, including Tory prime ministers, have flourished and still flourish. But the great landed families collectively could not have a political future, given economic and social trends. Disraeli might have been better advised to concentrate more wholeheartedly on securing the allegiance of the middle classes, something that the Tories then and later did only with much reluctance.

But what of the final cause, national prestige? Here Disraeli did set Britain and the Conservative Party on a new path, one previously trodden by Palmerston and before him Canning, but not by conventional Conservatives. As Salisbury said in the Lords in tribute to his old chief – a man he increasingly grew to respect, though never to like: 'Zeal for the greatness of England was the passion of his life.' When the mythology is stripped away – the overwritten novels, the overwrought expressions, the mysterious allusions, all later wrapped up in the hugely successful and highly eccentric trappings of the Primrose League – that simple core remains.[70] 'The greatness of England' (by which Disraeli meant Britain, but never thought it necessary to explain) is his decisive contribution to the idea which the Conservative Party has of itself, and which, down through the decades, it has wanted others to have of it too.

THE FINISH.

*Salisbury's triumph over Gladstone in the 1886 general election fundamentally
shifted the base of British politics. Gladstone's embrace of Irish Home
Rule irretrievably split his party: the alienated Liberal Unionists
first supported and then joined a coalition with the Conservatives.*

6

SALISBURY'S PARTY, I –
ACHIEVING DOMINANCE

Robert Gascoyne-Cecil, third Marquess of Salisbury, was almost as unlikely a leader of the Conservative Party as Beaconsfield had been, albeit in an entirely different way.[1] Disraeli had, for all his oddities, served an obvious purpose. He provided the rhetorical firepower and the tactical virtuosity which the party needed in its long, dark days in the wilderness; he then reached the top because the party was stuck with him – and because, the Conservatives being already in government, it was the Queen who made the final decision.

Salisbury was not so obviously indispensable. He was, of course, intellectually gifted and hugely experienced, and he possessed, like Disraeli, enormous courage and tenacity. But when the leadership fell vacant he was in the Lords, not the Commons, which was a large disadvantage when it came to popular politics and factional manoeuvring. More seriously, he was mistrusted, partly because of his still remembered past as a right-wing rebel, and partly because even his like-minded fellow peers doubted his capacity to make necessary compromises. They particularly dreaded his incapacity or unwillingness to control a ferocious tongue, surprising in one who was otherwise so courteous. A contemporary remarked: 'The combination of such genuine amiability in private life with such calculated brutality in public utterance constitutes a psychological problem which might profitably be made the subject of a Romanes Lecture.'[2]

The 'brutality' was not always well calculated. Salisbury's public remarks frequently delighted the Opposition. The Liberal MP John Morley would joke: 'I am very glad when Lord Salisbury makes a great speech, it is sure to contain at least one *blazing indiscretion* which it is a delight to remember.'[3]

Having a rare degree of self-knowledge, Salisbury fully recognized the problem which his own mentality posed. Writing to a well-wisher in 1884, he frankly observed: 'To be leader of a large party – still more to be the leader of anything resembling a Coalition – requires in a large measure the gifts of pliancy and optimism; and I, unfortunately, am very poorly endowed in either respect.'[4]

Salisbury could not in 1881 be denied the leadership of the Conservatives in the Upper House, though some Tory peers were initially minded to try. But it is equally clear that, had the Tories been in power on Beaconsfield's death or come to it shortly afterwards, Northcote, not Salisbury, would have been asked by the Queen to form a Government – as she more or less told him. (This explains the depth of Northcote's disappointment when Salisbury, and not he, was summoned to the Palace in 1885.)[5] The party thus embarked on an uneasy experiment in dual leadership.

It was hardly an unqualified success. Tory backbenchers were often highly critical of it. But it could have been a spectacular disaster if both Salisbury and Northcote, despite their rivalry, had not at the important moments acted with courtesy and honour. Salisbury, who was the more ambitious, vigorous and talented, showed consideration for Northcote's sensibilities, even while eclipsing him. 'The Goat's' persecutors were to be found elsewhere – in the so-called Fourth Party – though Salisbury prudently ensured that Northcote's losses materialized as his own gains.[6]

In the House of Commons, Randolph Churchill, Gorst and Wolff, with Arthur Balfour (Salisbury's nephew) as a semi-detached member of the group, repeatedly showed up Northcote by their brilliance and aggression in debate. (Churchill also cruelly and snobbishly mocked the bourgeois duo of Smith and Cross as 'Marshall and Snelgrove'.)[7] Churchill and his friends also captured the imagination of the wider Conservative Party, through startling interventions in the *Morning Post* and *Vanity Fair*. The Fourth Party members' aims were, though, by no means identical. Churchill was an ambitious young aristocrat, not just on the make but in a hurry, because of the mortal illness that first unbalanced his mind and then paralysed his body. (Salisbury knew his man. Writing to his friend Lady John Manners in 1884, he noted: 'Randolph and the Mahdi have occupied my thoughts about equally. The Mahdi pretends to be half mad, and is very sane in reality; Randolph occupies exactly the converse position.')[8]

Churchill never gave substance to the phrase 'Tory democracy' with which he became so strongly associated. He did not, in fact, use it often, anyway. When asked in private what it meant, he described it as 'principally opportunism', and on the public platform explained, somewhat circuitously: 'the Tory democracy is a democracy which has embraced the principles of the Tory Party.' As *The Times* noted, this did not get one very far.[9] Wolff made his main impact through his ideas for the Primrose League (on which more in Chapter 7 below). He was later neutralized by Salisbury by being sent on diplomatic missions. Balfour was always more Salisbury's agent than a mere *frondeur*. It was, in fact, Gorst whose schemes posed the greatest danger to the Tory hierarchy, even though Churchill was to be the chief beneficiary – and agent of those schemes' ultimate undoing.

In so far as the Fourth Party's activities destabilized Northcote, they assisted Salisbury. But the latter's main problem during these years of opposition was to rally the party – and even his fellow peers – to the strategy of obstruction which he favoured. Ireland was the initial focus. Gladstone's efforts to appease Irish nationalism were doomed. The tactics he adopted to end the so-called Land War disruptions were deemed humiliating – not least the behind-the-scenes horse-trading with the briefly imprisoned leader of the Irish Nationalists, Charles Stewart Parnell. The Liberal Chief Secretary of Ireland and Irish Viceroy resigned in protest. Shortly afterwards, on 6 May 1882, the new Chief Secretary, Lord Frederick Cavendish, and the veteran under-secretary, Thomas Henry Burke, were horribly assassinated in Phoenix Park, Dublin. In these circumstances Salisbury believed that he would have no difficulty in rallying the peers to oppose Gladstone's Irish Arrears Bill.[10] Initially, he found them enthusiastic. But the Irish land-owners, who saw a useful state hand-out to troublemakers where Salisbury saw a threat to property, then crumbled, and finally the rest of the party, intimidated by Gladstone's threat of a dissolution, also walked away. Salisbury angrily stood his ground but was left humiliated in the vote. It was the lowest point during the dual leadership. But Salisbury recovered. He did so because the same ruthless and unflinching resistance to liberalism that worried his fellow Tories soon started to look respectable and managed to worry the Liberal Government even more.

Ever since 1867, a further electoral reform measure had been inevitable. Salisbury understood this better than anyone. It was why he saw the first steps towards democracy in the boroughs as so inherently dangerous. He never changed his view of the principle, but he substantially modified his practical response. In any case, what mattered to him, as a realistic rather than a nostalgic Conservative, was to adapt to inevitable changes in the least socially damaging – and most politically advantageous – way. It was one of the many paradoxes that characterized his outlook. His pessimism was so deep that he found himself perpetually and pleasantly surprised when the worst was avoided. He had long envisaged that Britain would have to face a revolutionary convulsion of the sort endured by France in 1848. When it did not happen, and when instead Conservative Governments were elected, he modified his judgement, without ever entirely losing his apprehension. He merely wondered at the outcome. As he would reflect to the National Union on 16 November 1897: 'No doubt the history of recent times as it will be written is a very strange history.'[11]

Salisbury was also extremely interested in the nuts and bolts of electoral arithmetic. It was why he had caused so much difficulty to Disraeli and Derby in the run-up to the Second Reform Bill. Now, though, he adopted the earlier Disraeli–Derby view that re-distribution of seats was the best way to reduce the damage done by widening the county franchise. Ensuring that the two changes were introduced simultaneously was, he believed, the key to future Conservative victories. It was a high-risk strategy. It depended on blackmailing Gladstone, by threatening to stop the 1884 Reform Bill in its tracks. But first he had to ensure that his fellow Tories faced down Gladstone's threats of a dissolution, as they had failed to do in 1882.

It was a war of nerves, and Salisbury eventually won it. This was despite a riot in Birmingham – when a rally was attacked by furniture-throwing Liberals in what a Tory wag described a 'redistribution of seats' – and despite embarrassing pressure from the Queen to compromise.[12] When the details of redistribution were thrashed out in Downing Street by the two sides in November 1884, Salisbury demonstrated bravura and skill that put other Tories in the shade – including Northcote. The detailed negotiation was between Dilke and Salisbury, though the latter significantly shifted his view towards that of Beach, who favoured the radical option of single-member constituencies and roughly equal electoral districts. The fact remains that the outcome seemed to vindicate Salisbury's judgement (even though the Conservatives failed to win the first election held on the new franchise).

The Redistribution Bill received its second reading in the Commons on 4 December. The third reading of the Reform Bill, which Salisbury now allowed through, passed the Lords on 5 December and received Royal Assent on 6 December. As a result of the measure, nearly two million new voters were added to the existing register of three million. Some 60 per cent of male adults were henceforth eligible to vote. There were complications. Not all potential voters finished up on the register, of course, and 7 per cent of voters were able to vote in more than one constituency – this was significant because of the Irish vote in English seats. But the most important effect from the Conservative Party's point of view was the creation of a pattern of single-member seats surrounding the country's conurbations. This supplemented the larger trends working in the Conservatives' favour. It allowed 'islands' of Tory support to add to the number of Tory MPs returned. The electoral geography established by the combination of franchise and distribution reforms is still recognizable today. In election after election it has served the Conservative Party remarkably well – allowing it to gain significantly from the same trend of migration from inner to outer urban areas that has otherwise, in between further redistributions, proportionately benefited the party's opponents on the left.[13]

Salisbury had not been focusing his gaze on parliamentary tactics and numbers alone. He was acutely aware of the shortcomings of Gladstone's foreign policy. In particular, he watched – and warned about – Gladstone's inexplicable paralysis in the face of the Mahdi's revolt in Sudan. When he read in the evening paper of the decision to send General Gordon unaccompanied to Khartoum, Salisbury exclaimed: 'They must be quite mad!'[14] On 5 February 1885 news of Gordon's death reached England. A wave of obloquy descended on the Government. A motion of censure failed narrowly in the Commons – a failure for which Northcote was blamed – but was passed in the Lords, where Salisbury was devastating. It was then the Tory *frondeurs* – not the leaders – who managed to trap the Government into defeat in the Commons on a budget measure, when the Irish felt able to troop into the opposition lobby. Gladstone promptly resigned and Salisbury, travelling third class to escape detection by the press, made the train journey to Balmoral to kiss hands.

Northcote almost alone seems to have imagined he was still regarded as effective party leader, and was duly upset. But Salisbury was not particularly enthusiastic about acquiring the post of Prime Minister in such circumstances. Indeed, he might well have followed Disraeli's example and refused it, had he not been desperate to restore credibility to British foreign policy. (He complained of Gladstone's approach, based on support for a 'Concert of Europe', that it had only managed to unite Europe against Britain.) Salisbury did, in fact, prove remarkably sure-footed in the limited time available: by a quick reversal of position on the vexed Bulgarian issue, he helped keep the peace, while frustrating Russian ambitions.[15] But his ministry looked likely to be short-lived. A general election on the new franchise was unlikely to return it to power. And settling the fate of Northcote was still an unpleasant dilemma, linked to a still more intractable problem – coping with Randolph Churchill.

Churchill was in an immensely powerful position, or so it seemed. Under Gorst's direction, he had managed to take control of the voluntary party organization and turn it into a weapon against the leadership. Gorst's replacement as principal agent, G. C. T. Bartley, was sympathetic to the aims (such as they were) of Tory democracy. So, to a large extent, was Abergavenny. Churchill had himself elected to the Council of the National Union in July 1883 on a wave of exasperation with Northcote and the 'old gang', by which he meant the parliamentary party leadership which constituted the Central Committee. (Salisbury was left out of the insults for tactical reasons.) Churchill launched a fierce and direct attack at the annual National Union conference in Birmingham. Cranbrook was sent down to restore some order. But Churchill was now out of control. Improbably for the son of the Duke of Marlborough and incumbent of one of the last pocket boroughs, Churchill demanded that the 'working classes' be given a share in the direction of the party. The outcome of the conference was inconclusive. But Churchill also had a grip on the Organization Committee of the National Union, recently set up in response to the grumbling. His supporters threw the compliant Lord Percy out of the chair, which Churchill now took. He and his colleagues demanded to air their grievances with Salisbury, though they had to tolerate Northcote's presence for part of the meeting.

Churchill went away unappeased. His public utterances became steadily wilder. But what he really wanted was to gain control of the party funds, without which his agitation was bound to be fruitless. The donors, however, were unimpressed. The weakness of the National Union as a base was demonstrated when the party leaders ordered Bartley to expel its organization from Central Office.

The row reached its peak at the National Union conference in Sheffield in July 1884. Both Salisbury and Churchill spoke, but Churchill was acclaimed. He roundly attacked the 'county element', which he accused of blocking necessary party reform. Churchill himself came top in the elections to the Council, though Gorst failed to be elected.[16] It was not quite stalemate, because despite widespread alarm at his behaviour in the upper reaches of the party, Churchill had momentum. But how could he use it? In fact, he struck a deal.

His manner of doing so was deplored, and was indeed deplorable. He did not even inform, let alone consult, Gorst, whose career prospects never recovered and whose bitterness never abated.[17]

Churchill gained a few organizational concessions, but that was all. In exchange, he gave up his calls for Tory democracy, at least until he finally lost his job and his salary some years later. But if the whole enterprise was simply a way to force himself to the top in record time and with maximum popular support – which it was – he was wise to settle when he did.

Each of the two major players – Salisbury and Churchill – (Northcote's fortunes were by now plummeting fast) – needed the other. As long as Salisbury held his nerve he could not be threatened by Churchill, only embarrassed. This was because the choice of leader fell to the parliamentary party and the parliamentary party regarded Churchill as far too young, highly unbalanced and generally insufferable. But Salisbury also needed Churchill if he was to be Prime Minister. If Churchill were to carry through his threat of flouncing out, perhaps to ally with the Radicals under Joe Chamberlain, Salisbury's and the Conservative Party's interests would inevitably be jeopardized. Northcote sometimes longingly considered a fusion of conservative-minded Whigs with moderate Conservatives confronting the Radicals of both parties. But Salisbury knew perfectly well that in such a system he himself had no future.

The deed was done at a Marlborough House garden party on 26 July, for which Wolff and Balfour had paved the way. The Central Committee was wound up. The Primrose League was officially recognized. Northcote was to go to the Lords. Gorst would be rewarded in some capacity. The most important, probably unspoken, concession was that Churchill would be in Salisbury's Cabinet. Afterwards Salisbury reassured his nephew Balfour, now Churchill's rival, that this deal with Churchill was 'a temporary retreat on account of the peculiar circumstances of the moment, not compromising any future action'.[18] So it eventually proved.

But now, in June 1885, it was time for Salisbury to deliver. He appointed a large Cabinet for the day, with twenty-two members.

Northcote was duly, and painfully, 'kicked up stairs' (the origin of the phrase) to the Lords as the Earl of Iddesleigh, with the odd addition of being First Lord of the Treasury. His nemesis, Churchill, became Secretary of State for India. Beach, a friend of Churchill's, was Chancellor of the Exchequer and Leader of the House. Cross, despite Churchill's objections, was back at the Home Office. W. H. Smith, another of Churchill's *bêtes noires*, was Secretary for War. Lord Halsbury took the place intended for the recently deceased Cairns as Lord Chancellor. Carnarvon was made Viceroy of Ireland – in which role he would play a large if ambiguous role in decisive events.

It is difficult to defend the Irish policy of Salisbury's first Government in its own right. But it undoubtedly paved the way for his later extraordinarily tight grip on power.[19] Carnarvon, who was as keen as ever to promote a vision of Empire based upon federated self-governing colonies, had now become convinced that Home Rule for Ireland fitted neatly into that conception. It is hard to imagine that Salisbury was completely unaware of this. The Conservatives had already indicated to Parnell – through Churchill, who had been brought up in Ireland and was at this stage close to the Home Rulers – that they would not renew the Irish Coercion measures (emergency powers, including suspension of habeas corpus). Without telling the Queen or the Cabinet, Salisbury now authorized Carnarvon to hold a private meeting with Parnell. The latter subsequently revealed – to maximum embarrassment, during the debates on the Home Rule Bill in June 1886 – one (admittedly disputed) version of what occurred. Salisbury would always subsequently maintain that he had not authorized Carnarvon's proposal of what amounted to an Irish Parliament. But by agreeing to the meeting at all he had gone to dubious lengths to win Nationalist support at Westminster, and Irish votes at the following general election.

He also, perhaps deliberately, gave Gladstone the impression that the Conservatives might themselves introduce Home Rule of some sort – the term was subject to large differences of interpretation. (Gladstone would have learned of what transpired between Carnarvon and Parnell through his association with Kitty O'Shea, Parnell's mistress.) This provided Gladstone with a double motive to advance his own initiative. First, he could hope that Salisbury would be prepared to fall on his sword, as Peel had done over repeal of the Corn Laws, in order to help resolve a great national issue.[20] Second, it also made sense that, while hoping this, he should act at once. It was clear to any experienced politician that Home Rule would not be quickly or easily achieved. The initial plan was likely to be modified many times and, indeed, by different governments. But for Gladstone to assert his grip on the Liberals at the expense of other factions he had to take the lead with a dramatic gesture – a course which, anyway, suited his messianic temperament.[21]

In the meantime, the general election of November–December 1885, fought on the new franchise, was lost by the Conservatives. The outcome was expected, and it was in significant respects better than had been feared. The party gained about a dozen seats: 250 Conservatives now faced 334 Liberals, with 86 Parnellite Irish Nationalists in the wings. The Irish question was thus inevitably central, despite its having occupied a relatively minor role in the campaign. From Gladstone's viewpoint it was clear, too, that adding Home Rulers and Tories together in any combination would prevent the Liberals exercising an effective overall majority.

And so was flown the 'Hawarden Kite' (the memorable phrase, as usual, was Salisbury's). Gladstone approached the Conservatives via Balfour in December to see if the Irish problem could be resolved on the basis of Home Rule by the Conservatives with Liberal support. Perhaps he was sincere, perhaps not. In any case, Gladstone had his son Herbert write a short letter from the family's country home, Hawarden Castle, to *The Times* in which, presumably speaking on his father's behalf, he declared: 'Nothing could induce me to countenance separation, but if five-sixths of the Irish people wish to have a Parliament in Dublin, for the management of their own local affairs, let them have it.' In fact, it was less the proportion of the Irish people who wanted an Irish Parliament than the size of the Irish Home Rule contingent in the British Parliament which tempted him to make such a declaration. Salisbury's response was dismissive: 'His hypocrisy makes me sick.'[22]

Of greater political moment, however, was the queasiness that quickly now afflicted a large section of Gladstone's own party, which he had entirely failed to prepare for the announcement. It was, in fact, one of the most catastrophic misjudgements in British political history, similar to that of Peel in his volte-face on the Corn Laws. Gladstone appalled the Whigs, led by the aristocratic Hartington (later Devonshire, and ubiquitously known as 'Harty-Tarty'). The assassination of Hartington's brother, Lord Frederick Cavendish, Chief Secretary for Ireland, some three years earlier gave a personal edge to his already strong conviction that order and investment, not legislative reform or constitutional change, offered the only way forward in Ireland. Like other Whig moderates, he was anyway highly uneasy about the influence of Joseph Chamberlain. He already thought in the early 1880s that Gladstone was 'in a fool's paradise about everything'.[23] But on Ireland there could be no compromise. And when Hartington moved, so did an important section of British political society.

Gladstone also upset the economic conservatives, represented by the financier Goschen. Goschen was anyway moving towards the Conservative position out of dislike for the Radicals, who seemed to threaten property, and for Gladstone's foreign policy, particularly the humiliation of General Gordon's death. But his consuming interest was sound finance. He was destined to be one of Britain's most brilliant and successful Chancellors of the Exchequer. (It was Goschen whose conversion of the National Debt in 1888 from 3 per cent to 2.5 per cent effectively underwrote the expansion of British naval strength in the ensuing years.) Now the announcement of Gladstone's Home Rule proposals was a bombshell which exploded any remaining confidence in the ministry. Goschen would bring economic liberalism and financial understanding towards the Conservative camp – which he can be said finally to have entered in 1893, when he joined the party and the Carlton Club.[24]

The most significant repercussion of Gladstone's Home Rule announcement was the resignation and then the opposition of Joe Chamberlain and his patriotic Radical supporters. Chamberlain was initially sympathetic to the cause of Irish agrarian reform. He had even offered Parnell a scheme for devolved government in Ireland; but in this he had been turned down and outbid by Gladstone, whose own radical Home Rule ideas Chamberlain regarded as a threat to the Empire. For reasons of both principle and pique, then, he flounced out – with ruinous implications for the Liberals.

Thus it came about that Hartington, Goschen and Chamberlain, the Liberal Unionist leaders, would support Salisbury's ministry – first outside the Government and later as part of a formal coalition – and thereby turn the last years of the nineteenth century into the historic high point of Conservative dominance.

The immediate consequences of Gladstone's démarche were less clear. The Conservatives were also split about how to deal with Ireland, though not (barring Carnarvon, who resigned) about any version of Home Rule on offer, which they opposed. Salisbury himself wanted a renewal of Coercion, always his preferred policy, now that the Home Rule vote was irredeemably lost. Above all, he was eager to be out of Government. The expected defeat came on agricultural reform rather than Ireland, but the real cause was clear enough. On Saturday, 6 February 1886 Salisbury surrendered the seals of office to the Queen, who could no longer avoid summoning Gladstone – though, somewhat improperly, she kept closely in touch with Salisbury.

The introduction of Gladstone's Home Rule Bill precipitated the political revolution that the Hawarden Kite had tentatively signalled. Salisbury was in his element and so, still less scrupulously and even more aggressively, was Churchill. Salisbury, in one of his more memorable 'blazing indiscretions', explained to the National Union conference in May that while 'what is called self-government, but is really government by the majority – works admirably when it is confided to people of Teutonic race you will find that it does not work so well when people of other races are called upon to join it'. The Irish, like Hottentots, he elaborated, fell into the latter category. He also suggested that Irish emigration to Manitoba would yield benefits. In a less noticed but more significant passage, he also described the rationale of his future approach to Ireland, and it is worth quoting:

> My alternative policy is that Parliament should enable the Government of England to govern Ireland. Apply that receipt honestly, consistently, and resolutely for twenty years and at the end of that time you will find that Ireland will be fit to accept any gifts in the way of local government or repeal of coercion laws that you may wish to give her. What she wants is government – government that does not flinch, that does not vary; government that she cannot hope to beat down by agitations at Westminster.[25]

Both Salisbury and Churchill addressed rallies in Ulster, where Protestant resistance to Home Rule had begun to figure on Westminster's political radar. But it was Churchill who went furthest in playing the 'Orange Card', explicitly inviting the Loyalists in Belfast in February to be prepared to go beyond the 'lines of what we are accustomed to look upon as constitutional action'. In May he declared in a public letter: 'Ulster will fight; Ulster will be right' – this from the man who, but a few months earlier, had opposed in Cabinet the renewal of Coercion and who had been notoriously close to Parnell. But, for all that, in mainland

Britain, too, the catchy expression 'Home Rule is Rome Rule' had plenty of useful resonance in an increasingly heated and hysterical political climate.

The Liberal Unionists – as they can now be called – were the key. They played their role quietly, for the most part, in the understandable hope that the schism which the Grand Old Man or 'G.O.M' ('God's Only Mistake', quipped the Cecils) had created might somehow be healed when passions abated. Naturally, it was in the Conservative interest that they should not so abate, and they did not. But Salisbury was capable of subtlety as well as aggression. He now adroitly pulled the Liberal Unionist rebels into the Tory camp. Hartington had indicated as early as 6 December 1885 that he would be open to collaboration. But the most important public demonstration of the new alliance came at a rally on 14 April 1886 at Her Majesty's Theatre, where Salisbury appeared on the platform with Hartington and Goschen.

The development of the great Unionist Alliance, which constitutes one of the few significant and enduring seismic shifts in the history of British party politics, was a slow business. Its slowness helped make it secure. Salisbury was a patient man. Patience was part of his political philosophy. 'They will not leave time for trees to grow,' he would complain.[26] Goschen would enter the Cabinet in 1887 (replacing Churchill). But it was not till 1895 that a Unionist Coalition Government was formed; and only in 1911 did Liberal Unionists become eligible to join the Carlton Club, though by then the distinction between them and the Conservatives had already lost its meaning.

For now, Chamberlain still played his own game. He was not at the 1886 London demonstration. He had to keep his credibility with his supporters. But he was to prove, in practice, the most politically reliable of the Unionists, as well as ultimately the most influential. Through Balfour's good offices, Salisbury established with Chamberlain a relationship based on mutual respect and mutual understanding of how far each could push the other. As Balfour reported to his uncle, the Conservatives would 'find in [Chamberlain], so long as he agrees with us, a very different kind of ally from the *lukewarm* and slippery Whig [Hartington] whom it is difficult to differ from and so impossible to act with'.[27] A psychologically crucial moment was when Salisbury invited Chamberlain and his wife to Hatfield.

In the event, Gladstone's Home Rule Bill was defeated in the Commons on 8 June by a combination of 250 Conservatives and 93 Liberal Unionists against 228 Liberals and 85 Parnellites. Gladstone immediately sought and obtained a dissolution. The election was a test of popular feeling on the Irish question, of course, but it was also a test of how well the new Unionist allies could work together. In both respects, it was a Unionist triumph. By now the Conservative Party organization – whose evolution will be discussed shortly – was both efficient and disciplined. That was a special boon at this juncture, because it meant that grass-roots Tory resentment in the constituencies at nationally arranged carve-ups could be contained with relatively little embarrassment. A separate Liberal Unionist Management Committee had been set up on 24 April. The principle was now agreed by Salisbury and given effect by the Tory Chief Whip, Aretas Akers-Douglas, that no Liberal MP who voted against Home Rule would be opposed by a Conservative. A greater difficulty was where a Conservative and a Liberal Unionist might both claim to have the better chance against a Gladstonian. But Salisbury's continued pressure for accommodation successfully avoided serious trouble. As for the West Midlands, here Chamberlain, reigning from Birmingham, was understood to be the master. These understandings would later come under some strain, but for the moment, with Ireland the great issue, they held.

The result was decisive. The Conservatives made net gains of 38 county and 26 borough divisions. They swept the metropolis.

Salisbury wrote to Cranbrook: 'When you and I were first in the House of Commons how little we should have expected that you should even be able to write "London is really the base of Tory principles".'[28] (Again, this wider trend will be examined in the next chapter.) The elections returned 316 Conservatives and 77 Liberal Unionists, who faced 192 Liberals and 85 Home Rulers. This gave the Unionists – on Ireland, at any rate, because on other matters the Liberal Unionist element was fissiparous – a majority of 116. The turnout was substantially lower than in 1885, probably as a result of the agricultural labourers staying at home – because of the harvest, because the novelty of voting had worn off and because they did not care much about Ireland. The middle classes did care, however. They cared, above all, because Irish Home Rule was seen as constituting a challenge to property, having manifestly been forced on Westminster by violent disorder, and because it was a challenge to the Empire, which must be endangered by a hostile quasi-state established across the Irish Sea.

Salisbury was now prepared to offer Hartington the role of Prime Minister, as the price of cementing the new Unionist alliance and transforming it into a formal coalition. But Hartington, strongly advised to this effect by Chamberlain, refused. The clear risk was that the Liberal Unionists would have split had he joined the Government in any capacity. (Naturally, the Conservatives, too, were pleased when Hartington declined.) So Salisbury returned as Prime Minister of a Conservative ministry, supported by the Liberal Unionists. Iddesleigh got the Foreign Office, which Salisbury – ill from overwork – felt currently unable to manage himself. Churchill took over from Beach as Leader of the House of Commons and Chancellor of the Exchequer. He was just thirty-six years old. He had told Wolff that he would not live beyond forty-five.[29] This, in fact, encapsulated the Conservative Party's problem. For it was Randolph Churchill, not the Liberal Unionist leaders, nor even Gladstone, who now constituted Salisbury's biggest headache. The hostility was all one way. Salisbury's exasperation was to the end tempered by regard for Churchill's brilliance and the slender hope that he might mature. Only late in the day did Salisbury give up on him, though having done so he would under no circumstances have him back.[30]

Churchill was soon being difficult, advocating a more radical social programme in public, interfering in foreign policy in (semi-) private. In the latter case, the presence of the despised Iddesleigh at the Foreign Office was too tempting to resist. But Churchill made two miscalculations. He thought that his own position was invulnerable because of his popularity in the party; and he thought that Salisbury's tolerance of his behaviour – for which the Prime Minister was criticized by loyal colleagues (Cranbrook complained of his 'self-renunciation') was limitless. Salisbury was, indeed, temperamentally disinclined to grubby personal, as opposed to gloriously public, confrontations. But he was, at the same time, determined that Britain's national interests, as he perceived them, should be upheld abroad. It was the most important continuing theme of his ministerial career, and he would not abandon it.

So when Churchill, having settled upon a radical tax-cutting budget, chose a confrontation with Smith at the War Department, he could not have picked his ground worse. Britain at this juncture (December 1886) was faced with trouble in the Balkans and in Egypt. Large defence cuts were unthinkable. Public pressure was in the opposite direction. This, though, did not stop Churchill from demanding them, and threatening to resign if he did not get them. The Cabinet would not back down, and so Churchill wrote from Windsor – without telling his host, the Queen – declaring to Salisbury he intended to go. To his surprise, the resignation was accepted. To his still greater surprise, he discovered he attracted little sympathy and none at all where it mattered. He later tried to shift his ground, justifying his departure on wider policy disagreements. But his career was finished. He had no press support. His friends had already abandoned him. He was a physical wreck by 1893 and dead by 1895.

Adroitly, Salisbury now solidified the Unionist Government by first offering, once again, to stand aside for Hartington as Prime Minister, from which Hartington, again, demurred, and then by inducing Goschen to take over as Chancellor of the Exchequer. Churchill would later say: 'I forgot Goschen.' He would have plenty of occasions to remember him thereafter, because Goschen was so successful. Smith took over Churchill's other job, Leader of the House, which required a Tory, albeit a plodding one. Salisbury took back the Foreign Office, to the discomfiture of Iddesleigh, who first heard about it in the press. Salisbury was then himself discomfited when Iddesleigh, having refused other places offered, arrived at Downing Street and died of a heart attack in front of a horrified Prime Minister (who was not, understandably, invited to the funeral).

Salisbury also consolidated his power by unapologetic, and in this case literal, nepotism. Arthur Balfour had joined the Government, outside the Cabinet, as president of the Local Government Board in 1885. He became Secretary for Scotland the following year, first outside and then (from November) inside the Cabinet. In March 1887 he was promoted to Chief Secretary for Ireland, on Beach's withdrawal for health reasons. It was the post which seemed least likely to suit him, but the one that made his name – and eventually made him his uncle's successor, as Prime Minister.

Salisbury, ageing but still in his formidable prime,
as depicted by 'Spy' in 1895.

7

SALISBURY'S PARTY, II – DOMINANCE AND DECLINE

The destruction of Churchill and the parallel rise of Balfour offer a suitable juncture at which to consider the party that Salisbury led, the nature of his leadership and (no less important) the evolving relationship between the two. The posturings associated with the proponents of Tory democracy died away remarkable quickly. But they had reflected, as well as frustrated ambitions, real shifts in the Conservative political landscape. The Third Reform Act (1884) greatly extended the franchise, thus creating one set of uncertainties. The Corrupt and Illegal Practices Act (1883) had created another. By limiting expenditure on campaigns, but imposing no limit on party spending unrelated to particular constituencies, that Act reinforced both the importance of voluntary effort locally and the role of fund-raising and organization centrally. These were the twin conditions under which national parties on recognizable modern lines were induced to develop, and upon which (despite controversy) they still continue to depend. On the face of it, the Liberal Party – with its Radical caucus, its urban base, the increasing role of trade unions, and the bedrock of Dissenting societies and chapels – might have expected to emerge as the principal beneficiary from these changes. But, for several reasons, it did not.

One reason was that the Conservatives were, as they had always been, even in the darkest times, a good deal richer. That significant indicator, the party Central Fund, doubled in size from £50,000 in 1880 to £100,000 by the end of the century.[1] But there was more to it than that. The Conservative Party also managed to recruit and deploy a huge army of volunteers, slightly (but only slightly) detached from its central organization, in the shape of the Primrose League. The League, though ostensibly designed to perpetuate the memory of Disraeli, was conceived as yet another Fourth Party machination. It was established at a small meeting held in the Carlton Club on 17 November 1883 by the Fourth Party leaders, who constituted themselves the 'Grand Council' of the new body. Gorst then went abroad, which prevented the League from emerging, as it might have done, as a challenge to the National Union. Meanwhile, Churchill's ambitions came to focus on the National Union itself. This, then, left the creative work to Wolff, who productively employed his romantic imagination on its symbolism and structure. It was, indeed, to be a League, that is, a mass movement, and not yet another Tory Club. It was modelled loosely on freemasonry (though women were admitted – a radical departure), with terminology of 'knights' and 'dames' adapted whimsically from chivalric history.

During its first six months, it was very small. Only after the establishment of associate membership, in April 1885, did the League mushroom into a national force. Two general elections in quick succession and the heightened political tension over Home Rule ensured rapid recruitment. By 1887 half a million men and women were members, and the numbers kept on growing. Herbert Gladstone snobbishly mocked the League as 'only fit for duchesses and scullery maids'. But Lady Salisbury's response was apposite:

'Vulgar? Of course it is vulgar, but that is why we have done so well.'[2] In time, the League offered a comforting 'cradle to the grave' existence to its thousands of patriotic members. Children gathered to march to the 'Hymn of the Primrose Buds'. Contributors to the League's Benefit Society made provision against life's misfortunes, and indeed death. The League gave support to building cheap houses for working men.[3]

At the same time, the official Conservative Party organization made progress in a less showy but also more enduring manner than it had under the influence of the mercurial Gorst. Here the main credit must go jointly to the Tory Chief Whip, Aretas Akers-Douglas, and the (later legendary) principal agent, Captain ('Skipper') Richard Middleton. Both had an excellent political pedigree as sons of Kent, with its strong Tory tradition nurtured by patrons Hart Dyke, Abergavenny and Cranbrook. Akers-Douglas became Deputy Chief Whip in 1884 and succeeded as Chief Whip the following year. Middleton, a retired but still young naval officer, had earlier served as an agent in Kent.[4] In 1885 he succeeded the politically ambitious and (as it soon turned out) grossly disloyal Bartley as principal agent, to general relief. Middleton was a disciplined professional rather than a would-be politician, which was a break from the recent past. But he was not a solicitor, which was a break from the more distant one. He was certainly lucky in that political conditions favoured a Conservative revival – and he proceeded to exploit every opportunity offered. For example, though the franchise was much wider, the registration arrangements – the gateway to the franchise – were unreformed. This allowed effective Tory agents to gain advantage for the party by keeping registers tight and, consequently, polls low. (From now on high turnouts became in Tory folklore ominous harbingers of a bad result.)

Middleton worked closely with Akers-Douglas and with Salisbury's private secretary, Schomberg ('Pom') McDonnell, in coordinating the party's affairs. The National Union was brought firmly under control, where it would largely stay. It was henceforth destined to be the structure through which the leadership cajoled, encouraged and directed the party, not a means by which the party bossed the leader. Its annual conferences were stage-managed – because that is what they provided, a stage.

Despite his Olympian demeanour, and reflecting his years as an MP, Salisbury took a close interest in the nuts and bolts of party business. After the Lords had risen for the day, the 'Old Man' (as Middleton referred to him) would come round to Central Office (at this point in St Stephen's Chambers, Westminster Bridge) to receive reports and to discuss patronage. Gossiping about the constituencies was, indeed, one of the Prime Minister's favourite recreations, which he greatly preferred to talking public affairs with his senior colleagues. He referred to Middleton as 'the chief wire puller of the party', which was a compliment, and when Middleton, with his large family and limited savings, was thought to be needing encouragement to stay at his post, it was Salisbury who in 1896 presented him with a cheque for £10,000 raised by four thousand grateful subscribers.

Middleton was the champion of the professional Tory party agent, promoting his social status, improving his training (through the newly established Society of Conservative Agents) and ensuring his pension benefits (through the agents' superannuation scheme). Beyond that, he took a hand (again with Salisbury) in cultivating the press, not least the 'new journalism' of the Harmsworth papers. (Salisbury described the *Daily Mail* as a newspaper 'written by office-boys, for office-boys', but he read it and the rest of the press avidly all the same.[5])

Salisbury fully recognized the importance of 'villa Toryism', and not merely in retrospect. He noted to Northcote as early as 1882 that there was 'a great deal of Villa Toryism which requires organisation'.[6] Speaking to the National Union conference in 1900, he observed as a matter of fact that 'the villas outside London are the principal seed-plots of Conservatism'.[7] Why this should be so was a mystery to him, albeit a welcome one. Having a quasi-Marxist view of the inevitable clash of the propertied and the unpropertied classes, Tory *embourgeoisement* did not easily fit into his frame of understanding. That said, given the lack of available data, above all of psephological data, the contributing factors are, even now, difficult to weigh.

Nevertheless, some aspects are clear enough. The Conservative vote was, for example, generally and significantly 'harder' than the Liberal vote. Hence a lack of Liberal enthusiasm, rather than universal Conservative approbation, was a major factor when Conservatives won elections – hence also the already mentioned attraction in Tory eyes of a low national poll. (Conservative Party managers also favoured elections held at harvest time, to ensure the agricultural workers were out in the fields, not contributing to the ballot.)

As we would nowadays expect, but in a manner that had not previously been grasped, money clearly mattered in determining voter geography. Looking specifically at London, there was a consistent pattern of a higher Tory vote in constituencies which had richer voters (measured by rateable value per head of population). Where different metropolitan constituencies were equally rich, those that were less populous were more likely to be Tory, as were those further out, and those with the highest population of non-residents.[8]

London's suburbia was growing at a phenomenal rate, in large part fuelled by the opportunities to commute provided by railways. The population of Surbiton, for example, rose from 20,000 to 130,000 between 1851 and 1901. After the Third Reform Act it was one of the largest single-member constituencies. It proceeded to return Conservative MPs at every election from 1885 to the inter-war period. It was heavily populated by white-collar workers:

natural Tory voters perhaps, but because of the degree of mobility not easy to organize.[9] Precisely why the growth of the suburban commuter belt resulted so directly in a growth of Conservative representation is not obvious. The values of Charles Pooter – in far from upwardly mobile Holloway, the backcloth to George and Weedon Grossmith's classic *Diary of a Nobody* – were clearly a more important part of the answer than his modest income and fragile economic status.[10] Another classic from roughly the same era, *Three Men on the Bummel*, in which Jerome K. Jerome's Uncle Podger runs, along with a crowd of other overweight men, clutching papers and black bags, to catch the morning train from Ealing to the City, provides a further clue.[11] Rich or struggling, or just middling – the white-collar dwellers of suburbia were, above all, dependent upon the City of London for their livelihood; and, by and large, the City has always been a conservative institution. What is clear, in any case, is that in this period the Conservatives became the party of middle-class respectability and general affluence, and that both were in the ascendant.

The effects of social and economic polarization on politics became ever starker. Evidence of this trend preceded the Liberal split over Home Rule – in its beginnings, indeed, as has been noted, it preceded Salisbury – but it became steadily more marked in the 1880s and 1890s. For example, in 1885, that year of Tory defeat, Manchester still went Conservative, Balfour being returned in its eastern division. Lancashire, was, of course, a Tory hotbed, but these urban results astonished the party organizers. The triumph of 1886 extended earlier urban gains and reversed county losses. The defeat of 1892 – when the party lost a net 48 seats in England – did not involve the loss of its English heartland; and though the Liberal Unionists dropped a further 24 English seats, Chamberlain's fiefdom in the West Midlands was similarly secure. These were the decisive conditions for future advance.

On learning of his majority after the 1892 poll, Gladstone

lamented: 'Too small, too small!' And so it proved. Even with the Home Rulers he could muster a Commons majority of only 40. Given the ferocity of opposition in the Commons and Salisbury's refusal to bend in the Lords, his modified Home Rule measure would not pass. But, looking beyond Home Rule, neither were Liberal gains enough to reverse the long-term anti-Liberal tide in the country.

The Conservative landslides of 1895 and 1900 (the 'Khaki Election') appeared, indeed, to seal the Liberal Party's fate. That impression was, of course, misleading. Soon other issues than Ireland were in the forefront of politics. The Unionist vote had slipped badly in by-elections. The Khaki Election was a piece of brilliant opportunism, a matter of riding a wave, not catching a tide. It was, in truth the beginning of the end of a Conservative era.[12]

It was also the beginning of the end of Salisbury. He was a conservative, with a small as well as a big 'C', and probably the most recognizably and intelligently conservative leader the party has ever had. In this he was untypical – not only in that Conservative Party leaders are by no means always philosophical conservatives, but in that, even in his own day, Salisbury's conservatism was untypical in important respects. It was expressed in a dark, sometimes mischievous, sometimes emollient, sometimes shocking, but always distinctive tone. Salisbury's thinking was given early, public – though unacknowledged – expression in the 608 unsigned articles he wrote between 1856 and 1868, most famously in the *Quarterly Review* but most lucratively in the *Saturday Review*, which was owned by his brother-in-law. He was forced to earn his living by journalism, having been effectively cut off by his father, the second Marquess, for what was deemed an unsuitable marriage. Any attempt to judge his later views from these polemical pieces is of limited use, since, while his convictions remained in essence much the same, their practical implementation was modified greatly by his pragmatism and his ambition once he returned to office in 1874, and still more so as Prime Minister after 1885.[13]

Salisbury's last article in the *Quarterly Review*, with the eminently Salisburian title of 'Disintegration', was published in October 1883. It focused on Ireland, but claimed to perceive a wider threat of collapse, both foreign and domestic. The tone is still recognizably apocalyptic: 'Half a century ago, the first feeling of all Englishmen was for England. Now, the sympathies of a powerful party are instinctively given to whatever is against England.'[14] Salisbury's authorship, unsurprisingly, was leaked and, furious, he never wrote for that journal again.

One constant element in Salisbury's thought was his pessimism – which, as with many Tory pessimists, did not prevent his enjoying life, or impinge on his sense of humour. The pessimism was thus philosophical rather than merely temperamental. It began with a view of Man in which Original Sin was prominent, and it extended directly into politics. Its main conclusions were unsettling, at least for anyone with political ambitions. Salisbury concluded that democracy was ultimately incompatible with progress or liberty, both of which he valued highly, and that the fight for property and the struggle to Christianize society, which mattered more to him than anything else, were both destined to be lost.

He continued essentially to believe what he had written when supporting the losing side in the American Civil War: 'Every community has natural leaders, to whom if they are not misled by the insane passion for equality, they will instinctively defer. Always wealth, in some countries birth, in all intellectual power and culture, mark out the men to whom, in a healthy state of feeling, a community looks to undertake its government.'[15] This authentically Whiggish view had been abandoned by the Whigs, now barely distinguishable from Liberals, which was one reason why he so despised them. But it had also been overtaken by events, namely the Second and Third Reform Acts. Mass democracy was, undeniably, a fact. Salisbury prided himself on his scientific mind. (He was fascinated by chemistry, physics and biology, and dabbled know-ledgeably in all three.[16]) Facts mattered greatly to him. Despite democratic pressures, some important areas of state policy could be more or less isolated from the mob. That was what he successfully did with foreign policy. But, more generally, the great political question in late Victorian England was how to use democracy and, in so far as possible, tame it and ameliorate its effects. He wearily but determinedly accepted the challenge.

'In this task Salisbury, unlike Disraeli, was rigorously un-sentimental and even more calculating. It did not matter to him if the means adopted to foil demagogic measures – whether aimed at the constitution, or at property, or at the Church – were popular, or even in line with tradition. What mattered was whether they were likely to be effective. He was, in public as in private life, what might be described as a conservative innovator. Thus he supported a pro-posal for the introduction of life peers, in order to increase the standing of the Upper House. Naturally, it failed. Even more con-troversially, he advocated giving the vote to women, who he correctly thought (at least in those times) would act as a socially conservative counterweight to the male members of the working classes, now newly enfranchised.[17] In this, too, he was before his time.

The best-known example of Salisbury's innovative approach to the problems raised by mass democracy is, however, his doctrine of the 'mandate', by which he justified the Lords rejecting measures passed by the Commons that had not previously been laid before the electorate. In such circumstances, the peers were acting, he argued, in the high capacity of true representative of the people. He was even attracted by the principle of the referendum, though when pressed by Dicey he prudently and perhaps self-interestedly preferred that function of referring back to be played by the Upper House forcing an election. In practice, he was more prudent than the 'Salisbury doctrine' implied. Under his leadership the Lords never wielded the veto, unless he espied a future Unionist victory. Nor, of course, was he – even in theory – greatly attached to democratic mandates of any sort, since he considered the country in the throes of a 'bloodless civil war' in which, 'to loot somebody or something is the common object, under a thick varnish of pious phrases'. In any case, as he mockingly observed after the 1895 election: 'When the great oracle speaks, we are never quite certain what the great oracle said.'[18]

Balancing his cynicism, Salisbury had a strong sense of partisanship, which extended to appreciation of what would nowadays be called the Conservative 'core vote'. He always worried about measures he thought would disorientate supporters: 'You may say that they can't vote against you, but they won't trouble to vote for you, and they won't work for you, and you'll find it out at the polls.'[19] Salisbury was naturally averse to splitting the difference, and sought, instead, to polarize issues, at least where polarization created a Conservative majority. But whenever it would serve better he sought alliances and stuck to them – as with the Liberal Unionists.

His conservatism in practice balanced retreat with doggedness. He made concessions to demands for social reform, with very little grumbling – indeed, in some areas, notably slum clearance, with some originality and imagination. At home, he upheld the Church of England, in so far as he could (it was the only institution in which he really believed: he grew to respect the Queen, but no one with any great reverence for monarchy could have written: 'If we are doomed for ever to have German royalties, it is better to have such as have learned the use of the tub by residence in this country'[20]). Abroad, he devoted his energy to upholding the interests of Britain (or 'England', as he pointedly insisted on saying), administering its growing Empire and – partly because it was in British interests and partly because he foresightedly dreaded a European war – to maintaining peace.

Salisbury was, in many respects, fortunate. His elder brother was born sickly and died young, and so he succeeded to the marquessate, a great house (Hatfield) and a very large income (fortunately invested in urban, not just agricultural property). He was fortunate, too, in his happy marriage to Georgina Alderson (who, though daughter of a baron of the Court of Exchequer, was considered not nearly grand enough for even the second adult son of the second Marquess). He was politically lucky that Churchill was so keen to destroy Northcote, Salisbury's rival, and that Churchill then destroyed himself. He was more or less made a present of Middle England and of a large section of the parliamentary Liberal Party by Gladstone's misjudgement on Home Rule.

By equal good luck, he looked the part he was called upon to play. He was tall, in later years broad, and had a deceptive air of benignity. His temperament was adequate both for a party and for a coalition leader. He got on well with colleagues – perhaps too well, because he was even weaker in controlling his Cabinet than Disraeli, whom he had criticized for that defect.[21] He won and kept their confidence, even though he took remarkably little interest in their persons – he failed, for example, even to recognize his long-term colleague W. H. Smith at a breakfast meeting and had to ask his name.[22]

Salisbury was, despite a personal shyness and dislike of cant, no less adept at politics outdoors. He deplored in principle the requirement for public speaking but in practice accepted and even relished it: he warned his son, Cranborne, in 1881, that 'power is more and more leaving Parliament and going to the platform'.[23] He acted on that admonition. Salisbury practised public oratory with great aplomb, speaking without notes, in clear, powerful, language, to audiences which, even if he did not respect them, respected him, partly perhaps because he saw no need to flatter them.

If there was a single key, though, to Salisbury's personal outlook it was his religion. This also constituted the largest temperamental difference between him and the rising generation of Conservatives, who were becoming more secular, more doctrinally liberal and more materialistic – the backbenchers refused, for example, to support his attempt to bolster Church voluntary schools in his 1896 Education Bill.[24] Anti-socialism, not anti-liberalism, was the newer Tory outlook.

Salisbury's Christian faith was characteristically English, in that it involved a sharp division between the interior and exterior. Thus, while he was influenced by Tractarianism, he was hostile to Rome and critical of its tendency to (as he put it) 'pigeon hole the mysteries of the faith'.[25] Indeed, his emphasis on 'mystery', by which he meant what was inexplicable to reason, was not only a tendency of mind but also a useful fallback. It meant that, unlike many Anglo-Catholics, he was unbothered by ecclesiological questions relating to the disputed Catholicity of the Church of England. 'If I myself am satisfied that I believe what is true, what can it matter to me what others worshipping beside me believe!', he would protest.[26] This, in turn, meant that he felt in good conscience able to pursue in ecclesiastical patronage a policy aimed at balancing the opposing factions, rather than at favouring the group whose theology he personally favoured. Arguably, this policy helped preserve Anglican unity at a critical time. It certainly allowed him to pursue, with the support of all Anglican factions, a policy of reinforcing the Church's claim to a major role in mass education – also at a critical time.[27]

Foreign policy, on which most of his energy in government was expended, also felt the impact of Salisbury's religious convictions. But not in the way of Gladstone's. For Salisbury, foreign policy was not a way of doing good; it was a way of keeping afloat. God's will was inscrutable, which truth, along with His omnipotence, offered an ultimate answer to the fiddling, hesitant, self-righteous scrupulosity which he regarded as the root of Liberal foreign policy failure. A well-known exchange, recorded by Lady Gwendolen, is here to the point. Salisbury, then Foreign Secretary, and faced with some international crisis, had been entertaining guests. Before leaving Hatfield, they had condoled with him about his burden of responsibility:

> He was about to start upon a walk and was standing at the moment at the open door, looking out upon the threatening clouds of an autumn afternoon. 'I don't understand', he repeated, 'what people mean when they talk of the burden of responsibility. I should understand if they spoke of the burden of decision – I feel it now, trying to make up my mind whether or no to take a greatcoat with me. I feel it in exactly the same way, but no more, when I am writing a despatch upon which peace or war may depend. Its degree depends upon the materials for decision that are available and not in the least upon the magnitude of the results which may follow'. Then, after a moment's pause and in a lower tone, he added, 'With the results I have nothing to do.'[28]

For most of its term, Salisbury's ministry of 1886–1892 was a strong and effective one. And if the Prime Minister's own focus was more on foreign than domestic affairs, it was he who asserted his priorities in Ireland and education, as well as skilfully navigating, with Balfour's assistance, a way through the reefs that always potentially threatened relations with the Liberal Unionists. Dispatching Balfour to Ireland proved a stroke of genius. Whether the Balfour–Salisbury policy of 'resolute government' was in the long-term interests of either Ireland or Britain is certainly questionable. Balfour himself promised the Commons: 'I shall be as relentless as Cromwell in enforcing obedience to the law, but at the same time, I shall be as radical as any reformer in redressing grievances, and especially in removing every cause of complaint in regard to land.'[29] Partly thanks to the Liberal Unionists, a Land Bill was indeed introduced, and a start made to providing encouragement for tenant land purchase. This would reach its culmination in the Wyndham Land Act of 1903. But in practice it was repression, rather than reform, which marked Balfour's approach. Coercion was, for the first time, skilfully and consistently applied, and it proved effective. Under Balfour's Crimes Bill of 1887 the Irish National League was banned and, with help from the Vatican, the Land War campaign in just a few years defeated. Criminal acts were punished and deterred, and more than a few intimidated tenants also breathed a sigh of relief. In all this, Balfour was robustly supported by the young Dublin prosecutor Edward Carson. (Balfour later showed his gratitude by finding Carson the seat for Trinity College, Dublin, which Carson would hold for twenty-six years as he rose to national prominence.)

Salisbury had no sympathy with losers of any kind; and in his eyes the Irish as a whole fell into that category. On one occasion he even joked, on admiring a particularly harrowing depiction by a society painter, that he wished he could take part in an Irish eviction himself. He was also keen to see Parnell discredited on the basis of what turned out to be forged documents. When a special commission discovered in 1890 that Parnell was wrongly accused of complicity in the Phoenix Park murders, this was a bad moment – though Parnell's damaging links with militancy were also exposed. Fortunately, Parnell's disgrace in the O'Shea divorce case later that year split the Nationalists and made Salisbury's and Balfour's task a great deal easier.[30] One drawback of this success would become apparent only much later. When Gerald Balfour – Arthur's brother – was appointed Chief Secretary for Ireland in 1895 and, much against Salisbury's instincts, pursued greater engagement with the Irish majority community, his reforms were judged too little, too late – at least by the Irish: many Conservatives considered them too much, too soon. By that point attitudes had, in fact, irrevocably hardened. The days for constructive Unionism had gone – to which

Salisbury might have replied that they had never existed anyway. This was, admittedly, not quite what his formal policy suggested. But when he wrote in his *Quarterly Review* article on 'Disintegration' that 'possession of Ireland is our peculiar punishment, our unique affliction, among the family of nations', it was from the heart, and it was perhaps inherent in that analysis that to this particular malady there could be no lasting cure.[31]

In domestic policy the pressure for measures of social reform was unceasing. It reflected in part the need to keep Chamberlain happy, but to a larger extent the demands of public opinion and the press. In October 1891, in a speech at Carmarthen, Chamberlain listed the Conservative Government's measures, concluding: 'Lord Salisbury's Government has done far more for the solid improvement of the masses of the population than any Government has done before in the present century in a similar period.'[32] This assertion was self-justificatory, of course, because, in answer to Gladstone's and the Liberals' radical Newcastle Programme, it provided an argument for Chamberlain and the Radical Unionists keeping the Tories in power. It was also a message that the Conservatives, in their post-Disraelian phase, liked to parrot in their own propaganda. For example, the 1900 Conservative *Campaign Guide* soberly declared: 'It is a matter of easy demonstration that the real practical legislation which has affected for good the daily lives of our working population, and which has given them the means of helping themselves, is mainly the work of Conservative Government, and of the Conservative Party in Parliament.'[33]

Two of the measures listed by Chamberlain concerned working-class housing, and these can be seen as in some degree pursuing Salisbury's interest in a subject he had first addressed in the pages of the *National Review* in his 1883 article on 'Labourers' and Artisans' Dwellings' – written partly to outflank Churchill, but containing some serious proposals for all that. A further measure to institute county councils (in the Local Government Act of 1888) was in part a response to Liberal Unionist pressure and in part designed to pre-empt a worse solution by a Liberal Government. But Salisbury had regrets about it, particularly when the Liberals swept the board in the new London County Council – though in the counties Tory JPs moved effortlessly into their role of elected councillors.

There were also Conservative complaints about the Government's 1891 Education Act. Understandably, perhaps, some critics deemed free education socialistic. But on this Salisbury had no regrets. On one view, the introduction of free universal elementary education was simply inevitable, a matter of moving with the times, keeping out the Liberals, and also – looking further afield – keeping up with the Germans. What Salisbury himself wanted to do was ensure that, when it came, the system propped up Church voluntary schools, and did not exclusively favour their board school competitors. It was also, of course, a shameless pre-electoral bribe. But in this matter Salisbury had less shame than usual. He even argued in Cabinet for paying labourers to send their children to school as the best means to enthuse them. This early plan for an education voucher, though, was resisted by his colleagues.[34]

Foreign affairs constituted in some respects even more of a paradox. Salisbury had a great distaste for jingoism. He scathingly observed after some concession on the route to a larger diplomatic success: 'The Jingoes will lie egregiously, as is their habit.'[35] But he also presided over the Empire's greatest expansion. The list of territories acquired at this time is long: Bechuanaland (1885), Burma and Nigeria (1886), Somaliland and Zululand (1887), Kenya and Sarawak (1888), Rhodesia (1889) and Zanzibar (1890).[36] Salisbury avenged the defeat and death of Gordon at Khartoum (1885) by Kitchener's victory at Omdurman (1898); in the same year he dramatically asserted British power at the expense of

France in the Fashoda Crisis, securing control over the Upper Nile; he eventually and unconditionally prevailed over the Boers, with the memory of the defeat of Majuba Hill (1881) purged by the imposed Treaty of Vereeniging (1902). He also presided over the largest ever peacetime expansion of British naval power, under the terms of the Naval Defence Act of 1889.

The key to Salisbury's premiership, at least in his view, was his ability to prevent the Treasury starving his foreign policy – mainly by starving the War Department – of the required resources. Combining the posts of Prime Minister and Foreign Secretary for the great majority of his time in office, he was able to pursue a more independent line than any other British Foreign Secretary before or since. (Hence the foolishness, incidentally, of Churchill's picking a quarrel on the defence estimates.) Salisbury was not himself either particularly knowledgeable about or interested in military matters – a weakness acknowledged by his daughter.[37] He also distrusted military men even more than he distrusted other experts, on one occasion advising Sir Evelyn Baring, whom he rightly trusted to run Egypt, to beware military advisers: 'If they were allowed full scope they would insist on the importance of garrisoning the moon in order to protect us from Mars.'[38] But Salisbury was not merely bending to public pressure fuelled by a 'naval scare' when he – or, more precisely, Lord George Hamilton at the Admiralty – devised the formula for the Naval Defence Act. It was a mature policy. It formally established the unofficial benchmark of the 'Two Power Standard', which required that the Royal Navy be as strong as the combined forces of the next two largest navies in the world. The programme for seventy new warships was largely financed as Salisbury wished, by borrowing (more cheaply, because of Goschen's efforts) against a limited, seven-year rise in hypothecated taxation, while – an extra bonus for Salisbury – binding Parliament and, in practice, his likely Liberal successors, to honour the engagement.[39]

All of this might suggest that Salisbury was a believer in a heavily armed Empire with a vocation for global expansion. But, whatever intellectuals, subordinates or colleagues believed, that was not at all his view, as will shortly be demonstrated. He was even quickly disappointed by the naval programme. In 1892 the Admiralty told him that without the neutrality of the French fleet, it would be too dangerous to force the Dardanelles. Salisbury complained: 'What our huge fleet is doing or expected to do in the Mediterranean is one of the mysteries of official strategy.'[40] In 1895 the rest of the Cabinet lined up to prevent his trying to send in the fleet to frighten the Sultan into preventing Turkish atrocities against the Armenians.

What this acknowledged impotence meant, as he saw, was that his old prejudice against shoring up the Ottoman Empire had been finally proved correct. Turkey was now more likely to collaborate with Russia, supported by France, than with Britain, and there was nothing Britain could do to improve the Porte's behaviour. Loss of influence over Constantinople meant that Egypt acquired still more importance, as Salisbury had also foreseen, while the Cyprus base, obtained earlier through Salisbury's own efforts, became even more vital. In these circumstances, he felt he could come clean about his long-held view of the 'Eastern Question'. In one of his 'blazing indiscretions', in January 1897, he declared to the House of Lords that in refusing Russian proposals of 1853 to carve up Turkey and in choosing to fight instead for the Ottoman Empire's survival in the Crimean War, Britain had, in truth, backed 'the wrong horse'.[41]

As this episode demonstrates, the portrayal of Salisbury's foreign policy in Europe as one of 'splendid isolation' is, in important respects, inaccurate. The phrase itself did not originate with him – it did not even originate in Britain. When Salisbury later used it, he did so with irony and in a purely geographical sense – unlike Chamberlain, who alluded to the concept with imperialistic defiance.[42] To the contrary, Salisbury was quite willing to admit, as he did in 1888, that 'we are part of the community of Europe and we must do our duty as such'.[43] In the face of a possibly catastrophic war between the great powers, he even spoke (in 1897) of the need for an 'inchoate federation of Europe'.[44]

The reality of British concerns for what happened in mainland Europe, however, could not easily be expressed in public. Salisbury believed in giving as little away about foreign policy as possible. He was secretive with the public, with his colleagues, and even with his Foreign Office officials. He never delegated or divulged important matters, if he could help it.[45] On occasion, he might warn: 'Never jog a man's elbow when he is holding the reins'.[46] But only a few, like Baring in Egypt, were allowed to hold the reins. Still more important to the obscurity of British policy than Salisbury's work patterns was the reality that Britain could, anyway, afford no clarity about its intentions in Europe.

In the last two decades of the nineteenth century, the country was simply unable to contribute sufficiently to the European balance of power to secure corresponding benefits from treaty commitments. So it perforce avoided them. The Royal Navy could defend most of the Empire and the trade routes upon which Britain's financial and economic power depended. But Britain's army was not a credible force for European intervention. That had been shown when, in 1864, Palmerston and Russell had threatened to intervene in support of Denmark against Prussia, and their bluff had been called. (Bismarck responded that if they did intervene, he would send the Berlin police to arrest the expedition.) Salisbury never forgot the lessons involved – he had written about them at the time.[47] The British army's deficiencies were also, of course, demonstrated by the humiliating failures of the Boer War.

One charge that can be levelled against Salisbury is that he failed to pursue with any vigour the numerous proposals for army reform. But, in any case, he would have been foolish indeed had he not recognized the implications of the crippling British military imbalance

– a behemoth on the seas, a dwarf on land – for the objects of British diplomacy. It appealed to him to place much of the blame for Britain's inability to enter into treaty commitments on the waywardness of the democratic electorate. He liked to say that there was 'no means whatever of knowing what may be the humour of our people' at the time when any such treaty had to be honoured.[48] But the truth is that, in the circumstances in which he found himself, he had chosen a different and, for others, more perplexing route than either isolation on the one hand or commitment on the other – he had settled, instead, on a policy of conditional and flexible European engagement.

What this meant above all, in practice, was engagement with Germany, the dominant European power. Germany – despite occasional upsets, and at least while Bismarck ensured that German policy remained rational – took the place previously (and again later) filled by France as Britain's ally of default. Salisbury at this point regarded France and Russia – the main 'dissatisfied powers' – as the country's potential enemies. Germany, as satisfied as it could be, shared satisfied Britain's interest in stability. But to Bismarck's frustration, and despite the clumsy pressure exerted by Randolph Churchill and later the personal diplomacy practised by Joseph Chamberlain, the Anglo-German understanding would never become a formal alliance. It took, instead, the form of undertakings to Germany's closest allies, in the form of the secret 'Mediterranean Agreements' reached by Britain with Austria and Italy in 1887 and aimed at preserving the status quo in the Near East.

Salisbury would not commit the country to the German–Austrian–Italian Triple Alliance. He thought that if Bismarck had to choose between Britain, with its maritime power, and Russia, with its army to Germany's east, the German Chancellor would always choose Russia. Bismarck sought to reassure him by revealing the contents of Germany's secret guarantee of 1879 to Austria (for which it would, indeed, go to war against Russia in 1914).[49] But the gesture was to no avail. Salisbury was impressed but he would not be drawn further. At one point, Salisbury flew his own kite – in the form of a letter to the *Standard* in February 1887, signed 'Diplomaticus' (in fact written by Alfred Austin, Salisbury's favourite press crony). Diplomaticus urged the Government to withdraw Britain from its 1839 guarantee to Belgium. Germany, after all, was now Britain's ally. And Germany might need to take pre-emptive action against a revanchist France, by coming through Belgium. Had the kite-flying had some practical consequence, it is just possible that Britain might not have entered so precipitately – or perhaps at all – into the First World War.[50]

The relationship between Britain's policy in Europe and its imperial policy – notably during the 'Scramble for Africa' among the European powers – was carefully and expertly weighed by Salisbury, with concessions or assertions in one field being balanced by countervailing assertions or concessions in another. Salisbury's imperial policy generally lagged behind the patriotic ambitions of his fellow countrymen – until something went wrong, of course, when public opinion panicked. He had no ambition to civilize or dominate the world. The spread of formal, in place of informal, control over large swathes of Africa was for Salisbury a pragmatic response to the requirements of the moment. This might have made him a reluctant imperialist. But in practice it did not. His conviction that the maintenance of British prestige and the punishment of Britain's enemies were essentials of diplomacy ensured that. He was, therefore, more often than not a proponent of a forward policy, even though he might regret the events that made it necessary.

Salisbury's bleak view of international relations reflected his bleak view of human nature. There was a remorseless struggle for survival among the nations. He was a political Darwinian. He told the Primrose League in 1898 that the world was divided between the 'living and the dying', and that the living – growing in 'power . . . wealth . . . perfection of organisation', and benefiting from railways and 'weapons ever growing in their efficacy of destruction' – would 'encroach on the territory of the dying'. The speech caused uproar, especially from those powers like the southern Europeans, and Turkey, which reckoned they were depicted in the moribund category. The advancing powers were evidently Germany – which Salisbury adroitly managed – and the United States – to which he realistically made concessions.[51] But the larger question was, of course: in which category, ultimately, lay Britain?

It was a question on many minds, but one which few – of any party, let alone among the Conservatives – had, as yet, any interest in answering. Some far-sighted imperialists were already quite aware of the dangers. The impulse towards federation with the predominantly white-settled colonies was not just jingoism. In his influential lectures delivered in Cambridge in 1883, and published under the title of *The Expansion of England*, the historian J. R. Seeley urged the creation of what (borrowing Sir Charles Dilke's expression) he called a 'Greater Britain'. The country should cast off its 'indifference', recognize the direction and opportunities of history, and acknowledge that 'England has left Europe altogether behind it and become a world state'. Not the least persuasive reason for doing so was that, 'if the United States and Russia hold together for another half century, they will at the end of that time completely dwarf such old European states as France and Germany, and . . . they will do the same to Britain' unless 'Greater Britain' were to become 'not only a reality but a robust reality'.[52] Seeley's influence was deep and broad, though not universal. Joseph Chamberlain and Balfour carried his book around with them. Tennyson even gave a copy to Gladstone, who did not appreciate it.

The Second Boer War (1899–1902) was not Salisbury's war of choice, but, once he had embarked upon it, no one was more ruthlessly determined on victory. Despite Milner's having worked hard to provoke it when he did (see below), it was anyway more or less inevitable. The discovery of massive gold deposits in 1886 in the Witwatersrand, some 30 miles outside Pretoria, attracted British economic migrants and with them British financial and political interest. It also sharpened British dissatisfaction with the terms that had ended the First Boer War (1880–1), which had granted effective independence to the Transvaal.

Salisbury found it convenient to overlook Chamberlain's covert involvement in the humiliating Jameson Raid (1895–6) and to allow those directly involved to shoulder the blame for the failure. But popular sentiment wanted revenge, particular once the Kaiser sent a provocative telegram of congratulation to President Kruger. In any case, Salisbury had no time for the Boers. He despised their treatment of the blacks and, above all, he shared the national resentment at their exclusion of the British immigrant 'Uitlanders', now a majority in the new mining city of Johannesburg, from any meaningful political representation.

The Jameson Raid had an even greater impact on the Boers. It drew together the Transvaal and Orange Free State in defence of their independence and prompted them to acquire modern weaponry. Meanwhile, Sir Alfred Milner, Cape Governor and South African High Commissioner, on the spot and, under his influence, Chamberlain as Colonial Secretary in London worried that events were moving in the Boers' direction, and wanted to precipitate the inevitable confrontation. British terms accordingly hardened, even as the Boers seemed willing to compromise. In the end, to Britain's surprise, the Boers attacked first, and so the war began. The British should have won easily. But their generalship was incompetent, their training inadequate and their methods unsuitable. The Boers conceivably might have won too, if their strategy had been as good as their tactics. But they expended energy on besieging centres which they failed to take, rather than on the war of movement in which they excelled. In the end, numbers told.

By the beginning of December 1900, General Roberts could blithely assure an audience that the war was 'practically over'. It was not – though it suited the politicians as well as the military men to believe it was. Thirty thousand Boer soldiers were still at large, preparing a new kind of war, one not of set-piece battles but of raids and counter-insurgency operations that was equally bloody and even more bitter.[53]

By the time the final surrender terms were signed in Pretoria in May 1902, the balance sheet of war had been transformed. Britain had subdued and absorbed the two Boer republics. But the conflict had proved the most prodigal in lives lost of any British war since 1815, with 22,000 imperial and colonial troops dead (7,000 Boers died in battle, and anything between 18,000 and 28,000 civilians in badly run British concentration camps). The war cost more than £200 million, several times what had been expected.[54] It piled up debt, and it would push up tax. It thus represented a dramatic reversal of Gladstone's parsimony and was one of the more difficult features of Salisbury's legacy to his successor.

The importance of the Boer War in terms of British politics was greater than anyone foresaw. At the time it was the high point of imperial enthusiasm; but in the aftermath it stained the British imperial ethic. By the end of the nineteenth century, the Unionists (both Conservative and ex-Liberal) epitomized the politics of Empire, so their fortunes also rose sharply, and then equally sharply sank. The *Campaign Guide* of 1892 had boasted, reversing an earlier boast of Gladstone's: 'We have heard little of Foreign Affairs, and less of warfare' under the Conservative Government, and, in explanation, pointed to Salisbury's 'bloodless triumphs' in Africa.[55] Imperial expansion on the cheap was a vote-winner. The problem arose when it required the sacrifice of blood and treasure – as it now had in South Africa.

Popular imperialism was powerful, under ordinary circumstances more powerful than anti-imperialism. From the nursery to adulthood, in the press and on public occasions, the values and virtues that made the British race and their Empire were instilled. In intellectual circles, and on the political and religious left, the rationale for colonialism was challenged. But still nothing was more likely to find an answering echo in all classes – and particularly the Conservative-voting middle and working-classes – than the summons to give a good thrashing to the foreigner who insulted Britain's honour or threatened its interests. (As Lord Harmsworth observed, his *Daily Mail* readers liked 'a good hate'.)

The ceremonial high point of Empire was, of course, the Queen's Diamond Jubilee of 1897. It was, though, the manifestations of popular joy at the relief of Mafeking in May 1900, after 217 days of siege by the Boers, which showed how closely the nation followed the fortunes of its soldiers – and which, incidentally, contributed a new verb to the English language, to 'maffick'.[56]

With the 'Khaki Election' won, though, the mafficking mood went quickly sour. Salisbury's ministry declined into discredit, and his political legacy to the Conservative Party looked poisoned. In this process, however, one must distinguish between passing problems and deeper adverse changes.

To take the second category first, Salisbury perfectly understood the paradox. While the Empire was at its greatest, it was also at its most vulnerable. It was a classic problem of what would now be described as 'imperial overstretch'. In 1900 Britain possessed the most extensive empire the world had ever known: some 12 million square miles of it, encompassing a quarter of the globe's population. Unlike Spain and Portugal in an earlier age, it had used its wealth to create a formidable system of global defence and communications – the world's largest navy (the Two Power Standard was maintained, though sometimes only by a whisker); a network of naval bases from which its fleets could resupply; and a web of cable stations, allowing London to learn almost instantly about sudden threats. The British merchant navy far surpassed any other. These

221

assets were needed, not only because of the far-flung character of Britain's imperial possessions but also because of the dependence of British industry and, above all, British finance, based on the City of London, on unfettered movement of trade and capital.

Moreover, Britain's position was, indeed, under threat – as Seeley prophesied. There was the underlying problem of relative economic decline. For reasons which, despite all the ink expended on them, can more easily be listed than evaluated – and even the list is debatable – British growth rates were sluggish, while those of the country's main competitors, America and Germany, were not. Britain held its own more easily in the older industries, coal, textiles and ironware, than in the newer sectors of steel, chemicals, machine tools and electrical goods. Unease on this score was still limited, though the political class was aware of it. (The Conservative response is a theme of the next chapter.) But of greater immediate impact was relative military decline.

Again, one should neither exaggerate nor anticipate. Britain was the world colossus, and the giant continued to grow; but the advantage it once enjoyed was shrinking. The change had already occurred in Europe, where a united and self-confident Germany was the dominant power, and Britain was insignificant. (So was France, but it was also unpredictable, often unstable, resentful, and too close to Britain for military comfort – not that any of this prevented the Cecils from choosing to spend their holidays there.)[57]

Outside Europe the changes were more alarming. The need for a huge commitment of imperial troops in South Africa at the height of the Boer War exposed India as all but indefensible in the event of Russian attack. The British had earlier done well by bullying a weak China and grabbing the lion's share of its trade. But Chinese collapse, in the face of threats from Germany and Russia in the late 1890s, left Britain in a fragile position. Only a decisive break with Salisbury's preferred policy of non-committal, in the form of the 1902 treaty with Japan, could ultimately secure British interests where the Royal Navy's writ no longer reliably ran. Similarly, the challenge posed by a newly assertive, populous, economically productive United States was full of danger for Britain. Canada, the Caribbean and Latin America all saw clashes of interest between the two nations. Even the 'Scramble for Africa' – although Salisbury managed it with aplomb – was forced on Britain by the ambitions of other powers, not Britain's own.[58] The fall-out from the Boer War, casting doubt on the validity and solidity of Britain's imperial achievement, sharpened awareness of such worrying realities.

As in Disraeli's last years, it was the combination of disappointed jingoism with an onset of high-mindedness that did the political damage. The revelation both of the poor physical state of the British soldiers sent to fight in South Africa and of conditions in the concentration camps inflicted damage on the Government from both political directions. Meanwhile, the most important lesson offered by the war – revelation of the inadequacy of commanders and equipment – was, if not lost, at least submerged.

Was there a further reason for the wave of unpopularity that suddenly struck the Unionists? Arguably, the most persistent factor in the politics of the last two decades of the century was the advance of collectivism, that is, belief in a wider role for the state in the search for solutions to social problems. The Conservatives could override this trend – the argument runs – when some great 'national question' (like Ireland, or the Empire) loomed sufficiently large. They were also helped by self-inflicted damage from the Liberals. But the Tories could not, or at least would not, go far enough in assuaging the desire for more government intervention; and so the crash under Salisbury's successor was, on this calculus, inevitable.[59] Subsequent events suggest that the desire, for example, for old-age pensions was strong. Chamberlain was never able to deliver them under a Unionist Government; and once the Boer War had to be paid for they could not be afforded anyway. Even his important Workmen's Compensation Act of 1897, which did get through, thanks to Salisbury's support, was not the comprehensive measure he initially envisaged.[60] So if collectivism was the national demand, the Unionists would always be outbid.

But the most evident political demand for intervention the Tories faced was for action to protect British goods and products, and so incomes and jobs, from foreign competition. Here they could more easily respond – at a price. The pressure came both from manufacturers – above all, at this juncture, the Lancashire cotton interests – and from agriculture.

One complicated option offered by the cognoscenti was 'bimetallism'. This became the subject of a well-supported movement. The goal was to accord silver a fixed value alongside gold, creating a bimetallic standard. Exclusive adherence to gold, the supply of which was limited, was blamed for what would now be called a monetary squeeze. Bimetallism was, in essence, a way to inflate and devalue, and so secure markets. Salisbury was not sympathetic – though Balfour was – and, decisively, nor were the sound money men (Goschen and Beach) who consistently occupied the Treasury under the Unionists.[61]

More tempting, and more easily comprehensible, was the case for the raising of tariffs against foreign imports. Salisbury was not, himself, a doctrinaire free trader; but he ruled out any return to the Corn Laws, and he was (usually) aware of the electoral dangers of adopting policies that would lead, as the slogan had it, to the 'dear loaf'. He was, though, in favour of retaliation against tariffs applied against Britain. Of course, as other 'fair traders' have found, it is a moot point where retaliation stops and protection starts.

The erection by both Germany and the United States of protective tariffs provoked great hostility in Britain. In particular, the McKinley tariff – introduced by the US in 1890 – gave an impetus to demands for counter-measures. From 1887 onwards the National Union conferences repeatedly passed resolutions calling for protection. Salisbury usually managed to tread the line dexterously enough. But in a speech to the conference in Hastings, on the eve of the 1892 election, he went beyond his usual compromise, declaring: 'You must be prepared, if need be, to inflict upon the nations which injure you the penalty which is in your hands, that of refusing them access to your markets.'

The conference roared its approval. But when the disappointing election results came in, Chamberlain – of all people – observed, probably rightly, that Salisbury's utterance had cost 'a dozen seats in the counties'.[62] This, however, was a lesson which neither the Conservatives nor indeed Chamberlain seemed capable of absorbing. The reasons for such purblindness will be discussed later, in the context of tariff reform. Suffice it to say that though Salisbury moderated the protectionist momentum, he did nothing to counter it. It was an error – though an understandable one, given his failing powers and declining health.

Salisbury's performance in the Boer War revealed his deficiencies. He had doubts about the military preparedness for the campaign, and he thought that the Cabinet underrated the Boers; but he said nothing, and did nothing, effective in respect of either. Then, when things went wrong, he adopted what other ministers considered a culpably semi-detached attitude, complaining about shortcomings publicly, as if he were in Opposition.[63] He was, by common consent, insufficiently assertive as well as insufficiently collegiate: a bad combination, but one for which shrewdness, intelligence and courage usually provided compensation. Now the compensation looked increasingly inadequate. Personal loss then drained him. The death of his beloved wife, on 20 November 1899, was a blow from which he never properly recovered.

The Khaki Election the following year, which he entertained doubts about calling until he became convinced that it was required to demoralize the Boers, offered little consolation. It was Chamberlain, not Salisbury, who made the running. In terms of votes cast the contest was close, but in seats it was anything but, returning 402 Unionists to face 184 Liberals, 82 Irish Nationalists and 2 Labour Members. Salisbury did not share the rejoicing. His pessimism resurfaced: 'I am not sure whether I can consider the omens altogether favourable.' This is not what a victorious party wants to hear from its leader.[64] And the Boer War turned out not to have been finally won at all.

The subsequent reconstruction of the Cabinet was felt to have been botched. Salisbury knew his health was no longer good enough to combine the Foreign Office with the premiership, though it took the Queen's intervention to persuade him to relinquish it. The post went to Lansdowne. This did nothing to restore confidence, since Lansdowne had been Secretary for War against the Boers. The most damaging charge against the ministry was not, however, 'more of the same', but 'more of the Cecils'. The Radical Henry Labouchere described the grouping as 'the Hotel Cecil', after the grand building of that name built on Cecil land south of the Strand. Its political occupants (to prolong the metaphor) were: Salisbury's nephew, Arthur Balfour (First Lord of the Treasury and Leader of the House of Commons); another nephew, Gerald Balfour (President of the Board of Trade); yet another nephew, Evelyn Cecil (Prime Minister's parliamentary private secretary); Salisbury's nephew–in–law, James Lowther (Chairman of the Commons Ways and Means Committee); Salisbury's son-in-law, Lord Selborne (First Lord of the Admiralty); and Salisbury's eldest son, Lord Cranborne (Under-Secretary at the Foreign Office). Disgruntled Tories, not just the Liberal Opposition, expressed anger at such blatant nepotism – even going so far as to seek to amend the Loyal Address to that effect. Salisbury, himself, was unmoved. In answer to the complaints, relayed by Balfour, he explained:

Exactly the same number of 'relations' (minus Jim [i.e. Cranborne]) were in the Government in July 1895 as there are

now. The arrangement has therefore been before the country
during two general elections without provoking any adverse
comment. Herbert Gladstone may pair off with Jim. No doubt
one or two have been promoted. But they cannot be treated as a
class apart who can be employed but not promoted, like second
division clerks.[65]

The trouble was, of course, that whatever the Cecil arithmetic
strictly showed, the public and the party had other expectations.

The death of the Queen in January 1901 signalled, more than
anything else, that well-worn but unavoidable cliché, 'the end of an
era'. Salisbury rose to the occasion with a memorable tribute, which
was also characteristic in containing an important but not obvious
insight: 'She had an extraordinary knowledge of what her people
would think – extraordinary because it could not have come from
any personal intercourse. I have said for years that when I knew
what the Queen thought I knew pretty certainly what views
her subjects would take, and especially the middle classes of her
subjects.'[66]

Over the years, Queen Victoria had been a great, if sometimes
qualified, asset to the party. From the time she threw off, under the
Prince Consort's influence, her infatuation with Melbourne, she
was with varying degrees of enthusiasm supportive of the
Conservatives' claims. She highly respected Peel. She adored
Disraeli. She developed a relationship of the greatest trust in her
old age with Salisbury, who reciprocated. Even more importantly,
she detested first Palmerston and then, to still greater effect,
Gladstone. The drawbacks were real, though manageable. She
conceived strong likes and dislikes for particular ministers and
generals. She was, like most of the country, also strongly inclined to
the Latitudinarian wing of the Church, whereas most politicians
and clergy were not. She conceived a furious hatred of foreign
powers that were presumptuous enough to threaten British

interests – especially Russia – and even Disraeli, on occasion, had to issue a rebuke on this subject. But Salisbury had political, as well as personal, reasons to mourn her departure. His uneasy relations with his new sovereign, Edward VII, increased his inclination to step down.

The main reason for his departure, though, was his health. After a severe illness back in 1880, he had been transformed – whether by bad habits or metabolic change – from a tall thin man into a tall fat one. At six feet four and 18 stone, probably more in the end, he certainly looked the part of an elder statesman. But his refusal to take much exercise – in his last years he rode a tricycle, but that was the limit – and very long hours of work, which he maintained even during his frequent illnesses, combined with a Victorian diet and banquets, had their effect. His excess weight slowed him further, at an age when he was bound to slow down anyway. As a young man he had been afflicted by nervous complaints. Later he was inconvenienced by dreadful eczema, when under strain. Also during his last years, recurrent influenza weakened him.

When the coronation was postponed because Edward developed peritonitis, Salisbury decided he could not wait. On 11 July 1902 he resigned as Prime Minister. His timing was, as usual, excellent, and so were his dispositions. He knew that he would be criticized again for nepotism. But neither he nor his senior Conservative colleagues thought that anyone but his nephew, Arthur Balfour, should succeed him (significantly, he did not consult the Liberal Unionist Devonshire, who might have asserted a claim). The fact that Chamberlain, another rival, was currently in hospital after a cab accident added to the impression of stealth. But Chamberlain would not, anyway, have been acceptable to the Conservatives. So the Queen took Salisbury's advice and asked his nephew to head the Government.

Salisbury's health quickly declined further. Having slipped off the special chair on which he slept – to relieve the pressure on his chest from his huge weight – he suffered a heart attack. In the night of 22 August 1903 he died.

Without being greatly loved, outside his family, nor vividly remembered, except by acquaintances, he had stamped his personality on his times, and the Conservative Party was, for most of them, the beneficiary. The fact that the Tories were in office for fourteen of Salisbury's seventeen years as party leader is evidence of it. No Conservative has equalled that record, nor looks likely to do so.[67] At least as significant is his achievement in leading the first government since the Second Reform Act to be re-elected. To halt, or at least temporarily arrest, the 'pendulum', whose swing Disraeli had regarded as an immutable law of politics, was in itself extraordinary. To do so under a leader who scorned democracy seems deliciously ironic. Too ironic, perhaps, because it may help explain why no later generation of Conservatives, so willing when occasion suits to exalt Disraeli, or even seek inspiration from a not obviously inspiring Peel, has sought to lionize and emulate Robert Arthur Talbot Gascoyne-Cecil, third Marquess of Salisbury.

The unbearable lightness of being . . . Balfour at the Dispatch Box in 1907 – full of polished intelligence but strangely lacking in ballast.

8

THE PRECIPICE

Arthur Balfour's succession to the premiership, and thus to the leadership of the Conservative Party, was not just smooth: it was also proof that a succession can be too smooth. Once Joe Chamberlain and Devonshire had agreed, Salisbury's laying on of hands was sufficient. To ease the transition symbolically, Balfour was already First Lord of the Treasury. The monarch's commission to form a government merely formalized things. The meeting at which the Conservative Party endorsed Balfour's leadership was genuinely enthusiastic. But, as events soon showed, that support was, as the phrase is, wide rather than deep. The unanimity of welcome represented a peculiarly Conservative mix of good manners, complacency, self-delusion and hypocrisy. There was clearly trouble ahead, some inherited, some still forming, and contrary to appearances Balfour was unsuited to lead his party and the Unionist coalition through it.[1]

George Dangerfield's much mentioned study of the period, *The Strange Death of Liberal England*, is wrong about nearly all that matters. Liberal England did not 'die', though the Liberal Party (more or less) did. The rise of Labour to take the place of the Liberals was not inevitable. The great challenges of the time – constitutional upheaval, the suffragettes, Ireland, labour militancy – were neither inherently connected nor fundamentally unmanageable. But Dangerfield's description of Balfour as one for whom 'politics was little more than a serious game [that he] played . . . with the faintly supercilious finesse which belongs to a bachelor of breeding, and with a bitterly polite sarcasm,' definitely hits the mark.[2]

Balfour was intelligent and no coward, as his 'Bloody Balfour' Irish period demonstrated; and when he roused himself he could perform well in the House of Commons. It was this ability which ensured that he alone was trusted with piloting through the Government's contentious education measures. Even in the House, though, his manner was often deemed flippant, and as the years went by was criticized as ill-judged by enemies at both ends of the spectrum. When, after the 1906 Unionist smash, he was chastised in the Commons for his old style by the new Liberal Prime Minister, Sir Henry Campbell-Bannerman, with the words, 'I say enough of this foolery!', Balfour was silent, and his backbenchers crestfallen.[3] The Unionists, too, became increasingly exasperated, not just by his shifts and nuances but by his apparent inability to rise to the seriousness that issues required. Writing in the *National Review*, the Tariff Reform enthusiast Leopold Maxse complained: 'The old game between the ins and the outs may be very amusing – like lawn tennis [Balfour's favourite game] – but after all it is only a game. It is not business . . . People ask themselves what is the use of all this marvellous sword-play, and the unrivalled dialectics.'[4]

The obvious conclusion might be that it was Balfour's background that was the problem. He was a representative of the Hotel Cecil. He was the beneficiary of nepotism. He was old-fashioned in speech, manner and tastes. But that democratically informed insight is, for the most part, ill-informed. The proof is that, while

Salisbury would have been hard pressed to rise to or stay at the top in the generation about to fight the First World War, Balfour's uncle at least had the qualities that would have given him a chance – and these the nephew lacked. Salisbury, unlike Balfour, had had to earn his own living for a number of years. This probably helped. He was also more brutal, and a substantial figure in his own right. Balfour shared some of his uncle's interests – his fascination with science and technology, for instance – but in him, Salisbury's eccentricities acquired a certain aspect of silliness and self-indulgence. Balfour was fascinated by flight, he had a motorcycle, he above all loved cars. On his eightieth birthday he would be presented with a Rolls-Royce by his political friends, on his last visit to the Palace of Westminster.[5] It was all a bit childish.

Balfour was a more civilized man, aesthetically speaking. He enjoyed Handel and the opera, while Salisbury had no interest in music at all. Balfour collected paintings, notably the Pre-Raphaelites; art left the Marquess cold. Balfour was an entertaining talker in society – above all that of the preciously self-absorbed group called the 'Souls', who met at great houses to discuss books, philosophy and politics. Salisbury preferred to talk at home with family and close friends, to whom he delivered his rambling, witty monologues.

Salisbury was a serious and (at least by English standards) orthodox Christian of settled, hardened views. Balfour was fascinated by belief, but as a problem rather than a commitment or a bulwark. It was perhaps unfair that so much attention should have been paid to the first half of the title of his book *A Defence of Philosophic Doubt*, and so little to the second, *Being an Essay on the Foundations of Belief* (1879). It was, after all, a defence of the reasonableness of faith in an age that dogmatized Darwin's theories. But Balfour was, in truth, plagued by the consequences of open-mindedness, which his uncle rejected. It led him, among other things, to the silliness of the Society for Psychical Research, of

233

which he was a founder. At the height of the constitutional crisis of 1911 Balfour invited the famous spiritualist Annie Besant to Carlton Gardens 'to talk occultism with Gerald [Balfour] and me'.[6]

Perhaps the most important political difference between Salisbury and Balfour lies, however, in their attitudes to the party they led. Salisbury took a close interest in the workings of the party machine. Balfour took none, unless it was to protect his own prerogatives – which Salisbury never needed to do, and Balfour ultimately failed to do. Salisbury was grand and knew it, but he reserved his sneers for his opponents, and he flattered those whom he needed – like Chamberlain – whatever their status or behaviour. He was a good manager of men. Balfour, time and again, was not. Salisbury was not a club man, as Balfour, a lifelong bachelor, was; but it is, for all that, impossible to imagine Salisbury describing the Carlton Club, in his nephew's words, as 'a beastly Club: infested by the worst species viz: – the political bore'.[7] When Balfour, or any other Conservative leader, lost the bores, he lost the party.

In 1902, though, this fate lay far in the future. It is also important not to overlook either the successes of Balfour's Government or the scale of the difficulties he and his colleagues faced. Among the achievements must certainly be numbered the creation of the Committee of Imperial Defence, a development which Salisbury, with his dislike of bureaucratic innovation, had stubbornly impeded. The committee brought together the Prime Minister, the service chiefs and senior military advisers to oversee the defence of the Empire. From 1903, when Devonshire resigned, Balfour took the chair, as did his successors in the premiership. The result was better oversight – but not a shift in military priorities, which remained, as previously, maintenance of naval supremacy and limitation of the army to protection of the Empire. The First World War would expose the shortcomings of that approach. But it was not now seriously challenged, and it is anyway doubtful whether the alternative could have been afforded, even had it been politically acceptable.[8]

The other substantial achievement, though it came at a very high political price, was Balfour's Education Act. This, again, grasped a nettle from which Salisbury, faced with party opposition, had prudently backed away. The Act provided a logical answer to the anomaly whereby voluntary (i.e. Church) schools were regarded as the main source of national schooling, but were unsupported by the rates and operated outside the ambit of local councils. The 1902 Act transferred all local primary and secondary schools to the county and borough authorities and at the same time enabled the voluntary schools to receive rate aid. This latter provision quietened opposition within the ranks of the Conservatives. But it provoked outrage among the Nonconformists, whose political profile was in any case rising. It forced them into the ranks of the Liberals and caused substantial difficulties for Joe Chamberlain – who, in turn, was forced to find a new cause around which to stake his claim to Radical national support, with what turned out to be ominous consequences.

The outcome of the Boer War caused, as has been discussed, a malaise which extended into domestic as well as foreign policy. Politicians have, of course, to react to such realities, but there is a danger of overreacting; and this Chamberlain, under pressure from several quarters, certainly did.

Joe Chamberlain did not ask for the post of Chancellor of the Exchequer in the new Government, and Balfour did not offer it. This was the beginning of the trouble. By appointing C. T. Ritchie, a former protectionist become dogmatic free trader, Balfour stored up problems, and Chamberlain, who stayed as Colonial Secretary, did not see them coming. On 16 May 1902 Chamberlain spoke to his party in Birmingham. The timing was tactically astute. The outgoing Chancellor, Sir Michael Hicks Beach, though a free trader himself, had introduced revenue tariffs on corn, grain, meal and flour to help pay for the war. The policy was attacked by Campbell-Bannerman as the start of a return to protection. This was not the original intention. Balfour took pains to stress that there was no connection, either, with the forthcoming Colonial Conference. But Chamberlain had other ideas. Diverting his audience from worries about education policy, and setting out a benchmark for imperial policy, he now declared: 'At the present moment, the Empire is being attacked on all sides, and, in our isolation, we must look to ourselves . . . The days are for great Empires, not for little states.' He added, in code which hardly needed deciphering, that the challenges of the modern world would not be met by adherence to 'old shibboleths'.[9]

Chamberlain was disappointed by the meagre results of the Colonial Conference. He had hoped for a stronger push by the self-governing colonies towards an imperial trading union. But he thought that he had at least secured Cabinet's agreement that the corn duty would not be repealed. This, he believed, would be a bargaining chip when negotiating the system of Imperial Preference which, he envisaged, would bind the mother country to the colonies by economic ties. Chamberlain then, in November, departed for South Africa. While there, his enthusiasm for imperial economic union grew, along with his enthusiasm for Milner's South African dreams. But at home the rats, in the form of the four free trading Cabinet ministers, Ritchie, Devonshire, Hamilton and Balfour of Burleigh (no relation), successfully gnawed away at what Chamberlain thought – but they disputed – had been agreed.

Arthur Balfour now displayed the mixture of cunning and weakness that so often earned him the contempt of others. He privately inclined to Chamberlain. But he could not afford to lose Ritchie on the eve of the latter's budget. Chamberlain, tired and disappointed with developments in his absence, did not on his homecoming directly threaten resignation. This was certainly a mistake. Ritchie's budget was accordingly delivered, and it contained not just repeal of the duties but an embarrassing encomium on the merits of free trade.

But Balfour now shifted again. Unlike the other members of the Cecil clan, he was not, himself, a free trader. He merely feared the political cost of imposing duties – or 'food taxes' as they were damagingly called – which threatened a 'dear loaf'. His manoeuvrings were ridiculed after he admitted in the House of Commons that he had no 'settled convictions on the tariff question'. A Liberal, Sir Wilfrid Lawson, composed his commentary in verse:

> I'm not for Free Trade, and I'm not for Protection;
> I approve of them both, and to both have objections.
> In going through life, I continually find
> It's a terrible business to make up one's mind.
> And it's always the best in political fray
> To take up the line of the Vicar of Bray.
> So, in spite of all comments, reproach, and predictions,
> I firmly adhere to Unsettled Convictions.[10]

Chamberlain, though, did have convictions, and he resolved to educate public opinion in favour of them. He had, anyway, come to the conclusion that a re-alignment in British politics was necessary. The Coalition looked tired and the political climate seemed stale. It was time to shake them up. Adhering to the agreed, vague policy parameters – but in an entirely different spirit from Balfour, who the same day (15 May 1903) was addressing a deputation of Unionist MPs – Chamberlain delivered a speech in his constituency that constituted what Leo Amery described as 'a challenge to free trade as direct and provocative as the theses Luther nailed to the Church door in Wittenberg'.[11] Nor, one can add in retrospect, were the results much less disruptive.

Balfour still seemed resolved on a middle way. In the summer of 1903 he tried to rally the Cabinet around what seemed to both wings ambiguous and possibly contradictory proposals. An autumn reshuffle looked increasingly necessary. But which way to turn – or, more importantly, which faction to eject? In the end, he managed to achieve the worst of all possible outcomes.

Chamberlain offered to resign in order to be free to argue his case without inhibition. Balfour would have been better rejecting the offer and espousing the 'Whole Hog' protectionist case, whatever the risks. Instead, he accepted the loss of Chamberlain. But he thought that he would get rid of the free traders too, and effectively sacked Ritchie and Balfour of Burleigh, rightly assuming that Hamilton would follow. He wanted, though, to keep Devonshire, a far more powerful figure. And he failed. After some resentful reflection, the Duke went as well. So Balfour had lost both the free traders, who now hated him, and the protectionists, who despised him.

The protectionists formed a Tariff Reform League, which quickly gained an ascendancy. Chamberlain campaigned up and down the country. He enjoyed the support of almost the whole Unionist press. Only the *Standard*, of the London dailies, and the *Spectator*, of the weeklies, stood out against protectionism, and the *Standard* later capitulated. Balfour's compromise policy was publicly endorsed, but constituency parties often went further. For their part, the free traders formed a Free Food League, which caused trouble and eventually benefited the Liberals, but could not mount any serious challenge within the Unionist ranks. It was the leadership's worries about the electoral consequences, not lack of support for the official line among the rank and file, that modified policy. In Edinburgh, on 3 October 1904, Balfour thus announced that the Unionists would not introduce Imperial Preference until a second general election. Chamberlain grudgingly agreed.

By then, the free traders were only a small minority. Out of 392 Unionist MPs, just 65 joined the Free Food League, and 47 voted with the Liberals on one or more occasion in 1904–5. The successor to the League, the Unionist Free Trade Club, founded in April 1905, had only 29 MPs, and of these 11 went over to the Liberals before 1906 – including, most famously, Winston Churchill. In the end, Lord Hugh Cecil remained the only prominent Unionist Free Trade MP.

By contrast, the number of declared 'Whole Hog' tariff reformers steadily increased. In July 1904, 177 Unionist MPs gathered to celebrate Chamberlain's birthday. Chamberlain himself became increasingly frustrated by Balfour's equivocation and restarted his public campaign the following year.[12] But by now it was too late for tariff reform, for Balfour, for the Unionists and, tragically, for Chamberlain.

This muddle was not just the worst outcome for Balfour. It was probably the worst outcome for the party. The results of a long run of subsequent general elections and by-elections seem to confirm that tariff reform was a vote-loser. It might have been less so, as Chamberlain argued, if it had been expounded with conviction. But the problems with it were insuperable. Only duties on imported foodstuffs would make Imperial Preference attractive to the colonies (and this attraction would diminish once they developed indigenous industries). Yet these 'food taxes' were a political incubus. The short-term benefits of industrial protection could not outweigh that – and there could be no long-term economic benefits, for reasons to be discussed later. So, by rejecting free trade, the Conservatives made it difficult for themselves to win elections. Yet, equally, by failing to rally round tariff reform as a fully developed programme, the party was left flailing and faction-ridden. Tariff reform always seemed to resurface at odd moments as part of the answer to the economic, social and international problems of the day; but it could never be explained too fully, or embraced too warmly. It remained an issue about which to disagree – and frequently to quarrel in public.

Moreover, while the Unionists continued their struggle about protection, wider public opinion moved strongly against them. The scandal of 'Chinese slavery' – the use and abuse of Chinese indentured servants, authorized by Milner in South Africa – gave opposition to the Government a moral cause. The Nonconformist conscience – much outraged anyway by the awful thought of Anglican schools on the rates – was now dangerously stirred. For their part, the Liberals performed a skilful balancing act on religious matters, bringing out the Nonconformist vote but also enjoying the benefit of the Irish Catholic vote in mainland constituencies.[13]

Not much discussed at the time – which itself shows how out of touch the Unionists had become – but greatly talked of later and, indeed, of seminal importance, was the mobilization of trade union and working-class electors as a result of the Taff Vale verdict (1901). This judicial ruling effectively challenged the right of a union to organize a strike at all. The Government's failure to reverse or modify it became a rallying point for the Labour Representation Committee (LRC). A secret agreement between the Liberal Chief Whip, Herbert Gladstone, and the LRC secretary, Ramsay MacDonald, in 1903, turned this directly to the Unionists' disadvantage. In return for a free run for LRC candidates in some 35 seats, the LRC would not split the anti-Unionist vote in the rest of England and Wales. This pact inflicted damage at the 1906 and 1910 elections – significantly, its ending in 1918 coincided with a big Conservative revival.[14]

Probably the last point at which Balfour might have called an election with any chance of winning, or even of avoiding a rout, was early 1904. But, to his credit, he wanted to see through the new Entente agreement with France and the provision of new weaponry for the army; so he resisted Chamberlain's urging. The 1904 session saw a return to bad by-election results, more argument about protection, and, most seriously, the ruin of the Irish Secretary, Balfour's friend George Wyndham, when it was discovered that his (Catholic) under-secretary had been preparing a plan for Irish Home Rule. By suggesting that Balfour had gone soft on Ireland, this episode removed what would have been a useful prop as the

Unionists struggled against what looked increasingly like a Liberal landslide.

Balfour's final misjudgement was to resign voluntarily at the end of 1905 – the last Prime Minister to install the Opposition in power while still retaining a majority in the House. He was tired of office and even more tired of the sniping. But he also thought that the Liberals might split and be unable to govern. He had some reason to think this, because of a high-profile public clash between the Liberal imperialist Lord Rosebery and Campbell-Bannerman over Home Rule. There were also unsuccessful attempts to push the ageing Campbell-Bannerman to the Lords.[15] But, as usual, Balfour miscalculated. It all went wrong. The Liberals did not split. Campbell-Bannerman took office and then called an election himself, making clear that there would be no move to Irish Home Rule before a further election.

In the meantime, the Conservative Party and Liberal Unionist organizations had grown as slack as their politics, while the Liberal organization had been making strides. The tell-tale signs of late nominations and uncontested seats illustrated deeper problems. The Unionists campaigned on tariff reform, but neither coherently nor effectively. In the final stages they concentrated on fear of Labour, but there had been no preparation of the ground for a scare. Beach had forecast 'the very greatest smash that any party has had in my time'. That turned out to be an understatement.[16]

Balfour now achieved a further record, in being the only Conservative leader to lose his seat at an election. He was defeated in Manchester, where, to add salt to the wound, the turncoat Churchill was successful. Balfour had tried, and failed, to dispel in traditionally free trade Lancashire the fear that tariff reform would destroy the advantage on price which was believed essential in fiercely contested export markets. Nor was the Government able to come up with any convincing answer to the question why retaliation against the United States would not endanger Lancashire's supply of US cotton. The Manchester Free Trade League, including a number of leading Conservatives, was active against Balfour and in support of Churchill.[17] It was the same, to varying degrees, elsewhere.

At the 1906 general election the Unionists lost a catastrophic 245 seats. The new House of Commons, therefore, contained just 157 Unionists (out of a total of 670 Members), and only three of Balfour's outgoing Cabinet. Every part of the country shared in the disaster. There was now no Unionist representation in Wales. In London 31 seats were lost, along with 27 in the south-east, 25 in the south-west and 22 in Lancashire. Chamberlain's support held on in Birmingham, though the span of his West Midlands kingdom was reduced. Indeed, by and large, the Unionist vote had held up generally. But it was swamped by a huge increase in Liberal support. The adage that high turnouts were bad for the Tories certainly held true on this occasion. It was a truly terrible defeat.[18]

Few other routs in Conservative history are comparable. The collapse over the Corn Laws, though equally severe, was the result of a formal party split, so in a different category. The 1832 election is, of course, not quite parallel either, because at that point the Conservative Party did not yet exist, although recognizably conservative or 'Tory' interests did. The 1997 election defeat offers a closer comparison. A fag-end Conservative Government, a weak and unlucky leader, a discontented and divided party – all are recognizable, too, in 1906. The reactions, though, were different. In 1997 there was, as will be described, a near-fatal loss of self-confidence. Nothing like this happened in 1906. The response was not happy or, in the short run, particularly productive, certainly not for the country. But it was not a nervous breakdown either. If anything, the party reaction was too self-confident, when there was little enough to be confident about.

One further obvious difference is that Balfour survived as party leader, even though he was not even in Parliament (an anomaly soon rectified by his return for the City of London). There was, naturally, no formal process of removing a failed leader. But that was not the root of the difficulty. This was the fact that the obvious and, in a sense, real leader of the party, Chamberlain, was, as in 1902, simply unacceptable, as he himself realized. So Balfour sauntered on.

This did not stop Chamberlain's supporters from taking over the party institutions. A re-organization in 1906 managed to inflict the maximum harm. The National Union, by now in the hands of the tariff reformers, engaged in a rerun – but more bitter, more substantial and much more successful – of the struggle waged earlier against Central Office by the advocates of Tory democracy led by Randolph Churchill.

. A sort of armed truce then prevailed. While the party leadership retained control of Central Office, it lost all authority over the National Union and, for all practical purposes, over the party in the country. So provincial divisions were abolished and counties became fully autonomous. A National Union Organisation Committee took over the supervision of agents. Even central party literature was henceforth under the National Union's control. A final nonsense was that, while most of the spending was in the hands of the National Union, party funds remained under the control of the Chief Whip, Balfour's nominee. It would have made more sense to abolish Central Office altogether and give the National Union its head. If Chamberlain and his people had been granted total control, at least some professionalism would probably have been introduced.[19]

But in July 1906, after public celebrations of his seventieth birthday, Chamberlain suffered a disabling stroke. He would never return to the House of Commons and rarely be seen in public. His son Austen acted as his agent. Joe's spirit did not fail. He was as determined as ever to maintain the imperial cause and to resist sellout in Ireland. His last words, on his deathbed to Austen in June

1914, were: 'Somebody has got to give way, but I don't see why it should be always us.'[20] The chance to reshape Unionism in Chamberlain's image had, however, been lost eight years earlier.

The decisive political battles would initially be in Parliament. There were opportunities for new men to make a mark after the clean-out of Conservative MPs at the election. No one ever made more of a mark in a maiden speech than F. E. Smith. It was scathing and hysterically funny and argued the (quite unsustainable) case that tariff reform had not damaged the Unionists. F.E. was later almost alone in eviscerating that year's Trade Disputes Act, which overturned the Taff Vale judgment and established the legal right to picket. The arguments Smith deployed against the intimidatory purposes of picketing could have been taken from the 1980s.[21] But the Unionist leadership of the day was too intellectually lazy to adopt them.

Balfour thought that measures which were pressed by the Labour contingent of MPs (now an alarming thirty strong) should not be defeated in the Lords. But others could be. In a basic misreading of Salisbury's doctrine of the 'mandate', he also intended that on matters affecting property and the constitution – as he imprudently boasted – the Unionists 'should control, whether in power or opposition, the destinies of this great Empire'.[22] (Salisbury, though he adopted such language, knew perfectly well the dangers of acting on it, unless a Commons majority could be obtained in an early election: Balfour and Lansdowne conspicuously missed that point.[23]) The result was a constitutional crisis, and eventually Balfour's departure.

It was not just F. E. Smith's rhetoric that kept up Unionist spirits in the early opposition years. The party even started to look on top of events. Naval scares helped, and Balfour was good on defence. The economy also slipped, creating discontent. The Unionists made some policy gestures towards social reform. When, in 1908, the Government brought forward a scheme for old-age retirement pensions it looked as if they could not be afforded, unless at the expense of the naval building programme. The tariff reform enthusiasts then said that this proved that only revenue from duties could fill the gap. But Conservative crowing was short-lived.

Lloyd George's 1909 budget now proposed paying for the plans with swingeing tax increases, skilfully aimed at the Unionist aristocrats' solar plexus. His 'supertax' on those with incomes above £5,000 a year, his increase in death duties and his land taxes were undisguisedly class-driven attacks on the wealthy. The howls from the Unionist benches, particularly in the Lords, were predictable, the party leadership's reaction less so. Initially, it seemed, the Opposition would choose to put up a fight, but then accept defeat. Lloyd George's inflammatory Limehouse speech on 30 July, with its sneers at the aristocracy, changed that. Balfour, with extraordinarily poor judgement, reverted to the hardest line and, on the grounds that the budget was an unconstitutional measure, being more than a mere finance bill, he plunged the country and his party into a constitutional crisis. Balfour urged the Unionist peers to throw the budget out, which, by 350 to 75 votes, they duly did. The peers claimed that a general election alone could give the budget measures legitimacy. Asquith (who had succeeded Campbell-Bannerman in 1908) gave them one. He promptly dissolved and a long, ferocious campaign ensued.

The January 1910 election outcome was, on the face of it, quite encouraging for the Unionists. It was also, by the same token, bad news for the Liberals. The Unionists gained 116 seats and, with a total of 273, were now just two short of the Liberal tally. The Liberals were henceforth in historic decline. They would never have a parliamentary majority again in their own right. Labour, once more benefiting from the Lib–Lab electoral pact, secured 40 seats. But it was the implication for the two major parties of the 82 Irish Nationalist seats which was most alarming. For the Unionists, it meant that even if they now accepted the nation's verdict on the budget, Irish Home Rule was back on the agenda. This would have been good news in an earlier era, because it was a fine issue on which to campaign in England. Now, though, with the Liberals likely to introduce a new Parliament Bill to curb the powers of the Lords, the breaking of the Union, with all that meant for the Empire, looked all too likely. Some Conservative supporters were tempted by compromise. The *Observer*, though loyal to Balfour, pushed the case for a federal solution, with powers devolved to Ireland, Scotland and Wales. But Balfour was not having it, and neither would most of the party have gone along with it.[24] For the Liberals, dependence on the Irish vote in Parliament was, arguably, even more problematic. It threatened to derail the attempts of the 'New Liberalism' to re-establish the party as one of radical social reform. It would also bring it up against, in the Ulster Unionists, some of the hardest men it was ever the misfortune of an elected government to try to coerce.

The death of Edward VII and succession of George V imposed a potentially useful truce. Lloyd George's budget passed. The question of the day now became Lords reform. Since 1907, the Unionist peers had been attracted by the idea of altering the composition of the Upper House to increase its legitimacy. This became the party's answer to Asquith's plans to abolish the Lords' veto. With the King's support, the two sides negotiated. The real sticking point was always Ireland. The Unionists could not concede a measure which would prevent the peers throwing out a Home Rule Bill. But the Liberals, dependent on the Irish, could not offer a measure which would allow that to occur – given the unpopularity of Irish Home Rule in the subsequent election that would have to be fought on it. Significantly for the future, Lloyd George came up with a secret plan for a Liberal–Unionist coalition, which would have offered, on Ireland at least, a way forward. But neither side could accept. The Liberals returned to their proposals to abolish the veto and squeezed out of the King guarantees that he would, if necessary, create enough Liberal peers to secure such a measure's passage.

In order to divert attention from the unpromising theme of 'peers versus the people', the Unionists demanded a referendum on Home Rule. Balfour added, in answer to Liberal jeers, that he would accept a referendum on tariff reform, if they accepted one on Ireland. It was a typically Balfourian ploy, and it did not help. It mollified those worried about the unpopularity of food taxes, but it outraged the protectionists, to such an extent that Balfour tried to shift authorship of the proposal to Andrew Bonar Law, one of the party's coming men.[25] Nor did it, anyway, convince the electorate.

The party had high hopes of the second (December) 1910 election, but they were disappointed. The Unionists lost one seat overall. The balance between the different parties was almost unchanged. But the most important loser was Balfour. His authority as leader was shattered. There was now no hope of stopping a Parliament Bill, if Asquith pressed the King to create the promised peers. And without the Lords' veto there was no chance of stopping a Home Rule Bill passing before any new election. This hopelessness might have led to compromise. But, given the mood in the Unionist ranks and Balfour's incapacity to lead, it pushed the party towards dangerous misbehaviour.

On 24 July the House was suspended, as the result of a group of Conservative MPs, led by Lord Hugh Cecil, shouting down the Prime Minister. The next day Balfour announced that he intended to draw back from out-and-out opposition to the Parliament Bill. This enraged the hard-liners further. The following day a dinner for Lord Halsbury, the former Lord Chancellor, attended by several hundred MPs and peers, marked the foundation of the 'Halsbury Club'. Other groups of 'ditchers' (as opposed to the 'hedgers') in the shape of the 'Confederacy' and 'Reveille' also took up the charge. Almost as much venom was expended against Balfour as against the Government. The party was rapidly disintegrating. It was increasingly characterized by 'leagues' promoting different causes – including, of course, tariff reform – which largely escaped the leadership's control.

One should add that tariff reform itself was by now, in the eyes of its more radical proponents, about much more than reforming tariffs. It was a flag beneath which, it was felt, the Unionists could rediscover their purpose and offer a social vision to repel the advances of Labour. From 1906, Conservatives were conscious that they were operating in a rapidly developing three-party system. They feared the loss of working-class votes. This was sensible. But they undoubtedly exaggerated the effect. It was, indeed, one of the damaging aspects of the myths of Tory social reform attached to Disraeli's name. Progressive-minded Conservatives suffered excessive fears, and nourished inordinate hopes, in their preoccupation with the Tory working man at the expense of the Tory middle class. Maxse, writing in the *National Review* in September 1906, lamented: 'Outside Birmingham [Chamberlain's fiefdom], the Labour Party is robbing us of the Tory democracy which has been the mainstay of the Unionist cause for the past twenty years.'[26] This was, at least under the existing franchise, electoral nonsense. But it was a widespread sentiment. Certainly, any attempt to turn the party into a truly democratic party, with a powerful appeal to the lower orders, was likely to find in Balfour, with or without his nuanced policies on tariff reform, an improbable champion.

The circumstances under which the Parliament Bill finally passed the Lords dug deep into what little remained of party loyalty and restraint. Lord Curzon, Balfour's one-time friend, fellow 'Soul' and disgruntled former Viceroy of India, was prevailed upon to do the right thing, for which he was roundly hated: he led 37 Unionist peers into the 'yes' lobby to get the Bill through. Diehards resentful at Balfour's tactics, frustrated tariff reformers, and all those who simply longed for some direction from the top came together to demand change. The *National Review* had devised the slogan 'Balfour Must Go' or, in shorthand, 'BMG'.[27] It was now popular in all quarters.

Yet, as is the way of the Tory Party, such opposition was at first channelled into demands for party re-organization. This Balfour was in no position to resist. The changes now enacted constitute his only – modest – contribution to the future of the party he led for so many fruitless years.

After the second election defeat of 1910 there was unstoppable pressure for an inquiry into the party's failures. A committee chaired by the former Chief Whip, Aretas Akers-Douglas, was appointed. Its main proposals were that two new posts be created – that of party treasurer and that of chairman of the party (enjoying 'Cabinet rank') – and that Central Office and the National Union should be re-merged, with the former having all executive authority. Balfour accepted the changes but tried to reduce the status of the chairman, which he significantly (and permanently) re-titled 'chairman of the party organization'. He also concealed, as long as he could, the 'Cabinet rank' pledge. Finally, he appointed a rather junior but, as it turned out, vigorous and assertive Birmingham MP, Arthur Steel-Maitland, to the chairmanship. The far from vigorous Chief Whip, Sir Alexander Acland-Hood, was kicked upstairs and replaced by Lord Balcarres. The new team was a clear improvement and the new organization was much more rational.[28]

It is, though, hard to know how much difference either really made, because they were not to be put to any early test. The outbreak of the First World War saw to that. Moreover, the Unionists were in any case on an electoral upswing, which reflected national mood rather than party mobilization. The best tribute to the committee's work is that the new structure was not significantly altered, despite recurring criticism over the years of how the party was being run.

And Balfour finally stepped down. He was not much missed. The protestations of regret were loud but hollow. He would enjoy influence and sometimes office for many years. His legacy, though, had little to commend it. Not the least of the party's problems was the lack of an obvious successor. The two leading candidates were Austen Chamberlain and Walter Long. Each had more to be said against than for him.

Chamberlain's main problem was his name; but there were others. He was not, in fact, much like his father, whose opinions he parroted and whose appearance he aped. Paradoxically, and unlike Joe, he was very much a Conservative. This might have helped. But he lacked both flair and fight, and he was not particularly intelligent. He was stiff, and grew steadily stiffer and more pompous with age. Despite his background, he lacked any trace of the 'common touch'. He was certainly honest, but in a self-righteously plodding manner.[29] His most famous epitaph is provided by the waspish words of F. E. Smith: 'Austen always played the game, and always lost it.' (The remark, made apparently in 1923, also provides a commentary on F.E. It was in large measure out of consideration for Smith – now Lord Birkenhead – that Chamberlain refused to rejoin the Government in 1923. Doing so – and ditching Birkenhead – would have established him as the terminally ill Bonar Law's heir apparent.)[30] Chamberlain was also capable of annoying his fellow Unionists by his insistence on stating what would be best left unsaid. He had recently done it when declaring that Balfour's referendum pledge on tariff reform applied only to a single election, thus re-opening many wounds.[31] It was an untimely gaffe.

Walter Long represented the Tory squires. Wiltshire to Chamberlain's Birmingham, he was thought by many to be the stronger candidate. Whereas Chamberlain had been Chancellor of the Exchequer (albeit briefly), Long had twenty-five years' ministerial experience. He was strongly associated with Irish

Unionism, a useful cause, and only moderately associated with protectionism, a prudent stance. His bluffness concealed a good deal of cunning, if no great intellect. He might have seemed that eternally attractive option for Conservatives, 'a safe pair of hands', had it not been for his unrestrained outbursts of filthy temper. He was accordingly disliked, if also feared, by the senior people in the party.[32]

In the event, neither of the two main candidates seemed likely to secure a sufficient majority. (Of course, a vote, let alone a secret ballot, was the last thing the party wanted: also, the party conference was rapidly approaching and it was felt that uncertainty, let alone campaigning, at such an occasion, was unseemly.) So attention turned to the two outsiders. One, Edward Carson, though not without admirers, was too divisive, and he did not, in the event, put his name forward. But Bonar Law, the other outsider, did. Chamberlain surprised his supporters by offering to withdraw, if Long did too, in favour of Law. As a result, with Water Long proposing him, and another 'squire', Henry Chaplin, in the chair, Bonar Law was unanimously chosen by the party, meeting in the Carlton Club on Monday, 13 November, as its new leader.

Law's rise to the top had been steady rather than spectacular. His claims to the leadership were based more on who he was than on what he had done. He had never been a Cabinet minister. He had not expected to win, but he wanted to make a political mark for the future. His genuine modesty was compensated for by the enthusiasm and ambition of his closest friend and adviser, Max Beaverbrook. Born in Canada of Ulster–Scottish stock, Law had made his name and his money as a businessman – an iron factor – in Glasgow. He won the hearts of Unionists when he resigned his safe Dulwich seat to fight – and lose – a seat in Manchester in December 1910. (He was quickly found another, in Bootle.) He was possessed of reserves of grit and common sense that were at a premium. He spoke in an unpolished but persuasively direct manner, usually without notes, learning his speeches word for word beforehand. He had a formidable grasp of figures, acquired in business. When challenged on a point in the Commons, he would reach into his pocket to produce a small notebook containing statistics or Hansard references. As a result, the challenges were very few.[33] Law was a tactically cautious but intellectually committed tariff reformer. Chamberlain remembered his saying that he 'cared intensely for only two things: Tariff Reform and Ulster: all the rest was only a game'.[34] This was true, as long as we add that he also cared intensely about his family and about winning the war.

Importantly, and unlike Austen Chamberlain, Law had been loyal to Balfour. But it would certainly be difficult to find a more temperamentally different party leader, or indeed one more different from the current Prime Minister, Asquith. Law was teetotal. His favourite meal was roast chicken followed by rice pudding, washed down with ginger beer. His only vice was tobacco, which probably killed him. He was uninterested in music. He did play golf, but he was not an outdoors enthusiast, and he had no appreciation of nature. He preferred chess and, above all, bridge. He laughed and joked laconically with friends, especially Beaverbrook, but otherwise he had no small talk. He disliked entertaining or being entertained, particularly after his adored wife's premature death in 1909. He was not deliberately discourteous, though his directness could appear rude: the King found his manner alarmingly direct. He was not smooth.

Law was a merciless debater. As they walked together at the State Opening of Parliament in 1912, he apparently told Asquith: 'I am afraid I shall have to show myself very vicious, Mr Asquith, in this session. I hope you will understand.' He fulfilled his promise. The extreme language he used about Ulster was all the more chilling because of his low-key manner. He looked and often was melancholy. (The loss of his two sons in the war finally destroyed any last joy he had in life.) His greatest political asset was his well-deserved reputation for integrity. But he was, no less, a calculating tactician. His stance, quite the opposite of Balfour's, was to align himself with the most extreme elements in the party, and then try to control them. (Sometimes, though, they controlled him.) Under other circumstances his strategy, above all over Ulster, could have destroyed the party. As it turned out, he has a good claim to have saved it – and twice.

Bonar Law's term at the head of the party was very nearly cut short by yet another miscalculation by the leadership on tariff reform. Law and his colleagues decided to abandon Balfour's referendum pledge and return to the full tariff reform policy, a decision announced by Lord Lansdowne (leader in the Lords) and then confirmed by Law at the end of 1912. The satisfaction this evoked on one side was more than matched by the fury exhibited on the other. Moderates, too, were appalled at the ill-considered manner in which the change was made. But Law felt unable to back down. He and Lansdowne threatened to resign unless they were supported. Had there been a credible successor, Law would have been not merely (in Asquith's expression) the 'Unknown Prime Minister' but also (as Austen Chamberlain was fated to become) the 'Unknown Leader'. A compromise was found by that least likely compromiser, Carson. A 'memorial' he drafted, signed by nearly all the party backbenchers, expressed confidence in the leadership, and on the basis of tariff reform – but with the crucial qualification that food taxes would only be introduced after a second general election.[35]

Carson's role is significant. He had succeeded Long as leader of the Ulster Unionist MPs in 1910. He and others now regarded Law as indispensable, despite his blunders or shortcomings, because Law was the man for the fight over Ireland. And it was this, rather than any of the other questions that agitated Unionists, which would determine the party's fate. The paradox lies in the fact that, on the face of it, this was also a battle which could not be won. The passing of the Parliament Act meant that if the Government wished to press ahead – and Asquith confirmed to the King that he did – a Home Rule Bill would be on the statute book before the (presumed) date of the next general election.

This, though, had two further implications, which Asquith was apparently incapable of grasping. It meant that the Government would have to be prepared for the coercion of the Ulster Protestants; and it also meant that the Unionist Opposition had every reason to play up rather than play down the threat which resistance to coercion posed to constitutional and civil order, in order to frighten the Government into modifying its plans. Law was specially well equipped for the struggle. He knew Ulster well. He would, therefore, be satisfied, as some old-fashioned diehard Unionists would not, if the six (or possibly nine) counties of Ulster were extracted from the Irish deal. He was also capable of taking enormous risks. As even Balfour's aide Jack Sandars admitted: 'It was the hour, and he was the man.'[36]

The Unionists had some constitutional arguments. These, though sincerely held, have sometimes been given rather more weight than they should. Few Liberals had explicitly campaigned for Home Rule, so it was arguable whether the Government had a mandate. Similarly, the 1911 Parliament Act had been presented as an interim measure. Its preamble promised further reform. But this promise, unsurprisingly, remained unfulfilled. Law argued that the constitution was thus in suspense, and unconstitutional opposition was, therefore, justified. Neither argument can survive close scrutiny. In a three-party system the doctrine of the mandate cannot be strictly applied. And in the case of the Parliament Act, provisional or not, it was on the statute book.

There was, though, a moral and indeed practical argument for excluding Ulster from any Home Rule settlement. Clearly, the case for self-determination (Home Rule) for a minority (Irish Nationalists) wanting to leave the Union could hardly exclude the case for self-determination for another minority (the largely Ulster-based Protestants) which wanted to stay. Above all, the price of coercing the latter would be disproportionate. It threatened an armed conflict in which it seemed likely that the army would refuse to fight. On these larger grounds, refusing to budge on Home Rule, as Asquith did, in order to retain the support of Irish MPs, was at least as irresponsible as were the Unionists under Bonar Law. Not that either side comes out of the comparison well.

Four days before the Home Rule Bill was to be introduced in the House, on 11 April 1912, Law travelled to Ulster. He and Carson addressed a huge, silent crowd, beneath an enormous Union Jack, at Balmoral, near Belfast. Law joined in as the crowd, at Carson's urging, swore never to 'submit to Home Rule'.[37] Back in England, at a rally at Blenheim Palace on 27 July, accompanied by Carson, Chamberlain, Long, Smith, the Cecil brothers, most of the Unionist MPs and leading peers, Law issued unmistakable threats:

[Referring to the promise by the Liberal Chief Whip that the Home Rule Bill would be carried through the Commons by Christmas:]

Perhaps it will . . . I do not know. But I do know this – that we do not acknowledge their right to carry such a revolution by such means . . . We regard them as a revolutionary committee which has seized by fraud upon despotic power . . . We shall use any means to deprive them of the power which they have usurped . . . [Referring to and enlarging on an earlier threat, made before he became leader:]

I said that in my opinion if any attempt were made, without the clearly expressed will of the people of this country, and as part of a corrupt parliamentary bargain, to deprive these men [the Loyalists] of their birthright, they would be justified in resisting by all means, including force. I said so then, and I say so now, with a full sense of the responsibility which attaches to my position, that if the attempt be made under present conditions, I can imagine no length of resistance to which Ulster will go, in which I shall not be ready to support them, and in which they will not be supported by the overwhelming majority of the British people.[38]

While the Bill made its way through Parliament, the tumult in Ulster took increasingly dangerous form. Paramilitary organization was rapidly taking over from politics. The talk was of a 'provisional government', led by Carson. On 18 September 1912, Carson and a vast assembly of supporters signed a new 'Solemn League and Covenant', pledging defiance. F. E. Smith, henceforth derisively referred to as 'Galloper', was throughout these demonstrations at Carson's side, often on horseback. The King, deeply worried, tried to reason with Law, but was simply and bluntly told where the Unionists stood and warned about the attitude of his subjects if he should ever assent to the Bill.

George V now embarked upon an attempt to bring the party leaders to compromise. This was not impossible. The Unionists had indicated in the House of Commons, by reluctantly supporting an amendment which would have excluded the six heavily Protestant counties of Ulster, that modified Home Rule might be a possibility. More important – because Law could not have withstood his opposition – Carson, despite his Dublin background, indicated that he too could accept such a compromise. Balfour and 'Galloper' Smith concurred. Others were not convinced. Yet if there were a split on this amendment it would be a manageable one for the leadership. Asquith, too, left to his own devices, would have accepted such a compromise, though there was never agreement about whether the exclusion was to be permanent (the Unionist demand) or for a six-year period (the Government's position). But Asquith feared the Nationalists too much. The negotiations got nowhere.

Meanwhile, in 1913 the Unionist scorn for the Government had been deepened by the Marconi scandal, in which the Attorney General, Rufus Isaacs, and Lloyd George had both been implicated in (what amounts to) insider trading of shares. Both escaped formal censure, but there was outrage when the tainted Isaacs then became Lord Chief Justice.

Home Rule passed the Commons in January 1913 and again in July. It was, therefore, on course to become law in the autumn of 1914. So time did not seem to be on the Unionist side. To some that might have been an argument for flexibility. To Bonar Law it suggested raising the stakes further. The Unionists had backed the formation of the paramilitary Ulster Volunteers, the formation of a provisional government and the acquisition of arms through gun-running. There was only one possible further step open to them, and that was to prevent the army coercing the Ulstermen. Consideration was now given to amending the Army Bill in the Lords to prevent the use of troops to coerce Ulster, amounting to a direct challenge to Government control of the military. There was concern at the implications, even among the Unionist leaders. But Law was enthusiastic. Suddenly, though, news of the so-called 'Curragh Mutiny' – not in fact a mutiny, but the next worst thing and almost equally alarming – reached London. So the Army Bill stratagem was never tested.

In fact, the events in question were the result of incompetence and confusion, not malice or calculation. The rumours that the army was about to be deployed to arrest the Ulster leaders and coerce Ulster were false. The Government was expecting trouble but not (with the possible exception of Churchill) trying to precipitate it. The planned reinforcements were intended to make existing stores in the province safe from attack. But, fearing their allegiance, and as a precaution, officers domiciled in Ulster were to be excused. Following a misunderstanding of orders, the commanding officer at the Curragh camp in County Kildare and fifty-seven other officers declared that they would choose dismissal rather than act against Ulster. The Government was humiliated. Churchill's provocative deployment of warships to Northern Ireland was rescinded. The Secretary of War, Sir John Seely, was removed, to be replaced, improbably, by Asquith.

Law was back in the ascendant. He had been kept fully informed of events by Major-General Henry Wilson, Director of Military Operations at the War Office, Irishman by origin and Unionist by conviction. The overall impression was that the army could not be relied upon, and that it was more likely to look to the Opposition than the Government for its orders. Liberal politicians were shown as inadequately grappling with events.

The Palace tried a further intervention. The King opened a conference of the key participants in July. Neither Law nor Asquith could go further than their already adumbrated positions. There was disagreement about the disposal of Tyrone and Fermanagh. There was not even any discussion at the Buckingham Palace conference of the most likely way through – a time-limited exclusion of the North (which the Nationalists offered, but which the Unionists insisted be permanent).[39] The talks were deadlocked and fruitless. The King told John Redmond, the Nationalist leader, in a private audience that 'he looked forward to the time when the Irish people would be amongst his most devoted supporters, and that he knew that Ireland would be the greatest recruiting ground in the whole Empire'.[40] The former expectation seemed optimistic; the latter would soon be tested.

The Irish issue was due to come once more to the House of Commons at the end of July. It never did. On 28 June Archduke Franz Ferdinand, heir to the throne of Austria-Hungary, was assassinated in Sarajevo. The Austrians' demands of Serbia were deemed to be an ultimatum with only one possible outcome. At the end of July Law offered a truce on Ulster. The Unionists wanted the legislation frozen, on which they eventually had to accept defeat. They had to settle, with much resentment, for postponement of the Act's implementation. But other matters would not wait. On 4 August 1914 Britain declared war on Germany.

Bonar Law's achievement was to have saved the party from disintegration at a crucially dangerous period of inter-party flux. He had given the Unionists a cause around which to rally, the future of Ulster. Without it, and without him, it is easy to imagine the party squabbling interminably and damagingly over the election-losing issue of protection. He had then neutralized the diehards by adopting their approach, at least in public. Precisely the utterances that shocked the Liberals most were those which cemented his backbench support and secured the party's core vote.

But if Law had saved the party, the war saved Bonar Law. It is hard to know where UDI by the Ulstermen would have led the Unionists otherwise. The less likely option was some kind of coup. The more likely scenario was being discredited and suffering the electoral consequences of fomenting revolt. Coming as and when it did, the war precluded either unpleasantness.

Unless they are blamed for starting or mishandling them, the Conservatives generally do well from wars, while Liberals and socialists do badly. (The Second World War is a notable exception, but then Labour politicians were given a free hand to promote socialism at home – see below.) Why conflict brings out the best in Tories and casts them in a favourable light is no secret. Conservatives are, by instinct, less squeamish about force, less interested in the social cost of conflict, more inclined to apply and accept discipline, and, though the assertion may be indelicate, recognized to be more patriotic than their political opponents.

In the case of the First World War there were also specific reasons why the Unionists benefited. They had been pressing the argument for National Service for some years, though not formally through the party. As the case looked unanswerable, once the first wave of volunteers was exhausted, the party gained advantage from Liberal divisions on the question. The Unionists had also consistently called for more military spending in the face of German armament. They had now been proved right.

The party's links with the armed forces were also much closer than those enjoyed by the Liberals. Many more Unionist MPs had military backgrounds. Many served in the Yeomanry. This involved a cost. Unionist MPs and their sons were more likely to be in the front line. The class from which the Unionists drew their strongest support were more likely to volunteer, and more likely to die.[41] By January 1915 139 Unionist MPs had volunteered compared with 41 Liberals. Most of the remaining Unionists were beyond military age.[42] Admittedly, not all those who went were consigned to the trenches. F. E. Smith secured the unlikely and undemanding role of 'Recording Officer' for the Indian Corps in France in 1914–15. His sybaritic tastes were met by a liberal supply of cigars, oysters and brandy from home.[43]

Ordinary party politics was suspended for the duration of the war. Initially, it was the Unionists who had most reason to feel resentment at the effects of this dispensation, having no share in decisions but being unable to criticize them. Even attempts to use the party organization for recruitment of volunteers were initially frustrated for fear of annoying the less bellicose Liberals. The Unionist Business Committee was formed as a sounding-board for protests on this and other matters relating to the conduct of the war. Finally, after pressure from the National Union, in November 1915 Derby's scheme whereby agents of both parties were used for recruiting was accepted. But by then the Government had anyway been reconstructed to form a coalition.

This was the result of an agreement between Bonar Law and Lloyd George, subsequently imposed on Asquith, which the reluctant Prime Minister announced to the House of Commons on 17 May. The main beneficiary was Lloyd George, who, Law believed, alone had the drive to reform the sluggish supply of war munitions. Law himself was fobbed off with the minor Cabinet job of Colonial Secretary, which offended Unionist pride even as it demonstrated his own humility. In the new Cabinet of twenty-two, twelve were Liberals, one was Labour (Arthur Henderson), another (Lord Kitchener at the War Department) was non-political and eight were Unionists. These included Chamberlain, Curzon, Selborne and Balfour (already a member of the Imperial Defence Committee), who replaced the hated and, since the Dardanelles fiasco, discredited Churchill at the Admiralty.[44] This unequal and uneasy compromise was hardly a recipe for harmony, given that by now the Unionists had thirty more MPs than the Liberals, as a result of by-election victories. And indeed it could not last.

The war continued to go badly. The Government's and the Prime Minister's stock continued to fall. Carson, who had resigned from the Cabinet ostensibly over the Dardanelles, also started to look an increasingly serious threat to Law. He was now at the head of a Unionist War Committee. Conscription was the burning issue. Unionists inside and outside the Government were now totally convinced of the need for it. Asquith wriggled but eventually accepted a partial scheme (limited to unmarried men), which was introduced in January 1916. It looked and was inadequate, and Unionist pressure to expand it mounted. Asquith was humiliated in the Commons and in May had to bring in a general scheme.

In the meantime, the Dublin 'Easter Rising', in the spring of 1916, had been met with a rushed plan for implementation of Home Rule. This produced uproar in the Unionist ranks, which Bonar Law struggled to control. The plan had to be dropped. As the year went on, the multi-sided crisis gained momentum. Crucially, in November, Bonar Law himself had to face down a full-blown Unionist rebellion on a minor question relating to the sale of German assets in Nigeria. It was as Colonial Secretary that he had to answer the debate, but it was as Unionist leader that he now felt threatened. He found himself pushed into the not entirely reassuring embrace of Lloyd George.

Eventually, Law took the initiative. In joint discussions with Carson and Lloyd George it was agreed that the latter be entrusted with the chairmanship of a small group dedicated to effective pursuit of the war. The proposal was put in the form of a draft memorandum for Asquith's signature. The Prime Minister now ensured his own downfall. He at first accepted the scheme, but then, egged on by his Liberal colleagues and furious about an unpleasantly worded leak in *The Times* (for which he wrongly blamed Lloyd George), reversed his position and rejected the plan. Lloyd George immediately resigned, and Asquith accepted his resignation. Law, however, himself now under pressure from mistrustful Unionist colleagues, was not going to back down. He wrote to Asquith insisting on the original scheme. It was, therefore, Asquith who resigned.[45]

Bonar Law gave up any attempt to form a Government himself when it was clear that Asquith would not serve under him. In any case, Law now had no doubt that Lloyd George should be Prime Minister and smoothed the way for him. In the new Government, Law was Chancellor of the Exchequer and Leader of the House. He was, effectively, Deputy Prime Minister. He was also – along with Lloyd George, Curzon, Milner and Henderson – a member of the War Cabinet. Carson had been excluded in favour of Milner. The Unionists also kept Churchill out of the Cabinet altogether. Max Beaverbrook got a peerage. There was much Unionist relief.

Lloyd George's style of governing was a good deal more conducive to fighting a war than Asquith's. But it was not to everyone's taste, and it could not be described as seemly. The presence of the former proconsuls Curzon and Milner symbolized how little democracy counted in the arrangement. Lloyd George relied heavily on businessmen and press barons. He created his own personal apparatus of government. This fuelled tensions, but they only surfaced later. Indeed, during the last two years of the war the arrangements worked well. The Unionists – or at least, those who were not at the front – were both happier with Lloyd George than they had been with Asquith, and happier too that they were playing a part in decision-making. True, Lloyd George was the initiator. But he consulted and trusted Law, who acted as his sounding board. If Law was persuaded, then so too would the Unionists be, so would Parliament and, to the limited extent it mattered in wartime, so would the country.

There were disagreements. The Unionists were always on the side of greater belligerence. (They were thus especially mortified when one of their own – Lansdowne – publicly called for a negotiated peace in 1917). Unionist opinion was inclined to side with the military men against the Prime Minister in his quarrels with them. They saved Haig from dismissal. But in the end they rallied to Lloyd George, for the simple reason that they believed that he alone could ensure the war was won.[46]

As late as the summer of 1918, that happy outcome still looked a long way off. In May, prompted by accusations from the deposed Director of Military Operations, Major-General Maurice, Lloyd George and Bonar Law faced accusations of incompetence and lying. For the first and last time, Asquith divided the House against Lloyd George. The motion failed, and it hardened the Liberal split. Its timing also proved unlucky. In June and July the German offensive suddenly started to fail. Asquith's final misjudgement was to refuse to rejoin Lloyd George's Government on the return of peace.

The postponed general election, when it finally came in December 1918, was held amid celebrations of victory. There was little doubt who would be the immediate beneficiaries. There was, though, considerable doubt about what that meant for the shape of British politics.

*Bonar Law, dour, thorough, and with sufficient courage (or recklessness)
to play the political game for the very highest stakes. Law deserves Tory
gratitude because he twice saved the party from itself.*

9

1922

The year 1922 is one of unusual significance for the Conservative Party. The widespread assumption that today's '1922 Committee', consisting of all Conservative backbench MPs (but excluding ministers, as David Cameron was recently forced to recognize), commemorates that year's party rebellion is, in fact, false. The title, rather, reflects the decision of the Conservative intake resulting from the 1922 general election to organize themselves: a move which, once accepted by the whips, resulted in much better coordination of the parliamentary party.[1] The fact remains that the backbench revolt of 1922 was a milestone, comparable to the earlier upheaval that destroyed Peel on the issue of the Corn Laws in 1846 and the later rebellion that demolished Edward Heath in favour of Margaret Thatcher in 1974–5. Like these revolts, that of 1922 reshaped Conservative/Unionist politics and propelled both the party and the country in a new and hitherto largely unpredicted direction.

It was not inevitable. As the war came to an end, such an outcome did not even seem remotely likely. Conservative MPs, though now in a relative majority, were still apprehensive and defensive.[2] There was widespread acceptance that the experience of total war had transformed the country. This raised many questions about future policy, but it had a decisive impact upon arguments about the franchise. Democracy was even more of a 'leap in the dark' than the Second Reform Bill; but Conservatives accepted that the leap was now inevitable. This did not, though, prevent the party putting its own stamp on proposals.

The Conservatives would accept universal male suffrage (and women's suffrage too, for those over thirty and with property), as long as the new franchise included all the troops, and as long as some plural voting was retained. On the same usefully patriotic theme, the party sought to deny the vote to conscientious objectors. (In the end, the Act withheld the franchise from them for five years and gave the vote to all those serving in the armed forces, even if they were under 21.) The party also pressed for a scheme to reconstitute and strengthen the Lords. This failed, though that was not immediately apparent. The Conservatives' main success was in achieving a major redistribution of seats – the classic way in which the party has looked to recover any losses from widening or otherwise altering the franchise.[3]

The National Union was unhappy with some of the concessions the leaders made. Conservative MPs spoke – but did not vote – against these in the Commons. Amendments then marginally improved the deal. The most historically interesting and politically revealing disagreement came over the question of proportional representation, which was now proposed for cities. It was understandable, and in its way attractive, as an attempt to keep Labour out. For that reason, the Tory peers supported it in successive votes, as the proposals went back and forth between the two Houses. (In the end the single transferable vote was, somewhat illogically, applied to just four of the seven university constituencies.) But the Conservative Party organization was, in any case, not having proportional representation – nor even the less disruptive alternative vote system, which has since, once again, come briefly to prominence.

In the short term, the Conservative aim was protection of the business vote in urban constituencies. The National Union's priorities also reflected a deeper difference between it and the parliamentary party leadership. The party as a whole was more confident than the leaders about the future – and, as events turned out, rightly so. The first-past-the-post system would allow the Conservatives to rule alone, or as the dominant force in coalitions, for most of the twentieth century. (The great losers, by contrast, would be the Liberals, who at this juncture rejected proportional representation as a threat to party discipline: the decision would help lead to their elimination as a major political force.) There was another difference between the Conservative leadership and the rank and file. The party leaders were ready to sacrifice party interests in order to fight the threat of socialism. Grass-roots Tory opinion, more partisan and even now much less sympathetic to Lloyd George, was quite definitely not.[4]

The Representation of the People Act (1918) duly expanded the electorate from 7.7 million, in 1910, to 21.4 million. More than three-quarters of these electors had not voted before. The Conservatives were less fearful of the effects than they would have been in earlier times, and with good reason. They probably benefited from the women's vote. They certainly benefited from redistribution, which registered the effects of the continuing movement of the new middle classes out of the cities into gently sprawling suburbia. The net result was a gain of thirty seats. On top of that came the unconnected withdrawal of Sinn Fein MPs from Westminster after 1918. This was then consolidated by the Government of Ireland Act's redistribution of 1921, which permanently removed about seventy of the Conservatives' Irish Nationalist opponents from the House of Commons. These changes together established the Conservatives as the natural majority party.[5]

The December 1918 election became known as the 'Coupon Election', thanks to Asquith's description of Lloyd George's and Law's letter endorsing approved candidates as the 'Coupon'. The endorsement mattered much more to Lloyd George Liberals than to the Conservatives. Conservatives had successes where no Coupon applied, and even against the Coupon. Bonar Law and the other party senior figures had, rightly or wrongly, been convinced that they needed Lloyd George. He was still very popular in the country. But the results of the election showed the hard-headed men in the party organization that he would soon be dispensable. He had served his purpose, not just nationally but in terms of political alignment.

The Asquith Liberals were utterly crushed, down to 28 seats – Asquith lost his – and 12 per cent of the vote. Ten Coalition Labour MPs were returned. But the official Labour Party, with 63 seats and 22 per cent of the vote, was now the Conservatives' main enemy. It remained so, eating away at Lloyd George's support. The impact of Labour's success was, among other things, to prove to the Conservatives that Lloyd George could be destroyed. This in turn meant that the frustrated second rank in the Conservative hierarchy felt that they could afford to overthrow their leaders, who wanted to cling to the Coalition Prime Minister.[6]

The electoral changes of 1918 would, therefore, pose an irresolvable problem for both sets of Liberals, who anyway proved surprisingly ill equipped to campaign successfully in a mass democracy. Lloyd George's radicalism was, in theory, one possible answer to Labour. But the Labour Party was deeply rooted in the trade unions and had been left to champion labour issues for too long now to be outbid. The Liberal bedrock of Nonconformist opinion was also less important in the new mass electorate. A reunited Liberal Party could possibly have thrown in its lot with the

Conservatives in a common front against Labour. This, indeed, happened at a local level in many municipalities. But in a national choice between the Conservatives and the Liberals, each judged as the better means of resisting socialism, the Conservatives would always have the edge. In these conditions, the Liberal Party was squeezed out as a contender for power.

It was Labour which, directly and indirectly, did most of the squeezing. Its share of the vote rose from 1.8 per cent in 1900 to 33 per cent in 1923, when it secured 191 seats, enough to form a minority government. The explanation of why this happened has several elements, only some of which are relevant to the themes of this book. The war was an important factor, but probably not all-important. At one level, indeed, Labour had had a bad war, split between supporters of it (with Arthur Henderson in the Cabinet) and opponents (with Ramsay MacDonald at their head). Conscientious objectors and those who simply managed to avoid serving at the front by other means became the object of unpleasant but successful Conservative smears.

More important in the long run were the gains to Labour that flowed from the collectivization of the wartime economy, largely promoted by Lloyd George. By contrast with what occurred at the end of the Second World War, when the planned economy of war was deliberately applied to the problems of peace, the Coalition did not after 1918 go down the route of collectivism as a matter of policy. Most direct government controls were quickly dismantled. But collectivism had made headway at a deeper level – that of the workforce. Trade union membership was encouraged during the war as a means of combating the threat of wildcat stoppages and in order to mobilize resources. Union membership accordingly doubled, from four million in 1913 to more than eight million in 1919. Between a third and a half of British workers were now trade union members. Unemployment insurance was expanded. The Trade Boards Act of 1918 extended the scope of labour-management councils, setting minimum wages and regulating 'sweated labour'. At the same time, the shortage of manpower – a result of wartime losses of 600,000 killed and 1.6 million wounded – reduced the labour supply. The removal of price controls pushed up inflation. In these conditions the balance of industrial power shifted sharply in favour of unionized labour and against the employers.[7]

This helped the Labour Party, which had anyway been doing quite well in local elections in the years before the war. A condition for breakthrough was the reversal of the Osborne judgment of 1909. This, alongside the reversal of the Taff Vale judgment of 1901, was of seminal importance to the future shape of British politics on the left. Walter Osborne, who brought the case, was a branch secretary of the Amalgamated Society of Railway Servants (ASRS) and, significantly, a Liberal Party supporter. The judgment had ruled unlawful the political funds which unions had been setting up for Labour's benefit. The system was, indeed, unfair. Not only were union members compelled to contribute to a party they might not support; the Labour Party also required a pledge from its candidates that they would take its instructions. Since there was no pay for MPs this meant that Labour MPs were effectively dependent party delegates, not representatives of their constituents. The degree of short-term effect of the Osborne judgment on Labour is debatable. But it was clearly a blow to Labour hopes of encouraging more candidates to stand. Partly as a result, in the December 1910 general election the Labour Party was able to field only fifty-eight candidates.

Neither Lloyd George nor the Conservatives really wanted to reverse the Osborne judgment, knowing the likely consequences. But nor did they feel strong enough to leave matters as they were. Change, therefore, came gradually. In 1911 the House of Commons decided by budget resolution to begin the payment of MPs. In the same year the Labour party conference agreed to amend the party constitution, which had demanded that candidates abide by party decisions. Finally, in 1913, the Trade Union Act legalized the financing of political action by trade unions, provided that such payments came out of a special fund, and provided that each member had the freedom to contract out of his contribution to it, without loss of other privileges of membership. Such funds could only be established on the basis of a majority vote by the union members. This last provision never, in fact, caused any problems. The unions now won their ballots and set up funds, and the days of Labour as the other parties' poor relation were at an end.[8]

Two other developments paved the way for the rise of Labour. The first has been mentioned: the widening of the franchise. The second, ironically, was a partial reversal of those economic conditions which had led to Labour's wartime and early post-war advance. The boom turned into bust very sharply in Britain in 1920, more sharply than elsewhere. The immediate redeployment of war resources had come to an end. So had the upsurge in previously repressed consumer demand. But government policy was also important.

Contradicting the early cries for 'homes fit for heroes' were equally strident yells for retrenchment. The Rothermere press was at the front of demands for cuts. Its Anti-Waste campaign put up successful candidates at by-elections, and first the Conservatives and then Lloyd George, too, took fright. In a typically flamboyant and empty gesture, which won time but not much else, Lloyd George in 1921 appointed the all-purpose political businessman Sir Eric Geddes to wield the 'Geddes Axe'. But the hard work had already been done. Public spending was cut by no less than 75 per cent between 1918 and 1920.

As Chancellor of the Exchequer, Bonar Law had pursued orthodox financing as far as was compatible with the war effort. This meant large increases in income tax, which rose fivefold in five years. It went up again in 1919. This fiscal tightening had its effect.

But the most serious cause of the downturn was the monetary squeeze. Faced with record inflation, the authorities raised interest rates sharply to 7 per cent. Rates then remained high, despite the economic slowdown and rising unemployment, because of the Government's determination that sterling should rejoin the gold standard at the pre-war rate of $4.86. This eventually occurred, with severe consequences, in 1925. But it had also been the basis of the policy of high interest rates for the previous four years.[9] The failure of the British economy to adapt to the squeeze through lower labour costs, higher productivity or more efficient allocation of resources was the result of supply-side failings, including the growth of union power and the extension of cartels. But it was the Government, and the big employers, which received the blame.

The response was a rash of strikes, energized by a real if exaggerated input of communist ideology and agitation. What was happening abroad – the apparently inexorable outwash of waves from the Bolshevik Revolution – affected both ambitions and perceptions. In January 1919, while the German Government was suppressing its Spartacist Revolt, Britain faced two major strikes. In Belfast, strikers founded a 'soviet'. In Glasgow, 100,000 workers held the city for months, until suppressed by the military, using tanks. In 1920 and 1921 there were threatened nationwide strikes by the 'Triple Alliance' of miners, railwaymen and transport workers. In the longer term, the scares about Labour's extreme socialism proved unfounded, as the Governments of 1924 and 1929–31 showed. But this was far from clear at the time.

It was, therefore, the common concern of Conservative and Liberal politicians to keep Labour out, and the militants down. The debate about how this should be done was the first of three main issues that lay behind the highly personalized drama played out on 19 October 1922.

The second issue was the character and conduct of Lloyd George. In 1918, as noted above, the Conservatives thought they needed him. Four years later, they were anxious for him to be gone. Leading Conservatives who worked with Lloyd George by and large admired him. But he did not inspire affection, nor did he seek to do so. He was remembered by many in his earlier Radical incarnation and for his sneering Limehouse speech. He was (as he once boasted) a 'disruptive influence' – and while his disruptions were required to win the war, they quickly became less acceptable afterwards.

That said, the Conservative leadership never seriously envisaged fighting the 1918 election without him. Nor did the idea of coalition seem at all unpalatable per se. What had worked for the past two years of conflict should surely work for reconstruction. Bonar Law was the ideal partner in these circumstances. He had the standing to bring his backbenchers with him. He had a good personal and professional relationship with Lloyd George. He was humble enough to defer, but strong enough to instil respect. With Bonar Law in charge of the Conservatives, the much mooted project of 'fusion' with the Lloyd George Liberals might even have worked. In 1920 a large body of mainly newly elected Conservatives was pressing the idea. It had obvious appeal to Lloyd George himself, who also began to push the project. But when he found his Coalition Liberal colleagues objected, he quickly resiled from it – envisaging merely closer cooperation. This also provided the Conservatives with an opportunity for second thoughts. Law was never, in truth, as enthusiastic as were Churchill, Birkenhead and others, but he had backed the plan. Afterwards he observed, writing to Balfour in March 1920: 'I do not like the idea of complete fusion if it can be avoided, but I had come to think, as you had also, that it was really inevitable if the Coalition were to continue.'[10]

In any case, the moment never returned. The sudden retirement of Law from ill health a year later and his replacement by Austen Chamberlain was a blow to Lloyd George, as the Prime Minister very well understood. Even though Chamberlain quickly fell under

Lloyd George's spell, he lacked Law's qualities and his prestige in the party. A cipher was not enough.

The Coalition was by now unpopular, and the unpopularity focused heavily on Lloyd George personally. He was hardly responsible – or at least no more than his senior colleagues – for the deeper malaise. It was, rather, the association between his style of governing and the wider discontent that, as with other powerful leaders, proved so damaging. The appearance was of inordinate but incoherent activity, inconsistency and self-contradiction, and an egotistical obsession with gestures and initiatives which led nowhere. That appearance had some roots in reality, but it was also to some degree an unfair picture, because it reflected the circumstances in which Lloyd George had perforce to govern. He had on paper a huge majority; but it was fragile and unreliable and he had to shift his ground repeatedly to get his way with it. In domestic policy, he took up and then abandoned policies for housing and agricultural support: the second greatly annoyed key Conservatives, including Arthur Griffith-Boscawen, the agriculture minister, who became one of the strongest anti-coalitionists. In foreign policy, what was described as Lloyd George's 'pro-German' policy (one of moderation over war reparations) was roundly denounced by the Northcliffe press. His attempt to normalize relations and do business with Soviet Russia was suspect on the right. His European policy, by which he set great public store, failed miserably at the Genoa Conference, in April 1922, as the French continued to take a hard line on reparations; and the Germans and Russians reached a separate deal at Rapallo.[11] That year of 1922 was, indeed, to be Lloyd George's *annus horribilis*.

Despite the strains and splits in the Cabinet, the position was not yet hopeless. Lloyd George's and Austen Chamberlain's errors, however, made it so.[12] The 1922 Honours List and the scandal that followed brought into the public gaze Lloyd George's use of (what amounted to) the sale of political honours to reward supporters. He was not the first to do it. But he did it with abandon and, apparently, without shame. Of course, lacking other means of financial support, he needed the money. But it confirmed in public eyes his reputation as a crook. The moral disgust felt by his severest critics – such as Stanley Baldwin – must not be forgotten when explaining Lloyd George's destruction.

The Prime Minister's high-handed threatening of Turkey with war, as Turkish troops advanced on the allied base at Chanak, near the Dardanelles, also caused great unease. Traditionally pro-Turkish Conservatives were angry at Lloyd George's championing of Greece in any case. Many more suspected that he wanted a crisis to improve his standing and ward off political trouble. The Foreign Secretary, Lord Curzon – a dangerous enemy at this juncture – was furious, and had to go to Paris to try and sort out the diplomatic mess. The single worst blow, however, because it highlighted the issue on which the Coalition was most at odds with the Conservative right, was delivered by the assassination, on the doorstep of his house in London on 22 June, of Sir Henry Wilson, the former Chief of the Imperial General Staff – murdered by two Irish Republican terrorists.

Ireland played a significant and continuing role in alienating the Coalition from hardline Unionists. Lloyd George's policy seemed to veer waywardly and unpredictably between compromise and repression. The repression, by use of the notorious Black and Tan auxiliaries in 1920–1, horrified even unflinching supporters of the Union, and finally discredited British rule in the South. But it was the compromises that inflicted most political pain. In particular, the decision to negotiate with the IRA in 1921, in which Birkenhead became closely involved, did the Coalition serious harm. The results – the treaty of 1921, the creation of the Irish Free State, the split in IRA ranks and resulting civil war, followed by de facto acceptance of the separation of Ulster – can probably be described as a conditional success, at least from the British point of view.[13] But

Lloyd George's wider achievement was secured at a political price which he himself could not afford.

Above all, it was Ireland that prompted the return of an apparently healthy and rested Bonar Law to front-line politics. Law had reluctantly supported the Irish treaty, though later, in the wake of Wilson's assassination, he openly regretted it. His first act of public dissent from Coalition policy was a letter of 7 October to *The Times*, criticizing policy in the Chanak episode, in which he noted that Britain 'cannot act as the policeman of the world'.[14] It was a signal, perhaps unwitting, perhaps not, of his availability.

The third issue underlying the fall of the Coalition, however, was the failed relationship between the Conservative leadership and the rest of the party. This too began to fall apart in the summer of 1922. Chamberlain had succeeded to the leadership on Law's withdrawal without opposition, though without much enthusiasm. He was chosen because he had waited a long time and because Birkenhead, Curzon, Salisbury (now emerging as the diehards' champion) and Derby were all peers. Events two years later would show that being a peer did not automatically rule a candidate out. But being in the Commons certainly helped Chamberlain now. He handed over the Exchequer to Robert Horne and became Leader of the House and Lord Privy Seal. One other factor helped. This was the false idea that Chamberlain was, as both family name and reputation as a hardline tariff reformer suggested, a strong-minded politician. The death of his father in 1914 had allowed him to be his own man. And this was not an improvement. He had not mellowed, but he had softened. This was not widely grasped. He was in awe of Lloyd George, and he was a coalitionist by conviction rather than, like Law, by circumstance. Indeed, his behaviour from the beginning of his short leadership suggested that he had a profound distaste for the Conservatives on the back benches and in the National Union, and a particular animus against the diehards. It was two months before he addressed Tory backbenchers at all, and then only as a part of a wider Coalition gathering. He attended only a tiny number of regional party meetings. He took apparent delight in publicly scolding those he considered were culpably rocking the Coalition boat. His manner, which he may have thought dignified, was in reality extremely rude. In June 1921, for example, he declared: 'Those men [i.e. his own MPs] who at the present time would deliberately break up a national coalition and a national government in face of all the difficulties, foreign and domestic, with which we are confronted, would deserve ill of their countrymen, and would meet with condemnation at the hands of their fellow countrymen.'[15] This was foolish, because of its tone. It was unfair, because those who objected to the Irish policy did so for patriotic reasons, whether misguided or not. Finally, it was inaccurate. Even at the fateful 1922 meeting, which sealed Chamberlain's and Lloyd George's fate, the critics were not ruling out a coalition after an election; they were objecting to an election fought as a coalition, particularly one with Lloyd George at the head of it.

Austen Chamberlain neither reassured in Cabinet nor performed well in the Commons. Above all, he allowed himself to become too closely involved in Lloyd George's Irish policy, which was anathema to a section of his backbenchers. On this matter he personally held moderate and somewhat muddled views. But it was widely assumed that he was cast in his father's extreme Unionist mould, and that therefore he was now being weak or opportunistic. This helped destroy the reputation for honesty that was his main strength. So did his closeness to Churchill and, especially, Birkenhead. Indeed, Birkenhead's role in what transpired can hardly be overstated.

F. E. Smith might have become leader of the party. But he had decided to jump off the *cursus honorum* and plump, as Birkenhead, for the Lord Chancellorship instead. He was, indeed, a superb Lord Chancellor, a great reforming law officer. But when he realized what he had sacrificed he increasingly let himself go. He began to drink a great deal more, and as he grew older, unlike his closest friend Winston Churchill, he just could not hold it.[16] He was still brilliant, but now also dangerous, out of control; able to run rings around the rest of the party leadership, but ever more distrusted and disliked by most Conservatives.

Churchill's moving posthumous portrait of him is embellished, as was Churchill's wont. One wonders whether even F.E. would appreciate the suggestion that 'he had all the canine virtues in a remarkable degree – courage, fidelity, vigilance, love of the chase'. And could he have read without a smile that he had been a 'sober minded statesman'? But Churchill was right when he observed: 'The idea of a national party or government always appealed to [F.E.]. Indeed, it excited him.'[17]

Birkenhead, like Churchill and, to some extent, Curzon, believed that brains and talent – particularly their own – should be rewarded. They were, to this extent, natural coalitionists, where the coalition represented the best people, a coalition of all the talents employed within a Caesarist framework. (Curzon retained the instincts and ambitions of a party man to a greater extent, as his last-minute defection from the Coalitionist leadership confirmed.) Lloyd George's willingness to cut corners, his preference for playing against the system, his delight in the unconventional option, his isolation from inhibiting party connections, all made him the perfect leader around which such a group could assemble. Birkenhead, though, was its ideologue and propagandist. To a large extent he was also its undoing.

It was, it seems, Birkenhead's idea to push for an early election, straight after the diplomatic success of the Irish treaty, so as to catch out the Coalition's opponents. It was a typically bold wheeze, and Lloyd George was also greatly attracted by the prospect. They managed to persuade the rest of the Cabinet. Only Chamberlain stood out against a dissolution in January 1922. He was rightly worried about his party's reaction. But in his inconsequential fashion he hid behind the fact that it was for the Prime Minister – not for him, Chamberlain, though he was leader of the majority party – to make the decision. Chamberlain then wrote to a number of party colleagues, including his brother Neville, seeking their views. The variety of responses allowed him to continue to sit on the fence. The consultation exercise did, however, unleash passions which were already boiling on the subject of going into an election tied to Lloyd George.

A debate broke out in the press in which, in defiance of Austen Chamberlain and the Coalition ministers, the party's principal agent, Sir Malcolm Fraser, and the party chairman, Sir George Younger, campaigned against an early election or any agreement with Lloyd George. Younger sent a tendentious letter out to the constituencies and received the negative response he wanted. The replies were then forwarded to the unhappy and forlorn party leader. This stopped the early election ploy in its tracks. Lloyd George thought about resigning but opted to carry on.[18] Unfortunately for the Coalition, the political atmosphere during the summer and early autumn of 1922 became – as described above – markedly worse.

An immediate election had apparently been ruled out. But sooner rather than later one would have to be faced. No progress was made on the issue of Lords reform, which continued to agitate the party. Disgruntlement grew in the lower ranks of the Government. Junior ministers, who in a one-party administration might have hoped for promotion and who, at the same time, were close to backbench sentiment, started to act together. At two meetings with Chamberlain they demanded assurances that a Conservative majority after the next election would result in a Conservative Prime Minister – but in vain. This request could hardly be described as disloyal, but Chamberlain would not budge. A third meeting with Chamberlain, Balfour and Birkenhead, held in F.E.'s rooms in the Lords, was a disaster. Chamberlain was remote, Balfour irrelevant and Birkenhead insultingly dismissive.[19]

It was not just the junior ministers who gave Chamberlain the benefit of their objections. A meeting of more than seventy back-benchers gathered, and a delegation of Samuel Hoare, Ernest Pretyman and George Lane-Fox went to see Chamberlain on 18 October. He was visibly shocked by some of the names on the list of objectors, but his response was (in Hoare's words) 'completely wooden'.[20]

By letting Birkenhead take the lead, Chamberlain was quickly using up all his remaining support. Nor did it stop there. The two adventurers of the Coalition, Birkenhead and Churchill, now resolved to take the initiative and revive the idea of an early election. The plan was to avoid the Conservative party conference being dominated by criticism of the Coalition. They would thus bounce the Conservatives into closing ranks behind their leaders. Resolve would be enough to win, and Birkenhead and Churchill, whatever they lacked in judgement, had no lack of resolve. They certainly managed to bounce Chamberlain, who, despite all the representations amounting to barely veiled threats which he had received from the party, now fell into line. This misjudgement was crucial. From now on, he was committed to a course of action which his party would not support.

The question remains why? Perhaps he was genuinely convinced that without Lloyd George the party was lost. As he told one correspondent: 'Those who think that the Conservative ... Party, standing as such and disowning its Liberal allies, could return with a working majority are living in a fool's paradise.'[21] Events would shortly demonstrate who was the fool. And perhaps, in the end, that is sufficient explanation. Austen Chamberlain also thought – or had been persuaded to think – that he and his colleagues were in-dispensable. He complacently told Birkenhead, animator of the plot, that he had decided to seize the initiative by calling a meeting of Conservative MPs, 'to tell them bluntly that they must either

Disraeli's Cabinet in 1876: *left to right, standing*, Derby, Cairns, Sir Stafford Northcote and Gathorne-Hardy; *seated*, Disraeli and the Marquess of Salisbury.

RD DERBY LORD CAIRNS SIR S NORTHCOTE GATHORNE HARDY

EARL BEACONSFIELD

MARQUIS OF SALISBU

COPYRIGHT

The House of Commons in 1878 (*above*): Northcote, Chancellor of the Exchequer, is at the Dispatch Box. This year saw the culmination of a series of successes for Disraeli. In 1875 he had bought a controlling interest in the Suez Canal company, in the face of some French suspicion (*left*); the following year he had successfully seen the title Empress of India conferred on the Queen (*with Disraeli, far right*); and in 1878 his achievements at the Congress of Berlin were toasted at a celebratory banquet (*right*).

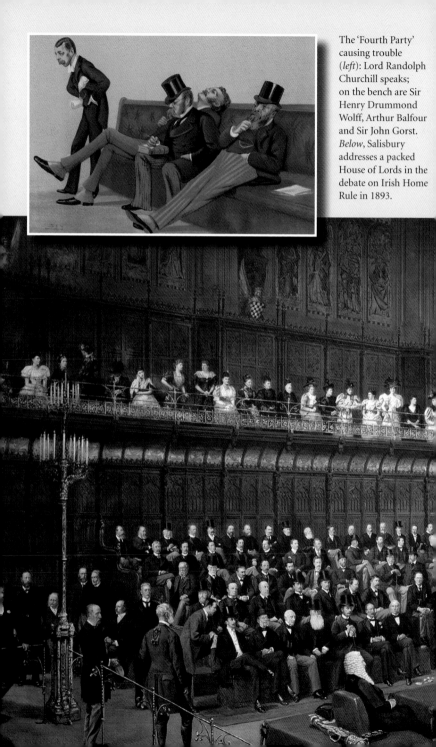

The 'Fourth Party' causing trouble (*left*): Lord Randolph Churchill speaks; on the bench are Sir Henry Drummond Wolff, Arthur Balfour and Sir John Gorst. *Below*, Salisbury addresses a packed House of Lords in the debate on Irish Home Rule in 1893.

Left: a Primrose League enamelled badge from *c.*1889, inscribed 'PL Imperium et Libertas'. Right: Captain 'Skipper' Richard Middleton, legendary Tory chief agent under Salisbury.

Joseph Chamberlain (*top left*) regales an audience with the case for tariff reform in his native Birmingham in 1903. Already propaganda was on the move, as in this Conservative Party poster van on the election trail in 1906 (*above*). In 1910, blaming free trade for unemployment was a favourite Tory theme (*bottom left*).

Two Conservative orators. Balfour (*above*) poses indoors, c.1900, and F. E. Smith (*below*) outdoors – at an anti-Home Rule rally in Ulster in 1912.

Above: The Great War Coalition Cabinet – notably (*counting from left to right*) Austen Chamberlain (2), Winston Churchill (4), Bonar Law (5), Kitchener (6), Asquith (7), Lloyd George (9); Lord Curzon (*far right*); Balfour and Lord Lansdowne (*seated, foreground*). *Below*: Balfour (*second from left*), as Foreign Secretary, arrives in Washington in 1917, after US entry into the war.

follow our advice or do without us', in which case 'they must find their own chief and form a government *at once*. They would be in a d—d fix!'[22]

Despite the naïveté which this assertion reveals, a certain amount of cunning went into the arrangements. Chamberlain had reason to think that he would be supported by leading parliamentary figures. He was not to know that Curzon would jump ship. Of the more senior ministers, only Baldwin had openly expressed opposition to Lloyd George. Chamberlain – or perhaps Birkenhead – seems to have timed the meeting to coincide with the predicted absence abroad of some of the right-wing rebels. He also excluded non-Government peers, to minimize the troublesome elements.

Most cynically, Chamberlain delayed the meeting to a time when the result of the Newport by-election would be known. An anti-Coalition Conservative was standing against a Liberal, and it was expected that Labour would, therefore, win the seat. The party in London clearly did not understand much about the politics of Newport, or it would have grasped that even the Liberal candidate was hardly a supporter of the Coalition and that local issues were more important than national ones. But Austen Chamberlain's own attitude is damningly clear from a letter he wrote at the time to Sir Malcolm Fraser at Conservative Central Office:

> Newport is giving us a beautiful illustration of the results of a split ... but ... we must not allow Newport to land us in a general engagement all along the line. I should say, therefore, in reply to your enquiry: Do the least that you can without making a breach with our Conservative friends. They are going to be beaten whatever you do, but I do not want them to attribute their defeat to you. I want you to be in a position to point the real moral when the election is over and the seat is lost.[23]

As David Cameron discovered during the Oldham East and

Saddleworth by-election in January 2011, when Central Office seemed to be under instruction from the leadership to help the Coalition Liberal at the expense of the Tory, this sort of tactic creates a bad impression. The difference is that in 2011 the Tory lost (though the Liberal did not win). Another difference is, of course, that Mr Cameron is more skilful at covering his tracks, and more skilful generally than Austen Chamberlain.

In any case, like everything else that Austen Chamberlain touched at this time, the ploy went disastrously wrong. The independent Conservative won with a large margin. In these circumstances, the Conservative Party assembled to decide its own future, and its leaders' fate.

The line-up of forces was well enough known before the meeting. It was bound to be dangerous for Chamberlain and the Coalitionist ministers. They had not just the diehards but most moderates and the party chiefs against them. They were, on paper, in a minority. On their side, though, they had the prestige of leadership, the traditional deference of Conservative MPs and fear of splitting the party. But, one by one, these remaining advantages fell away.

Chamberlain's conviction that he was irreplaceable was, in fact, already subject to one gnawing doubt – that Bonar Law might return to challenge him. 'Bonar Law tries on the crown,' he had earlier observed, 'but can't make up his mind to attempt to seize it.'[24] This was only half true. Law did not really want to return, despite his disagreements with the Coalition. But his sense of duty, sharpened by the urgings of advisers like Beaverbrook, forced him towards it. He felt much recovered, but he was still not physically strong. The decisive pressure was exerted by the party organizers, who would not authorize another joint electoral ticket with Lloyd George, despaired of Chamberlain, and looked for salvation in Law. Bonar Law was visited by a number of Conservative politicians the day before the meeting, and he finally resolved to appear. But still, on the morning of the meeting (Thursday, 19 October), when Sir

George Younger arrived he found him at home in his carpet slippers in front of the fire. 'I'm not coming,' said Law. Younger prevailed. He helped Law on with his boots, and they departed for the Carlton Club.[25]

The meeting was surprisingly good-humoured. Bonar Law arrived early and was cheered loudly. Chamberlain and Birkenhead then arrived and were not. They were, instead, the victim of a prank. Someone asked a Club servant to place two large glasses of brandy on the table in front of them. Chamberlain eyed the liquid through his monocle, gave a start, and, reaching for a chair, hid his tumbler behind it. Birkenhead took his glass – and downed it.[26]

Chamberlain, in the chair, now opened the proceedings with an over-long, unpersuasive speech, reiterating his view that it was essential to keep up the Coalition to stop Labour. The tone was hectoring. But the worst aspect was that it seemed to rule out the compromise that most Conservative MPs would have wanted. This was fighting the election as a separate entity, then deciding afterwards whether to enter into coalition again (which, at the time, seemed probable) – and, in that event, doing so under a Conservative Prime Minister, namely Chamberlain, rather than under Lloyd George. Chamberlain's harangue left open the awful prospect of a continuing Coalition led by Lloyd George and even fusion with the Lloyd George Liberals. The speech was badly received.

Baldwin spoke next. He was not, during his long career, to acquire much of a reputation for courage, but now his intervention was brave, because he knew that it might finish him. His short speech may or may not have been decisive in the outcome – analysis suggests that the great majority had made up their minds before the meeting.[27] But the speech was loudly applauded, as summing up the frustrations of the meeting, and it propelled Baldwin himself into the ranks of the party's leaders. Playing cleverly on Birkenhead's recent description of Lloyd George as a 'dynamic force', Baldwin noted the dangers of such dynamism. This particular 'dynamic force' had, he observed, smashed the Liberal Party and threatened to smash the Conservative Party too.[28]

The genie of revolt was now well and truly uncorked. The name alone of the next speaker, Ernest Pretyman, showed how far resentment of Chamberlain had gone, since Pretyman – who now proposed a motion urging that the Conservatives resume independent action – had been Chamberlain's own proposer for the leadership. Chamberlain could have accepted the motion and still left open the possibility of a future Coalition. But he signalled that he would not. Lane-Fox seconded the motion. Balfour later spoke in support of Chamberlain, to little effect.

It was Bonar Law whose intervention ensured that Chamberlain's stubbornness proved fatal. Law's was not technically a good speech. It rambled somewhat. His voice was weak. But in his concerns for retaining the unity and identity of the party he spoke sincerely and movingly. He warned that the party faced the risk of another schism, as under Peel. He drew a conclusion which does much to explain his own tactics in earlier years. He believed that it was crucial that the hard-liners should not be left in charge of the rump of the party – which, whatever happened, would be the continuing party – while all the leaders abandoned it. The party had to come first. With that low-key brutality which was often effective and which its victims (not least the thin-skinned Chamberlain) never forgot, Law added: 'The Party elects a Leader, and that Leader chooses the policy, and if the Party does not like it, they have to get another Leader.'[29]

Chamberlain was furious with Law. But he was apoplectic about the final speaker, and justly so, for it was none other than his own Chief Whip, Leslie Wilson, who now supported Law against the leadership.

Chamberlain was given one last chance. The suggestion was made that the meeting adjourn and the leadership be given time to come up with a compromise. But Chamberlain refused. He insisted on a vote. And he lost: 187 voted for Pretyman's motion, and 88 against.

Chamberlain at once resigned as party leader. As soon as he heard the result, Lloyd George also resigned as Prime Minister. The King sent for Bonar Law. But Law insisted that before he could take office he must be re-elected as Conservative Party leader. This was in recognition of the extraordinary circumstances, and of the existence of other potential leaders – Derby, Curzon, Salisbury. But it signified, above all, Law's understanding that the formal support of the parliamentary party was crucial to his wider political legitimacy. The Conservative Party was not as yet democratic in its procedures. But without adumbrating any new doctrine, the Carlton Club meeting had imposed a new quasi-democratic reality, one which no leader would be able to overlook. At a further party meeting held on Monday, 23 October at the Hotel Cecil, Law was proposed by Curzon, seconded by Baldwin, and duly elected by unanimity. Later that day he took office as Prime Minister.

Bonar Law had now twice saved the Conservative Party, first from fatal marginalization before the war, by skilfully exploiting the Ulster question, and second from fatal division four years after it, by breaking with Lloyd George and his Coalition. Such services were more appreciated at the time than later. But Law's reputation has suffered, above all, from the fact that he died so soon after rising to the top, thus becoming, in Asquith's unpleasant expression, 'the Unknown Prime Minister'.[30] In fact, Law was probably not well suited temperamentally to the task of running the country's government, which requires more than instinct and diligence. In any case, he now had a difficult hand to play.

Within hours of the Carlton Club meeting, 13 ministers (including 9 Cabinet ministers) had signed an agreement supporting Chamberlain. At a dinner at Chamberlain's house at the end of November, 49 Conservative MPs attended – a notable shrinkage, though, from the 88 Coalitionists at the Carlton meeting. Some Tories continued to be besotted with Lloyd George, but not many. In any case, it was not the backbenchers who presented the problem. It was the unreconciled former leaders. These, not least Chamberlain, had high hopes that the revolt against them would be undone by an imminent general election. If there was once more need for a coalition, who better than the old coalitionist Conservatives to dominate it? Nor was this mere opportunism. Even someone like Birkenhead, the blackness of whose moral character was now widely accepted, could plausibly argue that the need to resist socialism was paramount, and that a union between the non-socialist parties was required for it. The trouble was, first, that the dislodged coalitionists, notably Birkenhead, did not argue plausibly but, rather, behaved extremely badly, and second that the Conservatives then won a healthy majority at the general election.

Birkenhead let himself go in public utterances which were doubt-less enjoyable – and still read well – but whose effects were wholly counter-productive. He savaged Leslie Wilson. He rebuked Curzon. (He did not hold a grudge against Bonar Law; but Lloyd George sufficiently summed up the coalitionists' view when he ill-advisedly described Law on the campaign trail as 'honest up to the verge of simplicity'.) While Churchill spoke of 'a Government of the second eleven', Birkenhead warned that Law would be con-fronting 'first class problems' with 'second class brains'. Lord Robert Cecil's riposte that second class brains were better than 'second class character' struck home. Birkenhead also belittled Wilson and Younger as the Conservative Party's 'Cabin Boys'. But he was on his weakest ground in the role of principled victim. When F.E. boasted, in a continuation of the maritime metaphor, that though he had lost the Woolsack, he was 'still the Captain of [his] own soul', some wag put round the clubs the reply that this was 'a small command of which no-one will want to deprive him'.[31]

Law's problems, though, were principally caused not by Birkenhead's tantrums but by the fact that the decapitation of the Conservative Party left him with a limited number of candidates for senior posts in his Government. Law was not a skilful constructor of Cabinets. His parliamentary private secretary J. C. C. Davidson drew up a list of names and posts to be filled, which Law held in open view while asking his embarrassed potential colleagues whether they might like this post, or possibly that.[32] Baldwin was rewarded for his former service, becoming Chancellor of the Exchequer. As he had been Financial Secretary to the Treasury, it was a natural appointment. But Law had doubts – which were, indeed, amply fulfilled. Baldwin's clumsy handling of the vexed question of negotiating the interest on American war debt would almost lead to Law's own resignation, which would have been disastrous.[33] Curzon stayed as Foreign Secretary and, naturally, altogether dominated his portfolio. Derby took the War Office. Of the party hard-liners only Salisbury entered the Cabinet, as Lord President. The main obvious weaknesses – a recurrence of those which had plagued the Conservatives for much of the previous century – were a lack of high-profile Commons performers and an excess of peers. The less obvious, but much more serious, weakness was the state of the Prime Minister's health.

Bonar Law had defused two traditional Tory time bombs – Ireland, by refusing to re-open the matter of the treaty, and protection, by restating the pledge that there would be no food taxes without a second general election. Polling day was set for 15 November. The Conservatives, like the other non-socialist parties, offered a dearth of policies. Law emphasized the need for 'tranquillity', at once a rebuke to Lloyd George's unsettling activism and a warning of the socialist threat. The latter offered an excellent opportunity for red-baiting and many Conservatives sank to the opportunity with relish.[34] Oliver Locker-Lampson, for example, Chamberlain's private secretary, toured his Birmingham constituency brandishing his mascot of a 'Bolshie' hanging from a miniature gibbet.

There was not, in fact, much Conservative national campaigning, nor indeed much money, because the party treasurer thought it should all go to the coalitionists. But the other parties hardly fought distinguished campaigns either. After his gaffe about Law's 'simplicity', Lloyd George went uncharacteristically quiet. Any difficulties with the press proved equally manageable. *The Times* was purchased at the beginning of the campaign with Astor money and henceforth backed the Conservatives reliably. Law's best friend Beaverbrook controlled the *Daily Express*.[35] The Rothermere papers were problematic, because of the eccentric arrogance of their owner. Lord Rothermere visited Law to demand an earldom for himself and a Cabinet post for his son as the price of his support. Law was disgusted and refused, but Rothermere's papers supported the Conservatives all the same.[36]

Malcolm Fraser ensured that Conservative candidates stood against all the Liberal ex-ministers whenever he saw a chance of winning. This was a matter less of sweet revenge than of cold calculation, because the party was pessimistic about gaining an overall majority: every seat counted. The organizers need not have worried. The Conservatives won 344 seats out of 615, an overall majority of 75, obtaining 38 per cent of the vote in what had effectively been a four-party election. Labour was close behind in terms of share of the vote with 30 per cent, and won 142 seats. Lloyd George's National Liberals won 62 seats with 12 per cent and the Asquith Liberals 54 with 18 per cent.

The Government which got down to work in the New Year did not show much of the vigour that a substantial election victory should bestow. There was the overblown dispute between Law and the rest of the Cabinet over war debt. There was the inevitable sense of let-down which follows a campaign where policy questions have been largely avoided. Above all, there was mounting evidence that Law was gravely ill. He could no longer even speak in the House. A period of absence and recuperation was inevitable. On 1 May he sailed with his son to the Mediterranean on what was to be a restorative cruise. His health then worsened further. Back in Paris, Law's doctor, summoned by Beaverbrook, confirmed terminal throat cancer. On Saturday, 19 May Law arrived back at Victoria Station. His resignation must quickly follow and the issue of the succession – and of the outgoing Prime Minister's recommendation to the sovereign – must be resolved. This proved problematic.

Mister Baldwin

LOW

*Judged as party leader, Baldwin was by some measures among
the most successful the Conservative Party has had. He was
also – as suggested in this depiction by David Low in 1933 –
probably the most reassuring. But ambitious claims for his
statesmanship are less easy to defend.*

10

BALDWIN'S PARTY

Bonar Law declined to recommend any particular successor to the King. His desire to leave the matters to others is understandable. He was in pain, depressed and dying. But what was his underlying preference? His thoughts are not easy to penetrate. In any case, his career was full of indecision, so perhaps he was genuinely undecided.

The two obvious candidates were Curzon and Baldwin. Bonar Law certainly had his doubts about both. He had had plenty of experience of Curzon's quirks and bad behaviour. On one occasion, Law was wryly amused when an indignant Curzon protested that the French Interior Minister had refused to stop the trams in Clermont-Ferrand to allow him to sleep at night.[1] Less amusing, no doubt, was the insensitive letter which Curzon wrote to Law – now mortally stricken with cancer, though still not resolved to resign – reciting his claims to the premiership at length, with indignation, and with no apparent sympathy. On the other hand, disliking Curzon, which was easy, was not the same as disregarding him, which was hard. When Law departed for what was expected to be a restorative foreign tour, he had appointed Curzon his deputy, and done so in terms suggesting he considered him his successor.[2]

The key factor weighing against Curzon in the mind of the King, his advisers, and some senior Conservatives – perhaps including Law – was that Labour, led from the Commons, was now the main opposition party, and Curzon was a peer. To have the Prime Minister in the Lords, while constitutionally proper, could also prove constitutionally dangerous.

Stanley Baldwin, though, in all probability did not inspire Law's confidence either. He had, it is true, introduced a well-received budget. But Law must have doubted his basic competence. He could hardly forget that what he considered Baldwin's bungling of debt negotiations in the United States had recently almost precipitated his own resignation. Baldwin had not, indeed, greatly distinguished himself in anyone's eyes. He had entered the Commons at the relatively late age of forty-one, succeeding his father as MP for Bewdley in 1908. He background was in the family firm, a successful ironworks. (This would in future years be useful to his reputation: he made much play of the paternalistic management and good labour relations in Baldwins Ltd.) Baldwin delivered sensible and low-key speeches in the House. He had later risen up the hierarchical ladder on two occasions, mainly because other, better options were absent. First, with many MPs at the front, and thus a depleted pool of candidates, he had been chosen by Bonar Law, at this juncture Chancellor of the Exchequer, as his PPS in 1916. Later he became Financial Secretary to the Treasury, first jointly, and then in 1919 uniquely. It was in that capacity that he made an initiative which helped enhance his standing, but which might also have led to doubts about his judgement. Baldwin wrote to *The Times* – the letter was signed simply 'F.S.T.' – to announce that he was giving 20 per cent of his wealth (£120,000) to the Exchequer to help reduce the public debt incurred by the war.

The sum would purchase £150,000 of the new war loan, which he then sent to the Government for cancellation. 'F.S.T.' urged others to follow his lead, not just as a patriotic gesture, and to avoid the necessity of a capital levy, but also to defy what he called 'a wave of extravagance and materialism' sweeping the country. It was sincere. It turned out in the long run to be good politics. But as a practical initiative it was quite useless. Good example is not always contagious. Only some £500,000 in total was ever raised.[3]

Baldwin's next lucky break – though he had also earned it and courageously exploited it – was the role he played as a junior Cabinet minister at the time of the revolt of 1922. If there was ever a member of Churchill's 'second eleven' who benefited from the top-slicing of the Conservative Party, it was Baldwin. Simply because of that calculation and its consequences, in 1923 Baldwin was definitely *papabile*.

Crucially, Baldwin, for all his dreamy idealism, was guileful, which Curzon was not. Baldwin's role in the business of Law's non-recommendation is obscure; but on the basis of circumstantial evidence, and by application of the not always reliable principle of *cui bono?*, it was probably important. Law's PPS, J. C. C. Davidson, and his wife, Mimi, were Baldwin's closest and lifelong friends. Davidson now drafted a memorandum for the King which was taken to reflect Law's wishes. It did not have and did not formally claim Law's authority. But this was assumed at the Palace. The memorandum strongly endorsed Baldwin.[4] On top of that, Curzon's one-time friend but now enemy, the acidulous Balfour, also advised in Baldwin's favour. (On returning from the Palace he was asked by one lady if 'dear George' would become Prime Minister. 'No,' he replied. 'Dear George will not.')[5]

Curzon was at his country house, Montacute, on Whit Monday when he received Law's letter informing him of his resignation. Having grandly but impractically declined to install a telephone, he could not ring anyone to find out how the land lay. He thus simply assumed, when he subsequently received a telegram from the monarch's private secretary, Lord Stamfordham, summoning him to London, that the post of Prime Minister was his. He spent the train journey making plans for his ministry, greeting the press with a confident smile at Paddington. It was not to be. By the time Curzon actually met Stamfordham the following day, Baldwin had been chosen. Historians have generally lauded the decision. One, for example, goes so far as to judge that the choice 'would prove to be one of the best ever made for the party's shape and development'.[6] There is, however, another possible view.

Curzon had had a far more distinguished career. He was highly intelligent and industrious, neither of which could be said of Baldwin. Curzon would probably have been a better choice on internal party grounds as well, because he was better equipped to bring back Austen Chamberlain and the other coalitionists. He would not have been so lacking in self-confidence as to precipitate an unnecessary general election, which was then lost. Above all, he had a grasp of and feel for foreign affairs, which Baldwin disastrously lacked.[7]

Of course, Curzon would soon be dead, so the speculations of virtual history have limited value. But they do cast light on the wider, more important question of Baldwin's significance. His most recent biographer warns that 'more nonsense has been written about him than about any other modern Prime Minister'.[8] This is because Baldwin's reputation has been the subject of revisionism and counter-revisionism, processes themselves reflecting the ebb and flow of arguments about appeasement (considered in the following chapter). Baldwin was also, like Neville Chamberlain, scorched in the glorious fires of Winston Churchill's wartime and post-war reputation. Churchill himself contributed to this singeing, famously noting under the entry for Baldwin in the index of *The Gathering Storm*, the first volume of his war memoirs:

'confesses putting party before country'. Churchill's observations in the body of the text were, by contrast, nuanced and full of insight. In a shrewd comparison with Neville Chamberlain, he notes:

> Stanley Baldwin was the wiser, more comprehending personality, but without executive capacity. He was largely detached from foreign and military affairs. He knew little of Europe, and disliked what he knew. He had a deep knowledge of British party politics, and represented in a broad way some of the strengths and many of the infirmities of our Island race ... He had a genius for waiting upon events.[9]

Publicly, after 1940 Churchill treated Baldwin with respect. But whereas the regard he expressed for Chamberlain was real, if conditional, it is clear that any expressed esteem for Baldwin was not real at all. Churchill was not ungenerous. He contributed to Baldwin's memorial. At its unveiling he spoke of him as 'the most formidable politician I have ever known'.[10] But the epithet is ambiguous. To James Stuart, his Chief Whip, Churchill provided a useful gloss: 'Baldwin', said Churchill, 'was the best Party manager the Tories ever had.'[11] Churchill's private jokes were also revelatory. Informed that the Luftwaffe had bombed one of Baldwin's factories, he remarked: 'Very ungrateful of them.'[12]

A minor contribution towards the restoration of Baldwin's reputation has, correspondingly, been made by those critical of the Churchill legend. It is, of course, established that Winston Churchill used his writing to magnify his own achievement and, when necessary, belittle that of others. In this he was assisted by the fact that none of the three prime ministers of the 1930s (Ramsay MacDonald, Stanley Baldwin and Neville Chamberlain) wrote his memoirs.[13] Churchill was further assisted, it must be added, by the fact that he wrote so well. More specifically, and of some importance in the rather closed world of Conservative myth-makers and debunkers, there are those who have their own reasons for dislike of Churchill enthusiasts. John Major, on becoming Prime Minister in 1991, attempted to project a more consensual identity than his predecessor, Margaret Thatcher (a well-known worshipper at the Churchill shrine), by, for example, praising Baldwin's 'capacity . . . to still a nation that was socially adrift'.[14]

Reconciliation is, indeed, the foundation on which Baldwin and his admirers have based his claims to greatness. Assessing the soundness of these claims – alongside Baldwin's more evident, though not indisputable, reputation for astuteness as a party politician – is the purpose of much of what follows. But it is worth observing, beforehand, just how far-reaching the claims for his statesmanship in domestic policy are.

As already noted, Baldwin, though cunning, was, in his way, an idealist. His ideals were shared by large numbers of well-intentioned men inside and outside politics. This made them comprehensible and potent. They were, in their origin, a reaction to the harrowing experience of the Great War. On learning of the Armistice, Baldwin had observed: 'I find three impressions strongest: thankfulness that the slaughter is stopped, the thought of the millions of dead and the vision of Europe in ruins; and now to work. Pick up the bits.'[15]

Reconstruction and restoration, on a new social basis, was the guiding idea. But it did not offer much useful direction in public policy. At this point, politics entered. Baldwin's politics consisted of what would today be considered a mildly left-of-centre paternalism, though in his day they were more difficult to classify – which, arguably, helped. Reflecting on the much-criticized concessions he made to avoid the General Strike (which, of course, he did not in the end avoid), Baldwin observed: 'I still think we were right in buying off the strike in 1925, though it proved once more the cost of teaching democracy. *Democracy has arrived at a gallop in*

England and I feel all the time it is a race for life. Can we educate them before the crash comes?[16]

In one sense this was just stating the obvious. Baldwin was the first Conservative leader to cope over any length of time (Law having so quickly succumbed) with both universal suffrage – votes at twenty-one for both sexes were finally introduced by the Conservatives in 1928 – and Labour as the alternative party of government. The idea that democracy can function only if the electorate is educated for it is a distinctively Conservative notion, with overtones of Disraeli and Salisbury – and, even more pessimistically, of Burke. What was unusual about Baldwin's version was that it led him to conclude first, that a series of concessions from the distinctive Conservative position were required and, second, that the process could not at all be hurried – indeed, that in no positive sense could it even be led. In his old age he justified his approach – in this case over appeasement – by observing: 'The English will only learn by example.'[17]

The question arose from this intuitive view of what was and was not politically possible: who was to judge, and how? There was no longer a traditional, educated élite with the power to do so. Democratic institutions were untested under the new conditions. Some guiding principle was required, be it intellectual or spiritual. For Baldwin, who was not at all intellectual but was in his way extremely spiritual, the answer was clear. It lay in his own vocation to be the authentic voice of England.

The comparison is sometimes made between Baldwin and Salisbury.[18] Both had conservative dispositions and both were devout Christians. But the differences are more important by far than the similarities. For Salisbury, his pessimism was a spur to action and his faith was the ground of humility. For Baldwin, the first played to his lethargy and the second to a large, if well-disguised, degree of messianic illusion. Baldwin was, for his day, an accomplished mass media performer on radio and newsreel. He was temperamentally well equipped for the 'fireside chat', and he practised the technique. But he also felt – as no previous Conservative leader seems to have done – that he was, in some mysterious, even mystical sense, speaking for the people. As he put it in 1925: 'I give expression, in some unaccountable way, to what the English people think. For some reason that appeals to me and gives me strength.'[19]

Baldwin practised the arts of national flattery, and the response also flattered him:

> The Englishman is all right as long as he is content to be what God made him, an Englishman, but gets into trouble when he tries to be something else ... [W]e grumble, and we have always grumbled, but we never worry ... The Englishman is made for a time of crisis, and for a time of emergency ... It is in staying power that he is supreme ... I think that the English people are at heart and in practice the kindest people in the world.

He also romanticized the notion of England, which he perceived forcefully and memorably as existing in a halo of rural nostalgia: 'To me, England is the country, and the country is England ... the sounds of England, the tinkle of the hammer on the anvil in the country smithy, the corncrake on a dewy morning, the sound of the scythe against the whetstone.'[20]

Baldwin had considered becoming an Anglican cleric. It showed. He preached. Baldwin repeatedly urged on others a spirit of service. The word 'service' was always turning up. His final speeches were published under the title *Service of Our Lives*. The last of these addresses, delivered in May 1937, characteristically urged his young audience – who within three years would, indeed, be called to serve to the death – 'from tonight onwards and all your lives put your duty first, and think about your rights afterwards'.[21]

Baldwin was devout. His wife, Lucy, informed the Swedish ambassador at Curzon's funeral that she and her husband knelt together each morning commending the day to God and asking that some good work should be done by them.[22] Such devotion can lead, within the Protestant tradition from which Baldwin emerged, either to great resolution or to great complacency.[23] In July 1940, when he had lost his reputation, and even lost the iron gates of his house at Astley for scrap, and when, perhaps, in the light of events in France, a few grains of self-doubt might have emerged, the old man revealed his inner thinking to another believer, Lord Halifax. Baldwin said he had prayed:

> 'And I thought what mites we all are and how we can never see God's plan, a plan on such a scale that it *must* be incomprehensible.
>
> 'Then suddenly, for what must have been a couple of minutes, I seemed to see with extraordinary and vivid clarity, and to hear someone else speaking to me . . . "You cannot see the plan", then "Have you not thought there is a purpose in stripping you, one by one, of all the human props on which you depend, that you are being left alone in the world? You have now one upon whom to lean and I have chosen you as my instrument to work with my will."'[24]

The implications of this final reflection – inspired or not – are of psychological significance in explaining Baldwin's political successes and strategic failures, his tenacity and supineness, his self-satisfaction and hesitation, during the fourteen years he served as Conservative leader and his three spells as Prime Minister. At the end of this period, as from the beginning, his claim to statesmanship was that he had allowed mass democracy to emerge in safety. Even G. M. Young, Baldwin's 'authorized biographer' whose unsympathetic and inadequate book greatly harmed its subject's reputation, records this not only as Baldwin's own conviction but as one which he, the biographer, saw borne out by the moderation of the 1945 Labour Government.[25] A. J. P. Taylor goes even further: 'Baldwin and his counterpart, Ramsay MacDonald, were the two men who brought about reconciliation in British public life, who took the bitterness out of the class war, who made the British people more tolerant, more of a single community.'[26] These are large claims, and they must be tested against events.

Baldwin's first premiership did not offer much reason to think that he was destined for political longevity, let alone greatness. His first Cabinet excluded the coalitionists – he clumsily mismanaged the prickly Austen Chamberlain in the process, and not for the last time. Austen's half-brother, Neville, though, after a short delay, became Chancellor of the Exchequer.[27] Economic conditions were unfavourable and political conditions reflected the fact. It seemed to most Conservatives, including those operating the party machine, to be a time for consolidation. But Baldwin had other thoughts.

Tariffs were back on the agenda, and Baldwin himself was a long-standing protectionist. With Law out of office – he died in October 1923 – it was theoretically possible to revisit the question, unbound by the pledge of an election before the introduction of food taxes. But none of this seemed obviously pressing. Baldwin, however, announced to a largely unprepared Cabinet that he had concluded that tariffs were a necessity. He then proceeded to announce the decision to the party conference. Whatever he intended, the momentum for an early election to test the policy quickly became unstoppable. Baldwin again took a risk. He declared on 13 November that Parliament would be dissolved and a general election held on 6 December.

Baldwin later offered different explanations and justifications of his action. He had been worried about the prospect of rising unemployment. He thought that if the election were left until later Labour would do even better. He had heard (wrongly, in fact) that Lloyd George – his abiding *bête noire* – was poised to announce his conversion to tariff reform. An early election would re-unify the party, forcing the coalitionists back into line.[28] All of these arguments may be accorded a certain amount of weight, even though they were clearly polished in hindsight. The truth, though, is that Baldwin was uneasy about his authority. He wanted to strengthen it by an election victory. He felt he needed a personal mandate. He misread the political signs, ignored advice, and consequently made an unforced and quite extraordinary blunder. The later suggestion by 'Cato' in *Guilty Men* that Baldwin had 'fallen once from the Premiership by reason of doing a foolish thing' and that he thenceforth resolved to get by and 'do absolutely nothing' is one of the few accusations in that tract that has solid substance.[29] Baldwin's future career is, indeed, inexplicable without understanding the shock he received when he took a risk.

The election campaign was a shambles. Although free trade arguments were little heard on the Conservative side, there were large differences about the desirable scale of protection and a deep unease even among protectionists at the electoral impact of anything sounding like food taxes. The Beaverbrook and Rothermere papers were hostile for reasons of their own (or, more precisely, of their proprietors'). Baldwin himself was a modest success. He became known and liked and was henceforth viewed as an asset. But the party went down hard, with a net loss of eighty-eight seats. It would, of course, have been a much worse result without the impact on the electoral arithmetic that followed from the establishment of the Irish Free State, discussed earlier. The Conservatives still won 38 per cent of the vote.

Baldwin was determined to avoid any return of Lloyd George, for which Birkenhead briefly intrigued. This meant letting Labour in and avoiding talk of coalitions. He was also, it seems, less worried about Labour than many Tories. He shrewdly allowed Asquith, however, to take the blame for actually putting Labour in. On 17 January a Labour amendment to the Loyal Address was duly carried by seventy-two votes, and Baldwin made way for Britain's first (minority) Labour Government.[30]

Baldwin was not a natural Opposition leader, as events would later confirm, but the Conservatives behaved shrewdly at this juncture. They waited. The aim was to watch – and allow the country to watch – the inexperienced Labour leadership tie itself into parliamentary knots, and then to find the right occasion to let the Government unravel. In the meantime, Baldwin took advantage of the fact that the coalitionist ministers, deprived of rescue by Lloyd George, wanted to rejoin the Conservative majority on acceptable terms. Baldwin had every reason to permit this. He was widely, and rightly, blamed for the decision to dissolve and for the loss of office. He needed to neutralize his enemies quickly. So, when he called a meeting of the Shadow Cabinet, Baldwin simply summoned Austen Chamberlain, Birkenhead and Balfour to join the others. Austen Chamberlain then proceeded to lead the discussion on the vexed question of the tariff. It was agreed to return to the previous position of 1922. Limited protection of certain sectors of industry under the existing Safeguarding of Industry Act was the new policy. A revolt against Baldwin in free-trading Tory Lancashire, encouraged at a distance by Derby, quickly fizzled out, and Baldwin's leadership, along with the new policy, was endorsed at a party meeting held at the Hotel Cecil.

The 1923 election had been lost not through organizational deficiency but rather because of wider political failures. But the loss provided, as usual, and more usefully than on many occasions, an opportunity for organizational rethinking. For the first time, a secretariat was appointed for the Shadow Cabinet, and recognizably modern processes of policy formation were adopted. The secretariat was lodged along with Baldwin's personal staff at Central Office. Policy committees consisting of MPs and advisers met – each under a shadow minister – and reported to Baldwin and Austen Chamberlain. The conclusions were summarized in a pamphlet by Austen's brother Neville and then propounded by Baldwin in speeches.[31]

Indeed, through his speeches and through party literature disseminating them, Baldwin now put a distinctive stamp on Conservative strategy – though this is to use an over-precise term for the 'New Conservatism', which was always a mood or message rather than a programme. It embodied a call for moderate social reform, for the rejection of class war and for cooperation in industry. But representatives of the old politics were Baldwin's more immediate source of concern.

Churchill, who had briefly halted his return towards the Conservative Party when Baldwin revived protection, was again anxious to stand as an official party candidate. But knowing that he might very well be rejected by a selection committee, he wanted to be manoeuvred straight into a seat by Central Office. Unfortunately, this proved difficult, and so when he stood at the Westminster Abbey by-election in March 1924 it was as an independent against the official Conservative candidate. The party leaders now split. Balfour was initially persuaded by Baldwin not to send a letter of support to Churchill – who had, in fact, been persuaded to stand by Birkenhead. But then a letter of support from Leo Amery for his opponent, the official candidate, was published.

It is notable, as an aside, that this was just one of many inter-sections between Amery's career and Churchill's. From their first encounter at Harrow, when Churchill pushed Amery into the school swimming pool, during their rift over tariff reform, through their conflicting views about how to maintain the Empire, even later still when they both opposed appeasement, there was, as now, a mutually respectful but always distrustful rivalry. Amery's view of Churchill, expressed in 1932 after a heart-to-heart conversation aboard ship, is to the point: 'I have always said that the key to Winston is to realise that he is a mid-Victorian, steeped in the politics of his father's period, and unable to get the modern point of view.'[32]

In any case, with Amery's letter in print, Balfour's had to go out too. It was a mess. In fact, Churchill narrowly failed at Abbey. But he was then found Epping, where he would stand successfully as a 'Constitutionalist', with Conservative Party support.[33]

Whatever Amery thought of it all, Churchill's allegiances were politically important because, as the Conservative leadership was well aware, the next election would hang on where the Liberal vote – briefly revived by Baldwin's flirtation with protection – finished up. It was widely envisaged that the left liberals would go back to Labour. But this meant that the Conservatives must split off the right and moderate Liberals to their advantage. Whether Baldwin's bonhomie contributed to this, and if so how much, is unclear. But, in the event, it was a Red Scare, the classic means of frightening moderates into the Tory camp, which really did the trick.

MacDonald's Government walked a tightrope between meeting the radical expectations of its supporters and striving to appear acceptable to moderate opinion. It slipped over on the left. The Government first announced the intention to prosecute the communist editor of *Workers' Weekly* for inciting mutiny in the armed forces, and then under pressure from the left backed away. The Conservatives supported a Liberal motion of no confidence and the Government fell. It was a perfect issue, and it was now perfectly exploited.

Conservative Party propaganda had been distributing evidence of Labour's links with Soviet communism well in advance of publication of the so-called 'Zinoviev Letter'. The ground was thus well prepared for the scandal that now erupted. The extent of the party's covert involvement in the affair is still obscure. Probably Baldwin and Central Office did not know – any more than the Foreign Office or MI5 knew – that the letter itself was a forgery. But the party obtained it early on and was then able to manipulate it to maximum advantage through the *Daily Mail*, which published it four days before polling day. Very probably, a key role was played in this process by the intelligence officer Joseph Ball. Ball soon became dissatisfied with his MI5 pay and conditions and was recruited in 1927 by Davidson (now party chairman) ostensibly to manage the party's literature but also to conduct spying operations against Labour. It is highly likely that he was already involved with Central Office at the time of the Zinoviev affair and that he enabled the letter's transmission and organized its exploitation. (In 1930 Ball would become the first director of the Conservative Research Department.[34] He was, in truth, a sinister figure, and later still editor of the sometimes anti-semitic and always anti-Churchill *Truth* magazine – a devotee beyond the call of duty to Neville Chamberlain, and suspiciously sympathetic to the Third Reich.[35])

Baldwin's own comments at this juncture were studiously moderate. But those of other Conservatives were not. And it was not moderation but rather outrage that prevailed. Labour's vote actually increased (though its share fell). What governed the result, however, was a big increase in the Conservative vote at the expense of the Liberals. When the votes were counted, 419 Conservatives (including 'Constitutionalists') were returned. The Labour Party had 151 seats, and the Liberals just 40. It was the greatest Conservative Party victory – indeed, the greatest election triumph by any party – in modern times.

With such a mandate, Baldwin could do what he wanted. But what he wanted was much clearer in general (advancing the 'New Conservatism') than in particular (the legislative and policy programme). The latter was, from the first, largely in the capable but fidgety hands of Neville Chamberlain.[36] It is a common lament from apologists for Neville Chamberlain that his achievements in government – as a social reformer, Chancellor of the Exchequer and general administrator – have been overlooked because of his association with the outbreak of the war. The complaint is, in one sense, beside the point. Prime ministers must expect to be judged by their decisions on matters of war and peace. Policies for sanitation and social insurance simply do not weigh so heavily in the historic scales. In Chamberlain's case, however, the point has some validity, partly because his enemies sneered at his background in humdrum local government to belittle his abilities – Lloyd George scathingly described him as 'a good mayor of Birmingham in an off year' – and partly because those abilities in domestic affairs were truly exceptional.

Neville Chamberlain, as Austen's younger half-brother, was intended by his father for business, not politics. But he was more able, and he proved a better politician too, than Austen. He also inherited more of his father's social radicalism. After an early overseas business failure – for which he blamed himself – he concentrated on business, culture, welfare and politics in his native Birmingham, where he was in his element. He drove through the first two town planning schemes in Britain and committed himself as Lord Mayor (in 1915) to future ambitious plans of improvement. This was why – notwithstanding his own sneer – Lloyd George snatched him away the following year to become Director-General of National Service.

The post was not properly defined – Lloyd George was notoriously chaotic – and gave no real scope to Neville Chamberlain's administrative abilities. In 1917 Chamberlain resigned, again feeling a failure, but now, like many others, also with a well-developed animus against Lloyd George. Entering the Commons in 1918 for Birmingham Ladywood, Chamberlain was suddenly propelled towards the top of Conservative politics by the coup of 1922. Bonar Law offered him the non-Cabinet job of Postmaster-General, which, despite fear of offending Austen, he accepted. After the election victory he was unexpectedly promoted to become Minister of Health in March 1923. Here he was given a free hand. Housing, his main interest, was within the Health portfolio and Chamberlain now began the sorry story of statutory rent restriction and the politically necessary promotion of subsidized house-building and slum clearance. Later the Labour Party shifted the emphasis from private to public housing, but Chamberlain's legislation provided the pattern.

The replacement of Law, who was ill, by Baldwin, who was lazy, left Chamberlain with further enhanced authority. His brief spell as Chancellor was useful preparation for his long tenure of that post under the National Government. But it was only with his return to Health, after the landslide Conservative victory of 1924, that he was able to continue his programme of social reform, for which Baldwin's rhetoric gave political cover. It was the high point of Chamberlain's achievements in office.[37]

Baldwin's other and more risky key appointment was of Churchill as Chancellor. Churchill was still highly mistrusted and only recently returned to the party fold. For Baldwin, though, it was useful to have him inside rather than outside, fully immersed in this most time- and energy-consuming post, and well away from his obsessions of defence and foreign policy. During the years that followed, Churchill and Chamberlain collaborated to great effect, notably in the Widows, Orphans and Old Age Pension Act of 1925. Another bold measure was the National Health Insurance Act of 1928, which extended and improved health insurance benefits.

The most far-reaching, and most politically fraught, of Chamberlain's reforms was the Local Government Act of 1929. It was radical in just the sort of ways that get overconfident, long-standing governments into trouble – the Balfour Education Act of 1902 and the Thatcher Government's community charge/poll tax measure of 1989 are obvious parallels. In this instance, the collaboration of Churchill and Chamberlain caused problems, because the Bill contained too much. It abolished what remained of the old poor law system and placed the responsibilities for relieving destitution on local councils. This annoyed a number of Tory vested interests. The Bill also reformed local authority finance, increasing Treasury control. On top of that, special relief was given to agriculture and industry – exemptions which displeased others who faced higher bills. The timing was terrible, too: the Act came into effect on the eve of the 1929 general election.[38]

The economy in general and the labour question in particular were, however, the crucial areas in which the main battles of Baldwin's Government were fought. Here Baldwin himself was at the centre of events. The General Strike of 1926 was the test, and one which the Government was, by the end, generally thought to have passed. But it is important not to lose sight of the economic background, because it was the Baldwin Government's (and its predecessor's and successor's) failings here that provided the background to labour unrest.

As noted in the previous chapter, the British economy between the wars was suffering from what would today be described as an unplanned monetary squeeze and a series of supply-side failings. Looking ahead, the squeeze abated when the National Government was forced off the gold standard in September 1931. Thenceforth, to the astonishment of Labour ex-ministers, who had uncomprehendingly submitted to Treasury orthodoxy, the economy recovered. Many other European countries (notably Germany), terrified of inflation because of their earlier experiences of hyperinflation, still pursued exchange-rate oriented, tight money policies. These fuelled the rise of political extremism, whereas in Britain Oswald Mosley's initiatives gained no traction. The Bank of

England cut the interest rate to 2 per cent and held it there. Domestic demand recovered, exports increased, unemployment (though high) became essentially a regional problem. The incomes of those in work rose sharply. At the same time, the prudent fiscal policies pursued by Neville Chamberlain, the National Government's Chancellor, kept taxes down. Budget deficits remained firmly under control, only growing significantly under the impact of higher defence spending from 1936/7.

This summary suggests two important conclusions, both bearing on the record of Baldwin's Government. First, given this broader perspective on events, much of Baldwin's preoccupation with Britain's social fragility and his incessant search for compromise seem misplaced. Getting the economic fundamentals right, rather than pursuing a mild and muddled paternalism, was the main condition for order and stability.

The second conclusion, however, is more damning. This is that the Baldwin years saw no progress in solving the underlying structural problems which held the British economy back. Indeed, the remedies offered could only make matters worse. As noted earlier, the trend after the end of the First World War was towards industrial cartels and collectivization of labour. The rigidities thus imposed made it much more politically difficult to cut real wages, which a mixture of international conditions and domestic recession now required. A vigorously interventionist approach might possibly have promoted a shift away from the core, outmoded industries of coal, iron, steel, textiles and shipbuilding towards the developing sectors of chemicals, electrical goods and mechanical engineering. A determinedly non-interventionist government, on the other hand, might have created a framework of monetary and fiscal policies and labour laws which would have allowed the necessary process of adaptation to occur in a market-led manner. Instead, the Conservative Government of the day intervened haphazardly, always inclining towards the less disruptive option, while demonstrating no imaginative understanding – Keynesian or otherwise – of economic conditions.

Beyond this, and reflecting a deep ambivalence about the outside world and the new conditions prevailing there, Conservatives repeatedly offered the prospect of industrial protection within the context of imperial (later Commonwealth) integration. It is hard to imagine a message less likely to induce economic realism and promote the energy of those managing or working in industry and commerce.[39]

Baldwin and Chamberlain were at one in their commitment to protection. Both had industrial backgrounds. But for both sentiment was also important. For Baldwin, protection offered a cushion against economically harsh conditions. For Chamberlain, it offered a means of fulfilling his filial duty to his late father. Significantly – and once more to jump ahead in time – almost the only distinctive element brought by the Conservative Party to the 1931 election, fought on a generally policy-free 'doctor's mandate' justified by economic crisis, was protection.[40] The following year, the Cabinet agreed a general tariff of 10 per cent, to be linked to preference for the Dominions. The policy was endorsed at the British Empire Economic Conference, attended by Baldwin in Ottawa that August. Neville Chamberlain duly told the House of Commons: 'There can have been few occasions in all our long political history when to the son of a man who counted for something in his day and generation has been vouchsafed the privilege of setting the seal on the work which the father began but had perforce to leave unfinished.'[41]

This self-referencing and self-important manner would become ever more distinctly, and gratingly, Chamberlain's. But the serious objections to the policy itself – apart from that noted above, namely its offering an illusive security to British industry – were twofold. First, by giving preferential treatment to the Dominions it locked Britain into a limited, slow-growing market. Second, it gave strong encouragement to the current worldwide trend towards protection and economic self-sufficiency. That trend, reinforcing national aggressive ambitions, was a contributor to the outbreak of world war in 1939.[42]

The defeat of Labour, particularly in the circumstances of the Red Scare of 1924, was always likely to provoke a reaction by militants in the unions. The 'Triple Alliance' had already flexed its muscles. It now felt less inhibition about using them. The coal industry's problems would now, as in later national conflicts, be the *casus belli*.

Baldwin's preferred approach to the threat of labour militancy was compromise. In this he was in a minority in his Cabinet and an even smaller minority in his party. It did not bother him. Indeed, it seems to have further convinced him that he was right. He took high political risks in the endeavour.

In March 1925 what was technically a Private Member's Bill (in the name of the Scottish Conservative MP F. A. Macquisten) but was, in fact, supported by the Conservative Party and reflected established party policy, was introduced. Its aim was to replace the existing system of contracting out of the trade union political levy with one of contracting in.[43] Baldwin decided to resist the change, as he informed an astonished but eventually acquiescent Cabinet. He then did so in a powerful speech in the House of Commons. Baldwin accepted the principle of the measure, but called for the proposal to be withdrawn in the interests of industrial peace. The tone of magnanimity he struck was widely praised in the Commons and in the country, though not in much of the party. It was a fillip to his authority and has won praise from commentators since.[44] Three speeches on his approach to labour relations were published as a booklet entitled *Peace in Industry*, which sold half a million copies.[45]

That said, like his interventions in the developing crisis in the mining industry, this initiative did nothing to change industrial realities. It perpetuated a system of party finance which provided a large, coercively secured income for the Labour Party. When the system was changed (temporarily) to contracting in, under the Trade Disputes and Trade Unions Act (1927), a third of trade unionists decided not to renew their political subscriptions.

The difficulties of the coal industry were acute. It faced new competition from Germany, after the French evacuation of the coal-producing Ruhr. There was also a slump in home demand. The industry's underlying problems of low productivity and high costs were insoluble without radical re-organization. This had long been in the wind. The Sankey Commission (set up under Sir John Sankey in 1919) had recommended nationalization; but Lloyd George prudently rejected it – and when it finally came under Attlee it was, of course, a failure. The Samuel Commission (under Sir Herbert Samuel) was now set up by Baldwin as part of a twofold initiative to avert a threatened national miners' strike. The other, more controversial part, much disliked in Conservative circles, was the announcement of a special nine-month subsidy to stave off the wage cuts demanded by the employers. 'Red Friday' (31 July 1925) – when both climbdowns were announced – was as severe a humiliation for the Government as it was a cause for crowing on the left, and it provoked much Tory soul-searching.

The Samuel Commission duly recommended wage cuts (alongside some re-organization). The miners' union would not agree, and received the backing of the Trades Union Congress. The subsidy had now come to an end and the owners, despite intensive discussions, implemented a lock-out. For the Government, the breaking point came when unionized printers at the *Daily Mail* refused to print an editorial condemning the planned General Strike. The Government was by now well prepared. A remarkably efficient system to ensure vital services, and even to circulate news and propaganda (the *British Gazette* under Churchill), was mobilized.

The TUC, like the Labour Party leadership, was horrified at the politically dangerous waters the movement had entered. The General Strike was condemned as a revolutionary attack on the constitution and resisted not only by the authorities but by volunteers drawn from a united middle class and a large section of the non-unionized working class as well. It took just ten days for it to be called off. The miners' union kept up the struggle for six more months after which, facing poverty and certain failure, the miners drifted and then flooded back to work.

In the immediate aftermath, Baldwin's and the Government's standing was high. But the strike was also a clear and, indeed, final defeat for his personal strategy of industrial consensus. His health was badly affected by the strain, and his self-confidence and energy never fully returned.[46] The 1927 Act, whose proposals he only reluctantly accepted, banned sympathetic strikes and intimidatory mass picketing – like the Thatcher legislation of the 1980s. It also went further than she would go in tackling the political levy.[47] But, unlike Mrs Thatcher, Baldwin was not disposed to call for a national drive for discipline, effort and efficiency. He would not articulate the policy, and since articulation, rather than execution, was his greatest political strength, for the Tories this was a great political loss. As a result, the policy seemed to be dictated by unpopular vested interests, which helped make the Government unpopular too. Thus victory over the country's only national strike generated no lasting political benefit for the Conservatives.

From 1927 there was, indeed, a falling away in Conservative support to the benefit of the Liberals. More importantly, and more permanently, there was a revival of Labour, which now had, in the new Act, something to campaign against. Uncertainty was also increased, because the next election would be fought on a new franchise. In 1924 Baldwin had promised to equalise the franchise between men and women, and in practice this meant giving all women, like men, the vote at twenty-one. The measure was implemented, against Conservative Central Office's advice, in 1928.

There is, in fact, no reason to believe that extending the women's vote worked against the Conservative interest. Evidence over time suggests the contrary. But it was a further niggling source of dissent among elements of the party, which was increasingly distrustful of Baldwin's instincts and would become more so. Nor did Davidson as party chairman – Baldwin's nominee to succeed Stanley Jackson in 1926 – fail to stir up a good deal of personal enmity by his suspicion and quarrelling.

The 1929 campaign was not nearly as well prepared as that of 1924. There was no overarching theme, except the general assertion that Baldwin was an asset and should be returned to Downing Street. The policies were put together within the Government, without significant input from the party staff – always a recipe for blandness. But neither can the party itself escape blame, since the uninspiring slogan of 'Safety First' was its creation, albeit largely by default.

There was no shortage of money.[48] There was a competent principal agent in Robert Topping, appointed in February 1928. (As the first holder of the post to have been a Central Office area agent, he certainly knew the party. Although he would shortly demonstrate an alarming degree of disloyalty, he was clearly respected enough to hold his post, under one nomenclature or another, till 1945.[49]) In any case, few elections are lost by the party's organizational wing: that privilege usually, as in this case, falls to the politicians. Perhaps the most important explanation of the result is that, by contrast with 1924, there was nothing of which to be scared. David Low's cartoon in the *Evening Standard*, depicting Baldwin, Churchill and Davidson desolately waiting by a printing press for a new Zinoviev letter, has it about right. The letter never arrived, and neither did the votes.

The 1929 election was the party's worst electoral performance in the inter-war years. Compared with 1924, the Conservatives were down from 419 to 260 seats, the Liberals up from 40 to 59, and Labour up from 151 to 288 – the largest party. MacDonald duly formed his second Government.

The odds against Baldwin's surviving as Conservative leader hardly looked favourable. He had lost two out three elections. He was tired, and he was distrusted – at least within the party. But he proved surprisingly tenacious. He would stay as leader. He would again become Prime Minister. Any of the crises he faced might now have engulfed him. But none did. As Maurice Cowling observed, this reveals the other side of the man:

> Baldwin had moral, social and aesthetic beliefs, and also a religion
> . . . [H]is interests were spiritual and atmospheric, his instrument
> of demonstration the wand rather than the baton . . . What
> he wanted to express were the feelings of a 'decent Englishman'
> . . . All this, however moving, was also misleading. Baldwin
> was a tough operator of long experience and high
> accomplishment.[50]

This he now proved.

Within the parliamentary party as a whole, Baldwin's position after the 1929 election was weakened because a number of the younger, more left-leaning Conservatives, known without affection as the 'YMCA' – including Harold Macmillan and Duff Cooper – had lost their seats. Baldwin's performance as Opposition leader was also unsatisfactory, whatever one's ideological standpoint. He was sluggish and often silent. Following precedent, critics of the party's performance blamed his failures on his adherents. Under sustained attack, and on Neville Chamberlain's advice, Davidson stood down as party chairman, to be succeeded by none other than the ambitious and energetic Chamberlain.[51] The right of the party were not so easily appeased. They were angered because of Baldwin's positions on issues that mattered to them. The right, though, were not united, which helped Baldwin through.

The battle over India created a great stir. This was partly because the leadership's chief antagonist was Winston Churchill (who, however, was strongly opposed by other imperialists, such as Amery). The issue was dangerous because it went to the heart of what the Conservative Party traditionally stood for. The assumption made in the time of Salisbury and Balfour was that Britain's great power status depended on holding India. This proposition was not now directly denied, but it was finessed in a way that looked, to the critics, increasingly bogus.

The Simon Commission had been set up in 1927, under Sir John Simon, to report on how to involve Indian nationalist opinion in devising a stable role for India within the Empire. But Indian nationalists boycotted it. The Viceroy, Lord Irwin – previously the Conservative MP Edward Wood, and later the Foreign Secretary Lord Halifax – decided on 31 October 1929 to jump this particular gun by making a statement in favour of Dominion status for India. Baldwin and his successor as Prime Minister, MacDonald, both agreed with the sentiments expressed; but the statement was un-authorized, and it provoked an explosion of anger among the already suspicious Tory right. Baldwin, now in opposition, was forced to come out openly, at a difficult time, in favour of the proposal. The debate became personalized. Churchill publicly attacked the policy at the end of 1930, and then, in apparent resent-ment at a patronizing slight from Baldwin in a speech the following January – but also, doubtless, with a view to ousting Baldwin – resigned from the Shadow Cabinet to lead a frontal assault.

The rebels would fight on, in the country, in the party institutions and in Parliament, until the 1935 Government of India Act finally reached the statute book. By then, opposition was a lost and minority cause. But the bitterness of the debate, worsened by Churchill's unrestrained language and tactics, had two consequences, one long-term and one short-term. The long-term consequence, even worse for the country than the party, was to discredit Churchill in the eyes of most of his parliamentary colleagues. This allowed the party leadership to discount him later, when he was right and they were wrong. The shorter-term impact – that is, in the period 1929–31 – was on Baldwin's standing, because hostility within the party over India overlapped with hostility over what protectionists and press barons saw as his weakness on tariff reform.

Baldwin's lassitude, alongside the new conditions of mass democracy and a popular press, contributed to a sharp increase in the power and public profile of the newspaper proprietors, notably Lords Beaverbrook and Rothermere. The Conservative Party's conventional wisdom was that Beaverbrook (the *Express*) was an instinctive Tory who might be controlled through compromise and negotiation, whereas Rothermere (the *Mail*) was impossible. This analysis was broadly correct, though Baldwin hated both. The two press barons had somewhat differing agendas, and Rothermere was the more subject to whim. But for reasons of common interest they usually hunted together, and they did so now in destabilizing Baldwin.

Beaverbrook agitated through his 'Empire Crusade' for what he called 'Empire Free Trade', a useful disguise for protection. He was supported by Rothermere. From a loyalist perspective, Leo Amery also strongly pressed the case for tariffs. Press attacks were followed by private negotiations, which, however, broke down. Rothermere went ahead and decided to set up his own party. Meanwhile, Beaverbrook would offer support to the Conservatives only if they caused no difficulties for his own independent campaign.

Baldwin adjusted his position – being a protectionist himself, it was only for him a question of tactics, in any case. He gained the agreement of the Shadow Cabinet to a referendum on tariffs and announced it at a party meeting in the Hotel Cecil on 4 March 1930. Rothermere, though, would not accept the compromise, and Beaverbrook, not wishing to be isolated, accordingly also withdrew support for it. The two now backed United Empire candidates in by-elections against Conservatives. Baldwin gained a temporary respite by reading out to a Conservative Party meeting on 24 June a manically arrogant letter from Rothermere. The party rallied.

A further explicit shift towards protection, suggested by the Canadian Prime Minister, Richard Bennett, in the form of commitment to a 10 per cent tariff on all goods from outside the Empire, also helped consolidate Baldwin's position within his party. But he was still looking vulnerable. Beaverbrook's candidate won a by-election at South Paddington. The press lords, thus encouraged, resolved to fight every by-election that arose. Matters came to a head when a contest in the St George's division of Westminster coincided with what looks like – though cannot be proved to be – a plot by Neville Chamberlain to seize the party leadership.[52]

So great was the momentum behind Beaverbrook's Empire Crusade campaign that no Conservative could be found to fight the seat against his candidate. Meanwhile, on 26 February 1931, Robert Topping, in what without Chamberlain's secret approval would have been an astonishing piece of impudence, presented him, as party chairman, with a memorandum on the state of the party. This noted that the revival of Baldwin's popularity after the party's meeting which he had addressed in Caxton Hall (at the time of South Paddington) had not lasted. It concluded 'that it would be in the interests of the party that the Leader should reconsider his position' – in layman's language, resign. Chamberlain then, almost equally astonishingly, circulated the memorandum to others, including his brother Austen, who anyway despised Baldwin. The intention was to present the memorandum to Baldwin himself after he had delivered a scheduled speech on 6 March. But Beaverbrook's campaign in St George's made it necessary to do so sooner. It also, however, made it more difficult to ditch Baldwin without appearing to bow to Beaverbrook, and this none of the party leadership (including Neville Chamberlain) wanted.

Baldwin was duly handed the memorandum by Chamberlain, who told him that he agreed with its analysis. Shaken, Baldwin replied that he would announce his resignation to the Shadow Cabinet the next day. But Lord Bridgeman (formerly Home Secretary, and an old ally since 1922) and Davidson persuaded him out of it. At Davidson's prompting, Baldwin decided that he would resign his seat and himself contest St George's, breaking the news to a dumbfounded Chamberlain prior to Shadow Cabinet the following morning. Chamberlain lamely urged that he couldn't do that, he should think of the effect on his successor. Baldwin replied: 'I don't give a damn about my successor.'

In the event, Baldwin's threat was not realized. Duff Cooper stood instead. Baldwin spoke on his behalf. He condemned a venomous and untrue article about himself in the *Daily Mail*. Then, applying a phrase coined by his cousin Rudyard Kipling, he went further: 'What the proprietorship of these papers is aiming at is power, and power without responsibility – the prerogative of the harlot through the ages.' Duff Cooper won the by-election. The press barons were humiliated. Baldwin survived. Baldwin and Chamberlain made up, though Chamberlain renounced the chairmanship.[53] Beaverbrook made terms, but did not forget his encounters. He reflected: '[Baldwin] always won – he always beat me – the toughest and most unscrupulous politician you could find – cold, merciless in his dislikes.'[54]

Having survived as Conservative party leader, Baldwin found himself once more on the threshold of power, for the MacDonald Government's credibility had been destroyed along with its economic policy. Local election results suggested a swing against Labour sufficient to give the Conservatives victory in any early election. MacDonald had been calling for opposition party support in the economic crisis, but Baldwin was unreceptive. Of course, he had his own problems at the time. But, in any case, he had come to power through leading a revolt against one coalition, and he saw no immediate attraction in joining another.

Publication that summer of the majority May Commission Report on public expenditure, which revealed unmanageable public finances and proposed cuts in public sector wages and welfare, heightened the crisis. The Government was faced with a run on the (overvalued) pound. The Labour Cabinet could not agree on cuts in unemployment benefits, and the requirement for a National Government to restore credibility suddenly became immediate. Baldwin, though, was on holiday in Aix and returned to London reluctantly and only briefly on 11 August to meet MacDonald, Philip Snowden (the Chancellor) and Chamberlain at Downing Street. Having agreed to discussions on a coalition, he then returned to his holiday, leaving Chamberlain – along with Samuel Hoare, a Tory banker – to negotiate terms. Baldwin still hoped for an early election and a Conservative Government. But in his absence the King asked MacDonald to form a National Government, and then asked Baldwin to serve under him, to which Baldwin felt obliged to agree. The final terms of the arrangement were settled by Baldwin, MacDonald, Sir John Simon and Neville Chamberlain. There were to be just four Conservative Cabinet ministers, and of the forty-six ministerial posts only twenty-one went to Conservatives. Churchill and Amery were not included, which would have consequences. All in all, it was not very satisfactory in Conservative Party terms, though it had the enormous advantage of splitting Labour. Nor did it immediately end the crisis.

What was billed as 'mutiny' by naval ratings at Invergordon, though it was much less than that, precipitated another run on sterling and the abandonment of the link with gold – a blessing in disguise, as it turned out. The Shadow Cabinet and the 1922 Committee had been reassured by Baldwin that coalition was a temporary arrangement to deal with the crisis and that it would mean the implementation of tariffs – but there must be an election.

The October 1931 campaign had similarities with that of 1924, with much the same result. It was fought on the basis of fear, in this case rather more justified, relating to the threat of economic collapse if the National Government's candidates were not returned. Overwhelmingly, they were. In the new Parliament there sat 473 Conservative MPs, who alongside National Labour (under MacDonald), Liberal Nationals (under Simon) and Liberals (under Samuel) constituted a National Government majority of 554. Labour (now under Arthur Henderson) was smashed – down from 288 seats in 1929 to 52. The difference between 1931 and 1924 was, of course, that there was to be a Labour Prime Minister, leading but also the prisoner of a huge, largely Conservative majority.

In party terms, this arrangement worked. It worked because, despite his early doubts, Baldwin ensured that it did. He reverted to type, content to leave to others the task of policy-making, glad not to shoulder too much responsibility, all the while playing the political game with dexterity in the House of Commons. He remained as Lord President. MacDonald busied himself with foreign affairs, to no one's obvious benefit. Simon was Foreign Secretary. Samuel stayed on temporarily as Home Secretary, though when the tariff was introduced he and his fellow Liberals withdrew.

The most important appointment was of Neville Chamberlain as Chancellor. Chamberlain ran economic policy in its entirety – the Liberal, Runciman, at the Board of Trade proving compliant. But Chamberlain also increasingly ran the Government as a whole. The Treasury is always the department most ready to swallow the initiative of other departments. This usually occurs in an economic crisis – as, in modern times, in the 1980s and after the 2010 election. But the economic crisis of 1931 was quickly over.

The policy was agreed. The conditions seemed benign. Chamberlain's ascendancy under the National Government, headed first by MacDonald and after 1935 by Baldwin, was the result of Chamberlain's own administrative energy and the inadequacy of his colleagues. Well before Neville Chamberlain became Prime Minister, therefore, he had achieved a decisive role not just in domestic but also in foreign and defence policy.

Baldwin made every effort to keep MacDonald from resigning. He considered the coalition congenial and it fitted his idea of what government existed to do. It also allowed him to keep his own right wing at bay, particularly on India. (Parallels with David Cameron in coalition after the 2010 election are almost too obvious to mention.) MacDonald began as a prisoner and finished as a cipher; in public and in the House of Commons he was also frequently an embarrassment as his mental powers declined. The Simon Liberals, the Liberal Nationals, moved so close to the Conservatives as to be all but indistinguishable from them. As with the Liberal Unionists during Salisbury's premiership, formal association followed more slowly than practical fusion. The Liberal Nationals only finally lost their own whip in 1966.[55]

Sir John Simon himself was unpopular. Almost everyone could agree on how disagreeable they found him. Neville Chamberlain, no obvious charmer himself, remarked of Simon: 'He hasn't a friend even in his own Party.' Simon was a brilliant lawyer, with what the Civil Service mandarin and Baldwin intimate Thomas Jones called a 'Rolls-Royce' brain. But Simon's ambitions and the power he wielded as head of his own political faction usually saw him in posts for which he was temperamentally unsuited – Foreign Secretary, Home Secretary, Chancellor of the Exchequer, and it was only under Churchill – when he was largely discredited by his association with appeasement – that he became Lord Chancellor, serving until the end of the war. His worst and, indeed, fatal drawbacks were that he lacked decisiveness and that he could not inspire confidence.[56]

As in Simon's case, ministerial posts were shared out to the disproportionate benefit of the Conservatives' minority allies. Despite that, the National Government aroused in the Conservative Party none of the resentments and frustrations that coalition with Lloyd George had done. At one level this was a matter of personalities. Ramsay MacDonald was neither as formidable nor as irritating as David Lloyd George. Stanley Baldwin was a far subtler Conservative leader than Austen Chamberlain. But other differences, which reflect less well on government in the 1930s, were also at work. The Conservative Party, or at least the Conservative leadership and party establishment, had largely abandoned the politics of idealism or, perhaps, ideology. Foreign affairs mattered, as will be discussed, to only a small minority of Tories. In domestic affairs they were happy to have sterilized Labour and seen the Liberals disintegrate. They had the symbolically important tariff. It was at one level a National Government. But everyone who mattered knew who pulled the strings, and it was not MacDonald.

When Baldwin finally replaced MacDonald as Prime Minister in 1935 there was no change of direction or even of tone. The Conservatives were more or less united, once the India question was resolved. The party was well prepared for the forthcoming contest. As will be described, during the election Baldwin handled with dexterity, if hardly statesmanship, the question of re-armament. The 1935 election could never replicate the landslide of 1931. But it was a substantial victory all the same. Conservative representation in the new House of Commons was now 432. Labour recovered sharply to 154. The Liberal vote slumped. The 1935 general election, therefore, confirmed the apparently stable and – from the Conservative point of view – reassuring outlook.

Baldwin's final term as Prime Minister is, with one exception, best considered against the background of foreign policy, and Neville Chamberlain's wholly so. This will be done in the next chapter. But the exception – the Abdication crisis – served, as

Baldwin himself was acutely aware, as an important restorative to his by then somewhat dented reputation. The details of Edward VIII's involvement with Mrs Simpson and of Baldwin's role in forcing the monarch to confront realities are not part of the Conservative Party's story. Three aspects only are important here. First, Baldwin skilfully kept within the precise limits of constitutional convention. The Cabinet only formally offered its advice on the question of whether the King should contract a morganatic marriage with Mrs Simpson. It advised against.[57] This meant that it was the King, himself, not Baldwin, who set the pace and who decided on abdication. Second, Baldwin was given the opportunity to convey a morally upright and commonsensical impression to the House of Commons and the nation, which reminded people why they had voted for him, and made them miss him when he left. Third, Churchill's championing of Edward VIII's cause, impelled by a mixture of imprudent chivalry and ill-suppressed ambition, reminded people – and above all reminded his fellow Conservatives – why his judgement was so suspect. It was another hurdle to overcome when the nation found itself facing a struggle for survival.

A popular cartoon of the day in *Punch*, 'The Worcestershire Lad', shows Baldwin dressed as a ploughman, holding his inevitable pipe, being congratulated by John Bull: 'Well done, Stanley: a long day and a rare straight furrow.' The evening glow of national recognition would quickly fade. But the warmly complacent atmosphere accompanying Baldwin's departure from the scene is an historical fact.

Baldwin's national achievements do not constitute a long list and most lack specificity. His statesmanship can at best be described as atmospheric rather than practical. But of his political acumen (at least after 1924) there can be no doubt. He understood and, more successfully than any previous Prime Minister, manipulated the national mood, partly by instinct and partly through using techniques that were newly available. Under Baldwin, the

Conservatives (in whatever 'National' disguise) became the natural party of government. Baldwin won huge majorities. He just did know what to do with them. At a deeper level, undoubtedly he reflected the mood of the times. This, in fact, was the problem. He reflected it too well. In Baldwin the country got what it wanted and, arguably, and to stray into more disputable territory, it got what it deserved. But it did not get what it needed. Baldwin's success as the Conservative Party's leader serves as a reminder, were one necessary, that what is good for the party is not always good for everyone else.

PUNCH OR THE LONDON CHARIVARI—SEPTEMBER 21 1938

STILL HOPE

*Neville Chamberlain was at home in domestic policy-making, where
his reputation stood high. But notwithstanding the optimism of this
Punch cartoon from 1938, his misjudgement and mishandling of
Hitler unmade him, and nearly the country.*

11

THE APPEASEMENT PARTY

Neville Chamberlain finally became Prime Minister in May 1937. At sixty-eight, he was one of the oldest new occupants of Number Ten. Yet, except for gout, his health was good, his faculties undimmed, his experience large, his self-confidence undented. One disadvantage, compared with Baldwin, was that he was intensely disliked by the Labour Party. This was the result of his manner rather than his policies. Baldwin had warned him about the problem, but to no avail. It would matter if a great crisis, such as a war, required an all-party Government.

Despite the darkly clouded horizon, Neville Chamberlain himself believed that war was eminently avoidable. (So, paradoxically, did Winston Churchill, at least in retrospect: both were almost certainly wrong, albeit from opposite perspectives.[1]) Contrary to the impression given by his dour and frosty appearance, Chamberlain was a great optimist. He thought that improvement was possible and that he had a calling to bring it about. For Chamberlain was unashamedly an old-style Liberal or, in the parlance, 'Unionist', rather than a Conservative. This was literally true. In Birmingham, following Joe Chamberlain's tradition, the candidates were indeed called Unionists. Neville even, perhaps imprudently, joked about his non-Conservative origins when he was elected Conservative Party leader. In 1931 he had hoped to dispense altogether with what he termed the 'odious title of Conservative'. But, as others before and since (including his immediate successor) have found, its adhesive qualities are enormous: it stuck.[2] More importantly, and at a deeper level, Neville (unlike Austen) Chamberlain also had the distinctive liberal mindset. He was, as already noted, optimistic, even utopian, with a deep-seated conviction that rational argument would prevail. He was not, despite that, on the left, even of his party. Like his nemesis, Winston Churchill, Neville Chamberlain was, for example, viscerally anti-communist, and though he believed in social reform he also believed in small government and balanced budgets. He had, in fact, the merits and demerits of a thoroughly staid, bourgeois outlook. He was thus of a different stamp from the more socially and doctrinally obtuse and elusive Baldwin.

For that reason, and especially because it gave him some hope of a return to high office, Churchill welcomed the change. He even seconded Chamberlain's nomination as party leader. Churchill's observations about the new Prime Minister – the comparison is with Baldwin – are apt, and as always worth quoting: '[He] . . . was alert, businesslike, opinionated and self-confident in a very high degree. Unlike Baldwin, he conceived himself able to comprehend the whole field of Europe, and indeed the world. Instead of a vague but none the less deep-seated intuition, we had now a narrow sharp-edged efficiency within the limits of the policy in which he believed.'[3]

Stanley Baldwin's attitude towards the dangers confronting the country was one of exasperated incomprehension, combined with underlying smugness. In 1933, after Hitler's accession to power in Germany, Baldwin wrote to Thomas Jones: 'Walking alone among the hills I have come to the conclusion the world is stark mad. I have no idea what is the matter with it but it's all wrong and at times I am sick of being an asylum attendant. I think we are the sanest but the disease is catching.'⁴ Both Chamberlain and Halifax on different occasions professed the view that the Führer was mad or half-mad, though this did not prevent their trying to do business with him, and with considerable naïveté. But Baldwin's response to the Hitler business was a mental shrug.

Chamberlain intended to change all that. He wanted to pursue an active rather than a passive appeasement. Despite the folklore, Chamberlain invented neither the term nor the concept. Appeasement, in a general sense, had been the policy of Britain from at least the time of Salisbury, who had based his whole foreign policy on an awareness of the Empire's overstretched vulnerability (though Salisbury, of course, balanced compliance with steel in several major colonial wars). Britain was, as has been observed, the archetypical satisfied power. Satisfied powers have an overriding interest in appeasing the desire of dissatisfied powers to cause trouble. To that extent, Britain was bound to be in the forefront of the appeasers.

In a more specific sense, however – that in which it was used in the 1920s and 1930s – the term 'appeasement' referred to a policy of removing, primarily, those grounds for grievance on Germany's part which stemmed from the Versailles treaties, and, secondarily, occasions for the dissatisfaction of Italy, which was (or claimed to be) offended that it had not been better rewarded for its wartime efforts. The main sources of German grievance were the terms of reparations, the insistence on disarmament, exclusion from acquiring colonies, demilitarization (notably of the Rhineland), the prohibition of union with Austria (whatever the Austrians wanted), and the contentious frontiers of Czechoslovakia and Poland. In the 1920s, some progress was made, in fact, towards alleviating these perceived inequities. It was admittedly slow, mainly because France was, quite rightly, afraid of what a strong Germany might do.

The old French strategy of alliance with Russia had been destroyed by the Bolshevik Revolution and Soviet quasi-isolation. The new French strategy of trying to hem Germany in by alliances in eastern Europe never looked promising, and over time looked even less so. Moreover, it ran contrary to the French military concentration on defensive warfare (based heavily on the Maginot Line of fortifications). Such a strategy precluded providing any effective aid – even by way of distraction – for France's east European allies, who were too weak and divided to look after themselves. France thus tried, after a fashion, to hold the line against appeasing Germany. But because of its underlying weakness, France needed Britain, and Britain wanted appeasement. And so appeasement was pursued, with some modest benefits to show for it. The Dawes Plan was applied to make reparations payable without bankrupting the Germans. Locarno was agreed (see below). Germany entered the League of Nations. There were no acts of aggression or serious breaches of the Versailles terms.

Until 1929 such an approach seemed, indeed, quite sensible. Then came the Wall Street Crash. The economic revival of Germany proved to have been too dependent on American loans, which were now called in, bringing renewed convulsions and the rise of extremism.[5] Even so, up to 1933 appeasement as a policy option looked at least as good as anything else. Then came Hitler's triumph in the German elections and the post-election revolution, which imposed the Nazi totalitarian system. From this point on, the balance of advantage changed. Each act of appeasement towards Germany, however carefully calculated, gave a fillip to Hitler which, in turn, strengthened him against his internal opponents. And since Hitler's plans could not be fulfilled without war, these international concessions brought war closer and on what for Britain were (until the very end) increasingly disadvantageous terms. Such clarity in respect of dates and interests is, of course, possible only with the benefit of hindsight. No one – not even Churchill – had complete foresight at the time.

Specifically, Hitler wanted – among other things which are still subject to historical debate – a free hand in eastern Europe. But France and, more reluctantly, Britain would not and could not accord him one. In exchange, Hitler would, initially at least, have acknowledged Britain's maritime and imperial supremacy. The British, though, could not finally decide whether this was acceptable. They gave out contrary and conflicting signals, and Hitler became impatient. This is the background to the final period of appeasement played out under Chamberlain.[6]

There is, though, another essential background to this period, relating not directly to traditional perceptions of political and state interest, but rather to ideas. Viewed in the context of the intellectual and sentimental atmosphere prevailing in Britain, western Europe and the United States, the misjudgements made become explicable. They flowed, via different rivulets, from an all-encompassing torrent of reaction, indeed revulsion, against the Great War. They took the specific forms of a determination to avoid diplomatic entanglements, a preference for multilateral (preferably global) rather than bilateral commitments, a rejection of solutions based on the balance of power, and a conviction that 'large armaments' (in Baldwin's phrase) were the real cause of wars. The practical conclusions drawn from such analysis varied. For the idealistic left (and for the larger number who pretended to an idealism which they did not altogether share), the League of Nations and the League Covenant were the arch-stones of the new order. For the democratic right, which was now everywhere on the back foot, isolationism was the preferred response – within the hemisphere in America, within the Empire in Britain. Thus America stayed out of the League altogether and so condemned it to ultimate futility. In Britain, despite the reservations of Conservatives like Amery and Churchill, lip service was paid by the

National Government to the League, while in practice a cautious and qualified policy was followed.

It might, of course, have been possible to strike out more boldly and offer a completely different analysis. But the consequences of doing so were illustrated by the obloquy visited on Birkenhead for his notorious rectorial address at Glasgow University on 7 November 1923. Admittedly, F.E. might have put the point more tactfully and used language which was less likely to be turned against him. But that was not his way:

> For as long a time as the records of history have been preserved, human societies passed through a ceaseless process of evolution and adjustment. This process has sometimes been pacific; but more often it has resulted from warlike disturbance. The strength of different nations, measured in terms of arms, varies from century to century. The world continues to offer glittering prizes to those who have stout hearts and sharp swords; it is, therefore, extremely improbable that the experience of future ages will differ in any material respect from that which has happened since the twilight of the human race. It is for us, therefore, who in our history have proved ourselves a martial, rather than a military, people to abstain, as has been our habit, from provocation; but to maintain in our own hand the adequate means of our own protection; and, so equipped, to march with heads erect and bright eyes along the road of our Imperial destiny. [7]

Birkenhead sinned, not just by being his notorious self, but by daring to articulate the recognizably conservative view, which was shared by his friend Churchill, that the law of the jungle, not the law of the League, would prevail in international affairs, and that only the fittest and strongest would survive. Instead, the dictators dealt with Sir Samuel Hoare, Lord Halifax and Neville Chamberlain.

Foreign policy under Baldwin was always a mixture of contradictions and compromises. The nearest these came to coalescing in
a settled approach was when Austen Chamberlain was Foreign
Secretary at the time of the Locarno Pact in 1925. The approach
Chamberlain evolved, which resulted in Locarno, was the result of
another compromise. Austen would not go along with the so-called
Geneva Protocol, which further tightened up the obligations of
collective security established under Article 16 of the Covenant of
the League of Nations. British policy was, rather, to loosen them.
The Government would not have Britain become (in a frequently
used phrase) the 'world's policeman'. But Austen Chamberlain did
not want, either, to bow to isolationists in his party. Moreover, unusually among Conservative politicians (another exception being
Churchill), he felt a strong sympathy for France. A proposal from
Germany presented by Gustav Stresemann for the demilitarization
of the Rhineland as a quid pro quo for German re-engagement in a
new European settlement within the framework of the League provided, he thought, an international opportunity. Under the
resulting treaties, initialled at Locarno in October, Britain, France,
Germany, Belgium and Italy jointly agreed to observe the demilitarization of the Rhineland, to defend the existing borders
between Germany and France and Germany and Belgium, and to
render military assistance to any signatory which fell victim to a
flagrant violation of these undertakings. The Pact also included
arbitration agreements between Germany and its neighbours –
France, Belgium, Poland and Czechoslovakia. The following year
Germany was admitted to the League.

At least as important, however, was what Locarno did not do. It
did not guarantee by threat of force the borders of Germany and its
eastern neighbours. The Poles and Czechs were acutely aware of
this. So, of course, were the Germans, who even before Hitler's rise
to power were keen to revise these borders in their own interests.
Britain was also aware of the implications, though Chamberlain

pooh-poohed the danger. The real purpose of Locarno, from London's viewpoint, was to impose a model of national interest, limiting British involvement, upon the utopian framework of the League. This, in itself, made sense. But giving even a flickering green light to German ambitions in the east did not. These implications were not immediately apparent. George V insisted on the Garter for Austen Chamberlain, and confided to his diary: 'I pray that this may mean peace for many years. Why not for ever?'[8]

In the years that followed there was much talk by Austen Chamberlain of the 'Spirit of Locarno'. Locarno was his only achievement as a statesman and he intended to hold on to it. Informal meetings between the representatives of the signatories continued. More practically important were the management of the difficult reparations issue and the establishment of solid currencies in France and Germany. The League, meanwhile, apparently prospered. By 1928 every European state, except the Soviet Union, was a member, though, of course, the United States was still not. One should, incidentally, also note the involvement of Fascist Italy in these arrangements. Mussolini had come to power in 1922. His regime was disagreeable in many ways. But – to begin with, at least – he played the game much as other Italian leaders had.

The League of Nations was not, though, just a network of institutions. It was something like a religion. The precise contents of the faith changed somewhat over time, but the fervour – and the accompanying irrationality – did not. Both were particularly evident in the early 1930s, utopianism ruling even as challenges to the new order multiplied. In 1931 the Japanese occupied Manchuria. In February 1932 the World Disarmament Conference opened in Geneva, chaired by the former Labour Foreign Secretary Arthur Henderson; in October the following year Hitler withdrew from both the Conference and the League. In 1932 Britain finally abandoned the 'Ten Year Rule' (initiated in 1919 and reinforced in 1928), by which defence planning had been conducted on the assumption of no major war within ten years. Even so, despite the dangers, Britain and France did not risk publishing plans for rearmament while the Conference was sitting.[9] Illusion and reality marched together.

In Britain, the summer of 1935 saw the Peace Ballot, organized by the League of Nations Union. Eleven million people voted. The vast majority not only backed the League of Nations but agreed with international disarmament, the abolition by international agreement of military aircraft, and an end to the private manufacture of armaments. At the same time, strong assent in the Ballot to the use of economic and military measures to stop aggression served as a fig-leaf behind which the National Government and the Conservatives were able to hide. Indeed, the League was now increasingly viewed by Conservative politicians as a framework within which force might be applied, rather than one within which to promote global pacifism. As such, even sceptics like Churchill would eventually begin to see that it could be a help rather than a hindrance to rearmament. But this was not the national mood, and it was not at all the intention of the Ballot organizers.

It was the East Fulham by-election of October 1933, rather than the general election of 1935, that Baldwin had in mind – contrary to Churchill's insinuation – when in November 1936 he imprudently referred in the Commons, with what he called 'appalling frankness', to the earlier impossibility of winning political support for rearmament. (At East Fulham a Labour candidate had won the otherwise safe Tory seat on a disarmament platform.) In fact, in 1935 Baldwin had signalled, far too strongly for the arms-cutting Labour and Liberal parties, the need to rebuild Britain's defence. Even then, he felt he had to give assurances that there would 'be no great armaments'.[10] Hoare, rather cheekily, later suggested that Baldwin had received a clear mandate for rearmament and criticized him for failing to act on it.[11] But this is to exaggerate the speed of what was, in reality, a very slow turn-round in pacifist public opinion.

Hoare's own difficulties, as the new Foreign Secretary, over Italy and Abyssinia, undoubtedly, though inadvertently, helped prompt the change. The politicians were largely of one mind on the fundamentals. It was clearly in Britain's interest to detach Italy from Germany, given that Germany was the main threat and that Italy also posed a challenge to British interests in the Mediterranean and the Middle East. France had an even stronger interest in dividing Fascist Italy and Nazi Germany. Secret Franco-Italian military agreements, reached in May and June 1935, guaranteed the withdrawal of Italian troops from the French frontier in exchange for a free hand for Italy in Abyssinia, even envisaging possible joint military action against Germany.

This was not as unrealistic as its seems. Mussolini's ambitions preceded Hitler's rise to power. They were based on realpolitik with an added, unpredictable element of nationalistic theatre (*sacro egoismo*). If Italy's aims could be fulfilled, or at least not openly thwarted, the (limited) ideological similarities between Fascism and National Socialism might be subordinated to old-fashioned state interest. What stood in the way of this policy solution, suggested by the 'old diplomacy', was the new primacy of the League of Nations – though even the League, when the crunch came, was keen to see a compromise with Italy. The other alternative, of course, was that which Hitler later cynically suggested to Britain's ambassador, Neville Henderson, namely that London might have called Mussolini's bluff. Britain now disastrously managed to combine the worst of both policies.

In 1935 Italy made no secret of its designs on Abyssinia, the focus of Italy's plans for East African colonial expansion. All that was in doubt was how much Italy would settle for, and how difficult it would be to limit its ambitions. The war duly began, though the Italians initially faced setbacks. Samuel Hoare, on the advice of the influential and anti-German Permanent Secretary at the Foreign Office, Robert Vansittart, addressed the League of Nations in September in such robust language that it was widely expected that Britain would take the lead in applying League sanctions.[12] But Britain was also keen not to alienate Mussolini, and the French were even keener – so keen, indeed, that if Britain were to take the risk of war in the Mediterranean it would have to fight alone. The Cabinet, therefore, agreed the principles of a compromise, and Hoare was left to sort out the details with the French foreign minister, Pierre Laval. Hoare himself was ill and badly needed a holiday, but he signed off on the terms in Paris en route to Switzerland. These then embarrassingly appeared, first in the form of a leak to the French press, and then all over the British newspapers on 10 December.

Uproar ensued. Hoare was abandoned by Baldwin and the Cabinet and had to resign. Baldwin grovelled publicly and survived. Italy was furious and drew closer to a supportive Germany. The prospect of any reassurance for an increasingly shaky France disappeared. Abyssinia duly fell into Italian hands and Haile Selassie, its ruler, fled Djibouti in a British warship the following May.[13]

Meanwhile, Hitler used the international disarray for his own purposes. On 7 March 1936 German troops entered the Rhineland. Britain had already privately accepted that the demilitarization of the Rhineland zone – imposed under the Treaty of Versailles and reaffirmed under the Treaty of Locarno – would end. But the Government hoped that when that happened it could be as part of a negotiated replacement for Locarno, which Hitler would honour.

The French political situation at this juncture was fluid. French public opinion was unreliable, but certainly unprepared for conflict on this particular question. In the event, the French generals suffered a severe attack of cold feet, exaggerating the threat French forces would face if they did march against Germany. The sudden declaration by Belgium of its neutrality at this time also threw the French high command's plans for the defence of the French northern frontier from within Belgium into disarray.[14]

Meanwhile, the general feeling in Britain, not least in the Conservative Party, echoed in the Conservative-leaning press, was that the Germans were merely re-entering 'their own backyard'.[15] Indeed, majority Conservative opinion was moderately pro-German and sympathetic to righting alleged grievances, at least until the Austrian Anschluss of March 1938, and perhaps later.[16]

French protests were, therefore, greeted coldly in London. But Britain too was the loser. France had given up a significant buffer zone protecting its border, and done so with no significant reaction. Internationally, France was humiliated. In reaction, French politicians put all the blame on Britain and became even more committed to the doomed strategy of hemming Germany in by alliances to the east.

Hitler, by contrast, had taken a gamble against advice and been proved right. His support and his confidence rose. So did his standing with his own previously sceptical diplomats and generals. He was, in fact, significantly further along the road to war.

Anthony Eden had been appointed by Baldwin to succeed Hoare. (Austen Chamberlain, having temporized about the Hoare–Laval Pact, hoped he would be rewarded with Hoare's job, and was given reason to hope by Baldwin: but he was, yet again, disappointed.) Eden's selection, despite his tender years (at thirty-eight, he was Britain's youngest Foreign Secretary), was a politically shrewd move. Eden was the darling of League-obsessed liberal, and even left-wing, opinion. He was progressive, attractive and in sympathy with internationalism.[17] Although he and his supporters would eventually join forces with Churchill and his much smaller group, their outlook and interests were at this point very different. Churchill had no backing at any time from the progressive wing of the Conservative Party, nor, indeed, from progressives anywhere else.[18] Eden was more preoccupied with Italy. Churchill was prepared to overlook Italy's misbehaviour in the interests of a stronger policy against the real threat, Germany. Eden's claims to be a principled opponent of appeasement in all its forms have also to be qualified.

Eden was always greatly concerned with his reputation. It is the key to his behaviour. When he eventually resigned as Foreign Secretary in February 1938, Lloyd George observed: 'Eden has today paid a big cheque into the bank on which he can draw in the future.' This was a fair assessment, and draw he did. Churchill's own later account, based on incomplete knowledge of detailed discussions within Government, also reinforced Eden's heroic status.

In fact, there was only a marginal difference between Eden and either Baldwin or Neville Chamberlain on the question of appeasement of Italy, which all accepted – in some form – was necessary. Eden was more enthusiastic than the other two about the League, but he could hardly ignore realities. Eden also wanted to see Mussolini fulfil his promise to withdraw his 'volunteers' from Spain before recognizing Italy's conquest. But, crucially, Eden, like Chamberlain, recognized that after the Abyssinian fiasco some way of drawing Italy back into the anti-Hitler orbit had to be found, and sanctions would sooner or later have to be dropped. Eden was annoyed that now and later Chamberlain took too much on himself in personal initiatives and did not consult his self-important young Foreign Secretary enough. Chamberlain thought that greater urgency was required, and he also thought that Eden's highly personalized dislike of Mussolini was a problem. Nor did he share Eden's curious belief that there was a possibility of drawing the United States much further into the anti-German camp.[19] (The possible creation of a 'Grand Alliance' including the United States and the Soviet Union – to which Eden was also more sympathetic than Chamberlain – would receive eloquent but unpersuasive attention from Churchill in two great speeches in the Commons in March, after Eden's departure.[20]) Eden thought that Chamberlain should have responded positively, rather than sceptically, to Roosevelt's opaque proposal for a world conference on peace. That may be true. Arguably, even the slimmest opportunity to lure America back into collective security was worth seizing. But Chamberlain had a surer grasp of the real limits to what Roosevelt would or could do. So when Eden finally announced his resignation at Cabinet because of 'fundamental differences of policy' no one else was clear what they were.[21] Nor were many MPs, when he later explained his reasons to the House of Commons, and his subsequent studious avoidance of direct criticism confused them further.

Neville Chamberlain's becoming Prime Minister did not change direction, but gave earlier policies a more vigorous impetus. This, paradoxically, only exposed their underlying flaws. Chamberlain did not behave improperly. He consulted the Cabinet. But he also fell into the trap, to which his vanity anyway predisposed him, of relying excessively in making the big decisions on his own personal qualities and efforts, seconded by a very limited number of aides and advisers. On the other hand, the constraints he inherited and under which he operated, from 1937 to the outbreak of war, must also be remembered in any assessment. These bear on more than Chamberlain's reputation: they also set benchmarks by which the Conservative Party, in its attitudes to the least palatable features of appeasement, should be judged. Within the scope of such a book as this, such considerations can be only briefly enumerated. But there were five.

First, it was an unchallenged and apparently unchallengeable assumption in British defence policy that the protection of the Empire had priority. This, in turn, influenced the relative attention given to the different branches of the services: it also particularly impinged on the advice given by the Admiralty. Throughout the 1930s Britain was concerned about Japan, which launched its move against Manchuria in 1931, and with which, under American pressure, Britain had ended its traditional alliance. The Anglo-German naval agreement of 1935 did little to reduce British anxiety on this front. The army, too, was primarily envisaged as at the service of imperial defence. The Chiefs of Staff warned the Government after Locarno that there was nothing to spare to honour the obligations undertaken to defend France and Belgium. This gap between capabilities and undertakings exposes, of course, the lack of realism with which British diplomacy as a whole was conducted at the time.[22]

The second constraint was fear of Britain's vulnerability to air raids. Baldwin came up with the most memorably depressing observation in the Commons on 10 November 1932: 'the bomber will always get through'.[23] In Cabinet he proposed an end to all new military aircraft building as a route to the abolition of air forces. This proposal was, thankfully, not accepted. Baldwin himself had second thoughts, though he remained obsessed with the threat of bombing. Re-armament, including air armament, began. Indeed, the RAF, championed by both ministers and their critics, received a disproportionate share of the available resources. Technically speaking, the assumption that the bomber could not be stopped was at this point correct (though that hardly justifies broadcasting the fact, as Baldwin did). But the accompanying strategic assumption that bombing might act as a deterrent to Hitler, so that he did not bomb Britain, was plain wrong. Germany did not itself ever regard the Luftwaffe as a deterrent strike force, and, rightly, did not fear at this stage Britain's capability for bombing military or civilian targets in the Third Reich.

Chamberlain, partly on grounds of cost but wisely all the same, shifted the emphasis from bombers to fighters, once it was clear that Germany's advantage in the former – previously denied – was unassailable. From 1937, the build-up of fighter aircraft and the development, and finally deployment, of radar offered rational hope, and indeed expectation, that the bomber would not always 'get through'. A realistic and historically informed concept of military conflict would, naturally, have prepared British policy-makers for the alternating shifts between offensive and defensive advantage. Instead, emotions dictated policy, with predictably unhappy results. Even in 1938 Chamberlain was obsessed by the bomber. The presumed effects on London were at the forefront of his mind as he flew back along the Thames, over the sprawling suburbs of the metropolis, after his failed meeting with Hitler at Godesberg; and he spoke of his fears again to Cabinet. It was a nightmare; and it could never come true. In the event, Britain's total civilian casualties during the Second World War barely exceeded those predicted for London during the first week of air bombardment.[24]

Meanwhile, the British army languished. By February 1938 the Contingency Expeditionary Force had shrunk to two infantry divisions and one mobile division. Imperial commitments were still envisaged as having priority. The Austrian Anschluss and the start of the Czech crisis prompted warnings from the Chiefs of Staff that Britain could not defend Czechoslovakia without waging war on Germany, adding that this would probably involve fighting both Italy and Japan. Such advice obviously weighed heavily with Chamberlain at Munich. Finally, in a report to Cabinet in February 1939 the Chiefs of Staff admitted: 'It is difficult to say how the security of the United Kingdom could be maintained if France were forced to capitulate and therefore the defence of the former may have to include a share in the land defence of French territory.' Cabinet now agreed to create a full continental army of thirty-two divisions. It was far too late.[25] For the shambolic campaign in France, Britain was only able to commit 4 divisions, the basis of the new British Expeditionary Force. The French fielded 84 and the Germans 103.

The third constraint was money. Chamberlain, as Chancellor and then as Prime Minister, brought to the debate about re-armament a strong conviction of the need to keep Britain's economy from being overburdened by military spending. This, in turn, reflected his entirely correct understanding of the country's economic vulnerability. Britain had substantial overseas assets, but British governments had to be – and were – worried about running balance of payments deficits. Unlike the German command economy under Nazism, Britain did not aim for self-sufficiency to withstand the threats which war would pose. But it was well understood that Britain's best hope of survival was to use its navy to keep the sea lanes open and ensure that the British economy was capable of out-lasting Germany's. Unlike during the First World War, Britain in such straits could hope for no financial support from the United States. A succession of US Neutrality Acts ruled this out. Britain, as a sovereign defaulter, could not even, under the US Johnson Act (1934), raise loans there. All of this meant that the country could not just spend what it liked on armaments – though, clearly, it should have spent more and earlier.

The fourth constraint was faulty intelligence. It is debatable whether – had such a thing been possible – British politicians might not have made better decisions without any intelligence at all about German aims and conditions than with the intelligence they received in the years prior to the Second World War.[26] 'Cato' was wrong in suggesting that Chamberlain and his clique of advisers ignored the advice of the Foreign Office and intelligence experts.[27] The experts were part of the problem. More generally, intelligence concentrated over-much on second-guessing German intentions, while taking insufficient notice of either ideology or technology. Up to 1936, British intelligence tended to underrate the threat from Germany. But then its assessments shifted dramatically and con-sistently overrated the state of German preparedness and efficiency. By 1939 the (real but exaggerated) problems faced by the German economy were being reported. This intelligence combined with (real but exaggerated) confidence in British re-armament con-vinced the politicians, including Chamberlain, that they should press Germany harder, in the erroneous belief that Hitler could at this stage be deterred by guarantees to Poland. (These guarantees, it is sometimes forgotten, did not, as Chamberlain emphasized in

Cabinet, extend to Poland's territorial integrity, only its independence.)

Hitler, according to Chamberlain, who liked the ill-advised expression and used it right into 1940, had now 'missed the bus'. When war was declared, despite Chamberlain's and Halifax's attempts to delay it, the Prime Minister lamented in the Commons, and later on the airwaves: 'Everything that I have worked for, everything that I have hoped for, everything that I have believed in during my public life, has crashed in ruins.' Yet at one level, like the guarantees and the ultimatum, it was all a kind of bluff. Hitler would still draw back, it was hoped. The phoney war appeared to offer that possibility. Chamberlain wrote to his sister Ida on 23 September: 'The way to win the war is to convince the Germans that they cannot win it.' This, of course, was taking the approach to a delusional conclusion, but the experts had previously encouraged it.[28]

Finally, there was the lack of allies. The suggestion that Chamberlain failed to create a grand alliance against Hitler because of prejudice or lack of imagination was at one time widely accepted. Propagated both by the left, anxious to demonstrate Stalin's good intentions, despite the Nazi–Soviet Pact, and by the right (notably Churchill), it played particularly well to Americans, who liked to imagine that they were more enthusiastic to fight Nazism than they were. It still enjoys the nuanced support of some leading historians.[29] Of course, Chamberlain might have made more of an effort to secure alliances and less of an effort to satisfy Hitler; but it is difficult to believe that he would have been any more successful with the one than the other, and the attempt might well have precipitated the war earlier, when Britain was less prepared. (This is not, of course, to suggest that Chamberlain was pursuing the policy sometimes suggested by his defenders of merely buying time – see below.)

The three main allies to which Britain might theoretically look were France, the United States and the Soviet Union. For reasons having as much to do with domestic social and political conditions

The Treaty of Versailles, 1919 (*above*): in the centre is Georges Clemenceau (France), with Lloyd George on his left; Law looks on. Opposite him, with his back to the viewer, is Woodrow Wilson (US). The Treaties of Locarno (1925) amended the Versailles terms, with apparent success: here (*right*) signatories and spouses gather at Downing Street for a photo-call.

Three political adventurers (*above, left to right*): Lloyd George, F. E. Smith and Churchill in 1921. *Below* (*left to right*), F.E., Neville Chamberlain and Walter Guinness arrive at Downing Street for a meeting during the General Strike of 1926.

Top: A mortally ill Bonar Law (*right*) takes the air at Aix-les-Bains with his friend Max Beaverbrook (*left*) in 1923. Stanley Baldwin (*above*) looks vigorously avuncular for the cameras in the garden at No. 10 in 1928. A firm hand on the tiller (*left*) – or on to the rocks? The Conservatives focused on Baldwin in 1929, but they lost the election.

TRUST BALDWIN

He will steer you to safety!

As Foreign Secretary, Austen Chamberlain (*above, left*) found Mussolini quite amenable, here at a League of Nations meeting in Rome in 1929. That would change. *Below,* Austen's half-brother Neville, Conservative chairman, arrives at Caxton Hall, London, for a party meeting in 1930.

The crisis conditions of 1931 led to the emergence of the National Government (*above*) – notably (*counting from left to right*) Ramsay MacDonald, Prime Minister (1), Baldwin, Lord President (4) and Philip Snowden, Chancellor (5). Conservative posters for the 1931 election emphasized a protectionist theme, whether aimed at the agricultural vote (*below left*) or at trade and industrial interests (*below right*).

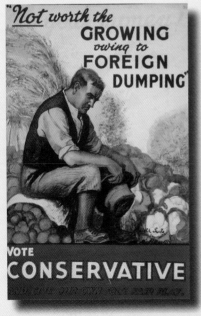

In 1935 Sir John Simon, Foreign Secretary (*left*), and Anthony Eden (*right*) hold talks with Hitler in Berlin (*above*). The Tory-dominated National Government seeks a balance between strength and appeasement, as illustrated by that year's election poster (*left*). Churchill, at this stage with little influence, campaigns in his constituency (*below*).

GRIP THE KEY TO PEACE

LEAGUE OF NATIONS

VOTE NATIONAL

VOTE FOR CHURCHILL

A STRONG BRITAIN MEANS A WORLD AT PEACE VOTE NATIONAL

Draining the dregs of appeasement: Chamberlain dines with Hitler on his mission to Munich in 1938 (*above*). In September the following year, a few days after the declaration of war, Eden, the new Dominions Secretary, is pictured in Downing Street (*left*) with gas mask slung over his shoulder.

Churchill, broadcasting
on 13 May 1940, promises
'blood, toil, tears and sweat'
on the road to victory
(*above*); on the evening
of VE-Day, 8 May 1945
(*right*), he appears on the
balcony of the Ministry
of Health.

as foreign policy, France was unreliable. Neville Chamberlain (unlike Austen) always believed this. Indeed, in the event the French collapse proved even the pessimists optimistic. As for the United States, there could be no realistic expectation – despite Eden's hopes – of any effective help in that quarter. American policy had even ruled out any prospect of Britain's trying to relieve pressure in the Far East through a continuing agreement with Japan, which would have allowed it to concentrate on the European theatre. And although Churchill in 1939 argued strongly for an alliance with the Soviet Union – a proposal which had obvious appeal and enjoyed the support of 87 per cent of the public – he knew why it was so difficult to pursue.[30] This was because the distrust which Chamberlain felt for Moscow was dwarfed by that felt by Britain's east European allies, who rightly judged themselves to be the Soviets' intended victims. This was particularly strongly felt by the Poles. In any case, Stalin had much more to hope for and fear from Hitler than he did for and from the British or French. And Stalin was altogether unprepared for war.[31]

Even within these tight constraints, however, Neville Chamberlain's policy must be accounted a culpable failure, notably from the onset of the Czechoslovakian crisis in 1938 to the outbreak of war. The reasons, less ideological and certainly less Machiavellian than those advanced by some of his critics, are not difficult to perceive. If Chamberlain's objective had been to postpone the evil day until Britain was strong enough to face it, that would have been a convincing defence of his action. But it was not his goal. He believed he could avoid war altogether, and he held to that belief. It is certainly true that, even when he returned from Munich and meeting Hitler, to be greeted by ecstatically enthusiastic crowds, he was not as sure as he seemed that he had truly guaranteed 'peace for our time'. In the car he turned to Halifax and said: 'Edward, we must hope for the best and prepare for the worst.' But 'the worst', even then, never seemed to encompass war, a prospect so mad and so horrible that he could not envisage that anyone – even Hitler, whom he sometimes believed 'half mad' – would plan or provoke it.[32]

Chamberlain simply did not understand Hitler. This would not have mattered so much, had he not thought that he did. He also thought that Hitler respected him and that Hitler, in turn, could therefore be trusted. Jock Colville, Chamberlain's (and later Churchill's) PPS, summed up the problem: '[Chamberlain's] sin was vanity.'[33] Thus the Prime Minister confidently told the Cabinet after his return from Godesberg that Hitler was only interested in redrawing frontiers in eastern Europe in so far as this would bring German minorities back within the Fatherland, misunderstanding that this traditional (but aggressive) objective was merely a part of a revolutionary dynamism with global objectives.[34] The right questions for British statesmen to ask were how to defeat Hitler, and when. Chamberlain never asked them.

Accordingly, with a regularity and predictability that are striking in retrospect, Chamberlain's policy failed. He exerted what proved irresistible pressure on the Czechs to concede the demands of the Sudeten Germans, even though doing so must make Czechoslovakia unsustainable as a state. He took it upon himself, intermittently consulting his own Cabinet but not the Czech Government, to work out a solution with Hitler at Berchtesgaden, on 15 September 1938. He then found himself faced with what amounted to an ultimatum on different terms when he visited Hitler at Godesberg on 22–3 September. At the two leaders' final conference in Munich (in which Italy and France also participated) Chamberlain thought that he had achieved a wider breakthrough, with Hitler offering, at the expense of the Czechoslovakian carve-up, the prospect of a new and peaceful start. Then, on 15 March 1939, came the Prague coup and German occupation of Bohemia and Moravia. This marked the end of appeasement. It was followed by a half-baked policy of deterrence via unenforceable guarantees to Germany's neighbours, which Hitler did not anyway take seriously. This policy was popular, but it was arguably even more frivolous and irresponsible than what preceded it.

At least Chamberlain was not alone in his misjudgements. His policy of appeasement was for most of the time very well supported, by all parties and all classes. Monthly opinion polling by Gallup, which began in October 1938, showed solid support for Chamberlain's Government until February 1940. The (less reliable) Mass-Observation polling detected a large surge of opinion in Chamberlain's favour at the time of Munich. Chamberlain was wildly, indeed hysterically, cheered in the House of Commons when he announced that he would accept Hitler's invitation.

However, it seems that when the actual terms of Munich became known, they were not popular.[35] A gulf opened up, and steadily widened, between Chamberlain and public opinion in perceptions of Hitler. In October 1938, when Chamberlain still seems to have trusted Hitler's assurances that his demands were satisfied, polling evidence suggests that 93 per cent of the public did not.[36] The more that was learned about Hitler's regime, the less it was liked. The Kristallnacht attacks on Jews and Jewish property in November 1938 were well reported. That said, the desire to avoid war remained intense. When war came, the mood was resolute, not enthusiastic. The disappointments after Munich had convinced opinion, including in the Dominions, that Hitler had to be fought. But the mood was not at all like that of 1914, doubtless because 1914 was by no means a distant memory.

For two obvious reasons, it was more than likely that the Conservative Party as a whole would support appeasement. First, nearly the whole political class and, to the extent they were aware of it, the great majority of the electorate did so. The scandal occasioned by the leak of the Hoare–Laval Pact was the exception, and, significantly it did not involve the terrible prospect of war with Germany, only standing up to Mussolini.

Second, appeasement was strongly supported by a variety of powerful individuals, institutions and interests with links to the Conservative Party. Not the least of these were the monarchy and the court. George V and his family were firmly in the appeasement camp. Edward VIII's sympathies were briefly an embarrassment and later (after the Abdication) a potential danger. But George VI's closeness to Hoare, admiration for Chamberlain and hearty dislike for Churchill (whose past – this time his championing of Edward VIII – again caught up with him) were more seriously problematic. The Queen even discouraged Chamberlain from taking Churchill into his Government. Naturally, the royal family were equally disappointed when Churchill, rather than their friend Halifax, became Prime Minister in May 1940.[37]

The Conservative-inclined press was also largely in favour of appeasement, at least until the policy manifestly unravelled. Chamberlain's return from Munich was the high (or, viewed differently, the low) point. *The Times* proclaimed that 'no conqueror returning from a victory on the battlefield had come adorned with nobler laurels' and attacked Churchill's 'dismal sincerity'. The *Daily Express* was equally enthusiastic about Chamberlain – and vitriolically dismissive of Beaverbrook's old sparring partner (and now sacked political commentator) Churchill. It sneered at his great speech in the debate as 'an alarmist oration by a man whose mind is soaked in the conquests of Marlborough'. Just the *Daily Telegraph* was openly critical of the policy.[38] Only from the turn of the year and into 1939 did press opinion shift. In any case, the press was by no means a wholly independent force. It was heavily influenced by Tory press management in favour of Chamberlain and against his critics. Strong pressures, resulting in a high degree of self-censorship, were applied by Joseph Ball, from the party, and by George Steward, who briefed the lobby from Number Ten.[39]

The period during which Conservative critics of appeasement faced greatest intimidation from the leadership and party organization was between Chamberlain's 'triumph' at Munich at the end of September 1938 and the Prague coup in mid-March 1939. The prospect of an early general election provided an incentive, and also an excuse, for loyalist party members to insist on a reckoning with rebel MPs. (In fact, Halifax had dissuaded Chamberlain from going to the country on the back of Munich, but this was not widely known.) Even Churchill was put under heavy pressure at Epping. He fought back successfully, but did so on the grounds of his right to free speech as a Member of Parliament, rather than by tapping sympathy for his views.[40]

Partly because of this pressure to support appeasement, and even more because of the temptation to downplay, deny or disown earlier pro-appeasement opinions once war broke out, it is difficult now to weigh the precise balance of feeling within the party. On one reading, the decisive moment came at the climax of what has been called 'the greatest, and the most portentous, of all parliamentary occasions in the twentieth century'.[41] The confidence debate of 7–8 May 1940, prompted by the Norway fiasco (for which Churchill was mainly responsible, but for which Chamberlain took the blame and subsequently had to resign), was indeed a great occasion. But with Churchill and Eden already back in Government, it is not very revealing of party opinion. In any case, only 38 MPs in receipt of the Government whip voted with the Opposition. Deliberate abstentions were probably fewer than 25. Chamberlain survived with a majority of 81. He then hoped to hang on once news came through of the German attack on France. The Cabinet stopped that. What was decisive was not the vote in the Commons, or the speeches that preceded it, but the fact that the Labour Party would not enter a coalition with Chamberlain as Prime Minister.[42] What was also decisive was that Churchill wanted the top job more than did the otherwise favoured candidate, Halifax. (And what avoided embarrassing argument involving the King was Chamberlain's decision to bring together the two candidates, in the presence of the

Chief Whip, to sort it out, so that one name only – Churchill's – went to the Palace.[43])

Abandoning the snapshot approach, there are, in fact, few fail-safe generalizations about who in the Conservative Party, in Parliament and outside it, fell into the pro- and anti-appeasement camps and why. The critics of appeasement tended to be younger, representing constituencies in the south-east (so safer and presumably less biddable by Central Office); they were also more likely to be connected to the aristocracy, and public school and Oxbridge educated. Beyond providing a useful antidote to the sloppy suggestion made by some on the left that appeasement was a mere 'Establishment' phenomenon, this does not get one very far.[44]

Ideology, indeed, hardly came into it. Anti-appeasers, always a minority, were to be found on both left and right and, indeed, in the centre of the party. A number of appeasers (such as Neville Chamberlain or Simon) were Liberal rather than Tory in background and outlook, but the rule does not always hold good – as the cases of the anti-appeaser Austen Chamberlain and, more obviously still, Churchill suggest. The common factors were, as Robert Blake observed, those which define all serious-minded political groupings, namely 'ones of temperament, outlook and judgement'.[45] Churchill's small band of devotees, the 'Eden Group' (chaired by Leo Amery when Eden returned to office, and sneered at by the whips as the 'Glamour Boys'), and Salisbury's less glamorous 'Watching Committee' were the three most important elements consistently challenging the Chamberlain party line.[46]

Nor is it a simple matter to classify all those who broadly followed that line and so must, with varying degrees of emphasis, be classed as 'appeasers'. A desire to uphold the pure doctrine of the League of Nations and collective security was not necessarily indicative of a desire to stand up to Hitler. Churchill, for example, like Austen Chamberlain, was sceptical of the League and not unsympathetic, at least in the early stages, to Mussolini and Fascism. A large number of Conservative MPs felt the same way. But Fascism was seen as an answer to chaotic communist-threatened Italy's needs, not to those of Britain.[47] Similar reasoning lay behind the widespread sympathy, both on the Conservative back benches and within the Government, to the Nationalist side in the Spanish Civil War. Franco and the army were seen as the way to keep the communists out.[48] Naturally, the left disagreed. Schism on this question rendered still-born attempts by Churchill to reach out in 1936 and 1937 to anti-appeasers on the left. But the left were anyway at the time involved in an internecine factional struggle over Spain.

Some Conservatives were also positively enthusiastic about Hitler. But these, though occasionally influential, were neither a coherent nor a representative grouping. Difficult as it is to credit, Hitler was clearly capable of exerting a strange, mesmeric charm over certain sorts of Englishmen (and occasionally Englishwomen). He had hoped to exert it over Baldwin. But the British Prime Minister, despite urging from Ribbentrop, was too lazy or too canny (or both) to make the required visit. (Ribbentrop improbably but optimistically confided in Tom Jones: 'I want Mr. Baldwin to meet Hitler. He is not the Dictator in conversation. He is like Mr. Baldwin.') Lloyd George did go, and at his meeting in Munich on 4 September 1936 proved himself a classically useful fool. He later described Hitler in glowing terms in the *Express* as a 'born leader of men'. He also lamented: 'I wish Neville Chamberlain could be closeted with him for an hour.'[49] Less than three years later the wish was granted. But in the meantime that sophisticated man of the world and future Foreign Secretary, Lord Halifax, had even more egregiously fallen into the trap.

The account of Halifax's encounter with Nazi Germany in November 1937 illustrates how a particular Conservative mentality was prone to falling for Hitler's crude mendacity. Even when the exaggerations of *Guilty Men* are discounted, Halifax's reactions show why the impression of Conservative complicity in the rise and advance of Hitler stuck and, at an important psychological level, was well founded. The bizarre occasion was an invitation to a hunting exhibition in Berlin, which Halifax (a great huntsman) accepted, apparently with Eden's encouragement. It was no mere goodwill gesture. Before he went, Halifax read carefully the line proposed by Britain's self-assured but out-of-his-depth ambassador in Berlin, Neville Henderson, on cultivating Anglo-German relations.[50] Halifax was then invited to see Hitler at Berchtesgaden. On arrival, he mistook Hitler for a footman, though the ultimate *faux pas* of asking him to take his coat was avoided. It was Halifax, not Hitler, who then in discussion proceeded to list the areas where the Versailles Treaty terms might be adjusted to Germany's benefit – Danzig, Austria and Czechoslovakia. The following day Halifax was entertained by Goering at his estate; he discussed Germany's desire for colonies with the economist, Schacht; and he concluded his visit by taking tea with Dr Goebbels and his wife. Eden was furious after the visit, but only because he had been upstaged: in Cabinet he congratulated Halifax on his negotiating acumen.[51]

Beside such a combination of cynicism and gullibility the odd, even treasonable behaviour of a small minority of right-wing Hitler enthusiasts seems almost beside the point. The case of the popular historian Sir Arthur Bryant, who sailed as close as possible to the cause of the Third Reich before tacking sharply away in time to rescue his reputation, is probably not untypical of the group.[52] The majority of the Tory right, faced with the choice between imperial isolation and anti-communism on the one hand, and sacrificing Britain's interests and risking its security with Nazi Germany on the other, joined Churchill in resisting Hitler. A few did not. At one time a dozen Tory MPs belonged to Captain Archibald Maule Ramsay MP's murky 'Right Club'. Ramsay himself was interned as a security risk under Regulation 18B.[53]

The main reason why Conservative MPs continued to be restive after Chamberlain's resignation and replacement by Churchill was not so much because of the policy – hardly anyone now believed that war could have been avoided or doubted that it needed to be won – but because of Churchill and those around him. He was much mistrusted because of his past, both distant and recent: he was wrongly thought to have plotted Chamberlain's overthrow after entering the Government on 1 September 1939.[54] There was much Tory sympathy, tinged with guilt, for Chamberlain, who remained party leader. In any event, it was the Labour benches which loudly applauded Churchill when the new Prime Minister entered the House on 13 May 1940. 'Chips' Channon records in his diary the contrasting reaction of his fellow Tory Members:

> After Prayers, [Winston Churchill, as Prime Minister] went into the Chamber and was greeted with some cheers but when, a moment later, Neville entered with his usual shy retiring little manner, [Tory] MPs lost their heads; they shouted; they cheered; they waved their order papers, and his reception was a regular ovation. The new PM spoke well, even dramatically, in support of the new all-party Government, but he was not well received.[55]

Even Channon reluctantly began, in due course, to perceive Churchill's strengths – though Chips's passionate snobberies (alongside other passions) always distorted his judgement. Moreover, the Tory Party's tears for the leaders it has consumed, as later in the case of Margaret Thatcher, need to be appreciated for their crocodilian quality. But the reaction was a serious warning to Churchill – and he, despite his bluster, was careful to heed it.

Neville Chamberlain himself was thereafter conscientiously loyal, though his followers were often not. Churchill, for his part, protected Chamberlain, both in his own interests and from a genuine magnanimity, when public blame was heaped upon the former Prime Minister and, as disasters multiplied, demands for Chamberlain's removal from his Cabinet post of Lord President grew. Chamberlain's resignation on health grounds in October – he died from cancer in November – would remove the main source of tension. Churchill then succeeded as party leader. He did so with some reluctance and against the strong urging of his wife, Clementine. But Beaverbrook's and Brendan Bracken's advice prevailed, and rightly so.[56] Churchill's candidature was, despite grumbles, unopposed. He was formally nominated by Halifax in a speech which dwelt a good deal more on Chamberlain's merits than on Churchill's.

Dislike of Churchill and his clique was from the first, and long remained, personal, visceral and intense. Baldwin's crony J. C. C. Davidson considered that under the new order 'the crooks are on top as they were in the last War' (a well-rehearsed Baldwinian theme). The deepest contempt was reserved for Brendan Bracken, Duff Cooper, Robert Boothby and Beaverbrook. Lord Dunglass (the future Sir Alec Douglas-Home and Lord Home of the Hirsel, previously Chamberlain's PPS, who accompanied him to Munich) expressed his thoughts over lunch at Prunier's in St James's: 'In the last fortnight, and indeed since Winston came in, the House of Commons had stunk in the nostrils of decent people. The kind of people surrounding Winston are the scum and the peak came when Brendan [Bracken] was made a Privy Councillor.'

R. A. ('Rab') Butler, who had been Halifax's second-in-command at the Foreign Office during appeasement and would in due course be shunted off to domestic policy, worried that Conservative 'virtues and values' were now under threat.[57] As for Churchill himself, Butler thought him 'a half-breed American whose main support was that of inefficient but talkative people of a similar type'.[58] Hostility to Churchill and his intimates is not, of itself, necessarily proof of nostalgia for appeasement. But it is at least significant as an indicator of how deeply attached most Conservative MPs were to the reputation of appeasement's practitioners.

Of course, the last line of Tory defence in the wider argument –

and by no means a weak one – is that the Conservative Party belatedly reversed policy. Not least under Chamberlain's influence, it began to re-arm the country, albeit from a very low level, and at key points the Conservative Cabinet and a minority of Conservative backbenchers forced Chamberlain (and Halifax) to stand up to Hitler's threats. By contrast, the Labour Party consistently opposed rearmament. It wholly embraced the pacifist mentality in the early 1930s, which made it all but impossible for even timid advocates of re-armament to get a hearing. *Guilty Men* makes much of Ernest Bevin's demolition of Labour's pacifist leader, George Lansbury, at the 1935 Labour party conference. But even after Lansbury was succeeded by Clement Attlee, the party opposed re-armament measures; and it decisively turned against appeasement only in the course of 1937. All this is particularly relevant because of the devastating impact of *Guilty Men* on both Chamberlain's and the Conservative Party's reputation. Its publication in 1940 was not, moreover, an isolated initiative, but one in a sequence of left-wing propagandist polemics which preceded the war and continued after it. Its publisher, Victor Gollancz, was ruthlessly but covertly engaged in pressing a pro-communist agenda.[59] So why, one might ask, should its analysis be accepted?

There are, unfortunately, three good reasons to avoid this convenient escape route from Tory culpability. In the first place, Conservatives should have known – and many in fact did know – better. In the second place, the Conservatives (under National Government colours) were in power, not Labour. In the third place, even pacifism, the folly of the left, has a better intellectual and moral pedigree than defeatism, the temptation of the right, to which the Conservative leadership and most of the party succumbed. Churchill alone – unloved by the Conservatives, and out of love with the party himself – would salvage Conservative honour and, though not immediately, help save its political bacon.

ALL BEHIND YOU, WINSTON

The cartoonist Low shows leading politicians in 1940 marching shoulder to shoulder with Winston Churchill in the war effort. But politics was only ever partly suspended – and the Conservatives lost out as a result.

12

CHURCHILL'S PARTY, I – WAR

Churchill's succession, first to the premiership and then to the leadership, had been a severe blow to powerful interests in the Conservative Party, especially in Parliament. For the best part of two years he was their master on sufferance, despite intermittent public acclaim. Churchill and his enemies in the party were well aware of their respective vulnerabilities, and manoeuvred accordingly. If he should lose public confidence, because of the way the war went, then key colleagues might turn against him, and disaffected Tory backbenchers, including ex-ministers, would seize their chance for a coup. For their part, his opponents were in awe of Churchill's personality (while despising his habits and mistrusting his advisers). They knew that – once Halifax was discarded – he remained the most acceptable Conservative Prime Minister to lead a coalition with Labour and Liberals. Above all, they feared national sentiment, which stayed far more supportive of the war and of Churchill's conduct of it than the professional political class as a whole assumed. Of course, if Britain had ever actually faced defeat it would have been different. The parallel with France, for example, suggests that all sorts of peace-advocating would-be collaborators would have emerged from across the political spectrum to overthrow not just Churchill but the political system from which he emerged and by which he was sustained. But this never happened. 'Fighting on [British] beaches' thus safely remained a rhetorical flourish.

Although the attempt must be made, there is inevitably something artificial in considering Churchill's political leadership in these years apart from his war leadership.[1] The latter was, after all, his constant, consuming preoccupation; the former intruded only at unwelcome moments, and almost always when the war itself was going badly. The failure of the Dakar raid in September 1940, for example, brought Conservative critics of Churchill's long-doubted judgement out in force. Significantly, Halifax, a key figure in any move against Churchill, privately distanced himself from the Dakar operation. The reshuffle which then followed Chamberlain's resignation on health grounds did not significantly strengthen Churchill's hand, because Halifax insisted on remaining at the Foreign Office, with that other appeasement veteran, R. A. Butler, at his side.[2]

Chamberlainite backbench resentment was particularly strong against David Margesson, the Chief Whip.[3] It was, in the circumstances, understandable. Margesson had implacably forced Tory MPs into the division lobby in support of Chamberlain's appeasement policies. Now he was retained by Churchill to apply discipline in the other direction and did so, in the classic Tory machine manner, without apology or embarrassment. In the reshuffle at the end of 1940 Margesson replaced Eden as Secretary for War, where he stayed until the fiasco of the fall of Singapore in 1942 required his head. Also in December 1940, Halifax was finally, and reluctantly, sent to Washington as ambassador and replaced as Foreign Secretary by Eden.

Margesson's own replacement as Chief Whip was James Stuart.

Stuart would be a formidably efficient manager of men. But he had been fiercely loyal to Chamberlain and, as Scottish Whip, had delivered a severe rebuke to Churchill when the latter supported the Duchess of Atholl, standing (against appeasement and against the official Tory candidate) in West Perthshire. Churchill now accepted the utility of having such a figure to keep the back-benchers in line. But there was mutual antipathy and distrust. Not until July 1941, in fact, did Stuart feel that he enjoyed the Prime Minister's confidence; and then it was only because Churchill was by that time more securely in charge of the party. Stuart would admire the great man, but he never altered his view that he 'was without doubt one of the most difficult men imaginable to deal with'.[4]

Churchill had few friends in the party organization. When in October 1940 Oliver Lyttelton – financier, businessman, and a First World War comrade of the Prime Minister – was looking for a seat, to join Churchill's administration, he approached Lord Windlesham, the Conservative vice-chairman in charge of candidates.[5] Asked by Windlesham if he was 'backed by Winston', Lyttelton confirmed the fact, only to be told that this was 'a great mistake, but it can't be helped'. Windlesham was sacked, as a result of Bracken's influence, but not until June 1941.

In July 1941 – fourteen months after becoming Prime Minister – Churchill could reshape his Government with a freer hand. Bracken became Minister of Information, replacing the ineffective Duff Cooper. Richard Law replaced Butler, who was despatched to what might have been, but turned out not to be, the backwater of the Board of Education. Law was himself replaced by Churchill's son-in-law, Duncan Sandys, as Financial Secretary at the War Office.[6] The reshuffle was unpopular with sections of the parlia-mentary party. Parliament itself was anyway now less effective as a check on the executive, with 200 MPs in some government role and another 116 serving in the armed forces.[7]

But there had been – and would be – some bad moments.

Setbacks in North Africa and then in Greece and Crete in 1941 stirred up the 1922 Committee, and defeats in the Mediterranean provoked criticism. Still, though, Churchill received the overwhelming backing of the House of Commons whenever the issue was forced. The Japanese attack on Pearl Harbor on 7 December 1941 can now be seen as the turning point of the war. But at the time it initiated months of dismally bad news. The warships *Prince of Wales* and *Repulse* were sunk by the Japanese three days later. In early 1942 collapse in the Far East, above all the humiliating loss of Singapore, raised public alarm. Three German warships, the *Scharnhorst*, *Gneisenau* and *Prinz Eugen*, then broke out of port. If this was possible, what else was? A full-scale invasion scare duly shook confidence and prompted accusations of misconduct of the war. These were not explicitly directed at Churchill as overall war leader; the critics concentrated on the desirability, as they saw it, of relieving him of day-to-day war management. But Churchill was not having it, and easily faced them down. The autumn saw a further change – first in the direction of the war and then in the direction of politics. The British victory at El Alamein in November and increasingly evident German reverses in Russia, culminating in the defeat at Stalingrad in February 1943, altered perceptions. The war, it seemed, would, indeed, be won. The important political question, though, was who would reap the benefit.

It is easy to see why Churchill, grappling with the terrible dangers facing the country, throughout this period paid little heed to his own party's sensibilities. There had been a suggestion at the time of his election as leader that a deputy leader should be appointed. But it had never happened. And since the only acceptable candidate would have been Eden – who was even more disliked, and almost as tied into the war effort – the proposal was still-born. The impulse behind it, though, was sensible and all too perceptive.

Churchill's reliance on non-party figures was even more of a problem than the promotion of Labour politicians. After all, the Conservatives were meant to be men of the world, who could make things happen. Bringing in outsiders was a kind of reproach. Even when Churchill did rely on Tories, they were from outside the established hierarchy. This disrupted accepted paths of promotion and disheartened those who relied on them. Eden was unclubbable, and far from mainstream. Sir John Anderson (Lord President) never even called himself a Conservative. Lyttelton, though a right-wing Tory by instinct, had no party track record. Kingsley Wood, the Chancellor, as an all-purpose opportunist who judiciously supported appeasement but then helped topple Chamberlain, was at least identifiably a party man. But he did not carry weight. Anyway, he was removed from the War Cabinet in 1942, and died the following year. Then there were the three talented eccentrics. Beaverbrook was, of course, anathema to most Conservative politicians – particularly to the Chief Whip, Stuart – despite the strident Toryism of the *Express*. Bracken, a genuine Tory, but not genuine in many other respects, was heartily despised. Lord Cherwell (Frederick Lindemann), 'the Prof', was proudly un-political – and he and Beaverbrook, as peers, were even less accountable to politicians than were Churchill's other cronies.

The career of Churchill himself was also, of course, that of an outsider's outsider – was he a Tory at all? Winston Churchill's personal style echoed that of Lloyd George during the Great War. Churchill's shortcomings in this respect were perhaps more excusable, because the pressures on him were greater. But unlike Lloyd George, Churchill was supposed to be a party leader. Whereas Bonar Law had protected Conservative interests in the Great War coalition, Churchill now showed no inclination to do so. Indeed, the balance of party advantage in the First World War was altogether reversed in the Second. The Labour Party was able to take the initiative in domestic affairs – through the efforts of

Clement Attlee, Stafford Cripps, Herbert Morrison and Ernest Bevin – while sharing in the ultimate kudos of military victory. This, indeed, is the key to politics during the war, and provides a partial explanation of the aftermath.

In theory, a party truce prevailed throughout the war years. But Conservatives interpreted it far more strictly than others. There was, for example, no Conservative party conference until 1943, and then not again till March 1945. Labour, though, held conferences each year. Conservative Central Office advised constituency parties to avoid anything provocative. In practice, this became a veto on local campaigning.

Not that there were many Conservatives to campaign. Conservatives did much more than their fair share in fighting and winning the War. By the start of 1941, 184 Conservative Party agents and organizers were in the armed forces, along with 135 Conservative MPs – more than a third of the parliamentary party, and a very high proportion of those of military age. This compares with 14 Labour MPs and 4 Liberals. Fourteen Tory MPs were killed in action, and 17 decorated.[8]

For the first half of the war the formal inter-party truce was reasonably successful. By-election turnouts were very low and fringe candidates easily defeated. But from 1942 conditions became more difficult. Anti-Government (and especially anti-Conservative) opinion rallied first around independent candidates and then around candidates standing in the name of the left-wing Common Wealth Party. Labour and Liberal voters supported these candidates, with a nudge and wink from local parties. Four Conservative seats were lost in 1942 and poor results registered elsewhere. There were no losses in 1943; but opinion, to the extent it could be gauged, was still strongly anti-Tory.[9]

The reasons for this leftward shift in public opinion during the war are not difficult to enumerate, but nor are they easy to rank in relative importance. The Conservative Party, though it was now the party of Churchill, had also been the party of Baldwin, Chamberlain and appeasement. Campaigners on the left were careful to disengage Churchill, who was (for now) beyond public criticism, from the party which he led. *Guilty Men* has already been mentioned. But its thesis was far from novel or unique. It was part of a series. It fitted in with the evocation (by the communist journalist Claud Cockburn) of a quasi-mythical 'Cliveden Set' – assembled there by the Astors with a view to stitching up British foreign policy. The successors of *Guilty Men* were no less splenetic in their propaganda. Aneurin Bevan ('Celticus') wrote *Why not Trust the Tories?* to explain how the appeasement of the dictators was really part and parcel of enduring Conservative attitudes to world politics.[10] In *We Were Not All Wrong*, Geoffrey Mander, a Liberal MP (and later Labour supporter), asserted that the Conservatives bore the blame for appeasement.[11] Such charges were answered by Quintin Hogg in *The Left Was Never Right*, but in defensive manner.[12] (This doubtless reflected, in part, Hogg's own equivocation: he won his Oxford seat at a by-election as a defender of Munich, which he called 'a great deliverance', but then went into the lobby against Chamberlain on the crucial division in May 1940.[13])

More subtle and probably more effective was the way in which left-wing intellectuals and activists used the public media. (And the fact that this was – as it regularly is – exaggerated by dyed-in-the-wool Conservatives seeking to excuse their own inadequacy as propagandists does not make it any less true.) The BBC did its bit by broadcasting J. B. Priestley's wireless 'Postscripts', provoking the ire of the 1922 Committee. When Priestley was removed, the objectionable tone of reporting remained. Probably more important, though, was the Army Bureau of Current Affairs, whose lecturers' left-wing slant on social and economic questions annoyed even Ernest Bevin. Within Bevin's own bailiwick, the unionized workforce – whose wages doubled in real terms during the war, and whose numerous industrial stoppages went unreported through censorship – the Workers' Educational Association, for its part, increased political awareness in a manner which could not but harm the Tories. Churchill was aware of what was happening, but he could not stop it. Politically unsympathetic messages from public bodies were then reinforced in the press, notably with the increasing circulation of the *Daily Mirror*.[14]

A particularly sore point for Tories was attitudes to the Soviet Union. The culpability of Stalin in the events leading to the outbreak of war was almost entirely ignored once the USSR in June 1941 became Hitler's victim. Churchill publicly praised 'Russia' (as the country was tactfully misnamed), but privately managed to prevent the 'Internationale' being played on the wireless for six months. He instructed the Ministry of Information 'to consider what action was required to counter the present tendency of the British public to forget the dangers of Communism in their enthusiasm over the resistance of Russia'. It was wasted effort. In February 1943, the twenty-fifth anniversary of the formation of the Red Army was celebrated up and down the country – with Government backing, for fear it would otherwise be hijacked by the Communist Party. The most prominent enthusiasts for 'Russia' were Cripps and Beaverbrook. Cripps was (wrongly) credited, when ambassador in Moscow, for helping bring the Soviet Union into the war. But he was outdone in bravura and cynicism by Beaverbrook, who on a visit to Moscow struck up a close relationship with Stalin. Beaverbrook resigned from the War Cabinet in February 1942 in order to campaign for the opening of a 'second front' in Europe, to take the strain from the Russians. The plan would, at this juncture, have been disastrous; and Churchill, who generally listened too much to Beaverbrook, was unmoved. Beaverbrook's first speech on the subject justified the Soviet show trials of the 1930s and denied the existence of religious or racial persecution in the USSR.[15] No paid agent could have done more.

This love affair with the Soviet Union was important – and damaging for the Conservative cause – because it fitted into a wider framework. It meant that now there were no acknowledged enemies on the left. It opened the way for the argument, which Labour would put to good use, that only the left (at home) could deal with the left (abroad). It subliminally weakened all criticisms of nationalization and government controls and intervention, because the system was thought to work so well in Russia. But most importantly it strengthened the sense that only a totally planned economy and society could rise to the challenges of war and peace. This sense, along with that of the Tory-dominated 1930s as a lost 'locust' decade, swung the mood towards socialism.

The Conservative Party under Churchill's leadership was unable to react effectively. It might have tried openly to combat state planning and spell out a coherent economic and social alternative. But Churchill was too tired and too preoccupied. It might even have gone along with the tide and sought to be swept to power by it. But Churchill, true to his own classic liberal instincts, could not accept that course either. Instead, the party slithered haltingly and unpersuasively towards collectivism, but without gaining any credit.

Churchill publicly insisted, even as late as March 1943, that it was still too early to think about post-war policy. But a good deal of thinking had, in fact, already gone on. Most of it was done by William Beveridge. This, for the Conservatives, was very much a mixed blessing. Beveridge used his multiple talents as a politically acute and propaganda-savvy bureaucrat of formidable intellect not just to devise a reform of social insurance, but also to gain widespread agreement to the establishment of what would come to be called the 'welfare state'.[16] The goal was to cover the loss of earning power caused by unemployment, sickness or retirement. The means was a single system of benefits at subsistence level, financed by flat-rate individual contributions. Alongside, there was to be a complementary system of National Assistance, financed out of taxation, to help those without sufficient contributions or cover. National Assistance would be means-tested. It was envisaged as temporary; but like many temporary innovations it became permanent; and it swelled to an extent which would have shocked its originator. Beveridge, as a relatively old-school Liberal, was always conscious of the dangers of dependency on the state. It was these sentiments, finding their way into his report in December 1942, that later made Margaret Thatcher sympathetic to his vision.[17] But those who thought like her at the time most certainly were not. The open-ended nature of Beveridge's plans shocked them. And these critics were vindicated, albeit too late. Beveridge's assumptions were wrong – not just about social insurance, but about the implications of providing what he insisted was required in order that his plans should work: a comprehensive National Health Service, universal child allowances and government-maintained full employment.

The Chancellor, Kingsley Wood, sent a memorandum to Churchill on 17 November 1942, spelling out why Beveridge's proposals were unaffordable. A committee of Conservative MPs, meeting in secret under the free-market-minded Ralph Assheton, was equally critical.[18] But the Labour Party, especially Herbert Morrison, kept up the pressure. Moreover, as the contents leaked out, it became clear that they were extremely popular. A government committee, chaired by Sir John Anderson, accepted Treasury warnings on cost. But no alternative reforms were advanced. The predictable – but unsatisfactory – outcome was agreement that the Government would welcome as much of the report as possible, but offer no commitment to implementation. While the war continued in earnest, this line was just about sustainable. But as peace approached, the competition to assert social reforming credentials grew. In the House of Commons, Labour MPs voted against a Government motion, because they considered it too weak. Forty-five Conservative MPs from the progressively minded Tory

Reform Committee, led by Hogg and Lord Hinchingbrooke, put down an amendment calling for the immediate creation of a Minister of Social Security. The cry of 'Beveridge Now!' was widely heard.

Churchill, a champion of national insurance in his early political life, and anyway still able to tell the way the wind blew and adjust to it, gave a broadcast on 21 March 1943 in what he hoped would be a reassuring manner. Without explicitly mentioning Beveridge, he declared his support for 'national compulsory insurance for all classes, for all purposes, from the cradle to the grave'.[19] It was not, though, enough. Beveridge's report had a massive sale and the popular reaction was damaging to the Conservatives, who were rightly perceived to be most sceptical towards its proposals.

There was, indeed, more than scepticism. Not everyone agreed even with the general direction. The opponents of Beveridge lost. Their objections were then tactfully forgotten. But the Tory Reform Committee did not reflect majority party opinion. The Progress Trust, set up in November 1944 to combat what Tories considered 'back-door socialism', probably has a better claim to do so. Universal benefits were seen by many Tories as inherently dangerous. Conservative social thinking had always favoured selectivity – that is, concentration on those in greatest need. Ralph Assheton noted: 'One of the chief troubles about the Beveridge Report is that whereas the diagnosis relates to Want, his proposals are very largely devoted to giving money to people who are not in Want.'[20] That was the heart of the welfare problem, and arguably still is.

Beveridge's plans seemed, in fact, only the thin end of a very thick wedge. In this too the critics were proved right, not least because the post-war Labour Government pushed up pension and benefit levels. Proposals for a National Health Service followed on, as observed, from Beveridge's original assumptions. But the NHS, in its final form, was very much the creation of Aneurin Bevan and the Attlee Government.

The emerging NHS was, as a result, significantly different from anything that a Tory-led coalition, let alone a Conservative Government, would have introduced. Many subsequent problems reflect the command economy model then adopted. The alternative model, though still comprehensive, universal, free at the point of consumption and tax-financed, would have been significantly different. The Conservative Health Minister, Henry Willink, worked up a blueprint. It involved separation between different service suppliers (revived under the later Thatcher 'internal market' reforms), as well as keeping the voluntary and local hospitals, which Bevan abolished. Consultation with the British Medical Authority (BMA) then pushed back regulatory powers somewhat further.[21] But these internal debates had no political impact. The general public was largely unaware of them. For his part, Churchill did not think it served any political purpose to be fighting such a battle.[22] Whether this was good or bad politics in 1945 is debatable. But it made the later conduct of Opposition more difficult. The Conservatives had not properly explained their own approach to public health by the time they came to vote against Bevan's Bill. This did lasting harm to the party's reputation. When Margaret Thatcher (unconvincingly) declared in 1982 that 'The National Health Service is safe with us,' and David Cameron (illogically) in 2010 promised to protect its growing spending against a background of wider spending cuts, both leaders were, in their different ways, trying to live down the same poisoned legacy from the 1940s.[23]

The one area in which the Coalition Government did legislate, and with a Conservative minister shaping that legislation, was education. Butler's 1944 Education Act was a long, complicated measure. It involved him in an enormous amount of negotiation and compromise. It remained the basic statutory framework –

subject to an emphasis on comprehensive schools in the 1960s and 1970s – until the Thatcher Government's Education Reform Act of 1988. Longevity constitutes merit of a sort. But it is otherwise hard to ascribe to the Act much importance, except in one rather backward-looking respect. Recognizing the financial difficulties faced by Church of England schools, Butler's Act established a new financial and legal basis for them. This finally ended the conflicts between the respective advocates of secular and religious education which had been such a recurring headache for previous Conservative governments. A kind of draw, but on very different terms, was reached with the Catholic Church, whose leaders (to Churchill's amusement) made Butler's life extremely uncomfortable.[24] The rest of the Act's measures for re-organization, with their vain attempts to achieve 'parity of esteem' between different types of secondary school, and to overcome the long-recognized weakness in Britain's technical education, were largely rendered nugatory by lack of resources. (Butler himself in retrospect claimed that the 'Comprehensive idea' was also contained in his proposals: to the extent it is true, and it may be on one reading, it is not necessarily a recommendation.[25]) Above all, whatever else the Act did, it certainly did not prepare Britain to compete successfully in the modern world. Nor, at a less elevated but hardly less important level, is there any evidence that Butler's efforts won the Conservatives votes at the 1945 election.

Butler's role might have been developed so as to give a stronger impression of Conservative seriousness about domestic policy. But it was not, because Churchill stopped it. Butler had been appointed Chairman of the Post-War Problems Central Committee. The seeds of the later work on industrial policy were now sown. But apart from the Education Act the committee's work had no immediate legislative result; its pronouncements received no official endorsement; and it had no impact, either, on the 1945 manifesto, which, couched in the traditional form of a personal declaration of policy by the party leader, was written by Churchill with contributions from Assheton, Bracken and Beaverbrook.[26]

The 1945 election was fought by the Conservatives under difficult conditions, made worse by bad tactics. Churchill had wanted the Coalition to continue. But the Labour leaders had made clear that it must end with the war in Europe. Eventually, the Labour party conference, rejecting Attlee's advice, voted to call for an immediate election. Labour and Liberal ministers then resigned, in May 1945, and Churchill continued with a Conservative or technocrat 'caretaker' administration. The Conservatives sought to blame Labour for their desertion. But it was the Conservative Party which really lost out. Until almost the last moment, it had been hoped that a Conservative-led National Coalition might coast to victory, as in the Coupon Election of 1918. This always unrealistic hope was now shattered. But what strategy to put in its place? Would there be time to find one?

Butler, who had more knowledge of the lamentable state of party affairs than his colleagues, alone argued, face to face with Churchill, against an early (summer) election. He was taken to task by Beaverbrook for his impertinence.[27] But Butler was right. The sudden return to party strife exposed the fact that during the war years the Conservative Party had become a shell. There was no organization to speak of, and no systematic canvass was even attempted. From June 1943 (when regular Gallup polling recommenced) the Conservatives were substantially behind Labour in popular support – though remarkably little attention was paid to the fact.[28]

Churchill himself should have been the party's passport to victory. But he was not. He was at the centre of the publicity campaign. The main Tory poster was a picture of the old warhorse with the slogan 'Help him finish the job – Vote National'. The word 'Conservative' did not even appear.[29] If it had been a presidential election, perhaps Churchill could have won. But such was not the system, and Churchill understood that. Somehow he had to drag the Conservative Party back to power in order to retain his own. Reverting to aggressive type, he overreacted, resulting in his notorious opening election broadcast on 4 June 1945, in which he spoke of the need for any 'Socialist Government . . . to fall back on some form of Gestapo' to repress public criticism of the system. Beaverbrook was blamed for it. But it was all Churchill's work.[30] It was badly received. The Chief Whip, James Stuart, rang Jock Colville, Churchill's private secretary, to say: 'If that is the way he wants to conduct the campaign he must decide. He is the Leader of the Party. But it is not my idea of how to win the election.'[31]

Other comment was even more critical, and Attlee was effective in his rebuttal. The broadcast was, indeed, an error – though it is worth noting that, according to Gallup, the party sharply picked up support during the campaign; so it cannot have lost many votes. But even viewed as an error, it was a more interesting and significant one than is usually noticed. The section in which Churchill inserted his explosive suggestion that a 'political police' would be introduced was not the logical consequence of the preceding sections, in which he had criticized the socialist tendency to extend controls until freedom itself was endangered – a contentious, but intellectually sustainable, argument that would be put effectively in the late 1970s.[32] The germ of an alternative Conservative case was present in 1945, even though it was crushed. It seems to have come from Friedrich Hayek (guru to a later generation of Conservatives), via Ralph Assheton. Assheton had obtained, with great difficulty, fifty copies of Hayek's *The Road to Serfdom* (published in 1944), which he sent to leading politicians. Whether Churchill had read Hayek is doubtful; but he had certainly read Assheton's summary of Hayek, delivered in a speech in April 1945, because he wrote back a note of congratulation.[33] Churchill's vulgarization of the Hayek thesis, and the notoriety which he attached to it, was one of several intellectual disservices he rendered to the Conservative cause in the later years of his career.

But despite this gaffe, which was not repeated, Churchill was more or less the Conservative Party's only asset. Labour had both the climate of opinion and the state of its party organization in its favour. It also had more of the press. The *Daily Herald* and the *Daily Mirror* were vociferous in its favour, the *Daily Telegraph* defensive, *The Times* uncommitted and the *Daily Express* wild. Unlike in 1918, it was not possible to capitalize effectively on the war record of Conservative candidates. Churchill's attempt to allow them to campaign in uniform was stopped by the War Office. More seriously, the rank and file of the armed services had been much more effectively politicized than in the First World War.

How far this had gone was still unclear. Indeed, a lack of clarity about opinion generally encouraged wishful thinking on the Conservative side. Not until early 1945 was the new electoral register, with the first phase of new electoral arrangements (agreed in 1944), in place. The absence of many servicemen and the disorientation of evacuations made opinion difficult to test. And, as noted, the Conservative machine was not anyway equipped to test it. So projection amounted to hunch. Churchill was told by the party to expect a majority of thirty-eight seats. But this advice seems to have been framed so as to err on the side of caution. Consequently, the results, when they eventually came out on 26 July, constituted a terrible shock.[34]

The Conservatives suffered what at the time (that is, before 1997) was their worst defeat since the rout of 1906. Together with National Liberals and other allies, they won just 213 seats. Five Cabinet ministers lost their seats. The Liberals were smashed, nearly beyond redemption, with just 12 seats. Labour had 392, including 79 gains in seats they had never held before. The Conservatives were especially badly beaten in the outer London boroughs. There was a strong shift against them in their traditional suburban redoubts in south-eastern England. Accompanying the collapse of the Liberals, this shift was enough to secure a Labour landslide. One can try to minimize the scale of the catastrophe by pointing to the fact that the Conservatives still won 40 per cent of the vote. The position was, therefore, not irrecoverable. But such statistics tell only part of the story. In every sense that mattered, the 1945 election marked a great shift leftwards in the British polity, and constituted a devastating blow to the Conservative Party's claims to be the natural party of government.

HOT SEAT

Despite its problematic inheritance, suggested by Low's cartoon of 1951, Churchill's peacetime government relaxed economic controls and living standards duly rose. But it also put off risky reforms, reflecting the ageing Prime Minister's aim of 'not being scuppered'.

13

CHURCHILL'S PARTY, II – PEACE

The Conservative Party was broken and humiliated. But Churchill, himself, after a bout of depression, quite quickly recovered from the shock of defeat. In 1947 a group of powerful party figures – though Eden, the successor in the wings, stayed clear – met at the house of Harry Crookshank, an obstreperous and frustrated backbencher, to discuss how to get Churchill to stand down. The Chief Whip was also summoned and deputed by his colleagues to tell the old man that it was time to go. When James Stuart delivered the message, Churchill was furious, shouting about plots and banging his stick on the floor. Stuart was only forgiven because he was known to dislike Eden, whom Churchill blamed. Shortly afterwards, he informed his constituents that he would 'soldier on' as leader in order to defeat the Labour Party – which, against expectations, he finally did.[1]

Churchill was able to face down such pressure because, despite his role in the 1945 election defeat and his advancing age, he was not just a party icon but a national hero. As the years went by his reputation steadily increased, until he could without exaggeration be called 'the Greatest Living Englishman', or just 'G.L.E.' (parallel-ing 'G.O.M.'), as Macmillan cheekily described him.[2] Reputation, though, was almost all that he did have to offer the party for the first two years, as he concentrated on his lucrative memoirs project and on overseas speaking tours.

Domestic affairs, by contrast, received little or none of Churchill's attention. He did not speak in the key economic debates. Nor was he active on the social policy front. This might seem surprising. Churchill was proud of his credentials as a social reformer, and with good reason. In the period 1911–14 (as a Liberal, of course) he had enjoyed, indeed, the reputation of a radical, before his interests increasingly turned towards military matters. Later still, he was not ill-disposed towards the Beveridge programme. But essentially he believed, in later life, that social reform was an achievement to be proud of, not a programme to be pursued. What needed to be done by way of policy had been done. Beyond that, he was vaguely paternalistic. Herbert Morrison's thoughts about Churchill, though predictable, are probably not far from the mark: 'He's the old benevolent Tory squire, who does all he can for the people – provided always that they are a good obedient people and loyally recognise his position, and theirs.'[3] This was not, in fact, a bad reputation among more conservative-minded voters. But it was not the basis for an active policy.

That said, the benefit to the party of both Churchill's magisterial memoirs and his impressive overseas speeches rubbed off: they pro-vided some consolation, when little else did. *The Gathering Storm* appeared in 1948. Two years earlier, Churchill's speech in Fulton, Missouri, had proclaimed a similar message, though in con-temporary circumstances: 'From Stettin in the Baltic to Trieste in the Adriatic, an Iron Curtain has descended across the Continent.' The speech was denounced by the American press, disowned by President Truman (who had seen and approved it, but timorously denied the fact), and condemned by Labour MPs in an Early Day

Motion in the House of Commons. But, announcing as it did the reality of the Cold War – rapidly confirmed by unfolding events in eastern Europe – Fulton re-established Churchill as a statesman with prophetic insight.[4] His still widely, if selectively, quoted addresses on Europe – especially those delivered in Zürich (1946) and The Hague (1946) – also received great public attention. Quite what he meant by them is disputable. Despite the language, he does not seem ever to have envisaged any 'United States of Europe' of which Britain, at least, could be part. Similarly, his later actions – and lack of action – in government disappointed the still relatively few Euro-enthusiasts in the party. But his advocacy of reconciliation between France and Germany, so soon after the exposure of the latter's egregious crimes, favourably impressed and rather astonished observers.[5] His reputation was further burnished.

The revival of Conservative Party fortunes depended in the first instance, however, on matters closer to home. Topping, the general director at Central Office, finally departed at the age of sixty-eight and was succeeded by Stephen Pierssené. But who would be chairman? Ralph Assheton wanted to leave, and Churchill does not seem to have wanted to keep him. Eden would have liked to replace him with the vice-chairman in charge of candidates, his friend J. P. L. Thomas; but Churchill did not agree. Churchill would have liked a full inquiry into Central Office by Lyttelton and then Macmillan as chairman; but Eden stymied that.

In these circumstances, Churchill's eye fell on Lord ('Fred') Woolton, a generally acceptable but on the face of it improbable choice. Woolton (earlier Frederick Marquis) had won his reputation at the interface between business and government. He had been recommended for a peerage to Chamberlain, with a view to wartime administrative work, but then found himself serving under Churchill. In April 1940 he was Minister of Food, the public face – a presentable one – of rationing, and would for ever be associated with that meat-free delectable, the 'Woolton Pie'. Woolton was throughout the war period determinedly non-political. He did not join the Conservative Party until Churchill made him its chairman – after much arm-twisting – in July 1946. But by then he was at least a Conservative of sorts, alarmed by Labour's attacks on free enterprise.[6]

Woolton later recalled: 'The organization of the Conservative Party was the most topsy-like arrangement that I had ever come across.'[7] But he made the most of what he found and, with allowances for a tendency to exaggerate his own importance, he greatly improved its effectiveness. He and Churchill would have liked, as others before and since, to change the party's name. They favoured the 'Union' party. In Woolton's case (though not Churchill's, given his past), this was with a view to distancing it from what Woolton called the individualism of 'the last stalwarts of the Asquithian Liberals', and to appealing instead to trade unionist support. Corporatism was in the air. But nothing came of the name change, nor indeed of the social refocusing. Woolton's sensitivity to political nomenclature was also – and more usefully – behind the decision to refer to the Labour Party always as 'Socialists', thus stressing its allegedly alien ideology.

Having Labour in power and energetically pursuing a pro-gramme of controls and nationalization created an excellent backdrop for Tory fund-raising. Here Woolton's shrewdly judged tactic of asking for outrageously large sums paid off. He believed it easier to stand on a public platform and demand a million than a lesser figure, and results proved him right.[8] He set similarly ambitious targets for party membership. A hundred and fifty paid 'missioners' were dispatched into the constituencies to spearhead the proselytizing effort. Between the end of 1947 and the summer of 1948 membership rose by a million, to two and a quarter million.[9]

The creation of the Young Conservative organization was also an astonishing success. It had its pre-war precedents but nothing of the scale had previously been achieved. It appealed to younger people in search of social activity, as well as to a smaller, more seriously political element – like the young Margaret Hilda Roberts (later Thatcher) – who saw the YCs as a ladder leading to the Commons. When Woolton described the Young Conservatives, in his memoirs, as 'probably the most powerful political youth organization in the free countries of the world' it was a slightly ludicrous claim; but, if one associates numbers with power, it was also probably true.[10]

Meanwhile, Conservative Party finances, which, despite promises of transparency repeated almost annually, remained conveniently opaque, became very healthy. The party's Central Board of Finance controlled the money, while fund-raising from business largely took place, at one remove, through the United Industrialists Association. Some of these funds went towards strengthening the central organization of the party. The staff of area offices, whose function it was to support and bully the weaker or idler constituencies so as to maximize the local vote, was substantially increased. (The Conservative Research Department, paid for through Central Office, but otherwise keeping itself jealously separate, will be discussed shortly.) On Butler's initiative, a new Conservative Political Centre (CPC) was created. It was intended to educate the local activists about party policy, through discussion groups and papers. It also issued questionnaires seeking members' views – of which the party centrally took no obvious notice. Most local parties soon had their CPC groups. The CPC nationally also published pamphlets and books. Its attempts to run bookshops were less successful, though one remained at Central Office, subsidized by the party.

A party educational and training college at Ashridge, dedicated to the memory of Bonar Law, had functioned before the war but had then fallen into disuse, finally passing out of the party's control. In 1947 Lord Swinton donated part of his own house to the party for a 'Conservative College of the North' at Masham in North Yorkshire. By 1949 it was operating courses and hosting conferences throughout the year. It was later known as Swinton Conservative College, and later still just 'Swinton'.[11] In the 1970s it was still serving as a hub for Conservative political education, its effectiveness being such that it came to cause the party leader of the day, Edward Heath, considerable irritation.[12] This, along with money worries, probably helps explain its demise.

It is easy, of course – as noted earlier – to exaggerate the impact of all such organizational change on election results. A study of three key marginal constituencies in the south-east of England – all returning Conservative Members by the time of the 1955 election – suggests that good organization, whether reflected in campaigning, membership, or CPC or Conservative trade unionist activity, was not the obvious key to victory. Moreover, official party membership was overstated (as it usually is). Non-subscribers lingered on lists from one year to another, a testimony to sloth and wishful thinking. And once the Conservatives got back into power in 1951, the efforts flagged (as, again, they usually do).[13] The fact remains that in the country as a whole, by the time of Woolton's retirement as chairman in 1955, the Conservative Party had been transformed. It looked, in fact, very much as it would look right into the 1970s, at which time Woolton's era was still regarded as the exemplary high point by many party professionals.

Still more difficult to assess is the impact of developments in post-war Tory policy-making. As with organization, those responsible for policy formulation have an interest in exaggerating not just their own personal importance but that of their function. This tendency must be borne in mind when considering, respectively, the roles of Butler, the Industrial Policy Committee and the Conservative Research Department (CRD). The CRD has been usefully described (by its current chairman, Oliver Letwin) as 'a collection of talented young impresarios, contributing intellectual energy to the party while acquiring for themselves a knowledge of policy and high politics on their way to something else'.[14] The careers of Reginald Maudling, Iain Macleod, Enoch Powell and, most recently, David Cameron confirm this – though it is worth recalling that, at least until the 1980s, a sizeable detachment of older, more seasoned, less frenetically ambitious senior staff was also present.

Mention has been made of the CRD's beginnings. It was formally set up by the Shadow Cabinet on 23 October 1929. But it gained direction only when Neville Chamberlain took it in hand, as its chairman, in 1930. Chamberlain kept the post when he became party chairman in place of Davidson. The Department followed Chamberlain's practical preference for politically useful rather than rarefied technical work. It provided the material for his 'Unauthorised Programme' of reforms. He had it concentrate on his preoccupations of unemployment insurance and tariffs. In the form of Joseph Ball, its shadowy director, it was inevitably involved in the promotion of appeasement. It was then largely shut down during the war. Churchill, in any case, felt no need for party research services: he relied on Lord Cherwell as his all-purpose technical adviser. It was Butler's appointment as chairman of the Post-War Policy Central Committee that opened the way for the Research Department's political resurrection.[15]

Also noted earlier was the formation in 1924, before the Research Department's creation, of a short-lived parliamentary secretariat to brief party committees and the Shadow Cabinet. The need for such a body was felt again in the war years, and in 1944 David Clarke, a pre-war CRD desk officer, was persuaded by Assheton to take on the task. Among the secretariat's early recruits were Reginald Maudling, Iain Macleod and Enoch Powell. But only in 1946 was Clarke able to concentrate on re-forming the CRD itself. The separation of functions between the secretariat and research was maintained, with the political operators in the first and the policy analysts in the second. But since the two groups shared offices in Old Queen Street (the CRD's home since 1930) and its officers often collaborated, the real relationship was closer than this suggests. Then, in 1948, the logical decision was made to bring policy-making and information services together. The CRD and the secretariat were united within a new organization, along with a third element – the Library and Information Department from Central Office. That November Butler became chairman of the Research Department – an obvious choice, though Churchill would have preferred his son-in-law, Duncan Sandys. Some of the old administrative distinctness remained for a while. But in 1950 Clarke became director of both the CRD and the secretariat, and finally, in 1959, Clarke's successor Michael Fraser became director of the whole, integrated Conservative Research Department.[16]

Butler, like his hero Chamberlain, believed that the Department's priorities should be politically relevant. He accordingly gave instructions to concentrate on taxation and industrial policy. The latter quickly emerged as the topic on which Butler and those on the 'progressive' wing of the party sought to reshape its image.

Mounting exasperation with Churchill's refusal to make explicit policy commitments had come to a head at the party conference in 1946. Churchill would not budge during the conference itself; but afterwards it was announced that he had set up an Industrial Policy Committee under Butler's chairmanship. The other frontbench members were Macmillan (who had publicly called for an 'Industrial Charter'), David Maxwell Fyfe, Oliver Stanley and Lyttelton.[17] The Charter itself, when it appeared, served the purpose which Quintin Hogg – another progressive enthusiast – had urged on Butler, namely to be a second 'Tamworth Manifesto'. It was, accordingly, dull, centrist and respectable, though unlike the Tamworth document rather long. It was later followed by a series of other Charters on different topics – an Agricultural Charter, an Imperial Charter and (most daringly) a Workers' Charter. The publication of the last of these was the occasion for a tantrum by the leadership. The minutes of the Leader's Consultative

Committee (Shadow Cabinet) meeting on 12 May 1948 record:

> The question of the Party Organisation was raised. This had become acute in view of the Workers' Charter pamphlet with its sentence on employment.
>
> It was stated that no one reviews pamphlets before they are issued; propaganda is bad and the machinery for dealing with it slow and creaking.[18]

The exact cause of complaint is not elaborated. But distrust of the party machine's machinations is palpable.

Assheton and Lyttelton, among others, were highly critical of the Industrial Charter. Churchill himself was not very interested; but, when told by Maudling that the Charter had received Shadow Cabinet authorization and party conference approval, he was prepared to deliver a passage in his leader's speech in 1947 endorsing the contents. These were somewhat corporatist in tone compared with Conservative policy statements of the 1930s, though less extravagantly so than Macmillan, in his inter-war period, would have liked. In retrospect, the talk of 'co-partnership' in industry seems more of a political smokescreen than a policy intent, and when the time for implementation arrived the mood had altered again.

The Conservative Research Department was set to work in 1949, under the supervision of a committee chaired by Eden, on a full policy review exercise. Hogg was then entrusted with drafting the final document, which was agreed by Shadow Cabinet and published as *The Right Road for Britain*. It sold two million copies – a sign of the party's increasing relevance and improving fortunes. It served as the basis for the 1950 election manifesto, *This is the Road*.[19]

The other significant changes made in the party's operation at this time are those contained in the so-called Maxwell Fyfe reforms. (The title is, in fact, a misnomer, because the ubiquitous, ambitious and industrious Maxwell Fyfe was entrusted only with pulling together the proposals, not devising them.[20]) These reforms appeared on the surface technical, but they were, in truth, quite far-reaching and intended to alter the nature of the Conservative Party, in both social and constitutional terms. They thus sought to draw candidates from outside the prevailing limited, wealthy élite, and they also sought to reinforce central control over money. To the former end, new rules were introduced limiting the permissible financial contribution made by parliamentary candidates. Any candidate adopted after 31 December 1948 was forbidden to pay anything toward his election expenses. Nor could he make any payment to the constituency agent. Maxima were also introduced of £25 for a candidate's annual subscription and £50 for that of an MP. It would take some time before the intended democratizing effect was felt. But appearances, after all, mattered too. The change immediately felt good in the party and looked good in the country. The other reform was that a financial 'quota' was henceforth to be paid by local associations to help cover the expenses of the central party organization. It would be calculated on presumed Conservative strength in the constituency, assessed broadly on the level of Tory vote at the previous general election.[21] Though a continuing subject of recrimination and indignation, the quota system provided the party organization with some needed stability.

More important than anything done by the Conservatives in opposition was what Labour was doing in power to alienate opinion. Arrogance and incompetence seemed increasingly evident and were easy targets. Rationing, grumpily born in wartime, became increasingly intolerable in peace – particularly when it was reinforced: it was extended to bread in 1946. February 1947 saw a fuel crisis. There were power cuts, and unemployment rose to two million the following month. In July 1947 there was a sterling crisis, after Dalton made the pound freely convertible into dollars. In September 1949 Cripps, his successor as Chancellor, had to devalue sterling and impose a round of spending cuts and controls.

It was easier for the Conservatives to take advantage of the country's economic problems than to devise a policy to deal with them, and, not for the first or last time, they chose the easier option. The free-market-minded Oliver Lyttelton had, in a memorandum of 26 August 1947, urged Churchill to apply a combination of deflation, devaluation and decontrol when the Conservatives returned to power. But only the last element was ever put into effect. When the Labour Government devalued sterling in 1949, Churchill declared that the Opposition's attitude 'should be unitedly hostile'.[22] Lyttelton, for his pains, would be passed over in favour of Butler as Chancellor. Churchill had settled on an approach of minimum change in all fields of domestic policy. His preference, as in a speech of April 1948, was for trying to take as much credit as possible for the welfare state now taking shape.[23] In any case, in opposition he adopted the traditional (and lazy, if sometimes prudent) view that policy commitments should be avoided, and that the Opposition's job was 'to oppose'.

An exception to this passivity, one largely forced on the Conservatives by business interests rather than undertaken as a matter of choice, was the fight against steel nationalization. The party initially sought to oppose nationalization on pragmatic grounds, industry by industry. Coal, railways, gas and electricity were treated as particular cases. But iron and steel nationalization finally brought out some fighting spirit. Polling showed increasing majorities against it. Moreover, Labour's intentions became more ambitious, just as the wider project was becoming less popular. In 1950 the Labour Party published plans to nationalize sugar-refining, cement and insurance. Anti-nationalization also became a more attractive cause for the Conservatives, as industries affected began their own well-financed campaigning. It was carried on in more or less covert collaboration with the party machine. Aims of Industry, founded in 1942, became a significant anti-socialist player at all general elections. The threats to sugar and construction would also prove invaluable rallying cries for the party in fund-raising right into the 1970s. Tate & Lyle and the building trade were long the backbone of Tory industrial support. In this climate Churchill rediscovered his aggression, moved beyond the caution preferred by Eden, and took to denouncing the concept of nationalization in all shapes and sizes.[24] Sweeping aside the nuances of the reformulated Conservative industrial view, he told the Shadow Cabinet on 11 May 1949 that the 'real issue at the next General Election would be – more or less Nationalisation?'[25]

The February 1950 general election was fought under new electoral conditions, as the wartime franchise changes were fully implemented. Of these, redistribution of seats, as usual, helped the party. The abolition of business votes, the loss of the City of London's two seats and the abolition of university seats, by contrast, did not. The introduction of postal votes would prove of use, because of superior Tory organization. But a large recovery was on the cards in any case: the Conservative effort in 1945 had been so feeble, and Labour's actions since then had annoyed so many. The Conservatives gained a larger swing in their old stamping ground in the south-east, reversing the previous trend. The Liberal vote collapsed still further: only nine Liberal MPs were returned. In the event, Labour had an overall majority of six. It was disappointing, but not dispiriting. Churchill called for 'one more heave'.

Success in any early election was not, though, inevitable. The country's politics were now highly polarized between two almost equally powerful parties. Turnouts were thus likely to be high, and high turnouts were something the Conservatives had learned to fear. In the event, the outbreak of the Korean War, the rise in defence spending and an accompanying rise in inflation made matters more difficult for the Attlee Government. The election was held in October 1951. Fighting on the intellectually self-confident slogan 'Set the People Free', and brushing aside the question in the *Daily Mirror*'s leader, 'Whose finger on the trigger?' – Churchill sued, and the paper backed down – the Tories won the political argument. If Labour was still slightly ahead in votes, the Conservatives were ahead on seats, and the party secured a majority of fifteen.[26]

So Churchill was back in power.[27] But what would he do? As a preliminary question: what *could* he do? He was seventy-seven. He was too old to contemplate with equanimity radical departures from what his own long experience, including his political shifts, had taught him. This may be one reason for the degree of continuity with Attlee, though there are others.[28] Nevertheless, while well past his prime, Churchill was not, until his major stroke in June 1953, seriously incompetent. He could rise to most parliamentary and public occasions. He had always been chaotic in his work methods, relying on energy, inspiration and advice, and the combination still often worked. Even at the end of his term, it is hard to distinguish between real differences of opinion with his colleagues and objective criticism of his performance. What is clear is that he had by 1951 finished with taking risks, or at least any that seemed avoidable. He had experienced all too recently the waywardness of electors, and he intended not to over-estimate their thoughtfulness. As he put it to his son-in-law Christopher Soames and Jock Colville, his programme was: 'Houses and meat and not being scuppered.'[29] It was an outlook that militated against any serious grappling with Britain's enormous post-war problems. This, rather than age or inattention, is the gravamen of the case against Churchill's role in his last government.

An opportunity was thereby missed. A comparison of 1951 with 1979 and Margaret Thatcher – and in a different way 1970 and Edward Heath – is perhaps illuminating. On each of these occasions an incoming Tory government was faced with the choice between holding power and using power. Churchill chose simply to hold it.

Trying to do more, even given the slim majority, was not impossible. One could argue, of course, that it is difficult to gain support for marked changes of national direction until the opposite extreme has been tested to destruction (as it would be in the 1970s, but had not been in the 1950s). Against that, an earlier starting point is less perilous, because the decline endured is less steep. The attempt to sort out Britain's economic difficulties in the fifties, had it been successfully made, would also have had one other enormous benefit: it could have made the inevitable transition from Empire much less traumatic.

One reason why such hypotheses are worth considering is that there was Tory talent aplenty. Whatever else they were, the Conservatives were not now the 'stupid party'. They had restored their respectability in the universities and among (what would later be termed) the 'chattering classes'. Indeed, the Conservative parliamentary party had in its ranks the most exceptional political intellects of the day. The Tory intake of 1950 was regarded – and rather smugly regarded themselves – as above the ordinary. The 'One Nation Group' contained its most prominent members, many of whom were Conservative Research Department old boys.[30]

Iain Macleod was the moving force behind the group's first booklet, on the social services. Angus Maude, a former journalist, did the editing. Enoch Powell did much of the actual writing. Powell probably accurately describes its origin: 'Slinking out of the Chamber disconsolately after yet another failed frontal attack upon the Labour Party's welfare state, Iain Macleod and Angus (now Lord) Maude put their heads together and said "Let's write a book about One Nation".'[31] It was published at the 1950 party conference and made a large impression. The thinking was not exactly radical – which was not surprising, given the tactical political origin of the initiative. But, then, social services was traditional Labour territory and offering coherent Tory principles on it at all was a highly significant step. The One Nation Group contained MPs from both wings of the party, and perhaps its most interesting publication – it still interested Margaret Thatcher many years later, and this at least says something for its abiding relevance – was *Change is Our Ally*, published in 1954, in which the free market iconoclasm of Powell and Maude added some spice to the mix.[32] The change in approach also reflects the fact that, by this stage in the Churchill Government, improved economic circumstances had raised expectations – though these were not, in the short term, to be fulfilled.

Churchill tried to run his second Government along lines he had found congenial in wartime. He preferred to rely on a few advisers drawn from outside party politics. He sought to group government departments under the overall control of policy 'overlords'. Woolton was brought in to oversee food and agriculture. Lord Leathers (previously Minister of War Transport) covered transport and fuel and power. Cherwell was responsible for scientific research and development and statistics. But Cabinet ministers soon pushed the overlords aside and government reverted to its more logical form and practical rhythm. Churchill was equally frustrated in his attempts to induce the Liberals to form a coalition. Their leader, Clement Davies, was offered the education portfolio, but the rest of his party would not support his taking it.

Churchill's intentions were manifest in another way. He did not ask back Beaverbrook, which showed judgement, and Bracken refused the sideshow of the Colonial Office, ostensibly on grounds of health. Churchill was steering clear of the maverick right. But he steered equally clear of the more constructive right, when he avoided making Lyttelton Chancellor and gave the job instead to Butler.

David Maxwell Fyfe was similarly passed over as Minister of Labour in favour of Walter Monckton. Maxwell Fyfe's sin was to have hinted during the campaign at possible trade union legislation. Monckton, who had no obvious Conservative beliefs and was thus ideal for the task in hand, received direct instructions from

Churchill under no circumstances to oppose the unions. Monckton was a hard worker and a charmer. David Margesson called him 'the old oil can'.[33] It was, however, Churchill who insisted the oil be poured, and in such quantities that by the end even Monckton felt it had gone too far.

Churchill would typically grant the unions more than they expected, even more than they demanded, in order to secure industrial peace. Possibly he thought that he had to live down his past reputation as a hawk. Like many others, he seems to have become convinced that the Conservative Party could only win vital working-class support by pursuing good relations with organized labour. After his stroke in 1953 he became obsessively preoccupied with foreign policy, and his attitude to all troubles on the home front was just to buy them off. When a rail strike threatened in December 1953, he was even more anxious than Monckton to keep the trains running. The following year, Churchill's last decisive intervention in domestic policy was to overrule Monckton and the rest of the Cabinet as the railwaymen demanded a large settlement and threatened a strike. He had his way, and a court of inquiry was appointed, which duly ruled that the cost of running the railways should not enter into the question of what the employees were paid. The unions won, and on the worst possible terms for the economy.[34]

As his elliptical observation to Soames and Colville confirms, Churchill was keen on the house-building programme and on lifting rationing. So both proceeded vigorously. The 300,000-a-year house building target, into which the party stumbled by a mix of official prodding and spontaneous enthusiasm from the party conference, was more easily achieved than those who actually gave the pledge imagined. It usefully fitted in with the older notion of a 'property-owning democracy' – a concept framed by the Conservative MP Noel Skelton in the 1920s and then espoused by those progressive young Conservatives of the day in the 'YMCA'.[35] Among this group had been Eden and Macmillan. It was Eden who popularized the slogan at the 1946 conference and it was then Macmillan as housing minister in the early 1950s who gave it substance. But it was Churchill who overrode the objections.[36]

Churchill was equally bold in insisting on the end of rationing. A trencherman himself, he was much against cutting back on meat. He thought, specifically, that the nation should eat more pork. In 1954 bacon and red meat were finally removed from the state's clutches. That year, with rationing at an end, the Ministry of Food was merged with the Ministry of Agriculture and Fisheries.[37]

These were the easy tasks. Reversing Labour's nationalizations was bound to be much more difficult. The Government had, after all, only a small majority and Labour threatened renationalization if it were returned to office: so who would buy the assets? Moreover, even in iron and steel there was a long tradition of government intervention, which the industry seemed to like. In the event, Churchill insisted that long-distance road haulage should jump the denationalization queue. As for iron and steel, there was much debate in Cabinet. The Bill only received Royal Assent on 14 May 1953. The sale of assets under the legislation then took a decade and was completed just in time for the Labour Government to come in and renationalize them.[38] In fact, the only notable success in what later generations would describe as 'privatization' was the breaking of the BBC monopoly and the creation of commercial television. This measure was carried through by party and backbench opinion against the resistance of the Cabinet and the unconcern of the Prime Minister. It was the only socially transformative change over which Churchill's peacetime Government presided.[39]

The general characterization of the period's economic policy is that of consensus, popularised by a leading article in *The Economist* of February 1954, which ironically introduced to 'a wider audience' the figure of 'Mr Butskell'.[40] 'Butskellism' is in certain respects a misleading concept. The term was originally used in allusion to common ground allegedly shared by R. A. Butler and Hugh

Gaitskell (the Labour Chancellor/economic spokesman) in setting economic policy. But the two men had, in fact, quite different conceptions of the role of the state, as one might expect.[41] What is true is that the Conservative Government failed to break out of the broader consensual mould, and so failed either to meet many of its supporters' expectations or to create a new momentum.

There were two reasons for this, neither of which was fully understood at the time. The first was that taxation remained very high, and it bore very hard on the middle classes. This reflected not just the level of spending (which kept growing on social services, even when defence was cut after the Korean War). It also reflected the system itself. Higher earners were penalized. With the sharply progressive surtax, the marginal rate on incomes above £5,000 was 90 per cent.[42] Butler's budgets sought to regulate spending in the economy by what were now classic Keynesian demand management techniques. But they did nothing to alter the structure of taxation and incentives, where a socialistic rationale was accepted.

The second arm of the straitjacket into which Churchill's Government bound itself (and disastrously bound Eden's) consisted in refusing to allow sterling to float freely on the exchanges, seeking instead to maintain its parity against the dollar – and doing so, moreover, without the (limited, but at the time real) benefit of exchange controls. The flaws of that policy had been pointed out by Lyttelton. They were now even acknowledged by Butler.

Events had forced the pace. The incoming Conservative Government had faced a balance of payments crisis. In January 1952 a group of officials at the Treasury and the Bank of England – Otto Clarke, Leslie Rowan and George Bolton (from whose names would be derived the scheme's code name, 'Robot') – devised a radical shift of policy. It was put first to Butler and then to Churchill and the Cabinet.[43]

As background, it is worth recalling that more than half of world trade in the early 1950s was still conducted in sterling, even though

Britain's own economic power had sharply waned. The sterling area thus mattered to more than Britain. Robot would have reshaped it, and much else. It would have challenged the Bretton Woods fixed exchange rate system; it would have closed the door on the International Monetary Fund; and it would probably have aborted the European Payments Union. If successful, it might thus have struck a blow at European economic integration, while rescuing sterling from dependence on decisions made in Washington – both matters extending well beyond the technicalities of financial policy.

Robot envisaged that the Chancellor should announce the immediate convertibility of sterling for non-residents of the sterling area on a floating rate of exchange. Sterling balances (net sterling liabilities) would be frozen and funded with long-term Treasury bonds. It was envisaged that a number of European countries would wish to become part of a wider sterling area 'payments club', floating with sterling against the dollar. The scheme would both return to Britain freedom of monetary action and create a new international monetary order, to which Washington would have to adapt.

There would be a further benefit. The pound would fall to its market value. Prices would rise. So, it was accepted, would unemployment. Distortions of markets at home would be overcome. So would those in foreign trade. Businesses would have to compete globally with dollar-denominated goods and services. The economic shock involved in ending inefficiencies would kick-start the British economy into higher productivity and greater competitiveness. Such was the ambitious project. Cut free of the post-imperial overhang of considerations of the sterling area, what was essentially suggested was a radical step towards Thatcherism *avant la lettre*.[44]

Cabinet considered it, debated it – and rejected it. It also then rejected a second version. The risks – above all, the risk of much higher unemployment – were deemed too great. In the short term, the crisis was met by the classic measures of cuts in spending, a clampdown on imports, and a higher bank rate. The considered response was worse. The long-term goal of reintroducing sterling convertibility was met in February 1955 – but without floating. The scene was thus set for Britain's humiliation by the United States at Suez. Whether Robot's other objectives could ever have been met is unclear. Nothing would alter the real diminution of British economic power when compared with America's. But allowing the pound to float, under the conditions proposed in Robot in 1952, would have made a slump in sterling's value four years later far less terrifying for the authorities and the politicians. And it was panic (larded with mendacity and betrayal) that finally 'scuppered' Britain at Suez.

Churchill's stroke in 1953 convinced everyone except Churchill himself that the time had come – indeed, had come some while ago – for him to stand down. The old man, though, was determined to hang on, partly for the reasons that convince all ageing but assertive leaders that they are still needed, partly because he wanted to achieve a final success on the international front, and partly because of the complex and ultimately insoluble Eden problem.

Eden had been formally designated Churchill's preferred successor as early as 1942.[45] Churchill never reversed his decision, but he frequently regretted it. For his part, Eden was loyal, though he grumbled. It was his behaviour and his judgement that caused Churchill and others to have serious and growing doubts. For example, on one occasion, late in the course of the war, Eden had screamed hysterically at Churchill over the telephone – he preferred that cowardly medium for his rants – because of a paper that Cherwell had submitted and that Eden thought an affront.[46] Generally speaking, though, it was Eden's aides and officials who felt the force of his temper. Eden, not surprisingly, failed to inspire loyalty. He did, though, inspire a mixture of hatred and contempt, not least from Randolph Churchill, Winston's erratically destructive son, who first coined the phrase 'the Eden Terror'.[47]

Randolph's venom was not drained, merely bottled up, when in the summer of 1952 Eden married (as his second wife) Churchill's niece Clarissa. The marriage itself led to further problems. Eden was a divorcee, and not the innocent party either. The Archbishop of Canterbury and other churchmen strongly disapproved. (Later, and unjustly, Eden as Prime Minister was accused of hypocrisy when Princess Margaret was forbidden to marry Group Captain Peter Townsend, because of the latter's divorced status.[48]) Nor was Clarissa tactful. The days had gone when a Prime Minister's wife could object to another woman hanging out her washing where visiting dignitaries to Chequers could see it. But Clarissa did. The saga of the indignant Maud Butt's unsightly washing line was another irritant when Eden's problems mounted.[49]

In the winter of 1952–3 Eden's health broke. It had long been precarious: he had endured a complicated operation for appendicitis in 1948. Now, in April 1953, he was subject to an inexcusably botched gall-bladder operation and nearly died. Churchill insisted that he have rectifying surgery in the United States and that the Conservative Party should pay for it. In Eden's absence, Churchill delivered a speech in the House of Commons, of which Eden from his sickbed greatly disapproved, urging detente with the Soviet Union in the wake of Stalin's death in March. But then (on 23 June) Churchill had his stroke. So at this politically crucial juncture both the Prime Minister and his heir apparent were out of the picture – and another Salisbury, the fifth Marquess, quietly and effectively ran the country from the House of Lords.

In fact, Churchill's physical recovery was rather faster than Eden's. Churchill delivered an acclaimed speech at the Conservative party conference. Eden, when he returned from America, still looked disconcertingly frail. The two men, neither of them well, probably both unsuited now for high office, spent the rest of Churchill's tenure arguing bitterly about foreign policy, an area in which each was entirely convinced of his boundless sagacity.

On the question of how to deal with the Soviet Union, one can say without hesitation that Churchill was in the wrong. He over-personalized the role that Stalin had played. He underrated the degree to which the system and its ideology determined the Soviet leaders' actions. He therefore exaggerated the scope for what he called 'easement'. He also thought that the arrival of the hydrogen bomb had altered the whole dynamics of the Cold War, which it had not and did not. Eden, supported by the Foreign Office, most of the British Cabinet and the US State Department, was sceptical towards this analysis, regarding it as wishful thinking and also likely to undermine NATO – still in its infancy, having been created in 1949. Eden was right.

Churchill was, by contrast, correct about the other side of the Cold War equation. He sometimes lamented, but he never for a moment doubted, the predominance of the United States and the need to frame British policy in that light. His settled view on the matter is recorded by his doctor, Lord Moran:

'Up to July 1944 England had a considerable say in things; after that I was conscious that it was America who made the big decisions. She will make the big decisions now.'
Winston said this with an air of finality.
'We do not yet realize her immeasurable power. She could conquer Russia without any help . . . Without their help, England would be isolated; she might become, with France, a satellite of Russia.'
Winston's voice broke, and his eyes filled with tears.[50]

On a visit to Washington in July 1954 the question of relations both with America and with the Soviet Union arose. Churchill and Eden argued in front of the Americans about Guatemala, where an aggressive communist-orientated regime had temporarily come to power. Churchill supported the Americans in sorting out their own backyard. He thought Eden very foolish in not recognizing that the Americans would have their way. Eden felt abused. Then on the way back the two clashed about Churchill's intention to fire off a telegram to Molotov calling for talks. After mediation by Jock Colville, it was agreed that the matter would go to Cabinet. (In the end, the Soviets stymied the proposal themselves; had they not, there would have been resignations.[51])

The pressure on Churchill to go increased from all sides as the date for a general election approached. The logic that a new man should gain his own mandate for a new term was difficult to dispute, though Churchill was ingenious in finding excuses. Eden was, in any case, now more popular. He had shone at the Geneva Conference on South-East Asia. He had made current the phrase about a 'property-owning democracy', and home ownership among other measures of prosperity had flourished. He was attractive to women, particularly older women. Woolton told Churchill that it made no sense for him to undergo the strain of fighting another general election. Even Macmillan, from whom Churchill had hoped for support, told him that he should go. Churchill finally made up his mind in early 1955. He would resign in April after his eightieth birthday celebrations had been completed, and without undignified haste.[52]

On 4 April, the night before his resignation, the departing Prime Minister gave a dinner for the Queen and the Duke of Edinburgh in Downing Street. Afterwards, Colville accompanied him upstairs. Still dressed in black knee-breeches and wearing his decorations, Churchill opened the curtains, sat on the bed and stared silently out into the night. Suddenly he turned to Colville, 'with a penetrating, almost frightening stare', and said: 'I don't believe Anthony can do it.'[53]

"O, WHITHER HAST THOU LED ME, EGYPT?"

Eden, first (here, in 1953) as Foreign Secretary, and later as Prime Minister, was faced with the problem of how to secure British interests in Egypt and the Suez Canal. Unfortunately, neither inspiration from Disraeli (appearing as the Sphinx), nor Eden himself, could devise a solution, and Eden's botched attempt had catastrophic results.

14

SUEZ

Churchill was not alone in his forebodings about Anthony Eden's premiership. Bob Boothby told the lobby that 'the others will be watching Eden and he will be pole-axed in eighteen months' time'. Boothby was three months out in his prediction.[1] Among the 'others' must certainly be ranked Harold Macmillan. Despite both being Old Etonians, veterans of the First World War and Tory 'progressives' (though Macmillan was much more to the left), the two men had little in common. Eden found Macmillan's constant self-promotion, his heart-on-sleeve evocations of dole queues in Stockton and his dwelling on his (real enough) sufferings at the Front unbearably vulgar.[2] Macmillan, who was cleverer and more ambitious, but also three years older than Eden and so in a hurry, had excellent reasons for wanting his rival out of the way. Churchill certainly understood this. Shortly before he yielded to the pressure to go, and doubtless provoked by the expression in what he called 'Anthony's hungry eyes', he asked Eden how he got on with Macmillan.[3] Eden replied: 'Very well. Why?' Churchill said: 'Oh, he is very ambitious.' Eden laughed.[4]

Despite such omens, Eden's succession was never in doubt, and it was smoothly accomplished. Churchill resigned on 5 April 1955. Eden became Prime Minister the following day. His leadership was confirmed by a party meeting on 21 April. A week earlier the new Prime Minister, after an acute bout of dithering, had called an election. The manifesto was entitled *United for Peace and Progress*, which adequately summed up the enlightened Tory message. Churchill was frozen out of the campaign and Eden's face was everywhere. His polite and easy style was popular. The Government's record was good. The Labour Party's earlier predictions of Reaction, high unemployment, social spending cuts and risky belligerence had all been negated by events. Attlee, not Churchill, was now the ageing, past-it leader, Eden the one fronting a (relatively) young team. Eden was also an accomplished performer on television, a medium with which Churchill had always been uneasy. Four million saw the new Prime Minister's party election broadcast. The Conservative lead of 4 per cent shrank somewhat during the campaign. But the outcome was never in doubt. The Conservative majority rose from 15 to 58 and Eden secured almost 50 per cent of the popular vote, a post-war triumph.[5]

The hurrahs did not last long.

Eden was an unlucky Conservative leader. But it was not only bad luck that destroyed him: the Government's earlier mistakes played their part. Butler's fourth budget, on the eve of the election, was too loose. It contained large measures of tax relief, including sixpence off the standard rate of income tax. At a time of rapid expansion it was asking for trouble, and when remedial action had to be taken Gaitskell tore into Butler, and with good reason. Butler's emergency budget in October harmed not just his own but Eden's reputation. Dubbed the 'pots and pans budget', it contained not only spending cuts but an increase in and extension of purchase tax – hence the name.

Butler's job had already been promised to Macmillan, though

Butler did not know it. Eden would have moved him earlier except that Butler's wife had died after a distressing illness, and the new Prime Minister displayed what turned out to be ill-judged compassion. For this, Eden received no credit. But he was widely damned for mismanaging the economy. This, in turn, drew attention to his lack of competence and credibility in domestic affairs more generally.[6]

There was no honeymoon for Eden's Government. He was thought to have failed to make a sufficient break with Churchill in his first ministerial reshuffle. More importantly defective, though, were the choices he did make. He dropped Lord Swinton, a Churchill crony and no fan of Eden, from the Colonial Office. But he failed to put his friend, the well qualified 'Bobbety' Salisbury, into the Foreign Office – fearing that the appointment of a peer would be deemed improper (a fear later proved unfounded by the appointments of Lords Home and Carrington).[7] Instead, Eden appointed Macmillan, replacing him at Defence with Selwyn Lloyd. Macmillan was too strong a figure to do what Eden told him, and Eden could not resist – and showed no inclination to resist – interfering in what he regarded as his field of supreme expertise. In no time at all, he regretted moving Macmillan, and he regretted keeping Butler.

Eden was, indeed, a spectacularly inept picker. It is difficult, even now, to see why he chose William Clark as his Number Ten press secretary, a post requiring discretion, professionalism and loyalty. Clark was a left-wing, opinionated, homosexual journalist from the *Observer* who went on to have a great future in international circles. He may have started out with some affection for Eden, whose glamorous aura appealed to both sexes (though Eden's own inclinations were always unambiguous). Anyway, the regard did not last. Clark offered technically bad advice, soon disagreed with Eden's policies (notably over Suez), betrayed his confidence, and finally resigned at the most difficult moment imaginable. Not surprisingly, Eden was soon trying to sideline Clark in his own fumbling relations with the press. In these he largely concentrated on revealing but not very useful discussions with the editor of *The Times*, Sir William Haley.[8]

As the political climate worsened, the barely suppressed rivalry of Eden's colleagues and their shared disregard for the leader's character surfaced. On 20 December, Eden belatedly acted to move Macmillan, who went to the Treasury, replacing him at the Foreign Office with the pliable Selwyn Lloyd. Butler was notionally elevated, but in fact downgraded, as Lord Privy Seal and Leader of the House. Macmillan had flexed his muscles, insisting that he should have complete control of his economic brief, and effectively asserting his right to be seen as Eden's number two at the expense of Butler – who, he demanded, must not be de facto Deputy Prime Minister (as Butler had hoped to be).

Other changes failed to bolster Eden's position. Oliver Poole, a former MP, replaced Lord Woolton as very much a back-room, fund-raising party chairman. Edward Heath became Chief Whip. Iain Macleod joined the Cabinet. Neither Heath nor Macleod would agree with Eden on Suez, though both kept their counsel. Perhaps the most inappropriate appointment, though, was of the 'old oil can', Monckton, as Defence Minister. So agitated did he become over Suez that he had to be replaced during the struggle by Anthony Head. (With Mountbatten as First Sea Lord – an appointment made by Churchill, albeit with misgivings – Eden would be singularly unfortunate in those responsible for defence policy, since Mountbatten was also wholly against the Suez venture.)

The political atmosphere was bad. By-election failures made it worse. Any improvement in the economy, if and when it came, would be to the benefit of the Chancellor of the Exchequer, Macmillan. In the event, Macmillan's plans to raise income tax and cut defence were stopped by Eden; but the Chancellor managed to score a minor public relations triumph with the launch of Premium Bonds.

The crescendo of press criticism reached a peak after the December reshuffle. It was at this time that Maud Butt's washing enlivened the public debate about Eden's inadequacies. Eden could not rely on the Conservative press for help. Lady Pamela Berry, the wife of the chairman and editor-in-chief of the *Daily Telegraph* and a great political hostess, hated both Anthony and Clarissa Eden. It was the *Telegraph* which on 3 January 1956 published an article whose author, ridiculing a characteristic gesture of Eden – that of noiselessly striking with one fist the open palm of his other hand – called for 'the smack of firm government'. Eden was beside himself with rage when he read it. He foolishly referred to the matter in a speech, which naturally made him look petulant. He then, even more foolishly, and following the inept advice of William Clark, issued, in response to an article in the downmarket *People* newspaper, a denial that he was about to resign. The press feeding frenzy continued. Ambushed at the airport and asked for his views, Butler weakly replied that he was determined 'to support the Prime Minister in all his difficulties'. He then agreed with the proposition that Eden was 'the best Prime Minister we have'. It was perhaps the most famous Rab-ism and probably the most damaging. Whether Clark or Butler intended Eden harm is unclear. That they did him harm, and that they thereby reflected their inner feelings, is indisputable.[9]

In these circumstances, a besieged Prime Minister is best advised to pull up the drawbridge and sit it out. But Eden could not sit. He constantly and counter-productively fidgeted and fretted. As John Boyd-Carpenter, his pensions minister, records, Eden himself worried, and then he also worried his ministers, ringing them up with complaints at all hours.[10] This bilateral style of governing wasted energy, destroyed morale and made for bad feeling. It also encouraged the view that Eden was intent on bypassing the Cabinet. In fact, that was not the case. Unlike Churchill, Eden lacked personal cronies or close policy advisers. Even during Suez, and contrary to what was asserted later, he did not keep Cabinet in the dark. It was just that he was isolated, which was his weakness.

Under pressure at home, it was natural that Eden should strive to assert himself in the sphere of foreign affairs, where his reputation lay. But, unlike Churchill, he was an internationalist, not a warrior. His diplomacy was focused on the conference, not the gunboat. He thus fell into risks rather than courted them, and he was too highly strung then to face them with equanimity. This contrast between Churchill and Eden is, indeed, central to the personal and national tragedy of Suez.

Churchill had a low view of the Egyptians but, at the same time, an acute consciousness of the importance of Egypt. It was not just that 80 per cent of western Europe's oil supplies came through the Suez Canal. Britain's prestige in the Middle East, where its influence was under threat from Arab nationalism and American ambition, was bound up with Egypt as well. Churchill blamed the Labour Government's earlier weakness in Persia for creating an impression of drift. So he particularly wished to stand firm when the twenty-year Anglo-Egyptian Treaty of 1936 expired. By this treaty, Britain had acquired the right to station 10,000 troops in the Canal zone. In 1951 Egypt unilaterally abrogated the treaty. But British forces remained. Churchill had been seeking to bring the Americans into negotiations about the Canal's future; but, despite repeated requests, Eisenhower would not be drawn. At the end of 1953 the American President politely but firmly ended the correspondence.

Churchill recognized, in principle, the need for a negotiated settlement with Egypt. But it was only during his convalescence that year that Salisbury and General Sir Brian Robertson, British Commander-in-Chief of land forces in the Middle East, worked out the details. Then Eden managed to persuade Churchill to accept the proposed phased evacuation of British troops. Churchill rationalized his own about-face on the grounds that the new strategic situation created by the hydrogen bomb meant that the traditional priority given to overseas military bases had been superseded. He had previously sought to use the existence of the Suez Group of Tory MPs, led by Captain Charles Waterhouse and Julian Amery, to stiffen Eden's spine. But now Churchill robustly defended the Anglo-Egyptian settlement in the House of Commons against them. In the event, on 29 July 1954, twenty-six backbenchers still voted against ratification of the deal. The policy of retreat from Egypt was none the less, and rightly, perceived as Eden's. Eden trusted Nasser, or at least thought that he could be pressured to keep his word. Eden was wrong.

Churchill later remarked of the Suez adventure: 'I would never have dared to do it without squaring the Americans, and once I had started I would never have dared stop.' He would not, in fact, have been able to 'square' Eisenhower, but neither in all probability would Eisenhower have dared treat him as shabbily as he did Eden. That might, in the circumstances, have been enough. And Churchill would undoubtedly have gone in earlier, and held on longer – at least until British face had been saved.[11]

Unfortunately, as Churchill had earlier feared, Eden demonstrated a tin ear in his dealings with Washington.[12] Eden thought Eisenhower inept, and he disliked the US Secretary of State, John Foster Dulles, in a quite physical manner, particularly detesting his halitosis. At the Geneva Conference in 1954, Eden not only frustrated American policy towards Russia and China, he even upbraided Dulles on the steps of the Hôtel du Rhone: 'The trouble with you, Foster, is that you want World War Three.'[13] This was typical of what British Foreign Office types thought (and still think) about America. But saying so was (and is) tactless, at best.

Eden misunderstood the Americans. He also misunderstood what was happening in the Middle East. He knew a good deal about the people, states and interests. But he did not realize how explosive were the forces at work.

Paradoxically, in the light of what followed, Eden was regarded as an Arabist. In his Guildhall speech on 9 November 1955, he had publicly called on Israel to give up territory acquired in 1949. He was close to Anthony Nutting, Minister of State at the Foreign Office, who was even more inclined to the Arabs. Nutting was known as 'Eden's Eden', and his resignation later deeply wounded his mentor.

British policy, as Eden stressed when he and Lloyd visited Eisenhower in January 1956, was to uphold the Baghdad Pact of the previous year as the bulwark against Soviet penetration in the region. But the Americans were not interested. Washington was already concentrating on the presidential election later that year – another key factor that Eden and his advisers inexplicably over-looked in assessing American reactions.

The reception given to Selwyn Lloyd on his tour of the Middle East in March demonstrated Britain's weakness. The sudden dismissal of Glubb 'Pasha' (alias Lieutenant-General Sir John Bagot Glubb), Britain's man in Jordan, was a blow. Lloyd was the target of taunts by Nasser. His party was stoned in Bahrain. Nasser was now in the ascendant. He also had nothing to lose after the collapse of the American-led Anglo-American plan to finance his pet project, the Aswan High Dam. He turned still more openly to the Russians. He was confident enough – and angry enough – to prod the British lion in the eye.

Events now moved quickly. The last British troops left Port Said on 13 June. Ten days later Nasser became President in elections in which he was the sole candidate. On 26 July – in response to a coded injunction in Nasser's speech in Alexandria – Egyptian troops seized key points along the Canal. The news came through when Eden was hosting a dinner at Number Ten in honour of King Faisal of Iraq. After the dinner ended, Eden sought out Gaitskell and won his (later retracted) support for vigorous action. He then chaired a discussion in the Cabinet Room with Lloyd, Salisbury, Kilmuir

(Lord Chancellor, and thus the Government's chief legal adviser) and Home, who were later joined by the military and by French and American representatives. The polyglot attendance and disunited advice can, in retrospect, be seen to have set the tone for the débâcle.[14]

It did not seem so at the time. The press was all but unanimous in condemning Nasser. The left-wing news media were as vitriolic as the Tory papers. It was the *Daily Mirror*, not Eden, which first drew a parallel with Mussolini and Hitler. Eden was the hero of anti-appeasement. So the comparison came naturally and simplistically. He would not and could not back down. An 'Egypt Committee' of Cabinet ministers – effectively a War Cabinet – was formed consisting of Eden, Salisbury, Macmillan, Lloyd, Home and Monckton. The presence of Macmillan was significant. Ironically, Macmillan would later advise Margaret Thatcher, when faced with a similar crisis in the Falklands, to keep the Chancellor of the Exchequer (then Geoffrey Howe) off such a committee. But, anyway, Macmillan in 1955–6 was stronger than Howe in 1982.[15]

Contrary to what Eisenhower later claimed, Eden kept the US President fully informed of the intention to use force, if necessary. He repeatedly requested American assistance. Eisenhower's response would be equally clear – and negative. The Americans, like the British and French, wanted ultimately to see regime change in Egypt. But the issue now, said Ike, must be resolved by negotiation.

France, by contrast, saw an opportunity. The French wanted immediate military action. Guy Mollet, the French Socialist Prime Minister, was less concerned with the Canal, as such, than with getting rid of Nasser in short order, whom the French saw as standing in the way of suppressing their Algerian insurgency. France, too, was much closer than Britain to Israel, which the French had armed. French policy was now set on launching a joint but disavowed assault on Nasser in conjunction with the Israelis.

Israel's agenda was also different, and could be summed up in a single word: survival. Precisely which of Israel's surrounding Arab enemies, and in what order and combination, required defeating was wholly dependent on circumstances. One of the oddities, and complications, of the Suez venture was that until almost the last moment it seemed as if Jordan, to which Britain was bound by treaty, might be punished, rather than Egypt. This greatly alarmed the British. When Eden proclaimed in the crisis that Britain's aim was mediation, this was not, therefore, complete invention – though it certainly did not reflect the truth either. The prospect, however, of bringing French and British forces into a joint assault on Nasser was enough to convince the Israelis that Egypt should be the present target. The lightning Israeli Sinai campaign followed this logic. For Israel, the war of 1956 lasted no more than a hundred hours.[16] In fact, the speedy success of the Israelis and the slowness of the Anglo-French attack notably reduced the credibility of Eden's line that Britain was intervening as an honest broker.

So Eden's position was difficult. But he made it impossible. He could have acted militarily in agreement with France – with or without Israel – and in defiance of America. This, though, required speed. Or he could have relied on diplomacy, hoping that American pressure would be sufficient to make Nasser back down. This required persistence. In fact, he tried both, and failed. He delayed, to give negotiation time to work; but it did not. Then he acted in the face of inevitable American opposition; and he had to back down. He managed at the same time to involve himself in a policy of collusion with the Israelis, which he and Selwyn Lloyd both always denied, but which secret papers since released have confirmed. Even at the time, the denials convinced very few – not that most people cared either way.

Eden's failure abroad finished him at home, notably in the Cabinet. The pressure he had faced to act in the first place had stemmed in part from his domestic weakness. But if he had succeeded, or even not obviously failed, at Suez, he would have survived, for a while at least. The Cabinet certainly contained its doubters, like Butler and Macleod; but it did not rebel. Only Monckton had to be shifted sideways. The only ministers who resigned were Nutting and Edward Boyle.

The Conservative Party in the country was overwhelmingly and enthusiastically in favour of intervention, as the October party conference showed. In Parliament, although there was more unease on the back benches than surfaced at the time, Tory MPs were by and large thoroughly and militantly committed to destroying Nasser. The Suez Group, now feeling vindicated by events, rapidly expanded its numbers and consistently pressed the case for force. Only eight Conservative MPs abstained on a whipped vote on 8 November, the day after the ceasefire. These then came under great pressure from their constituencies. Four were de-selected permanently. Nutting was one whose career foundered, despite his later attempts to revive it. Those minded to oppose the policy had had the ground cut from under them when Gaitskell – who had now brazenly reversed direction – counter-productively called on dissident Tory MPs in a televised address, on 4 November, to bring Eden down.[17]

In all this, the Tory Party reflected wider opinion. Eden's approval rating was 40 per cent before Suez. But it now climbed. At the height of the crisis it was 52 per cent, against Gaitskell's 44 per cent. By December, as Eden's colleagues were contriving his euthanasia, his support stood at 56 per cent. And while it is doubtless true that there was a marked shift against Eden among intellectuals, it is also true that this group was in a small minority, despite its influence in the liberal media (the BBC and the *Economist* were both hostile) and the universities.[18]

Nasser outmanoeuvred Eden, but with a lot of help from the Americans. Obstruction from Washington was the main factor behind the two months of futile diplomacy which allowed Nasser to secure his position and his possession of the Canal. A first London Conference in August came up with a new plan for administration of the Canal, which Sir Robert Menzies, the Australian Prime Minister, tried to sell to Nasser. The Americans effectively ensured its rejection by meanwhile publicly ruling out the use of force. A second London Conference in September, following Dulles' initiative, now devised the idea of a 'Suez Canal Users' Association' (SCUA). Eden tried to persuade Dulles of the need to withhold dues to induce Nasser to cooperate and had hopes of succeeding. But Dulles's opacity at key moments provides no real excuse for British misunderstanding. Eisenhower again clearly warned against the use of force. Macmillan's account of a conversation with the American President in which the latter allegedly 'accepted' the argument that Britain '*must* win' (Macmillan's emphasis) and demonstrated his determination 'to bring Nasser down' was completely misleading. Macmillan's over-optimism at the start and panic at the end can be attributed to gross miscalculation – a belief that he could 'manage' the Americans – or to deviousness, or perhaps a complex mixture of both.[19] In any case, Ike could not, in fact, have been clearer. He was altogether against even the threat of force, and he was, therefore, wholly against the planned military operation. Nor was his motivation difficult to fathom. He was absolutely determined that nothing would embarrass his presidential campaign before the elections on 6 November. Indeed, he had clearly decided that he could gain politically by playing on American populist anti-colonialism.[20]

In any case, with the negotiations stalled, Eden went ahead. The French plan was put to him at Chequers on Sunday, 14 October. At Eden's insistence, no notes were to be taken. Israel would invade the Canal Zone and Britain and France were to intervene, in order to 'separate the combatants'. How Eden could have thought this would be convincing is difficult to discern. He doubtless wanted to act before winter made conditions difficult. But his judgement was so bad that it suggests he was already ill. (He had been laid low with a fever when visiting his wife in hospital, and his frail health would soon break entirely.) Selwyn Lloyd returned from the UN in New York optimistic about the diplomatic prospects, only to find that the deadline had been set for war. Lloyd went along with the plan only at Eden's urging. On 18 October, Cabinet discussed the implications of the attack.

Secret meetings between the British, French and Israeli sides then took place at Sèvres on 22 and 24 October.[21] Eden did not attend. Lloyd attended the first, though not the second, session. Cabinet discussed the proceedings on 23 October. Eden was later horrified to learn that notes had been taken of the final Sèvres agreement. The British version was destroyed. But French and Israeli copies were not.

Eden now sent messages to Eisenhower and made a statement to the Commons. At the end of the same day, midnight on 30 October, the British Seaborne Assault Force sailed from Malta. Passage took six days. British parachute drops then occurred at dawn on 5 November. Port Said was quickly captured and British forces advanced 23 miles down the Canal. In the meantime, though, the stuffing had been knocked out of the politicians at home.[22]

American anger, predictable but unpredicted, broke the British Government's will. The combination of diplomatic and economic pressure from the United States proved insuperable. It stemmed wholly from American interests, not from wider geopolitics. This needs to be emphasized. On 23 October, Moscow had sent in tanks to crush the Hungarian uprising. On 5 November, when the Anglo-French Operation Musketeer began, the Soviet Union issued a direct threat. But Washington's reaction had nothing to do with Hungary. Nor were Moscow's own plans influenced by Suez, except perhaps marginally in the timing.[23] It was the US presidential election of 6 November that mattered in the short term, and America's wish to supplant the European colonial powers in the Middle East (and elsewhere) that counted in the long run. In both regards, US policy at Suez was overwhelmingly successful – albeit at a high price.

When the Bank of England had made its assessments of the repercussions, it had identified American obstruction as the worst scenario. When this materialized in the form of outright hostility, panic set in; and it quickly spread. Sterling and the reserves were, of course, vulnerable because of the failure to follow through with Robot. De facto convertibility combined with a fixed exchange rate was a lethal combination in a crisis. The largest holders of transferable sterling included Arab countries, and Britain also customarily paid for its oil in sterling. But it now needed dollars. In these circumstances, Britain sought a waiver of interest payments on debt owed to the United States. This was not forthcoming. Indeed, America now openly worked for economic sanctions at the United Nations. On 6 November, Britain accepted a UN ceasefire, dismaying the French. Britain also sought massive financial assistance from the US, only to be further disappointed. It was made clear that this would not be available until Britain and France physically pulled out of Egypt. (American threats also forced Israeli evacuation of Sinai.) Only on 10 December, after this withdrawal, and with Anglo-French acceptance that Britain and France would not even be members of the planned UN Expeditionary Force, was a large American-backed IMF loan to Britain agreed.[24]

Harold Macmillan's role in these events provides the thread between what was happening abroad and Eden's fate at home. Having been one of the keenest on the original expedition, and having then misled Eden about Eisenhower's feelings, Macmillan went into sharp reverse. As Chancellor, he warned the Cabinet about the real outflow in gold currency reserves as the crisis developed. But he also greatly, and probably deliberately, exaggerated it.[25] From at least this point on, it seems clear that he was embarked on a stratagem to oust Eden and replace him as Prime Minister.

Eden was personally humiliated. He had gambled and failed. His health again broke. On 19 November, on his doctor's orders, he cancelled all engagements. Butler was left in effective charge while Eden, again with poor judgement, departed with his wife to the Caribbean to convalesce, leaving others to pick up the pieces while shivering through a British winter. Eden in Jamaica knew a little about Macmillan's activities, but not everything, and in any case was powerless to impede them.

In all this, Macmillan's relationship with the Americans was the key. He was known and liked by Eisenhower from the war years in North Africa and was the Administration's preferred candidate for British Prime Minister. In his financial negotiations Macmillan also had ample opportunity to prove himself useful. He exceeded his powers, let alone his duties, promising that he could command a sufficient majority of Tory MPs to vote for withdrawal, and even promising Eden's replacement (in which he was more successful). The contacts were close and constant. Macmillan held three meetings with the US ambassador in London in just three days.

Macmillan was equally adept in the forum of the Conservative Party. His only serious rival now was Butler, over whom he had anyway already gained a lead. The two addressed the 1922 Committee on 22 November – and it was Macmillan who shone, employing his well-known (and deeply misleading) parallel of ancient Greece and Rome as a future model for the relationship between Britain and America. Butler, allegedly the man in charge, was shown up and humiliated.

The following month Eden finally returned. He was still intent on defending his actions. He explicitly denied in the House any collusion with Israel. It was an ignominious coda to an honourable, if overstated, career. But renewed ill-health came to the rescue in his indignities. On 5 January Eden informed Salisbury that medical advice left him no alternative but to resign.[26]

Eden seems to have recommended Butler rather than Macmillan as his successor. Butler, the appeaser, he considered weak, but Macmillan he considered treacherous. A letter of commiseration from Clarissa to Rab suggests as much. But Eden must also have known, in his heart, that Macmillan would succeed. And this is presumably why his advice to the Queen was kept quiet.[27] Salisbury, with his aristocratic speech impediment, now had the task of sounding out the Cabinet. Should it be 'Wab or Hawold?' Hawold it overwhelmingly was. Macmillan was also Churchill's choice. Heath as Chief Whip and Oliver Poole as party chairman delivered the same verdict. Home, too, agreed. It was not just a matter of which the party preferred but which the party would accept. The parliamentary supporters of Butler would accept Macmillan. The partisans of Macmillan would not accept Butler. It was much the same in the country. Butler was disliked as an appeaser and as a wobbler. And he was, indeed, both. But had the full facts of Macmillan's conduct in the crisis been known, Macmillan would have looked worse. Luckily for him, they were not known. The message to the Palace was, in any case, clear; and on 10 January Harold Macmillan was duly summoned to succeed Anthony Eden as Prime Minister.[28]

Looking back on Suez many years later, Selwyn Lloyd suggests that, paradoxically, one result of Suez was closer cooperation between Britain and the United States, though he concedes that Eden could not have achieved this, while Macmillan could and did.[29] This rationalization of events contains some truth, but it is also misleading. Suez marked a huge and irreversible setback for British power and influence. It destroyed Britain's reputation as an independent force to be reckoned with in world affairs – one which would not be restored until the 1980s, and then only in part. If Suez made the Anglo-American 'Special Relationship' closer, it was because it ended any remaining Anglo-American rivalry by removing even the fig-leaf of pretended equality. The realities of power had discreetly changed under Churchill, as he realized. Appearances then humiliatingly followed suit under Eden.

Suez specifically marked an immediate shift of influence in the Middle East from Britain (and an already semi-eclipsed France) to America. It also probably speeded the progress of European decolonization and withdrawal, which America wanted. The problem, as Henry Kissinger has observed, was that America refused to face up to what this shift entailed. In retrospect, Richard Nixon (Eisenhower's Vice-President), Dulles and even Eisenhower himself – the key players, in fact – all seem to have regretted how things turned out. But this was only after Washington found it had succeeded too well; and found, too, something of the challenge that perpetual engagement in global trouble spots poses to domestic harmony. Suez cleared the way for American superpower dominance, and at the same time made that dominance lonelier and its burden harder to bear. Reaction to the crushing of France, in particular, found expression in the anti-American policies pursued under de Gaulle and his successors. As the West German Chancellor Konrad Adenauer, no enemy of America, merely a European realist, told the French foreign minister, Christian Pineau: 'Europe will be your revenge.' The French – at least until M. Sarkozy – have agreed.[30]

For Britain, the results were still more complex. Eden had shown little or no interest in the Messina Conference, held in June 1955 to discuss the possibility of developing the European Steel and Coal Community into a European Common Market. In this he was at the time wholly representative of wider British political opinion. Churchill's European outpourings in opposition had already been replaced by caution in government. The European enthusiasts in the Conservative Party were few and without influence – something which would change under Macmillan. This disengagement from European integration was a consequence not of over-confidence in the link with America, but of the psychological grip, for good and ill, of the historic links with the Commonwealth.

The feeling of isolation and impotence that followed Suez broke this pattern.[31] It stimulated a new search for closer relations with Europe, at the same time as it solidified a subordinate relationship with the United States. Macmillan's premiership would give expression to both. At first, the two goals seemed compatible, even mutually supporting. The tensions between them developed only later. But underlying each already was a deep unease about Britain's 'role' – a word that increasingly entered into quizzical, and often querulous, political discussion.

"ACCELERATOR ... BRAKES ... ACCELERATOR — AND, LOOK, NO HANDS!"

The cartoonist Vicky's creation of 'Supermac' unintentionally boosted the new Prime Minister's image. But this 1958 depiction of Macmillan throwing away the controls, as he and his terrified Chancellor, Heathcoat Amory, race ahead, accurately foresees the economic problems in store.

15

MACMILLAN'S PARTY

Harold Macmillan looked the part of Conservative Prime
Minister. As time went by, he contrived to look it more.
Having fixed his teeth, improved his hairstyle, smartened his
clothes, trimmed his moustache, changed his spectacles and become
more Edwardian than the Edwardians, he now personified – first for
better, later for worse – the nation's idea of what it was to be a
Conservative.[1] And even more than with other successful
politicians, certainly more than with any other Tory Prime
Minister, it was an act. Yet in Macmillan's early years it seemed
most improbable that he would ever get the part.

Harold Macmillan liked to play the grandson of a Scottish crofter
(when he was not playing the son-in-law of a duke), but what
mattered was that he was born into an already successful publishing
family. Throughout his life, his literary, business and political
interests intermeshed. He published Keynes before he ever became
his disciple. Equally important to his career was the influence of his
ambitious, domineering and beloved American mother Nellie.
Driven by Nellie, and driving himself in despair at the lengthy,

notorious sexual liaison conducted by his wife, Lady Dorothy Cavendish, with Robert Boothby, Macmillan owed much of his success, in a backhanded fashion, to women. This was despite the fact that, and perhaps helps explain why, he generally preferred the company of men. He later smugly confessed: 'I am, I think, what is called clubbable.'[2] This was true, both metaphorically and because he was a member of many clubs.

Macmillan was from the start a good political networker, but not someone who impressed his colleagues. That was unexpected, because by 1918 he had justly earned the invaluable reputation, at least for a Tory, of having fought 'a good war'. Macmillan was conspicuously brave and seriously wounded. He was an exact contemporary, at Eton and then in the Guards, of Oliver Lyttelton, Harry Crookshank (mentioned above as active in the attempt to hasten Churchill's retirement) and Bobbety Cranborne (later Salisbury) – the four of them politically conscious survivors of the trenches.[3] But whereas the others were more obviously conservative, Macmillan was unusual in being remarkably left-wing – even for that somewhat ideologically confused inter-war Tory generation.

To what extent this was fortuitous, being the result of his selection – and repeated return – for the northern industrial seat of Stockton-on-Tees, is unclear. (He stood unsuccessfully in 1923, won in 1924, lost in 1929, won in 1931 and 1935, lost in 1945, and then shifted permanently to the middle-class suburban seat of Bromley in South London.) Certainly, references to the hardships of Stockton, alongside the horrors of the trenches, all stuck together with some more or less banal references to Disraeli's style of socially conscious Toryism, became Harold Macmillan's trademarks. Thus when he was formally elected leader of the Conservative Party at a meeting in Church Hall, Westminster, on 22 January 1957, he declared in his acceptance speech: 'To use Disraeli's phrase, we must be conservative to conserve all that is good and radical to uproot all that is bad. So it is that we have never been, and I trust that while I am Leader we will never be, a Party of any class or sectional interest.'[4]

More than six years later, in his valedictory message to the 1963 Conservative party conference, which his own manipulations had thrown into destructive turbulence, he was still rehearsing the old themes:

> Since 1945, I have lived to see the Party of our dreams come into being . . . I have seen our policies develop into that pragmatic and sensible compromise between the extremes of collectivism and individualism for which our Party has always stood in its great periods. I have seen it bring to the people of our country a degree of comfort and well-being . . . such as I and my comrades could not have dreamed of when we slogged through the mud of Flanders nearly fifty years ago.[5]

By the 1950s Macmillan's views – at least the generalities – seemed orthodox. By the early sixties, they seemed stale. But in their raw form of the twenties and thirties they were very radical and, by almost any measure adopted, not at all conservative. As early as 1924, Macmillan had privately expressed a wish to see some sort of merger between 'the right Conservatives and the right Labourites' (and by right he did not mean right-wing).[6] Naturally, once in the Commons, he quickly gravitated towards the YMCA group inspired by Skelton. He co-authored a booklet urging collectivism and corporatism, albeit with ownership of industry remaining in private hands. This became a recurring interest which would influence the later 'Industrial Charter' undertaking. But Macmillan's radicalization went much further after he lost his seat in 1929. He openly supported the programme advanced by Oswald Mosley for massive Keynesian reflation and intervention to curb unemployment. After Mosley's resignation in May 1930,

Macmillan wrote to *The Times* attacking 'the reactionary immobility of parties alleged to be progressive' – a letter answered in
withering terms by Butler (with others), which was perhaps the
start of the bad blood between the two men.[7] Macmillan seriously
considered joining Mosley's New Party, but was persuaded out of it
– by Boothby. Instead, he prudently stood in 1931 as a National
candidate, though not before suffering a severe nervous breakdown.
Depressions and panics would accompany or precipitate many of
his future moves.

Once back in the Commons in 1931, Macmillan's radicalism was
just as evident. He collaborated with Labour Members in pressing
the case for industrial planning and, at this stage in second place,
Keynesian demand management. In November 1932 he told the
House of Commons: 'There is no alternative except a planned
economy.' Macmillan was a key supporter of the cross-party 'Next
Five Years' group, and in 1937 was urging collaboration with Lloyd
George's 'Council of Action'.[8] He had by now became a thorn in
the side of the leadership and was much disliked by the whips.
Unsurprisingly, when Baldwin became Prime Minister in June 1935
Macmillan found no place in the Government. In June 1938 he
published *The Middle Way*, his most serious and detailed exposition
of the case for a state-planned economy, which, however, he still
sought to differentiate from socialism.[9] (Such hair-splitting looks
now – as it did to many then – unconvincing: for example,
Macmillan even suggested that the Stock Exchange be replaced by
a National Investment Board.[10])

This background of dissent from the mild paternalism of the
Baldwin years in favour of economic interventionism and political
re-alignment is important if one wishes to understand the future
political leader. It marks out Macmillan's disagreement with the
Baldwin/Chamberlain Government's foreign policy, which also
manifested itself towards the end of the period, from that of other
Conservative opponents of appeasement – and not just from the

traditionalist Churchill, either, but from the rest of the liberal internationalist group around Eden, of which Macmillan was a member.
Macmillan was also unusual in going so far as to resign the Tory
whip – though briefly – over the question of sanctions against Italy
in 1936. Significantly, he was regarded by plotting Tory anti-
appeasers as the natural and best link with the Labour Party, and he
amply justified his reputation.[11]

The fall of Chamberlain and the succession of Churchill as
Prime Minister restarted Macmillan's political career, which had
hitherto been an undistinguished and eccentric failure. Churchill's
patronage and approval, as well as Macmillan's gifts as a diplomat,
evident during his postings in North Africa and Italy, were crucial
in transforming his political standing during the war – though at
the expense of continued controversy over the return in 1945 of
non-communist combatants and their families to the Soviet Union
and Yugoslavia. In the course of these war years, Macmillan forged
what turned out to be important links with Eisenhower and other
Americans and what might, under other circumstances, have been
equally useful contacts with de Gaulle, who owed him favours that
he had no intention of repaying. Spells at Housing and Defence
under Churchill, and in the Foreign Office and Treasury under
Eden, brought him within reach of the premiership, which he then
cunningly and unscrupulously seized under circumstances already
described.

Macmillan's aims were now to hang on, draw a line under Suez,
and create the conditions for an election victory – in that order,
both chronologically and in importance. He relied on Edward
Heath, as Chief Whip, and Oliver Poole, as deputy to the ebullient
new party chairman, Lord Hailsham, to keep his troops in order.
Brushing aside Butler's wish to be Foreign Secretary, Macmillan
sent him instead to the Home Office, where his liberal instincts
enraged the party faithful at successive conferences. Macmillan
made this decision partly because he felt that Lloyd had to stay on

after Suez ('one head on a charger should be enough'), and partly because his whole game plan depended on using, but also neutralizing, Butler. In any case, dealing with the aftermath of Suez, which involved re-establishing the Anglo-American relationship, would be Macmillan's responsibility, and one he would not contract out.

More problematic turned out to be the decision to appoint Peter Thorneycroft as Chancellor, supported by Nigel Birch (Economic Secretary) and Enoch Powell (Financial Secretary). Having a strong economic team to inspire confidence was one thing. Having an economic team which also believed in sound money and tight finance, neither of which suited Macmillan's political tactics or economic prejudices, was quite another. His own priorities were expressed revealingly in a note to Michael Fraser, director of the Conservative Research Department, in February 1957: 'I am always hearing about the Middle Classes. What is it they really want? Can you put it down on a sheet of notepaper, and then I will see whether we can give it to them?'[12]

There was, in fact, more than a little affectation – beside the cynicism – in this professed ignorance. Macmillan did know, or thought he knew; and the answer was prosperity. It is often, and correctly, observed that his speech to a crowd at Bedford football ground on 20 July 1957, though it contained the famous assertion that 'most of our people have never had it so good', continued with a different, more sober message: 'What is beginning to worry some of us is "Is it too good to be true?" or perhaps I should say "Is it too good to last?" For, amidst all this prosperity, there is one problem that has troubled us – in one way or another – ever since the War. It's the problem of rising prices.'[13] The warning against inflation was then linked to a more characteristic one of the impact on unemployment. But, as is often the case, the textual distortions homed in on the salient truth. The message under Macmillan was that affluence was assured with the Conservative Party in power – and only then. It reached its most pithy expression in the 1959 election slogan –

probably the most effective Tory slogan of all time – 'Life's better under the Conservatives. Don't let Labour ruin it.'

A year before that, Macmillan's fear was that his Treasury team would, indeed, ruin it. The circumstances of the Treasury ministers' resignation have been much debated – more in retrospect than at the time. The issue was, strictly speaking, one of public expenditure control rather than inflation, let alone 'monetarism'. Enoch Powell rightly believed that Macmillan was soft on inflation. He also rightly pointed out that from this point on, public spending as a share of national income began an inexorable rise. These reflections are, however, more important as part of a general analysis of the Macmillan Government's economic mistakes than in elucidating the specifics of the crisis of January 1958.[14] (Margaret Thatcher's appointment in 1975 of Lord Thorneycroft – long out of politics, though with the characteristically Tory advantage of being Willie Whitelaw's cousin – to be her party chairman was a symbolic acknowledgement of the episode's historic significance.[15])

Thorneycroft's first (and, as it turned out, only) budget in April 1957 was a mildly tax-cutting one and had Macmillan's approval. Macmillan had kept a close eye on economic policy, preventing, for example, Thorneycroft from replacing Macmillan's appointee, Sir Roger Makins, with his own man, Sir Frank Lee, to run the Treasury. Macmillan was also regularly receiving advice altogether contrary to his Chancellor's from his old friend, the hyper-Keynesian and Keynes biographer Sir Roy Harrod.

The economy now seemed to be over-heating and, to quell a run on the pound, on 19 September Thorneycroft, with Macmillan's reluctant agreement, raised the bank rate from 5 per cent to 7 per cent. Wage settlements, though, continued to surge. There was talk of a wages policy, which Macmillan instinctively favoured, and a committee of 'Three Wise Men' was appointed, whose more or less wise reports were largely ignored. There was also talk of cutting spending, which – apart from cutting spending on defence, a task entrusted to Duncan Sandys – Macmillan found less congenial. Initially the Prime Minister supported his Chancellor, circulating a memorandum telling ministers to keep their 1958/9 expenditure to the previous year's level. It was their failure to do this, rather than the eventual gap between Treasury demands and spending ministers' bids, that actually prompted Thorneycroft, Powell and Birch to resign. Macmillan then, faced with the unwillingness of ministers to find the extra £50 million or so required, and after some tactical pirouetting aimed at making Thorneycroft look petulant (in which it succeeded), accepted the Treasury team's resignation. He was due the following day to depart on a long Commonwealth tour, so time pressed; but whether he would have acted differently had it not is doubtful. As it was, he found the occasion useful as an opportunity to deliver his apparently ad lib, but in fact scripted, observation about 'little local difficulties' to journalists on the plane.

Events appeared to vindicate Macmillan. After the resignations, and under Derick Heathcoat Amory, Thorneycroft's personally respected, ostentatiously moderate but, above all, obedient successor, the economic situation actually improved.[16] Inflation stayed at 1 per cent, taxes were cut, unemployment fell and optimism increased – Macmillan could look back on the crisis of 1958 as one which enhanced his standing. (At the time he had, in one of his paranoid fantasies, thought it was part of a plot to oust him, but that too was quickly forgotten.[17])

Equally happy effects had ensued from confrontation of a further obstacle in the shape of Bobbety Salisbury. Salisbury was, by temperament and habit, a resigner. He was also, alongside Butler, Macmillan's equal in seniority and experience. He was not a threat, but his presence cramped the new Prime Minister's style. At the end of March 1957, Salisbury suddenly submitted his resignation over the obscure issue of the release from detention of Archbishop Makarios, whose liberation was a key demand of the EOKA Greek

Cypriot terrorists. Macmillan accepted Salisbury's resignation with alacrity. It meant that the most able opponent of the retreat from Empire, which Macmillan intended to be one of his Government's major undertakings, was safely out of the way before that project had even begun. It also meant delightful revenge for all the snubs and humiliations Macmillan thought he had had to endure from the aristocracy, whose manners he aped but of which he could never be a part. He commented nastily in his diary: 'All through history, the Cecils, when any friend or colleague has been in real trouble, have stabbed him in the back – attributing the crime to qualms of conscience.'[18] The reference is, of course, to 1867. Stung by Salisbury's criticism of Macleod and himself, and in another spasm of paranoia, Macmillan later had his former colleague put under close surveillance by MI5.[19]

Safe at home, Macmillan applied the finishing touches to his re-election strategy by adding some foreign policy kudos. Foreign affairs would, indeed, be the area in which Macmillan achieved his greatest success – as well as his most painful defeat. But what most mattered throughout, particularly now before an election, was appearance. Post-imperial Britain had to have 'a role', of some sort, in refutation of the view that it lacked one, tactlessly expressed by Dean Acheson (whom Macmillan considered 'a conceited ass').[20] Such a role was most likely to be achieved by acting as an honest – if not equidistant – broker between the two great Cold War powers. Arms control was ideal for the purpose.

Macmillan claimed that he had prayed for the success of his campaign to achieve a (partial) Nuclear Test Ban Treaty (initialled in July 1963), and that he wept when he told Lady Dorothy the news.[21] But, apart from fitting in with his general preoccupation with avoiding an arms race, it is hard to know what made the policy so strategically important. After all, how could Britain have a credible nuclear deterrent – another of Macmillan's preoccupations – without testing? It was, though, politically important, because it was a policy which allowed Macmillan and Britain to appear to wield influence.

In fact, when Macmillan embarked on his high-profile visit to Moscow in February 1959 there was no prospect of any East–West thaw, and no possible purpose for the visit other than to boost his status in domestic politics. The previous November, Khrushchev had precipitated a new crisis over the status of Berlin by threatening to end all Western rights there, with control over access passing to East Germany. Macmillan had acted the dove, to de Gaulle's hawk, and sought to use the crisis to press for a great power summit, for which he hoped to act as the long-distance impresario. This was a mistake, an error now confirmed by the visit to Moscow. Macmillan's failure to speak up for the West Germans at this juncture decisively shifted Adenauer into the French camp. And Adenauer's distrust of Macmillan emboldened de Gaulle, if more boldness were required, to veto Britain's application to the European Common Market, because de Gaulle knew he could build the Common Market on a Franco–German axis.[22]

The Soviet visit itself was televisually satisfactory. Macmillan dressed appropriately and looked statesmanlike. But it also included a public snub and a violently anti-capitalist speech from Khrushchev. This at one point had a flustered Macmillan about to pack his bags. Selwyn Lloyd helped calm him down. Intimidation was what passed for diplomacy in Khrushchev's political lexicon – as Kennedy learned to his cost at Geneva in 1961 – so the British visitors had little reason to complain. In any case, Macmillan had got his visit in before Gaitskell, and before the election.

Even more useful was Eisenhower's visit to Britain in August 1959. Ike knew that he was being used and privately resented it. But Macmillan had genuinely reset Anglo-US relations after Suez, a task facilitated by the fact that Washington had begun to wake up to the scale of the problems it faced upholding Western interests in the Middle East more or less single-handed. Anyway,

Eisenhower regarded Macmillan as his man, and he enjoyed reminiscing. Macmillan, for his part, ensured that the 'old buddies' act with the most powerful man in the world received the fullest and most obliging media coverage.

Above all, Macmillan did the three things which successful party leaders in power have to do: he got his timing right, he got the economy right (at least in political terms) and he got the Opposition right. Amory's first budget in 1958 had been produced in the austere shadow of Thorneycroft. His 1959 budget was more of a giveaway, cutting taxes and interest rates. It fuelled a boom which needed no fuelling – and which, under pressure from Macmillan, he later failed to cool in time – but made for a landslide result in the election on 8 October.

The British economy was, indeed, growing fast. Such growth dazzled the electorate, because it was unprecedented, at least in the democratic age, and because British electors lacked as yet any sense of how much Britain was underperforming by comparison with other countries. It was an age of plenty. The number of owner-occupiers for the first time outnumbered those who rented. The number of cars had doubled since 1952. The Mini was launched. Motorways were being built. White goods transformed the domestic drudgery of housewives. The general election of 1959 was the first in which television really mattered, partly because Macmillan had made the effort to look good on it, but above all because, for the first time, half the electorate had access to a television set.

The Conservatives raised and spent far more money than their opponents on slick and highly professional advertising devised by Colman, Prentis and Varley.[23] The Labour Party was poor, and so was its publicity. It was divided personally and ideologically. Gaitskell – whom Macmillan despised as a Wykehamist, and because he had no war medals – was, in truth, a leader of courage and integrity. But he was now trapped into a mistake by Tory attacks on his spending promises. Defending his plans, he pledged no rise in income tax, a promise rendered still less credible by an apparently unauthorized commitment from the Labour press conference at Transport House to cut purchase tax.[24] Labour's campaign never recovered.

But, as in 1955, the Tory record was what mattered most. The country basked in affluence and would not risk it. The electorate had forgotten Suez. It felt secure and reassured by Macmillan, for whom the result, when it was announced, was a personal triumph. The Conservatives won 365 seats (up 21), the Labour Party 258 (down 19) and the Liberals still had 6. The Tories, therefore, now enjoyed a majority of a hundred. Labour fell into an orgy of faction-ridden recrimination. There was a spate of comment suggesting that the party was finished, overtaken by social and economic change, and that the Conservatives would be in for ever, as the natural party of government.

Macmillan himself was now sixty-five. But he was at the height of his powers. A slow developer, he had learned from his own and others' failures, in particular those of Eden. He sought to live up, at least in public, to the notice he had placed on the door of the Cabinet Room: 'Quiet calm deliberation disentangles every knot.' It was a pose. He was often a bundle of nerves. He confessed to having to read a novel (Trollope, Scott, Dickens or Austen) for an hour before turning out the light at night, however late it was, because otherwise he would be too worked up to sleep. (This, though, was after he had written up his diaries, always intended for publication – for concern with historical reputation was another obsession.[25])

Macmillan chaired his Cabinets with courtesy and efficiency. Like Churchill, he was a late riser, but he did not conduct high-level business in bed. He had good personal staff, official and private, whom he treated well and who were loyal to him – a contrast with Eden. In John Wyndham, who acted as a resident jester, fixer and friend during much of Macmillan's public life, and all of his premiership, he had someone who could share his problems, in the absence of his otherwise distracted and usually distant wife.[26]

Macmillan's standing was now very high. The left-wing cartoonist 'Vicky' had intended no compliment when, in November 1958, he devised for the *Evening Standard* the character of 'Supermac'. But the image stuck, and it helped. Macmillan was thus portrayed as a mix of fogey and super-hero, tackling impossible problems with old-world brio and quasi-miraculous success.

After the election Macmillan reshuffled his team. Hailsham, who had taken too much of the limelight away from the Prime Minister at conferences, was moved to the new Department of Science and Technology. (The loss of favour was only temporary.) He was replaced as chairman by Butler, who also remained Home Secretary. This was bad for Butler, but also bad for the party, which needed a chairman with time and energy to keep its organization up to the mark. The most significant promotions were for Heath, who became Minister of Labour; Maudling, who became President of the Board of Trade and was entrusted with the creation of the European Free Trade Area, EFTA (see below); and Macleod, who took over from Alan Lennox-Boyd as Colonial Secretary.

Macleod's appointment signified a much swifter and more combative approach to decolonization. Lennox-Boyd's tenure had been honourable but unhappy, as the Government struggled to cope with upheaval in Nyasaland and insurgency and (over the Hola Camp 'massacre') scandal in Kenya. Outside the group around Salisbury, there was widespread acceptance of the need for a fairly rapid transfer of power, and no enthusiasm for prolonged suppression of nationalist movements. But the conflict of interest between the white settlers (especially in Southern Rhodesia) and black majorities remained.

On 5 January 1960 Macmillan and Dorothy departed for their African tour. They visited Ghana and Nigeria before stepping on to the more treacherous territories of the Central African Federation. Macmillan had promised to uphold the Federation. But he had probably already decided to see it dissolved, as it would be, into Northern Rhodesia (Zambia), Nyasaland (Malawi) and Southern Rhodesia (Zimbabwe). Macmillan's 'wind of change' speech was delivered not here, however, but to the South African parliament, meeting in Cape Town, where the gusts would not reach gale force till after Macmillan's death.

The speech itself rather bemused his listeners in the Cape. But at home it was widely regarded as precipitate and imprudent – including by Churchill. It led to the creation of the right-wing Tory Monday Club, soon headed by Salisbury, which was a thorn in the side of successive Conservative leaders. In November 1961, ninety Conservative MPs signed an Early Day Motion critical of government policy towards the Central African Federation. By a process that owed more to sentiment than logic, the right of the party, with the Monday Club playing an important role, came to focus less on decolonization and more on the problem of New Commonwealth (that is, coloured) immigration, where the party leadership proved slow to react – though the 1962 Commonwealth Immigrants Act provided a temporary sop.[27]

While it gained plaudits from non-Conservative opinion, accelerated decolonization turned a significant section of the party against the Government. Macmillan himself was buffeted between fear of the reaction of the white settlers and fear of the radicalism of Macleod, who pushed Macmillan further than he wanted to go and threatened resignation if he were held back (as would his equally radical successor Maudling). The Prime Minister's reputation for unflappability was in these conditions more than usually undeserved.[28] For his part, Macleod, a bold but not always prudent gambler, relished mocking and infuriating the policy's critics.[29] Salisbury's description of him in a debate in the Lords in March 1961 as 'too clever by half' was much deplored, but it stuck. The venom directed against Macleod ensured that when in 1963 the leadership suddenly fell vacant, and despite his own opinion of his suitability, he was not regarded as a credible candidate.

British disengagement from Africa also fitted in with the American world-view, as would re-engagement with Europe. It was, indeed, through his dealings with the Americans that Macmillan made his main contribution to Britain's national interests. Macmillan could speak patronizingly about Americans – the 'Romans' to Britain's 'Greeks'. He could expatiate with eloquence to de Gaulle, at his Birch Grove home in November 1961, upon the need to maintain European civilization, under pressure from, among other incursions, 'our Atlantic friends'.[30] But he understood at least as keenly as Churchill, and less regretfully, Britain's ultimate dependence on the United States. It was what Suez had demonstrated. Repair of the Special Relationship – a phrase as mocked then as now, but representing a kind of reality – was the first priority of his foreign policy.

The crux of the relationship was (and is) military. Macmillan's first success, though he was pressing on an open door, was to secure the repudiation of the McMahon Act, by which the US Congress in 1946 had forbidden the exchange of atomic information between the United States and any other country. Eisenhower went further. He established new structures for Anglo-American nuclear co-operation. Eisenhower and Macmillan also agreed on the deployment in Britain of sixty Thor missiles equipped with nuclear warheads, provided by the Americans but under joint US–UK control.

The Americans had been surprised to find how advanced the British nuclear programme was. The British problem was money for development. It had been intended that Britain would have its own delivery system for a strategic nuclear deterrent, in the form of the Blue Streak surface-to-surface long-range missile. But for technical and, mainly, financial reasons, the project was abandoned in February 1960. In its place, the following month, Eisenhower offered Britain Skybolt. This was a planned long-range, air-launched missile. As such, it had the advantage that it could be used from Britain's ageing V-bomber fleet. There was also a 'gentlemen's agreement' that if Skybolt did not prove suitable Britain would be able to purchase Polaris, the more sophisticated US submarine-based missile. As part of the deal, Polaris submarines would be based in a Scottish loch. So matters stood at the change of US Administration.

Macmillan had been impressed by John F. Kennedy, and not much impressed by Richard Nixon, and he foresaw the former's victory. But that did not make the changeover any less problematic for Britain. Expert opinion in Washington was pressing the case for squeezing out other Western nuclear deterrents in favour of an effective American monopoly, with, at a pinch, the remainder as part of a somewhat vaguely defined NATO (or European) 'Multilateral Force' (MLF). This, indeed, formed the political and strategic background to the decision, finally taken on financial and technical grounds, to cancel Skybolt. The decision leaked out in December 1962. But British ministers, including a theatrically out-raged Thorneycroft (now back as Defence Minister), must already have known what was in the wind.

Macmillan had, in the meantime, been cultivating Kennedy. His own account certainly exaggerates his influence over the President. (He rather absurdly pretended to think that he was like a son to Ike and like a father to Jack.) But he had built up a good deal of personal credit all the same. This was not because he was a robust supporter of American Cold War policy – far from it. He had, in fact, an exaggerated regard for the Soviet system and also un-realistic hopes for international summitry. His written analysis of the international scene ('The Grand Design' memorandum) received no welcome from Washington. But Macmillan was, in the old-fashioned sense, an excellent diplomat. He exerted charm. He also used connections, especially the important connection offered by David Ormsby-Gore, later Lord Harlech, his son Maurice's brother-in-law, and a close friend from his youth of Jack Kennedy. It was at the President's special request that Ormsby-Gore became British ambassador in Washington in May 1961.[31] During the October 1962 Cuban Missile Crisis, Macmillan and the British offered no useful advice and were, in fact, less robust than de Gaulle – but then Paris, unlike London, was never a likely target for a Soviet nuclear missile. That said, throughout the stand-off Ormsby-Gore was a support, and during hours of conversation with Kennedy on the telephone Macmillan proved himself a sympathetic listener.[32] He gave Kennedy reassurance.

The personal debt was now called in. At a tense encounter in Nassau at the end of 1962, Macmillan persuaded Kennedy to over-rule the advice of the Pentagon and the State Department and supply Britain, on remarkably favourable terms, with Polaris. The decision confirmed Britain's highly fragile great power status. It was, indeed, one of the most significant diplomatic coups achieved by any British Prime Minister. It arguably constitutes the only significant achievement, judged by the criterion of national interest, of Macmillan's Government.[33] It also came at a cost – of which the Americans, oddly enough, were more conscious than the British.

The result of the Nassau summit was not decisive in de Gaulle's veto of Britain's application to join the European Common Market. Defence was an important issue for France, but not in the way either Kennedy or, particularly, Macmillan seems to have believed. At Nassau Macmillan persuaded Kennedy to make a direct offer of Polaris to France on the same terms as that to Britain. He then sent the British ambassador in Paris, Sir Pierson Dixon, to see the General and learn his reaction. De Gaulle was unmoved. This was entirely predictable. France did not have the submarines or the warheads to enable it to take up the offer; the French had no interest in allowing the United States any say in French nuclear strategy; and the only terms on which de Gaulle would do business with the US were those of strategic equality, which were unavailable. He would, therefore, press ahead with the wholly independent *force de frappe*.[34] The General had, in fact, already made his decision and even indicated it. He had mocked, quasi-publicly, Macmillan's efforts at Rambouillet, just before the Nassau meeting, to press Britain's case for entry into the EEC, by quoting Edith Piaf: 'Ne pleurez pas milord!' This was before he knew what had happened at Nassau. But the outcome did make it easier for him to explain his reasons to the French public.[35]

Macmillan's keenness to have Britain join the Common Market stemmed, on the face of it, from mature strategic analysis. He was fond of forward-looking policy papers – he had earlier commissioned a sort of cost–benefit analysis of Britain's imperial commitments. His officials then embarked on a study of 'The Next Ten Years'. The conclusion was that Britain must get closer to Europe. But Macmillan was not, in fact, a strategic thinker at all. He just liked to juggle with grand-sounding initiatives. Back in 1955, when he was Foreign Secretary, he had not shown any great interest in the Messina Conference, crucial in the transition from the ECSC to the EEC. British hopes continued to rest on diluting the process of European integration by setting the Common Market within a wider free trade area. (This, though, misunderstood the venture itself, which was dependent on a tariff wall and – once de Gaulle took power – on subsidies for French agriculture.) The launch of a separate EFTA in 1960 was, therefore, in British eyes a second best. Maudling, its architect, was enthusiastic, and there were indeed potential trading benefits. But British official-dom was not convinced. Neither was a large section of the political class – including Macmillan. Moreover, American pressure was applied; and one uncontested lesson of Suez was that what America wanted from British foreign policy, America must get.

Entry into the European Common Market also offered, or appeared to offer, benefits in domestic policy. It would force British industry, weighed down by accumulated inefficiencies and hampered by union restrictive practices, to reform itself. It would also provide a new project around which to regroup, as decolonization stripped away British power, and, more specifically, as the Conservative Party looked increasingly tired and directionless.[36] Indeed, the momentum brought to the European project by these domestic political considerations would become part of the problem. Had entry been presented by the Government as an option among many, rather than the unique path to salvation, de Gaulle's veto would have been much less damaging. But so much else was going wrong by the time the veto came that there was nothing else to offer. That was a failure of political leadership, for which Macmillan was personally responsible.

Macmillan had used the Cabinet reshuffle of 27 July 1960, occasioned by Amory's insistence on retirement from the Treasury, to put in place his team for guiding the country into Europe. Selwyn Lloyd, who became Chancellor – securing a (subsequently broken) promise from Macmillan to keep him there till the next election – fitted the bill as a former Foreign Secretary. Lord Home, in a much-criticized appointment, became Foreign Secretary; but his number two in the Commons was to be Heath (also Lord Privy Seal). Heath was in charge of negotiating entry, and no more zealous Europhile could have been wished for. Two other Euro-enthusiasts were installed in important roles: Duncan Sandys at Commonwealth Relations (the Commonwealth would play up) and Christopher Soames at Agriculture (so would British farmers). Butler was the most Eurosceptic of the senior figures – typically, Macmillan thought this masked a plot against him personally – but Butler, true to form, now dutifully altered his view. Opposition on the Tory back benches was, in the light of later events, surprisingly muted. The main difficulty appeared to be with the

Commonwealth, which naturally viewed with dismay any end to preferential access to British markets. On this front Macmillan scored no more than a draw at the Commonwealth Conference of 1962.[37]

In fact, the difficulty was with France. Macmillan had no excuse for his illusions about French attitudes. But, as in the run-up to Suez, wishful thinking and a refusal to plan for damage limitation led him into terrible trouble. In their meetings de Gaulle had stated what kind of Europe he wanted for France, and there was no excuse for refusing to grasp that Britain – for all the reasons eloquently expressed in the General's press conference at the Elysée on 14 July 1963 – had no part in it.

Of course, by then much else was going wrong as well. To understand this one must take note of the economic background. During the 1950s an inconclusive and far from rigorously conducted debate was taking place among theorists, officials and politicians about inflation. Inflation was low. Yet it was worrisome because it was a threat to full employment, upon whose desirability and attainability almost everyone agreed. But was inflation (as the jargon had it) a 'cost-push' or a 'demand-pull' phenomenon? Adherents of the first view emphasized the cost of imported raw materials (about which nothing could be done, except for keeping up the value of sterling) and the cost of union-driven pay rises (about which not much could be done either, though hope sprang eternal, as experiments with incomes policy showed). Adherents of the second (demand-pull) view emphasized the effect of excess demand on limited capacity. Unless productivity growth improved – another vain hope – the proper response was to slow the economy by putting up interest rates (and cutting credit) or increasing taxes (so lowering consumption). This also meant accepting some unemployment – which counted against the whole approach.

These ruminations had only limited effect on policy for as long as politicians convinced themselves that Britain's relatively slow rate of economic growth reflected the process of catch-up by Europe and Japan after the war. By the early 1960s, however, this explanation was no longer convincing. Something needed to be done – but what? The Common Market was meant to provide a way out – though of course it did not (and, actually, could not). Otherwise, this final period of the Conservative Government was characterized by a dash for economic growth, with resort to a succession of 'voluntary' incomes policies to restrain inflation.

The Conservatives in 1951 inherited a balance of payments deficit of £700 million, largely for temporary reasons. They left behind them in 1964 a deficit of £750 million, for reasons reflecting the weakness of the unreformed British economy and its inability to sustain the prevailing exchange rate.[38] The Conservative economic experiment – to the extent that such a collection of ad hoc responses can be graced with such a title – had failed.

This, though, is to anticipate.

Selwyn Lloyd, who became Chancellor of the Exchequer in July 1960, was pliant. The consistent message from Number Ten was that there must be no economic contraction. In January 1961, restrictions on hire purchase were eased. That year's budget was preceded by a run on sterling and bad balance of payments figures. The budget introduced 'regulators', that is, discretionary powers to alter tax rates, of 10 per cent for purchase tax and national insurance, as a means of 'fine-tuning' demand – the implication being that the Treasury had matters under control, which it did not. Lloyd also raised the starting point for surtax. But conditions were already too loose. Pressure on sterling built up during the summer, and in July an emergency mini-budget had to be introduced. Consumption taxes were raised. So was the bank rate. Government spending was squeezed. The Chancellor declared that, in view of runaway wage settlements, a 'pay pause' was to be introduced. It was a damaging setback. The autumn also saw the creation of a new institution, the National Economic Development

Corporation (NEDC), to bring together employers and unions with the Government in setting the conditions for economic policy. Neddy and its offspring the little Neddies were to prove the country's most enduring expression of economic corporatism.

The impulse for tripartite discussion was concern with wages. Union leaders took no obvious notice of the 'pause'. Outside the public sector it was impossible to apply, and within the public sector it created plenty of bad feeling. In March 1962 it was succeeded by a 'guiding' light, attempting to limit wage demands to 2.5 per cent.[39] This had no obvious effect either.

Macmillan was already disillusioned with his Chancellor. He hankered after more expansion and thought Selwyn Lloyd had been captured by the Treasury. Lloyd's performances in attempting to explain his policy were widely judged inept. The Government was becoming unpopular; the next election was approaching; and something had to be done to win it.

In such conditions, prime ministers' minds turn to a reshuffle. And the more unpopular they are, the more radical they think it has to be. Lloyd was allowed to deliver his second and final budget on 9 April 1962. He thought he had received assurances from Macmillan about his future. He should have known better. In an extraordinary intervention, on 28 May Macmillan read out to Cabinet a six-thousand-word memorandum he had written. It called for a permanent incomes policy, based on cooperation, which was to be achieved by means of a National Incomes Commission – and for reflation. Lloyd meekly listened, and the rest of the Cabinet concurred without debate. But the fate of a third of them had been sealed by something other than economic dissertations.

The Liberals, benefiting from large-scale middle-class discontent with the Conservatives, did well in the local elections of 1961. But they made a breakthrough in March 1962. There were bad by-election results for the Tories in Lincoln and Blackpool North; then, on 14 March 1962, the Liberals took the London suburban constituency of Orpington with a huge swing of 27 per cent. The same day a Tory candidate barely saved his deposit in Middlesbrough East. Macmillan made an unscheduled visit to Central Council to still the panic. But the 1922 Committee panicked all the same. Nor was Macmillan immune. A National Opinion Poll survey found the Liberals at 35.9 per cent, Labour at 30.5 per cent and the Conservatives at 27.4 per cent. The outcome was so unbelievable that NOP suppressed it. A week later, a rerun showed the three parties nearly level. The bad news was thus confirmed.[40]

Macmillan had hoped to conduct a limited cull of Cabinet colleagues in his own time and in orderly fashion. In the event, it was neither limited, nor timely, nor orderly. He had decided to get rid of Lloyd and then take advantage of other semi-offers of retirement from other colleagues to bring in some new faces. But he handled everything atrociously.

First, he made the mistake of telling Butler. It was, of course, a dilemma. Butler's attitude was politically crucial. He served, as his biographer has commented, as Macmillan's 'personal breastplate'.[41] But he was also – particularly as Macmillan weakened – well placed, had he ever wished, to insert the dagger, though, to the frustration of his supporters, he refused to do so. And he was potentially dangerous in another way – in his indiscretion. This he now demonstrated by prematurely blabbing to a *Daily Mail* journalist over lunch that Macmillan intended to rid himself of Lloyd in a reshuffle. So Macmillan felt he had to act. His mask of adamantine calm cracked, and an air of panic then exuded from a fearful Cabinet out to the wider parliamentary party and into the public arena. This had a devastating, indeed irreversible, effect on Macmillan's image for competence and on his Government's credibility. His interview with Lloyd was poisoned by Macmillan's implication that the dismissed Chancellor was involved in a (non-existent) conspiracy. The pressure of time then meant there was no opportunity to allow colleagues who might have been eased out, rather than thrown out, to go gracefully. Macmillan's quips did him no obvious good. When Kilmuir was reported to object that a cook would have been given more notice, Macmillan retorted that it was easier to find Lord Chancellors than cooks. He told Harold Watkinson at Defence that he should make way for a younger man, and then appointed Thorneycroft who was older. In all, seven ministers were sacked, either because they had no choice, or because they refused alternative posts.[42]

So the reshuffle was botched. But the Cabinet that emerged from it was an improvement. Maudling at the Treasury, an able and convinced adherent of going for growth by fuelling demand, was at least technically capable of giving this (wrong-headed) policy, so dear to the Prime Minister, a final shot. Butler's appointment as Deputy Prime Minister, in name and not just fact, as well as his being given responsibility for winding up the Central African Federation, recognized at once his seniority and his abilities. Not only Thorneycroft but also Powell returned – the latter not officially to the Cabinet, but with effective Cabinet rank as Minister of Health. Duncan Sandys, with a brief combining the Colonial Office and Commonwealth Relations Office, was a steadier figure in party eyes than his more liberal predecessors, Macleod and Maudling. One who was not brought back was Nigel Birch, a dangerous enemy. Birch's letter to *The Times* after Lloyd's dismissal reminded critics of the policy issues beneath the personalities: 'For the second time the Prime Minister has got rid of a Chancellor of the Exchequer who tried to get expenditure under control. Once is more than enough.'[43]

Macmillan's 'Night of the Long Knives' dealt a blow to the Government's standing, but it was an accumulation of woes that brought it to its knees. The European fiasco has been mentioned. The handling by Macmillan of security scandals, none of which, in itself, would have been fatal, reinforced the public impression that the Prime Minister was out of touch with events and with the modern world.

In March 1963 John Profumo, the Secretary for War, told the Commons – though he had not told Macmillan, because he had not been asked – that there was no substance to the allegation that he had been sexually involved with a call-girl, Christine Keeler (who with her lover and pimp, a well-connected osteopath called Stephen Ward, had links with the Soviet naval attaché). In June Profumo had to admit that he had lied to the House and resigned. Macmillan's behaviour throughout the episode had been inexcusable, as the release of secret papers confirms. He was warned in February by Wyndham – unlike Macmillan, a man of the world – about the detailed rumours. He was then kept closely in touch with events. This makes his subsequent unsuccessful attempts to plead ignorance not just embarrassing but deceitful. Nor were other colleagues guiltless. The Chief Whip, Martin Redmayne, in particular, offered bad advice throughout, not least to Profumo.[44]

This humiliation came in the wake of the Vassall spy case of the previous year, which made the Profumo incident seem far more serious than it was, at least in security terms. John Vassall was a homosexually compromised cipher clerk who – blackmailed, recruited and rewarded by the Soviet Union – spied for Moscow. When exposed, the affair led to (false) allegations of a homosexual cover-up in the Government.

The Radcliffe Tribunal cleared ministers over Vassall. The Denning Report more or less cleared ministers over Profumo. But the impression of decay and disintegration remained. It was sedulously propagated by the press, in a collective fury of revenge for the gaoling of two journalists who had refused to reveal their sources. Open season was declared on Macmillan and the Tories.

How closely this breaking of the Government's authority can be connected – and by what strands – with the wider sense that the Tories and the Prime Minister were fundamentally out of kilter with the times is debatable. But the connection existed. It was a cruel paradox. Macmillan was, to the end, convinced of the need to demonstrate that he was a modernizer. It was central to his idea of himself and of the party that 'progress' was a beneficent reality, and that he and the Tories must strive to be progressive. It was, therefore, horrible to discover that the country, or at least those who moulded public opinion, found Macmillan a relic and the Conservatives ridiculous. Social, moral and cultural liberalism and a naïve and self-destructive obsession with novelty, the hallmarks of the sixties, were bound to create difficulties for a Conservative Government. They were all the more damaging when the party had been in power so long, when the material benefits generated during that period had been taken for granted, and when the Government was led by a man of almost seventy, who looked and spoke like a satirical comedy sketch, disseminated by television.[45]

The sudden death of Gaitskell in January 1963, to be replaced the following month by Harold Wilson as Labour leader, was much more of a blow to Macmillan – who liked the new arrival as much as he despised the man he replaced – than the Prime Minister grasped. Wilson was twenty-two years younger than Macmillan; he was a fresh face; he was the master of a different, sharper kind of Commons repartee; he was entirely at home with economics of the technical and pragmatic kind that people found fashionable and reassuring. He was also a genuine northerner – rather than a *de haut en bas* Stockton-adopted sentimentalist.[46]

Wilson epitomized the difference of classes at a time when class obsession was all the rage. Macmillan himself was always ready with Disraeli-style declarations on the matter – 'the class war is obsolete,' he pronounced in October 1959.[47] But it was not. A better answer would have been that the Conservative Party was now a party in which the sons of middle-class professionals – not soldiers and aristocrats – were making their way to the top, as shown by the careers of Macleod (son of a Scottish doctor) or Maudling (son of a suburban actuary). In fact, the Conservative Party's problem now was arguably a surfeit of professionals and a lack of those self-made businessmen who might have exerted a surer grasp on economic policy. But it was not just critics on the left who snarled about class. Many in the party did so too. Macleod's devastating article on the Tory 'magic circle', which he would claim had imposed Home as leader, included the observation that 'eight of the nine men' relied upon by Macmillan to garner advice had been to Eton.[48] It was noted that Macmillan's circle of friends consisted of 'mostly Etonians, aristocrats and relations'.[49] Not until the emergence of David Cameron would Tory Old Etonians be allowed back into the limelight.

In any case, Macmillan, personally, was now the problem. He was everything that the party did not think it ought to be, and, as the party usually does in such circumstances, it soon made him aware of the fact that he ought to go. April 1963 saw Reggie Maudling's first budget. The Chancellor went some of the way towards the expansion Macmillan demanded. Hoping to abate wage demands, he raised income tax thresholds rather than cutting rates – a strategy often applied and, as then, always disappointing. But it was well received. If Macmillan had gone at this stage, Maudling would almost certainly have been his successor – and the party might have made the leap of generation necessary to recast itself before an election, and so perhaps win it.[50] Also in April Macmillan brought back Oliver Poole to be joint chairman of the party with Macleod. Poole and Macleod disliked one another. But if Macmillan thought he could thus divide and rule he was to be disappointed. Poole told the Prime Minister in a memorandum in August that the party now faced the prospect of a defeat on the scale of 1945, and that the best chance of avoiding it was for Macmillan to retire before the end of the year.

It was not an entirely unwelcome message. Macmillan was tired; he had had an international success with the signing of the Test Ban

Treaty in Moscow (where his representative was his current favourite, the flamboyant and grotesquely unsuitable Hailsham); his support had risen: it was not a bad time to go. He was certainly tempted. But it was a wrench, and he would anyway like to engineer the succession. The chance of doing that had been afforded by a Bill to allow hereditary peers to renounce their peerages. Backed by the Labour Party, it was specifically intended to favour the MP Anthony Wedgwood Benn; the only question for the Government was precisely when it should take effect. If it applied immediately, then both Lord Home and Lord Hailsham could renounce their peerages, seek seats in the Commons, and so enter the stakes to succeed Macmillan. This is, indeed, what occurred, by means of an amendment in the Lords. The change was a blow to Maudling, whose star was anyway now waning. But it was probably fatal for Butler. Butler was still the best-known candidate – indeed, he would remain the bookies' favourite on the very eve of the outcome. But he would have to fight, and, as Powell later lamented, this by temperament he could not or would not do.[51]

By September Macmillan had decided to go.[52] He told the Queen that he would announce his decision at the October party conference. He informed Lord Swinton that Hailsham was his preferred successor. But then he changed his mind. He now resolved to stay on and fight the election, and resign a year or two into the next Parliament (assuming he won). Perhaps this was because he did not relish being – as he was already regarded in Washington – a lame duck leader. Perhaps he really thought he could recover the position. But on the night of 7 October he was taken ill with terrible bladder pain. A well-known hypochondriac, he had often been seen by colleagues quaffing medicine for real or imaginary ailments. But at the following day's Cabinet, which he had to leave several times, there was no doubt about his condition. When he was out of the room, all his colleagues – with the exception of Enoch Powell – declared, with varying degrees of insincerity, that

Macmillan should carry on, it being now pretty evident that he would not. Macmillan then summoned the strength to attended a staff cocktail party at 8.00 p.m., at which he told Butler and Home that he would have to resign. He left Butler, as Deputy Prime Minister, in charge. On the morning of 10 October Macmillan was operated on for a benign prostate tumour. He knew that it was benign before the operation, so he did not resign as Prime Minister believing he had cancer. He may, though, have thought that recovery would be more difficult than it actually was. Or may he have thought it was a good excuse to go after all.

Meanwhile, the party was meeting in Blackpool. As news of Macmillan's illness spread, it began to resemble an American convention more than a sedate seaside assembly. Hailsham campaigned vulgarly, openly and counter-productively. Maudling made a lacklustre, downbeat speech. Home spoke with authority on foreign affairs. Butler, who insisted on his prerogative of winding up the conference in lieu of Macmillan, delivered an address of unrelieved blandness. Any self-confidence he retained had been knocked by Home's telling him over lunch that he had consulted his doctor, which meant that he envisaged becoming Prime Minister.

Home was a dark horse, but his colleagues later made him out to be darker than he was. He had been entrusted by Macmillan with reading out to the faithful at Blackpool the Prime Minister's letter announcing his forthcoming departure. It was sheer chance that as chairman of the conference that year Home was officially in a position to do this. But his being entrusted with the letter was not chance. It signified that Macmillan had already decided – even before Hailsham made an ass of himself – that Home was the right successor. (Macmillan had resolved many years earlier, of course, that Butler could never be that.[53])

From his sickbed – where he chose to remain longer than he needed, because it was the best place to weave his web without interruption – Macmillan drew up a memorandum for Butler, setting out how consultations should be undertaken to establish who should be recommended to the Queen to succeed him. Macmillan liked to refer to 'customary processes'. But there were, in fact, no customary processes. That does not mean that the result was irrational or even illegitimate, though it was almost certainly politically mistaken. Because the party conference was in session and because of the detailed processes of consultation, there was more rather than less democratic pressure than in earlier Tory leadership selections. (This also meant that more outsiders were following it, which was a disadvantage when an unpopular choice was made.) A distinctive feature on this occasion was the emphasis on negative and not just positive opinion. The search for unity and the emergence of a compromise candidate was not, of course, new: that is how Bonar Law had beaten Austen Chamberlain and Walter Long. But the formulation of the enquiry was a novelty. MPs were now asked their preferred candidate, their second choice, and then the name of anyone they would oppose. The third point quickly emerged as the most important, and a fourth question was then put, as to how they would feel about Home.

Cabinet members' opinions were registered by the Lord Chancellor, Lord Dilhorne, who was regarded as impartial, but whose conclusions were later disputed. Dilhorne noted down that Macleod gave his support to Home. This was either a mistake or – more likely – proof of the cynical, ambitious and devious attitude that Macleod adopted towards the process. He may have assumed that Home would not, in fact, stand and that when the acknowledged candidates, Hailsham and Butler, were deemed too divisive, he (Macleod) might succeed by default. This, though, is speculation. In any case, the results clearly favoured Home. Hailsham was liked by the party faithful and by Macmillan, but was not acceptable otherwise. There was a strong, lingering distrust of Butler, and his succession was thought, therefore, too divisive. (Maudling, another undeclared but acknowledged candidate, seemed no longer in the picture.) The main proponents of Home apart from Macmillan were Selwyn Lloyd; Martin Redmayne, the Chief Whip; and John Morrison, the chairman of the 1922 Committee. The last was the most important. Morrison had already told Butler that the party would not have him, which helps explain why Butler did not avail himself of the backlash against Macmillan's recommendation of Home.[54]

On the night of 17 October news leaked out that Macmillan had plumped for Home. At Enoch Powell's house in South Eaton Place furious discussions lasted through the night. Macleod and Powell told Home on the telephone that they could not accept the decision. Other senior figures came and went. Redmayne was summoned to convey the views of the dissenters to Macmillan – who was not to be moved. It was a dangerous moment. Powell recorded:

> On Friday morning, 18 October 1963, the following declared, to Mr Butler and to one another, that they did not consider Lord Home should be Prime Minister, and that they would not serve under Lord Home unless Mr Butler had previously agreed to do so: Iain Macleod, Reginald Maudling, Quintin Hailsham, John Boyd-Carpenter, Frederick Errol [sic], Edward Boyle, Enoch Powell.[55]

Powell and Macleod had now created the conditions for Butler to stop Home. Had Butler held firm and refused to serve, Home would have had to tell the Queen he could not form a government.[56] But whether Butler would then have been Prime Minister himself, after all this undignified agitation, is quite another matter. It is more likely that Maudling would have re-emerged. Harold Wilson subsequently expressed the view that the Conservatives would have won the election the following year if they had had Butler not Home (or Sir Alec Douglas-Home, as he had by then become). But while Wilson was doubtless delighted to be confronting a fourteenth earl with no recent experience of the Commons, perhaps he would have been equally delighted to face a far from pugnacious Butler, surrounded by poisonous and fretful colleagues and undermined by Macmillan.

In any case, after some reflection, Butler did agree to serve, as did Hailsham and Maudling. But Macleod and Powell refused. This was embarrassing. Yet what turned embarrassment into something deeply – and, in Douglas-Home's view, fatally – damaging was Macleod's blow-by-fascinating-blow account of the affair on 31 January 1964, in the *Spectator*, of which he was now editor. Framed as a review of Randolph Churchill's book *The Fight for the Tory Leadership*, which Macleod described as 'Mr Macmillan's trailer for the screenplay of his memoirs', the piece was a far more effective challenge to the legitimacy of Alec Douglas-Home's succession than anything from the Labour Party. The remark that did most harm to the morale of the parliamentary party was one which Macleod had also made to Home at the time: 'We were now proposing to admit that after twelve years of Tory Government no one amongst the 363 members of the party in the House of Commons was acceptable as Prime Minister.'[57]

Home got himself elected as MP in a by-election for Kinross and West Perthshire. In the new Cabinet the main winner was Selwyn Lloyd, who now became Lord Privy Seal and Leader of the House. Heath would have liked to be Foreign Secretary but the job – finally – went to Butler. Heath as Trade and Industry Secretary was entrusted with the controversial Bill to abolish resale price maintenance, designed to prevent price-fixing and so to increase competition in the interests of the consumer. But the measure was hated by small shopkeepers and other traders, who saw it as a means of the big firms undercutting them and driving them out of business. Heath, with his natural inflexibility and a scorn for dissent hardened by years as Chief Whip, successfully drove through the measure – but at the cost, on 11 March 1964, of the largest revolt by Conservative MPs since the fall of Neville Chamberlain.[58]

Douglas-Home was an efficient dispatcher of business. He was liked by his colleagues. As Prime Minister, though not later as Leader of the Opposition, he even had a certain hold on the House. His perceived weakness was economics. Two years earlier, he had explained in an interview with the journalist Kenneth Harris that he used matchsticks in order to understand economic arguments.[59] Of course, at that stage he had no thought of becoming Prime Minister. But the damage was done. He was only at ease with foreign policy. He had started at Munich with Chamberlain, become a Cold Warrior by the time of Yalta, served as Commonwealth Secretary under Eden, and been appointed Foreign Secretary by Macmillan – as he would be again by Heath. This experience, joined to the old-world manners of bucolic Scottish aristocracy, did not fit easily into modern party politics. Nor did it equip Douglas-Home to second-guess his ministers.

Maudling thus had a free hand in the sordid matter of trying to keep the boom going long enough to win an election. In fact, he had already done it too well, or at least for too long. By 1964 he was well aware that the economy could not safely continue growing at 6 per cent. He knew public spending was also out of control. It was only a question of how much, and how soon, to rein in. Maudling's budget did so lightly, with £100 million of tax increases. But, worried about how long the boom could last, he urged an early general election that summer. Labour at this point was well ahead. So Douglas-Home sensibly rejected Maudling's advice and plumped for October – he wished in the event he had chosen November. By then Maudling was in a sulk, but the polls, at least, looked better, even registering a modest Tory lead.[60]

The election was probably, in fact, winnable. Labour was still not greatly trusted, and the fragility of the country's prosperity was not yet grasped – though bad balance of payments figures during the campaign were an indicator, and a blow. But the Conservative campaign was not good enough, and Alec Douglas-Home did not perform well. He wanted to talk about Labour's failings on the nuclear deterrent rather than its follies on economic policy. And he looked bedraggled and beaten when he was all but shouted down at a meeting in the Birmingham Bull Ring.[61]

The results were not as bad as many had feared. Labour's share of the vote, at 44.1 per cent, was only just up on 1959, but the party's tally of seats rose from 258 to 317. The Conservative share was down from the historic high of 49.4 per cent to 43.4 per cent, which gave them 304 seats. The Liberals were the main beneficiaries, up from 5.9 per cent to 11.2 per cent, but still with a total of only 9 seats. So Labour formed a Government with a wafer-thin majority, but with greater expectations. The Conservatives entered Opposition, and with decidedly worse ones.

The result was not thought to be the fault of Alec Douglas-Home. (It was his inadequacies as Leader of the Opposition, rather than his shortcomings as Prime Minister, that sealed his fate a few months later.[62]) But he was not a credible candidate for a further election. He represented exactly what the Conservative Party had to avoid being, if it wanted to win. He looked, and he was, old-fashioned. The way he had been selected was also used against him and against the party.

Yet when blame is apportioned for the Conservative Party's short- and long-term failure in the 1960s and 1970s, it must mainly fall on Harold Macmillan – just as to Macmillan, personally, must go the credit for the party's landslide victory in 1959. It is not just Macmillan's mistreatment of colleagues, his misreading of trends and his mishandling of crises which constitute his poisoned legacy. It is the policies, above all the economic policies, which he pursued and which his later successor and in many respects disciple, Edward Heath, would systematize and strive to implement, that caused the trouble.

Macmillan himself never repented. A recently unearthed

memorandum which he wrote to Margaret Thatcher as Prime Minister in 1980 shows the same confidence that all that was required to solve Britain's economic problems was another dose of demand, this time on an international scale, and a contemptuous disregard for controlling the supply of money.[63] From the 'little local difficulties' of 1958 to the 'sale of the family silver' of which he spoke to the Tory Reform Group in 1984, the sneer about bothering with grubby realities is a constant. Macmillan was sometimes described as a Whig.[64] By some definitions, and by analogy with Disraeli, he could just about count as a Tory. But, by no known definition was he philosophically speaking a conservative. This, through his legacy to the Conservative Party, was a problem – nor necessarily one that is extinct.[65]

Edward Heath's ungracious demeanour and musical interests came to define his image in the eyes of the press and public. But it was the way he conducted economic policy that destroyed his government.

16

HEATH'S PARTY

Alec Douglas-Home could not last. He, apparently, did not immediately realize this, and others, through loyalty or politeness, did not say it; but, despite his success in reducing what had looked like being a humiliating wipe-out to a marginal defeat, his departure was inevitable. The party wanted a new face and needed a new image. There was rather less enthusiasm to take on the job than would have been the case had anyone imagined that the next election would propel the Conservatives back to power. But a start must be made before too long.

Douglas-Home's appointment of Heath as his Shadow Chancellor was decisive. Maudling, now Shadow Foreign Secretary, had no opportunity to shine. And while Powell and Macleod also returned, Powell was little known and Macleod deeply unpopular with much of the party. Heath, by contrast, earned for himself in short order what turned out to be an undeserved reputation as an effective debater, by his well-prepared attacks on the new Labour Government's Finance Bill. The MPs wanted to see some fight. They thought he was a bruiser, which, of course, he was – but not in the way they hoped.

Heath also gained prestige within the party through his appointment by Douglas-Home as chairman of the Advisory Committee on Policy (ACP) in place of the now ageing Butler. From this vantage point he would exert a Chamberlain-like grip on policy initiatives for the next few years.[1] His appetite for detailed policy prescriptions had been more than satisfied by the time he handed charge of the ACP to the more lackadaisical Maudling in 1969. Brendon Sewill, director of CRD, could boast that more than fifty major policy groups had met and over two thousand papers produced.[2] In fact, Heath tried to do too much, both now and, later, in government. (In opposition in the 1970s Sir Keith Joseph also set up numerous policy groups, but Mrs Thatcher took little notice of them, and as party chairman Lord Thorneycroft was also highly sceptical.)

As the dust from the recent election defeat settled, Heath was thus definitely the coming man. It was his supporters who, without his prodding but presumably also without his disapproval, set about undermining Douglas-Home. Having efficiently overseen rules for an openly democratic election of his successor by the party's MPs, the old leader gracefully bowed out in July.[3]

On the face of it, Heath was still behind his main rival. A *Daily Express* opinion poll showed that the public preferred Maudling to him by 44 per cent to 28 per cent, a scale of preference replicated among Tory voters. But from the start Heath had momentum. He had the support of the press and, when the vote came, of most of the Shadow Cabinet, as well (probably) of the activists.

Heath was already, it is true, disliked by Edward du Cann, the party chairman appointed by Douglas-Home. Du Cann had been effective and he was popular. After a certain amount of public pressure, Heath would manage to get rid of him in 1967, apparently intimating that he could expect a post in the Cabinet. This promise, if given, was not honoured.[4] Du Cann became chairman of the 1922 Committee in 1972. But in 1965 he was more of a problem of the future than the present.

The three nominated candidates were Maudling, Heath and Powell. Powell wanted to make a point about policy – as will be discussed – and to register his ambitions for the future (to leave his 'visiting card', as he put it).[5] The other two were out to win. Maudling, right to the end, thought he would. The new rules required more than a simple majority. To succeed on the first ballot, the successful candidate had to win a super-majority, with a margin of 15 per cent of the votes cast. But Maudling was, in any case, supremely confident. The results were, therefore, a devastating shock to him: Heath 150; Maudling 133; Powell 15. Maudling did the decent thing, as did Powell, by quickly conceding, without a second round. But Maudling then went and sat in the Commons Smoking Room on his own, getting drunk and falling apart with self-pity for everyone to see. From this point on, despite his intellect and experience, he was a growing liability to the party and a tragedy in the making. (He would resign in disgrace in 1972 over allegations of corruption, enjoy – if that is the word – a return to frontline politics as Mrs Thatcher's rancorous and mistrusted Shadow Foreign Secretary in 1975–6, and then die in 1979, aged sixty-one, of the consequences of alcoholism.[6])

The Conservative Party never learned to love Edward Heath, though it respected him and stuck with him. He managed to lose three out of four general elections, and still it was only with a traumatic wrench that he was finally prised out, when a rather junior colleague – and a woman – stood against him. Heath's selection and retention at the head of the party raises pertinent questions about why colleagues first so misjudged and then so feared him – to which one must return. But another question, rarely asked by historians, is whether the party, in the light of its experience with Heath, is nearly as good at pursuing power as its many critics, and a few inexperienced enthusiasts, often suggest.

On paper, Heath was ideally suited. He was, above all, the opposite of Douglas-Home, being distinctly low-born, the precocious son of a carpenter (become small businessman) and a lady's maid. (His mother was the main influence in his life, and proved irreplaceable in it on her death, when he was thirty-five. Thereafter no woman – or man – would become truly an intimate.[7]) Like Margaret Thatcher (née Roberts), Heath went to grammar school, not public school, and by hard work got into Oxford. Like her, it was thanks to the generosity of others – and in his case a Balliol organ scholarship – that he had enough to get by. But the social and not just the obvious sexual distinction between the two is worth emphasizing, because in class-conscious Britain, and especially the class-conscious Conservative Party, it mattered. Margaret Roberts learned from her father the attitudes of bourgeois England. Edward Heath imbibed from his mother those of the less self-confident and more pliant respectable working class. She spoiled him. He was the centre of the family universe. It was accepted that he, not his brother, represented the future. His parents saved up to buy him a piano. Music was to be his outlet, indeed his only non-political interest – until he took up sailing, which, despite attempts to suggest otherwise, always seemed to be done with political impressions in mind.[8] Music, though, certainly mattered deeply to Heath. So, remarkably quickly, did international and especially European politics.

While at Balliol, Heath visited Germany and Spain and saw enough of Nazism and fascism to turn him into a virulent and informed critic of both systems. He was the most senior Conservative undergraduate at Oxford to oppose appeasement, campaigning vigorously (like Macmillan) against Hogg and for the Master of Balliol, the socialist A. D. ('Sandy') Lindsay, in the famous 'Munich' by-election.[9] On the eve of the war he was with his lifelong friend (and future MEP) Madron Seligman in Poland and was lucky to get back to England. Naturally, Heath immediately joined up. He had a 'good war', though most of it was spent frustratingly in training; only from July 1944 did he see action.

This social, educational and political background explains much about the future Conservative leader and Prime Minister – his solitariness, his sensitivity to rebuffs received (despite insensitivity to snubs given), his self-reliant single-mindedness, his genuine idealism, his easy acceptance of an internationalism usually associated with the left of politics and, finally, his obsession with Europe. On top of which, it is suggested that because of his humble background he suffered such a surfeit of snobbery from sections of the Tory Party that he was at some point turned from a pleasantly amenable individual into an anti-social monster.[10] That he finished a most unpleasant human being is hardly disputable. That he started off something essentially different and was poisonously transformed by the party he led is neither proven nor, despite some testimony, at all likely. As Tory Chief Whip under Eden and Macmillan he may, indeed, have been no more authoritarian than other tenants of that terrifying role. (Margaret Thatcher remembered him as distinctly aloof, though not hostile, as an adjoining candidate in Kent.[11]) But it is inherently unlikely that his increasingly bad manners and off-putting rudeness from the time he became leader reflected earlier ill-treatment, and much more likely that they reflected the fact that he had a high idea of himself and thought he could get away with being a bully. (The characters of most Tory leaders – especially Tory prime ministers – bear out the fact that power easily goes to a politician's head: probably, only Bonar Law and Alec Douglas-Home can be said to have remained genuinely modest in demeanour when in office.)

But there is a danger in attributing Heath's failure – and by all the usual criteria even sympathetic analysts (though not Heath himself) would accept that he failed – merely or even mainly to personality. As with the comparable case of Robert Peel, psychological flaws offer only part of the explanation. In both instances, stubbornness and an inability or perhaps unwillingness to carry colleagues along sharpened the splits and magnified the final crash. Yet it was the policies which did the political damage – the difference being that in Peel's case the policies, though untimely, were right and coherent, whereas in Heath's (for reasons to be discussed) their timeliness or lack of it was immaterial: it was the prescriptions themselves, and their contradictions, which caused the collapse.[12]

To understand why this is so, one must recall, in the first instance, how much Heath owed to Macmillan. Macmillan had celebrated his victory in the party leadership in 1957 with the Chief Whip of the day, one Edward Heath, at the Turf Club over champagne, oysters and game pie, and from then on the two men remained personally and ideologically close.[13] On two points, admittedly, they differed. Heath believed that Macmillan was wrong at Nassau to choose the American option for Britain's independent nuclear deterrent. He would even toy in office with collaboration with France on an alternative: he managed to have seriously and continuously bad relations with Washington.[14] Secondly, Heath, unlike Macmillan, became convinced that radical reform of the trade unions was required, to reduce their obstructive power and to modernize industry – though he also, rather oddly, envisaged that the unions would fit into a cooperative, corporatist model of economic management achieved through the NEDC.

What Heath and Macmillan shared was a commitment to full employment. This concept had, at least by the 1960s, very little to do with the actual balance between the number of jobs and the demand for them. It was, rather, the talismanic touchstone for running the economy. It ruled out anything more than tweaks of demand management to cool down overheating, usually manifested in a sterling crisis. (This particular constraint fell away when the pound was floated freely in June 1972, but the implications were not grasped.) It also implied that job creation was in the hands of government rather than, as Keith Joseph and Margaret Thatcher would later argue, being the result of producers supplying customers with the goods and services they wanted, that is, the operation of markets. Heath's sensitivity to the unemployment level, unlike Macmillan's, did not stem from personal or even second-hand experience. It reflected the degree to which, though socially an outsider, he was – and had been from the very beginning of his career – politically on the inside. He had been made a whip within months of entering Parliament and he remained close to the party power-brokers ever after. It was for his traditional mindset, his lack of questioning imagination, that his seniors valued and promoted him, as much as for his energy and ability. This same mindset, disguised by an unswerving and remorseless commitment to what he considered modernization, ill equipped him to face up to the challenges of the 1970s. He could not set Britain on a new course, though he started out wanting to do so.

Douglas Hurd, then Heath's political secretary, recalls that the 'short and angry' passage in the leader's foreword to the 1970 Conservative manifesto was very much Heath's own, reflecting a heartfelt personal condemnation of Harold Wilson's approach to government.[15]

> Once a decision is made, once a policy is established, the Prime Minister and his colleagues should have the courage to stick to it. Nothing has done Britain more harm in the world than the endless backing and filling which we have seen in recent years. Whether it be our defence commitments, or our financial policies, or the reform of industrial relations, the story is the same. At the first sign of difficulty the Labour Government has sounded the retreat, covering its withdrawal with a smokescreen of unlikely excuses. But courage and intellectual honesty are essential qualities in politics, and in the interests of our country it is high time that we saw them again.[16]

It is not by chance that the U-turns which made a much-mocked mockery of this dogmatic, even hubristic, statement of intent, began in January 1972, when the headline unemployment figure reached what was thought to be the scandalous level of one million. After the first phase of what now looks like, though was always less than, proto-Thatcherism, Heath reverted to the approach, inherited from Macmillan, of running the economy at full throttle to boost demand and jobs, and relying on incomes policy, voluntary or (if and when necessary) statutory, to control inflation. Finally, of course, Heath shared with Macmillan an unconditional commitment to membership of the European Common Market, the *deus ex machina* offering Britain, at one and the same time, economic prosperity and strategic significance.

Heath was given a very free hand to fight the 1966 election, which Wilson called, on the crest of good by-election and opinion poll results, for 31 March. The conclusions of the policy review conducted under Heath's own oversight had appeared in the form of an unusually detailed set of commitments contained in a party document entitled *Putting Britain Right Ahead*, published at the 1965 party conference. (Maudling sensibly suggested the addition of the word 'Ahead', because otherwise it might be asked who, in power, had been getting 'Britain Wrong' – an echo of a wider problem.) The document formed the basis of the party election manifesto. Conservative candidates duly registered the new emphasis on trade union reform (mentioned in 60 per cent of election addresses, compared with 24 per cent in 1964) and on Europe (mentioned by 50 per cent, compared with 10 per cent in 1964).[17] But it was to little avail.

The 1966 election returned a Labour Government with an overall majority of 96. The Conservatives lost 51 seats. Expectations and morale had been so low that the result was greeted with relief rather than recrimination. Heath's position, despite his repeated trouncing by Wilson in the House and his unpopularity – at the election his standing in the polls was lower than Douglas-Home's fourteen months earlier – was even felt to have been strengthened.[18]

He now reshaped his Shadow team. Out went Lord Dilhorne, Selwyn Lloyd, Boyd-Carpenter and Ernest Marples. In came Geoffrey Rippon, Peter Walker and Anthony Barber. Rippon, a short-tempered, right-of-centre barrister, would be entrusted with negotiating entry into Europe, which he did successfully, though on what were later widely deemed unsatisfactory terms. Walker, a financier and businessman, and by far the most talented of the three, had been Heath's campaign manager for the leadership in 1965, and would be again, when he failed to hold on to it a decade later.[19] Barber, a tax lawyer, would be entrusted in government, as Chancellor, with implementing Heath's prolonged reflation and then sharp deflation of the economy. The two most important figures, however, were already in post, and stayed there: Macleod and Powell.

Macleod was Shadow Chancellor. He was not an economist and he had no strong views about how an economy should be run. He was combative, however, and this inclined him to reject compromise with Labour's policies. In this case, it made him a fierce opponent of the Labour Government's National Plan and its various attempts at an incomes policy. (It was, doubtless, regard for the same forensic aggression in Margaret Thatcher that prompted him to take her on as his deputy to cover tax, and then to protect and promote her.) Macleod and Powell were the party's finest orators. The two largely agreed on economics, albeit in Macleod's case for opportunistic reasons. Unlike Powell, though, Macleod was a liberal on social matters, particularly anything smacking of race. In 1968 Macleod would be as much a rebel against the party compromise on immigration control as was Powell from the other direction, though he kept his place and his respectability. Had he not died shortly after the Conservatives took office in 1970, Macleod might have been able to keep economic policy on track. He would certainly not have allowed Heath and his claque of advisers to take it out of the Treasury's hands, as Barber did. Since it was ultimately economics

– not the other two conflict points of immigration and Europe – which sank the 1970–4 Conservative Government, Macleod's survival might also have avoided the shipwreck.

Enoch Powell's decision to take the Shadow Defence portfolio when Heath became leader, while appearing merely quirky – he thought Britain should withdraw from east of Suez, although remaining there was the dearest wish of most Tory backbenchers – was, in fact, doubly revealing. First, it illustrated why he was such a difficult colleague. He thought of his role, at least out of government (where he was fated to stay), as being primarily that of educator. He wanted to persuade, and he argued that this was anyway what politics was largely about – on which he differed fundamentally from Heath, who (like Peel) believed above all in the executive function. Second, his taking defence – in other words, not taking an economic department – reflected a growing despair at making any headway on the subjects which mattered most to him. A freely floating exchange rate, rejection of indicative planning (regional or national) and of incomes policies – all to be underpinned, as he would propose in his alternative 'Morecambe Budget' in 1968, by large public spending cuts and denationalization, in order to slash income tax – this was the radical course he wanted to take.[20] But he already knew it was not going to happen without an earthquake. This meant intimidating or destabilizing or removing Heath. Without this background, it is impossible to understand why Powell chose to take the risk he did with his Birmingham speech on immigration in April 1968.

The clash between Powell and Heath was not just intellectual but temperamental. This was despite superficial similarities. They had both entered the House of Commons in 1950. They were both ambitious, both impatient with what they saw as a culture of mediocrity, both proud, both self-reliant and both self-regarding. They both came from modest backgrounds.

Powell's parents were teachers, who admired cerebral rather than social achievement. Powell was, in fact, an extraordinarily brilliant polymath, having been the youngest Professor of Greek in the British Commonwealth (at Sydney) and later the youngest brigadier in the British army, with a romantic fixation on India. Powell's views evolved. From being an atheist he became a High Anglican, and from being an imperialist he became scornful of post-imperial illusions. But he was now and he would remain an angular right-wing intellectual. Right-wing intellectuals are distrusted as habitually dangerous, and with some reason, by the establishment of the Conservative Party. Like the third Marquess of Salisbury (or later, with qualifications, Keith Joseph), they seem made to lead it or to destroy it. Powell did not achieve the former; but, with more than a little help from Heath, he came near to achieving the latter.[21]

Enoch Powell's speech on immigration, delivered in Birmingham on 20 April 1968, was (with Margaret Thatcher's Bruges speech on Europe in 1988) one of the very few speeches that changed the course of British politics. His colleagues were taken by surprise, as he must have intended, and outraged by his tactics, as he should have foreseen. Powell had already practised the device of using a public speech to exert pressure before putting in a policy paper in his own field of defence. He had also discovered, when the Shadow Cabinet remained unconvinced by his arguments, that there were limits to its efficacy.[22] On this occasion, he gave no indication of the way his mind was working. In April the previous year, he had intervened in discussion at Shadow Cabinet to warn about the danger of a new wave of hostility to immigrants – and paradoxically received support from the Shadow Cabinet's most liberal member, Edward Boyle.[23] But Powell had since fallen strangely silent on this and on other matters that would previously have exercised him, as his new Shadow Cabinet colleague, Margaret Thatcher, remembered.[24] Remarkably, and not creditably, Powell expressed no reservations about Shadow Cabinet policy when the Government's Race

Relations Bill was discussed by Shadow ministers on Wednesday 10 April and Monday 22 April. These were substantive discussions. Hogg had described the Bill – which made it illegal to refuse housing, employment or public services to anyone on grounds of race – as 'a curate's egg' and one which would do 'more harm than good'. Edward Boyle, Keith Joseph and Robert Carr had all raised objections to the compromise plan to put down a reasoned amendment. All were objecting from the liberal wing. Boyle stated firmly that he would abstain.[25] This pattern of response replicated the split exposed at the earlier Shadow Cabinet meeting on 26 February, when the Government's Commonwealth Immigration Bill was discussed. Then Macleod had said he would vote against the measure to control the inflow.[26] In none of these discussions did Powell register dissent.

Even so, the Birmingham speech did not come quite out of the blue. The immigration issue was causing tremors. Like other MPs with large New Commonwealth immigrant populations in their constituencies, Powell had been worrying quasi-publicly about the problem for some while. He had recently spoken on it in Walsall, without receiving much attention. His concern, as he always insisted, was immigration and not 'race'. That did not stop the Birmingham speech as being so described. It was equally misdescribed – and still is – as his 'rivers of blood' speech. Powell included a passage from Virgil's *Aeneid* in his peroration: 'As I look ahead, I am filled with foreboding. Like the Roman, I seem to see "the River Tiber foaming with much blood".' This was strong, but not as strong as if he had been warning of a blood-bath in the Thames.[27]

The extreme wording of the Birmingham speech was, presumably, adopted to ensure it did not suffer the fate of his earlier overlooked forays on the subject. In this it succeeded. In fact, though, it went much too far, not just because it unwisely quoted the contents of an anonymous letter containing language about 'wide-grinning piccaninnies' which sounded offensively racist (and Powell, though nationalist, even by most definitions an extreme nationalist, was not himself racially prejudiced). It also went too far in another respect, because it exceeded the political limits of what Powell intended. He had clearly planned to shake Heath, but to stay inside the Shadow Cabinet. Instead, as the press furore grew, he was unceremoniously sacked; and if he had not been, several other Shadow Cabinet ministers would have walked out. The enthusiastic popular reaction from sections of the public not usually supportive of the Conservative Party turned him into a national figure – in many eyes, a hero, a martyr to speaking the truth about a threat that no one had hitherto addressed.[28] The speech also made him a life-long leper in the eyes of others.

The row was extremely galling for the Tory leadership, which had seen the credibility of the Government's economic policy collapse along with the pound in November 1967 – when Wilson had foolishly denied any effect on the 'pound . . . in your pocket' – and had since enjoyed the adverse reaction to Roy Jenkins's first austerity budget in March. And it was deeply humiliating for Heath personally, because his own popularity still lagged behind that of his party and behind Wilson's, while Powell's soared.[29]

But Heath hung on. The Conservative Party does not like revolutions, as Randolph Churchill had discovered. And the party hierarchy now united around Heath. The leadership adapted enough to cover its vulnerable right flank by sharpening the party's rhetoric on immigration. Similarly, at the next election, the party adopted an economic line that echoed closely that taken by Powell. Hence the 1970 manifesto noted: 'We utterly reject the philosophy of compulsory wage control.' Unfortunately, this concession was not matched by any recognition that some other means of controlling inflation was required, despite repeated attempts by advisers to make Heath and his colleagues focus on the gap.[30] Instead, the manifesto merely observed: 'Britain now faces the worst inflation for twenty years. This is mainly the result of tax increases and devaluation. In implementing all our policies, the need to curb inflation will come first.' This tritely mendacious assertion – blaming higher prices on higher taxes and weak sterling – was intended to cover up the lack of policy. When put under pressure, it collapsed into the damaging formula, actually contained in party briefings rather than a formal pledge, that the Government would 'cut prices at a stroke'.

The Conservatives were not expected to win the June 1970 election. Only one poll at the end of the campaign suggested they might. They, themselves, did not believe they would. It is still not clear why they did.

Wilson had probably helped, when he launched what he thought to be a clever attack on 'Selsdon Man', the personification of primitive Tory egotism. The reference was to the Shadow Cabinet weekend meeting at Selsdon Park of 31 January–1 February 1970. These innocuous and pedestrian discussions – a matter of tidying up loose ends and no more – hardly qualified for their assigned place in the political Chamber of Horrors. They ranged over defence costs, family allowances, reform of local government structures, housing finance and the National Health Service. The pressing problem of what to do about wages and inflation was treated only briefly and inconclusively. The one notable disagreement was a sharp spat between Heath and Mrs Thatcher about her proposal to mention in the manifesto support for the proposed private university of Buckingham, which Heath opposed. (It suggests a clash of temperaments significant for the future.)[31] The decision to highlight law and order – a subject which had not even been discussed – in the press conference afterwards was, it seems, the fortunate mistake that gave life to Wilson's invention.[32] The caricature assisted the Conservatives because it suggested a degree of strategic coherence which, despite a plethora of individual policies, hardly matched the reality. The party now briefly moved ahead in the opinion polls, though the lead dropped away in the spring.

During the election campaign itself, Powell's well-publicized speeches, which brought out the Conservative vote, particularly in the West Midlands, and the appearance of some bad trade figures, which raised doubts about the Labour Government's economic policy, certainly helped the Tories. But accumulated tiredness with Wilson's antics was probably most important. The results, when they came in, were certainly a surprise. The Conservatives won with a majority of thirty-one seats.[33] The very unexpectedness of the victory worked in Heath's favour. It seemed his personal achievement. It was now, truly, Heath's party.

It was also, and remained, Heath's Government. He was completely dominant.[34] Despite his policy twists and turns, not a single Cabinet minister resigned or threatened to resign. Only Nicholas Ridley, a junior minister at the Department of Trade and Industry, and certainly a fervent critic of the Government's then interventionist mode, claimed to have done so.[35] But Heath himself maintained that Ridley was effectively faced down and sacked from the DTI.[36] Either way, Heath is perfectly correct in stating that, beyond a few gripes on particular details, Keith Joseph and Margaret Thatcher, the duo who would unseat him and reverse his policies, stayed silent.[37]

It was not just Heath's personality that intimidated his colleagues – the brusque put-down, the stony glower, the ominous silences. So did his method of working. Most strong prime ministers – and Heath was strong – are blamed for being secretive and operating by the back stairs in order to bypass Cabinet. Cabinet government is, in truth, always more of a theoretical than a practical concept. But Heath – like Mrs Thatcher and unlike Tony Blair – did maintain the constitutional forms.[38] On the other hand, he also increasingly used smaller groups of Cabinet ministers who were close to him – like Peter Walker, James Prior, Lord Carrington and Willie

Whitelaw – to devise approaches to difficult issues (and to prepare U-turns), on matters ranging from industrial policy to Ulster.

Heath also made use of the Civil Service in a way rarely observed before or since. His closeness to the head of the Civil Service, Sir William Armstrong, was notorious among his colleagues. (Armstrong was sometimes unappreciatively described as the 'Deputy Prime Minister'.) Heath was also even more heavily reliant than is usual for a Prime Minister on his principal private secretary, Robert Armstrong (no relation). Among other officials wielding great influence was Sir Con O'Neill, who controlled the negotiations for entry into the European Common Market.

Heath at once distrusted and approved of the Civil Service – the first because it seemed too conservative, and the second because it was non-political. Increasingly the second consideration overcame the first. His idea was, in fact, to reduce politics to the minimum and adopt the best policy, arrived at by experts thinking logically. (He hoped, for the same reason, to bring businessmen into government, but recruited only the hapless John Davies, former director general of the CBI, who proved politically out of his depth at the DTI.) Heath's distaste for political argument, in turn, helps explain his creation of the Central Policy Review Staff (CPRS or 'Think Tank'), intended to devise bright ideas and analyse policy programmes, alongside the process of Policy Analysis and Review (PAR), an idea conceived in business and then transferred to and emasculated by the British bureaucracy. Heath's anti-political, technocratic outlook also explains his innovation of joint committees of ministers and civil servants sitting together to resolve policy conundrums.[39] Finally, it explains his obsession with the processes of decision-making, often at the expense of the contents of decisions, which were soon proving hard to explain or defend in public.

A full account of the Heath Government's travails from the time of its election to that of its demise, as a result of the election defeat of February 1974, would be inappropriate here. Only the main phases can be sketched.

The first phase, which can be dated approximately to between June 1970 and January 1972, was fraught but broadly successful. Taxes were cut and some public spending savings made. There was trouble when Mrs Thatcher, at Education, stopped free school milk. (Heath stood by her, which he need not have done.) The nationalization of the insolvent but strategically vital Rolls-Royce company was denounced by some as an early U-turn. It was embarrassing for a Government expected to denationalize. But it was an emergency means of saving the aero-engine giant from bankruptcy, which neither security nor industrial considerations permitted.

In August 1971 the ambitious Industrial Relations Act became law. This was, on the face of it, a remarkable achievement, and stood in sharp contrast to Wilson's retreat on the previous Government's *In Place of Strife* proposals for union reform in 1969. Collective bargaining agreements were to be legally enforceable and union immunities from civil action were to be narrowed and confined to those unions which met certain criteria. 'Cooling off' periods – enforced suspension of strikes – and secret ballots could under certain circumstances be imposed. Unfortunately, it did too much too quickly. The system was overcomplicated. It relied on new institutions, including a National Industrial Relations Court. Crucially, its provisions depended on trade unions registering, which under TUC direction they refused to do. It was discredited when it proved useless in the February 1972 miners' strike and counter-productive in the summer, when dockers were threatened with gaol and had to be saved by the intervention of the Official Solicitor. By then the second, inglorious phase of the Heath Government was well under way.

As suggested earlier, the turning point (introducing the second phase) was when unemployment passed a million at the start of

1972. By now the coal miners were on strike. For all the talk of preparedness, the Government proved entirely unprepared for this. The most humiliating moment was when on 10 February mass picketing closed the Saltley coke depot; it was also a moment of triumph for the militants and, in particular, for the local NUM leader Arthur Scargill, who would try in vain to repeat it against Mrs Thatcher in 1984–5. Heath appointed a court of inquiry under the politically respected judge Lord Wilberforce, which awarded a massive pay rise. Also in February came an equally embarrassing U-turn when the Government's policy of austerely refusing subsidies for 'lame ducks' went into reverse at Upper Clyde Shipbuilders. Industrial blackmail by militants was shown to pay, which did the militants' standing no end of good in the trade unions. The Government now really had two options. It could try to find a tactical way forward which left the proclaimed non-interventionist strategy of 1970 intact. Or it could simply reverse direction. Heath had no doubt about choosing the second, because his heart had never been in the first.

The different components of the strategic U-turn were quickly in place. Barber's – or more precisely Heath's – budget on 21 March employed tax cuts and spending increases to stoke the fires of demand. The following day the Industry White Paper (the basis of that year's Industry Act – also Heath's personal policy) was published. This instituted an interventionist industrial strategy, theoretically based on picking winners but, as is always the case, keeping in business many a loser along the way. The summer and autumn saw tripartite talks with the CBI and the TUC in search of a voluntary incomes policy to control the inflation that monetary and fiscal profligacy, under union pressure, were encouraging. The talks came to nothing. On 6 November Heath announced Stage One of a statutory pay policy. Stages Two and Three would follow in 1973, until the whole complicated structure collapsed before the juggernaut of another miners' strike.

The issue of 'Europe' – the single word at about this time took over in public parlance from earlier more technical formulations – straddles all three phases of the Heath Government's turbulent life. A majority of the population and a vociferous minority of Tories opposed Common Market entry. But it was Heath's dream. He was not bluffing when he told backbenchers on the eve of the second reading vote on the European Communities Bill that it would be treated as a matter of confidence. Defeat, and the Government would fall. Even then, the majority was only eight, and fifteen Tories defied the whips. Heath had been fortunate in that before he came to tread the path of supplicant to the Elysée Palace the occupant had changed. Pompidou, de Gaulle's successor, was happy, if the terms were right, to withdraw the French veto, and Heath was prepared to offer almost any terms. Yet it was an achievement, all the same, and so in October 1971 was the large majority in favour of entry on a Commons free vote – which embarrassed a deeply split Labour Party. For Heath there was an added bonus. Enoch Powell's increasingly obsessive focus on Europe, where his views had less resonance than on the economy or immigration, helped isolate him within the party. This worked in Heath's favour – though arguably not in the party's, as it drove Powell and his supporters further towards the edge and, finally, over it. The main problem posed by Europe for Heath was deeper but less obvious. The anti-European rebels became the hard core of repeated and habitual dissent within the ranks of the Conservative parliamentary party. This dissent went wider than Europe, but even then it was focused, above all, on questions where Heath's personal decisions were most controversially at stake. Measured from the division lobbies, it reached a level never experienced in the party since the fall of Chamberlain.[40]

The third phase can be considered as stretching from the summer of 1973 to the election of February 1974. By May 1973 it was clear that the economy was dangerously overheating. Inflation (and not just in Britain) was again a problem. That month's budget started to trim back spending. But the Yom Kippur War in October, in reaction to which the Arab states applied an oil embargo that sent oil prices soaring – in fact, they quadrupled – forced the Government into rapid retreat. Nothing like the current levels of planned public expenditure could now be afforded. In December an emergency budget implemented sharp cuts. The higher price of energy also gave the coal miners an opportunity to press their demands, which they relished immoderately. After fevered attempts by the Government to find a way out within the rules of Stage Three (published on 8 October), the NUM staged an overtime ban. The Government then responded by imposing a three-day working week to save energy.

The air of emergency this created proved politically helpful. The Conservatives at last felt they had something to fight for, or at least against. The Labour Party was in disarray. The country was sharply polarized, but the polarization for the moment was in the Government's favour. A touch of Dunkirk spirit over Christmas was reassuring. Party officials started to consider an early election and enthusiasm for it grew when in January 1974, for the first time in three years, the Conservatives edged two points ahead of Labour in the polls. Heath himself did not want an election. He liked being Prime Minister. He had hopes that his model of collaboration, cooperation and consensus would somehow prevail. All that was needed was a technical solution achieved and implemented by rational people. (Unfortunately, even the bureaucracy let him down in the end when, at a disastrously inopportune moment, a leak from the Pay Board, set up under Stage Three, suggested that the miners' demands could have been accommodated within the rules, and so the election was unnecessary.)

In any case, when the NUM voted to strike on 5 February even Heath had had enough. The election was called for 28 February. The question 'Who Governs Britain?' on which the Conservatives fought the campaign might perhaps have yielded an answer beneficial to the party. But it was not the only question asked: there were also questions about the Government's record, which received less flattering replies. In any case, what Heath would have done with his victory is unclear – and theoretical, because he lost.

The Pay Board leak was one contributory factor. Powell's public announcement that he was resigning his seat and voting Labour was another. Heath's rebarbative personality over the years was certainly a third.

Afterwards, there were those who argued that the result was not too bad. This, though, overlooks the fact of Labour's own weakness and incoherence during the crisis. The Tories should have won. They did indeed – on a high turnout – secure 38 per cent of the vote, against Labour's 37 per cent. (The Liberals more than doubled their share at 19 per cent, which provided Heath in the aftermath with arguments for a Con–Lib 'moderate' coalition.) But the number of seats was what ultimately mattered, and here Labour, with 301 against the Conservatives' 297, though lacking an overall majority, were clearly ahead. The only hope the Conservatives might have had of staying in power would have been through a deal with the Ulster Unionists. But Heath's Ulster policy, since the suspension of the Northern Ireland Parliament in March 1972, had fatally alienated Unionist opinion, and so excluded that possibility. After three days of much-criticized procrastination, while messages went back and forth between Heath and Jeremy Thorpe, the Liberal leader, who might have liked to come in but could not persuade his colleagues, Heath finally resigned. The experiment was over.

What had it proved? On this there were major disagreements. Heath had, in truth, successively pursued two incompatible strategies, though he never admitted it.[41] Had the second just been a rational recognition of the flaws of the first? Or had the first, despite its flaws, been more or less on the right lines? Would another attempt at reducing the role of the state, removing controls, promoting efficiency, reforming trade unions and relying on private enterprise to create jobs be doomed – as Heath and his followers now maintained – or would it work in different hands and under different conditions? Douglas Hurd concluded: 'Britain cannot be governed dogmatically or by the use of willpower.'[42] Mrs Thatcher disagreed, and proved his analysis wrong, at least to her own and the electorate's general satisfaction.

One thing which ought to have been evident was that Heath should hand over the leadership to someone else, just as Douglas-Home had to him. This, though, he considered out of the question. The fact that he was the first elected party leader probably strengthened his authority: it certainly disorientated his opponents, who now had to manoeuvre not discreetly within inner circles ('magic' or otherwise) but under the spotlight of publicity.

Heath insisted on deducing from the February 1974 result that there was a widespread desire for a 'National' Government, based on a coalition of experts and moderates, and that he was the man to lead it. This was an incredible proposition, in the literal sense that no one outside his immediate circle could believe it. The failure to convince the electorate of the thesis – even when it was sugared by such irresponsible pledges as that made (with some brio) by Margaret Thatcher, now holding the Tory Environment brief, arbitrarily to limit mortgage rates – is not at this distance in time at all surprising. Electors were, with good reason, sceptical of the ability of Wilson's Government to tackle the country's economic problems, but insufficiently so to put Heath back in Downing Street. At that October's election Labour were returned with 319 seats against the Conservatives' 277, 13 Liberals and 26 'Others' – Scottish and Welsh Nationalists and Northern Irish. Labour thus had an overall majority of 3 seats, too small to last a Parliament, but enough, given horse-trading with the small parties, to survive most of it. In any case, the Conservatives were out.

With historical perspective, what seems surprising is neither that by the summer of 1974 the flag of intellectual revolt had been raised by Keith Joseph in his speeches on the economy, nor that by the autumn the 1922 Committee executive, now chaired by Heath's deadly enemy du Cann, were pressing for a leadership election. It is that Heath and his praetorian guard really thought that he could ride out the discontent. What is even more surprising is that he was almost right, because he almost won. And if he had been even slightly less of an egomaniac, he could have assured the succession of someone like the charming and acceptably establishment Willie Whitelaw, who would have burnished his memory, venerated his legacy and continued his policies. The explanation is that the Conservative Party at all levels – the Shadow ministers, the MPs, the party grandees and officials, even the party faithful – were over-whelmingly in favour of a non-confrontational approach. Since only confrontation would remove Heath, and since only his removal would allow a fundamental rethinking of policy and re-invigoration of the leadership with new blood, it does not say much for the party's instinct for survival that what has been nicely christened the 'Peasants' Revolt' was initially so hesitant and took so long in coming.[43]

The Conservative Party was at this juncture in a fragile and uncertain state, for a number of reasons. Losing two successive general elections is always traumatic. But the loss of the February 1974 election was especially so, because most Conservatives believed – rather as in 1945 – that they were speaking for the nation, and the nation had not recognized their voice. There was, on top of that, a certain amount of shame, difficult to pinpoint but present all the same. Conservative rhetoric, while strong in attacking militancy and the Red Menace, had all but given up on defending the twists and turns of Conservative policy.

The party was also split. At the top, the grip exerted by Heath seemed unshakable. The Shadow Cabinet contained only two strong critics, Joseph and Mrs Thatcher, who had long bided their time. The rest strongly supported Heath's continued leadership. This reflected not just his psychological dominance (already mentioned) but also the fact that the old Cabinet and now Shadow Cabinet had remained remarkably untouched by resignations or dismissals. It was a kind of *corpus separatum* – part of the parliamentary party and yet isolated from it. The immobility had increased solidarity within the élite but also, by denying opportunities for patronage and promotion, increased resentments among those kept outside it on the back benches.[44] This was reflected in the membership of the 1922 executive which was strongly, though discreetly, anti-Heath. The extent of this alienation, concealed by du Cann's combination of suppressed ambition and oleaginous diplomacy, really became clear to the Heath camp only when the vote was taken. The party organization and, in so far as their views can be gauged, the party members were also divided from their MPs in their opinions about Heath, because they still admired him and did not want to throw him over. This is what was reported by Conservative Central Office (more precisely, the National Union) at the time of the contest, and though the source was hardly unbiased, or even reliable, the assessment was almost certainly accurate.

But the most important aspect of the split in the Conservative Party now was ideological. In the conflicts over immigration, economics and Europe, a new right (interested mainly in economics and individual liberty) had come into existence alongside the recognizably old right (interested mainly in Rhodesia, immigration and law and order), with Powell as the link between the two.[45] Both Powell and Joseph (along with Geoffrey Howe and Margaret Thatcher on an intermittent basis) had been close to the Institute of Economic Affairs, run by Ralph Harris and Arthur Seldon. Through the IEA, the thinking of Hayek – and, more peripherally at this stage, the economics of Milton Friedman – provided a yeast of ideas to leaven the stolid, unpalatable dough served up by

478

Central Office and the Conservative Research Department.[46] This trend became sharper, and much more dangerous for Heath, when he foolishly agreed to Keith Joseph's proposal to set up the Centre for Policy Studies in May 1974. The CPS, driven by the intellect and animus of the journalist Alfred Sherman, its director, but acting as the hub of a much wider group of right-of-centre dissidents, was active first in counter-revolution and then in the fully fledged 'Thatcher revolution'. Naturally, it and all its works were soon hated by Heath and his allies.

The soul-searching had also started in press comment. T. E. ('Peter') Utley in the leader columns of the *Daily Telegraph* was just the most well-known of a range of journalists who were keen to revive old Tory values and advance free market policies, and to provide a fresh philosophical underpinning for that combination.[47]

Keith Joseph's Upminster speech of June 1974 (which talked of 'thirty years of socialistic fashions') and his Preston speech that September (which blamed monetary incontinence for inflation) had so powerful an effect because they fitted into this framework of public reflection. Indeed, although he lacked the aggression (and judgement) required to command the heights of politics, Joseph was ideally placed to prompt the required debate. His conversion to an unashamedly free market position was all the more convincing for his having started on the left of the party – he opposed Suez – and having a well-deserved reputation for social reform. (The fact that it was really a reconversion, since he had adopted the IEA analysis once before and then abandoned it, was forgotten, except by the IEA.) Joseph now openly questioned the policies of the Government in which he had served and suggested that it, along with previous governments, bore the blame for what was amiss. But he then spectacularly destroyed his leadership prospects with an ill-judged speech in Edgbaston in October, in which his speculations about threats to 'the human stock' from proletarian overbreeding led to disastrous headlines.

On the same day that Keith Joseph pulled out of the undeclared leadership race Margaret Thatcher jumped in. Along with her own courage, she enjoyed two crucial assets. The first was the guile of her campaign manager, Airey Neave, a war hero with strong intelligence connections, whose hope of advancement had been rudely quashed by Heath. The second was the fact that so many back-benchers, whatever they thought of Mrs Thatcher, desperately wanted to give Heath a shock. When the contest was formally declared she duly knocked out Heath on the first ballot (Thatcher 130; Heath 119; Hugh Fraser 16) on 4 February 1975, and gained the momentum to win against a wider field on 11 February (Thatcher 146; Whitelaw 79; Prior and Howe 19 each; John Peyton 11).

One is tempted to say, in the well-used cliché, that with the accession of Margaret Thatcher to the party leadership, 'the rest is history'. In fact, it is not history at all. It is still, in a sense, part of current affairs. Mrs (now Baroness) Thatcher herself is still alive, and her merits and demerits, achievements and failures, are so much a part of the continuing discussion of contemporary events that the years after 1975 must be treated in the next two chapters in a different fashion from those historical developments which preceded them.[48]

But what of Edward Heath, who lumbered grumpily on, discrediting every argument he espoused, while discrediting himself by association with Saddam Hussein and communist China (he was supportive even after Tiananmen Square)? A final observation is in order. Heath's only significant achievement as Prime Minister was to secure British entry into the European Economic Community. Views of that outcome differ. But even for enthusiasts of the European project it must be hard to deny that the way in which he did it was harmful. Following Macmillan's example, Heath played up all the benefits, without discussing the costs. He suggested that entry would bring about reform of the British economy, by implication without any pain or effort. It did not. He settled on bad terms, particularly as regards future financial contributions, but also in respect of fishing and agriculture, and he glossed over losses of parliamentary and legal sovereignty. These issues were bound to come back to haunt successive governments, even governments that wanted a collaborative engagement with Europe, and they provided the material for future damaging Tory splits, which are still not resolved.

Nor did Heath's failures even do the party any good. As noted, there was still after 1974 room for argument about the role of prices and incomes policies, monetary policy and trade union reform, and the arguments would continue well into the early years of the Thatcher Government, a decade later. The real turn-round in broader economic thinking came about not in reaction against Heath but in consequence of the International Monetary Fund's intervention in 1975–6, which finally dispelled the Keynesian illusions. It was the Labour Prime Minister, James Callaghan, who ran down the political curtain by telling his supporters in 1976: 'We used to think that you could just spend your way out of a recession and increase employment by cutting taxes and boosting government spending. I tell you, in all candour, that this option no longer exists.'[49] (Of course, the Labour Party did not heed the lesson for long, and Mrs Thatcher would then be called upon to apply it systematically.)

Heath's attempts to secure his personal historical reputation have, by and large, fared badly. He used a legal loophole to obtain the freehold of his beautiful house in Salisbury on the cheap from the Dean and Chapter of the Cathedral. Bar a few small donations, he then used his fortune to turn it into a posthumous shrine to himself.[50] The money has since run out, and it is to be sold. Enoch Powell's observation (of Joseph Chamberlain) that 'all political lives unless they are cut off in midstream at a happy juncture end in failure' is doubtless of general application.[51] But few political lives in modern Britain brought such unhappy consequences as the life of Edward Heath.

Margaret Thatcher's knockout blows to Europe in pursuit of 'our money' contributed, along with victory in the Falklands War, to her image as the strongest British Prime Minister in modern times.

17

THATCHER'S PARTY

The year 1975 has enormous importance for the Conservative Party and for British politics more widely, but the benefit of hindsight is required fully to appreciate it. At the time, Margaret Thatcher's victory in the party leadership election had mainly negative significance. It represented the overthrow of Heath and the party hierarchy which had backed him. By implication, it also suggested a challenge to the economic orthodoxy and to the approach which he and they had favoured. But only in retrospect does it mark the start of a reframing of political debate, with new criteria applied and new parameters accepted. In 1975 it was not just difficult to foresee the 'Iron Lady'. It was entirely impossible to envisage Tony Blair. In fact, at this early juncture Mrs Thatcher's hold on the leadership was fragile; the scope for patronage of her few supporters was limited; and the implications of what would become known as monetarism and supply-side economics were as yet barely grasped – even by well-informed commentators. These constraints were very much in evidence over the next four years.[1]

Margaret Thatcher's problems stemmed much less from being a

483

woman than from being an outsider – though her sex made it less easy to fit (or be fitted by others) into the clubby atmosphere of traditional Tory politics. She was not (as yet) disliked by many. But she lacked political friends. In the Shadow Cabinet she could rely on Willie Whitelaw, whose speciality was loyalty, but who did not understand her ideas. Airey Neave's interests were, of course, completely bound up with hers. But he had little influence. She could always trust Keith Joseph (first in charge of policy, then shadowing Industry), who remained a mentor as well as a devotee. As Shadow Chancellor, Geoffrey Howe, though not a personal friend, was committed to reining in government and restoring enterprise, both of which she too believed essential. Lord Thorneycroft, as party chairman, usefully imposed his authority, though he was also quite capable of challenging hers. That said, in varying degrees, on different issues, and under shifting conditions, most of the rest of the Shadow Cabinet – let alone those recently excluded from it – would have liked to abandon the economic strategy and, if pushed, see the back of her as well.[2]

Over the parliamentary party as a whole, however, she established a much firmer hold. This was despite the fact she was frequently worsted in the House of Commons, first by Wilson and then, from April 1976, by the formidable James Callaghan. The Tory party activists were also very quickly won over. Instinctive loyalty to the leader had, as always, much to do with it. But Mrs Thatcher's party conference speeches – especially the first in 1975 – created enormous excitement. Anger at the Labour Government, the trade unions and, in the near distance, the Soviet Union, was a potent force in these years. For the first time since Bonar Law, the party was led by someone who, the rank and file were fully and correctly confident, was at least as angry as they were.

Mrs Thatcher faced personal problems, of course – not least from Edward Heath, who thought he could make a comeback. His stock rose with the endorsement of European Community membership in the referendum in the summer of 1975. He was convinced he would return at the head, or at least as part of, a government of national unity. But he made no attempt to win over support or even to stay in touch with his old allies. In the end, his curmudgeonly demeanour helped secure his enemy's position.[3]

There were also secondary policy distractions, which led to short-term rows and splits. The issue of Scottish devolution – though it would ultimately inflict terminal damage on Callaghan's government – was one such, prompting resignations from the Shadow Cabinet in 1976. There was a mighty row with right-wing backbenchers over the line to take on Rhodesian sanctions in 1978.

But economic strategy was, naturally enough, the focus of the sharpest conflict. This had a theoretical background in the disputed cause of and cure for inflation. The arguments themselves had not greatly changed since Powell and Maudling fought over them in the 1960s, though the writings of Milton Friedman had helped shift the intellectual balance and added technical refinement. The debate now centred, in practice, on the role – if any – of prices and incomes policy in curbing the alarmingly spiralling wage inflation, and, specifically, on how much support to give to Government attempts to apply such a policy. In this respect, the imposition of the proto-monetarist programme devised by the IMF in 1975–6 proved a politically mixed blessing. On the one hand, the programme's success – the world did not end, inflation fell, growth resumed – suggested that getting the finances right should have primacy over keeping unemployment down. On the other hand, the experience of the last two years of Callaghan's Labour Government suggested that sensible financial policy of itself was not enough. This insight was, indeed, well founded. Structural reform of the economy, which successive governments had avoided and unions and employers resisted, was required if British economic decline was to be checked and reversed. What happened in the short term, however, was that Heath and his supporters simply demanded a return to prices and incomes policy.

This period – 1977–8 – was particularly dangerous for Mrs Thatcher. Conservative popular support fell. Conservative internal dissent became public.[4] The Conservative leadership was seriously divided from most Conservative opinion over what to do about inflation. Meanwhile, the economy seemed sufficiently strong after its dose of IMF medicine to suggest to many of the uncommitted that Labour, under the reassuring leadership of Callaghan, deserved another chance.

These were the tricky circumstances prevailing when the Lib–Lab Pact, which had kept Labour in power since March 1977, finally broke down in May 1978. A general election in the autumn of 1978 was then widely expected. Had it in fact been held then, it is probable that the Conservatives would have lost. If that had happened, Mrs Thatcher would have been replaced, and the later 'Thatcher experiment' would never have occurred. If the Conservatives had nonetheless won an autumn election, but with a very small majority, the resulting Government would probably have proved too weak to press on in 1981, when obstacles mounted – with the same result. But now it was Callaghan who flinched and postponed the election. This gave the Labour Government's economic and political strategy just enough time to fall apart.

Trade union militancy and arrogance, exposed during the 'Winter of Discontent' of 1978–9, did not in themselves destroy the Government. What they did was to make Callaghan and his colleagues look weak and floundering. Most significantly, that winter's strikes allowed Mrs Thatcher to shift the public debate away from the thorny issue of price and wage control to the curbing of trade union power. The strikes made her analysis look respectable and her arguments seem realistic. They thus allowed the Conservatives to return to the terrain abandoned after the February 1974 defeat, but this time with solutions, and with a wary, competent, resolved leader to apply them.

The defeat of the Labour Government's proposals for devolution to Scotland and Wales in referendums on 1 March 1979 meant that there was nothing it could usefully offer the nationalist parties. An embarrassing scramble by Callaghan to bid for Irish support ensued. It, too, eventually failed on 28 March, when the Government was defeated in the House of Commons by one vote on a motion of confidence. By and large, Labour then conducted the better general election campaign. The Conservatives, though benefiting from highly effective advertising and a strong organizational effort, were on the defensive and far from fleet of foot. There was a palpable lack of confidence in Mrs Thatcher, whom the party chairman and others tried to muzzle – though to limited effect. The result, anyway, left everyone on the Tory side feeling vindicated. The Conservatives secured an overall majority of forty-three seats, having gained the largest swing of any party since 1945.[5]

A full account of the eleven and a half years of Margaret Thatcher's premiership is far beyond the scope of this book.[6] All that can be done here is to outline the highlights (and lowlights), assess the results and clear up some misunderstandings before, finally, considering the Thatcher legacy, into which John Major's leadership and premiership can most appropriately be fitted.[7]

The early period of the Thatcher Government was almost wholly dominated by the stresses imposed by economic policy. One should not imagine that this was because the Government concerned itself only with economics. Large increases in police pay stopped the fall in numbers, and doubtless also helped ensure crucial police support when industrial and social disorder and Irish Republican terrorism surfaced. Of great long-term significance was the 1980 Housing Act, which gave council tenants the right to buy their homes at large discounts reflecting their length of tenure. This resulted in the largest increase in home ownership in modern times. And while the initial attempts at education reform now look timid, they were the first steps away from the egalitarian and coercive system which had grown up since the 1960s. Economic concerns, though, certainly overshadowed everything.

The economic inheritance from the Labour Government was not just bad and deteriorating, but worse and deteriorating faster than even incoming ministers, let along the wider public, properly understood. It was necessary to deal with a swollen budget deficit and rapidly rising public sector pay as a result of the settlements by which Callaghan had bought off the trade unions. Inflation was rising, and would be given a sharp upward kick by the increase in VAT introduced in the first Conservative budget. The world was going into a new recession, driven by the oil price rises consequent on the Iranian Revolution. Sterling (now a petro-currency) also rose. This, combined with disinflation, increased the pressure on industry, and British industry – overmanned, ill-managed, un-competitive – could not cope.

Significant deregulation began early. Controls on prices, incomes, dividends, industrial development and, most radically, foreign exchange went in the first year. Cuts in the basic and upper rates of income tax from their previously penal levels would help recreate incentives in the longer run. (In 1979 the standard rate was cut from 33 to 30 per cent and the top rate from 83 to 60 per cent; the rate on so-called 'unearned', i.e. investment, income had been 98 and fell to 75 per cent.) But it was the economic squeeze which now made the headlines.

The primacy of controlling inflation was determined less by what critics liked to deride as monetarist dogma – and it should be remembered that monetarists themselves had quite strong mutual disagreements – than by ingrained past experience. Consciousness of the failure of Conservative Governments since the fifties and sixties to achieve a sustainable economic strategy was part of this. But more important was awareness of the Heath Government's

Lord ('Fred') Woolton, Conservative Party chairman, poses in front of party campaign posters in 1949.

Quintin Hogg (later Lord Hailsham) campaigns exuberantly in Oxford during the close-fought 1950 election campaign (*left*), while babies and bulldogs turn out the Tory vote in Westminster (*below*).

VOTE CONSERVATIVE

Make Britain great again

for fair wages

VOTE CONSERVATIVE

Churchill, wearing the Garter, escorts the Queen to her car after his long-delayed farewell banquet in Downing Street in 1955 (*above*). Tory election posters that year (*bottom left*) give prominence to the new leader, Eden, whose appeal to women 'of a certain age' is exerted on a 91-year-old voter (*bottom right*).

Harold Macmillan (*top left*) basks in the Kennedy glamour at the White House in 1961. A rare moment of happiness for Sir Alec Douglas-Home on the campaign trail in October 1964 (*top right*). In 1970 Edward Heath's optimism was not shared by many in the party, but later proved justified: here he arrives for the count in Bexley in June (*bottom right*). Enoch Powell (*above, in Wolverhampton*) probably helped secure the Conservative victory.

Conservative and Unionist Central Office, 32 Smith Square. In the warren of poky rooms and dingy corridors behind this imposing façade almost fifty years of campaigning triumphs and disasters were planned and executed: the building was sold in 2004.

LABOUR ISN'T WORKING.

UNEMPLOYMENT OFFICE

BRITAIN'S BETTER OFF WITH THE CONSERVATIVES.

Margaret Thatcher, Tory Environment spokesman, holds the floor, while Peter Carrington and Heath laugh, at an October 1974 election press conference (*top*). Heath's smile soon faded. In the summer of 1978 Saatchi & Saatchi produced an effective poster (*above*) which may have caused James Callaghan to postpone an autumn election that he might (just) have won. October 1984 brought devastation at the hands of the Provisional IRA that reduced the Grand Hotel, Brighton, to a bomb-blasted shell (*left*).

A warm embrace for Mrs Thatcher from Willie Whitelaw in October 1989 (*above*).
A year later he would be less supportive. The understated personality of her successor,
John Major (*below*), was an asset in the 1992 election, which the Tories unexpectedly won.

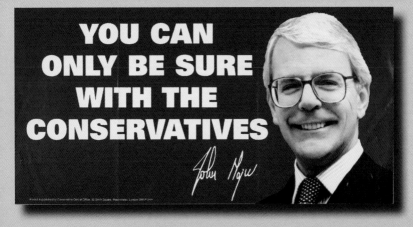

**YOU CAN
ONLY BE SURE
WITH THE
CONSERVATIVES**

All change? David Cameron's final rally during the 2010 election campaign.

U-turns. Not for nothing is the most famous Thatcher line 'the lady's not for turning'.[8] Mrs Thatcher could not afford to alter course, because the assumption was that any such alteration implied an abandonment of the whole approach – a return, in short, to 1971–2. This assumption was, in fact, correct, because a return to reflation – lower interest rates, higher borrowing, more spending, accompanied by varying degrees of industrial subsidy and exchange rate intervention – was precisely what the critics wanted. Varieties of the same prescription came from many quarters and were voiced in different tones, from that of the 364 economists who wrote to *The Times* protesting about the 1981 budget, to the Conservative Party 'Wets' (including Heath), through the newly created SDP, with Roy Jenkins articulating the consensual wisdom, out into the far reaches of an increasingly left-wing Labour Party under Michael Foot.

The significant change from the stop–go policies of previous governments was to try to bring the money supply and the government deficit down over the medium term. This was what the much-mocked Medium Term Financial Strategy (MTFS), formally launched in 1980, was all about. The aim was to squeeze out inflation without squeezing industry to death through excessively high interest rates, while providing a stable background against which managers and wage bargainers could operate. The MTFS was a major step forward, but it did not work out as smoothly as that. Despite the debate about what particular monetary indicators did or did not show, it served well enough against inflation. Over the period when the MTFS was most consistently applied, inflation was brought down from a high point of 21.9 per cent in May 1980 to a low point of 2.4 per cent in the summer of 1986. Its failure was that it did not much influence economic behaviour. Unions priced their members out of jobs until high unemployment forced them to accept reality, and until workers stopped listening to trade union leaders.

The decisive year in economic policy was 1981. The March budget, which put up income tax in order to bring down government borrowing (and so interest rates) in the depths of a recession, was decisive. It was a break with post-war policy and with traditional Tory Party economic pragmatism. It marked a decisive break, too, with the habit of excessive borrowing that had grown up under the previous Labour Government – at least until Gordon Brown again let rip in the face of the banking crisis and recession in 2007–9. When the Thatcher Government took power, government borrowing stood at over 5 per cent of GDP. From 1981 it fell steadily. In Mrs Thatcher's last three years the Government was running a surplus and repaid £27 billion of debt.

That year was even more decisive in political terms. The September Cabinet reshuffle cleared the decks, both to protect what had been achieved in changing macroeconomic policy and also to permit embarkation on the crucial microeconomic, structural changes required.[9] Specifically, the replacement of Jim Prior with Norman Tebbit signalled the introduction of significant reforms of labour law which curbed trade union power and allowed industry, forcibly slimmed down by recession, to improve productivity. The key here was the 1982 Employment Act which substantially cut back trade union immunities – immunities which the Conservative Party from Disraeli onwards had either increased or accepted its opponents increasing. The overall approach was, in contrast to the failed blockbuster approach of Heath's Industrial Relations Act, described as being 'step by step'. The 1982 Act marked the biggest step. And it paved the way for other useful steps – notably the 1984 Trade Union Act, which required the use of secret ballots before strikes and for the election of union officials, and the 1988 Employment Act, which abolished what remained of the old union 'closed shop'.

The first signs of economic recovery came through in early 1982. Then the successful outcome of the Falklands War consolidated the upturn in Tory support. Of course, it might not have turned out like that. The Falklands crisis could at almost any stage of its nail-biting duration have finished Mrs Thatcher. There was also a threefold link with the economy. First, the fact that the public finances were in such good order allowed the war to be fought without any increases in planned public spending and without any run on the pound, all of which, like the victory itself, stood out in marked contrast to the Suez fiasco of 1956. Second, the outcome of the war made Government claims that the worst of the economic tribulations was over much more credible. If Mrs Thatcher was capable of beating the Argentines, the subliminal reckoning was, then the same iron-willed approach was applicable to domestic economic dangers too. Third, and finally, by helping secure her a second term, the Falklands War allowed the Government's economic reforms to take root. Lamentable leadership of the Opposition Labour Party by Michael Foot and the fact that the SDP–Liberal Alliance (as it turned out) split the anti-Conservative vote did the rest. The June 1983 election gave Mrs Thatcher an overall majority of 144.[10]

The second Thatcher Government was, in terms of achievement rather than drama, the most significant, despite having been fought on a rather tame manifesto. Nigel Lawson replaced Geoffrey Howe as Chancellor, while Howe went to the Foreign Office. Economic recovery continued and accelerated. Unemployment – having reached what a decade earlier would have been regarded as the unthinkable figure of over three million – gradually started to fall. Large-scale privatization of previously loss-making, state-owned industries proceeded at a swift pace, beginning with businesses operating in competitive markets and ending with the public utilities. Altogether some forty-four major businesses were privatized. Among the most notable sales were Cable and Wireless (1981), British Aerospace (1981), British Telecom (1984), British Gas (1986), British Airways (1987), Rolls-Royce (1987),

British Steel (1988), water (1989) and electricity (1990). Losses were replaced by profits, which benefited the taxpayer. Wider share ownership flowing from the sale of these companies supplemented the large social changes already introduced by the sale of council houses to their tenants under the 'right to buy'. Ministers started to explain the Government's aims less in terms of dry economic statistics and more by reference to the established Tory goal of a 'property-owning democracy'.

The fundamental shift in industry, however – involving also an historic reckoning with the Tories' old enemy, the National Union of Mineworkers – came with the defeat of the year-long coal miners' strike of 1984–5. There was an almost apocalyptic feel to events at this time. Organized violence on a scale unprecedented in twentieth-century Britain, with mass pickets attacking the police and police counter-charges, shocked the whole nation. The attempt by the Provisional IRA to assassinate the Prime Minister and her Cabinet in a deadly bomb blast at the Grand Hotel in Brighton, the party conference hotel, at 2.54 a.m. on 12 October 1984 was equally unprecedented and equally shocking.

Despite its successes, this second Thatcher term also witnessed some politically ominous developments. In Europe, 1985 saw Britain's agreement to the single market proposals which took shape in the form of the Single European Act: the powers now given to the European Commission would be used to go beyond what Mrs Thatcher had envisaged. In turn, her resentment would underlie the international quarrel and internal Government split over Europe. The following year saw a huge row, about the future of the Westland helicopter company, between Mrs Thatcher and Michael Heseltine, resulting in the latter's resignation and very nearly her own. From now on Heseltine pursued a cunning, remorseless and ultimately successful strategy to destabilize her. During that year and into 1987 the (later accelerating) trend towards looser financial policies began, with the result that inflation rose once more.[11] The same period saw the publication of proposals for a community charge, or poll tax, whose implementation would be the main cause of the unpopularity that finally helped sweep Mrs Thatcher out of Downing Street.

Cold War tension also reached a new pitch. Cruise missiles had been deployed in the face of Soviet threats in November 1983. There followed a dangerous stand-off. Neither side had much idea of what the other's intentions were. In fact, the Kremlin secretly buckled. Mikhail Gorbachev – declared by Mrs Thatcher to be a man with whom the West could 'do business' – accordingly succeeded as Soviet leader in March 1985. The seriousness of the Soviet foreign policy shift towards accommodation which underlay this change was not immediately apparent in the West. But close personal relations between the Soviet and British leaders during Mrs Thatcher's visit to the USSR in March 1987 certainly were. As with Macmillan, the perception did no electoral harm, and unlike with Macmillan, the closeness was not illusory. The June 1987 Conservative general election campaign which followed shortly was a fraught affair: Mrs Thatcher's nerves were bad, and she got on other people's even more than usual. But after a violent wobble, when the opinion polls looked shaky, the Tories won another large majority – of 101.[12]

The intention was to use the third Thatcher term to introduce reforms in the welfare state – promoting grant-maintained (independent state) schools, an internal market in the health service, and the break-up and improvement of sink housing estates.[13] It did not work out like this. Progress in devolving power to schools was more than countered by the way in which the new National Curriculum was used by interests within the Department of Education and the teaching profession to tie up schools in central regulation. The health service reforms – introducing self-governing hospitals and budgets for GPs, distinguishing between buyers and providers of health care, and having money follow the patients – were a start. But they were only a start, and a belated one, in reforming the system's all but unreformable structures. They, too, were to a large degree undermined by scare stories and obstruction. The attempt to devolve housing management from councils to charitable or private enterprises (via Housing Action Trusts or HATs) was similarly blocked when a mixture of judicial intervention and local campaigning ensured its frustration. Finally, of course, the equally successful tactics pursued by mainly Labour-controlled local authorities to sabotage the new community charge – pushing up spending and then blaming Mrs Thatcher and the poll tax for the bills – wrecked the whole reform programme.

The greatest step forward in domestic policy in the third Thatcher term was in tax reform. Nigel Lawson was the most successful tax-reforming Tory Chancellor Britain has had, though his reputation was – sadly for him, and no less sadly for the Government – destroyed by his failures in macroeconomic management. In 1984 Lawson had restructured corporate taxation, phasing out tax reliefs and cutting tax rates, so improving the direction and quality of business investment, while abolishing the investment income surcharge, which discriminated against savings. In 1988 he reshaped income tax in a still more radical fashion. The standard rate of income tax was reduced to 25 pence (from 27 per cent) and the top rate to 40 per cent (from 60 per cent). The reduction in the top rate was highly controversial and proved itself highly beneficial. Not only did it increase incentives for higher earners to stay and work in Britain, rather than seek relief through avoidance or absence; it also increased the flow of revenue into the Treasury – and even increased the share paid by those re-energized wealthier taxpayers.

Unfortunately, the tax changes of the 1988 budget, which can be numbered as among the Thatcher Government's most significant economic achievements, were swallowed up by, and possibly in the short run worsened, the overheating that now became very evident. From June 1988 the brakes were applied. Interest rates rose steadily. Political problems mounted too. The deteriorating economy, dramatically symbolized by Lawson's resignation in October 1989, weakened an otherwise highly defensible record. Mishandling of poll tax implementation outraged many traditional supporters, as well as provoking a full-scale riot in March 1990. The fall of the Berlin Wall in November 1989, which should have triumphantly vindicated Mrs Thatcher's Cold War statesmanship, did not, because it became submerged in a dispute about German re-unification, on which she was left looking out of touch and isolated.

More seriously, Britain was left behind the game on European Union matters, as the pace of integration sharply quickened. The timing could hardly have been worse. The shift in Conservative rhetoric from mild Euro-enthusiasm to hard-line Euroscepticism, marked by Mrs Thatcher's Bruges speech of September 1988 – though in the long run transformative of party and national opinion – proved too radical now for a weakened Government. It was easy in the autumn of 1990, when relations with the other European heads of government and the Commission broke down entirely, to portray the dispute as the result of one woman's pig-headed obsession, rather than a clash of philosophies and of national interests. The long-delayed entry of sterling into the European Exchange Rate Mechanism in October did not relieve either the pressure to accept a Single European currency or that to get rid of Mrs Thatcher. At home, the seething ambitions of frustrated Cabinet colleagues, opportunistically eyeing Michael Heseltine's non-stop leadership campaign, provided an inflammable backdrop; Geoffrey Howe's resignation on 1 November provided the spark. In the first round of the Conservative leadership election on 20 November Mrs Thatcher won against Heseltine, but without securing the necessary plurality of votes.[14] Two days later, under Cabinet pressure, she withdrew. Her – recently adopted – preferred successor, John Major, emerged as a unity candidate and duly defeated Heseltine. On 28 November Margaret Thatcher resigned as Prime Minister and was succeeded by Major.

John Major was in some respects a better politician than his predecessor.[15] He was even in some respects a more typical Conservative. His temperament was more even. He was good at perceiving an opponent's weakness. There was, initially at least, no large difference of policy between her and him. He was a typical middle-of-the-road Tory, who accepted the Thatcher achievement but disliked the Thatcher methods. Unfortunately, methods and achievement were more closely connected than he realized. Major's surprise election victory of 1992 can be attributed in roughly equal measure to public approval of the Thatcher record, relief at her recent removal, tentative satisfaction with her replacement, and profound distrust of the competence and character of Neil Kinnock, the Labour Party leader and alternative Prime Minister.

Major had, at least by the summer of 1992, an enviable political inheritance. The worst of the necessary economic pain, resulting from inflation and the high interest rates necessary to deal with it, seemed over. Michael Heseltine's ambitions were stilled and in large part satisfied. (He even became Deputy Prime Minister in 1995, apparently in exchange for supporting Major when the latter took the risk of putting himself up for re-election.) The left of the Tory Party were pacified by the execution of their Demon Queen. Mrs Thatcher's supporters, by and large, still considered Major their man, despite some doubts about his loyalty at crucial moments.

The Major Government's economic policy as a whole did not greatly differ from that of Mrs Thatcher. Spending and taxes rose somewhat, but borrowing was controlled, and deregulation and privatization continued. Privatization of the railways proved, politically speaking, a step too far. (It is one of the few privatizations that never subsequently gained acceptance.) But it was European policy that sank the Government.

Mrs Thatcher had been strategically correct about the nature of the European dilemma. Britain was, indeed, confronted by an emerging United States of Europe, and it had to accept it or fight it. What she had got wrong were tactics and timing – to the extent she had leeway in either. By contrast, Major, as he proved at the time of the Maastricht Treaty in 1991–2, was tactically adept but altogether lacking in strategic sense. Nor did he understand, more generally, that some issues of high policy are simply not amenable to splitting the difference. On these questions, leadership is required.[16]

Major was proud of his achievement at Maastricht and he seems to have been genuinely hurt, surprised and then very angry that others did not share that assessment. He could point to the two opt-outs – from economic and monetary union and from the regulations of the Social Chapter – which he had obtained for Britain.[17] The Government also tried to argue, less convincingly, for the merits of the principle of 'subsidiarity', built into the treaty, which was supposed to check centralization and even return powers to individual states, but which, naturally, did neither.[18] Major's critics, including Mrs Thatcher, could argue that he should have vetoed the treaty and prevented the creation of a structure – with social, judicial and defence implications as well as a new European citizenship of a new European Union – into which Britain would increasingly be drawn.[19]

The deep split on the Maastricht Treaty – a split magnified by the need to drive the measure through the House of Commons on a wafer-thin majority – irrecoverably fractured the parliamentary Conservative Party and, indeed, the Cabinet, though all its members, for their own purposes, stayed on board. The contrast between venomous disloyalty behind the scenes and public protestations of support was as corrosive of trust and as corrupting of respect as it always is.[20] The recessionary fall-out from an over-valued pound and too high interest rates, themselves flowing from Major's determination to keep sterling within the narrow band of the ERM – followed by sterling's chaotic exodus from the system on 16 September 1992 ('Black Wednesday') – irreversibly destroyed the Government's record for economic competence.[21] Major bought himself some time and room for manoeuvre when his quixotic decision to resign and stand for re-election as leader in June 1995 paid off. John Redwood's candidacy – in place of what might have been Michael Portillo's, had he not at the last minute funked the challenge – was not sufficiently credible to destroy a sitting Prime Minister.[22] And so Major went on.

The Conservative election defeat of 1997, when it came, was hardly unexpected; but the scale of the rout was. A long period with a single party in power tends to engender boredom, complacency, small- and large-scale corruption, cynicism, tiredness, reward of mediocrities and a depletion of talent. It did so in the eighteen years before 1997, as it did in the thirteen years before 1964. Moreover, in 1997 (even more than was true in 1964) there was a highly presentable Labour leader, in the form of Tony Blair, exuding moderation and promising 'change'. But the wipe-out clearly reflected more than personalities. The dispute about what it did reflect has bedevilled the Conservative Party to some extent ever since.

The consequences of that dispute must be considered in the next and final chapter of this book. But here it is necessary to offer some assessment of the unevenly virtuoso Thatcher performance, and its downbeat Major coda.

Mrs Thatcher was the first Conservative Prime Minister since Robert Peel to devote pride of place to economic policy over other aspects of governing.[23] After decades during which Conservative governments had favoured hiding behind a tariff wall or using soft money and subsidies to cushion change, she deliberately made

British industry and British workers face reality and adapt to it. Assisting and prodding her to do this were advisers like Alfred Sherman at the CPS and John Hoskyns and Alan Walters at Number Ten, who in turn drew on intellectual and technical arguments put outside government. Despite the setbacks and occasional (in retrospect, minor) deviations, there was a clear and consistent strategy to revive Britain's economic strength and so – something that mattered especially to the Prime Minister herself – to revive Britain's international standing. This strategy was overwhelmingly successful. An array of statistics, but above all the figures for relative productivity growth, confirm this success.[24] Britain's economy was restructured and Britain's economic decline began to be reversed. The most decisive political recognition of this is that Tony Blair made great public play both in opposition and in government of continuing the broad economic policies instituted by the Thatcher governments – though he and his successor later moved away from them.[25] Further confirmation of the rightness of those economic policies is provided by the fact that such policies, wherever and whenever they have been applied, have had similarly positive outcomes.[26]

Britain's revival was, of course, more than economic. Between 1980, when Ronald Reagan took up the US presidency, until 1988 when he left it, Britain under Mrs Thatcher wielded more influence in world affairs than under any Conservative leader since the Second World War. This was partly because of the close personal relationship between the two leaders, partly because of their remarkably similar ideological standpoint, and partly because of the enduring strategic interests of the US–UK 'special relationship'. It did not mean that they always agreed. There was a strong though always politely expressed disagreement about the role of the nuclear deterrent, which Reagan wished to abolish and Mrs Thatcher wished to retain and, if possible, strengthen. (They both agreed on the importance of the Strategic Defense Initiative, popularly known as 'Star Wars', but for rather different reasons.) There was also an uncomfortable spat over the US invasion of the Caribbean island of Grenada in 1983. But, despite such occasions on which real reluctance and hesitations reflected assessments of different national interests, the US and Britain supported each other in emergencies. Reagan, finally and importantly, 'tilted' US support away from neutrality to support for Britain in the Falklands War in 1982; and Mrs Thatcher, after initial dismay at the implications, gave the US permission to use British bases and airspace to bomb Colonel Gaddafi's Libya in 1986. The Reagan–Thatcher combination was notably triumphant in securing the key concessions that resulted in Western victory in the Cold War. Both leaders, of course, were unusually committed Cold Warriors. It is an oversimplification to suggest that America provided the brawns and Britain the brain – because Reagan was a great deal cleverer than his critics suggested – but there is something in this formulation. As a result, the names of Reagan and Thatcher are still specially venerated – along with the name of Pope John Paul II – in eastern Europe as liberators, which shows that those who have the deepest personal insight into what communism meant also have a very clear view of who actually helped them out of it.[27]

Britain's standing was certainly far higher during the period of Margaret Thatcher's premiership than under that of Macmillan – the nearest modern comparison. Moreover, unlike in the 1960s, it was based on a strengthened economy, a credible defence, and a restored international reputation (notably since the Falklands War). Mrs Thatcher dominated and frequently disrupted the international summits she attended with as much flair as General de Gaulle, while because of the closeness she had established with America she more frequently got her way. Some of the international causes she championed have been discredited, which has harmed her reputation and done no good to Britain's. Her long struggle to prevent international economic sanctions against white-ruled South Africa failed, though this outcome should be seen in the context of the changed conditions which accompanied the end of the Cold War. Europe is still limping towards institutionally closer union, though there is plenty of political disunion too, and Britain has some protection against the worst features of both. Margaret Thatcher's downfall will always be linked to her final defeats and humiliation in Europe. But despite the bad taste left behind as a result of her attitude towards German re-unification, she and Britain still emerged from the Cold War as prominent among the victors. On the wider international stage, the first Gulf War waged against Saddam Hussein in 1990–1, begun under Mrs Thatcher and continued under John Major, solidified Britain's position as the principal ally of the world's new hyper-power, the United States.

One can argue, of course, about whether the economic strategy was implemented at too high a price. One can debate whether Britain's emergence as America's chief ally put the country where it should have positioned itself. But it is difficult to argue that these achievements, taken as a whole, were anything other than startling, when compared with the record of other modern British governments – not least modern Conservative governments.

One of the commoner, but most quickly dated, arguments of Mrs Thatcher's critics was the suggestion that she was somehow not a Conservative at all. Her 'dogmatism' and the 'ideological' basis of her policies were common complaints from the more articulate Tory 'Wets'.[28] She was certainly, it is true, not in the mould of Baldwin or Macmillan. Although she had some affection for Disraeli, she never took seriously the social message which, with varying degrees of ignorance and insincerity, Tory politicians and propagandists down the years have affected to believe is his legacy. Mrs Thatcher's temperament was probably most similar to Winston Churchill's. Her instincts were probably most like Bonar Law's. But the most illuminating comparison is perhaps with the third Marquess of Salisbury.

Mrs Thatcher is the party's most successful leader, if one counts continuous years in Number Ten (eleven and a half) and election victories (three won, none lost). But Salisbury holds the record for total years in office – over thirteen and a half years as Prime Minister. Despite the obvious differences – sex, class, education, sophistication, energy – there are also certain similarities. Both were notably unsentimental and unsqueamish, unfashionably high-principled, imbued with strategic sense and common sense, and possessed of a hardness of mind and harshness of speech that people respected but found off-putting. In slightly different circumstances, either could have failed completely, which is another way of saying that both were lucky, and that so was the Conservative Party.

Far from damaging the Conservative Party, as was contended at the time, Margaret Thatcher rescued it and strengthened it. She was, herself, very much a partisan Tory. She even enjoyed the annual party conference, which most leaders detest. The Conservative Party organization, by and large, worked well during her leadership. In Cecil Parkinson (1981–3) and Norman Tebbit (1985–7) the party had two of its most high-profile, politically successful chairmen, and in Alistair McAlpine (1975–90) probably its most financially successful treasurer. The tendency to complacency within the organization was not absent. It never is when the party is in office. But the membership level, in so far as the unreliable figures meant much, was always apparently healthy. Indeed, one can now say that this period was the high-water mark of membership as the basis for party strength. With the rise of internet campaigning and the weakening of party allegiances in favour of single-issue politics, a new world has since dawned: coping with and adapting to it is work in progress. A start, though, was made in the 1980s in the professional use of targeted direct mail, using American models. Most importantly, in the 1980s the money kept on coming in. Despite hostility from the CBI in the early years, individual business leaders strongly backed the Thatcher policies. As a result of this largesse, the professionalism and number of the party's agents was perfectly satisfactory. There was also plenty of money for political advertising, and it was well spent. Saatchi & Saatchi's posters, press advertising and televised party political broadcasts broke new creative ground and put the Conservative Party's self-marketing far ahead of Labour's – an achievement in which Tim (now Lord) Bell had the key role.

Meanwhile, the Conservative Research Department operated more or less as required, though in the later 1980s and early 1990s it nurtured within it what would become a young cadre for a very different brand of politics.[29] Mrs Thatcher's greatest achievement in that sphere was perhaps to create a wave of enthusiasm on the party's youth wing, though this did sometimes lead to embarrassment.[30] The long-term effect of her influence on the young is to be found in the opinions of those entering Parliament twenty years after her departure, which can broadly be termed libertarian Eurosceptic. A survey in the spring of 2009 concluded that the likely new intake were 'to a large extent followers of Margaret Thatcher and her revolution'.[31]

Despite the trauma of Margaret Thatcher's defenestration, remarkably little harm was done in the immediate aftermath to the self-confidence of the wider party or the support it attracted. The grass roots had, after all, not been involved in the decision. Activists had cheered her wildly at her last conference, a month before her removal. The coup, when it came, was narrowly focused on the Cabinet.[32]

In fact, the wider party's problems began under John Major. He was popular – even after the terrible defeat of 1997 – with the party in the country. He had a good understanding of what they wanted to hear and feel. But it was not enough. The near wipe-out of the Conservative Party in local government, following the collapse of public support after 'Black Wednesday', destroyed the party's traditional base. After the 1996 local elections there were only 4,700 Conservative councillors compared with 5,100 Liberal Democrats and 10,800 Labour.[33] This hollowing out of the constituency parties undermined, probably irreversibly, the national Tory campaign in 1997, with well-known results.

Perhaps the most substantial criticism of Mrs Thatcher's own leadership is that she left no successor able to grasp, continue or develop her legacy. This is undeniable, and it was not just a matter of personnel. It went also to the root of what 'Thatcherism' was. There was always an uneasy jostling between the two strands of libertarianism and conservatism – the one focused on individuals, the other on institutions – in the philosophy she embodied and pro-pounded.[34] Not being a philosopher herself was, in this respect, usually a help to her. She was uninterested in nuances or hypothe-ses. Unlike Balfour, she just got on with the job, and did it all the better for that. Yet some Balfour-like reflection might have been in order, at least in the latter stages.[35] Too much of Thatcherism has had to be refined in retrospect, which always brings the danger of distortion.[36]

David Cameron's elevated origins and privileged education, portrayed here by Gerald Scarfe in 2010, present a problem for a government which stresses that 'we are all in this together'. Meanwhile, Nick Clegg plays the obstreperous glove-puppet.

18

CAMERON'S PARTY?

The 1997 general election delivered a blow to the Conservative Party from which it has still not fully recovered. This is less because of the scale of the defeat – great though that was – than because of the pathology of the defeated.[1] In any case, the swift resignation of John Major meant that mature reflection on what had gone so profoundly wrong was overtaken by the instant reactions required in a leadership election. No one truly shouldered the responsibility – Major did so only momentarily at the party conference, and then as a ruse to shift it quickly on to others.[2] No policy approach was singled out as inadequate. No political strategy was held deficient. And because the blame was unfocused, it spread, sapping confidence in the party, its record and even its identity.

At this point another identity crisis intervened: that of Michael Portillo. Portillo's loss of his Enfield Southgate seat radically unnerved him. Again, the worst damage was done not so much by the fact of the loss as by the reaction to it – first of Portillo himself, and then of his many admirers. Portillo was embarrassed about aspects of his personal life and shaken by the hatred he faced for his former right-wing rhetoric. For whatever mix of reasons, he deter-mined on a very public self-reinvention. This was then seized upon by his supporters in politics and the media as offering a prescription for the still undiagnosed ailments of the Conservative Party. Everything was to be challenged. Only counter-intuitive positions henceforth seemed clever. Self-effacement and self-abasement were the accepted marks of insight. Self-confidence was ridiculed as self-denial. Not since the 1960s has neophilia swept any institution as it did the Conservative Party at the turn of the twentieth and twenty-first centuries.[3]

This turbulent maelstrom, into which a flotsam of other ambitions and interests was quickly sucked, would have posed a severe challenge to any new party leader's authority. Of the potential leaders available, only Michael Howard – a successful Home Secretary in Major's otherwise unsuccessful Government, a moderate Eurosceptic, experienced but energetic, intelligent but pugnacious – probably had the qualities required at this perilous juncture. But his leadership campaign was holed below the water-line by his former colleague and now enemy, Ann Widdecombe, who attacked him as tainted by 'something of the night'. The electoral deal which Howard made with the young and ambitious William Hague also fell through, when Hague's allies persuaded him that he could win on his own.[4] They were, in fact, right about that, and Hague did win eventually – defeating an unholy alliance of Tory left and right when Kenneth Clarke and John Redwood joined forces.[5] Hague's circle were wrong, however, about his suit-ability to lead the Conservative Party at this juncture. He was chosen because he was young and thought to be quite right-wing and because he was not Kenneth Clarke. (Margaret Thatcher's last-minute public endorsement also greatly helped.) Hague would prove an able debater in the Commons, repeatedly outshining Tony Blair at the Dispatch Box. Perhaps he would have later made a good leader, had he waited and matured. But this was a young man in a hurry, surrounded by other young men, also in a hurry, who were untried and unseasoned and who thought they were a great deal cleverer than they were. Hague's period as leader was one of acute unhappiness and discredit for almost everyone concerned, and the party made no significant headway in the course of it.

Initially, Hague tried to press a message of change. With his fresh face, his Yorkshire vowels and his jauntily sported baseball cap, he could certainly claim to embody it. The party, too, felt it needed the change, though it did not appreciate the cap. It was very soon uneasy about more significant shifts. Picking a row with Norman Tebbit at the time of the new leader's first party conference proved a predictably bad idea. Signalling a dismissive break with the Thatcher years on the occasion of celebrations of the twentieth anniversary of her becoming Prime Minister proved a step too far for many more – including key members of the Shadow Cabinet, who were furious.[6] The pressure to advance ever further into this treacherous morass of proto-modernization had been sharply increased when Michael Portillo re-entered the Commons in November 1999 – just when Hague was starting to resile. Portillo became Shadow Chancellor, displacing Francis Maude (Angus's son, and previously a low-profile right-winger), who might have resented it, but who instead became Portillo's chief cheerleader. ('Cheer' is used metaphorically: furious tantrums were rather more in evidence.[7]) Maude would also be the principal link between Portillo's personal campaign and the wider modernizing movement which developed out of and eventually superseded it.

Disowning the past annoyed Tory core voters, without winning over new support. Nor did Mrs Thatcher stay obligingly silent as her legacy was dismissed. The party leadership shivered and shook at her interventions. It squirmed with embarrassment at her championing of ex-President Pinochet of Chile when he was arrested in 1998. It dreaded her politically incorrect remarks. This was not at all what the new Conservative Party was meant to be about. With the polls bad and criticism rife, there was a crisis of confidence. This was, effectively, the end of Hague Mark One.

In 1999–2000 Hague and his supporters sharply reversed course. There were no half-measures. They adopted, in so far as Portillo and Maude allowed, a crude right-wing populism, far cruder than anything practised by Mrs Thatcher. This consisted of sneers about the allegedly dominant 'liberal élite', promises of tax cuts whatever the state of the economy (the much mocked 'tax guarantee'), heavy emphasis on law and order and on restricting immigration, and, above all, a strident anti-European rhetoric, which stupidly and mendaciously claimed that only a Conservative victory at the 2001 general election would 'save the pound'. (In fact, both major parties, under pressure from Sir James Goldsmith's Referendum Party, had already pledged a referendum before any adoption of the euro.)

The arrival of Hague Mark Two saved his leadership, but only until the election defeat. This, when it came in 2001, was a body blow, as depressing in its way as 1997. The Conservatives gained just one seat overall (to 166). Labour were down 6 (to 412) from their tally in 1997. The Liberal Democrats won 52, their highest total since 1929. After that humiliation, and sick of the sniping, and like Major before him, Hague resigned immediately.[8] So there was, once more, no proper post mortem. (An insight into the vagaries of Tory politics at this juncture is provided by the fact that some of those who had been the most enthusiastic advocates of Tory populism quickly transmogrified, once it had failed, into high-minded critics of anything that even suggested it.[9]) One change that Hague did achieve, though its merits are debatable, was an alteration to the party leadership election rules in 1998 that restricted Conservative MPs to expressing their preferences in the early rounds, giving the final say to Conservative Party members in the country. This was an important factor in future events, because henceforth even MPs would be influenced in their choices by the knowledge that there were certain candidates whom the grass roots would be unlikely to tolerate.

The Conservative Party now passed through what must surely rank as the historic nadir of its fortunes. It was widely expected that Michael Portillo would win the ensuing leadership election. He stood. But he lost. Perhaps he did not in the end want the position, now it seemed within his grasp. Perhaps he had become alienated not merely from the Conservative Party, whose MPs and activists he wearily lectured and chided, but from politics altogether. In any case, while Portillo came out top in the first round, he then lost momentum for the second, and Iain Duncan Smith came out of the Tory undergrowth to defeat him in the third – by just one vote. IDS then decisively beat Kenneth Clarke in the final round, when the choice fell to party members, by 61 per cent to 39 per cent. This, however, was not the end of the party's woes. It was not even the beginning of the end.

Portillo himself flounced out of front-line politics and pursued a successful media career. But his followers joined forces with other alienated elements of the party to spread mayhem. Duncan Smith was entirely out of his depth. He was a natural backbencher. At this stage he was a single-issue man, known for his ceaseless campaigning against more powers for the European Union.[10] Yet on becoming leader he chose to talk about anything except Europe (on which the party was now, in fact, fairly united). He misunderstood his position. He could have been a respected transitional figure, stabilizing the position before handing over to someone abler. Instead, he tried to take on the mantle of change. It did not suit him. He had few loyal advisers, and they often gave bad advice. He preferred, anyway, to listen to the modernizers. They initially professed loyalty to him personally, but all the while they were redefining the party's agenda in a way that made IDS an anachronism, and finally an intolerable incubus.[11] Not only did he listen to them, he also appointed them to top positions. They then proceeded to let him down. Indeed, IDS was in receipt of a degree of publicly expressed contempt and disloyalty from his own people never previously shown towards a Tory party leader.[12] As time went by, he looked increasingly isolated and vulnerable. His standing with the parliamentary party was poor, because of his faltering performances against Tony Blair at Prime Minister's Questions. But it was the farce of the last party conference he addressed as leader, in 2003, that finished him. The false applause and arranged demonstrations of support were just too much. Once it was understood that Michael Howard was available to rescue the party's dignity, IDS was doomed. He was duly voted out by Tory MPs.

Howard was then elected unanimously in November 2003 when his main potential opponent, David Davis, withdrew. (It was, indeed, the condition of his taking over at all.) Howard now knocked sense into the party. He had the qualities required. He was a senior party man, dragged back out of the wilderness, a kind of metropolitan Cincinnatus. He had, importantly, good and long-standing personal links with many other senior Tories, not all of them from his own wing of the party.[13] He had gravitas. He was widely feared – even by Blair. The Tory factions were now aware that a return of order was needed if the party was to be in a state to fight the forthcoming election. Attention was also beginning to be drawn by a previously rapt media to the Labour Government's policy failures. The increasingly awful outcome of the Iraq War would only later draw these strands together. But opinion was at least starting to shift by the time of the 2005 election.

As with Hague in 2001, so with Howard in 2005, it was the people who advised on election strategy at the time who were later most vociferous in proclaiming the need for 'change' afterwards. (David Cameron himself drafted the 2005 Conservative manifesto.[14]) The Tory campaign was weakened not by the heavy emphasis placed on immigration, a key issue with the Conservative base and a source of concern for many others, but by its failure to say anything substantial about the economy, except to note the need for less debt. As a rule of thumb, it is impossible for the Conservatives to win elections unless they also win the economic argument. They did not now seriously engage in it. This omission reflected, in part, the priorities of the leader himself – a sound money man rather than a tax-cutter. Underlying the approach was also the belief that any talk of providing incentives through tax cuts would open the party up to accusations that it intended to cut spending on public services. No way was found or, indeed, sought, out of this self-imposed constraint. (The refusal to face up to it is one of the less widely remarked but most significant elements of continuity between the Howard and Cameron regimes.)

That said, the election result was not too bad.[15] Labour were on the way down, its majority dropping to 66 from 167, and its share of the vote to just 36.2 per cent. No previous Labour Government had suffered so sharp a loss of support during its term in office. Admittedly, the main beneficiaries in terms of vote share were the Liberal Democrats (who obtained 22.7 per cent of the vote and 62 seats), not the Conservatives (with 33.2 per cent and a net gain of 33 seats, giving the party 198). But stage one of Conservative recovery, the decay in Labour's support, was clearly well advanced. Stage two, a Conservative victory, was the likely result, given time – because the Conservative base had held, memories of the Tories in power would fade further, the already perceived inadequacies of the incoming Gordon Brown would assist, and the electoral system would do the rest. The shift in support now required for victory, though large, was not unthinkable. The 2005 election outcome provided, therefore, what had for so long been lacking – it provided hope.

But, again, there was no reflection, just a swift leadership election, with Michael Howard staying on only long enough to ensure that his favoured candidate, David Cameron, succeeded him to put into practice the modernizing agenda. Before describing the mechanics of how this occurred and what followed, it is worth considering in slightly greater depth the group which now gained a decisive hold on the party leadership, and which then proceeded to put through, with results that are as yet still uncertain, its own distinctive brand of revolution.[16]

The word 'revolution' is appropriate here, as is another: 'brand'. 'Branding', a process whose terminology and techniques are borrowed from marketing, was at one level what the modernization project was about. There was widespread acceptance that the Conservative Party's image was very bad by 1997, and had deteriorated since. There was also widespread acceptance that it needed to be fixed by experts. Within their different fields, the young modernizers claimed such expertise.[17] Their analysis was that the party's identity needed to be 'detoxified' or 'decontaminated'.[18]

Much attention was later paid to the social identity of the key figures – the number of Old Etonians, their fashionably relaxed lifestyles, the fact that they lived near each other and met socially, and other gossip-worthy features. At least as significant, however, was the number who had worked in the Conservative Research Department. There is, of course, nothing inherently surprising about that. From the late 1940s to the 1970s the CRD had been a natural recruiting ground for party talent. But the CRD has its own variety of *déformation professionnelle*.[19] Like marketing, it emphasizes technique rather than ideas.

Yet the modernizing project was not only a rebranding. It was also a revolution. This was not widely grasped within the party at the time.[20] The objective was, in fact, a total change in the Conservative Party, and not just a change in its appearance. This change would be imposed from the centre. Obstruction from the parliamentary party or the constituencies would be overridden. That required the removal of older MPs (unless they were fully part of the project) and, through the manipulation of selection processes, the substitution of socially liberal young people and representatives of ethnic and sexual minorities. It also implied – at different times and with variation between different modernizing sub-groups – the discarding of what were regarded as old shibboleths, such as commitment to a small state (a banned phrase), low taxes, business interests and hostility to Europe. In their place the emphasis was to be on concern for green issues, social and sexual equality, quality of life – GWB (General Well Being) rather than GNP (Gross National Product) – and on government's social functions and spending (above all, the NHS) rather than on government's security functions and spending (on defence or the police).[21] The fact that almost all of this, despite a few blue tints, was profoundly different from what the Conservative Party – let alone conservatism – had traditionally stood for is obvious. In fact, some key figures in this project had never been Conservative (let alone conservative). They hailed from the SDP.[22] Of the rest, hardly any had fond recollections of Conservative success. Most admired Tony Blair without reserve. They thought that he had provided an applicable template for Tory problems by the invention of New Labour. (When David Cameron declared that he considered himself the 'heir to Blair', he was only saying what these people hoped and desired.[23])

A comparison with three earlier, in some respects similar, movements within the Conservative Party is moderately instructive. The 'YMCA' group of MPs in the time of Baldwin in the 1920s – described in earlier chapters – were also young, rather embarrassed by the prevailing stuffy Tory image, keen to reposition themselves and the party away from big business and towards the left. But they did not (with the exception of that eccentric radical Harold Macmillan) offend the mainstream or seek to leave it. Their ultimate aim was power – their own and the party's – which they thought would be achieved by stressing a commitment to social improvement, most imaginatively through a 'property-owning democracy'.

More similar to the twenty-first-century modernizers were the Tory Reform Committee MPs and their associates in the 1940s. These were very self-conscious progressives. They were listened to then, as the modernizers were some half a century later, because the Tory Party was reeling from defeat at the hands of Labour. Yet there the similarities end. The Tory Reformers were, on occasion, considered a thorough nuisance by the party leadership.[24] But the Tory Reform Committee were also used by the leadership, as well as, when necessary, stopped or dropped or taught a lesson by it. They were always definitely in a minority, and the majority fought back hard. In any case, neither the Tory Reform Committee nor the One Nation Group which followed in its footsteps (with more results to show for itself) was ever more than a parliamentary pressure group. Neither was a commando unit intent on seizing the commanding heights. And when members did, individually, scale a peak or two, they obligingly left their ideological baggage and their collective loyalties back at base camp.

In some ways, today's Tory modernizing project has more in common with the Thatcherite movement than with any of these previous groups. This is not surprising, since a number of young radical Thatcherites performed key functions in the early stages of modernization, and they brought their mindsets with them. Like the modernizers, the thinkers and campaigners who backed Mrs Thatcher in the late 1970s unashamedly wanted to take over the party: otherwise, there would be no chance of changing the country's economic direction, which was the objective. So far, so similar; but it is not quite as far as it seems.

By contrast with the Thatcher revolution, the modernizing project lacks intellectual ballast. Some of those involved were and are extremely clever. They know the literature. But they have lacked a directing idea. Game theory, evolutionary biology and neurology have all been invoked to fill the void.[25] The fashionable American notion of 'nudge', described by its inventors as (that strange contradiction) 'libertarian paternalism', is one such example: it now energizes and perplexes the ministers and civil servants called upon to apply it.[26] More practically useful has been the creation of a well-funded and effective right-of-centre think tank, Policy Exchange. Yet 'modernization' itself remains an oddly empty revolution. It has no core doctrine. Its messages were assembled ad hoc from a mix of socially liberal assumptions and marketing research. And the result is usually embarrassment, when the practitioners are expected to defend the project against those for whom image enhancement is not enough. Hence the search for a modernizing Big Idea.

No one in the Thatcherite 1970s or 1980s felt that they needed to invent a big idea, or even to devise small ideas. The ideas were already in existence, as powerful ideas have a habit of being. The difficulty was in applying them. By contrast, David Cameron and his advisers have had to work in the opposite direction. They knew what they wanted to do. But they then had to try to explain why they were doing it in the first place. Like George H. W. Bush, they lacked the 'vision thing'; but, unlike John Major, they thought they needed it. After various earlier misfired shots, they devised the notion of the Big Society.[27]

David Cameron has said that the Big Society is more important to him than anything else in Government: that it is his 'mission'.[28] He is the more to be believed since as a slogan it is hardly a success. It is not widely understood, though when explained it seems to most people fair enough. Unfortunately, it is too diffuse to excite enthusiasm.[29] The Big Society involves – depending on the interpreter – localism, volunteering and deregulation.[30] It is in essence, though, yet another 'Third Way' strategy – in this case, a third way between the Scylla of Thatcherite individualism ('There is such a thing as society,' intones Cameron, as if Mrs Thatcher thought otherwise, which she did not) and the Charybdis of Big Government socialism.[31] Think-tank members, government officials, Conservative advisers, MPs and journalists have been drafted in to promote it. The fortunes of political figures are, apparently, made or broken by deemed commitment to it.[32] Yet, despite this, it is far from universally accepted that the Big Society is an idea whose time has come.[33]

David Cameron owes his leadership of the party to Michael Howard's patronage, David Davis's errors and his own talents, in roughly that order. Howard used his last reshuffle as leader to promote Cameron to shadow Education and George Osborne to shadow the Chancellor. (In fact, Howard seems initially to have preferred Osborne as his successor, but then to have settled for Cameron.[34]) The outgoing leader had become convinced that a complete overhaul of the party was required and that David Cameron alone could provide it. Liam Fox, the joint party chairman and Howard's former leadership campaign manager and PPS, and an obvious contender, was sidelined. David Davis, whom Howard disliked and distrusted, was still more conspicuously cold-shouldered. Cameron's fortunes duly rose. Howard hoped to have the rules of the leadership election changed so as to give the final say back to MPs – who, it was thought, were more likely to pick a candidate on the liberal wing than the activists, whom the modernizers saw as half the trouble. But this ploy failed. Not that it mattered in the end.[35]

Davis started off the leadership campaign as the favourite, with broad support across the parliamentary party. This turned out to be his undoing. He never developed a distinctive message, because he wanted to please everyone. He fell back in campaigning on his lowly social origins, in contrast to Cameron's upper-class background and Eton education. But inverted snobbery was not enough. Davis had, in any case, many old enemies. Then, at the crucial juncture – the 2005 party conference – he delivered a poorly received speech. For his part, Liam Fox was slow off the mark. Had he started his campaign earlier, he might have got into the final round. He did knock out Kenneth Clarke in the first. As a talented speaker, with a clear, populist message that appealed to the party faithful, who still had the final say, Fox might even then have beaten Cameron. Cameron, though, went up against Davis in the final round. David Cameron spoke well. He looked safe. He was polished. He was young and, despite his upbringing, he had an insight into proletarian culture. He thus represented hope against experience. And he won handsomely.[36]

Relatively little needs to be said of the years between 2005 and 2010. It is all too recent. Rhetoric and, to a lesser extent, policy shifted away from rugged capitalism and towards a more socially liberal identity. The leader did not devote much time to economics. Nor did the Shadow Chancellor, George Osborne, who busied himself with party strategy and finance. The assumption was that the economy was safe, and so largely irrelevant as an issue. Policy was kept in the softest focus. Green issues took centre stage. A tree replaced the torch of freedom as the party symbol. Much media coverage was obtained for the Cameron family's joys and (tragically real) sorrows, in a manner that no party leader, let alone Tory Party leader, had hitherto attempted. The guiding assumption was that the Conservative Party, not the Labour Government, was the problem, and so the Conservative Party had to change. The Tory image was too negative, too pessimistic, too unappreciative of modernity, too hostile to diversity. David Cameron cultivated his own image as the opposite. 'Let sunshine win the day!' he exhorted the party conference – and, whatever that meant, his audience seemed happy to go along.[37]

More than happy were sections of the media usually hostile to the Tories. To the *Guardian*, the *Independent* and, above all, the BBC, Cameron's message seemed uniquely sympathetic, and their coverage showed it. *The Times*, with its Blairites and Tory modernizers, was enthusiastic. The doubts of the *Telegraph* and *Mail* were muffled, because the owners and editors wanted to see the Conservatives back, and the back of Labour. Conservative commentators swooned even more than usual over the reigning party leader, with the exception of one or two unpersuadables. Events moved in the right direction. Blair was humiliatingly forced out. Brown's accession looked inevitable. An air of complacency descended on the Tory Party, which looked forward to early redivision of the spoils of office.

Unfortunately, when in June 2007 Gordon Brown actually stepped into Downing Street, the fragility of Cameron's position was exposed – though Brown's own fragilities later made up for that. Labour briefly leapt into a double-digit opinion poll lead. There was talk of an early election. This precipitated a full-scale Tory crisis. The wave of criticism took Cameron and his colleagues by surprise. But at that year's Conservative conference the leadership fought back effectively. George Osborne threw red meat to the party rank and file by pledging to take all except millionaires out of inheritance tax (a pledge that was not fulfilled). While Brown dithered, Cameron counter-attacked, and the moment passed. From now on, Labour could only lose.

The sudden prominence of economic policy, though, had found Cameron and Osborne struggling to cope. Until late in 2008, the party was pledged to match Labour's public spending plans and relied in summing up its approach on a confusing and increasingly unrealistic formula of 'sharing the proceeds of growth' (between tax cuts and spending increases). Then, after some public agonizing, Cameron denounced the deficit, promised spending cuts and announced an 'age of austerity'. But the polling evidence suggested that this stance was poorly received. So the party played down the deficit reduction plans, backed away from its promise of detailed spending reductions, and focused instead on the traditional Opposition pledge of eliminating 'waste'. This remained the line during the 2010 election campaign.

The Tory campaign itself was widely judged a failure.[38] When asked, 62 per cent of Conservative Party members deemed it 'poor', while just 20 per cent thought it 'good' or 'excellent'. This critical view was confirmed in a survey of Conservative parliamentary candidates. The campaign failed to highlight important populist issues – like immigration, on which the modernizers were squeamish; it was not credible on the economy; and it was, arguably, more 'presidential' – too focused on David Cameron – than was sensible in the British system. The worst mistake was to agree to Britain's first ever televised debates. These, as previous Conservative leaders and their advisers had grasped, served to give equal coverage to the third party, the Liberal Democrats, and so now provided a priceless opportunity for their leader, the smoothly plausible Nick Clegg. In the event, Liberal Democrat support fell back, and the party actually lost seats. But the final stage of the Tory campaign was taken up with frantic attacks on Clegg, rather than devoted to exposing the Labour Government's record. Such diversion of activity probably forfeited votes and seats.[39]

The Conservatives secured a swing against Labour of 5.1 per cent.[40] This was the third largest swing since 1945, and the party gained ninety-seven seats; but it was not enough. Cameron rejected the option of a minority Government and swiftly set out to form a coalition with the Liberal Democrats. He showed enthusiasm, rather than reluctance. Observers remarked on how much more at ease he was with the new Deputy Prime Minister, Nick Clegg, than with some of his own colleagues. Cameron portrayed the coalition as an ideal, not a necessity, and a welcome change to single-party government. It was, he told the Conservative conference, 'a shared way of trying to do business, reasonable debate, not tribal dividing lines, give and take, respect when you disagree, trust'.[41] The suspicion has duly grown among Tory MPs and party members that the leadership wishes, despite denials, to make coalition with the Liberal Democrats a permanent feature. Cameron's closest advisers and trusted senior figures such as Sir John Major have acted as sounding boards for that course.[42]

Which party has gained more from coalition is debatable. The Liberal Democrats had to sign up to an accelerated programme of budget deficit reduction and large spending cuts. They also accepted – with dire electoral impact – university tuition fees, levied at a much higher level. In principle, they also accepted the continuation of Britain's independent nuclear deterrent, though the postponement of the final decision on the Trident submarine upgrade means that this support will not be tested.

The Conservatives also made sacrifices. The promised cut in inheritance tax was dropped. The commitment to a 'United Kingdom Sovereignty Bill', intended to curb the inroads of European Union law, was diluted. The pledged 'Bill of Rights' intended to define in domestic law – and thus limit – 'human rights', as currently defined according to the European Convention on Human Rights through Tony Blair's 1998 Human Rights Act, has effectively been abandoned. Defence cuts replaced promised defence increases, while overseas aid was sharply increased. These priorities were always likely to prove politically risky, and indeed they have done so. There were repeated allegations that the Anglo-French-led campaign to overthrow Colonel Gaddafi's regime in Libya was hamstrung by shortages. Attempts to persuade the public of the merits of increased overseas aid have not gained traction.

In general, Cameron and his colleagues are felt to have shown too much concern for their coalition partners and too little for their own side. This was predictable, but the leadership seems not to have predicted it, and then not to wake up to it. One of Cameron's first acts as Prime Minister was to pick – and then lose – a fight to change the rules of the 1922 Committee, so as to allow ministers to vote. This was, apparently, a clumsy way of trying to ensure that the awkward squad did not get elected to the 1922 executive. It had the opposite effect: they now dominate it. The wider parliamentary party was already more fractious than one would expect. There were serious rebellions on a range of issues, involving not just the usual suspects but the new arrivals too. Trivia contributed. Resentment at the way in which the parliamentary expenses scandal was handled continued to fester. MPs complained that the whips demanded onerous attendance from Tories, while coddling Liberal Democrats. There was frustration about the lack of opportunities for promotion. (In response, large numbers of PPSs were appointed, but this is just the small beer of patronage.) Moves to reduce the number of MPs have threatened Tory discipline and morale.

The leadership's failure to take the party seriously in Parliament has been matched by lack of regard for the constituency stalwarts.[43] Candidates deemed favourable to Cameron's plans were pushed into winnable seats by the centre, overriding local wishes. There was nothing new about that. But it caused tensions. All was clearly not well out in the country. Party membership figures suggest a marked decline since David Cameron became leader.[44] The same lack of feel was manifest in the choice of the two party joint chairmen. One, Andrew (Lord) Feldman, a wealthy university friend of the Prime Minister's, is to keep the party financially afloat. The other, Baroness Warsi, given the sort of views she holds, may yet sink it.[45] Past party chairmen have – in Norman Tebbit's words – served as lightning conductors. But neither Lady Warsi nor Lord Feldman could protect the leadership from party trouble. And party trouble is the abiding headache of coalition government.

On this matter of living with (and, when necessary, escaping from) coalitions, the Conservative Party's history offers some useful insight. Disraeli famously observed, in December 1852, that 'England does not love coalitions'. Disraeli was wrong about many things, and this may be one of them. He was certainly wrong when he predicted: 'Coalitions, although successful, have always found this, that their triumph has been brief.'[46] The coalition of Peelites and Liberals which confronted him that night would, indeed, not last long in government, discredited by its handling of the Crimean War. But between the mid-1880s and 1945 Britain was consistently, with the exception of a decade or so, governed by Conservative-led (or at least Conservative-dominated) parliamentary coalitions of one sort or another.[47] There is also some evidence, given the size of the third party vote since the 1970s, of an underlying return to that system, which – the argument goes – should strengthen the case for electoral reform.[48] (The dismal polling of the Liberal Democrats under Nick Clegg may yet demolish the credibility of that one.)

In general, the Tories as a party have probably benefited from coalition, whereas the Liberals have not. In the late nineteenth century Salisbury cleverly manipulated the Liberal Unionists into the Conservative fold while making remarkably few concessions to them. The case of the National Government from 1931 to 1940 is less clear-cut. It was doubtless useful for the Conservatives to be able to shelter behind National Labour and, to a somewhat lesser extent, the National Liberals. But there was a cost. Coalitions favour safety first, and safety-seeking leaders shrink from radical remedies. Muddling through in the face of failure acquires an irresistible attraction. Unremedied economic decline and the pursuit of appeasement arguably hurt the country more than they did the Conservatives – but the Conservatives suffered too, in the end.

The wartime coalitions of 1915–18 and 1940–5 were, naturally, different. Both were responses to grave and present danger. But they had different political outcomes: the Conservatives emerged strengthened from the First World War and weakened from the Second. It is the attempt to prolong and, indeed, renew the First World War coalition with Lloyd George's National Liberals which is most suggestive.

The events that led to the end of the coalition, the fall of Lloyd George and the defenestration of Austen Chamberlain as Conservative Party leader in 1922 have been discussed earlier in this book. There are some parallels with conditions in the parliamentary Conservative Party today. There are also large differences. So far, the differences still outweigh the parallels. The present governing coalition is led by a Conservative, not a Liberal. David Cameron is a much better politician than Austen Chamberlain was. And Nick Clegg is less obnoxious – as well as far less significant – than Lloyd George. The parallels would seem closer if, as in 1922, it were concluded that an out-of-touch group of senior ministers wanted to force the party to fight a further election on a common slate with its coalition partners, and possibly merge with them. At that point, the frustrations of those denied promotion could coalesce with the resentment of MPs (fearing the loss of their seats) and draw in the anger of constituency activists. The decisive loss of the referendum of 5 May 2011 on the alternative vote, which was seen as ending the prospect of any move to proportional representation (of any kind) for at least a generation, has reduced the fears of Conservative backbenchers that they may be forced into a permanent shotgun marriage with the Liberal Democrats. It thus also relieved the pressure on David Cameron, whose position if AV had gone through would have been at some risk from furious Tory MPs with nothing to lose by revolt. That said, the position is far from stable. It is still possible, for example, that anger with the Liberal Democrats, if they were to be seen as standing in the way of a strong, popular reaction against the August riots, could threaten the coalition. The European issue remains explosive and could become more so. At some point, Mr Cameron and his closest colleagues will probably have to face the choice they most dread: whether to side with the Conservative Party on the back benches and in the country, or whether to cling to their coalition partners. On this, at least, party history offers a warning which any party leader would be foolish to ignore.

Whether the history offers any other useful insights or tips to a modern Conservative leader is less clear. At a superficial level, it may appear to do so. It is easy enough to say that (*pace* Peel) a leader should avoid splits in his own party and instead, like Salisbury, take advantages of splits in others. This notional leader must master the Commons (like Disraeli). He should be strategically decisive (as Mrs Thatcher was, and as Major was not). He should not allow a single issue to preoccupy the party so that other matters of broader interest are forgotten – as happened with tariff reform in the 1920s and Europe, more debatably, in the 1990s. He should be prepared for wars (as Baldwin and Neville Chamberlain were not), and win any that have to be fought (as Churchill did) – while keeping a wary eye on home front developments (as Churchill failed to do). He should try to ensure that the economic and political cycles remain correctly synchronized (as Macmillan largely did). At the same time, he should not forget that governments are principally judged on economic competence, not just passing prosperity (as, by contrast with Macmillan, Cameron and Osborne seem to understand). But all such sage exhortations overlook the inexorable fact that governments, by and large, come to power expecting one set of problems only to be faced with quite another. Edward Heath's administration was, in the sense of detailed policy work, probably better prepared than any other. It was also probably the least successful.

As to the periods of greatest achievement, and the greatest leaders, opinions will surely differ. Baldwin's long tenure of power (in and out of coalition) counts as a political but hardly a national triumph, given the economic and diplomatic record. Baldwin had a kind of magic in his day, though it soon faded. Winston Churchill's national leadership in the country's 'Finest Hour' brooks no comparison; but his failures as a party politician – in either party – were legion, and his legacy is mixed.

On higher plinths, within the Tory pantheon, stand three other figures. Disraeli has often been misunderstood, his governmental achievement exaggerated, his views and priorities distorted. But without him the party would not be what it is. He was the greatest Leader of the Opposition, and the greatest weaver of national legend. These count for much. His successor, Salisbury, can lay still better claim – though he would think it vulgar – to both national and political laurels. By the measure of years in office, support widened, enemies defeated, allies absorbed, and great power ruthlessly but intelligently wielded, Salisbury was surely the greatest Tory master of his craft. And it is perhaps reassuring for those who are conservative, as well as just Conservative, that Salisbury himself was both. But in modern times, and therefore different circumstances, Margaret Thatcher's achievement in winning three elections, remoulding the economy and re-establishing the country's reputation is unlikely to be eclipsed. Her legacy is fresh and still difficult to evaluate. But she, too, fundamentally altered the base of the Tory Party; and she altered the shape of British politics even more.

Disraeli, the Jewish outsider who championed traditional institutions, Salisbury, the fastidious aristocrat who won over the bourgeoisie, and Thatcher, the woman who crushed the unions, the Argentine Junta and most of the Cabinet, and restored the economy to health, are all, in their different ways, completely surprising. It matters to the country that the Conservative Party should retain its capacity to produce surprises, and so harness the eccentric, distinctive qualities of British national greatness.

CHRONOLOGY

1770	Edmund Burke's *Thoughts on the Cause of the Present Discontents*
1783	William Pitt the Younger becomes Prime Minister
1789	French Revolution begins
1790	Burke's *Reflections on the Revolution in France*
1794	The Duke of Portland Whigs join Pitt's ministry
1800	Act of Union with Ireland
1812–27	Lord Liverpool's ministry
1815	Battle of Waterloo and Congress of Vienna
1819	Peterloo Massacre
1820	Death of George III and succession of George IV
1822	Suicide of Lord Castlereagh
1827	George Canning's ministry
1828	Duke of Wellington becomes Prime Minister
1830	Death of George IV and succession of William IV
1830	Overthrow of Charles X of France
1832	Great Reform Act
1834	Robert Peel's first Government
1837	Death of William IV and accession of Victoria
1841	Peel's second Government
1846	Repeal of the Corn Laws and resignation of Peel
1848	Revolution in France, fall of the July Monarchy
1850	Death of Peel

1852	Derby's first Government
1853–6	Crimean War
1858	Derby's second Government
1865	Death of Palmerston
1866	Derby's third Government
1867	Second Reform Bill enacted by Conservatives
1868	Benjamin Disraeli succeeds Derby as Prime Minister
1869	Death of Derby
1870–1	Franco–Prussian War
1874	Disraeli succeeds Gladstone as Prime Minister
1876	Bulgarian Atrocity agitation
1878	Congress of Berlin
1880	Conservative defeat in general election
1881	Death of Disraeli
1884	Third Reform Act
1885	Salisbury's first ('caretaker') Government
1886	Salisbury's second Government (with Liberal Unionist support) to 1892
1895	Salisbury's third Government (henceforth in Coalition with the Liberal Unionists) to 1900
1899–1902	(Second) Boer War
1900	Conservatives win 'Khaki Election': Salisbury's fourth Government (to 1902)
1901	Death of Victoria and accession of Edward VII
1902	Arthur Balfour becomes Prime Minister
1903	Death of Salisbury
1906	Heavy Conservative defeat in general election; death of Chamberlain
1910	Death of Edward VII and accession of George V; two general elections
1911	Balfour replaced as Conservative leader by Bonar Law
1914	First World War begins
1915	Conservatives enter Coalition Government
1916	David Lloyd George becomes Prime Minister
1918	First World War ends; 'Coupon' general election won by Coalition
1921	Law resigns as Conservative leader, succeeded by Austen Chamberlain
1922	Conservative Party revolt against Lloyd George and Coalition leaders; Chamberlain steps down as party leader; Law becomes leader again and Prime Minister, and wins general election
1923	Law succeeded as Prime Minister by Stanley Baldwin;

	Conservatives lose general election; minority Labour Government takes office under Ramsay MacDonald; death of Law
1924	Conservative landslide in general election; Baldwin again becomes Prime Minister
1925	Locarno Treaties
1926	General Strike
1929	Conservative defeat at general election, MacDonald's second Government; in US, Wall Street Crash
1931	Formation of National Government under MacDonald; Conservative/National Government landslide in general election
1933	Hitler becomes German Chancellor
1935	Baldwin begins third term as Prime Minister; Conservative/National Government election victory; Hoare–Laval Pact; Peace Ballot
1936	German troops re-occupy the Rhineland; death of George V; accession and abdication of Edward VIII, succeeded by George VI
1937	Neville Chamberlain succeeds Baldwin as Prime Minister
1938	Munich Conference
1939	Prague coup; German attack on Poland; Second World War begins; Winston Churchill joins the Cabinet
1940	Churchill replaces Chamberlain as Prime Minister; Churchill becomes Conservative party leader; death of Chamberlain
1945	Victory in Europe; heavy Conservative defeat in general election
1946	Churchill's 'Iron Curtain' speech in Fulton, Missouri
1950	Labour returned in general election with small majority
1951	Conservative general election victory; Churchill again becomes Prime Minister
1955	Anthony Eden succeeds Churchill as Prime Minister; Conservative general election victory
1956	Suez crisis
1957	Harold Macmillan succeeds Eden as Prime Minister
1958	Resignation of Peter Thorneycroft, Enoch Powell and Nigel Birch ('little local difficulties')
1959	Conservative victory in general election
1960	Macmillan's 'Wind of Change' speech
1963	President de Gaulle vetoes British entry into the Common Market; Profumo scandal; Macmillan resigns and is succeeded by Lord Home (Alec Douglas-Home)

1964	Conservative defeat in general election
1965	Edward Heath becomes Conservative leader
1966	Conservative defeat in general election
1968	Powell's speech on immigration in Birmingham
1970	Conservative victory in general election; Heath becomes Prime Minister
1973	Britain joins the EEC
1974	Conservative defeats in general elections (February and October)
1975	Margaret Thatcher becomes Conservative leader; referendum on EEC membership
1979	Conservative victory in general election; Mrs Thatcher becomes Prime Minister
1982	Falklands War
1983	Conservative victory in general election
1984	Provisional IRA bomb in Brighton during Conservative party conference
1984–5	National miners' strike
1987	Conservative victory in general election
1988	Thatcher's Bruges speech on Europe
1990	Sterling joins the ERM; Thatcher replaced as Conservative leader and Prime Minister by John Major
1992	Conservative victory in general election
1995	Major resigns as party leader and is re-elected
1997	Heavy Conservative defeat in general election; Tony Blair becomes Prime Minister; Major replaced as Conservative Leader by William Hague
2001	Conservative defeat in general election; Hague succeeded as Conservative leader by Iain Duncan Smith
2003	Duncan Smith replaced as Conservative leader by Michael Howard
2005	Conservative defeat in general election; Howard succeeded as party leader by David Cameron
2007	Gordon Brown succeeds Blair as Labour Prime Minister
2010	General election; Cameron becomes Prime Minister, leading a Conservative–Liberal Democrat Coalition Government

NOTES

Introduction

1 See listed in the bibliography the individual works by Robert Stewart (Peel and Derby – one volume), Richard Shannon (Disraeli and Salisbury – two volumes) and John Ramsden (from Balfour to Heath – three volumes).

2 Robert Blake, *The Conservative Party from Peel to Churchill* (London: Eyre & Spottiswoode, 1970); see also John Ramsden, *An Appetite for Power: A History of the Conservative Party since 1930* (London: Harper Collins, 1998).

3 I have also made much use of that magnificent source, the *Oxford Dictionary of National Biography* (Oxford: Oxford University Press, 2004–; hereafter *Oxford DNB*), as the bibliography shows.

4 Michael Oakeshott, 'On Being Conservative', in *Rationalism in Politics and Other Essays* (London: Methuen, 1962), p. 98. Oakeshott was uninterested in party politics, at least in later life, and though he probably voted Conservative he refused the offer of appointment as a Companion of Honour under Margaret Thatcher, because he did not wish to be considered political.

Chapter 1: Tory Beginnings

1 Edmund Burke, *The Writings and Speeches of Edmund Burke*, vol. 8: *The French Revolution 1790–1794*, ed. L. G. Mitchell (Oxford: Clarendon Press, 1990), p. 83.

2 Benjamin Disraeli, *Sybil or The Two Nations* (Oxford: Oxford University Press, 2008), pp. 272–3. I standardize or, where necessary, modernize

spelling and punctuation. I also use capitals for Tory and Toryism, whereas many contemporaries and some modern historians use lower-case.

3 Roger Scruton, *A Dictionary of Political Thought* (London: Macmillan, 1996), pp. 552, 587.

4 Charles I's speech from the scaffold of 30 Jan. 1649, in David Lagomarsino and Charles J. Wood, eds, *The Trial of Charles I: A Documentary History* (Hanover: University Press of New England, 1989), p. 142 (emphasis added).

5 See Roger Scruton, *The Meaning of Conservatism* (London: Penguin, 1980), pp. 27–35.

6 'Unquestionably there was at the Revolution, in the person of King William, a small and a temporary deviation from the strict order of regular hereditary succession': Burke, *Writings and Speeches*, vol. 8: *The French Revolution 1790–1794*, p. 68.

7 See for all this J. C. D. Clark, 'A General Theory of Party, Opposition and Government, 1688–1832', *Historical Journal*, 23/2 (1980), pp. 295–325.

8 The King's refusal to agree to the abolition of the Anglican episcopacy was, indeed, the immediate cause of his trial.

9 Keith Feiling, *A History of the Tory Party 1640–1714* (Oxford: Clarendon Press, 1924), pp. 24, 42.

10 H. T. Dickinson, *Bolingbroke* (London: Constable, 1970), pp. 17–23, 309–11. See also H. T. Dickinson, 'Henry St John, first Viscount Bolingbroke (1678–1751)', *Oxford DNB*.

11 Benjamin Disraeli, 'Vindication of the English Constitution in a Letter to a Noble and Learned Lord by Disraeli the Younger', in *Whigs and Whiggism: Political Writings*, ed. William Hutcheon (London: John Murray, 1913), pp. 210–25.

12 F. P. Lock, *Edmund Burke*, vol. 1: *1730–1784* (Oxford: Clarendon Press, 2008), pp. 82–5. See also Burke, 'A Vindication of Natural Society' (1756), in *The Writings and Speeches of Edmund Burke*, vol. 1: *The Early Writings*, ed. T. O. McCloughlin and James J. Boulton (Oxford: Clarendon Press, 1997), pp. 132–84. St John's works had been published posthumously in 1754 so Burke was not at all tilting at historic windmills when he wrote. Burke's rhetorical question is from the *Reflections* (*Writings and Speeches*, vol. 8: *The French Revolution*, p. 140).

13 See the assessment of Isaac Kramnick, *Bolingbroke and his Circle: The Politics of Nostalgia in the Age of Walpole* (London: Oxford University Press, 1968), pp. 264–265.

14 Henry Fielding, *The History of Tom Jones, a Foundling*, in *The Works of Henry Fielding Esq.*, ed. Leslie Stephen, vol. 1 (London: Smith, Elder, 1882), p. 251.

15 J. C. D. Clark, 'The Heartfelt Toryism of Dr. Johnson', *Times Literary*

Supplement, 14 Oct. 1994, pp. 17–18; J. C. D. Clark, *Samuel Johnson: Literature, Religion and English Cultural Politics from the Restoration to Romanticism* (Cambridge: Cambridge University Press, 1994), pp. 141–210.

16 Namier's thesis, supported by minute prosopographical analysis of members of the mid-eighteenth-century House of Commons, downplays (though it does not logically negate) the role of party and emphasizes instead that of three groups – royal servants, independent country gentlemen and the small number of political professionals. For an account of how well the thesis has stood the test of time, see Linda Colley, *Lewis Namier* (London: Weidenfeld & Nicolson, 1989), pp. 53–89.

17 Edmund Burke, *The Writings and Speeches of Edmund Burke*, vol. 2: *Party, Parliament, and the American Crisis*, ed. Paul Langford (Oxford: Clarendon Press, 1981), p. 317.

18 Ibid., p. 314.

19 Rockingham's first ministry (1765–6) was also short-lived.

20 See William Hague, *William Pitt the Younger* (London: Harper Perennial, 2005), pp. 136–74.

21 For example, T. E. Kebbel, *A History of Toryism: From the Accession of Mr. Pitt to Power in 1783 to the Death of Lord Beaconsfield in 1881* (London: W. H. Allen, 1886): 'The Conservative Party of the present day still runs upon the old lines which were traced out by the Younger Pitt' (p. 2).

22 Burke was not the only, though he was the most interesting and influential, British intellectual critic of the Revolution: T. P. Schofield, 'Conservative Political Thought in Britain in Response to the French Revolution', *Historical Journal*, 29/3 (1986), pp. 601–22.

23 Richard Pares, *King George III and the Politicians* (Oxford: Clarendon Press, 1953), p. 194.

24 Burke had a particular dislike of the Unitarians, whom he regarded as out to subvert Christianity. The fact that some of their leaders, such as Richard Price, against whom Burke launched his great philippic, were also agitating for what Burke suspected was republicanism just added to the flames.

25 How Dr Johnson would have judged the politics of the later Burke – the Burke of the campaign against the French Revolution – is unclear, Johnson having died in 1784.

26 Edmund Burke, 'Speech at the Conclusion of the Poll', 3 Nov. 1774, in *The Writings and Speeches of Edmund Burke*, vol. 3: *Party, Parliament, and the American War 1774–1780*, ed. W. M. Elofson and John A. Woods (Oxford: Clarendon Press, 1996), p. 69.

27 L. B. Namier, 'The Character of Burke', *The Spectator*, 19 Dec. 1958, pp. 395–6.

28 This is the substance of Burke's pamphlet *Appeal from the New to the Old Whigs* (1791), but Burke's method of answering his opponents – a comparison with the arguments of the Whigs at the trial of the polemical Tory cleric Henry Sacheverell for seditious libel (1710) – was not particularly well chosen. For an explanation of Burke's approach, see F. P. Lock, *Edmund Burke*, vol. 2, *1784–1797* (Oxford: Clarendon Press, 2006), pp. 380–7.

29 John Ehrman, *The Younger Pitt*, vol. 2: *The Reluctant Transition* (London: Constable, 1983), p. 80.

30 J. J. Sack, 'The Memory of Burke and the Memory of Pitt: English Conservatism Confronts its Past', *Historical Journal*, 30/3 (1987), pp. 623–40.

31 Edmund Burke, 'First Letter on a Regicide Peace', in *The Writings and Speeches of Edmund Burke*, vol. 9, part 1: *The Revolutionary War*, ed. R. B. McDowell (Oxford: Clarendon Press, 1991), p. 199.

32 Burke, *Writings and Speeches*, vol. 8: *The French Revolution 1790–1794*, p. 138.

33 This point is regularly misrepresented by Conservative and even non-Conservative politicians. Burke is talking of a man's social status, not the local conditions in which he lives. His is a social not a communitarian point; a justification of class, not a prefiguring of the 'Big Society' – which does not, of course, preclude the idea's extension into other spheres. The full passage runs: 'Turbulent, discontented men of quality, in proportion as they are puffed up with personal pride and arrogance, generally despise their own order. One of the first symptoms they discover of a selfish and mischievous ambition is a profligate disregard of a dignity which they partake with others. To be attached to the subdivision, to love the little platoon we belong to in society, is the first principle (the germ as it were) of public affections. It is the first link in the series by which we proceed towards a love of our country and to mankind' (Burke, *Writings and Speeches*, vol. 8: *The French Revolution 1790–1794*, p. 97).

34 Burke regards man as a 'religious animal', but he is a sociologist of religion rather than a Christian zealot. For example, he regarded, with greater enthusiasm than knowledge, Hinduism in India as performing a similar role to Anglican Protestantism in England and (Gallican) Catholicism in France (Lock, *Edmund Burke*, vol. 2, p. 164).

35 For example, Russell Kirk's 'Summary' in Peter J. Stanlis, ed., *The Relevance of Edmund Burke* (New York: P. J. Kennedy & Sons, 1964): 'Thus in our own time of troubles, when the role of America is so much like that of Britain in the French Revolution, America and the civilization of which America is a part turn to Burke for normative understanding' (p. 133).

36 For example, Hernando de Soto, *The Mystery of Capital: Why Capitalism Triumphs in the West and Fails Everywhere Else* (London: Bantam, 2000). The book's thesis is that lack of secure property rights is the fundamental cause of underdevelopment.

37 Burke, 'First Letter on a Regicide Peace', p. 242.

38 Burke, *Writings and Speeches*, vol. 8: *The French Revolution 1790–1794*, p. 72.

39 Ibid., pp. 101, 130. Burke was ferociously attacked for the 'swinish multitude'.

40 Frank O'Gorman, *Edmund Burke: His Political Philosophy* (London: George Allen & Unwin, 1973), p. 37.

41 Asa Briggs, *The Age of Improvement 1783–1867* (London: Longman, 1971), pp. 134–47.

42 Burke, *Writings and Speeches*, vol. 8: *The French Revolution 1790–1794*, p. 146.

43 The Test Act of 1673 required all office-holders and members of the House of Commons to take an oath against the *de fide* Catholic doctrine of transubstantiation, and an Act of 1678 extended this stipulation to peers. Other aspects of the discriminatory system against Catholics through the penal code had largely been ameliorated or removed.

44 See the survey by R. F. Foster, 'Ascendancy and Union', in R. F. Foster, ed., *The Oxford History of Ireland* (Oxford: Oxford University Press, 2001), pp. 134–73.

45 Boyd Hilton, *A Mad, Bad, and Dangerous People? England 1783–1846* (Oxford: Clarendon Press, 2006), pp. 195–6. Even then, Toryism cannot be taken as a scientifically precise description of the anti-Catholic right: for example, Lords Newcastle and Eldon, two of that group's most important members, both called themselves Whigs.

46 Robert Stewart, *The Foundation of the Conservative Party 1830–1867* (London: Longman, 1978), pp. 15–18.

47 See W. H. Greenleaf, *The British Political Tradition*, vol. 2: *The Ideological Heritage* (London: Methuen, 1983), pp. 19–102.

48 Hilton, *Mad, Bad, and Dangerous People?*, pp. 314–28.

49 Charles Greville, *The Greville Memoirs: A Journal of the Reigns of King George IV and King William IV by the Late Charles Greville, Esq., Clerk of the Council to the Sovereign*, ed. Henry Reeve, vol. 1 (London: Longmans, Green, 1875), p. 122.

50 Benjamin Disraeli, *Coningsby* (Dublin: Nonsuch, 2007), p. 77. John Williams, Dean of Westminster and later Bishop of Lincoln, was Lord Keeper of the Great Seal under James I.

51 Harriett Arbuthnot, *The Journals of Mrs. Arbuthnot 1820–1832*, ed. Francis Bamford and the Duke of Wellington (London: Macmillan,

1950), vol. 2, pp. 140–1. Winston Churchill was also a great weeper.

52 Norman Gash, *Lord Liverpool: The Life and Political Career of Robert Banks Jenkinson, Second Earl of Liverpool 1770–1825* (London: Weidenfeld & Nicolson, 1984), p. 251. Gash's biography and his essay 'Robert Banks Jenkinson, second earl of Liverpool (1770–1828)', *Oxford DNB*, are the factual sources for what follows unless otherwise indicated.

53 Hilton, *Mad, Bad, and Dangerous People?*, p. 200.

54 Ministers acknowledged that the local authorities had overreacted but felt they must not be undermined. The Acts were in the circumstances quite mild and partly based on Pitt's earlier legislation: they limited public meetings, increased the penalties against blasphemy and seditious libel, and increased stamp duty on newspapers and pamphlets (ibid., p. 252).

55 Although from now on the term 'Prime Minister' is used for convenience, it was not current until much later. Indeed, the first time that a serving British First Lord of the Treasury so signed himself in a public document was when Disraeli signed the treaty concluding the Congress of Berlin in 1878.

56 See Derek Beales, 'George Canning (1770–1827)', *Oxford DNB*, on which what follows is based, unless otherwise signalled.

57 Greville, *Memoirs: George IV and William IV*, vol. 1, p. 107.

58 In the 1810s the *Edinburgh Review* had 13,500 subscribers and the *Quarterly Review* 14,000 – very high circulations for the day. See Jeremy Black, *The English Press 1621–1861* (London: Sutton, 2001), p. 199.

59 From 'New Morality', published in the *Anti-Jacobin*, quoted in Wendy Hinde, *George Canning* (London: Collins, 1973), p. 62. Canning's friend J. H. Frere also wrote part of it. I have slightly modernized and simplified the punctuation.

60 For comparison of the black legend with reality, see John W. Derry, *Castlereagh* (London: Allen Lane, 1971), pp. 1–25. There is no full length, authoritative biography of Castlereagh, to complete the account by H. Montgomery Hyde, *The Rise of Castlereagh* (London: Macmillan, 1933).

61 The failure of the expedition to the Dutch island of Walcheren in 1809 – several thousand British troops died of malaria by the time of the force's humiliating withdrawal – was, in fact, equally the fault of the politicians and the military.

62 Giles Hunt, *The Duel: Castlereagh, Canning and Deadly Cabinet Rivalry* (London: I. B. Tauris, 2008), pp. 109–54. For the evidence that Castlereagh may now and later have been suffering from syphilis acquired at Cambridge, see ibid., appendix 1, pp. 187–91.

63 Harold Temperley, *The Foreign Policy of Canning 1822–1827: England, the Neo-Holy Alliance and the New World* (London: G. Bell & Sons, 1925),

pp. 447–8. Castlereagh may have had more sympathy with the Holy Alliance powers than did Canning – at least, those powers thought so – but he would not have substantially dissented from Canning's approach, as expressed to his cousin Stratford in 1824: 'Great Britain maintains a policy of her own, suited to her position and constitution. She will be no party to a general interference in the concerns of other states; though prepared to intervene on *special* concerns in her opinion justifying such interference.'

64 Cf. Greville, *Memoirs: George IV and William IV*, vol. 1, p. 19.
65 Arbuthnot, *Journals*, vol. 1, p. 179.
66 Greville, *Memoirs: George IV and William IV*, vol. 1, pp. 51–2.
67 Quoted by Derry, *Castlereagh*, p. 5.
68 The fullest discussion of Canning's style of politics is to be found in Stephen M. Lee, *George Canning and Liberal Toryism, 1801–1827* (Woodbridge: Royal Historical Society, 2008).
69 The contents of Canning's foreign policy are beyond the scope of this book but have been thoroughly examined by Temperley.
70 See H. C. G. Matthew, 'Sir John Gladstone (1764–1851)', *Oxford DNB*.
71 Canning's Cabinet all had to pledge not to propose either parliamentary reform or the repeal of the Test Act, but this did not reassure the Tory critics.
72 Greville, *Memoirs: George IV and William IV*, vol. 1, p. 89.
73 Robert Blake, *Disraeli* (London: Methuen, 1969), p. 240.
74 Arbuthnot, *Journals*, vol. 2, p. 93 (emphasis added).
75 Ibid., p. 109 (emphasis added).
76 Ibid., p. 134 (emphasis added).

Chapter 2: Peel's Party

1 Elizabeth Longford, *Wellington: Pillar of State* (London: Weidenfeld & Nicolson, 1972), p. 147.
2 Greville, *Memoirs: George IV and William IV*, vol. 1, p. 214; ibid., vol. p. 83.
3 Richard Holmes, *Wellington: The Iron Duke* (London: Harper Perennial, 2007), pp. 121–4.
4 The doctor's mistreatment probably did most of the damage: Longford, *Wellington*, pp. 100–1.
5 Greville, *Memoirs: George IV and William IV*, vol. 1, p. 256.
6 Longford, *Wellington*, pp. 119–20.
7 The Association had been founded in 1823, suppressed in 1825, and refounded exploiting a loophole the same year. It was the first successful mass organization aimed at promoting Catholic emancipation.
8 The classic biography of Peel is Norman Gash's two-volume work: *Mr Secretary Peel: The Life of Sir Robert Peel to 1830* (London: Longman,

1961) and *Sir Robert Peel: The Life of Sir Robert Peel after 1830* (London: Longman, 1972).

9 Walter Bagehot, *Biographical Studies*, ed. Richard Holt Hutton (London: Longmans, Green, 1889), p. 14.

10 Benjamin Disraeli, *Lord George Bentinck: A Political Biography* (London: Archibald Constable, 1905), p. 202.

11 M. Guizot, *Memoirs of Sir Robert Peel* (London: Richard Bentley, 1857), p. 374.

12 [G. W. E. Russell,] *Collections and Recollections by One Who has Kept a Diary* (London: Smith, Elder, 1898), p. 191.

13 Douglas Hurd, *Robert Peel: A Biography* (London: Phoenix, 2007), p. 168.

14 Bagehot, *Biographical Studies*, p. 27.

15 Guizot, *Memoirs of Sir Robert Peel*, p. 664.

16 Peel in 1847 broke with Croker after thirty-seven years of friendship because of a critical – though by no means insulting – article the latter had written in the *Quarterly Review*. Croker's letter to Peel speaks of his 'unalterable affection'. Peel's to Croker is of icy formality. They never spoke again. See John Wilson Croker, *The Correspondence of the Late Right Honourable John Wilson Croker, LL.D., FRS, Secretary to the Admiralty from 1809 to 1830*, ed. Louis J. Jennings, vol. 3 (London: John Murray, 1884), pp. 96–7.

17 Gash, *Sir Robert Peel*, pp. 167–70.

18 Ibid, p. 130.

19 Blake, *The Conservative Party from Peel to Churchill*, p. 18.

20 Gash, *Mr Secretary Peel*, pp. 205–18.

21 Michael Brock, *The Great Reform Act* (London: Hutchinson, 1973), pp. 56–7.

22 See W. P. Courtney, rev. Rita M. Gibbs, 'Sir Richard Rawlinson Vyvyan, eighth baronet (1800–1879)', *Oxford DNB*.

23 John Cannon, *Parliamentary Reform 1640–1832* (Cambridge: Cambridge University Press, 1973), p. 191.

24 See Hilton, *Mad, Bad, and Dangerous People?*, pp. 573–88.

25 Brock, *The Great Reform Act*, pp. 17–34.

26 Specifically, J. W. Croker urged that the seats of Grampound, a corrupt borough in Cornwall, and East Retford, Nottinghamshire, be given to Leeds, Sheffield, Manchester and Birmingham.

27 Cannon, *Parliamentary Reform*, pp. 194–9.

28 Longford, *Wellington*, pp. 226–8.

29 Greville, *Memoirs: George IV and William IV*, vol. 2, p. 55.

30 Arbuthnot, *Journals*, vol. 2, p. 397.

31 Ibid., p. 399.

32 Greville was close to them and put excessively high hopes in their

influence: Greville, *Memoirs: George IV and William IV*, vol. 2, pp. 213 et seq.

33 Arbuthnot, *Journals*, vol. 2, p. 423.

34 Greville, *Memoirs: George IV and William IV*, vol. 2, p. 299.

35 Cannon, *Parliamentary Reform*, p. 242.

36 Examination of this theme is beyond the scope of this book: for a useful summary see Geoffrey B. A. M. Finlayson, *England in the Eighteen Thirties: Decade of Reform* (London: Edward Arnold, 1969).

37 The expression was coined by O'Connell. It alluded to a poem by Canning and suggested that Stanley's 'party' could have been fitted with ease into a coach. Stanley became fourteenth Earl of Derby in 1851. He had gone to the Lords (as Lord Stanley) in 1844.

38 Greville, *Memoirs: George IV and William IV*, vol. 3, p. 109.

39 For a discussion of these points, see Cannon, *Parliamentary Reform*, pp. 257–9.

40 Brock, *The Great Reform Act*, p. 318.

41 Blake, *The Conservative Party from Peel to Churchill*, p. 7.

42 Croker, *Correspondence and Diaries*, vol. 2, p. 184.

43 Norman Gash, *Reaction and Reconstruction in English Politics 1832–1852* (Oxford: Clarendon Press, 1965), p. 130 n. 3. Haydon's politics were Liberal, but Peel was a patron.

44 Hurd, *Robert Peel*, p. 2.

45 Bagehot, *Biographical Studies*, p. 16.

46 Richard Shannon, 'Peel, Gladstone and Party', *Parliamentary History*, 18/3 (1999), pp. 317–20.

47 Disraeli, *Coningsby*, p. 105.

48 Stewart, *The Foundation of the Conservative Party*, p. 96 and n. 17.

49 Specifically, reform of the municipal corporations, relief of the Dissenters and re-organization (but not alienation) of Church assets.

50 Blake, *The Conservative Party from Peel to Churchill*, p. 6.

51 Robin Harris, *Talleyrand: Betrayer and Saviour of France* (London: John Murray, 2007), p. 305. Talleyrand had just retired as French ambassador to the Court of St James.

52 Stewart, *The Foundation of the Conservative Party*, p. 122.

53 Greville, *Memoirs: George IV and William IV*, vol. 2, p. 377 (11 June 1833).

54 Greville, *Greville Memoirs: George IV and William IV*, vol. 3, p. 263 (14 June 1835).

55 For what follows, see Sir Charles Petrie and Alistair Cooke, *The Carlton Club 1832–2007* (London: Carlton Club, 2007), pp. 4–10; Stewart, *The Foundation of the Conservative Party*, pp. 73, 121.

56 Norman Gash, 'Francis Bonham (1785–1863)', *Oxford DNB*.

57 For what follows, see Stewart, *The Foundation of the Conservative Party*, pp. 129–71.

58 Blake, *The Conservative Party from Peel to Churchill*, p. 2.

59 For what follows, see Hilton, *Mad, Bad, and Dangerous People?*, pp. 499–513.

60 See Miles Taylor, 'Richard Cobden (1804–1865)', and 'John Bright (1811–1889)', *Oxford DNB*.

61 Disraeli, *Lord George Bentinck*, p. 196.

62 See the assessment by Boyd Hilton, 'Peel: A Reappraisal', *Historical Journal*, 22/3 (1979), pp. 585–614.

63 For example, Greville notes that Peel 'is become very unpopular' (Charles Greville, *The Greville Memoirs: A Journal of the Reign of Queen Victoria from 1837–1852 by the Late Charles Greville, Esq., Clerk of the Council to the Sovereign*, ed. Henry Reeve (London: Longmans, Green, 1885), vol. 2, p. 161, 6 June 1843); 'Peel has fallen immensely in public opinion' (ibid., p. 189, 1 Aug. 1843); 'The Tories wish Peel out' (ibid., p. 280, 22 April 1845).

64 Gash, *Reaction and Reconstruction*, pp. 126–7.

65 R. F. Foster, *Modern Ireland 1600–1972* (London: Penguin, 1989), p. 315.

66 Hurd, *Robert Peel*, p. 397.

67 Sir William Fraser, *Disraeli and His Day* (London: Kegan Paul, Trench, Trübner & Co. Ltd, 1891), p. 187.

68 William Flavelle Monypenny and George Earle Buckle, *The Life of Benjamin Disraeli Earl of Beaconsfield* (London: John Murray, 1929), vol. 1, p. 749.

69 Ibid., p. 750.

70 Ibid., p. 752.

71 Ibid., p. 758.

72 Angus Hawkins, *The Forgotten Prime Minister: The 14th Earl of Derby*, vol. 1: *Ascent: 1799–1851* (Oxford: Oxford University Press, 2007), pp. 296–7.

73 Ibid., p. 302.

74 Cf. the observation of White House Chief of Staff Rahm Emanuel on using the financial crisis to introduce measures anyway favoured by President Obama: 'Rahm Emanuel: you never want a serious crisis to go to waste', http://www.youtube.com/watch?v=1yeA_kHHLow, 9 Feb. 2009.

75 Hawkins, *The Forgotten Prime Minister*, vol. 1, p. 311.

76 Greville found Peel 'elated' that he would be in Government and 'chuckling mightily' at the discomfiture of the Whigs (*Memoirs: Victoria*, vol. 2, pp. 340–1, 23 Dec. 1845); he was still 'in high spirits' on 2 Feb. 1846 (ibid., p. 365).

77 Quoted in Gash, *Reaction and Reconstruction*, p. 153.

78 *Sir Robert Peel – from his Private Papers*, ed. C. S. Parker, 3 vols (London: John Murray, 1899), pp. 473–4, letter to Lord Hardinge, 24 Sept. 1846.

79 Blake, *Disraeli*, pp. 164, 238–9. The remarkable parallel between Peel's treatment of Russell and of Disraeli is not often mentioned. Russell had sent a letter in 1835 opposing the election of Manners Sutton as Speaker. Peel had the letter and challenged him but Russell denied writing it. Peel did not reveal the letter. Its existence got into *The Times* and Russell apologized (Greville, *Memoirs: George IV and William IV*, vol. 3, p. 218).

80 Edward Stanley, *Disraeli, Derby and the Conservative Party: Journals and Memoirs of Edward Henry, Lord Stanley 1849–1869*, ed. John Vincent (Hassocks: Harvester Press, 1978), p. 23; Hurd, *Robert Peel*, pp. 385–6; Gash, *Sir Robert Peel*, pp. 702–3 n. 1.

Chapter 3: Derby's Party

1 Understanding of the significance of Stanley/Derby and of the period during which he dominated the Conservative Party has been revolutionized by Angus Hawkins's magisterial two-volume biography, *The Forgotten Prime Minister*.

2 Blake, *The Conservative Party from Peel to Churchill*, pp. 60–72.

3 Hawkins, *The Unknown Prime Minister*, vol. 1, p. 307.

4 Stanley, *Disraeli, Derby and the Conservative Party*, pp. 1–2.

5 Blake, *Disraeli*, p. 758.

6 For a useful collection of Disraeli's best lines, see Benjamin Disraeli, *The Sayings of Disraeli*, ed. Robert Blake (London: Duckworth, 2003).

7 Fraser, *Disraeli and His Day*, p. 343.

8 Ibid., pp. 81–2, 279.

9 Ibid., pp. 146, 148–9.

10 Ibid., p. 293.

11 Ibid., pp. 205–6.

12 Ibid., pp. 400–1.

13 Ibid., pp. 401–2.

14 Stanley, *Disraeli, Derby and the Conservative Party*, p. 76.

15 The 1851 census showed that for the first time rather more Englishmen lived in towns than the country.

16 Hawkins, *The Unknown Prime Minister*, vol. 2, p. 65.

17 Stewart, *The Foundation of the Conservative Party*, pp. 270–1.

18 Stanley, *Disraeli, Derby and the Conservative Party*, p. 8.

19 Ibid., pp. 42–52.

20 Hawkins, *The Unknown Prime Minister*, vol. 2, pp. 25–6.

21 Ibid., p. 55.

22 Blake, *Disraeli*, p. 345.

23 Stanley, *Disraeli, Derby and the Conservative Party*, p. 90.

24 Blake, *The Conservative Party from Peel to Churchill*, p. 82; Stewart, *The Foundation of the Conservative Party*, p. 238.

25 For the full list, see J. B. Conacher, *The Peelites and the Party System 1846–1852* (Newton Abbot: David & Charles, 1972), p. 16.

26 Ibid., pp. 176–7.

27 Stanley, *Disraeli, Derby and the Conservative Party*, p. 90.

28 Stewart, *The Foundation of the Conservative Party*, p. 261.

29 Hawkins, *The Unknown Prime Minister*, vol. 2, p. 97.

30 Stanley, *Disraeli, Derby and the Conservative Party*, p. 92; Hawkins, *The Unknown Prime Minister*, vol. 2, p. 119.

31 Fraser, *Disraeli and His Day*, pp. 156–7.

32 Hawkins, *The Unknown Prime Minister*, vol. 2, p. 122.

33 Ibid., pp. 67–8.

34 Fraser, *Disraeli and His Day*, p. 183.

35 Hawkins, *The Unknown Prime Minister*, vol. 2, p. 234.

36 Stanley, *Disraeli, Derby and the Conservative Party*, p. 90.

37 Stewart, *The Foundation of the Conservative Party*, p. 311.

38 Ibid., p. 310.

39 W. L. Burn, *The Age of Equipoise: A Study of the Mid-Victorian Generation* (London: Unwin, 1964), p. 55.

40 Hilton, *Mad, Bad, and Dangerous People?*, pp. 612–21.

41 See Roderick Floud and Paul Johnson, eds, *The Cambridge Economic History of Modern Britain*, vol. 1: *Industrialisation, 1700–1860* (Cambridge: Cambridge University Press, 2004), p. 4, table 1.1, 'Estimated annual rates of growth of real output 1700–1871', and p. 272, figure 10.1, 'Real earnings in Great Britain 1781–1855'.

42 James Chambers, *Palmerston: The People's Darling* (London: John Murray, 2004), pp. 484–6. For example, Palmerston justified hostile action against Brazil on the grounds of its complicity in slavery, but this did not prevent him smiling on the Confederacy's cause in the American Civil War.

43 Stanley, *Disraeli, Derby and the Conservative Party*, p. 77.

44 Fraser, *Disraeli and His Day*, p. 321.

45 Jasper Ridley, *Lord Palmerston* (New York: E. P. Dutton, 1971), pp. 386–9; Greville, *Memoirs: Victoria*, vol. 3, p. 348.

46 Hansard, vol. 112 (3rd ser.), 25 June 1850, cols 443–4.

47 E. D. Steele, 'Palmerston's Foreign Policy and Foreign Secretaries 1855–1865', in Keith M. Wilson, ed., *British Foreign Secretaries and Foreign Policy: From the Crimean War to the First World War* (London: Croom Helm, 1987), pp. 25–84.

48 Hawkins, *The Unknown Prime Minister*, vol. 2, p. 159.

49 Chambers, *Palmerston*, pp. 456–7.

50 Hawkins, *The Unknown Prime Minister*, vol. 2, pp. 246, 249, 252–4, 256–7.

51 Ibid., p. 297.

52 Stewart, *The Foundation of the Conservative Party*, pp. 278–80.

53 Ibid., pp. 325–31.
54 Ibid. pp. 333–7.
55 Ibid., p. 312.
56 See Jonathan Parry, 'Robert Lowe, Viscount Sherbrooke (1811–1892)', *Oxford DNB*.
57 This was demonstrated by Maurice Cowling in *1867: Disraeli, Gladstone and Revolution – The Passing of the Second Reform Bill* (Cambridge: Cambridge University Press, 1967): Cowling notes (p. 303) that 'Disraeli's was a policy of consistent opportunism'.
58 Andrew Roberts, *Salisbury: Victorian Titan* (London: Weidenfeld & Nicolson, 1999), pp. 97–8.
59 Stewart, *The Foundation of the Conservative Party*, pp. 359–5; Blake, *Disraeli*, pp. 452–77.
60 Fraser, *Disraeli and His Day*, p. 206.
61 *The Quarterly Review*, no. 123, July–Oct. 1867, pp. 533–65.
62 Hawkins, *The Unknown Prime Minister*, vol. 2, p. 353.
63 Shannon, *The Age of Disraeli*, pp. 10–12.
64 Blake, *Disraeli*, p. 460.
65 Hawkins, *The Unknown Prime Minister*, vol. 2, pp. 261–2.
66 Ibid., pp. 351–5.
67 Ibid., p. 364.
68 Shannon, *The Age of Disraeli*, pp. 29–32.
69 Fraser, *Disraeli and His Day*, p. 52.
70 Cf. the disapproval of Hawkins in *The Unknown Prime Minister*, vol. 2, p. 360.
71 Monypenny and Buckle, *Disraeli*, vol. 2, pp. 289, 291.
72 Hawkins, *The Unknown Prime Minister*, vol. 2, p. 386.

Chapter 4: Disraeli's Party, I – Leader of the Opposition

1 The term 'Fenian', while specifically relating to the mid-nineteenth-century Irish revolutionary brotherhoods, almost immediately gained wider application.
2 Richard Shannon, *Gladstone: Heroic Prime Minister 1865–1898* (London: Penguin, 1999), pp. 45–51.
3 Blake, *Disraeli*, pp. 495–506.
4 For the dour but often pivotal figure of Cairns, see David Steele, 'Hugh Cairns, first Earl Cairns (1819–1885), *Oxford DNB*.
5 *A Selection from the Diaries of Edward Henry Stanley, 15th Earl of Derby (1826–1893) between September 1869 and March 1878*, Royal Historical Society, Camden Fifth Series, vol. 4, ed. John Vincent (London: 1994), p. 11.
6 Stanley, *Disraeli, Derby and the Conservative Party*, p. 31.

7   The distinctions were much misunderstood. For example, Oxford Movement men like Salisbury (though he had his own theological eccentricities) had no time for what they thought were Ritualist excesses in the liturgy.

8   Monypenny and Buckle, *Disraeli*, vol. 2, p. 428.

9   Shannon, *The Age of Disraeli*, pp. 37–76.

10 Blake, *Disraeli*, p. 499.

11 Shannon, *The Age of Disraeli*, pp. 85–97.

12 Fraser, *Disraeli and His Day*, p. 455.

13 Ibid., p. 319.

14 For what follows see Jane Ridley, *The Young Disraeli* (London: Sinclair-Stevenson, 1995), pp. 5–78.

15 Monypenny and Buckle, *Disraeli*, vol. 1, pp. 388–9.

16 William Kuhn, *The Politics of Pleasure: A Portrait of Benjamin Disraeli* (London: Simon and Schuster, 2006), pp. 113–141. Despite Kuhn's evidence, Disraeli's sexual orientation is not altogether clear. He certainly patronized, helped and, in a manner, flirted with good-looking young aristocrats. He sometimes over-indulged their deficiencies and overlooked their foolishness (as in the case of the shallow and ungrateful Lord Henry Lennox). On other occasions his judgement was eminently sound (as in picking out as his indispensable, solid and talented secretary Monty Corry). For practical reasons, older politicians need younger ones, and always have. In any case, Disraeli certainly loved and made love to women, and they in turn loved him. There is no evidence that even his numerous embittered enemies thought or implied he was homosexual or even bisexual, which must carry some weight.

17 Monypenny and Buckle, *Disraeli*, vol. 1, p. 162, letter to Benjamin Austen [Oct. 1830].

18 Ridley, *Young Disraeli*, pp. 97.

19 Monypenny and Buckle, *Disraeli*, vol. 1, p. 281.

20 The full, unexpurgated text of Disraeli's extraordinary letter to Mary Anne dated 7 Feb, 1835 is to be found in Blake, *Disraeli*, appendix 1, pp. 769–71.

21 John Vincent, *Disraeli* (Oxford: Oxford University Press, 1990), p. 4.

22 Cf. Ridley, *Young Disraeli*, pp. 256, 342, who suggests otherwise.

23 Wilfrid Meynell, *The Man Disraeli* (London: Hutchinson, 1927), p. 213. The occasion was the Buckinghamshire election of 1847, when one of the Cavendishes was Disraeli's opponent.

24 Disraeli, *Lord George Bentinck*, p. 323.

25 Stanley Weintraub, *Disraeli: A Biography* (London: Hamish Hamilton, 1993), pp. 283–4.

26 Blake, *Disraeli*, p. 504.

27 For what follows, see Shannon, *The Age of Disraeli*, pp. 93–100.

28 Foster, *Modern Ireland*, pp. 390–9.

29 Shannon, *Gladstone: Heroic Prime Minister*, p. 85.

30 Roy Jenkins, 'Sir Charles Wentworth Dilke, second baronet (1843–1911)', *Oxford DNB*.

31 Monypenny and Buckle, *Disraeli*, vol. 2, pp. 472–4.

32 Gathorne Gathorne-Hardy, *The Diary of Gathorne-Hardy, later Lord Cranbrook, 1866–1892: Political Selections*, ed. Nancy E. Johnson (Oxford: Clarendon Press, 1981), p. 149.

33 See W. D. Rubinstein, 'Stafford Northcote, first earl of Iddesleigh (1818–1887)', *Oxford DNB*.

34 Fraser, *Disraeli and His Day*, pp. 374–6.

35 Liverpool, already fringing Knowsley Hall, was still more Derby home territory – and so less suitable for Disraeli's expedition.

36 Monypenny and Buckle, *Disraeli*, vol. 2, pp. 523–30.

37 P. R. Ghosh, 'Style and Substance in Disraelian Social Reform, c.1860–1880', in P. J. Waller, ed., *Politics and Social Change in Modern Britain: Essays Presented to A. F. Thompson* (Brighton: Harvester Press, 1987), pp. 62–8.

38 Monypenny and Buckle, *Disraeli*, vol. 2, pp. 531–2.

39 Cf. Blake, *Disraeli*, p. 665. The 'millstone' phrase, to be fair, stems from his days as Chancellor of the Exchequer. Nearly all Chancellors regard foreign commitments in this light. In this case, it occurs as one of a number of complaints in a moaning letter of 13 Aug. 1852 to Lord Malmesbury (Monypenny and Buckle, *Disraeli*, vol. 1, p. 1201).

40 Sarah Bradford, *Disraeli* (London: Weidenfeld & Nicolson, 1982), p. 296.

41 Fraser, *Disraeli and His Day*, p. 286.

42 Blake, *Disraeli*, pp. 414–21. She, like Mary Anne and later Disraeli himself, was buried at Hughenden.

43 Bradford, *Disraeli*, pp. 307–10.

44 Monypenny and Buckle, *Disraeli*, vol. 2, pp. 541–58.

45 Ibid., p. 602.

46 See E. J. Feuchtwanger, 'Sir John Eldon Gorst (1835–1916)', *Oxford DNB*.

47 Shannon, *The Age of Disraeli*, pp. 15–23.

48 Ibid., pp. 118–25.

49 Letter from Salisbury to Balfour, 10 April 1880, quoted by Shannon, *The Age of Disraeli*, p. 379.

50 Edgar Feuchtwanger, *Disraeli* (London: Arnold, 2000), p. 189.

51 Lord George Hamilton, *Parliamentary Reminiscences and Reflections*, vol. 1: *1868–1887* (London: John Murray, 1916), p. 11.

52 See Richard Davenport-Hines, 'William Henry Smith (1825–1891)', *Oxford DNB*.

53 See S. V. Fitz-Gerald, rev. Paul Smith, 'Richard Assheton Cross, first Viscount Cross (1823–1914)', *Oxford DNB*.

54 Stanley, *Selection from the Diaries*, pp. 7–8.

55 Monypenny and Buckle, *Disraeli*, vol. 2, p. 616.

56 Shannon, *The Age of Disraeli*, p. 174.

57 Ibid., pp. 127–8.

58 H. J. Hanham, *Elections and Party Management: Politics in the Time of Disraeli and Gladstone* (London: Longman, 1959), pp. 209, 225; J. P. D. Dunbabbin, 'Parliamentary Elections in Great Britain, 1868–1900: A Psephological Note', *English Historical Review*, no. 318, Jan. 1966, pp. 86–7.

59 Ireland was now represented by (1868 figures in brackets) 12 (67) Liberals, 34 (38) Conservatives and 57 Home Rulers.

Chapter 5: Disraeli's Party, II – In Power

1 Fraser, *Disraeli and His Day*, p. 318.

2 Meynell, *The Man Disraeli*, p. 47.

3 Blake, *Disraeli*, pp. 632–3. He was certainly less badly advised on his health than his predecessor, Derby.

4 Lady Gwendolen Cecil, *The Life of Robert Marquis of Salisbury*, vol. 2: *1868–1880* (London: Hodder & Stoughton, 1921), p. 44.

5 Salisbury believed that he had failed to cope with another such famine when first at the India Office and he was still racked with guilt about it.

6 Cecil, *Life of Salisbury*, vol. 2, pp. 49–50.

7 Roberts, *Salisbury*, 136–8.

8 Fraser, *Disraeli and His Day*, p. 253.

9 Monypenny and Buckle, *Disraeli*, vol. 2, p. 731.

10 Vincent, *Disraeli*, p. 11.

11 Stanley, *Selection from the Diaries*, p. 220.

12 Monypenny and Buckle, *Disraeli*, vol. 2, p. 711.

13 Benjamin Disraeli, *The Letters of Disraeli to Lady Bradford and Lady Chesterfield*, ed. Marquis of Zetland (London: Ernest Benn, 1929), vol. 1, p. 260.

14 Monypenny and Buckle, *Disraeli*, vol. 2, p. 709.

15 Conservative policy was to provide universal education as far as possible within the existing framework, predominantly based on church schools. Disraeli was forced – under pressure from Salisbury and backbenchers – to accept a new clause in the Bill providing for the dissolution of 'superfluous' board schools. See Shannon, *The Age of Disraeli*, pp. 218–20.

16 Ghosh, 'Style and Substance in Disraelian Social Reform', p. 60.

17 Shannon, *The Age of Disraeli*, pp. 107–10.

18 Ibid., pp. 211–12.

19 See e.g. the Conservative Research Department's publication: Charles E. Bellairs, *Conservative Social and Industrial Reform: A Record of Conservative Legislation between 1800 and 1945* (London: Conservative Political Centre, 1947). This was reissued as *Conservative Social and Industrial Reform: A Record of Conservative Legislation between 1800 and 1974* (London: Conservative Political Centre, 1977), with an introduction by Margaret Thatcher. In 1985 a short second volume was produced containing the Thatcher Government's own reforms.

20 For example, David Willetts, 'Benjamin Disraeli, My Hero. A pragmatist, and yet passionate believer in social responsibility and localism: what better model for modern Conservatives?', *Guardian*, 30 Sept. 2008. Similarly, Phillip Blond, sometimes described as David Cameron's guru, has founded an organization called ResPublica, the material on whose website (http://www.respublica.org.uk/) is full of Disraelian allusions – there is even a 'Disraeli Room'.

21 See Stewart A. Weaver, 'Michael Thomas Sadler (1780–1835)', Stewart A. Weaver, 'Richard Oastler (1789–1861)', John Wolffe, 'Anthony Ashley Cooper, seventh earl of Shaftesbury (1801–1885)', *Oxford DNB*.

22 Monypenny and Buckle, *Disraeli*, vol. 2, p. 709.

23 *The Times*, 18 April 1883.

24 Robert McKenzie and Allan Silver, *Angels in Marble: Working Class Conservatives in Urban England* (London: Heinemann, 1868), p. iii.

25 Monypenny and Buckle, *Disraeli*, vol. 2, pp. 1184.

26 One is repeatedly struck by the similarities, even of speech; for example, Disraeli's complaint that X was 'not redeemed by a single vice' (Fraser, *Disraeli and His Day*, p. 313).

27 Freda Harcourt, 'Disraeli's Imperialism, 1866–1868: A Question of Timing', *Historical Journal*, 23/1 (1980), pp. 87–109.

28 Blake, *Disraeli*, pp. 581–7.

29 Lowe claimed in a speech that Disraeli's predecessors as Prime Minister had resisted pressure from the Queen to change her Indian title. The Queen then allowed Disraeli to quote her in the House denying that she had ever made such approaches. Gladstone also denied the charge. Lowe had publicly to apologize. Humiliated, he was henceforth a broken man.

30 For an analysis of events on the Bosnian ground (rather than in the European chancelleries) see Noel Malcolm, *Bosnia: A Short History* (London: Papermac, 1994), pp. 131–5.

31 Monypenny and Buckle, *Disraeli*, vol. 2, p. 886.

32 Ibid., p. 885.

33 Blake, *Disraeli*, p. 636.

34 The question of how far the Derbys went and how much Disraeli exaggerated their indiscretions in his own interests – indeed, how

competent Derby was at any stage – is disputable. For the best gloss on Derby's performance, see John Vincent's comments in his introduction to Stanley, *Selection from the Diaries*, pp. 27–28. On another view, Derby was, as a whole but particularly during this crisis, one of the worst Foreign Secretaries Britain has ever had.

35 Cecil, *Life of Salisbury*, vol. 2, p. 145. The passage incidentally provides an interesting insight into Salisbury's kind of conservatism.

36 See the discussion of Salisbury's motives and thinking in Roberts, *Salisbury*, pp. 169–80.

37 Apart from the proximity of Hughenden, and Disraeli's earlier connection with Buckinghamshire, he probably chose the title because Burke had been offered it – and had turned it down.

38 Monypenny and Buckle, *Disraeli*, vol. 2, p. 862.

39 Weintraub, *Disraeli*, p. 568.

40 Cecil, *Life of Salisbury*, vol. 2, p. 91.

41 In a letter to Lord Lytton of 9 March 1877: see Cecil, *Salisbury*, vol. 2, p. 130.

42 Derby seems to have suffered a nervous collapse, whose effects were exacerbated by tiredness and alcohol. On the other hand, his problems may well have been exaggerated, like his and his wife's indiscretions, by Disraeli. See Stanley, *Selection from the Diaries*, pp. 30–1.

43 Roberts, *Salisbury*, pp. 184–5.

44 For the different interpretations that have been put on these events, see ibid., pp. 186–7, 206–8; Blake, *Disraeli*, pp. 640–1.

45 The chorus lines of the song run:
We don't want to fight, but by Jingo if we do,
We've got the ships, we've got the men, we've got the money too.
We've fought the Bear before, and while we're Britons true
The Russians shall not have Constantinople.

46 Gathorne-Hardy had been passed over in favour of Sir Stafford Northcote as Leader in the Commons in 1876 when Disraeli went to the Lords. See Jonathan Parry, 'Gathorne Gathorne-Hardy, first earl of Cranbrook (1814–1906)', *Oxford DNB*.

47 Blake, *Disraeli*, p. 670.

48 Ibid., p. 719.

49 Roderick Floud and Paul Johnson, eds, *The Cambridge Economic History of Modern Britain*, vol. 2: *Economic Maturity, 1860–1939* (Cambridge: Cambridge University Press, 2004), table 6.1, p. 135; table 6.4, p. 141.

50 Shannon, *The Age of Disraeli*, p. 364.

51 While Britain's share of global manufacturing remained more or less stable, British industrial growth rates were sluggish compared with those

of the United States and Germany, and only keeping pace with that of France. See Floud and Johnson, eds, *The Cambridge Economic History of Modern Britain*, vol. 2, tables 4.5 and 4.6, p. 81.

52 Shannon, *The Age of Disraeli*, pp. 323–31.

53 Hanham suggests that there is no reason to believe that a dissolution after the Congress 'would have secured the Ministry another term with *a safe majority*' (Hanham, *Elections and Party Management*, p. 228, emphasis added). But avoiding wipe-outs is just as much part of the political game as gaining 'safe' victories.

54 Dunbabbin, 'Parliamentary Elections', p. 87.

55 It was in the seat formerly held by the patriotic Radical J. A. Roebuck (on whom see S. A. Beaver, 'John Arthur Roebuck (1802–1879)', *Oxford DNB*). Sheffield, with its iron and steel industry, had good material reasons to approve of a Conservative foreign and military policy.

56 Blake, *Disraeli*, pp. 711–12.

57 These (slightly disputable) figures come from Blake, *The Conservative Party from Peel to Churchill*, p. 282.

58 Shannon, *The Age of Disraeli*, pp. 223–4.

59 The precise term exists only in French, *roman à clé*, though the ugly 'faction' is close.

60 Shannon, *The Age of Disraeli*, p. 403.

61 Monypenny and Buckle, *Disraeli*, vol. 2, p. 1467, letter from Disraeli to Salisbury, 27 Dec. 1880. Disraeli was not, though, above dangling the same prospect before Northcote (Roberts, *Salisbury*, p. 244).

62 Richard Shannon, *Gladstone: God and Politics* (London: Hambledon Continuum, 2007), p. 209.

63 Richard Aldous, *The Lion and the Unicorn: Gladstone vs. Disraeli* (London: Hutchinson, 2006), pp. 1–7.

64 Shannon, *Gladstone: God and Politics*, p. 209.

65 Shannon, 'Peel, Gladstone and Party', p. 321.

66 Monypenny and Buckle, *Disraeli*, vol. 2, pp. 1052–3.

67 Simon Heffer, 'How the Great Mr Gladstone Saved Our Country', *Daily Telegraph*, 22 Dec. 2009.

68 Peter Oborne, 'Cameron is Our Disraeli', *The Spectator*, 8 January 2010.

69 Monypenny and Buckle, *Disraeli*, vol. 2, p. 389.

70 For the Primrose League see the next chapter.

Chapter 6: Salisbury's Party, I – Achieving Dominance

1 As well as the two fine newer biographies (Roberts, *Salisbury*; David Steele, *Lord Salisbury: A Political Biography* (London: UCL Press, 1999), the magical but unfinished account of her father by Lady Gwendolen Cecil (*Life of Salisbury*) is indispensable. See also Paul Smith, 'Robert

Arthur Talbot Gascoyne-Cecil, third Marquess of Salisbury (1830–1903)', *Oxford DNB*.

2 [Russell,] *Collections and Recollections*, p. 192. The Romanes lectures are delivered annually by distinguished public figures in Oxford.

3 Quoted by Roberts, *Salisbury*, p. 251.

4 Letter to Canon MacColl of 11 July 1884 in Cecil, *Life of Salisbury*, vol. 3, p. 111.

5 Roberts, *Salisbury*, p. 254.

6 The 'Fourth Party' was not, of course, a party at all – just a small faction of trouble-makers. Apparently the name emerged as a result of exchanges in the Commons. One Member had referred to 'two great parties'. Parnell (for the Home Rulers) interjected: 'Three.' Lord Randolph Churchill then shouted 'Four!' Laughter followed. See Blake, *The Conservative Party from Peel to Churchill*, p. 135 n. 1.

7 The famous textile and clothing shop set up in London's Oxford Street in 1851. After the First World War it merged with Debenham & Freebody.

8 Cecil, *Life of Salisbury*, vol. 3, p. 88.

9 See R. E. Quinault, 'Lord Randolph Churchill and Tory Democracy, 1880–1885', *Historical Journal*, 22/1 (1979), pp. 141–65.

10 The Act was intended to pay off with government money the rent arrears of poorer Irish tenants.

11 Shannon, *The Age of Salisbury*, p. 107.

12 Ibid., pp. 89–92.

13 Ibid., pp. 95–106. The national benefit to Labour has, of course, been that Labour MPs have needed fewer votes to get elected than have Tory MPs.

14 Cecil, *Life of Salisbury*, vol. 3, p. 98.

15 See Roberts, *Salisbury*, pp. 352–6.

16 Shannon, *The Age of Salisbury*, pp. 19–42.

17 Harold E. Gorst, *The Fourth Party* (London: Smith, Elder, 1906), pp. 303–4. This account by Gorst's son reflects the father's view.

18 Quoted in R. F. Foster, *Lord Randolph Churchill: A Political Life* (Oxford: Clarendon Press, 1981), p. 160.

19 A good stab at defending Salisbury's honour is, however, made by Andrew Roberts: see *Salisbury*, pp. 348–51.

20 Ibid., pp. 363–4.

21 A. B. Cooke and John Vincent, *The Governing Passion: Cabinet Government and Party Politics in Britain 1885–86* (Brighton: Harvester Press, 1974), p. 163.

22 Roberts, *Salisbury*, pp. 362–4.

23 Jonathan Parry, 'Spencer Compton Cavendish, marquess of Hartington and eighth duke of Devonshire (1833–1908)', *Oxford DNB*.

24 Thomas J. Spinner jun., 'George Goschen, first Viscount Goschen (1831–1907)', *Oxford DNB*.

25 Cecil, *Life of Salisbury*, vol. 3, pp. 302–3.

26 Lady Gwendolen Cecil, *Biographical Studies of the Life and Political Character of Robert Third Marquis of Salisbury* (London: Hodder & Stoughton, n.d.), p. 76.

27 John France, 'Salisbury and the Unionist Alliance', in Lord [Robert] Blake and Hugh Cecil, eds, *Salisbury: The Man and his Policies* (London: Macmillan, 1987), p. 240.

28 Shannon, *The Age of Salisbury*, pp. 203–8.

29 Ibid., p. 222.

30 Cecil, *Life of Salisbury*, vol. 3, pp. 316–45.

Chapter 7: Salisbury's Party, II – Dominance and Decline

1 Shannon, *The Age of Salisbury*, pp. 76–82.

2 Martin Pugh, *The Tories and the People 1880–1935* (Oxford: Basil Blackwell, 1985), pp. 12–13, 27, 144, 157.

3 Alistair Cooke, *A Gift from the Churchills: The Primrose League, 1883–2004* (London: Carlton Club, 2010), p. 66.

4 For what follows see Richard Shannon, 'Richard Middleton (1846–1905)', *Oxford DNB*.

5 Roberts, *Salisbury*, p. 311.

6 James Cornford, 'The Transformation of Conservatism in the Late Nineteenth Century', *Victorian Studies*, 8/1 (Sept. 1963), p. 52.

7 Shannon, *The Age of Salisbury*, p. 109.

8 Cornford, 'The Transformation of Conservatism', pp. 54–9.

9 Frans Coetzee, 'Villa Toryism Reconsidered: Conservatism and Suburban Sensibilities in Late Victorian Croydon', in E. E. H. Green, ed., *An Age of Transition: British Politics 1880–1914* (Edinburgh: Edinburgh University Press, 1997), pp. 32–45.

10 See George and Weedon Grossmith, *The Diary of a Nobody* (London: Penguin, 1999), with a useful introduction about Holloway by Ed Glinert. The Pooters lived at 'The Laurels', Brickfield Terrace, a house with six rooms, a basement and a front garden with a path up to steps at the front door – which, however, was permanently locked, friends entering by a side door. There was a back garden running down to the railway. They had one servant and were afflicted by a host of rude, drunken and incompetent tradesmen.

11 Jerome K. Jerome, *Three Men on the Bummel* (London: Arrowsmith, 1942), p. 70.

12 Dunbabbin, 'Parliamentary Elections', pp. 98–9.

13 For these writings see Michael Pinto-Duschinsky, *The Political Thought of*

Lord Salisbury 1854–1868 (London: Constable, 1967).

14 'Disintegration', *Quarterly Review*, no. 156, July–Oct. 1883, p. 562.

15 Quoted in Michael Bentley, *Lord Salisbury's World: Conservative Environments in Late-Victorian Britain* (Cambridge: Cambridge University Press, 2001), p. 73.

16 Salisbury's appreciation of scientific advance is illustrated by his installation of electric lights and early telephones at Hatfield, as amusingly described by Gwendolen (Cecil, *Life of Salisbury*, vol. 3, pp. 3–8). She equally notes: 'His passion for liberty influenced him in every relation of life' (Cecil, *Biographical Studies*, p. 78). This is demonstrable at one extreme by his intense dislike of temperance legislation, and at the other by his anarchistic attitude to bringing up his family. Lady Salisbury once observed of her husband: 'He may be able to govern the country, but he is quite unfit to be left in charge of his children' (Cecil, *Life of Salisbury*, vol. 3, p. 13).

17 Shannon, *The Age of Salisbury*, p. 350.

18 Andrew Adonis, *Making Aristocracy Work: The Peerage and the Political System in Britain 1884–1914* (Oxford: Clarendon Press, 1993), pp. 111–16.

19 Quoted by Roberts, *Salisbury*, p. 576.

20 Quoted by Steele, *Lord Salisbury*, p. 2.

21 Cecil, *Life of Salisbury*, vol. 3, pp. 169–70.

22 Lady Gwendolen Cecil, 'Salisbury in Private Life', in Lord [Robert] Blake and Hugh Cecil, eds, Salisbury: *The Man and his Policies* (London: Macmillan, 1987), p. 34. He was short-sighted.

23 Quoted by Roberts, *Salisbury*, p. 248.

24 Shannon, *The Age of Salisbury*, pp. 443–4.

25 Cecil, *Life of Salisbury*, vol. 1, p. 116.

26 Ibid., p. 117.

27 See E. D. Steele, 'Salisbury and the Church', in Lord [Robert] Blake and Hugh Cecil, eds, Salisbury: *The Man and his Policies* (London: Macmillan, 1987), pp. 185–218.

28 Cecil, *Life of Salisbury*, vol. 1, p. 119.

29 Quoted by R. J. Q. Adams, *Balfour: The Last Grandee* (London: John Murray, 2007), p. 82.

30 Parnell was cited by Captain William O'Shea in divorcing his wife, Kitty. The case came for trial in November 1890. Mrs O'Shea had had three children by Parnell, but in Catholic Ireland divorce was a step too far. In the ensuing controversy, in which Parnell was denounced by the Irish hierarchy, a majority of Parnellites broke away. Parnell died the following year.

31 'Disintegration', *Quarterly Review*, no. 156, July–Oct. 1883, p. 563.

32 Roberts, *Salisbury*, pp. 569–70.

33 Conservative and Unionist Party, *The Campaign Guide 1900: A Handbook for Unionist Speakers* (Edinburgh: David Douglas, 1900), p. 147.
34 Roberts, *Salisbury*, pp. 556–8.
35 Steele, *Lord Salisbury*, p. 333.
36 Roberts, *Salisbury*, p. 465.
37 Cecil, *Biographical Studies*, p. 35.
38 Cecil, *Life of Salisbury*, vol. 3, p. 218, letter to Sir Evelyn Baring of 5 February 1892, about the defence of ports on the northern shore of the Red Sea. Baring became Lord Cromer later that year.
39 A. N. Porter, 'Lord Salisbury, Foreign Policy and Domestic Finance, 1860–1900', in Lord [Robert] Blake and Hugh Cecil, eds, *Salisbury: The Man and his Policies* (London: Macmillan 1987), pp. 148–84.
40 Steele, *Lord Salisbury*, p. 324.
41 Roberts, *Salisbury*, pp. 607–9, 645–6.
42 Ibid., pp. 629–30; Cecil, *Life of Salisbury*, vol. 4, pp. 85–6.
43 Cecil, *Life of Salisbury*, vol. 4, p. 90.
44 Steele, *Lord Salisbury*, p. 4.
45 Cecil, *Life of Salisbury*, vol. 2, pp. 234–5.
46 Ibid., p. 237.
47 Roberts, *Salisbury*, pp. 44–5.
48 C. J. Lowe, *The Reluctant Imperialists* (London: Routledge and Kegan Paul, 1967), vol. 1, p. 10.
49 Cecil, *Life of Salisbury*, vol. 4, pp. 72–3.
50 Roberts, *Salisbury*, pp. 438–40.
51 As when challenged by the United States over Venezuela's claims to British Guiana: ibid., pp. 691–2.
52 J. R. Seeley, *The Expansion of England: Two Courses of Lectures* (London: Macmillan, 1907), pp. 10, 88, 340.
53 Thomas Packenham, *The Boer War* (London: Abacus, 2009), pp. 458–9.
54 Ibid., pp. 572–3.
55 Conservative and Unionist Party, *The Campaign Guide: An Election Handbook for Unionist Speakers* (Edinburgh: David Douglas, 1892), pp. 10–11.
56 Lawrence James, *The Rise and Fall of the British Empire* (London: Little, Brown, 2000), pp. 200–16.
57 Salisbury built a neo-Gothic holiday home at Puys, near Dieppe – the 'Château Cecil' – though the climate of the Midi in Beaulieu-sur-Mer on the Côte d'Azur exerted greater appeal in his later years.
58 See the analysis of Paul Kennedy, *The Rise and Fall of the Great Powers: Economic Change and Military Conflict from 1500 to 2000* (London: Fontana, 1989), pp. 290–4.
59 Cf. Blake, *The Conservative Party from Peel to Churchill*, pp. 164–6.

60 Shannon, *The Age of Salisbury*, pp. 463–7. The measure faced strong Conservative opposition.

61 E. H. H. Green, 'Rentiers versus Producers? The Political Economy of the Bimetallic Controversy', *English Historical Review*, no. 406 (1988), pp. 588–612.

62 Shannon, *The Age of Salisbury*, pp. 374, 380.

63 David Steele, 'Salisbury and the Soldiers', in John Gooch, ed., *The Boer War: Direction, Experience and Image* (London: Frank Cass, 2000), pp. 3–20.

64 Roberts, *Salisbury*, pp. 778–9; Shannon, *The Age of Salisbury*, pp. 503–11.

65 Roberts, *Salisbury*, pp. 789–90.

66 Ibid., p. 795.

67 Lord Liverpool served longer as Prime Minister (fifteen years), but to describe Liverpool as a 'Conservative' is anachronistic. In the twentieth century, Margaret Thatcher, unlike Salisbury, won three consecutive victories. But she served eleven and a half rather than his fourteen years as Prime Minister.

Chapter 8: The Precipice

1 The word 'Unionist' here, when used of a party, is synonymous with 'Conservative'. The former term was at this time more frequently used, and this chapter follows that style. 'Unionism' refers to the ideology, shared by Conservative and Liberal Unionists, of commitment to the Union with Ireland. 'Ulster Unionists' refers to Unionist members from that province. From 1912 when the (already somewhat artificial) Liberal Unionist Party was officially merged with the Conservatives, against Joe Chamberlain's wishes but in line with those of his younger colleagues, the word 'Unionist' ceases to have any ambiguity. The unwieldy title of the party from that point – 'The National Unionist Association of Conservative and Unionist Associations' – bears witness to the contemporary problems of language, which also face historians and their readers: see Ramsden, *The Age of Balfour*, p. 71.

2 George Dangerfield, *The Strange Death of Liberal England* (London: Serif, 1997), pp. 24–5. Equally memorable and almost equally accurate is his description of Lloyd George as 'less a Liberal than a Welshman on the loose' (ibid., p. 29).

3 Adams, *Balfour*, pp. 231–32.

4 Quoted in Ramsden, *The Age of Balfour*, p. 29.

5 Blanche E. C. Dugdale, *Arthur James Balfour, First Earl of Balfour* (London: Hutchinson, 1936), vol. 2, p. 396.

6 Adams, *Balfour*, p. 114.

7 Ibid, pp. 111–12.

8 Ibid, pp. 184–6.
9 Richard Jay, *Joseph Chamberlain: A Political Life* (Oxford: Clarendon Press, 1981), pp. 259–60.
10 Quoted in Adams, *Balfour*, p. 209.
11 Jay, *Joseph Chamberlain*, pp. 271–3.
12 Ramsden, *The Age of Balfour*, pp. 10–15.
13 A. K. Russell, *Liberal Landslide: The General Election of 1906* (Newton Abbot: David & Charles, 1973), p. 182.
14 As noted by Blake, *The Conservative Party from Peel to Churchill*, pp. 175–6.
15 Élie Halévy, *Histoire du peuple anglais au xixe siècle, Épilogue*, vol. 2: *1905–1914* (Paris: Hachette, 1932), pp. 2–4.
16 Ramsden, *The Age of Balfour*, p. 18.
17 Russell, *Liberal Landslide*, pp. 173–4.
18 Ramsden, *The Age of Balfour*, p. 19. Subject to definitional ambiguities, I have generally used from this point on figures contained in David Butler and Anne Sloman, *British Political Facts 1900–1979* (London: Macmillan, 1980).
19 Ramsden, *The Age of Balfour*, p. 26.
20 Peter T. Marsh, *Joseph Chamberlain: Entrepreneur in Politics* (London: Yale University Press, 1994), p. 666.
21 John Campbell, *F. E. Smith, First Earl of Birkenhead* (London: Jonathan Cape, 1983), pp. 142–3, 155–7.
22 Adams, *Balfour*, p. 233.
23 Adonis, *Making Aristocracy Work*, p. 135.
24 Alfred M. Gollin, *The Observer and J. L. Garvin: A Study in a Great Editorship* (London: Oxford University Press, 1960), pp. 184, 204, 213–19. J. L. Garvin, the *Observer*'s editor, argued for 'a safe constructive compromise between the Gladstone Home Rule ... and the old Unionist position which has lost so much of its old basis' (ibid., p. 214).
25 In fact it was no more Bonar Law's proposal than a number of other people's, though Law favoured it. The most important promoters were the Unionist press. See R. J. Q. Adams, *Bonar Law* (London: John Murray, 1999), pp. 44–5.
26 Alan Sykes, *Tariff Reform in British Politics 1903–1913* (Oxford: Clarendon Press, 1979), p. 115.
27 Ramsden, *The Age of Balfour*, pp. 34–41.
28 Ibid., pp. 57–62.
29 For the contrast between his relatively pleasant private persona and his inability to communicate with colleagues, see David Dutton, *Austen Chamberlain: Gentleman in Politics* (Bolton: Ross Anderson, 1985), pp. 6–9. The similarities with another Tory leader, Edward Heath,

are striking, though Heath had no pleasant private persona.

30 Campbell, *F. E. Smith*, p. 628.

31 Dutton, *Austen Chamberlain*, p. 76.

32 See Alvin Jackson, 'Walter Hume Long, first Viscount Long (1854–1924)', *Oxford DNB*.

33 Robert Blake, *The Unknown Prime Minister: The Life and Times of Andrew Bonar Law, 1858–1923* (London: Eyre & Spottiswoode, 1955), p. 48.

34 Quoted in Adams, *Bonar Law*, p. 76.

35 Ramsden, *The Age of Balfour*, pp. 74–6.

36 Adams, *Bonar Law*, p. 119.

37 Ibid., p. 103.

38 Ibid., pp. 107–9.

39 Denis Gwynn, *The History of Partition (1912–1925)* (Dublin: Browne & Nolan, 1950), pp. 102–30.

40 Ibid., pp. 130–1.

41 Ramsden, *The Age of Balfour*, pp. 99, 111–12.

42 Adams, *Bonar Law*, p. 176.

43 Campbell, *F. E. Smith*, pp. 387–8.

44 The Dardanelles (or Gallipoli) campaign of 1915–16 against Turkey was initiated at the behest of Churchill, then First Lord of the Admiralty, but it became a major land engagement – and a humiliating, costly defeat – only when others invested ever more resources in a flawed strategy. Churchill, though, was personally blamed for the outcome.

45 Adams, *Bonar Law*, pp. 220–37; Blake, *The Unknown Prime Minister*, pp. 326–34.

46 Ramsden, *The Age of Balfour*, p. 115.

Chapter 9: 1922

1 The committee was in fact set up in April 1923. See Philip Goodhart with Ursula Branson, *The 1922: The Story of the Conservative Backbenchers' Parliamentary Committee* (London: Macmillan, 1973), pp. 15–20.

2 Despite the continued frequency of use of the term 'Unionist' in contemporary discussion, from this point on – somewhat artificially, but in the interests of clarity – I revert to use of the term 'Conservative' to describe the party and its members.

3 Martin Pugh, *Electoral Reform in War and Peace 1906–1918* (London: Routledge & Kegan Paul, 1978), pp. 103–18.

4 Ramsden, *The Age of Balfour*, pp. 119–22; Vernon Bogdanor, *The People and the Party System: The Referendum and Electoral Reform in British Politics* (Cambridge: Cambridge University Press, 1981), pp. 129–34.

5 Ramsden, *The Age of Balfour*, p. 122.

6 Maurice Cowling, *The Impact of Labour 1920–1924: The Beginning of*

Modern British Politics (Cambridge: Cambridge University Press, 1971), p. 429.

7 Floud and Johnson, eds, *The Cambridge Economic History of Modern Britain*, vol. 2, p. 320.

8 Keith Laybourn, 'The Rise of Labour and the Decline of Liberalism: The State of the Debate, *History*, 80 (1995), pp. 213–18; Henry Pelling, 'The Politics of the Osborne Judgement', *Historical Journal*, 25/4 (1982), pp. 889–909. The tortured history of the political levy – still a subject of controversy – is that in 1927, after the General Strike, contracting out was replaced by contracting in; contracting out recommenced in 1946; and the system was again shaken up in the 1980s. That shake-up might have been more severe – by reverting to contracting in rather than merely having review ballots – but the Conservatives were worried that over-radical reform might provide an unwelcome boost for the fortunes of the then apparently vibrant new left-of-centre Social Democratic Party.

9 Floud and Johnson, eds, *The Cambridge Economic History of Modern Britain*, vol. 2, p. 324.

10 Adams, *Bonar Law*, p. 290.

11 Michael Kinnear, *The Fall of Lloyd George: The Political Crisis of 1922* (London: Macmillan, 1973), pp. 3–19.

12 Kenneth O. Morgan, *Consensus and Disunity: The Lloyd George Coalition Government 1918–1922* (Oxford: Clarendon Press, 1979), pp. 344–6.

13 For events in Ireland, see Foster, *Modern Ireland*, pp. 495–515. The agreement of 1921 also made matters simpler for the Conservatives. Not only did they see the back of a large number of hostile Irish MPs, as noted earlier; they were also able to develop a less Irish-centred version of Unionism. See Stephen Evans, 'The Conservatives and the Redefinition of Unionism, 1912–1921', *Twentieth Century British History*, 9/1 (1998), pp. 1–27.

14 Adams, *Bonar Law*, p. 318.

15 Dutton, *Austen Chamberlain*, pp. 163–6.

16 Campbell, *F. E. Smith*, p. 529.

17 Winston Churchill, '"F. E." First Earl of Birkenhead', in *Great Contemporaries* (London: Thornton Butterworth, 1937), pp. 171–83.

18 Ramsden, *The Age of Balfour*, pp. 157–60.

19 Ibid., p. 163.

20 Dutton, *Austen Chamberlain*, p. 195.

21 Ibid., p. 193.

22 Ibid., p. 194.

23 John Ramsden, 'The Newport By-election and the Fall of the Coalition', in Chris Cook and John Ramsden, eds, *By-elections in British Politics* (London: UCL Press, 1997), pp. 13–36.

24 Dutton, *Austen Chamberlain*, p. 180.

25 Kinnear, *The Fall of Lloyd George*, pp. 123–4.

26 Lord [Max] Beaverbrook, *The Decline and Fall of Lloyd George – and Great was the Fall thereof* (London: Collins, 1963), pp. 200–1.

27 Kinnear, *The Fall of Lloyd George*, pp. 131–2 and Appendix I, pp. 221–42.

28 Beaverbrook, *The Decline and Fall of Lloyd George*, p. 201.

29 Adams, *Bonar Law*, p. 328.

30 Bonar Law's ashes were buried near the Tomb of the Unknown Warrior in Westminster Abbey. Asquith is said to have remarked when leaving: 'It is fitting that we should have buried the Unknown Prime Minister by the side of the Unknown Soldier' (ibid., p. 2).

31 Campbell, *F. E. Smith*, pp. 609–16.

32 J. C. C. Davidson, *Memoirs of a Conservative: J. C. C. Davidson's Memoirs and Papers, 1910–1937*, ed. Robert Rhodes James (London: Weidenfeld & Nicolson, 1969), p. 134.

33 The question of who was right – Balfour or Baldwin – in his assessment of the terms offered by America is debatable. See Adams, *Bonar Law*, pp. 347–51. For a view more sympathetic to Baldwin's analysis, see Keith Middlemas and John Barnes, *Baldwin: A Biography* (London: Weidenfeld & Nicolson, 1969), pp. 139–47.

34 Kinnear, *The Fall of Lloyd George*, p. 27.

35 Ramsden, *The Age of Balfour*, pp. 169–70.

36 Davidson, *Memoirs of a Conservative*, p. 135.

Chapter 10: Baldwin's Party

1 Davidson, *Memoirs of a Conservative*, p. 147.

2 David Gilmour, *Curzon* (London: Papermac, 1994), pp. 580–1.

3 Middlemas and Barnes, *Baldwin*, pp. 73–74.

4 The fullest recent analysis is to be found in Adams, *Bonar Law*, pp. 362–71.

5 Adams, *Balfour*, p. 364.

6 Ramsden, *An Appetite for Power*, p. 250.

7 Gilmour, *Curzon*, pp. 585–6. Curzon died on 20 March 1925.

8 Philip Williamson, *Stanley Baldwin: Conservative Leadership and National Values* (Cambridge: Cambridge University Press, 2007), p. 1. Williamson's book is a study of Baldwin's political rhetoric rather than a full-length biography. But pp. 21–60 provide an excellent summary of Baldwin's political career, which supplements the account in the *Oxford DNB*: Stuart Ball, 'Stanley Baldwin, first earl Baldwin of Bewdley (1867–1947)'.

9 Winston Churchill, *The Second World War*, vol. 1: *The Gathering Storm* (London: Penguin, 2005), p. 199. Unfortunately, the Penguin volume has a different index.

10 Middlemas and Barnes, *Baldwin*, p. 1072.

11 James Stuart, *Within the Fringe: An Autobiography* (London: Bodley Head, 1967), p. 75.

12 Andrew Roberts, *Eminent Churchillians* (London: Phoenix, 2004), p. 168.

13 David Reynolds, *In Command of History: Churchill Fighting and Writing the Second World War* (London: Allen Lane, 2004), p. 91.

14 Interview with Carol Kennedy, 'Top of the Classless', *The Director*, Nov. 1991. Admittedly, Major threw in Iain Macleod, Pitt the Younger, Gladstone and Neville Chamberlain, though 'not as Prime Minister'. But it was the coded message about Baldwin – in a list that notably excluded Churchill – which at the time created ripples.

15 Middlemas and Barnes, *Baldwin*, pp. 70-1.

16 Ibid., p. 390 (emphasis added).

17 Thomas Jones, *A Diary with Letters 1931-1950* (Oxford: Oxford University Press, 1954), p. 482. This was 1941.

18 Cf. Andrew Jones and Michael Bentley, 'Salisbury and Baldwin', in Maurice Cowling, ed., *Conservative Essays* (London: Cassell, 1978), pp. 25-40.

19 Williamson, *Stanley Baldwin*, p. 341.

20 Both passages from 'On England', speech to the Annual Dinner of the Royal Society of St George at the Hotel Cecil, 6 May 1924, in Stanley Baldwin, *On England and Other Addresses* (London: Philip Alan, 1933), pp. 1-7.

21 Speech delivered to the Empire Rally of Youth at the Royal Albert Hall, London, 18 May 1937, in Stanley Baldwin, *Service of Our Lives: Last Speeches as Prime Minister* (London: Hodder & Stoughton, 1937), p. 157.

22 Middlemas and Barnes, *Baldwin*, p. 168.

23 Baldwin's background was Methodist but he moved closer towards High Church Anglicanism, while refusing to attach himself to any particular tradition.

24 Middlemas and Barnes, *Baldwin*, pp. 1058-9.

25 G. M. Young, *Stanley Baldwin* (London: Rupert Hart-Davis, 1952), pp. 253-4.

26 A. J. P. Taylor, *British Prime Ministers and Other Essays*, ed. Chris Wrigley (London: Allen Lane, 1999), p. 51. This is the text of a televised lecture on Baldwin.

27 Baldwin himself held the Exchequer in expectation that the Liberal banker Reginald McKenna, at the time in America, would take the post. McKenna then declined and Chamberlain was appointed.

28 Middlemas and Barnes, *Baldwin*, pp. 212-13.

29 'Cato', *Guilty Men* (London: Victor Gollancz, 1940), p. 19. The authors sheltering behind the classical *nom de plume* were the left-wing journalists

Peter Howard, Frank Owen and Michael Foot, all paid by the Beaverbrook newspapers.

30 Ramsden, *The Age of Balfour*, pp. 181–3.

31 Ibid. pp. 194–5.

32 L. S. Amery, *My Political Life* (London: Hutchinson, 1953–5), vol. 1, p. 39; vol. 2, pp. 292–3; vol. 3, p. 510.

33 Ramsden, *The Age of Balfour*, pp. 187–92.

34 Christopher Andrew, *The Defence of the Realm: The Authorized History of MI5* (London: Penguin, 2010), pp. 126, 150.

35 An interesting indicator both of his success in covering his tracks and of the aura of fear he left behind him – he died in 1961 – is the bland and uncommunicative notice on him by Robert Blake in the *Oxford DNB*, 'Sir Joseph Ball (1885–1961)'.

36 There is no satisfactory full-length modern biography of Neville Chamberlain. Keith Feiling, *The Life of Neville Chamberlain* (London: Macmillan, 1946), the authorized biography, was written before most of the useful state papers were available. David Dilks, *Neville Chamberlain*, vol. 1: *Pioneering and Reform, 1869–1929* (Cambridge: Cambridge University Press, 1984) covers only the earlier period. Andrew Crozier, 'Neville Chamberlain (1869–1940)', summarizes the life in the *Oxford DNB*. The best overall account, emphasizing the debates about appeasement, is David Dutton, *Neville Chamberlain* (London: Hodder, 2001).

37 See Dilks, *Neville Chamberlain*, pp. 405–28, 446–57.

38 Ibid., pp. 577, 583.

39 Floud and Johnson, eds, *The Cambridge Economic History of Modern Britain*, vol. 2, pp. 331–41.

40 See the YouTube broadcast by Baldwin: 'Baldwin appeals for support for the national government (1931)', http://www.youtube.com/watch?v=0UL5AOgqWLQ.

41 Ramsden, *The Age of Balfour*, p. 321.

42 P. M. H. Bell, *The Origins of the Second World War* (London: Pearson Longman, 2007), pp. 151, 160.

43 It did not figure in the 1924 manifesto and Baldwin did not mention it in the election campaign – but neither had it been repudiated since it had been made in the wake of the 1913 Trades Union Act. To the contrary, even Baldwin had supported a Bill on similar lines in 1922 (Ramsden, *The Age of Balfour*, pp. 272–4).

44 Ibid., pp. 275–6.

45 Ibid. p. 277.

46 Middlemas and Barnes, *Baldwin*, pp. 462, 500.

47 Another subtle difference is that under the Thatcher reforms secondary picketing was dealt with under the civil law, while the existing criminal

(common) law, albeit clarified by government legal officers and the courts, was applied to mass picketing.

48 Ramsden, *The Age of Balfour*, pp. 290–2.
49 Blake, *The Conservative Party from Peel to Churchill*, pp. 231–2.
50 Maurice Cowling, *The Impact of Hitler: British Politics and British Policy 1933–1940* (Cambridge: Cambridge University Press, 1975), pp. 260–1.
51 Ramsden, *The Age of Balfour*, pp. 292–303.
52 That Chamberlain plotted is often denied, and he certainly protested his innocence. But Baldwin thought he had, and Baldwin knew how to make and read plots.
53 Ramsden, *The Age of Balfour*, pp. 311–14.
54 Middlemas and Barnes, *Baldwin*, p. 579.
55 Ramsden, *The Age of Balfour*, p. 329.
56 David Dutton, *Simon: A Political Biography of Sir John Simon* (London: Aurum Press, 1992), pp. 324–337.
57 A morganatic marriage would have meant that the divorced Mrs Simpson on her marriage to Edward VIII would not become Queen and her children would not succeed to the throne. It would have been an imported concept. The Commonwealth prime ministers, when consulted, also opposed. For the issues at stake, see Vernon Bogdanor, *The Monarchy and the Constitution* (Oxford: Clarendon Press, 1995), pp. 135–44.

Chapter 11: The Appeasement Party

1 Cf. Churchill, *The Second World War*, vol. 1, p. xiv. 'One day President Roosevelt told me that he was asking publicly for suggestions about what the war should be called. I said at once "the unnecessary war".'
2 Ramsden, *The Age of Balfour*, pp. 356–7.
3 Churchill, *The Second World War*, vol. 1, p. 199.
4 Letter dated 14 Sept., Aix, France, in Jones, *A Diary with Letters*, p. 115.
5 Bell, *The Origins of the Second World War*, p. 40.
6 R. A. C. Parker, *Chamberlain and Appeasement: British Policy and the Coming of the Second World War* (London: Macmillan, 1993), pp. 1, 19, 25.
7 Campbell, *F. E. Smith*, p. 640.
8 Dutton, *Austen Chamberlain*, pp. 230–52.
9 Bell, *The Origins of the Second World War*, p. 189.
10 Middlemas and Barnes, *Baldwin*, pp. 970–1.
11 Viscount Templewood [Samuel Hoare], *Nine Troubled Years* (London: Collins, 1954), p. 195.
12 See Norman Rose, 'Robert Vansittart, Baron Vansittart (1881–1957)' *Oxford DNB*.
13 For Hoare's persuasive account, see Templewood, *Nine Troubled Years*, pp. 149–92. See also the analysis by Norman Medlicott, 'The Hoare–Laval

Pact Reconsidered', in David Dilks, ed., *Retreat from Power: Studies in Britain's Foreign Policy in the Twentieth Century*, vol. 1: *1906–1939* (London: Macmillan, 1981), pp. 118–38.

14 James Thomas Emmerson, *The Rhineland Crisis 7 March 1936: A Study in Multilateral Diplomacy* (London: Maurice Temple Smith, 1977), pp. 226–37.

15 Richard Griffiths, *Fellow Travellers of the Right: British Enthusiasts for Nazi Germany 1933–9* (Oxford: Oxford University Press, 1983), p. 201.

16 N. J. Crowson, *Facing Fascism: The Conservative Party and the European Dictators, 1935–1940* (London: Routledge, 1997), p. 36.

17 Cowling, *The Impact of Hitler*, pp. 102–3.

18 Robert Rhodes James, *Churchill: A Study in Failure 1900–1939* (London: Weidenfeld & Nicolson, 1970), p. 299.

19 David Dutton, *Anthony Eden: A Life and Reputation* (London: Arnold, 1997), pp. 1–4, 73–4, 81–90, 99–101.

20 Parker, *Chamberlain and Appeasement*, p. 323.

21 Dutton, *Anthony Eden*, p. 107. For a more sympathetic interpretation of Eden's behaviour as Chamberlain's Foreign Secretary, see D. R. Thorpe, *Eden: The Life and Times of Anthony Eden First Earl of Avon, 1897–1977* (London: Pimlico, 2004), pp. 189–217.

22 Michael Howard, 'British Military Preparations for the Second World War', in David Dilks, ed., *Retreat from Power: Studies in Britain's Foreign Policy in the Twentieth Century*, vol. 1: *1906–1939* (London: Macmillan, 1981), pp. 102–3.

23 Middlemas and Barnes, *Baldwin*, p. 735.

24 Dutton, *Neville Chamberlain*, pp. 170–1.

25 Howard, 'British Military Preparations for the Second World War', pp. 104–115.

26 See David Dilks, 'Appeasement and "Intelligence"', in David Dilks, ed., *Retreat from Power: Studies in Britain's Foreign Policy in the Twentieth Century*, vol. 1: *1906–1939* (London: Macmillan, 1981), pp. 139–69.

27 'Cato', *Guilty Men*, p. 40.

28 Cowling, *The Impact of Hitler*, p. 355.

29 Cf. Parker, *Chamberlain and Appeasement*, p. 347: 'This book suggests that Chamberlain led the Government in 1938 and 1939, particularly in the months after Munich, into rejecting the option of a close Franco-British alliance, which might have dealt firmly with Mussolini's pretensions, and might have acted as a nucleus around which those states with reason to fight the Third Reich could assemble to resist it.'

30 R. A. C. Parker, *Churchill and Appeasement* (London: Macmillan, 2000), pp. 223–5.

31 Bell, *The Origins of the Second World War*, pp. 300–5.

32 David Dilks, ' "We must hope for the best and prepare for the worst": The Prime Minister, the Cabinet and Hitler's Germany, 1937–1939', *Proceedings of the British Academy*, 73 (1987), pp. 329–33.

33 John Colville, *Footsteps in Time* (London: Century Publishing, 1985), p. 74.

34 Dutton, *Neville Chamberlain*, p. 183.

35 Ibid., pp. 45–52.

36 Ibid., p. 57.

37 See Andrew Roberts's essay, 'The House of Windsor and the Politics of Appeasement', in *Eminent Churchillians*, pp. 5–53.

38 Dutton, *Neville Chamberlain*, p. 54; Graham Stewart, *Burying Caesar: Churchill, Chamberlain and the Battle for the Tory Party* (London: Weidenfeld & Nicolson, 1999), pp. 330–1. The allusion to Marlborough refers to Churchill's well-received biography of his ancestor John Churchill, first Duke of Marlborough and successful general.

39 Richard Cockett, *Twilight of Truth: Chamberlain, Appeasement and the Manipulation of the Press* (London: Weidenfeld & Nicolson, 1989), pp. 9–12.

40 Stewart, *Burying Caesar*, pp. 330–43; Andrew Roberts, *'The Holy Fox': The Life of Lord Halifax* (London: Phoenix, 1997), p. 123.

41 Alan Clark, *The Tories: Conservatives and the Nation State 1922–1997* (London: Phoenix, 1998), p. 204. Clark's volume gives a much fuller account of war politics – and indeed war fighting – than will be found here.

42 Dutton, *Neville Chamberlain*, pp. 62–3.

43 Halifax's decision to stand aside was explained to the King as being taken on the grounds that he was a peer. This was an excuse. Even the Labour leaders at this point would have preferred Halifax (Bogdanor, *The Monarchy and the Constitution*, pp. 99–103).

44 Stewart, *Burying Caesar*, pp. 331–3.

45 Blake, *The Conservative Party from Peel to Churchill*, pp. 242–3.

46 Cowling, *The Impact of Hitler*, pp. 375–8.

47 Griffiths, *Fellow Travellers of the Right*, pp. 14–15, 262–4.

48 Cowling, *The Impact of Hitler*, p. 266.

49 Jones, *A Diary with Letters*, pp. 197, 244–52.

50 On Henderson's shortcomings, see Felix Gilbert, 'Two Ambassadors: Perth and Henderson', in Gordon A. Craig and Felix Gilbert, eds, *The Diplomats 1919–1939* (Princeton: Princeton University Press, 1994), pp. 536–44.

51 Roberts, *'The Holy Fox'*, pp. 64–75.

52 See Andrew Roberts's essay, 'Patriotism: The Last Refuge of Sir Arthur Bryant', in *Eminent Churchillians*, pp. 287–322.

53 Roberts, *Eminent Churchillians*, p. 144.

54 Sheila Lawlor, *Churchill and the Politics of War, 1940–1941* (Cambridge: Cambridge University Press, 1994), pp. 33–44.

55 Channon, Sir Henry, *Chips: The Diaries of Sir Henry Channon*, ed. Robert Rhodes James (London: Weidenfeld & Nicolson, 1967), p. 252. Cf. the entry for 18 July: 'Winston was superb, magnificent, in the House' (ibid., p. 261). On 'Chips' himself see Richard Davenport-Hines, 'Sir Henry [Chips] Channon (1897–1958)', *Oxford DNB*.

56 For the strange but, for a brief time, important Brendan Bracken, see Jason Tomes, 'Brendan Bracken, Viscount Bracken (1901–1958)', *Oxford DNB*.

57 Roberts, *Eminent Churchillians*, pp. 146–47, 164. Dunglass's reported views are contained in a letter to Tommy Dugdale MP from his wife, Nancy.

58 Dutton, *Neville Chamberlain*, pp. 118–19.

59 Ibid. pp. 71–80. For Gollancz, see Paul Johnson, 'The Troubled Conscience of Victor Gollancz', in his *Intellectuals* (London: Weidenfeld & Nicolson, 1988), pp. 269–287.

Chapter 12: Churchill's Party, I – War

1 For a nearly persuasive critical analysis of Churchill's wider strategy, see John Charmley, *Churchill: The End of Glory* (London: Hodder & Stoughton, 1993). Charmley concludes: 'Churchill stood for the British Empire, for British independence and for an "anti-Socialist" vision of Britain. By July 1945 the first of these was on the skids, the second was dependent solely on the Americans and the third had just resulted in a Labour election victory. An appropriate moment to stop, for it was indeed the end of glory' (p. 649). For (to my mind) a fully persuasive rebuttal implicit in a recent study – and defence – of Churchill's conduct of the war, see Max Hastings, *Finest Years: Churchill as Warlord 1940–45* (London: HarperCollins, 2009). Hastings observes: 'No course of action existed which would have averted [Churchill's] nation's bankruptcy and exhaustion in 1945, nor its eclipse from world power and the new primacy of the United States and Russia' (p. 594).

2 Roberts, *Eminent Churchillians*, pp. 180–1.

3 See Robert Pearce, 'David Margesson, first Viscount Margesson (1890–1965)', *Oxford DNB*.

4 Stuart, *Within the Fringe*, pp. 88, 93–95, 11.

5 See Philip Murphy, 'Oliver Lyttelton, first Viscount Chandos (1893–1972)', *Oxford DNB*.

6 See N. Piers Ludlow, 'Duncan Sandys, Baron Duncan-Sandys (1908–1987)', *Oxford DNB*.

7 Roberts, *Eminent Churchillians*, pp. 181, 185–208.

8 John Ramsden, *The Age of Churchill and Eden, 1940–1957* (London: Longman, 1995), pp. 49–50.

9 Ibid., 56, 66–9.

10 'Celticus', *Why Not Trust the Tories?* (London: Victor Gollancz, 1944).

11 Geoffrey Mander, *We Were Not All Wrong* (London: Victor Gollancz, 1944).

12 Quintin Hogg, *The Left Was Never Right* (London: Faber & Faber, 1945).

13 See S. M. Cretney, 'Quintin Hogg, second Viscount Hailsham and Baron Hailsham of St. Marylebone (1907–2001)', *Oxford DNB*.

14 Ramsden, *The Age of Churchill*, p. 59.

15 Paul Addison, *The Road to 1945: British Politics and the Second World War* (London: Pimlico, 1994), pp. 134–9.

16 See Nicholas Timmins, *The Five Giants: A Biography of the Welfare State* (London: HarperCollins, 1995), pp. 11–25. On Beveridge himself, see Jose Harris, 'William Beveridge, Baron Beveridge (1879–1963)', *Oxford DNB*.

17 Margaret Thatcher, *The Path to Power* (London: HarperCollins, 1995), pp. 12–121.

18 Assheton, with his knowledge of the City and sympathy for liberal economics, was someone who would have flourished under Margaret Thatcher, but was consigned to early impotence under Butskellism, as noted by Julian Amery, 'Ralph Assheton, first Baron Clitheroe (1901–1984)', *Oxford DNB*.

19 Addison, *The Road to 1945*, pp. 221–7.

20 Ramsden, *The Age of Churchill*, p. 45.

21 Timmins, *The Five Giants*, pp. 110–30.

22 Ramsden, *The Age of Churchill*, p. 79.

23 Cf. Margaret Thatcher, speech to the Conservative Party Conference, Brighton, 8 Oct. 1982, and Conservative Party, *Invitation to Join the Government of Britain: The Conservative Manifesto 2010* (London, 2010).

24 Lord Butler, *The Art of the Possible: The Memoirs of Lord Butler* (London: Hamish Hamilton, 1971), pp. 96–107.

25 Ibid., p. 123.

26 Ramsden, *The Age of Churchill*, pp. 40–1.

27 Butler, *The Art of the Possible*, p. 127.

28 In February 1940 voting intentions as registered by Gallup were: Government 51 per cent, Opposition 27 per cent, Don't Know 22 per cent. Between June 1943 and June 1945, on a party basis, Labour's lead over the Conservatives varied between 8 and 20 per cent (Butler and Sloman, *British Political Facts*, p. 234; Anthony King, ed., *British Political Opinion 1937–2000: The Gallup Polls* (London: Politico's, 2001), table 1.1., p. 2).

29 Ramsden, *The Age of Churchill*, p. 79.

30 Colville, *Footsteps in Time*, p. 206.
31 Ibid., p. 207.
32 See the full text reproduced in Winston Churchill, *The Speeches of Winston Churchill*, ed. David Cannadine (London: Penguin, 1990), pp. 269–72.
33 Richard Cockett, *Thinking the Unthinkable: Think-Tanks and the Economic Counter-Revolution, 1931–1983* (London: HarperCollins, 1994), pp. 91–4.
34 Ramsden, *The Age of Churchill*, pp. 82–90.

Chapter 13: Churchill's Party, II – Peace

1 Stuart, *Within the Fringe*, pp. 145–7.
2 See John Ramsden, 'How Winston Churchill Became "The Greatest Living Englishman"', *Contemporary British History*, 12/3 (1998), pp. 1–40.
3 Paul Addison, 'Churchill and Social Reform', in Robert Blake and W. Roger Louis, eds, *Churchill* (Oxford: Clarendon Press, 1996), pp. 65–77.
4 For the text, see Churchill, *Speeches*, pp. 295–306. For the circumstances and reactions, see Martin Gilbert, *'Never Despair': Winston S. Churchill 1945–1965* (London: Heinemann, 1988), pp. 197–206.
5 Max Beloff, 'Churchill and Europe', in Robert Blake and W. Roger Louis, eds, *Churchill* (Oxford: Clarendon Press, 1996), pp. 443–55.
6 See Michael D. Kandiah, 'Frederick Marquis, first earl of Woolton (1883–1964)', *Oxford DNB*.
7 [Woolton, Lord], *The Memoirs of the Rt. Hon. the Earl Woolton* (London: Cassell, 1959), p. 331.
8 Ibid., pp. 336–7.
9 Ramsden, *The Age of Churchill*, p. 111.
10 Woolton, *Memoirs*, p. 338.
11 Ramsden, *The Age of Churchill*, pp. 117–118.
12 Philip Ziegler, *Edward Heath: The Authorised Biography* (London: Harper Press, 2010), p. 479. Swinton had became a 'hotbed for all [Heath] disliked most about his party'.
13 The three seats studied were Banbury, Lambeth Norwood and Gravesend. See Janet Johnson, 'Did Organization Really Matter? Party Organization and Conservative Electoral Recovery, 1945–59', *Twentieth Century British History*, 14/4 (2003), pp. 391–412.
14 From the introduction by Oliver Letwin to Alistair Cooke, ed., *Tory Policy-Making: The Conservative Research Department 1929 to 2009* (Eastbourne: Manor Creative, 2009), p. 4.
15 John Ramsden, *The Making of Conservative Party Policy: The Conservative Research Department since 1929* (London: Longman, 1980), pp. 23, 29, 33, 41–6, 63, 95–7.
16 Ibid., pp. 104–5, 106, 117, 129.

17 Stanley would have had a good chance of becoming Chancellor – he was even discussed as leadership material – had he not died in 1950. See Andrew Whitfield, 'Oliver Stanley (1896–1950)', *Oxford DNB*.
18 Conservative Party Archive, LCC 1/1/3.
19 Ramsden, *The Age of Churchill*, pp. 138–62.
20 See D. J. Dutton, 'David Maxwell Fyfe, earl of Kilmuir (1900–1967)', *Oxford DNB*.
21 Ramsden, *The Age of Churchill*, pp. 131–4.
22 Conservative Party Archive, LCC 1/1/4.
23 Paul Addison, *Churchill on the Home Front 1900–1955* (London: Jonathan Cape, 1992), pp. 396–402.
24 Ramsden, *The Age of Churchill*, pp. 190–4.
25 Conservative Party Archive, LCC 1/1/4.
26 Ramsden, *The Age of Churchill*, pp. 222, 228–30.
27 There are so many personal and thematic studies of Churchill that it is impossible to list them here. But the best short account is by Paul Addison, 'Sir Winston Churchill (1874–1965)', *Oxford DNB*.
28 Anthony Seldon, *Churchill's Indian Summer: The Conservative Government, 1951–55* (London: Hodder & Stoughton, 1981), p. 421.
29 John Colville, *The Fringes of Power: Downing Street Diaries 1939–1955* (London: Weidenfeld & Nicolson, 2004), entry for 22–3 March 1952, p. 604.
30 Others in the group were Robert Carr and Edward Heath.
31 Enoch Powell, 'A Strange Choice of Hero', *The Independent*, 27 March 1991, reproduced in *Reflections of a Statesman: The Writings and Speeches of Enoch Powell, selected by Rex Collings* (London: Bellew Publishing, 1991), p. 362. (The 'Hero' is Macleod.)
32 Thatcher, *The Path to Power*, pp. 86–7.
33 Roberts, 'Walter Monckton and the Retreat from Reality', in *Eminent Churchillians*, pp. 243, 246–7, 258.
34 Addison, *Churchill on the Home Front*, pp. 427–31.
35 See Philip Williamson, 'Noel Skelton (1880–1935)', *Oxford DNB*.
36 Addison, *Churchill on the Home Front*, pp. 405–6, 418.
37 Ibid., pp. 422–4.
38 Ibid., pp. 424–5.
39 Ibid., p. 421.
40 It was written (anonymously, of course) by Norman Macrae: 'Mr Butskell's Dilemma', *The Economist*, 13 Feb. 1954, pp. 439–41.
41 The term can also be used more widely to extend to social policy and the size of the state in the 1950s, but this is more misleading and is certainly not the subject of the article in question, which was intended as a warning to managers of economic demand that they must be tough enough to

deflate when necessary. For the large differences between Butler's and Gaitskell's views see Scott Kelly, *The Myth of Mr Butskell: The Politics of British Economic Policy, 1950–55* (Aldershot: Ashgate, 1988).

42 Addison, *Churchill on the Home Front*, p. 427.

43 'ROBOT' comes (more or less) from ROwan, BOlton and OTto.

44 See Peter Burnham, *Remaking the Postwar World Economy: Robot and British Policy in the 1950s* (London: Palgrave Macmillan, 2003), pp. 2–19, 157; Addison, *Churchill on the Home Front*, pp. 411–12; and, not least, Nigel Lawson, 'Robot and the Fork in the Road: How Churchill Might have Made Thatcher Unnecessary', *The Times Literary Supplement*, 21 Jan. 2005, pp. 11–12. Lord Lawson argues that had Robot been implemented, 'the Thatcherite revolution perhaps might never have been needed'.

45 Thorpe, *Eden*, pp. 271–2.

46 John Colville, *The Churchillians* (London: Weidenfeld & Nicolson, 1981), pp. 163–4.

47 Thorpe, *Eden*, p. 379.

48 Ibid., pp. 447–8.

49 Ibid. p. 459.

50 Lord Moran, *Winston Churchill: The Struggle for Survival 1940–1965* (London: Constable, 1966), p. 587.

51 Colville, *The Churchillians*, pp. 168–70. Churchill and Eden also quarrelled on the subject of the US wish to keep communist China out of negotiations on the future of Korea and Vietnam at Geneva. Churchill's view was that it was never in Britain's interest to oppose the United States on Far Eastern policy.

52 Ramsden, *The Age of Churchill*, p. 273.

53 Colville, *The Churchillians*, p. 171.

Chapter 14: Suez

1 Ramsden, *The Age of Churchill*, p. 273.

2 Thorpe, *Eden*, p. 456.

3 Colville, *The Churchillians*, p. 170.

4 Gilbert, *'Never Despair'*, p. 1085.

5 Ramsden, *The Age of Churchill*, pp. 278–81.

6 Thorpe, *Eden*, pp. 434, 438, 450.

7 For Bobbety, often underrated in modern accounts of the party, see David Goldsworthy, 'Robert Arthur James Gascoyne-Cecil, fifth marquess of Salisbury (1893–1972)', *Oxford DNB*.

8 Thorpe, *Eden*, pp. 443–4.

9 Ibid., pp. 459–60.

10 John Boyd-Carpenter, *Way of Life: The Memoirs of John Boyd-Carpenter* (London: Sidgwick & Jackson, 1980), pp. 123–5.

11 W. Roger Louis, 'Churchill and Egypt 1946–56', in Robert Blake and W. Roger Louis, eds, *Churchill* (Oxford: Clarendon Press, 1996), pp. 473–90.
12 Moran, *Winston Churchill*, pp. 559–60.
13 Thorpe, *Eden*, pp. 407, 411.
14 Ibid., pp. 473–8.
15 Margaret Thatcher, *The Downing Street Years* (London: HarperCollins, 1993), p. 188.
16 Martin Gilbert, *Israel: A History* (London: Doubleday, 1998), pp. 316–29.
17 Ramsden, *The Age of Churchill*, pp. 305, 307, 309–10, 318.
18 Thorpe, *Eden*, p. 503.
19 See the full account in D. R. Thorpe, *Supermac: The Life of Harold Macmillan* (London: Chatto & Windus, 2010), pp. 332–56. Thorpe gives Macmillan the benefit of the doubt. But doubt there must be. See also the next chapter of this book, in which Macmillan's character is discussed.
20 Thorpe, *Eden*, pp. 506–10.
21 The text of the Protocol of Sèvres of 24 October 1956, in so far as it can be reconstructed, is to be found (as an appendix) in Keith Kyle, *Suez* (London: Weidenfeld & Nicolson, 1991), pp. 565–7.
22 Thorpe, *Eden*, pp. 513–20.
23 John C. Campbell, 'The Soviet Union, the United States, and the Twin Crises of Hungary and Suez', in W. R. Louis and Roger Owen, eds, *Suez 1956: The Crisis and its Consequences* (Oxford: Clarendon Press, 1989), pp. 233–53.
24 Diane B. Kunz, 'The Importance of Having Money: The Economic Diplomacy of the Suez Crisis', in W. R. Louis and Roger Owen, eds, *Suez 1956: The Crisis and its Consequences* (Oxford: Clarendon Press, 1989), pp. 215–32.
25 Thorpe, *Eden*, p. 524.
26 Ibid., pp. 534–46.
27 Bogdanor, *The Monarchy and the Constitution*, pp. 93–5.
28 Thorpe, *Supermac*, pp. 356–67.
29 Lord Selwyn-Lloyd, *1956: A Personal Account* (London: Jonathan Cape, 1978), p. 257.
30 Henry Kissinger, *Diplomacy* (London: Simon & Schuster, 1994), pp. 544–9.
31 Eden's own position shifted towards what has been described as British Gaullism, based on a distrust of America, which did not, of course, preclude good relations with individual Americans. See David Carlton, 'Anthony Eden', in Vernon Bogdanor, ed., *From New Jerusalem to New Labour: British Prime Ministers from Attlee to Blair* (London: Macmillan, 2010), pp. 54–8.

Chapter 15: Macmillan's Party

1 Alistair Horne, *Macmillan: The Official Biography*, vol. 2: *1957–1986* (London: Macmillan, 1989), p. 145.
2 Ibid., p. 158.
3 See Simon Ball, *The Guardsmen: Harold Macmillan, Three Friends, and the World They Made* (London: HarperCollins, 2004). Macmillan and Salisbury would have a spectacularly vicious falling out over Africa (ibid., pp. 344–69). On Crookshank, see also S. J. Ball, 'Harry Crookshank, first Viscount Crookshank (1893–1961)', *Oxford DNB*.
4 Thorpe, *Supermac*, p. 375.
5 Ramsden, *The Winds of Change*, p. 1.
6 Thorpe, *Supermac*, p. 75.
7 Ibid., p. 103.
8 His characteristic desire to hark back to his radical past is demonstrated by the title of *The Next Five Years* given to the 1959 Tory manifesto.
9 Thorpe, *Supermac*, pp. 110–21.
10 Harold Macmillan, *The Middle Way: A Study of the Problem of Economic and Social Progress in a Free and Democratic Society* (London: Macmillan, 1966), pp. 260–2. A flavour of Macmillan's approach is given by the following passage: 'The weaknesses of partial planning seem to me to arise from the incomplete and limited application of the principles of planning. The lesson of these errors, which I regard as errors of limitation, is not that we should retreat. On the contrary, we must advance, more rapidly and still further, upon the road of conscious regulation' (ibid., p. 11).
11 Thorpe, *Supermac*, pp. 133–6.
12 Ibid., p. 385.
13 Horne, *Macmillan*, vol. 2, p. 64.
14 Ramsden, *The Winds of Change*, pp. 33–4.
15 For her own reflections on 1958, see Thatcher, *The Path to Power*, p. 92.
16 See John Ramsden, 'Derick Heathcoat Amory, first Viscount Amory (1899–1981)', *Oxford DNB*.
17 Thorpe, *Supermac*, pp. 395–410.
18 Ibid., p. 389.
19 Ibid., p. 479.
20 Horne, *Macmillan*, vol. 2, p. 429.
21 Ibid., p. 522.
22 Horne, *Macmillan*, vol. 2, pp. 120, 135–6.
23 Ramsden, *The Winds of Change*, p. 55.
24 D. E. Butler and Richard Rose, *The British General Election of 1959* (London: Macmillan, 1960), pp. 59–60. In response, Rab Butler suggested as an appropriate Labour Party slogan, 'a bribe a day keeps the Tories away'.

25 Harold Macmillan, *The Macmillan Diaries: The Cabinet Years, 1950–1957*, ed. Peter Catterall (London: Macmillan, 2003), pp. xvii–xix.

26 See Mark Garnett, 'John Wyndham, first Baron Egremont and sixth Baron Leconfield (1920–1972)', *Oxford DNB*.

27 Ramsden, *The Winds of Change*, pp. 148–52.

28 Richard Lamb, *The Macmillan Years 1957–1963: The Emerging Truth* (London: John Murray, 1995), p. 272.

29 For Macleod's character, see Robert Shepherd, *Iain Macleod* (London: Hutchinson, 1994), and David Goldsworthy, 'Iain Macleod (1913–1970)', *Oxford DNB*.

30 Horne, *Macmillan*, vol. 2, p. 315.

31 Roy Jenkins, 'David Ormsby Gore, fifth Baron Harlech (1918–1985)', *Oxford DNB*.

32 Horne, *Macmillan*, vol. 2, pp. 281–308, 362–85.

33 The above account of Anglo-American nuclear deliberation and collaboration is based on: John Baylis, *Anglo-American Defence Relations 1939–1984: The Special Relationship* (London: Macmillan, 1984), pp. 29–136; Alistair Horne, 'The Macmillan Years and Afterwards', in W. Roger Louis and Hedley Bull, eds, *The 'Special Relationship': Anglo-American Relations since 1945* (Oxford: Clarendon Press, 1986), pp. 87–102; C. J. Bartlett, *'The Special Relationship': A Political History of Anglo-American Relations since 1945* (London: Longman, 1992), pp. 20–100.

34 Lamb, *The Macmillan Years*, p. 319; Alan S. Milward, *The Rise and Fall of a National Strategy 1945–1963 (The UK and the European Community*, vol. 1) (London: Whitehall History Publishing, 2002), pp. 463–83. While remaining 'independent' – de Gaulle caused outrage in 1967 by publicly authorizing as French nuclear doctrine the achievement of a global system, able to fire in all directions (*à tous azimuts*), i.e. including, theoretically speaking, at the United States – the French deterrent has, in practice, over the years enjoyed the benefit of a good deal of US assistance.

35 Jean Lacouture, *De Gaulle*, vol. 3, *Le Souverain 1959–1970* (Paris: Seuil, 1986), pp. 334–5.

36 Thorpe, *Supermac*, pp. 452–3, 468.

37 Horne, *Macmillan*, vol. 2, pp. 356–7.

38 Peter Oppenheimer, 'Muddling Through: The Economy, 1951–1964', in Vernon Bogdanor and Robert Skidelsky, eds, *The Age of Affluence* (London: Macmillan, 1970), pp. 140–51.

39 The possibility that incomes policy might – along with a lower exchange rate – have allowed the British economy to make progress in these years was, interestingly, left open by Samuel Brittan, writing at the time: see Samuel Brittan, *The Treasury under the Tories 1951–1964* (London: Penguin, 1964), pp. 280–300. But twelve years later he concluded that

incomes policies do not work, and demonstrated why: see Samuel Brittan and Peter Lilley, *The Delusion of Incomes Policy* (London: Temple Smith, 1976).

40 Ramsden, *The Winds of Change*, p. 155.

41 Anthony Howard, *Rab: The Life of R. A. Butler* (London: Jonathan Cape, 1987), p. 308.

42 Thorpe, *Supermac*, pp. 521–4.

43 Ibid., p. 525.

44 Lamb, *The Macmillan Years*, pp. 457–76.

45 For these changes, see Christopher Booker, *The Neophiliacs: A Study of the Revolution in English Life in the Fifties and Sixties* (London: Collins, 1969).

46 See Roy Jenkins, 'Harold Wilson, Baron Wilson of Rievaulx (1916–1995)', *Oxford DNB*.

47 Booker, *The Neophiliacs*, p. 129.

48 Michael Pinto-Duschinsky, 'From Macmillan to Home, 1959–1964', in Peter Hennessy and Anthony Seldon, eds, *Ruling Performance: British Governments from Attlee to Thatcher* (Oxford: Basil Blackwell, 1987), pp. 170–2. For Macleod's *Spectator* article see n. 56 below.

49 Anthony Sampson, *Anatomy of Britain* (London: Hodder & Stoughton, 1962), p. 337.

50 In the wake of the Profumo scandal, when Maudling's chances were at their best, a poll of Tory MPs taken by Harry Boyne, the chief political correspondent of the *Daily Telegraph*, showed overwhelming support for him (Lamb, *The Macmillan Years*, p. 476).

51 Thorpe, *Supermac*, pp. 546–53.

52 For Macmillan's own account of his thinking and decisions in this period, see the recently published second volume of his diaries: *The Macmillan Diaries: Prime Minister and After, 1957–66*, ed. Peter Catterall (London: Macmillan, 2011), pp. 589–611.

53 Butler recalls in his memoirs how during Macmillan's foreign tours he invariably acted as head of the government:

> But to do him justice, the Prime Minister never gave me any impression that he wanted me to succeed him. The only time the subject was ever mentioned was late one night at Chequers when he said, 'At your age you had better be king-maker rather than king'. This seemed strange coming from a man nearly nine years my senior, but it was of course entirely consistent with the attitude he later adopted in the succession in 1963. (Butler, *The Art of the Possible*, p. 196)

54 Vernon Bogdanor, 'The Selection of the Party Leader', in Anthony

Seldon and Stuart Ball, eds, *Conservative Century: The Conservative Party since 1900* (Oxford: Oxford University Press, 1994), pp. 75–80. The chairman of the 1922 Executive, John Morrison, had bluntly told Butler: 'The chaps won't have you' (Goodhart, *The 1922*, p. 191).

55 Enoch Powell, 'How Macmillan Deceived the Queen', *The Spectator*, 13 Oct. 1973, reproduced in *Reflections of a Statesman*, p. 315.

56 Enoch Powell, 'Rab Butler: The Man Who Saw His Prize Snatched Away', *The Times*, 10 March 1982, reproduced in *Reflections of a Statesman*, p. 325.

57 Iain Macleod, 'The Tory Leadership', *The Spectator*, 17 Jan. 1964, pp. 65–7.

58 D. R. Thorpe, *Alec Douglas-Home* (London: Sinclair Stevenson, 1996), pp. 322–3, 331–2, 355–7.

59 Ibid., p. 366.

60 Lewis Baston, *Reggie: The Life of Reginald Maudling* (London: Sutton, 2004), pp. 224–37.

61 Thorpe, *Alec Douglas-Home*, pp. 367–72.

62 Robert Blake, *The Conservative Party from Peel to Major* (London: Heinemann, 1997), p. 297.

63 The memorandum was published under the thirty-year disclosure rule. But, contrary to what was written in the newspapers, it was indeed seen, studied, marked up and commented upon by Mrs Thatcher, who took what Macmillan thought seriously – perhaps too seriously. This is proved by the version, with additions, published on the Margaret Thatcher Foundation website:
http://www.margaretthatcher.org/PREM19/1980/THCR1–5–11.pdf.

64 To Enoch Powell, Macmillan fitted the description of Whig so well as to be a 'Superwhig'. This was not intended as a compliment since, according to Powell, Whiggism is characterized by 'cynicism, agnosticism, bread and circuses' (Enoch Powell, 'Superwhig?', *The Spectator*, 1 March 1980, reproduced in *Reflections of a Statesman*, pp. 318–19).

65 David Cameron, as Leader of the Opposition, chose to hang a portrait of Macmillan in his office. The significance of this is, of course, debatable.

Chapter 16: Heath's Party

1 Ramsden, *The Making of Conservative Party Policy*, pp. 236–7.

2 Brendon Sewill, 'Policy Making for Heath', in Alistair Cooke, ed., *Tory Policy-Making: The Conservative Research Department 1929 to 2009* (Eastbourne: Manor Creative, 2009), p. 68.

3 These provisions were significantly weakened at the expense of the sitting leader in 1975, under terms revised by a committee chaired by Lord Home. The 15 per cent majority rule thenceforth applied to all the

available votes, not just those cast. Provoked by Heath's obstruction in his last months, it was also provided that there be an election within twenty-eight days of the start of a new Parliament, i.e. in November, and that the election be held annually, whether the sitting leader had resigned or died or not, and whether the party was in power or not. These changes finished Mrs Thatcher in 1990. Heath, though, was finished in 1975 by a straight majority on the first ballot.

4 Edward du Cann, *Two Lives: The Political and Business Careers of Edward du Cann* (Malvern: Images, 1995), p. 126.

5 Simon Heffer, *Like the Roman: The Life of Enoch Powell* (London: Weidenfeld & Nicolson, 1998), p. 385.

6 Baston, *Reggie*, pp. 263, 504.

7 John Campbell, *Edward Heath: A Biography* (London: Jonathan Cape, 1993), pp. 1–8.

8 Cf. Ziegler, *Edward Heath*, pp. 164–5.

9 Campbell, *Edward Heath*, pp. 30–9.

10 Cf. Ziegler, *Edward Heath*, pp. 180–1.

11 Margaret Thatcher, *The Path to Power*, p. 68.

12 It would later be argued by those wishing tactfully to excuse Heath while professing support for his successor that the intellectual tide had not yet turned in 1970, whereas it would later. This is to ignore the fact there was an intellectual case made by Powell, among others, before 1970, but the party had refused to grasp it or adhere to it. Cf. Lord [Robert] Blake, 'A Changed Climate', in Lord Blake and John Patten, eds, *The Conservative Opportunity* (London: Macmillan, 1976), pp. 1–12.

13 Thorpe, *Supermac*, pp. 371–2, 378–9.

14 See Henry Kissinger, *Years of Renewal* (London: Simon & Schuster, 1999), pp. 602–3.

15 Douglas Hurd, *An End to Promises: Sketch of a Government 1970–74* (London: Collins, 1979), pp. 13–14.

16 Foreword, in Conservative and Unionist Party, *Conservative 1970 Manifesto: A Better Tomorrow* (London, 1970).

17 Ramsden, *The Winds of Change*, p. 264.

18 Ziegler, *Edward Heath*, p. 173.

19 Peter Walker, *Staying Power: An Autobiography* (London: Bloomsbury, 1991), pp. 42–3, 128–9.

20 Enoch Powell, *Income Tax at 4/3 in the £*, ed. Anthony Lejeune (London: Tom Stacey, 1968).

21 For Powell's intellectual evolution, see Heffer, *Like the Roman*, pp. 1–198.

22 Conservative Party Archive, LCC 1/2/8: discussion of Enoch Powell's defence policy paper on 23 Jan. 1967 and press release of his speech to Birkenhead Conservative Association on 21 Jan. 1967.

23 Conservative Party Archive, LCC 1/2/9: discussion of a paper from Quintin Hogg on race relations on 24 April 1967.

24 Thatcher, *The Path to Power*, p. 144. She joined the Shadow Cabinet, with the Fuel and Power portfolio, in October 1967.

25 Conservative Party Archive, LCC 1/2/12.

26 Conservative Party Archive, LCC 1/2/11.

27 Heffer, *Like the Roman*, p. 454. Actually, it was not a 'Roman' but rather the Sibyl (a rather unattractive legendary prophetess) who came up with the prediction. Powell originally quoted the verse in Latin, but then offered a translation – which he later claimed to regret.

28 For a full discussion, see ibid., pp. 444–68.

29 On Heath's unpopularity as registered in Gallup polls between 1966 and 1970, see the chart in David Butler and Michael Pinto-Duschinsky, *The British General Election of 1970* (London: Macmillan, 1971), p. 64.

30 Sewill, 'Policy Making for Heath', pp. 72–4.

31 Conservative Party Archive, CRD 3/9/93. This material is most easily accessed via the Margaret Thatcher website, http://www.margaretthatcher.org/.

32 Ziegler, *Edward Heath*, pp. 216–17.

33 The results were: Conservatives 330; Labour 287; Liberals 6; Scottish Nationalists 1; Others 6.

34 Dennis Kavanagh, 'The Heath Government 1970–1974', in Peter Hennessy and Anthony Seldon, eds, *Ruling Performance: British Governments from Attlee to Thatcher* (Oxford: Basil Blackwell, 1987), p. 218.

35 Nicholas Ridley, *My Style of Government* (London: Hutchinson, 1991), p. 4. Ridley had already incurred Heath's anger when he chaired a policy group on the nationalized industries which recommended denationalization (or privatization as it came to be known). Heath described the proposals as 'alarmingly naïve and even half-baked' (Ziegler, *Edward Heath*, p. 210).

36 Edward Heath, *The Course of My Life: My Autobiography* (London: Hodder & Stoughton, 1998), pp. 399–400. Heath claims he had told Ridley he was to leave the DTI but offered him Minister of Arts, which Ridley rejected.

37 Heath, *The Course of My Life*, p. 521. Cf. the explanation – which is not a refutation of Heath's point – in Thatcher, *The Path to Power*, pp. 200, 221.

38 The former Cabinet Secretaries, Lords Wilson of Dinton and Lord Turnbull, told the Iraq War inquiry that Tony Blair sidelined Cabinet, whereas Mrs Thatcher always maintained Cabinet government (Rosa Prince, 'Tony Blair Went to War Without Cabinet Consent, Senior Mandarins Say', *Daily Telegraph*, 25 Jan. 2011.

39 Ziegler, *Edward Heath*, pp. 246–51.

40 Philip Norton, *Conservative Dissidents: Dissent within the Parliamentary Conservative Party 1970–74* (London: Temple Smith, 1978), pp. 207, 223–4, 238.

41 For example, commenting on the Industry Act, which reversed his industrial policy in 1972: 'Some tried to make out that the Industry Act was a "socialist" measure, an abandonment of principle. This was unjustifiable. It was a sensible, pragmatic and practical response to a disappointing state of affairs' (Heath, *The Course of My Life*, p. 400).

42 Hurd, *An End to Promises*, p. 140.

43 The phrase was apparently coined by the Tory MP (and later Thatcher critic) Julian Critchley: see Hugo Young, *One of Us: A Biography of Margaret Thatcher* (London: Macmillan, 1989, p. 98).

44 Norton, *Conservative Dissidents*, pp. 230–2.

45 Powell published his speeches in a series of books, of which the most important are *Freedom and Reality* (London: Batsford, 1969) and *Still to Decide* (London: Batsford, 1972), both edited by John Wood. An early and not uninfluential example of the way in which old and new right thinking were bonded is Lord Coleraine, *For Conservatives Only: A Study of Conservative Leadership from Churchill to Heath* (London: Tom Stacey, 1970).

46 Cockett, *Thinking the Unthinkable*, pp. 163–76.

47 See T. E. Utley, *A Tory Seer: The Selected Journalism of T. E. Utley*, ed. Charles Moore and Simon Heffer (London: Hamish Hamilton, 1989), with a foreword by Margaret Thatcher and an introduction by Enoch Powell.

48 Moreover, I deal fully with Margaret Thatcher's life and works in my forthcoming biography.

49 Speech to the Labour party conference, Blackpool, 28 Sept. 1976. The speech continues: 'and that in so far as it ever did exist, it worked by injecting inflation into the economy. And each time that has happened, the average level of unemployment has risen. Higher inflation followed by higher unemployment. That is the history of the last twenty years.' The passage was apparently written by Callaghan's son-in-law, the economist and journalist Peter Jay.

50 Ziegler, *Edward Heath*, pp. 542–3, 588–9.

51 Enoch Powell, *Joseph Chamberlain* (London: Thames & Hudson, 1977), p. 151.

Chapter 17: Thatcher's Party

1 What follows is based upon – and is covered far more extensively in – Thatcher, *The Path to Power*, pp. 282–461.

2 Peter Thomas and Geoffrey Rippon declined to serve, the latter being

resolutely hostile. Robert Carr, Nicholas Scott and Peter Walker were all sacked. (Walker came back into government.) Of the first Shadow Cabinet, Ian Gilmour (shadowing Home Office; later Defence), James Prior (Employment), Timothy Raison (Environment), Reginald Maudling (Foreign Affairs, until sacked in November 1976), Michael Heseltine (Industry; later Environment) were all hostile to her and her economic policy. Others, like Lord Carrington and Francis Pym, disliked the policy but kept their heads down. Carrington finished up a friend. Pym's head would be raised (in government) in 1981, before being brutally removed in 1983.

3 Campbell, *Edward Heath*, pp. 689–90.

4 One should also note that a barely concealed civil war was taking place all the while within the Conservative Party on the back benches and in the country. This became, for a time, heavily focused on Tory pressure groups. The studiously high-minded, middle-of-the-road Bow Group (founded in 1951) had been overtaken, at least in terms of public profile, by the Monday Club on the right, which gave Mrs Thatcher support but received little appreciation from her. Closer to her way of thinking, though less well supported, was the right-of-centre free market Selsdon Group, founded in 1973, of which Nicholas Ridley was the key figure. While sheltering behind the legend created about the 1970 Selsdon conference's radicalism, it advanced, at least in the economic sphere, views mainly associated with Enoch Powell. The Tory Reform Group (which has no connection with the old Tory Reform Committee) was founded by Peter Walker out of several other left-of-centre Tory groups in 1975–6. The TRG's main battles were with the Monday Club in the universities, and in Westminster with the policies of Mrs Thatcher.

5 The results in terms of seats were: Conservatives 339; Labour 269; Liberal 11; Plaid Cymru 2; Scottish Nationalist 2; Others (Northern Ireland) 12.

6 Thatcher, *The Downing Street Years* remains by far the best available source. A critical antidote is provided by John Campbell, *Margaret Thatcher*, vol. 1: *The Grocer's Daughter* (London: Jonathan Cape, 2000) and *Margaret Thatcher*, vol. 2: *Iron Lady* (London: Jonathan Cape, 2003).

7 Sir John Major's biographer makes no high claims for his distinctness: 'He did not have room in 1990–97 to pursue a real Majorite agenda, nor did he have the time to develop his admittedly inchoate ideas'. See Anthony Seldon with Lewis Baston, *Major: A Political Life* (London: Weidenfeld & Nicolson, 1997), p. 74.

8 'To those waiting with bated breath for that favourite media catchphrase, the "U-turn", I have only one thing to say. You turn if you want to. The lady's not for turning.' Party conference speech, Brighton, 10 Oct. 1980, in Margaret Thatcher, *Collected Speeches*, ed. Robin Harris (London:

HarperCollins, 1997), p. 116.

9 Norman St John Stevas was removed in a mini-reshuffle in January 1981. In the September reshuffle Ian Gilmour, Mark Carlisle and Lord Soames were sacked and Prior was moved, after much grumbling, to Northern Ireland. Norman Tebbit and Cecil Parkinson joined the Cabinet. This was the only one of Mrs Thatcher's Cabinet reshuffles that decisively shifted the political balance of her Government.

10 Conservatives 397; Labour 209; SDP–Liberal Alliance 23; Others 21.

11 For differing accounts of when, why – and by whose fault – the anti-inflation policy failed, see Thatcher, *The Downing Street Years*, pp. 695–706, and Nigel Lawson, *The View from No. 11: Memoirs of a Tory Radical* (London: Bantam, 1992), pp. 638–57.

12 Conservatives 375; Labour 229; SDP–Liberal Alliance 22; Others 24.

13 See Thatcher, *The Downing Street Years*, pp. 589–624.

14 Thatcher 204; Heseltine 152; abstentions 16.

15 Lord Lamont, who was Major's campaign manager in 1990 and understood him probably better than anyone else, notes:

> John Major turned out to be the ideal leadership candidate in a way that I had not fully appreciated at the time. With hindsight it is clear. He had cultivated to quite an extraordinary level of execution the ability to encourage people on both sides of any question to believe that he was one of them. This facility was the secret of John Major's political success and his rapid rise. (Norman Lamont, *In Office*, London: Little, Brown, 1999, p. 496)

16 Or, as Lord Lamont puts it in the same passage, 'imparting a clear sense of direction' (ibid.).

17 John Major, *The Autobiography* (London: HarperCollins, 1999), pp. 286–7.

18 A sample of the high-flown claims – later dropped – for subsidiarity can be found in official Conservative Party propaganda. See Conservative and Unionist Party, *The Campaign Guide 1994: A Comprehensive Survey of Conservative Policy*, ed. Alistair B. Cooke (London: Conservative and Unionist Central Office, 1994), pp. 641–3.

19 See Thatcher, *The Path to Power*, pp. 481–8.

20 Major was notoriously caught out describing some of his colleagues in 1993 as 'bastards'. For a revealing insight into what one member of the Cabinet thought about – and was prepared to say to a journalist about – the Prime Minister and his policy, see the account by Hugo Young of a lunch with Michael Portillo in June 1995 (Hugo Young, *The Hugo Young Papers: Thirty Years of British Politics – Off the Record*, ed. Ion Trewin (London: Allen Lane, 2008), pp. 448–50).

21 Gallup's regular polling on the question of which party was considered best placed to handle the economy shows that in May 1992 the Conservatives had a strong lead over Labour (48.8 per cent to 30.3 per cent). By December the positions were totally reversed (28.3 per cent to 38.7 per cent). This remained the case right up to the 1997 election, despite a resumption of growth and strong finances. See King, ed., *British Political Opinion*, table 2.4, pp. 117–18. For a less than convincing and factually disputable attempt to put a favourable gloss on the ERM fiasco and his own role in events, see Sir John Major, 'The Limits of Power: Conservative Experience and Opportunity', speech at Churchill College, Cambridge, 26 Nov. 2010, http://www.telegraph.co.uk/news/politics/8163394/John-Major-The-Limits-of-Power.html#.

22 It came nearer to it than many thought at the time, because Major had privately decided he would go if had received just three votes fewer. The results were: Major 218; Redwood 89; Abstentions 8; Spoiled 12. See Major, *The Autobiography*, p. 645. Redwood's slogan of 'No Change, No Chance' at least turned out to be accurate.

23 Norman Gash even suggested in a laudatory essay to mark Mrs Thatcher's ten years as Prime Minister that she and Peel were a unique pair, as truly 'radical' Conservative leaders. See Norman Gash, 'The Supreme Tory Radical', in Conservative and Unionist Party, *The First Ten Years: A Perspective on the Conservative Era that began in 1979* (London: Conservative Central Office, 1989), pp. 9–14.

24 For some of the evidence, differently assessed but pointing to the same conclusions, see: Thatcher, *The Path to Power*, pp. 568–78; Lawson, *The View from No. 11*, pp. 976–83; Patrick Minford, *The Supply Side Revolution in Britain* (London: Edward Elgar/Institute of Economic Affairs, 1991); Nicholas Crafts, *The Conservative Government's Economic Record: An End of Term Report* (London: Institute of Economic Affairs, 1998).

25 Employment laws and the frontiers between private and public enterprises (at least until the big bank bail-outs of 2008) were left broadly as Mrs Thatcher bequeathed them. But public expenditure, after being checked for the first two years, started a rapid rise. Between 1999/2000 and 2005/6 spending was allowed to grow by 4.8 per cent a year in real terms, rising as a proportion of GDP to 43.1 per cent. As a result, government borrowing rose and so, in due course, did taxes.

26 This point is illustrated in general by the results of the annual Heritage Foundation and Wall Street Journal Index of Economic Freedom, which regularly confirms the close relationship between economic freedom and prosperity: see http://www.heritage.org/index/. A particularly striking example is that of Chile, which began along the road to economic freedom before Britain, when during the military government from 1973, under the

inspiration of Chicago-style economics, and has remained, under left-of-centre governments (and now a right-of-centre one), the pre-eminent economic success story of South America. See José Piñera, 'Why Chile is More Economically Free than the United States', Cato Institute, http://www.cato-at-liberty.org/why-chile-is-more-economically-free-than-the-united-states/.

27 On which see John O'Sullivan, *The President, the Pope and the Prime Minister: Three Who Changed the World* (Washington: Regnery, 2006).

28 For example, *de haut en bas*: 'Like all ideologies, Thatcherism is based on a simplistic view of human nature, which reflects more the qualities of the ideologist than any common attributes of mankind' (Ian Gilmour, *Dancing with Dogma: Britain under Thatcherism*, London: Simon & Schuster, 1992, p. 271); 'Of course, the Conservatism of the eighties and nineties had borne no relation to One-Nation Toryism: indeed, the Conservative Governments of 1979–97 had not even pursued One-British-Nation policies, but One-South-east-England policies. Such attitudes will probably be even less appropriate in the coming decades, when worship of the market is likely to be on the wane' (Ian Gilmour and Mark Garnett, *Whatever Happened to the Tories: The Conservative Party since 1945*, London: Fourth Estate, 1997, p. 384).

29 As director between 1985 and 1989, I inadvertently helped the nurturing. The CRD background of many current Tory modernizers is discussed briefly in the following chapter.

30 The Federation of Conservative Students was ultra-Thatcherite in an embarrassingly extreme libertarian sense. It was finally closed down by Norman Tebbit in 1986; in its place a Conservative Collegiate Forum was created. The leading lights of the FCS dispersed and their views diverged, some remaining recognizably right-wing and others forming a key element of the modernizing faction, while one – the present Speaker of the House of Commons, John Bercow – went so far to the left as to be rumoured to be planning to defect to the Labour Party, though so far he has not done so.

31 Tim Montgomerie, 'Margaret Thatcher Revolution Inspires this Generation', *The Times*, 30 April 2009, http://www.timesonline.co.uk/tol/news/politics/article6195108.ece.

32 See Thatcher, *The Downing Street Years*, pp. 829–55.

33 After good local election results in May 1992, each year brought new disasters. By the end of the Parliament the Conservatives had a clear majority in only one county council, five London boroughs and eight shire districts. In only three local authorities outside the Home Counties were the Tories in control. See David Butler and Dennis Kavanagh, *The British General Election of 1997* (London: Macmillan, 1997), p. 13.

34 For a by no means entirely successful contemporary attempt to harmonize and reconcile them, see Robin Harris, *The Conservative Community: The Roots of Thatcherism – and its Future* (London: Centre for Policy Studies, 1989).

35 That said, some of the criticisms levelled against Margaret Thatcher from a philosophical perspective are wide of the mark. For example, Phillip Blond, dubbed by many David Cameron's guru and apparently the foremost intellectual advocate of the 'Big Society' (addressed in the next chapter), has written:

> Mrs Thatcher, elected in 1979, instigated a much-needed modernisation of the British economy. Unfortunately, however, she threw the baby out with the bathwater by completely surrendering the entirety of British public life and its related values to the dictates of a neo-liberalism whose consequences she would not have supported and the operations of which she clearly did not understand. Instead of a popular capitalism with open and free markets, what she got instead was a capitalism captured by concentrations of capital and a market monopolised by vested interest and the dominance of the already wealthy. With the bottom half of the population progressively de-capitalised and subject to an ever-widening array of barriers to market entry, more and more people were unable to fulfil the promise of a capitalism for all ... If socialists laid waste to the private sphere, Mrs Thatcher completed the evisceration of British culture by allowing the same in the public realm. (Phillip Blond, *Red Tory: How Left and Right Have Broken Britain and How We Can Fix It*, London: Faber & Faber, 2010, pp. 18–19)

Much could be said of this analysis. But, briefly: (a) Phillip Blond is unrealistic about the state of Britain in the pre-Thatcher era, imagining a degree of community and public-spirited high-mindedness which did not exist – and which were certainly altogether absent from the nationalized industries that Mrs Thatcher denationalized and the union closed shops that she opened up; (b) he greatly exaggerates the power of government – any government, at least in a democracy – to change society; (c) consequently, he blames Mrs Thatcher for social and cultural trends over which she had no control and little influence; (d) in the service of his polemic, he gives a significance to artificial abstractions like 'neo-liberalism' (and its 'dictates') that they do not deserve in explaining what occurred; (e) he does not, therefore, accurately describe either how the free market system works in general or how it worked specifically in the 1980s;

(f) he apparently accepts the falsehood that the poor became poorer, and also implies, as the left did and does, that the fault lay in the Thatcher Government's unconcern with equality of outcomes; (g) he confuses the effect of welfare dependency – of which Mrs Thatcher was keenly aware and highly disapproving, though admittedly she did insufficient to check it – with what he describes as 'decapitalisation', an odd charge considering how many tenants bought their council houses and how many people acquired shares and savings; (h) finally, he does not seem to place value on the fact that people nowadays have, partly as a result of the market and of Mrs Thatcher's policies, but also as a result of global technological progress, much more control over their own lives. The results of this individual empowerment may, indeed, be messy and, on many occasions, aesthetically deplorable. No doubt there is a lack of civic spirit, and moral rearmament in all sorts of ways is required. But freedom is a good, all the same, and we should be glad that people have more of it.

36 Mrs Thatcher's own reflections on and application of her beliefs are to be found principally in Thatcher, *The Path to Power*, pp. 465–606; Margaret Thatcher, *The Collected Speeches*, ed. Robin Harris (London: HarperCollins, 1997); and Margaret Thatcher, *Statecraft: Strategies for a Changing World* (London: HarperCollins, 2002). For an analysis of Mrs Thatcher's message at a psychological and philosophical, even moral level, involving promotion of the 'vigorous virtues', see Shirley Letwin, *The Anatomy of Thatcherism* (London: Fontana, 1992).

Chapter 18: Cameron's Party?

1 It was a true landslide defeat. Labour won 419 seats (a record for the party). The Conservative total of 165 seats was the party's lowest number since 1906. The 10 per cent swing from Conservative to Labour was the largest swing since 1945. The Conservative share of the vote at 30.7 per cent was the lowest since the coming of mass democracy (Butler and Kavanagh, *The British General Election of 1997*, p. 244).

2 Major cleverly told the conference: 'Our defeat was not your defeat. Perhaps it was mine.' (Predictably, at this there were loud expressions of dissent.) 'Perhaps divided views – expressed without restraint – in the parliamentary party made our position impossible.' He also shifted some blame by implication on to his predecessor, pledging to give Hague 'the unqualified support – in public and in private – that he has a right to expect from his predecessor'. See Michael White, 'Conservatives in Blackpool: Major Accepts Election Blame. Swansong: Former PM Bows Out with Promise of Public Backing to Hague, in Pointed Reference to Thatcher and Tory Party Divisions', *Guardian*, 8 Oct. 1997.

3 An indispensable document illustrating this phase of manic modernization

is the collection of essays edited by Edward Vaizey, Nicholas Boles and Michael Gove, *A Blue Tomorrow: New Visions for Modern Conservatives* (London: Politico's, 2001). Of these contributions perhaps the most radical is that by Andrew Cooper, 'A Party in a Foreign Land: The Tory Failure to Understand How Britain Has Changed', pp. 9–29. He is dismissive of emphasis on marriage, chides Conservatives for intolerance towards homosexuals and racial minorities, admires Tony Blair's public blubbing on the death of Princess Diana, decries the 'Millwall tendency', the 'flat-earthers' and the 'face-lift faction' of Tories, and concludes with five reasons why an 'unchanged' Conservative Party 'cannot survive'. Mr Cooper is now David Cameron's Director of Strategy at 10 Downing Street.

4 This was one of the four failed Tory leadership campaigns of which I have personal experience – perhaps some sort of record. They were: Margaret Thatcher in 1990, John Redwood in 1995, Michael Howard in 1997 and David Davis in 2005. Howard's was the best organized, and also the least successful. He came last in the first round – Clarke 49; Hague 41; Redwood 27; Peter Lilley 24; Howard 23. For a good account, see Michael Crick, *In Search of Michael Howard* (London: Simon & Schuster, 2005), pp. 364–90.

5 Redwood could not, in the end, carry his forces with him. The final result (in the third round) was Hague 93; Clarke 70.

6 See Tim Bale, *The Conservative Party from Thatcher to Cameron* (Cambridge: Polity, 2010), pp. 88–93.

7 See Simon Walters, *Tory Wars* (London: Politico's, 2001), pp. 86–127.

8 He had apparently had his sights on a minimum of 240 to 260 seats if he were to stay on. This was hardly realistic, but it must have added to the shock. Cf. ibid., p. 6.

9 Several leading modernizers, including George Osborne (the current Chancellor) and Daniel Finkelstein (now a political columnist on *The Times*), served as key Hague advisers.

10 His earlier role in effectively opposing Maastricht ensured that not just the modernizers and Euro-enthusiasts but those who had supported Major's compromise detested him.

11 For a flavour of this, see Edward Vaizey, 'IDS: Rising from the Ashes?', *New Statesman*, 4 March 2002, http://www.newstatesman.com/200203040021.

12 Duncan Smith appointed Mark Macgregor, former chairman of the FCS (which, as noted above, had been disbanded by Norman Tebbit), as the chief executive of Central Office. Macgregor was now a Portillo supporter and a key modernizer. He was removed by Iain Duncan Smith in 2003, creating a huge row, in which Portillo unhelpfully intervened. The dispute

also became mixed up with false allegations of financial impropriety regarding IDS's wife – the contrived scandal of 'Betsygate'. A still worse misjudgement was IDS's appointment of Dominic Cummings as Director of Strategy. Cummings resigned in 2003 and promptly wrote an article in which he described Duncan Smith as 'incompetent' and said he 'must be replaced'. He added for good measure: 'the Party is a joke' (Dominic Cummings, 'Mr Duncan Smith is Incompetent and Must Go', *Sunday Telegraph*, 26 Oct. 2003).

13 Howard was part of a talented, ambitious set of Cambridge Tories who dominated the university's Conservative Association in the late 1950s and early 1960s, and which included Kenneth Clarke, Norman Lamont, Leon Brittan, John Gummer and Norman Fowler (Crick, I*n Search of Michael Howard*, pp. 58–81).

14 Francis Elliott and James Hanning, *Cameron: The Rise of the New Conservative* (London: Fourth Estate, 2007), p. 252.

15 Cf. Dennis Kavanagh and David Butler, *The British General Election of 2005* (London: Macmillan, 2005), pp. 196–202, 235–59.

16 What follows is no more than a sketch. A full account of the networks and tactics of the Conservative modernizers will only be written when one of them decides to reveal it, or it is prised out of the most significant people by an enterprising journalist. In any case, it would be out of place here.

17 Several, not least David Cameron himself and his most influential adviser, Steve Hilton, both worked in corporate relations/marketing.

18 This illustrates one of the puzzling contradictions about the modernization project. The modernizers often note that positions held by the Conservative Party are popular, but when it is explained to the public that they are Conservative positions, support for them falls. (The case of immigration control is one such: it is, indeed, the only case to which reference is usually made.) In other words, people dislike being associated with the Conservative Party. This may well be true. But it may also be the fact of politicization to which they object: i.e. they do not want to be bracketed with any party. Indeed, the reliability of the polling on which the modernizing approach rests has been challenged, persuasively and in detail. See Andrew Scholefield and Gerald Frost, *Too 'Nice' to be Tories? How the Modernizers have Damaged the Conservative Party* (London: Social Affairs Unit, 2011), pp. 26–32.

More importantly, it does not follow that the Conservative Party should cease to hold distinctively and traditionally conservative positions. Indeed, that would defeat the point. The positions the modernizers have urged the Conservatives to adopt – e.g. support for homosexual marriage and promotion of a green agenda – or those they have urged the party to forget – e.g. support for custodial punishments, for action against illegal immigrants, for restoration of powers from Europe – make no sense in terms of the opinion poll findings. They do, of course, make sense if these are positions which the modernizers hold because of their own ideological preferences rather than because of objective analysis of the Conservative Party's interests. Improving the Conservative Party's image should, logically, have been aimed at allowing it to promote important and popular policies, not at abandoning them for something else.

19 Notable ex-CRD modernizers (or participants in the Cameron leadership enterprise, which is not quite the same thing) include: Steve Hilton, George Osborne (Chancellor), Edward Vaizey (Culture Minister), Rachel Whetstone (wife of Steve Hilton, and former political secretary to Michael Howard) and Edward Llewellyn (Chief of Staff at 10 Downing Street). One should also mention Daniel Finkelstein, ex-director of CRD, journalist and Cameron apologist. The political commentator Bruce Anderson, of an earlier generation of CRD (mine), though a keen supporter of Cameron (as previously of Major and Hague), is not quite in the same category, but may for completeness be added here. Another over-lap is with the so-called 'Notting Hill set', a phrase devised, it seems, by the since disgraced MP (and David Davis supporter) Derek Conway. This includes Cameron, Osborne, Hilton, Vaizey and Whetstone, but also Nicholas Boles (now an MP; the founder of Policy Exchange), and Michael Gove (former journalist, now Education Secretary).

20 Not even, apparently, by some well-informed observers: cf. Janet Daley, 'The Battle is on for the Soul of the Tory Party', *Sunday Telegraph*, 9 Jan. 2011.

21 Speaking to a Google Zeitgeist Europe Conference in San Francisco on 22 May 2006, David Cameron stated:

> Too often in politics today, we behave as if the only thing that matters is the insider stuff that we politicians love to argue about – economic growth, budgets, GDP. GDP, Gross domestic product. Yes it's vital. It measures the wealth of our society [*sic*]. But it hardly tells the whole story. Wealth is about so much more than pounds, or euros or dollars can ever measure. It's time we admitted that there's more to life than money, and it's time we focused not just on GDP, but on GWB – general well-being.

It has now been decided that all government policies will be tested for their effect on people's 'well-being' so as to make 'individual happiness' an indicator of their success (Marie Woolf, 'Happy and You Know It? Make it Policy', *Sunday Times*, 20 March 2011).

22 Matthew D'Ancona, 'The Men Who Want to Save the Tories from

Themselves', *Sunday Telegraph*, 20 Feb. 2011. D'Ancona discusses the role of three key modernizers – Daniel Finkelstein, Rick Nye and Andrew Cooper – at the Social Market Foundation in the late 1990s.

23 Andrew Pierce, 'Horror as Cameron Brandishes the B Word', *Daily Telegraph*, 5 Oct. 2005.

24 Churchill was furious when in March 1944 Thelma Cazalet-Keir, on behalf of the Tory Reform Committee, amended Butler's Education Bill on the issue of equal pay for women teachers. Churchill treated the clause's deletion as a matter of confidence and made the Reformers file back into the lobby against their own proposal. See John Grigg, 'Thelma Cazalet Keir (1899–1989)', *Oxford DNB*.

25 For example, David Willetts, 'Renewing Civic Conservatism', The Oakeshott Lecture, London School of Economics, 20 Feb. 2008: http://www.conservativecoops.com/20022008_david_willetts_oakeshott _lecture.

26 Richard H. Thaler and Cass R. Sunstein, *Nudge: Improving Decisions about Health, Wealth and Happiness* (London: Penguin, 2009), p. 253. A 'Nudge Unit' (the Behavioural Insight Team) functions in the Cabinet Office. See Patrick Wintour, 'David Cameron's "Nudge Unit" Aims to Improve Economic Behaviour', *Guardian*, 9 Sept. 2010.

27 'Social responsibility' was tried out but never caught on. Cf. David Cameron, 'What I Believe in is Family, Responsibility and Opportunity', *Daily Telegraph*, 8 Sept. 2007.

28 Nigel Morris, 'Big Society is My Mission in Politics', *Independent*, 14 Feb. 2011.

29 Cameron's own contributions have sometimes increased the confusion. For example, in his 2010 party conference speech he included government debt repayment and public waste elimination as topics within the Big Society remit.

30 For an overall explanation of the Big Society philosophy by someone who has as good a claim as anyone to understand it, see Jesse Norman, *The Big Society: The Anatomy of the New Politics* (Buckingham: University of Buckingham Press, 2011).

31 For what Mrs Thatcher actually said – and actually meant – by her 'no such thing as society' observation, see Thatcher, *Statecraft*, p. 426.

32 Although Andy Coulson, the No. 10 Director of Communications, eventually left Downing Street for other reasons, he was apparently a marked man because he was thought insufficiently committed to the Big Society (Allegra Stratton, 'Andy Coulson Takes the Rap in the Big Society Blame Game', *Guardian*, 9 Feb. 2011).

33 There are six more fundamental reasons to believe that the Big Society programme will not fulfil expectations. First, as a general rule of thumb,

no powerful political idea was ever invented: and this one is obviously artificial. Second, the aspiration to mobilize private and charitable effort requires a consensus on what constitutes good works: today society has no common view on what constitutes meritorious activity, i.e. on the 'good' – as the effective exclusion of orthodox Christians from this area under the guise of human rights law confirms. Third, the link between the Big Society and Cameron's and his colleagues' plans to re-engineer society (increasing social mobility, promoting women and minorities, giving an extra advantage to children and students from poor families, etc.) will always lead to disappointment. This is because egalitarian strategies always involve state intervention, which squeezes out private initiative. (On which see e.g. Philip Collins, 'Progressive Tories Must Learn Their Own History', *The Times*, 28 Oct. 2009). Fourth, in practice, so much of the charitable sector depends directly or indirectly on government spending that its promotion is incompatible with severe restraint in public spending. Fifth, the essential component in volunteering is wealthy people with leisure: today's highly employed middle class just do not have the time for philanthropy (though they may donate to it). And finally, unluckily but unavoidably, the Big Society was and is bound to be attacked, and very effectively too, as a cover for those spending cuts that today's fiscal requirements demand.

34 Elliott and Hanning, *Cameron*, pp. 261–5.

35 The party members refused to accept euthanasia. The proposal was rejected by the party's constitutional college. For the changes to be approved, 50 per cent of those eligible to vote were required to vote in favour, along with 66% of MPs who voted and 66% of National Convention members who voted. This final threshold was not reached. The results were: MPs 71.4% for, 28.6% against; volunteers 58.4% for, 41.5% against; peers and MEPs 63.6% for, 36.5% against.

36 The results were: first round (MPs only), Davis 62, Cameron 56, Fox 42, Clarke 38; second round (MPs only), Cameron 90, Davis 57, Fox 51; third round (party members), Cameron 134,446 (68%), Davis 64,398 (32%).

37 Cameron's public embrace of optimism was better received by commentators on the left than by those on the right. See e.g. Andrew Rawnsley, 'David Cameron's Sunshine Could Put Labour in the Shade', *Observer*, 8 Oct. 2006.

38 For an assessment that suggests that the 'rebranding' and 'decontamination' elements of the Cameron strategy failed to deliver the expected gains, see John O'Sullivan, 'Cameron Capers: The Anatomy of the British Election', *National Review Online*, 15 June 2010, http://www.national-review.com/articles/229951/cameron-capers-john-osullivan.

39 See the Conservative Home Election Report, http://conservativehome.

blogs.com/generalelectionreview/, and subsequent comment. For a some-what less critical view see Dennis Kavanagh and Philip Cowley, *The British General Election of 2010* (London: Macmillan, 2010), pp. 334–9.

40 The results of the 2010 General Election were: Conservative 306, Labour 258, Liberal Democrat 57, Democratic Unionist 8, Scottish National 6, Sinn Fein 5, Plaid Cymru 3, Social Democratic and Labour 3, Alliance 1, Green 1, Independent 1, Speaker 1.

41 David Cameron, speech to Conservative party conference, *Daily Telegraph*, 6 Oct. 2010.

42 Simon Walters, 'Cameron Aide: Coalition Will Survive Tory Majority', *Mail on Sunday*, 24 Oct. 2010; James Kirkup, 'John Major: Let's Keep the Coalition After the Next Election', *Daily Telegraph*, 27 Nov. 2010.

43 Whether accurate or not, the suggestion that the new Director of Strategy at No. 10 once described the Tory grass-roots membership as 'vile' is also less than helpful in assuaging party worries: http://twitter.com/TimMontgomerie/status/37576508667207680.

44 Apparently, Conservative Party membership has dropped by 80,000 since David Cameron became leader: http://conservativehome.blogs.com/thetorydiary/2010/10/tory-membership-down-by-a-third-to-177000-since-cameron-became-leader.html.

45 Lady Warsi publicly defends wearing of the *burqa* and believes that Islamophobia is a serious problem at middle-class dinner parties. David Cameron pointedly refused to endorse her views. See James Kirkup, 'Tory Chief Attacks "Bigotry" Against Muslims', *Daily Telegraph*, 20 Jan. 2011, and 'Cameron Ducks Muslim Bigotry Row', *Daily Telegraph*, 21 Jan. 2011. It is difficult to imagine that many Conservative supporters agree with her.

46 Monypenny and Buckle, *Disraeli*, vol. 1, p. 1263.

47 The exact figures are debatable and depend on definitions of coalition. Salisbury's Government of 1886 to 1892 was supported by the Liberal Unionists, and from 1887 Goschen was a member of it, but it was not a formal coalition. That from 1895 to 1900, by contrast, was. By the end of Salisbury's premiership and during Balfour's the relations between the Conservatives and Liberal Unionists were so close as hardly to qualify as a coalition either. Similarly, by 1935, and arguably several years earlier, the coalition element of the National Government was rather notional. It was Conservative in all but name, though Baldwin liked to play up the cross-party façade. In 1935 MacDonald actually lost his seat and had to be found one by the Conservatives, standing at a by-election the following year and representing the Scottish universities.

48 See Geoffrey Wheatcroft, 'Clegg will Pray that Disraeli was Wrong about Loving Coalitions', *Guardian*, 29 June, 2010; also Kavanagh and Cowley, *The British General Election of 2010*, pp. 385–6.

BIBLIOGRAPHY

I list here only those sources that I found of direct use for the writing of this book and to which, therefore, reference is to be found in the notes. Essays that appear in a volume by the same author, and individual volumes of multi-volume works, are not listed individually here. Essays by different authors contained in a single volume are listed separately, as is the volume under the name of its editor(s).

Primary Sources
Archival
Conservative Party Archive, Oxford
The Margaret Thatcher Foundation Archive
  (http://www.margaretthatcher.org/)

Published
Butler, David, and Anne Sloman, *British Political Facts 1900–1979* (London: Macmillan, 1980)
King, Anthony, ed., *British Political Opinion 1937–2000: The Gallup Polls* (London: Politico's, 2001)

The Daily Telegraph
The Director
The Guardian
Hansard
The Mail on Sunday

BIBLIOGRAPHY

The National Review
The New Statesman
The Quarterly Review
The Spectator
The Sunday Telegraph
The Sunday Times
The Times Literary Supplement

Arbuthnot, Harriett, *The Journals of Mrs Arbuthnot 1820–1832*, ed. Francis Bamford and the Duke of Wellington, 2 vols (London: Macmillan, 1950)

Baldwin, Stanley, *On England and Other Addresses* (London: Philip Alan, 1933)

Baldwin, Stanley, *Service of Our Lives: Last Speeches as Prime Minister* (London: Hodder & Stoughton, 1937)

Burke, Edmund, *The Writings and Speeches of Edmund Burke*, vol. 1: *The Early Writings*, ed. T. O. McCloughlin and James J. Boulton (Oxford: Clarendon Press, 1997)

Burke, Edmund, *The Writings and Speeches of Edmund Burke*, vol. 2: *Party, Parliament and the American Crisis*, ed. Paul Langford (Oxford: Clarendon Press, 1981)

Burke, Edmund, *The Writings and Speeches of Edmund Burke*, vol. 3: *Party, Parliament and the American War 1774–1780*, ed. W. M. Elofson and John A. Woods (Oxford: Clarendon Press, 1996)

Burke, Edmund, *The Writings and Speeches of Edmund Burke*, vol. 8: *The French Revolution 1790–1794*, ed. L. G. Mitchell (Oxford: Clarendon Press, 1990)

Burke, Edmund, *The Writings and Speeches of Edmund Burke*, vol. 9, part 1: *The Revolutionary War*, ed. R. B. McDowell (Oxford: Clarendon Press, 1991)

Channon, Sir Henry, *Chips: The Diaries of Sir Henry Channon*, ed. Robert Rhodes James (London: Weidenfeld & Nicolson, 1967)

Churchill, Winston, *The Speeches of Winston Churchill*, ed. David Cannadine (London: Penguin, 1990)

Colville, John, *The Fringes of Power: Downing Street Diaries 1939–1955* (London: Weidenfeld & Nicolson, 2004)

Conservative and Unionist Party, *The Campaign Guide: An Election Handbook for Unionist Speakers* (Edinburgh: David Douglas, 1892)

Conservative and Unionist Party, *The Campaign Guide 1900: A Handbook for Unionist Speakers* (Edinburgh: David Douglas, 1900)

Conservative Party, *The Campaign Guide 1994: A Comprehensive Survey of Conservative Policy*, ed. Alistair B. Cooke (London, 1994)

Conservative Party, *Conservative Manifesto 1970: A Better Tomorrow* (London, 1970)

Conservative Party, *Invitation to Join the Government of Britain: The Conservative Manifesto 2010* (London, 2010)

Croker, John Wilson, *The Correspondence and Diaries of the Late Right Honourable John Wilson Croker, LL.D., FRS, Secretary to the Admiralty from 1809 to 1830*, ed. Louis J. Jennings, 3 vols (London: John Murray, 1884)

Davidson, J. C. C., *Memoirs of a Conservative: J. C. C. Davidson's Memoirs and Papers, 1910–1937*, ed. Robert Rhodes James (London: Weidenfeld & Nicolson, 1969)

Disraeli, Benjamin, *Coningsby* (Dublin: Nonsuch, 2007)

Disraeli, Benjamin, *The Letters of Disraeli to Lady Bradford and Lady Chesterfield*, ed. Marquis of Zetland, 2 vols (London: Ernest Benn, 1929)

Disraeli, Benjamin, *Lord George Bentinck: A Political Biography* (London: Archibald Constable, 1905)

Disraeli, Benjamin, *The Sayings of Disraeli*, ed. Robert Blake (London: Duckworth, 2003)

Disraeli, Benjamin, *Sybil or The Two Nations* (Oxford: Oxford University Press, 2008)

Disraeli, Benjamin, 'Vindication of the English Constitution in a Letter to a Noble and Revered Lord by Disraeli the Younger', in *Whigs and Whiggism: Political Writings*, ed. William Hutcheon (London: John Murray, 1913), pp. 111–232

Fielding, Henry, *The History of Tom Jones, a Foundling*, in *The Works of Henry Fielding Esq.*, ed. Leslie Stephen, 2 vols (London: Smith, Elder, 1882)

Fraser, Sir William, *Disraeli and His Day* (London: Kegan Paul, Trench, Trübner & Co. Ltd, 1891)

Gathorne-Hardy, Gathorne, *The Diary of Gathorne Hardy, later Lord Cranbrook, 1866–1892: Political Selections*, ed. Nancy E. Johnson (Oxford: Clarendon Press, 1981)

Greville, Charles, *The Greville Memoirs: A Journal of the Reign of Queen Victoria from 1837–1852 by the Late Charles Greville, Esq., Clerk of the Council to the Sovereign*, ed. Henry Reeve, 3 vols (London: Longmans, Green, 1885)

Greville, Charles, *The Greville Memoirs: A Journal of the Reigns of King George IV and King William IV by the Late Charles Greville, Esq., Clerk of the Council to the Sovereign*, ed. Henry Reeve, 3 vols (London: Longmans, Green, 1875)

Hamilton, Lord George, *Parliamentary Reminiscences and Reflections*, 2 vols (London: John Murray, 1916, 1922)

Jones, Thomas, *A Diary with Letters 1931–1950* (Oxford: Oxford University Press, 1954)

Macmillan, Harold, *The Macmillan Diaries: The Cabinet Years, 1950–1957*, ed. Peter Catterall (London: Macmillan, 2003)

Macmillan, Harold, *The Macmillan Diaries: Prime Minister and After, 1957–66*, ed. Peter Catterall (London: Macmillan, 2011)

Macmillan, Harold, *The Middle Way: A Study of the Problem of Economic and Social Progress in a Free and Democratic Society* (London: Macmillan, 1966)

Peel, Robert, *Sir Robert Peel – from his Private Papers*, ed. C. S. Parker, 3 vols (London: John Murray, 1899)

Powell, Enoch, *Freedom and Reality*, ed. John Wood (London: Batsford, 1969)

Powell, Enoch, *Income Tax at 4/3 in the £*, ed. Anthony Lejeune (London: Tom Stacey, 1968)

Powell, Enoch, *Reflections of a Statesman: The Writings and Speeches of Enoch Powell, selected by Rex Collings* (London: Bellew Publishing, 1991)

Powell, Enoch, *Still to Decide*, ed. John Wood (London: Batsford, 1972)

[Russell, G. W. E.,] *Collections and Recollections by One Who has Kept a Diary* (London: Smith, Elder, 1898)

Stanley, Edward, *Disraeli, Derby and the Conservative Party: Journals and Memoirs of Edward Henry, Lord Stanley 1849–1869*, ed. John Vincent (Hassocks: Harvester Press, 1978)

Stanley, Edward, *A Selection from the Diaries of Edward Henry Stanley, 15th Earl of Derby (1826–1893) between September 1869 and March 1878*, Royal Historical Society, Camden Fifth Series, vol. 4, ed. John Vincent (London: 1994)

Thatcher, Margaret, *The Collected Speeches*, ed. Robin Harris (London: HarperCollins, 1997)

Utley, T. E., *A Tory Seer: The Selected Journalism of T. E. Utley*, ed. Charles Moore and Simon Heffer (London: Hamish Hamilton, 1989)

Young, Hugo, *The Hugo Young Papers: Thirty Years of British Politics – Off the Record*, ed. Ion Trewin (London: Allen Lane, 2008)

Secondary Sources

Adams, R. J. Q., *Balfour: The Last Grandee* (London: John Murray, 2007)

Adams, R. J. Q., *Bonar Law* (London: John Murray, 1999)

Addison, Paul, 'Churchill and Social Reform', in Robert Blake and W. Roger Louis, eds, *Churchill* (Oxford: Clarendon Press, 1996), pp. 57–78

Addison, Paul, *Churchill on the Home Front 1900–1955* (London: Jonathan Cape, 1992)

Addison, Paul, *The Road to 1945: British Politics and the Second World War* (London: Pimlico, 1994)

Addison, Paul, 'Sir Winston Churchill (1874–1965)', *Oxford Dictionary of National Biography* (Oxford: Oxford University Press, 2004–): hereafter *Oxford DNB*

Adonis, Andrew, *Making Aristocracy Work: The Peerage and the Political System in Britain 1884–1914* (Oxford: Clarendon Press, 1993)

Aldous, Richard, *The Lion and the Unicorn: Gladstone vs. Disraeli* (London: Hutchinson, 2006)

Amery, L. S., *My Political Life*, 3 vols (London: Hutchinson, 1953–5)

Amery, Julian, 'Ralph Assheton, first Baron Clitheroe (1901–1984)', *Oxford DNB*

Andrew, Christopher, *The Defence of the Realm: The Authorized History of MI5* (London: Penguin, 2010)

Aspinall, A., *Politics and the Press c.1780–1850* (London: Home & Van Thal, 1949)

Bagehot, Walter, *Biographical Studies*, ed. Richard Holt Hutton (London: Longmans, Green, 1889)

Bale, Tim, *The Conservative Party from Thatcher to Cameron* (Cambridge: Polity, 2010)

Ball, S. J. 'Harry Crookshank, first Viscount Crookshank (1893–1961)', *Oxford DNB*

Ball, Simon, *The Guardsmen: Harold Macmillan, Three Friends, and the World They Made* (London: HarperCollins, 2004)

Ball, Stuart, 'Stanley Baldwin, first Earl Baldwin of Bewdley (1867–1947)', *Oxford DNB*

Bartlett, C. J., *'The Special Relationship': A Political History of Anglo-American Relations since 1945* (London: Longman, 1992)

Baston, Lewis, *Reggie: The Life of Reginald Maudling* (London: Sutton, 2004)

Baylis, John, *Anglo-American Defence Relations 1939–1984: The Special Relationship* (London: Macmillan, 1984)

Beales, Derek, 'George Canning (1770–1827)', *Oxford DNB*

Beaver, S. A., 'John Arthur Roebuck (1802–1879)', *Oxford DNB*

Beaverbrook, Lord [Max], *The Decline and Fall of Lloyd George – and Great was the Fall Thereof* (London: Collins, 1963)

Bell, P. M. H., *The Origins of the Second World War* (London: Pearson Longman, 2007)

Bellairs, Charles. E., *Conservative Social and Industrial Reform: A Record of Conservative Legislation between 1800 and 1945* (London: Conservative Political Centre, 1947)

Bellairs, Charles E., *Conservative Social and Industrial Reform: A Record of Conservative Legislation between 1800 and 1974* (London: Conservative Political Centre, 1977)

Beloff, Max, 'Churchill and Europe', in Robert Blake and W. Roger Louis, eds, *Churchill* (Oxford: Clarendon Press, 1996), pp. 443–5

Bentley, Michael, *Lord Salisbury's World: Conservative Environments in Late-Victorian Britain* (Cambridge: Cambridge University Press, 2001)

Black, Jeremy, *The English Press 1621–1861* (London: Sutton, 2001)

Blake, Lord [Robert], 'A Changed Climate', in Lord Blake and John Patten, eds, *The Conservative Opportunity* (London: Macmillan, 1976), pp. 1–12

Blake, Robert, *The Conservative Party from Peel to Churchill* (London: Eyre & Spottiswoode, 1970)

Blake, Robert, *The Conservative Party from Peel to Major* (London: Heinemann, 1997)

Blake, Robert, *Disraeli* (London: Methuen, 1969)

Blake, Robert, 'Sir Joseph Ball (1885–1961)', *Oxford DNB*

Blake, Robert, *The Unknown Prime Minister: The Life and Times of Andrew Bonar Law, 1858–1923* (London: Eyre & Spottiswoode, 1955)

Blake, Lord [Robert], and Hugh Cecil, eds, *Salisbury: The Man and his Policies* (London: Macmillan, 1987)

Blake, Robert, and W. Roger Louis, eds, *Churchill* (Oxford: Clarendon Press, 1996)

Blake, Lord [Robert] and John Patten, eds, *The Conservative Opportunity* (London: Macmillan, 1976)

Blond, Phillip, *Red Tory: How Left and Right Have Broken Britain and How We Can Fix It* (London: Faber & Faber, 2010)

Bogdanor, Vernon, *The Monarchy and the Constitution* (Oxford: Clarendon Press, 1995)

Bogdanor, Vernon, *The People and the Party System: The Referendum and Electoral Reform in British Politics* (Cambridge: Cambridge University Press, 1981)

Bogdanor, Vernon, 'The Selection of the Party Leader', in Anthony Seldon and Stuart Bell, eds, *Conservative Century: The Conservative Party since 1900* (Oxford: Oxford University Press, 1994), pp. 69–96

Bogdanor, Vernon, ed., *From New Jerusalem to New Labour: British Prime Ministers from Attlee to Blair* (London: Macmillan, 2010)

Bogdanor, Vernon, and Robert Skidelsky, eds, *The Age of Affluence* (London: Macmillan, 1970)

Booker, Christopher, *The Neophiliacs: A Study of the Revolution in English Life in the Fifties and Sixties* (London: Collins, 1969)

Boyd-Carpenter, John, *Way of Life: The Memoirs of John Boyd-Carpenter* (London: Sidgwick & Jackson, 1980)

Bradford, Sarah, *Disraeli* (London: Weidenfeld & Nicolson, 1982)

Briggs, Asa, *The Age of Improvement 1783–1867* (London: Longman, 1971)

Brittan, Samuel, *The Treasury under the Tories 1951–1964* (London: Penguin, 1964)

Brittan, Samuel, and Peter Lilley, *The Delusion of Incomes Policy* (London: Temple Smith, 1976)

Brock, Michael, *The Great Reform Act* (London: Hutchinson, 1973)

Burn, W. L., *The Age of Equipoise: A Study of the Mid-Victorian Generation* (London: Unwin, 1964)

Burnham, Peter, *Remaking the Postwar World Economy: Robot and British Policy in the 1950s* (London: Palgrave Macmillan, 2003)

Butler, David, and Dennis Kavanagh, *The British General Election of 1997* (London: Macmillan, 1997)

Butler, David, and Michael Pinto-Duschinsky, *The British General Election of 1970* (London: Macmillan, 1971)

Butler, D. E., and Richard Rose, *The British General Election of 1959* (London: Macmillan, 1960)

Butler, Lord, *The Art of the Possible: The Memoirs of Lord Butler* (London: Hamish Hamilton, 1971)

Campbell, John, *Edward Heath: A Biography* (London: Jonathan Cape, 1993)

Campbell, John, *F. E. Smith, First Earl of Birkenhead* (London: Jonathan Cape, 1983)

Campbell, John, *Margaret Thatcher, vol. 1: The Grocer's Daughter* (London: Jonathan Cape, 2000)

Campbell, John, *Margaret Thatcher*, vol. 2: *Iron Lady* (London: Jonathan Cape, 2003)

Cannon, John, *Parliamentary Reform 1640–1832* (Cambridge: Cambridge University Press, 1973)

Campbell, John C., 'The Soviet Union, the United States, and the Twin Crises of Hungary and Suez', in W. R. Louis and Roger Owen, eds, *Suez 1956: The Crisis and its Consequences* (Oxford: Clarendon Press, 1989), pp. 233–53

Carlton, David, 'Anthony Eden', in Vernon Bogdanor, ed., *From New Jerusalem to New Labour: British Prime Ministers from Attlee to Blair* (London: Macmillan, 2010), pp. 42–59

'Cato', *Guilty Men* (London: Victor Gollancz, 1940)

Cecil, Lady Gwendolen, *Biographical Studies of the Life and Political Character of Robert Third Marquis of Salisbury* (London: Hodder & Stoughton, n.d.)

Cecil, Lady Gwendolen, *Life of Robert Marquis of Salisbury*, 4 vols (London: Hodder & Stoughton, 1921–32)

Cecil, Lady Gwendolen, 'Salisbury in Private Life', in Lord [Robert] Blake and Hugh Cecil, eds, *Salisbury: The Man and his Politics* (London: Macmillan, 1987)

'Celticus', *Why Not Trust the Tories?* (London: Victor Gollancz, 1944)

Chambers, James, *Palmerston: The People's Darling* (London: John Murray, 2004)

Charmley, John, *Churchill: The End of Glory* (London: Hodder & Stoughton, 1993)

Churchill, Winston, *Great Contemporaries* (London: Thornton Butterworth, 1937)

Churchill, Winston, *The Second World War*, vol. 1: *The Gathering Storm* (London: Penguin, 2005)

Clark, Alan, *The Tories: Conservatives and the Nation State 1922–1997* (London: Phoenix, 1998)

Clark, J. C. D., 'A General Theory of Party, Opposition and Government, 1688–1832', *Historical Journal*, 23/2 (1980), pp. 295–325

Clark, J. C. D., *Samuel Johnson: Literature, Religion and English Cultural Politics from the Restoration to Romanticism* (Cambridge: Cambridge University Press, 1994)

Clark, Jonathan, 'The Heartfelt Toryism of Dr. Johnson', *Times Literary Supplement*, 14 Oct. 1994, pp. 17–18

Cockett, Richard, *Thinking the Unthinkable: Think Tanks and the Economic Counter-Revolution, 1931–1983* (London: HarperCollins, 1994)

Cockett, Richard, *Twilight of Truth: Chamberlain, Appeasement and the Manipulation of the Press* (London: Weidenfeld & Nicolson, 1989)

Coetzee, Frans, 'Villa Toryism Reconsidered: Conservatism and Suburban Sensibilities in Late Victorian Croydon', in E. H. H. Green, ed., *An Age of Transition: British Politics 1880–1914* (Edinburgh: Edinburgh University Press, 1997), pp. 29–47

Coleraine, Lord, *For Conservatives Only: A Study of Conservative Leadership from Churchill to Heath* (London: Tom Stacey, 1970)

Colley, Linda, *Lewis Namier* (London: Weidenfeld & Nicolson, 1989)

Colville, John, *The Churchillians* (London: Weidenfeld & Nicolson, 1981)

Colville, John, *Footsteps in Time* (London: Century Publishing, 1985)

Conacher, J. B., *The Peelites and the Party System 1846–1852* (Newton Abbot: David & Charles, 1972)

Conservative and Unionist Party, *The First Ten Years: A Perspective on the Conservative Era that began in 1979* (London: Conservative Central Office, 1989)

Cook, Chris, and John Ramsden, eds, *By-elections in British Politics* (London: UCL Press, 1997)

Cooke, Alistair, *A Gift from the Churchills: The Primrose League, 1883–2004* (London: Carlton Club, 2010)

Cooke, Alistair, ed., *Tory Policy-Making: The Conservative Research Department 1929 to 2009* (Eastbourne: Manor Creative, 2009)

Cooke, A. B., and John Vincent, *The Governing Passion: Cabinet Government and Party Politics in Britain 1885–86* (Brighton: Harvester Press, 1974)

Cooper, Andrew, 'A Party in a Foreign Land: The Tory Failure to Understand How Britain Has Changed', in Edward Vaizey, Nicholas Boles and Michael Gove, eds, *A Blue Tomorrow: New Visions for Modern Conservatives* (London: Politico's, 2001), pp. 9–29

Cornford, James, 'The Transformation of Conservatism in the Late Nineteenth Century', *Victorian Studies*, 8/1 (Sept. 1963), pp. 35–66

Courtney, W. P., rev. Rita M. Gibbs, 'Sir Richard Rawlinson Vyvyan, eighth baronet (1800–1879)', *Oxford DNB*

Cowling, Maurice, 1867: *Disraeli, Gladstone and Revolution – The Passing of the*

Second Reform Bill (Cambridge: Cambridge University Press, 1967)

Cowling, Maurice, *The Impact of Hitler: British Politics and British Policy 1933–1940* (Cambridge: Cambridge University Press, 1975)

Cowling, Maurice, *The Impact of Labour 1920–1924: The Beginning of Modern British Politics* (Cambridge: Cambridge University Press, 1971)

Cowling, Maurice, ed., *Conservative Essays* (London: Cassell, 1978)

Crafts, Nicholas, *The Conservative Government's Economic Record: An End of Term Report* (London: Institute of Economic Affairs, 1998)

Craig, Gordon A., and Felix Gilbert, eds, *The Diplomats 1919–1939* (Princeton: Princeton University Press, 1994)

Cretney, S. M., 'Quintin Hogg, second Viscount Hailsham and Baron Hailsham of St Marylebone (1907–2001)', *Oxford DNB*

Crick, Michael, *In Search of Michael Howard* (London: Simon & Schuster, 2005)

Crowson, N. J., *Facing Fascism: The Conservative Party and the European Dictators, 1935–1940* (London: Routledge, 1997)

Crozier, Andrew, 'Neville Chamberlain (1869–1940)', *Oxford DNB*

Dangerfield, George, *The Strange Death of Liberal England* (London: Serif, 1997)

Davenport-Hines, Richard, 'Sir Henry [Chips] Channon (1897–1958)', *Oxford DNB*

Davenport-Hines, Richard, 'William Henry Smith (1825–1891)', *Oxford DNB*

Derry, John W., *Castlereagh* (London: Allen Lane, 1971)

Dickinson, H. T., *Bolingbroke* (London: Constable, 1970)

Dickinson, H. T., 'Henry St John, first Viscount Bolingbroke (1678–1751)', *Oxford DNB*

Dilks, David, 'Appeasement and "Intelligence"', in David Dilks, ed., *Retreat from Power: Studies in Britain's Foreign Policy in the Twentieth Century*, vol. 1: *1906–1939* (London: Macmillan, 1981), pp. 139–69

Dilks, David, *Neville Chamberlain*, vol. 1: *Pioneering and Reform, 1869–1929* (Cambridge: Cambridge University Press, 1984)

Dilks, David, '"We must hope for the best and prepare for the worst": The Prime Minister, the Cabinet and Hitler's Germany, 1937–1939', *Proceedings of the British Academy*, 73 (1987), pp. 309–52

Dilks, David, ed., *Retreat from Power: Studies in Britain's Foreign Policy in the Twentieth Century*, vol. 1: *1906–1939* (London: Macmillan, 1981)

Du Cann, Edward, *Two Lives: The Political and Business Careers of Edward du Cann* (Malvern: Images, 1995)

Dugdale, Blanche E. C., *Arthur James Balfour, First Earl of Balfour*, 2 vols (London: Hutchinson, 1936)

Dunbabbin, J. P. D., 'Parliamentary Elections in Great Britain, 1868–1900: A Psephological Note', *English Historical Review*, 318 (Jan. 1966), pp. 82–99

Dutton, David, *Anthony Eden: A Life and Reputation* (London: Arnold, 1997)

Dutton, David, *Austen Chamberlain: Gentleman in Politics* (Bolton: Ross Anderson, 1985)

Dutton, D. J., 'David Maxwell Fyfe, earl of Kilmuir (1900–1967)', *Oxford DNB*

Dutton, David, *Neville Chamberlain* (London: Hodder, 2001)

Dutton, David, *Simon: A Political Biography of Sir John Simon* (London: Aurum Press, 1992)

Ehrman, John, *The Younger Pitt*, 3 vols (London: Constable, 1968–96)

Elliott, Francis, and James Hanning, *Cameron: The Rise of the New Conservative* (London: Fourth Estate, 2007)

Emmerson, James Thomas, *The Rhineland Crisis 7 March 1936: A Study in Multilateral Diplomacy* (London: Maurice Temple Smith, 1977)

Evans, Stephen, 'The Conservatives and the Redefinition of Unionism, 1912–1921', *Twentieth Century British History*, 9/1 (1998), pp. 1–27

Feiling, Keith, *A History of the Second Tory Party 1714–1832* (London: Macmillan, 1938)

Feiling, Keith, *A History of the Tory Party 1640–1714* (Oxford: Clarendon Press, 1924)

Feiling, Keith, *The Life of Neville Chamberlain* (London: Macmillan, 1946)

Feuchtwanger, E. J., 'Sir John Eldon Gorst (1835–1916)', *Oxford DNB*

Feuchtwanger, Edgar, *Disraeli* (London: Arnold, 2000)

Finlayson, Geoffrey B. A. M., *England in the Eighteen Thirties: Decade of Reform* (London: Edward Arnold, 1969)

Fitz-Gerald, S. V., rev. Paul Smith, 'Richard Assheton Cross, first Viscount Cross (1823–1914)', *Oxford DNB*

Floud, Roderick, ed., and Paul Johnson, *The Cambridge Economic History of Modern Britain*, vol. 1: *Industrialisation, 1700–1860* (Cambridge: Cambridge University Press, 2004)

Floud, Roderick, and Paul Johnson, eds, *The Cambridge Economic History of Modern Britain*, vol. 2: *Economic Maturity, 1860–1939* (Cambridge: Cambridge University Press, 2004)

Foster, R. F., *Lord Randolph Churchill: A Political Life* (Oxford: Clarendon Press, 1981)

Foster, R. F., *Modern Ireland 1600–1972* (London: Penguin, 1989)

Foster, R. F., ed., *The Oxford History of Ireland* (Oxford: Oxford University Press, 2001)

France, John, 'Salisbury and the Unionist Alliance', in Lord [Robert] Blake and Hugh Cecil, eds, *Salisbury: The Man and his Policies* (London: Macmillan, 1987), pp. 219–51

Garnett, Mark, 'John Wyndham, first Baron Egremont and sixth Baron Leconfield (1920–1972)', *Oxford DNB*

Gash, Norman, 'Francis Bonham (1785–1863)', *Oxford DNB*

Gash, Norman, *Lord Liverpool: The Life and Political Career of Robert Banks Jenkinson, Second Earl of Liverpool 1770–1828* (London: Weidenfeld & Nicolson, 1984)

Gash, Norman, *Mr Secretary Peel: The Life of Sir Robert Peel to 1830* (London: Longman, 1961)

Gash, Norman, *Reaction and Reconstruction in English Politics 1832–1852* (Oxford: Clarendon Press, 1965)

Gash, Norman, 'Robert Banks Jenkinson, second Earl of Liverpool (1770–1828)', *Oxford DNB*

Gash, Norman, *Sir Robert Peel: The Life of Sir Robert Peel after 1830* (London: Longman, 1972)

Gash, Norman, 'The Supreme Tory Radical', in Conservative and Unionist Party, *The First Ten Years: A Perspective on the Conservative Era that began in 1979* (London: Conservative Central Office, 1989), pp. 9–14

Ghosh, P. R., 'Style and Substance in Disraelian Social Reform, c.1860–1880', in P. J. Walker, ed., *Politics and Social Change in Modern Britain: Essays Presented to A. F. Thompson* (Brighton: Harvester Press, 1987), pp. 59–90

Gilbert, Felix, 'Two Ambassadors: Perth and Henderson', in Gordon A. Craig and Felix Gilbert, eds, *The Diplomats 1919–1939* (Princeton: Princeton University Press, 1994), pp. 537–54

Gilbert, Martin, *Israel: A History* (London: Doubleday, 1998)

Gilbert, Martin, *'Never Despair': Winston S. Churchill 1945–1965* (London: Heinemann, 1998)

Gilmour, David, *Curzon* (London: Papermac, 1994)

Gilmour, Ian, *Dancing with Dogma: Britain under Thatcherism* (London: Simon & Schuster, 1992)

Gilmour, Ian, and Mark Garnett, *Whatever Happened to the Tories: The Conservative Party since 1945* (London: Fourth Estate, 1997)

Goldsworthy, David, 'Iain Macleod (1913–1970)', *Oxford DNB*

Goldsworthy, David, 'Robert Arthur James Gascoyne-Cecil, fifth marquess of Salisbury (1893–1972)', *Oxford DNB*

Gollin, Alfred M., *The Observer and J. L. Garvin: A Study in a Great Editorship* (London: Oxford University Press, 1960)

Gooch, John, ed., *The Boer War: Direction, Experience and Image* (London: Frank Cass, 2000)

Goodhart, Philip, with Ursula Branson, *The 1922: The Story of the Conservative Backbenchers' Parliamentary Committee* (London: Macmillan, 1973)

Gorst, Harold E., *The Fourth Party* (London: Smith, Elder, 1906)

Green, E. H. H., ed., *An Age of Transition: British Politics 1880–1914* (Edinburgh: Edinburgh University Press, 1997)

Green, E. H. H., 'Rentiers versus Producers? The Political Economy of the Bimetallic Controversy', *English Historical Review*, no. 406 (1988), pp. 588–612

Greenleaf, W. H., *The British Political Tradition*, 3 vols (London: Methuen, 1983–7)

Griffiths, Richard, *Fellow Travellers of the Right: British Enthusiasts for Nazi Germany 1933–9* (Oxford: Oxford University Press, 1983)

Grigg, John, 'Thelma Cazalet Keir (1899–1989)', *Oxford DNB*

Grossmith, George and Weedon, *The Diary of a Nobody* (London: Penguin, 1999)

Guizot, M., *Memoirs of Sir Robert Peel* (London: Richard Bentley, 1857)

Gwynn, Denis, *The History of Partition (1912–1925)* (Dublin: Browne & Nolan, 1950)

Hague, William, *William Pitt the Younger* (London: Harper Perennial, 2005)

Halévy, Élie, *Histoire du peuple anglais au xixe siècle, Épilogue*, 2 vols (Paris: Hachette, 1926, 1932)

Hanham, H. J., *Elections and Party Management: Politics in the Time of Disraeli and Gladstone* (London: Longman, 1959)

Harcourt, Freda, 'Disraeli's Imperialism, 1866–1868: A Question of Timing', *Historical Journal*, 23/1 (1980), pp. 87–109

Harris, Jose, 'William Beveridge, Baron Beveridge (1879–1963)', *Oxford DNB*

Harris, Robin, *The Conservative Community: The Roots of Thatcherism – and its Future* (London: Centre for Policy Studies, 1989)

Harris, Robin, *Talleyrand: Betrayer and Saviour of France* (London: John Murray, 2007)

Hastings, Max, *Finest Years: Churchill as Warlord 1940–45* (London: HarperCollins, 2009)

Hawkins, Angus, 'Edward George Geoffrey Smith Stanley, fourteenth earl of Derby (1799–1869)', *Oxford DNB*

Hawkins, Angus, *The Forgotten Prime Minister: The 14th Earl of Derby*, 2 vols (Oxford: Oxford University Press, 2007–8)

Heath, Edward, *The Course of My Life: My Autobiography* (London: Hodder & Stoughton, 1998)

Heffer, Simon, *Like the Roman: The Life of Enoch Powell* (London: Weidenfeld & Nicolson, 1998)

Hennessy, Peter, and Anthony Seldon, eds, *Ruling Performance: British Governments from Attlee to Thatcher* (Oxford: Basil Blackwell, 1987)

Hilton, Boyd, *A Mad, Bad and Dangerous People? England 1783–1846* (Oxford: Clarendon Press, 2006)

Hilton, Boyd, 'Peel: A Reappraisal', *Historical Journal*, 22/3 (1979), pp. 584–614

Hinde, Wendy, *George Canning* (London: Collins, 1973)

Hogg, Quintin, *The Left Was Never Right* (London: Faber & Faber, 1945)

Holmes, Richard, *Wellington: The Iron Duke* (London: Harper Perennial, 2007)

Horne, Alistair, *Macmillan: The Official Biography*, 2 vols (London: Macmillan, 1989)

Horne, Alistair, 'The Macmillan Years and Afterwards', in W. Roger Louis and Hedley Bull, eds, *'The Special Relationship': Anglo-American Relations since 1945* (Oxford: Clarendon Press, 1986), pp. 87–102

Howard, Anthony, *Rab: The Life of R. A. Butler* (London: Jonathan Cape, 1987)

Howard, Michael, 'British Military Preparations for the Second World War', in David Dilks, ed., *Retreat from Power: Studies in Britain's Foreign Policy in the Twentieth Century*, vol. 1: *1906–1939* (London: Macmillan, 1981), pp. 102–17

Hunt, Giles, *The Duel: Castlereagh, Canning and Deadly Cabinet Rivalry* (London: I. B. Taurus, 2008)

Hurd, Douglas, *An End to Promises: Sketch of a Government 1970–74* (London: Collins, 1979)

Hurd, Douglas, *Robert Peel: A Biography* (London: Phoenix, 2007)

Hyde, H. Montgomery, *The Rise of Castlereagh* (London: Macmillan, 1933)

Jackson, Alvin, 'Walter Hume Long, first Viscount Long (1854–1924)', *Oxford DNB*

James, Lawrence, *The Rise and Fall of the British Empire* (London: Little, Brown, 2000)

Jay, Richard, *Joseph Chamberlain: A Political Life* (Oxford: Clarendon Press, 1981)

Jenkins, Roy, 'David Ormsby-Gore, fifth Baron Harlech (1918–1985)', *Oxford DNB*

Jenkins, Roy, 'Harold Wilson, Baron Wilson of Rievaulx (1916–1995)', *Oxford DNB*

Jenkins, Roy, 'Sir Charles Wentworth Dilke, second baronet (1843–1911)', *Oxford DNB*

Jerome, Jerome K., *Three Men on the Bummel* (London: Arrowsmith, 1942)

Johnson, Janet, 'Did Organization Really Matter? Party Organization and Conservative Electoral Recovery, 1945–59', *Twentieth Century British History*, 14/4 (2003), pp. 391–412

Johnson, Paul, *Intellectuals* (London: Weidenfeld & Nicolson, 1988)

Jones, Andrew, and Michael Bentley, 'Salisbury and Baldwin', in Maurice Cowling, ed., *Conservative Essays* (London: Cassell, 1978), pp. 25–40

Kandiah, Michael D., 'Frederick Marquis, first earl of Woolton (1883–1964)', *Oxford DNB*

Kavanagh, Dennis, 'The Heath Government 1970–1974', in Peter Hennessy and Anthony Seldon, eds, *Ruling Performance: British Governments from Attlee to Thatcher* (Oxford: Basil Blackwell, 1987), pp. 216–40

Kavanagh, Dennis, and David Butler, *The British General Election of 2005* (London: Macmillan, 2005)

Kavanagh, Dennis, and Philip Cowley, *The British General Election of 2010* (London: Macmillan, 2010)

Kebbel, T. E., *A History of Toryism: From the Accession of Mr. Pitt to Power in 1783 to the Death of Lord Beaconsfield in 1881* (London: W. H. Allen, 1886)

Kelly, Scott, *The Myth of Mr Butskell: The Politics of British Economic Policy, 1950–55* (Aldershot: Ashgate, 1988)

Kennedy, Paul, *The Rise and Fall of the Great Powers: Economic Change and Military Conflict from 1500 to 2000* (London: Fontana, 1989)

Kinnear, Michael, *The Fall of Lloyd George: The Political Crisis of 1922* (London: Macmillan, 1973)

Kissinger, Henry, *Diplomacy* (London: Simon & Schuster, 1994)

Kissinger, Henry, *Years of Renewal* (London: Simon & Schuster, 1999)

Kramnick, Isaac, *Bolingbroke and his Circle: The Politics of Nostalgia in the Age of Walpole* (London: Oxford University Press, 1968)

Kuhn, William, *The Politics of Pleasure: A Portrait of Benjamin Disraeli* (London: Simon & Schuster, 2006)

Kunz, Diane B., 'The Importance of Having Money: The Economic Diplomacy of Suez', in W. R. Louis and Roger Owen, eds, *Suez 1956: The Crisis and its Consequences* (Oxford: Clarendon Press, 1989), pp. 215–32

Kyle, Keith, *Suez* (London: Weidenfeld & Nicolson, 1991)

Lacouture, Jean, *De Gaulle*, 3 vols (Paris: Seuil, 1984–6)

Lagomarsino, David, and Charles J. Wood, eds, *The Trial of Charles I: A Documentary History* (Hanover: University Press of New England, 1989)

Lamb, Richard, *The Macmillan Years 1957–1963: The Emerging Truth* (London: John Murray, 1995)

Lamont, Norman, *In Office* (London: Little, Brown, 1999)

Lawlor, Sheila, *Churchill and the Politics of War, 1940–1941* (Cambridge: Cambridge University Press, 1994)

Lawson, Nigel, *The View from No. 11: Memoirs of a Tory Radical* (London: Bantam, 1992)

Laybourn, Keith, 'The Rise of Labour and the Decline of Liberalism: The State of the Debate', *History*, 80 (1995), pp. 207–26

Lee, Stephen M., *George Canning and Liberal Toryism, 1801–1827* (Woodbridge: Royal Historical Society, 2008)

Letwin, Shirley, *The Anatomy of Thatcherism* (London: Fontana, 1992)

Lock, F. P., *Edmund Burke*, 2 vols (Oxford: Clarendon Press, 1998, 2006)

Longford, Elizabeth, *Wellington: Pillar of State* (London: Weidenfeld & Nicolson, 1972)

Louis, W. Roger, and Hedley Bull, eds, *'The Special Relationship': Anglo-American Relations since 1945* (Oxford: Clarendon Press: 1986)

Louis, W. R., and Roger Owen, eds, *Suez 1956: The Crisis and its Consequences* (Oxford: Clarendon Press, 1989)

Lowe, C. J., *The Reluctant Imperialists*, 2 vols (London: Routledge & Kegan Paul, 1967)

Ludlow, N. Piers, 'Duncan Sandys, Baron Duncan-Sandys (1908–1987)', *Oxford DNB*

McKenzie, Robert, and Allan Silver, *Angels in Marble: Working Class Conservatives in Urban England* (London: Heinemann, 1968)

Major, John, *The Autobiography* (London: HarperCollins, 1999)

Malcolm, Noel, *Bosnia: A Short History* (London: Papermac, 1994)

Mander, Geoffrey, *We Were Not All Wrong* (London: Victor Gollancz, 1944)

Marsh, Peter T., *Joseph Chamberlain: Entrepreneur in Politics* (London: Yale University Press, 1994)

Matthew, H. C. G., 'Sir John Gladstone (1764–1851)', *Oxford DNB*.

Medlicott, Norman, 'The Hoare–Laval Pact Reconsidered', in David Dilks, ed., *Retreat from Power: Studies in Britain's Foreign Policy in the Twentieth Century, vol. 1: 1906–1939* (London: Macmillan, 1981), pp. 118–38

Meynell, Wilfrid, *The Man Disraeli* (London: Hutchinson, 1927)

Middlemas, Keith, and John Barnes, *Baldwin: A Biography* (London: Weidenfeld & Nicolson, 1969)

Milward, Alan S., *The Rise and Fall of a National Strategy 1945–1963 (The UK and the European Community*, vol. 1) (London: Whitehall History Publishing, 2002)

Minford, Patrick, *The Supply Side Revolution in Britain* (London: Edward Elgar/Institute of Economic Affairs, 1991)

Monypenny, William Flavelle, and George Earle Buckle, *The Life of Benjamin Disraeli Earl of Beaconsfield*, 2 vols (London: John Murray, 1929)

Moore, Charles, and Simon Heffer, eds, *A Tory Seer: The Selected Journalism of T. E. Utley* (London: Hamish Hamilton, 1989)

Moran, Lord [Charles], *Winston Churchill: The Struggle for Survival 1940–1965* (London: Constable, 1966)

Morgan, Kenneth O., *Consensus and Disunity: The Lloyd George Coalition Government 1918–1922* (Oxford: Clarendon Press, 1979)

Murphy, Philip, 'Oliver Lyttelton, first Viscount Chandos (1893–1972)', *Oxford DNB*

Namier, L. B., 'The Character of Burke', *The Spectator*, 19 Dec. 1958, pp. 395–6

Norman, Jesse, *The Big Society: The Anatomy of the New Politics* (Buckingham: University of Buckingham Press, 2011)

Norton, Philip, *Conservative Dissidents: Dissent within the Parliamentary Conservative Party 1970–74* (London: Temple Smith, 1978)

Oakeshott, Michael, *Rationalism in Politics and Other Essays* (London: Methuen, 1962)

O'Gorman, Frank, *Edmund Burke: His Political Philosophy* (London: George Allen & Unwin, 1973)

Oppenheimer, Peter, 'Muddling Through: The Economy, 1951–1964', in Vernon Bogdanor and Robert Skidelsky, eds, *The Age of Affluence* (London: Macmillan, 1970), pp. 117–67

O'Sullivan, John, *The President, the Pope and the Prime Minister: Three Who Changed the World* (Washington: Regnery, 2006)

Packenham, Thomas, *The Boer War* (London: Abacus, 2009)

Pares, Richard, *King George III and the Politicians* (Oxford: Clarendon Press, 1953)

Parker, R. A. C., *Chamberlain and Appeasement: British Policy and the Coming of the Second World War* (London: Macmillan, 1993)

Parker, R. A. C., *Churchill and Appeasement* (London: Macmillan, 2000)

Parry, Jonathan, 'Gathorne Gathorne-Hardy, first earl of Cranbrook (1814–1906)', *Oxford DNB*

Parry, Jonathan, 'Robert Lowe, Viscount Sherbrooke (1811–1892)', *Oxford DNB*

Parry, Jonathan, 'Spencer Compton Cavendish, marquess of Hartington and eighth duke of Devonshire (1833–1908)', *Oxford DNB*

Pearce, Robert, 'David Margesson, first Viscount Margesson (1890–1965)', *Oxford DNB*

Pelling, Henry, 'The Politics of the Osborne Judgement', *Historical Journal*, 25/4 (1982), pp. 889–909

Petrie, Sir Charles, and Alistair Cooke, *The Carlton Club 1832–2007* (London: Carlton Club, 2007)

Pinto-Duschinsky, Michael, 'From Macmillan to Home, 1959–1964', in Peter Hennessy and Anthony Seldon, eds, *Ruling Performance: British Governments from Attlee to Thatcher* (Oxford: Basil Blackwell, 1987), pp. 150–85

Pinto-Duschinsky, Michael, *The Political Thought of Lord Salisbury 1854–1868* (London: Constable, 1967)

Porter, A. N., 'Lord Salisbury, Foreign Policy and Domestic Finance, 1860–1900', in Lord [Robert] Blake and Hugh Cecil, eds, *Salisbury: The Man and his Policies* (London: Macmillan, 1987), pp. 148–84

Powell, Enoch, *Joseph Chamberlain* (London: Thames & Hudson, 1977)

Pugh, Martin, *Electoral Reform in War and Peace 1906–1918* (London: Routledge & Kegan Paul, 1978)

Pugh, Martin, *The Tories and the People 1880–1935* (Oxford: Basil Blackwell, 1985)

Quinault, R. E., 'Lord Randolph Churchill and Tory Democracy, 1880–1885',

Historical Journal, 22/1 (1979), pp. 141–65

Ramsden, John, *The Age of Balfour and Baldwin 1902–1940* (London: Longman, 1978)

Ramsden, John, *The Age of Churchill and Eden, 1940–1957* (London: Longman, 1995)

Ramsden, John, *An Appetite for Power: A History of the Conservative Party since 1830* (London: HarperCollins, 1998)

Ramsden, John, 'Derick Heathcoat Amory, first Viscount Amory (1899–1981)', *Oxford DNB*

Ramsden, John, 'How Winston Churchill became "The Greatest Living Englishman"', *Contemporary British History*, 12/3 (1998), pp. 1–40

Ramsden, John, *The Making of Conservative Party Policy: The Conservative Research Department since 1929* (London: Longman, 1980)

Ramsden, John, 'The Newport By-election and the Fall of the Coalition', in Chris Cook and John Ramsden, eds, *By-elections in British Politics* (London: UCL Press, 1997), pp. 13–36

Ramsden, John, *The Winds of Change: Macmillan to Heath, 1957–1975* (London: Longman, 1996)

Reynolds, David, *In Command of History: Churchill Fighting and Writing the Second World War* (London: Allen Lane, 2004)

Rhodes James, Robert, *Churchill: A Study in Failure 1900–1939* (London: Weidenfeld & Nicolson, 1970)

Ridley, Jane, *The Young Disraeli* (London: Sinclair-Stevenson, 1995)

Ridley, Jasper, *Lord Palmerston* (New York: E. P. Dutton, 1971)

Ridley, Nicholas, *My Style of Government* (London: Hutchinson, 1991)

Roberts, Andrew, *Eminent Churchillians* (London: Phoenix, 2004)

Roberts, Andrew, *'The Holy Fox': The Life of Lord Halifax* (London: Phoenix, 1997)

Roberts, Andrew, *Salisbury: Victorian Titan* (London: Weidenfeld & Nicolson, 1999)

Rose, Norman, 'Robert Vansittart, Baron Vansittart (1881–1957)', *Oxford DNB*

Rubinstein, W. D., 'Stafford Northcote, first earl of Iddesleigh (1818–1887)', *Oxford DNB*

Russell, A. K., *Liberal Landslide: The General Election of 1906* (Newton Abbot: David & Charles, 1973)

Sack, J. J., 'The Memory of Burke and the Memory of Pitt: English Conservatism Confronts its Past', *Historical Journal*, 30/3 (1987), pp. 623–40

Sampson, Anthony, *Anatomy of Britain* (London: Hodder & Stoughton, 1962)

Schofield, T. P., 'Conservative Political Thought in Britain in Response to the French Revolution', *Historical Journal*, 29/3 (1986), pp. 601–22

Scholefield, Andrew, and Gerald Frost, *Too 'Nice' to be Tories? How the Modernisers Have Damaged the Conservative Party* (London: Social Affairs Unit, 2011).

Scruton, Roger, *A Dictionary of Political Thought* (London: Macmillan, 1996)

Scruton, Roger, *The Meaning of Conservatism* (London: Penguin, 1980)

Seeley, J. R., *The Expansion of England: Two Courses of Lectures* (London: Macmillan, 1907)

Seldon, Anthony, *Churchill's Indian Summer: The Conservative Government, 1951–55* (London: Hodder & Stoughton, 1981)

Seldon, Anthony, with Lewis Baston, *Major: A Political Life* (London: Weidenfeld & Nicolson, 1997)

Seldon, Anthony and Stuart Ball, eds, *Conservative Century: The Conservative Party since 1900* (Oxford: Oxford University Press, 1994)

Selwyn-Lloyd, Lord, *1956: A Personal Account* (London: Jonathan Cape, 1978)

Sewill, Brendon, 'Policy Making for Heath', in Alistair Cooke, ed., *Tory Policy-Making: The Conservative Research Department 1929 to 2009* (Eastbourne: Manor Creative, 2009), pp. 55–78

Shannon, Richard, *The Age of Disraeli, 1868–1881: The Rise of Tory Democracy* (London: Longman, 1992)

Shannon, Richard, *The Age of Salisbury, 1881–1902: Unionism and Empire* (London: Longman, 1996)

Shannon, Richard, *Gladstone: God and Politics* (London: Hambledon Continuum, 2007)

Shannon, Richard, *Gladstone: Heroic Prime Minister 1865–1898* (London: Penguin, 1999)

Shannon, Richard, 'Peel, Gladstone and Party', *Parliamentary History*, 18/3 (1999), pp. 317–52

Shannon, Richard, 'Richard Middleton (1846–1905)', *Oxford DNB*

Shepherd, Robert, *Iain Macleod* (London: Hutchinson, 1994)

Smith, Paul, 'Robert Arthur Talbot Gascoyne-Cecil, third Marquess of Salisbury (1830–1903)', *Oxford DNB*

Soto, Hernando de, *The Mystery of Capital: Why Capitalism Triumphs in the West and Fails Everywhere Else* (London: Bantam, 2000)

Spinner, Thomas J., jun., 'George Goschen, first Viscount Goschen (1831–1907)', *Oxford DNB*

Stanlis, Peter J., ed., *The Relevance of Edmund Burke* (New York: P. J. Kennedy & Sons, 1964)

Steele, David, 'Henry John Temple, third Viscount Palmerston (1784–1865)', *Oxford DNB*

Steele, David, 'Hugh Cairns, first Earl Cairns (1819–1885)', *Oxford DNB*

Steele, David, *Lord Salisbury: A Political Biography* (London: UCL Press, 1999)

Steele, David, 'Salisbury and the Soldiers', in John Gooch, ed., *The Boer War: Direction, Experience and Image* (London: Frank Cass, 2000), pp. 3–20

Steele, E. D., 'Palmerston's Foreign Policy and Foreign Secretaries 1855–1865', in Keith M. Wilson, ed., *British Foreign Secretaries and Foreign Policy: From the Crimean War to the First World War* (London: Croom Helm, 1987), pp. 25–84

Steele, E. D., 'Salisbury and the Church', in Lord [Robert] Blake and Hugh Cecil, eds, *Salisbury: The Man and his Policies* (London: Macmillan, 1987), pp. 185–218

Stewart, Graham, *Burying Caesar: Churchill, Chamberlain and the Battle for the Tory Party* (London: Weidenfeld & Nicolson, 1999)

Stewart, Robert, *The Foundation of the Conservative Party 1830–1867* (London: Longman, 1978)

Stuart, James, *Within the Fringe: An Autobiography* (London: Bodley Head, 1967)

Sykes, Alan, *Tariff Reform in British Politics 1903–1913* (Oxford: Clarendon Press, 1979)

Taylor, A. J. P., *British Prime Ministers and Other Essays*, ed. Chris Wrigley (London: Allen Lane, 1999)

Taylor, Miles, 'John Bright (1811–1889)', *Oxford DNB*

Taylor, Miles, 'Richard Cobden (1804–1865)', *Oxford DNB*

Temperley, Harold, *The Foreign Policy of Canning 1822–1827: England, the Neo-Holy Alliance and the New World* (London: G. Bell & Sons, 1925)

Templewood, Viscount [Samuel Hoare], *Nine Troubled Years* (London: Collins, 1954)

Thaler, Richard H., and Cass R. Sunstein, *Nudge: Improving Decisions about Health, Wealth and Happiness* (London: Penguin, 2009)

Thatcher, Margaret, *The Downing Street Years* (London: HarperCollins, 1993)

Thatcher, Margaret, *The Path to Power* (London: HarperCollins, 1995)

Thatcher, Margaret, *Statecraft: Strategies for a Changing World* (London: HarperCollins, 2002)

Thorpe, D. R., *Alec Douglas-Home* (London: Sinclair Stevenson, 1996)

Thorpe, D. R., *Eden: The Life and Times of Anthony Eden First Earl of Avon, 1897–1977* (London: Pimlico, 2004)

Thorpe, D. R., *Supermac: The Life of Harold Macmillan* (London: Chatto & Windus, 2010)

Timmins, Nicholas, *The Five Giants: A Biography of the Welfare State* (London: HarperCollins, 1995)

Tomes, Jason, 'Brendan Bracken, Viscount Bracken (1901–1958)', *Oxford DNB*

Vaizey, Edward, Nicholas Boles and Michael Gove, eds, *A Blue Tomorrow: New Visions for Modern Conservatives* (London: Politico's, 2001)

Vincent, John, *Disraeli* (Oxford: Oxford University Press, 1990)

Walker, Peter, *Staying Power: An Autobiography* (London: Bloomsbury, 1991)

Walker, P. J., ed., *Politics and Social Change in Modern Britain: Essays Presented to A. F. Thompson* (Brighton: Harvester Press, 1987)

Walters, Simon, *Tory Wars* (London: Politico's, 2001)

Weaver, Stewart A., 'Michael Thomas Sadler (1780–1835)', *Oxford DNB*

Weaver, Stewart A., 'Richard Oastler (1789–1861)', *Oxford DNB*

Weintraub, Stanley, *Disraeli: A Biography* (London: Hamish Hamilton, 1993)

Whitfield, Andrew, 'Oliver Stanley (1896–1950)', *Oxford DNB*

Williamson, Philip, 'Noel Skelton (1880–1935)', *Oxford DNB*

Williamson, Philip, *Stanley Baldwin: Conservative Leadership and National Values* (Cambridge: Cambridge University Press, 2007)

Wilson, Keith M., ed., *British Foreign Secretaries and Foreign Policy: From the Crimean War to the First World War* (London: Croom Helm, 1987)

Wolffe, John, 'Anthony Ashley Cooper, seventh Earl of Shaftesbury (1801–1885)', *Oxford DNB*

[Woolton, Lord,] *The Memoirs of the Rt. Hon. the Earl Woolton* (London: Cassell, 1959)

Young, G. M., *Stanley Baldwin* (London: Rupert Hart-Davis, 1952)

Young, Hugo, *One of Us: A Biography of Margaret Thatcher* (London: Macmillan, 1989)

Ziegler, Philip, *Edward Heath: The Authorised Biography* (London: Harper Press, 2010)

PICTURE ACKNOWLEDGEMENTS

In-text illustrations

Pages 8, 196, 264: Getty Images; pages 40, 230: © Illustrated London News/Mary Evans; page 76: © The Print Collector/Alamy; page 106: Mary Evans Picture Library; pages 290, 374, 418: Solo Syndication/Associated Newspapers Ltd (Vicky, *Evening Standard*, 7 November 1958/British Cartoon Archive, University of Kent, www.cartoons.ac.uk); page 454: copyright Mark Boxer; page 482: Nicholas Garland (*The Independent*, British Cartoon Archive, University of Kent, www.cartoons.ac.uk); page 506: copyright © Gerald Scarfe.

Section one

A Uniform Whig, satire by James Gillray, 1791: © The Trustees of the British Museum [1868,0808.6122].

William Pitt the Younger by Robert Dighton: Palace of Westminster Collection; *William Pitt in the House of Commons on the French Declaration of War* by Anton Hickel, 1793: National Portrait Gallery, London/The Bridgeman Art Library; *George Canning* by Thomas Lawrence: © Christie's Images/The Bridgeman Art Library; *Arthur Wellesley, 1st Duke of Wellington with Sir Robert Peel* by Franz Xavier Winterhalter, 1844: The Royal Collection © 2011 Her Majesty Queen Elizabeth II/The Bridgeman Art Library; *The Reformers' Attack on the Old Rotten Tree, or the Foul Nests of the Cormorants in Danger*, satirical cartoon, *c.*1831: British Library, London, UK/© British Library Board, all rights reserved/The Bridgeman Art Library.

Modern Phoenix. The Bird Wot Exits Single And Rises Again Out Of its Own Ashes, political cartoon, 1841: courtesy Cowan's Auctions Inc., Cincinnati, OH; *The Stepping Stone, or John Bull peeping into Futurity!!!*, anonymous satire, *c.*1846: The Bridgeman Art Library; *A Race between the Old Protectionist Drag, and the Anti Corn Law League Fast Coach*, wood engraving, *c.*1846: © The Trustees of the British Museum [1868, 0808.13357]; Peel retires, 1846: © Mary Evans Picture Library/Alamy; *Benjamin Disraeli* after Alfred Edward Chalon: Palace of Westminster Collection.

The House of Commons by Joseph Nash, 1858: Palace of Westminster Collection; the Earl of Derby, 1858: Getty Images; *The Derby Cabinet of 1867* by Henry Gales, 1868: National Portrait Gallery, London; Reform League demonstration, 23 July 1866: Getty Images.

Caricature of Benjamin Disraeli by 'Ape' or 'Singe' (Carlo Pelligrini), 30 January 1869: Getty Images; Benjamin Disraeli and friends at Hughenden Manor, 1874: Getty Images.

Section two

'Politicians – Conservative', carte-de-visite, 1876: National Portrait Gallery, London.

The House of Commons, 1878 by William Morison Wyllie, 1878: The Palace of Westminster Collection; 'Alas, why does this path home not belong to me?, cartoon: akg-images; Drinking Disraeli's health at the Carlton Club banquet, 1878: © Illustrated London News/Mary Evans; *Queen Victoria and Benjamin Disraeli* by Tom Merry, 1879.

'The Fourth Party', caricature by Spy (Leslie Ward) from *Vanity Fair*, December 1880: © Mary Evans Picture Library/Alamy; *Marquis of Salisbury Speaking in the House of Lords during the Debate of Home Rule, 1893* by Foster Dickinson: Palace of Westminster Collection; Primrose League badge, 1889: © The Trustees of the British Museum [M8934]; caricature of Richard Middleton by Spy (Leslie Ward) for *Vanity Fair*, 18 April 1901: © Mary Evans Picture Library.

Joseph Chamberlain, Bingley Hall, Birmingham, 19 October 1903: Topham Picturepoint/Press Association Images; Conservative Party van, 10 December 1906: Getty Images; Conservative Party poster, 1910: Getty Images; *Arthur James Balfour* by George Reid, *c.*1900: Edinburgh University Library, Scotland, with kind permission of the University of Edinburgh/The Bridgeman Art Library; F. E. Smith, speaking in Ulster, September 1912: Getty Images.

PICTURE ACKNOWLEDGEMENTS

The Coalition Cabinet for the Great War after Samuel Beff, from 'The Illustrated War News': Private Collection/The Stapleton Collection/The Bridgeman Art Library; Arthur Balfour and Robert Lansing, Washington, 22 April 1917: AP/Press Association Images.

Section three

The Treaty of Versailles by William Orpen, 1919: Private Collection/The Bridgeman Art Library; signatories of the Locarno Treaties, December 1925: Hulton-Deutsch Collection/Corbis.

Lloyd George, F. E. Smith and Winston Churchill, Downing Street, 1921: Getty Images; F. E. Smith, Neville Chamberlain and Walter Guinness, May 1926: Getty Images; Bonar Law and Lord Beaverbrook, Aix-les-Bains, 1920s: © TopFoto.co.uk; Stanley Baldwin, Downing Street, August 1928: Getty Images, © TopfFoto.co.uk; Conservative Party poster, 1929: Getty Images.

Austen Chamberlain and Benito Mussolini, April 1929: Getty Images; Neville Chamberlain, Caxton Hall, 24 June 1930: Getty Images; National Cabinet in the garden at No. 10 Downing Street, 1931: private collection/The Stapleton Collection/The Bridgeman Art Library; Conservative Party posters, 1931: both Getty Images.

Sir John Simon, Adolf Hitler and Anthony Eden, 26 March 1935: Popperfoto/Getty Images; National Government poster, 1935: Getty Images; Winston Churchill, Epping, 14 November 1935: Popperfoto/Getty Images; Neville Chamberlain and Adolf Hitler, September 1938: Getty Images; Anthony Eden, Downing Street, 7 September 1939: Len Putnam/AP/Press Association Images.

Winston Churchill broadcasting, 13 May 1940: Gamma-Keystone via Getty Images; Winston Churchill, VE-Day, 8 May 1945: Popperfoto/Getty Images.

Section four

Lord Frederick Woolton, February 1949: Time & Life Pictures/Getty Images.

Quintin Hogg, Oxford, 25 February 1950: Getty Images; baby in pram, general election, 22 February 1950: Daily Mail/Rex Features; Winston Churchill and the Queen, Downing Street, 5 April 1955: mirrorpix; Conservative Central Office, 5 May 1955: Getty Images; Anthony Eden electioneering, 26 May 1955: Associated Newspapers/Rex Features.

Harold Macmillan and J. F. Kennedy, White House, April 1961: Time & Life Pictures/Getty Images; Alec Douglas-Home, Stockport, October 1964: mirrorpix; Enoch Powell electioneering, 9 June 1970: Getty Images; Edward Heath, Bexleyheath, 18 June 1970: mirrorpix; Conservative Central Office, Smith Square: Nicholas Bailey/Rex Features.

Margaret Thatcher, Peter Carrington and Edward Heath, press conference, October 1974: mirrorpix; Conservative Party poster: Pictorial Press/Alamy; Grand Hotel, Brighton, bomb damage, 12 October 1984: PA Photos/ Topfoto/TopFoto.co.uk; Margaret Thatcher and William Whitelaw, 13 October 1989: PA/PA Archive/PA Photos; Conservative Party poster: Getty Images.

David Cameron, party rally, 5 May 2010: Getty Images.

INDEX

INDEX